Ballentine's Thesaurus
for Legal Research & Writing

TITLES IN THE DELMAR LCP SERIES

Ransford C. Pyle, *Foundations of Law for Paralegals: Cases, Commentary, and Ethics,* 1992.

Peggy N. Kerley, Paul A. Sukys, Joanne Banker Hames, *Civil Litigation for the Paralegal,* 1992.

Jonathan Lynton, Donna Masinter, Terri Mick Lyndall, *Law Office Management for Paralegals,* 1992.

Daniel Hall, *Criminal Law and Procedure,* 1992.

Daniel Hall, *Survey of Criminal Law,* 1992.

Jonathan Lynton, Terri Mick Lyndall, *Legal Ethics and Professional Responsibility,* 1993.

Michael Kearns, *The Law of Real Property,* 1994.

Angela Schneeman, *The Law of Corporations, Partnerships, and Sole Proprietorships,* 1993.

William Buckley, *Torts and Personal Injury Law,* 1993.

Gordon Brown, *Administration of Wills, Trusts, and Estates,* 1993.

Richard Stim, *Intellectual Property: Patents, Copyrights, and Trademarks,* 1994.

Ransford C. Pyle, *Family Law,* 1994.

Daniel Hall, *Administrative Law,* 1994.

Jonathan Lynton, *Ballentine's Thesaurus for Legal Research & Writing,* 1994.

Jack Handler, *Ballentine's Law Dictionary: Legal Assistant Edition,* 1994.

Angela Schneeman, *Paralegals in American Law,* 1994.

BALLENTINE'S THESAURUS FOR LEGAL RESEARCH & WRITING

Jonathan S. Lynton, Ph.D., J.D.

Lawyers Cooperative Publishing

Delmar
Publishers Inc.

Cover design by Spiral Design Studio

Certain portions of this work edited by The University of Chicago Law Review and the University of Chicago Legal Forum.

Delmar Staff:

Administrative Editor: Jay Whitney
Developmental Editor: Christopher Anzalone
Project Editor: Andrea Edwards Myers
Production Coordinator: James Zayicek
Art/Design Coordinator: Karen Kunz Kemp

For information, address

Delmar Publishers Inc.
3 Columbia Circle
P.O. Box 15015
Albany, New York 12212-5015

Printed in the United States of America

1 2 3 4 5 6 7 8 9 10 XXX 00 99 98 97 96 95 94

Library of Congress Cataloging-in-Publication Data

Lynton, Jonathan S.
    Ballentine's thesaurus for legal reseach & writing / Jonathan S. Lynton,
        p.   cm. — (Delmar paralegal series)
    ISBN 0-8273-6208-0
    1. Law—United States—Terminology.   2. Law—Terminology.
I. Title.   II. Series.
KF156.L96   1994
349.73'0148—dc20
[347.300148]   93-13825
                                                            CIP
                                                            AC

DEDICATION

To Kim, Nicky, and Aaron,
my triad of hope and light;
and to Alexander,
the beloved, the sunset, the sun:

Caught by the sun's Western fire
it's loving you
that makes me fly higher.

AM JUR LEGAL FORMS 2D: A COMPILATION OF BUSINESS AND LEGAL FORMS DEALING WITH A VARIETY OF SUBJECT MATTERS.

AM JUR PLEADING AND PRACTICE FORMS, REV: MODEL PRACTICE FORMS FOR EVERY STAGE OF A LEGAL PROCEEDING.

AM JUR PROOF OF FACTS: A SERIES OF ARTICLES THAT GUIDE THE READER IN DETERMINING WHICH FACTS ARE ESSENTIAL TO A CASE AND HOW TO PROVE THEM.

AM JUR TRIALS: A SERIES OF ARTICLES DISCUSSING EVERY ASPECT OF PARTICULAR SETTLEMENTS AND TRIALS WRITTEN BY 180 CONSULTING SPECIALISTS.

UNITED STATES CODE SERVICE: A COMPLETE AND AUTHORITATIVE ANNOTATED FEDERAL CODE THAT FOLLOWS THE EXACT LANGUAGE OF THE STATUTES AT LARGE AND DIRECTS YOU TO THE COURT AND AGENCY DECISIONS CONSTRUING EACH PROVISION.

ALR AND ALR FEDERAL: SERIES OF ANNOTATIONS PROVIDING IN-DEPTH ANALYSES OF ALL THE CASE LAW ON PARTICULAR LEGAL ISSUES.

U.S. SUPREME COURT REPORTS, L ED 2D: EVERY REPORTED U.S. SUPREME COURT DECISION PLUS IN-DEPTH DISCUSSIONS OF LEADING ISSUES.

FEDERAL PROCEDURE, L ED: A COMPREHENSIVE, A—Z TREATISE ON FEDERAL PROCEDURE—CIVIL, CRIMINAL, AND ADMINISTRATIVE.

FEDERAL PROCEDURAL FORMS, L ED: STEP-BY-STEP GUIDANCE FOR DRAFTING FORMS FOR FEDERAL COURT OR FEDERAL AGENCY PROCEEDINGS.

FEDERAL RULES SERVICE, 2D AND 3D: REPORTS DECISIONS FROM ALL LEVELS OF THE FEDERAL SYSTEM INTERPRETING THE FEDERAL RULES OF CIVIL PROCEDURE AND THE FEDERAL RULES OF APPELLATE PROCEDURE.

FEDERAL RULES DIGEST, 3D: ORGANIZES HEADNOTES FOR THE DECISIONS REPORTED IN FEDERAL RULES SERVICE ACCORDING TO THE NUMBERING SYSTEMS OF THE FEDERAL RULES OF CIVIL PROCEDURE AND THE FEDERAL RULES OF APPELLATE PROCEDURE.

FEDERAL RULES OF EVIDENCE SERVICE: REPORTS DECISIONS FROM ALL LEVELS OF THE FEDERAL SYSTEM INTERPRETING THE FEDERAL RULES OF EVIDENCE.

FEDERAL RULES OF EVIDENCE NEWS

FEDERAL PROCEDURE RULES SERVICE

FEDERAL TRIAL HANDBOOK, 2D

FORM DRAFTING CHECKLISTS: AM JUR PRACTICE GUIDE

GOVERNMENT CONTRACTS: PROCEDURES AND FORMS

HOW TO GO DIRECTLY INTO YOUR OWN COMPUTERIZED SOLO PRACTICE WITHOUT MISSING A MEAL (OR A BYTE)

JONES ON EVIDENCE, CIVIL AND CRIMINAL, 7TH

LITIGATION CHECKISTS: AM JUR PRACTICE GUIDE

MEDICAL LIBRARY, LAWYERS EDITION

MEDICAL MALPRACTICE — ALR CASES AND ANNOTATIONS

MODERN APPELLATE PRACTICE: FEDERAL AND STATE CIVIL APPEALS

MODERN CONSTITUTIONAL LAW

NEGOTIATION AND SETTLEMENT

PATTERN DEPOSITION CHECKLISTS, 2D

QUALITY OF LIFE DAMAGES: CRITICAL ISSUES AND PROOFS

SHEPARD'S CITATIONS FOR ALR

SUCCESSFUL TECHNIQUES FOR CIVIL TRIALS, 2D

STORIES ET CETERA — A COUNTRY LAWYER LOOKS AT LIFE AND THE LAW

SUMMARY OF AMERICAN LAW

THE TRIAL LAWYER'S BOOK: PREPARING AND WINNING CASES

TRIAL PRACTICE CHECKLISTS

2000 CLASSIC LEGAL QUOTATIONS

WILLISTON ON CONTRACTS, 3D AND 4TH

FEDERAL RULES OF EVIDENCE DIGEST: ORGANIZES HEADNOTES FOR THE DECISIONS REPORTED IN FEDERAL RULES OF EVIDENCE SERVICE ACCORDING TO THE NUMBERING SYSTEM OF THE FEDERAL RULES OF EVIDENCE.

ADMINISTRATIVE LAW: PRACTICE AND PROCEDURE

AGE DISCRIMINATION: CRITICAL ISSUES AND PROOFS

ALR CRITICAL ISSUES: DRUNK DRIVING PROSECUTIONS

ALR CRITICAL ISSUES: FREEDOM OF INFORMATION ACTS

ALR CRITICAL ISSUES: TRADEMARKS

ALR CRITICAL ISSUES: WRONGFUL DEATH

AMERICANS WITH DISABILITIES: PRACTICE AND COMPLIANCE MANUAL

ATTORNEYS' FEES

BALLENTINE'S LAW DICTIONARY

CONSTITUTIONAL LAW DESKBOOK

CONSUMER AND BORROWER PROTECTION: AM JUR PRACTICE GUIDE

CONSUMER CREDIT: ALR ANNOTATIONS

DAMAGES: ALR ANNOTATIONS

EMPLOYEE DISMISSAL: CRITICAL ISSUES AND PROOFS

ENVIRONMENTAL LAW: ALR ANNOTATIONS

EXPERT WITNESS CHECKLISTS

EXPERT WITNESSES IN CIVIL TRIALS

FORFEITURES: ALR ANNOTATIONS

FEDERAL LOCAL COURT RULES

FEDERAL LOCAL COURT FORMS

FEDERAL CRIMINAL LAW AND PROCEDURE: ALR ANNOTATIONS

FEDERAL EVIDENCE

FEDERAL LITIGATION DESK SET: FORMS AND ANALYSIS

CONTENTS

PREFACE

It was the French novelist Gustave Flaubert who first coined the phrase *le mot juste,* describing every writer's yearning for that perfect word to describe exactly his or her thoughts and feelings. The Irish poet W. B. Yeats further describes the craft of writing in "Adam's Curse" (1902):

> A line will take us hours maybe;
> Yet if it does not seem a moment's thought,
> Our stitching and unstitching has been naught.

The right word, like the right line of poetry, therefore, feels natural in its exactness; it communicates with perfection.

Ballentine's Thesaurus for Legal Research & Writing is designed to help lawyers and paralegals write and reason effectively by providing a thesaurus aimed at the vocabulary used in legal work. Whether you are writing a memo, drafting a brief, presenting a proposal, accessing legal databases, using computerized legal research, or presenting your ideas to a jury, the way you express yourself often determines the result you will achieve. Like writers, lawyers, paralegals, and law students are continually in search of *le mot juste*— just the right word to communicate accurately, effectively, and persuasively.

This thorough, easy-to-use thesaurus is simply formatted and presented to make an efficient tool in the writing and editing process. Key words are presented alphabetically; for each key word, you will find the word's pronunciation and part of speech, followed by synonyms and, in come cases, sample usages and antonyms. If a word has more than one distinct meaning, synonyms for each meaning are separated by a semicolon.

Note that the pronunciations supplied here are intended only as a general guide for normal use. Regional variations and alternate pronunciations abound. Readers are cautioned that the syllabifications and pronunciations in this thesaurus are by no means authoritative; they are merely a general guide for everyday usage.

The synonyms offered differ from each other and from the key word in shading, tone, and usage. This reflects the flexibility and social context of language, and it is up to the writer to be sensitive to the nuances of meaning that should—or should not—be used to express a certain idea. Of course,

countless other synonyms exist for each key word, each with its own flavor, import, and weight. No such collection could hope to be exhaustive, but this thesaurus aims to present a good selection of common, useful, and varied words for use at the reader's discretion, as his or her need dictates. Choosing the right word, therefore, is not merely a matter of scientific precision but also an exercise of aesthetic appreciation. By using words effectively, you will discover options in language that will improve and enhance your communication.

The four included appendixes join with the thesaurus to make this book an invaluable aid to legal research and writing. Appendix A gives you a copy of the Constitution, obviously an essential reference document in the law because it is the ultimate authority upon which the law is based. Appendix B is a user-friendly overview of legal research written by Terri Lyndall, which will help you gain an understanding of the general process of legal research. Appendix C, *The Living Law,* is an indispensible aid to legal research. It contains a total introduction to the entire range of legal research materials published by Lawyers Coop. In addition to showing you how to use the research materials, this appendix also provides sample annotated pages from the research materials, thus giving you a thorough introduction to the materials and procedures necessary to perform legal research. Appendix D is a necessary tool for legal writing, *The University of Chicago Manual of Legal Citation.* This important volume for legal writers provides a thorough discussion of the rules and protocols governing the use of citations in legal writing. Taken together, *Ballentine's Thesaurus for Legal Research & Writing, The Living Law,* and *The University of Chicago Manual of Legal Citation* comprise an indispensable tool for legal research and writing.

Researching, writing, editing, and typing a thesaurus is a major project, and such an undertaking would not have been possible without the assistance of many people. Janiet Walker did an outstanding job of typing the manuscript, making sense and clarity of sometimes ragged drafts. Her promptness, efficiency, and positive attitude are greatly appreciated. I also appreciate the fine research and editing performed by the following paralegals, whose contribution to this project was invaluable: John Ritondo, Jo-Ann Cowan, Beth Geeslin, Sherrie Polson, Robin Tucker, Leigh Hayes, Carrie Gray, and Kathryn Hadden. Thank you all very much.

I cannot present a book of words without acknowledging those of my teachers whose love of words has inspired me. Alexander's mastery of words and language is a continuing inspiration. Michael Harper and Duncan Smith of Brown University taught me to love words, to feel their heart and their power. Law professors Paul Milich, James Bross, Mark Kadish, Steve Kaminshine, and Patrick Wiseman all showed great insight into the language of the law and how it shapes legal thinking. And I cannot think of words without remembering long hours with Steve Strasser, as we struggled to learn the lessons of "Lethal" Ethel Kapeloric, wordmeister extraordinaire.

My family, as usual, has been completely supportive of my work. Special thanks and appreciation are due my wife, Kim, and my sons, Nicky and Aaron. My publishing family at Delmar, expecially my managing editor, Jay Whitney, his delightful assistant, Glenna Stanfield, and my copyeditor, Brooke Graves, has been wonderful in every way. My DeVry family has given me valued support and uncommon freedom, and I am especially grateful to Ron Bush, Ray Bass, and Nick Vitterite for their enlightened leadership. My family at the National Center for Paralegal Training (NCPT) in Atlanta—Matt Cornick, Jennifer John, and Jerry Nelms—has been extremely supportive and encouraging. I appreciate the support of my sister, Vicki Sendele, and her family, Rick and Brooke, and my stepparents, William J. Klein and Joan L. Lynton. Thanks also to Sherrie, Bob, Gail, Maggie, and the gang at Mick's in Decatur. I also appreciate, more than you know, my "small circle of friends": Jerry, Dennis and Martha, Bob, Felix, Dr. Phil, Terri and Mike, Max, Cory, Paul, and Rick.

Finally, to my parents—my mother, Joan S. Lynton, and my father, Julian E. Lynton, who long ago pegged me as "Last Word Lynton"—I offer not only the last word but all the thousands of words preceding it. Having been told I "always had to have the last word," it is at last gratifying to have not only the last word (*zoom*, by the way) but the first word (*abaction*), as well as all the words in between. Thanks, Mom and Dad, for the excellent foundation (support, background, base, groundwork, infrastructure) you gave me.

abaction [ab · *ak* · shen] *n.* carrying away, larceny, robbery, stealing.

abandon [a · *ban* · den] *v.* give up, surrender, desert, quit, repudiate, abnegate, forsake, leave. *Ant.* maintain.

abandon [a · *ban* · den] *n.* wantonness, lawlessness ("wanton abandon").

abandonment [a · *ban* · den · ment] *n.* desertion, relinquishment, disavowal, renunciation, rejection, disownment, forsaking, yielding, withdrawal.

abatable [a · *bate* · abl] *adj.* impermanent, modifiable, revocable, destructive.

abate [a · *bate*] *v.* quash, decrease, reduce, beat down, diminish, do away with, eliminate, terminate, curtail, modify.

abatement [a · *bate* · ment] *n.* termination, eradication, curtailment, extermination, cessation ("abatement of a nuisance"); reduction, lessening, diminution, lowering, mitigation ("tax abatement").

abbrochment [a · *broach* · ment] *n.* stifling, forestalling, monopolizing.

abdicate [*ab* · di · kate] *v.* forsake, give up, renounce, throw off, disown, relinquish, cede ("The government has abdicated its taxing power").

abdication [ab · di · *kay* · shen] *n.* renunciation, resignation, abandonment, cessation, abjuration, relinquishment.

abduct [ab · *dukt*] *v.* kidnap, seize, shanghai, capture, steal.

abduction [ab · *duk* · shen] *n.* kidnapping, seizure, capture, arrogation.

aberemurder [*ay* · bur · mer · der] *n.* assassination, killing, homicide, extermination.

abet [a · *bet*] *v.* aid, assist, facilitate, spur, urge, exhort, foment, sustain, conspire.

abettor [a · *bet* · er] *n.* accessory, accomplice, advocate, prompter, instigator, partner, collaborator.

abeyance [a · *bay* · ense] *n.* latency, inaction, deadlock, repose, suspension, remission, quiescence ("held in abeyance").

abide [a · *bide*] *v.* obey, comply with, accept, observe, submit to ("abide by the decision of the court"); tolerate, endure, suffer ("He could not abide the new owner").

ability [a · *bil* · it · ee] *n.* capability, skill, capacity, faculty, acumen, proficiency, talent. *Ant.* limitation, incompetency, incompetence, ignorance.

abjudicate [ab · *joo* · di · kate] *v.* deprive, remove.

abjuration [ab · joo · *ray* · shen] *n.* renunciation, forswearing, abandonment, relinquishment, rejection, recantation.

A

abjure [ab · *joor*] *v.* retract, disclaim, renounce, repudiate. *Ant.* assert, inject, put forth.

able [*ay* · bul] *adj.* competent, proficient, capable, qualified. *Ant.* incompetent.

abnegate [*ab* · ne · gate] *v.* give up, surrender, renounce.

abnormal [ab · *nor* · mal] *adj.* uncommon, peculiar, odd, unnatural, idiosyncratic. *Ant.* regular, common, normal.

abode [a · *bode*] *n.* dwelling, residence, home, domicile, homestead ("usual place of abode").

abolish [a · *bol* · ish] *v.* repeal, recall, revoke, cancel, eliminate, erase, obliterate, dissolve. *Ant.* establish, confirm, legalize.

abolition [ab · o · *lish* · en] *n.* negation, nullification, cancellation, rescission, retraction, eradication, disestablishment. *Ant.* establishment, confirmation

aboriginal [ab · o · *rij* · in · el] *adj.* native, prehistoric, primeval, primal, indigenous, first, original. *Ant.* foreign, acquired, alien.

abort [a · *bort*] *v.* sever, miscarry, stop, terminate. *Ant.* continue, save.

abortion [a · *bore* · shen] *n.* destruction, miscarriage, aborticide, termination ("Abortion is a woman's choice"); failure, frustration, disaster, blunder ("the committees' work was an abortion").

about [a · *bout*] *adv.* approximately, nearly.

about [a · *bout*] *prep.* relating to, concerning, involving. *Ant.* exactly, precisely.

abridge [a · *brij*] *v.* reduce, cut down, curtail, condense, shorten, edit, cut ("The Constitution states that Congress shall make no law abridging freedom of speech"). *Ant.* increase, expand, lengthen.

abridgment [a · *brij* · ment] *n.* reduction, summary, synopsis, abstract, digest.

abrogate [*ab* · roh · gate] *v.* cancel, repeal, make void, annul, revoke, nullify ("The new statute abrogates most of the existing law on this subject"). *Ant.* ratify, establish, invoke, support.

abrogation [ab · roh · *gay* · shen] *n.* repeal, annulment, termination, rescission.

abscond [ab · *skond*] *v.* leave, hide, conceal, flee, retreat, escape, vanish, bolt, depart. *Ant.* remain, stay.

absence [ab · *sense*] *n.* nonpresence, withdrawal, avoidance, defection, nonappearance.

absenteeism [ab · sen · *tee* · izm] *n.* absence, nonpresence, nonappearance, truancy.

absolute [*ab* · so · loot] *adj.* unrestricted, unconditional, complete, unrestrained, entire, total, unimpeded ("absolute privilege").

absolution [*ab* · so · *loo* · shen] *n.* exoneration, discharge, acquittal, release, vindication, liberation, clearance.

absolve [ab · *zolv*] *v.* acquit, exculpate, exonerate, vindicate, free, liberate.

absorbed [ab · *zorbd*] *adv.* engaged, involved, occupied ("He was so absorbed in his work that he did not hear the telephone ring").

abstain [ab · *stane*] *v.* refrain, forbear, hold back, resist, forgo, refuse, spurn, decline.

abstention [ab · *sten* · shun] *n.* avoidance, nonparticipation, evasion, inaction.

abstract [*ab* · strakt] *adj.* theoretical, impractical, conceptual

abstract [*ab* · strakt] *n.* summary, synopsis, extract, analysis.

abstract [*ab* · strakt] *v.* steal, take away, detach, disengage, purloin.

abstraction [ab · *strak* · shen] *n.* taking, removal, larceny, theft ("the abstraction of money"); generalization, theory, concept, notion, hypothesis ("her bizarre abstraction").

A

abuse [a · *buze*] *v.* injure, damage, maltreat, molest, debase, misuse, mishandle.

abuse [a · *byooss*] *n.* mistreatment, disrespect, debasement, damage, harm, impairment, crime, molestation, injury. *Ant.* aid, respect, assist.

abut [a · *but*] *v.* end at, border on, adjoin, touch against, neighbor, conjoin ("This is the point at which the lot abuts the highway").

abutment [a · *but* · ment] *n.* connection, attachment, junction; support, buttress, prop.

academic [ak · e · *dem* · ik] *adj.* collegiate, learned, scholarly; abstract, theoretical, moot, hypothetical ("an academic question").

accede [ak · *seed*] *v.* give consent, assent, concede, concur, acquiesce; attain, succeed to, inherit, assume ("to accede to a position"). *Ant.* decline.

accelerate [ak · *sel* · e · rayt] *v.* hasten, rush, quicken, precipitate, stimulate. *Ant.* delay.

acceleration [ak · *sel* · er · ray · shun] *n.* expedition, quickening, hastening ("acceleration of payment").

accept [ak · *sept*] *v.* receive, gain, obtain, secure; assent to, admit, welcome, approve, adopt, ratify. *Ant.* reject, deny.

acceptance [ak · *sep* · tense] *n.* acquisition, reception, adoption, compliance, consent, acknowledgment. *Ant.* rejection, opposition.

access [*ak* · sess] *n.* opportunity, accessibility, availability ("access to the president"); entry, opening, ingress ("access to the records").

accession [ak · *sesh* · en] *n.* accretion, addition, enlargement; assumption, induction, succession; accedence, assent, concurrence.

accessory [ak · *sess* · e · ree] *n.* accomplice, abettor, conspirator, collaborator, consort, assistant ("accessory after the fact"); supplement, attachment, addition, extension.

accident [*ak* · se · dent] *n.* casualty, collision, misadventure, happenstance; mishap, calamity, fortuity.

accidental [*ak* · se · den · tul] *adj.* fortuitous, coincidental, inadvertent, unexpected, unintended. *Ant.* planned.

acclamation [ak · la · *may* · shen] *n.* approval, acclaim, ovation, plaudits, approbation.

accommodate [a · *kom* · o · date] *v.* oblige, aid, supply, shelter, assist, adjust, coordinate, integrate, adapt, acclimate.

accommodation [a · kom · o · *day* · shen] *n.* adaptation, compliance, conformity, modification; lodging, shelter; kindness, assistance.

accomplice [a · *kom* · pliss] *n.* accessory, abettor, conspirator, collaborator, partner, associate.

accord [a · *kord*] *v.* coincide with, conform with, agree with, ("That accords with what I have been told"); grant, confer, give ("We must accord the instructor the respect she is due").

accord [a · *kord*] *n.* agreement, settlement, adjustment, concurrence.

accost [a · *kost*] *v.* assail, approach, assault, attack, ambush.

account [a · *kount*] *n.* ledger, register, report, computation ("He audited the firm's accounts"); version, story, chronological explanation, narrative ("an account of the trial").

accountable [a · *kount* · a · bul] *adj.* responsible, liable, answerable, obligated, beholden, duty-bound.

accountant [a · *kount* · ant] *n.* auditor, bookkeeper, controller, actuary, analyst, CPA.

A

accounting [a · *kount* · ing] *n.* statement, report, description ("The partner received an accounting from an independent auditor").

accredit [a · *kre* · dit] *v.* license, authorize, certify, sanction ("accredit a school"); attribute, credit, assign, ascribe ("accredit the idea to Alexander").

accretion [a · *kree* · shen] *n.* accumulation, augmentation, increase; fusion, conference, consolidation.

accrual [a · *krew* · el] *n.* increase, expansion, accumulation, growth, development.

accrue [a · *krew*] *v.* increase, collect, amass, enlarge, heighten, multiply; flow, follow, proceed, acquire, result from. *Ant.* decrease, stagnate.

accumulate [a · *kyoo* · myoo · late] *v.* gather, amass, accrue, assemble, combine, increase. *Ant.* separate.

accurate [*ak* · yoo · ret] *adj.* precise, correct, reliable, faultless.

accusation [ak · yoo · *zay* · shen] *n.* charge, allegation, gravamen, indictment, complaint, aspersion, arraignment. *Ant.* exoneration.

accuse [a · *kuze*] *v.* charge, blame, attack, inculpate, indict, implicate.

accused [a · *kyoozd*] *n.* suspect, defendant, respondent.

acknowledge [ak · *now* · lej] *v.* certify, authenticate, endorse, attest to ("acknowledge the deed"); recognize, respond to, notice ("acknowledge counsel's presence").

acknowledgment [ak · *naw* · lej · ment] *n.* confirmation, admission, ratification, declaration, endorsement ("acknowledgment of paternity"); recognition, acceptance, assent, acquiescence ("acknowledgment of liability").

acquire [a · *kwire*] *v.* derive, gain, reap; assume, attain, obtain.

acquisition [ak · wi · *zish* · en] *n.* procurement, attainment, purchase, receipt, takeover.

acquit [a · *kwit*] *v.* absolve, exculpate, exonerate, liberate, release ("He was acquitted of the charge"); discharge, exempt, excuse ("acquitted of further responsibility").

acquittal [a · *kwit* · el] *n.* exoneration, clearance, dismissal, discharge, release.

acquittance [a · *kwit* · ense] *n.* release, discharge.

act *v.* perform, do, behave, enact, execute, transact.

act *n.* law, statute, bill, ordinance, ruling, determination, code, rule ("a legislative act"); pretense, sham, fraud ("We saw through his act"); performance.

acting [*ak* · ting] *adj.* interim, substitute, temporary, transient, provisional ("an acting director").

action [*ak* · shen] *n.* legal proceeding, lawsuit, dispute, litigation ("an action for divorce"); conduct, behavior, activity, performance, deed ("an unnecessary action").

actionable [*ak* · shen · a · bul] *adj.* justifiable, suable, litigable, remediable, chargeable.

active [*ak* · tiv] *adj.* functioning, performing, operational, engaged ("an active manager"). *Ant.* uninvolved, silent.

actual [*ak* · chew · el] *adj.* real, verifiable, objective, legitimate, undeniable.

acute [a · *kyoot*] *adj.* keen, sharp, penetrating, piercing, fine, discerning.

addicted [*a* · dik · ted] *adv.* dependent, habituated, attached, obsessed.

additional [a · *dish* · en · el] *adj.* extra, supplementary, further, increased ("the judge's additional instructions").

adduce [a · *dyooss*] *v.* present, offer, introduce, allege, declare, produce ("The prosecutor adduced evidence of the defendant's guilt").

adeem [a · *deem*] *v.* take away, revoke, withdraw, cancel, annul.

A

ademption [a · *demp* · shen] *n.* retraction, nullification, repudiation, recall, negation.

adequate [*ad* · e · kwet] *adj.* sufficient, suitable, satisfactory, ample, fitting, fair, commensurate ("adequate remedy").

adhere [ad · *here*] *v.* attach, cling, secure, join; comply, confirm, follow, espouse; persevere, maintain, sustain.

adhesion [ad · *hee* · zhun] *n.* fusion, contact, cohesiveness; allegiance, loyalty, devotion, fealty, support, fidelity.

adjacent [a · *jay* · sent] *adj.* adjoining, touching, contiguous, bordering, coterminous.

adjoin [ad · *join*] *v.* border, connect, neighbor, meet, touch.

adjoining [a · *join* · ing] *adj.* touching, contiguous, abutting, neighboring, joined ("Your lot and mine are not adjoining because they are separated by the highway").

adjourn [a · *jern*] *v.* postpone, suspend, defer, delay, recess, discontinue.

adjournment [a · *jern* · ment] *n.* suspension, discontinuation, deferral, postponement, recess, cessation.

adjudicate [a · *joo* · di · kate] *v.* decide, sentence, adjudge, decree, settle, arbitrate, decide, mediate.

adjudication [a · joo · di · *kay* · shen] *n.* decision, ruling, holding, disposition, pronouncement, verdict, judgment.

adjunct [*ad* · junkt] *adj.* corollary, supplemental, auxiliary.

adjure [a · *joor*] *v.* entreat, command, request, plead, aver.

adjust [a · *just*] *v.* correct, rectify, accord ("Our account has been adjusted"); adapt, accommodate, conform ("adjusted to the new circumstances").

adjuster [a · *just* · er] *n.* reconciler, arbitrator, intermediary, intervenor, mediator.

adjustment [a · *just* · ment] *n.* agreement, compensation, settlement ("acceptable adjustment"); adaptation, orientation, acclimatization ("His adjustment to the higher altitude was quick").

adjutant [*ad* · ju · tant] *n.* assistant, aide, auxiliary.

admeasurement [ad · *mezh* · er · ment] *n.* assignment, apportionment, partition, division.

administer [ad · *min* · is · ter] *v.* manage, supervise, oversee, steer, operate, take charge; give, supply, furnish, bestow, offer, extend ("administer an oath").

administration [ad · min · is · *tray* · shen] *n.* application, supplying ("the administration of justice"); government, governing authority, leadership, regime, presidency, bureaucracy ("The public does not support the fiscal policies of this administration").

administrative [ad · *min* · iss · tray · tiv] *adj.* regulatory, organizational, governmental, supervisory, ministerial, supporting.

administrator [ad · *min* · iss · tray · ter] *n.* representative, executor, trustee ("the estate's administrator"); manager, supervisor, director, facilitator, leader ("the administrator of the department").

admissible [ad · *miss* · uh · bul] *adj.* allowable, acceptable, just, fair, permissible, sanctioned, unobjectionable, proper. *Ant.* inadmissible.

admission [ad · *mish* · en] *n.* confession, acknowledgment, affirmation, declaration, disclosure ("his admission of guilt"); admittance, access, passage ("admission to the bar").

admit [ad · *mit*] *v.* accept, affirm, confirm, agree ("admit fault"); allow, induct, open, initiate ("admit into practice").

A

admonish [ad · *mon* · ish] *v.* advise, counsel, enjoin, instruct, recommend; warn, prewarn, forewarn, caution, reprehend.

adolescent [*ad* · o · less · ent] *n.* junior, juvenile, teenager, youth, youngster.

adopt [a · *dopt*] *v.* choose, foster, raise ("adopt a child"); accept, affirm, assent, endorse, embrace, assume ("adopt an inconsistent position").

adoption [a · *dop* · shen] *n.* acceptance, embracement, approval, assumption ("their adoption of a hostile stance"); fostering, fosterage, raising ("adoption of the homeless child").

adulteration [a · dul · ter · *ay* · shen] *n.* alteration, debasement, contamination, impurification, corruption ("adulteration of food products").

adultery [a · *dul* · ter · ee] *n.* infidelity, affair, unfaithfulness, cuckoldry.

advance [ad · *vanse*] *n.* loan, deposit, down payment, retainer ("a cash advance"); improvement, progress, development, enrichment ("an advance in the field"); promotion, elevation ("her advance into management").

advancement [ad · *vanse* · ment] *n.* improvement, development, progression, evolution. *Ant.* deterioration, stagnation.

adventure [ad · *ven* · choor] *n.* challenge, undertaking, experience, happening, event, venture.

adversary [*ad* · ver · sair · ee] *n.* opponent, enemy, competitor, foe, challenger, litigant, opposing party, adverse party.

adverse [ad · *verse*] *adj.* antagonistic, opposing, conflicting, antipathetic, counter, antithetical, contrary ("an adverse party"); unfavorable, destructive, harmful ("adverse circumstances").

advice [ad · *vice*] *n.* view, opinion, suggestion, counsel, guidance, recommendation, input ("a lawyer's advice to the client").

advise [ad · *vize*] *v.* counsel, commend, urge, recommend, encourage, suggest; inform, notify, update.

advisement [ad · *vize* · ment] *n.* consideration, deliberation ("take the matter under advisement").

adviser [ad · *vize* · er] *n.* confidante, counselor, consultant, expert, mentor.

advisory [ad · *vize* · e · ree] *adj.* informative, suggestive, recommending, advising ("an advisory opinion").

advocacy [*ad* · vo · ke · see] *n.* support, advancement, representation, defense, backing, endorsement, espousal.

advocate [*ad* · vo · kate] *v.* argue, plead, espouse, advance, urge.

advocate [*ad* · vo · ket] *n.* attorney, supporter, representative, adviser, counsel.

affair [a · *fare*] *n.* matter, concern, activity, transaction, lawsuit, business.

affect [a · *fekt*] *v.* act upon, influence, alter, stir, impact ("The rain always affects my mood"); change, weaken ("Alcohol seriously affects my judgment"); put on airs, imitate, pretend, fake, arrogate ("He always affects an English accent when he visits London").

affect [af · *ekt*] *n.* feeling, mood ("Dr. Jacobs is concerned about his patient's bizarre affect"). *Ant.* cognition.

affected [a · *fek* · ted] *adj.* fake, feigned, counterfeit, pompous, artificial ("affected mannerisms").

affiant [a · *fie* · ent] *n.* deponent.

affidavit [a · fi · *day* · vit] *n.* affirmation, oath, statement, testimony, avowal, averment, declaration, sworn statement.

affiliate [a · *fil* · ee · ate] *v.* join, ally, combine, connect, associate ("affiliate with a lodge").

affiliate [a · *fil* · ee · et] *n.* branch, offshoot, partner ("The Smith Company is an affiliate of the Jones Corporation").

affiliation [a · fil · ee · *ay* · shen] *n.* association, joining, merging, partnership, relationship ("His affiliation with mobsters hurt his credibility as a witness"); kinship, family, heredity.

affinity [a · *fin* · i · tee] *n.* kinship, lineage, propinquity, heritage ("A husband is in a closer degree of affinity with his wife's brother than with his wife's cousin"); attraction, propensity, proclivity, predisposition, penchant ("her affinity for mathematics").

affirm [a · *ferm*] *v.* uphold, validate, confirm, ratify ("The decision was affirmed"); declare, assert, maintain, allege ("He affirmed his innocence").

affirmance [a · *fer* · mense] *n.* confirmation, affirmation, approval, endorsement, substantiation.

affirmation [af · er · *may* · shen] *n.* statement, oath, declaration, assertion, avowal, confirmation ("out-of-court affirmation").

affirmative [a · *fer* · me · tiv] *adj.* affirming, approving, positive, endorsing.

affix [a · *fiks*] *v.* attach, unite, append, bond, add ("to affix one's name to a deed").

afforce [a · *forss*] *v.* add, increase, strengthen.

affray [a · *fray*] *n.* fight, brawl, altercation, fracas, mêlée, disorderly conduct, breach of the peace ("the barroom affray").

affront [a · *front*] *v.* afflict, disturb, grieve, offend, scorn, slight.

aforesaid [a · *fore* · sed] *adj.* preceding, aforementioned, previously described ("the aforesaid conduct").

aforethought [a · *fore* · thawt] *adj.* previously planned, premeditated, preconceived, planned, designed, calculated, deliberate, intended ("malice aforethought").

against [a · *genst*] *prep.* versus, counter, facing, in opposition to ("against public policy").

age *n.* period, time, epoch, phase, era ("the age of litigation"); seniority, maturity, venerableness, decrepitude ("The senior partner is showing his age").

age *v.* mature, ripen, develop, mellow, decline, deteriorate.

agency [*ay* · jen · see] *n.* bureau, department, organization ("an administrative agency").

agenda [a · *jen* · da] *n.* schedule, outline, plan, diary, docket, timetable.

agent [*ay* · jent] *n.* assistant, delegate, emissary, assignee, deputy, functionary, proxy, representative.

aggravate [*ag* · re · vayt] *v.* annoy, gall, pester, provoke, irritate; increase, deepen, complicate, intensify, worsen.

aggravated [*ag* · re · vay · ted] *adj.* exacerbated, heightened, deepened, intensified, inflamed ("aggravated assault").

aggravation [ag · re · *vay* · shen] *n.* annoyance, bother, irritation; worsening, exacerbation, deepening, intensification, heightening.

aggregate [*ag* · gre · gate] *v.* accumulate, assemble, collect, gather.

aggregate [*ag* · gre · get] *n.* assemblage, collection, entirety, whole, sum.

A

aggressor [a · *gress* · er] *n.* attacker, belligerent, initiator, combatant, provocateur, invader.

aggrieved [a · *greevd*] *adj.* distressed, afflicted, harmed, injured, wronged.

agree [a · *gree*] *v.* concur, assent, acquiesce, accede, endorse ("agree to new terms"); contract, settle, bargain, compromise.

agreement [a · *gree* · ment] *n.* contract, bargain, compact, arrangement, pact; concurrence, compliance, alliance.

aid *v.* support, help, assist, promote, subsidize.

aid *n.* help, support, assistance, encouragement.

akin [a · *kin*] *adj.* alike, analogous, similar, related, connected; fraternal, kindred.

alcoholic [al · ke · *hol* · ik] *adj.* intoxicating, inebriating, brewed.

alderman [*all* · der · man] *n.* councilman, legislator.

alias [*ay* · li · es] *n.* false name, pseudonym, moniker.

alibi [*al* · i · by] *n.* defense, excuse, explanation, proof, avowal.

alien [*ale* · yen] *n.* foreigner, immigrant, outsider, stranger, visitor.

alien [*ale* · yen] *adj.* foreign, different, exotic, remote, strange, unfamiliar.

alienable [*ale* · yen · a · bul] *adj.* lawfully transferable, severable, removable.

alienate [*ale* · yen · ate] *v.* transfer, convey, assign, deed ("alienate property"); estrange, separate ("The attorney's offensive manner alienated the jury").

alimony [*al* · i · moh · nee] *n.* support, maintenance, sustenance, allowance, settlement.

alive [a · *live*] *adj.* living, existing, extant, functioning, viable; animated, eager, energetic, spirited.

allay [a · lay] *v.* calm, lessen, mollify, pacify, decrease.

allegation [al · e · *gay* · shen] *n.* assertion, accusation, avowal, claim, charge.

allege [a · *lej*] *v.* declare, state, testify, assert, claim, advance, aver, cite.

alleged [a · *lej* · ed] *adj.* claimed, announced, asserted, propounded ("the alleged murderer").

allegiance [a · *leej* · ence] *n.* dedication, devotion, fealty, fidelity, homage, obedience.

allocation [al · o · *kay* · shen] *n.* distribution, allowance, allotment, assignment, share ("In distributing the income that will be earned by your estate, it is important that each heir's allocation be appropriate").

allonge [a · *lonj*] *n.* appendix, rider, addendum.

allotment [a · *lot* · ment] *n.* division, distribution, share, portion, quota, part.

allow [a · *low*] *v.* approve, authorize, accept, acquiesce ("The insurance company allowed my claim"); permit, consent to ("He was allowed to go home on a weekend pass").

allowance [a · *low* · ense] *n.* allotment, share, stipend, payment, allocation, recompense, pay, remittance.

allowed [a · *lowd*] *adj.* accepted, legal, lawful, rightful, authorized, legitimate.

alluvion [a · *loo* · vee · en] *n.* accretion, accumulation. *Ant.* erosion.

alter [*al* · ter] *v.* adjust, modify, vary, transform, rearrange, deviate.

alter ego [*all* · ter *ee* · go] *n.* other self, second self, double, stand-in, counterpart, twin.

alteration [all · ter · *ay* · shen] *n.* change, modification, conversion, reshaping, shift, switch, correction.

alternate [*all* · ter · net] *n.* backup, replacement, surrogate ("alternate juror").

alternate [*all* · ter · nayt] *v.* rotate, vary, exchange, shift, alter.

alternative [all · *ter* · ne · tiv] *n.* choice, opportunity, option, selection ("She chose the easier alternative").

alternative [all · *ter* · ne · tiv] *adj.* different, alternate, varying ("alternative lifestyle").

amalgamation [a · mal · ga · *may* · shen] *n.* consolidation, coalescence, commingling, fusion, integration, incorporation.

ambassador [am · *bass* · e · dor] *n.* delegate, emissary, consul.

ambiguity [am · bi · *gyoo* · i · tee] *n.* uncertainty, equivocation, ambivalence, obscurity, indefiniteness, incertitude, vagueness. *Ant.* clarity, lucidity.

ambiguous [am · *big* · yoo · us] *adj.* unclear, enigmatic, vague, uncertain, indefinite.

ambit [*am* · bit] *n.* boundary, limit, perimeter, extent, confiner, jurisdiction.

ambulatory [*am* · byoo · le · tore · ee] *adj.* changeable, revocable ("an ambulatory will"); walking, moving, roving, peripatetic ("The hospital patient was ambulatory").

ambush [*am* · bush] *v.* assail, attack, snare, trap.

ameliorate [a · *meel* · e · orate] *v.* improve, allay, better, enhance, palliate, mitigate.

amenable [a · *men* · ibl] *adj.* pliable, accessible, pliant, flexible, reasonable, yielding.

amend [a · *mend*] *v.* correct, remedy, adjust, change, revise, alter, modify.

amendment [a · *mend* · ment] *n.* correction, revision, betterment, reworking ("amendment of a document"); statute, act, measure, clause; attachment, appendix, addendum.

amercement [a · *merse* · ment] *n.* fine, penalty, punishment, chastisement.

amicable [*am* · i · kabl] *adj.* friendly, agreeing, cordial, civil, social, amiable, kind, understanding, like-minded.

ammunition [am · mu · *nish* · en] *n.* arms, weapons, munitions, defense.

amnesty [*am* · nes · tee] *n.* clemency, pardon, reprieve, dispensation, absolution.

amortize [*am* · er · tize] *v.* pay off, reduce, discharge; depreciate, write off.

amotion [a · *moh* · shen] *n.* removal, eviction, ouster ("the amotion of a tenant").

amount [a · *mount*] *n.* total, whole, aggregate, bulk, quantity, sum.

analogous [a · *nal* · e · gus] *adj.* similar, corresponding, comparable, akin ("an analogous case").

analysis [a · *nal* · uh · sis] *n.* critique, investigation, scrutiny, inquiry, examination.

analytical [an · e · *lit* · i · kel] *adj.* inquiring, interpretive, critical, judicious, questioning.

anarchist [*an* · er · kist] *n.* agitator, insurgent, rebel, revolutionary.

anarchy [*an* · er · kee] *n.* lawlessness, chaos, confusion, disorder, disorganization.

ancient [*ane* · shent] *adj.* old, aged, antiquated, dated, outmoded, venerable ("ancient civilization").

ancillary [*an* · sih · la · ree] *adj.* subordinate, auxiliary, secondary, dependent, collateral ("ancillary jurisdiction").

animal [*an* · i · mel] *adj.* coarse, vulgar, beastly, brutish.

annex [an · *eks*] *v.* attach, join, affix, bind, connect, append ("Please annex the defense to the application"); seize, take, appropriate, arrogate ("Annex the park").

annex [*an* · eks] *n.* extension, wing, addition, attachment.

A

annexation [an·ek·*say*·shen] *n.* takeover, appropriation, acquisition ("the annexation of territory"); merger, attachment, joining, addition.

annotate [*an*·o·tayte] *v.* comment, explain, note, elucidate, expound.

annotation [an·o·*tay*·shen] *n.* comment, commentary, explanation, exegesis, explication, footnote.

annoy [a·*noy*] *v.* irritate, offend, displease, grate, harass, upset, torment.

annuity [a·*nyoo*·i·tee] *n.* payment, income, pension, subsidy, stipend, allotment.

annul [a·*nul*] *v.* erase, nullify, wipe out, make void, expunge, cancel, revoke, abrogate.

annulment [a·*nul*·ment] *n.* cancellation, abrogation, voiding, invalidation, repeal, rescission, dissolution, nullification.

anonymous [a·*non*·i·mus] *adj.* unnamed, unknown, nameless, unclaimed, unacknowledged.

answer [*an*·ser] *v.* reply, respond, defend, controvert ("He answered the plaintiff's complaint by denying the allegations"); assume liability for, be obligated for ("I will answer for your debt to the bank").

answer [*an*·ser] *n.* defense, reply, denial, rebuttal, refutation, counterclaim ("file an answer to a complaint").

answerable [*an*·ser·abl] *adj.* liable, accountable.

antagonize [an·*tag*·o·nize] *v.* offend, embitter, estrange, displease, irritate, insult.

antecedent [an·te·*see*·dent] *n.* previous, preexisting, earlier.

antedate [*an*·te·date] *v.* predate, backdate.

antenuptial [an·te·*nup*·shel] *adj.* prenuptial, premarital.

anticipate [an·*tiss*·i·pate] *v.* contemplate, look forward to, await, envision ("anticipate the decision"); foresee, preconceive, augur, predict ("anticipate the problem").

anticipation [an·tiss·i·*pay*·shen] *n.* apprehension, anxiety, fear, anguish, dread ("He approached the jury with great anticipation").

apex [*ay*·peks] *n.* high point, pinnacle, climax, peak, zenith, summit, apogee, acme, crest, culmination. *Ant.* nadir.

apparent [a·*par*·ent] *adj.* clear, evident, obvious, distinct, likely, discernible.

appeal [a·*peel*] *n.* allure, pleasingness, attraction ("The witness had appeal"); petition, review, reexamination ("his appeal to a higher court").

appeal [a·*peel*] *v.* implore, beg, beseech, plead ("She appealed for assistance").

appear [a·*peer*] *v.* spring, surface, attend, arrive, come in, materialize ("appear in court").

appearance [a·*peer*·ense] *n.* actualization, entrance, exhibition, materialization, emergence ("The appearance of his attorney was timely"); form, bearing, look, demeanor ("the witness's calm appearance").

appellant [a·*pel*·ant] *n.* appealer, litigant, petitioner, party.

appellee [a·pel·*ee*] *n.* respondent, defendant.

append [a·*pend*] *v.* adjoin, annex, fasten, stack on, attach.

appendage [a·*pen*·dej] *n.* addition, supplement, extremity, member.

appendix [a·*pen*·diks] *n.* appendage, codicil, rider, attachment, insertion, pocket part.

appertain [a·per·*tane*] *v.* belong, apply, be proper, refer, pertain.

applicable [ap · lik · ebl] *adj.* appropriate, applicative, relevant, befitting, germane, fit, fitting, apt, befitting.

applicant [ap · li · kent] *n.* candidate, inquirer, petitioner, aspirer, seeker, suitor.

application [ap · li · *kay* · shun] *n.* proposal, request, submission, bid, motion.

apply [a · *ply*] *v.* use, utilize, exercise, employ; request, petition, pray, seek.

appoint [a · *point*] *v.* assign responsibility, furnish, allot, choose, commission.

appointee [a · poin · *tee*] *n.* beneficiary, deputy, representative, agent, delegate.

appointment [a · *point* · ment] *n.* authorization, certification, choice, designation, empowerment.

apportionment [a · *pore* · shen · ment] *n.* allocation, distribution, parceling out, administration ("apportionment of representatives").

appraisal [a · *pray* · zel] *n.* estimation, assessment, opinion, valuation, appraisement.

appreciable [a · *preesh* · able] *adj.* measurable, discernable, ascertainable, perceptible, recognizable, substantive.

appreciate [a · *pree* · she · ate] *v.* perceive, comprehend, understand ("I appreciate your point"); enhance, gain, inflate, increase in worth ("The property has appreciated a great deal"); value, respect, adore, savor, treasure ("appreciate the arts").

appreciation [a · pree · she · *ay* · shen] *n.* thankfulness, sensitivity, addition, testimonial, gratitude, gain, growth, inflation; recognition, regard, awareness, enjoyment, sensitivity.

apprehend [ap · re · *hend*] *v.* arrest, capture, detain, incarcerate, confine ("The prisoner was apprehended earlier that night"); conceive, fathom, grasp, comprehend ("apprehend an idea").

apprehension [ap · re · *hen* · shen] *n.* understanding, awareness, knowledge; seizure, arrest, detention, confinement ("the apprehension of the perpetrator").

apprentice [a · *pren* · tiss] *n.* novice, intern, neophyte, pupil, starter.

apprise [a · *prize*] *v.* advise, make aware, reveal, disclose.

appropriate [a · *proh* · pree · ate] *v.* set aside, allot, assign, disburse; steal, lift, pilfer, usurp, embezzle, filch.

appropriate [a · *proh* · pree · et] *adj.* fit, suitable, deserved, apt, belonging, befitting, felicitous, desired, pertinent ("very appropriate phrase").

appropriation [a · proh · pree · *ay* · shen] *n.* set-aside, apportionment, assignment, stipulation, allocation ("appropriation of funds for education"); conversion, misappropriation, embezzlement ("the appropriation of her savings").

approval [a · *proov* · el] *n.* authorization, assent, accord, assurance, endorsement, permit, sanction, confirmation, compliance.

approximately [a · *prok* · si · met · lee] *adv.* nearly, bordering, comparatively, in the vicinity of.

appurtenance [a · *per* · te · nense] *n.* accessory, auxiliary, extension, addendum.

appurtenant [a · *per* · te · nent] *adj.* belonging, attached, subsidiary, dependent ("an appurtentant easement").

arbiter [ar · bi · ter] *n.* referee, umpire, interceder, mediator, moderator, advisor, adjudicator.

arbitrarily [ar · bi · *trare* · i · lee] *adv.* unreasonably, randomly, whimsically.

arbitrary [ar · bi · trare · ee] *adj.* capricious, unreasoned, irrational, fanciful; dictatorial, domineering, bossy.

A

arbitration [ar · bi · *tray* · shen] *n.* adjustment, compromise, mediation, determination ("Compulsory arbitration is the name for arbitration required by law").

arbitrator [*ar* · bi · tray · ter] *n.* judge, umpire, mediator, intervenor, adjudicator.

argue [*ar* · gyoo] *v.* contend, debate, altercate, bicker, wrangle, oppose, challenge. *Ant.* concede.

argument [ar · gyoo · ment] *n.* disagreement, blow-up, dispute, debate, controversy ("a heated argument"); position, statement, rebuttal ("the attorney's argument to the bench").

argumentative [ar · gyoo · *men* · te · tiv] *adj.* belligerent, controversial, quarrelsome, litigious ("an argumentative question").

arise [a · *rize*] *v.* perceive, commence, derive, emerge, ensure, originate, materialize ("When did the cause of action arise?"); stand up, ascend, rise ("arise from your desk").

aristocracy [ar · is · *tok* · re · see] *n.* elite, gentry, nobility, upper class, gentility.

arms *n.* weapons, firearms, munitions, armament.

arraign [a · *rain*] *v.* accuse, blame, charge, implicate.

arraignment [a · *rain* · ment] *n.* accusation, incrimination, formal accusal, judicial charge.

array [a · *ray*] *n.* collection, arrangement, batch, design ("an array of clothing").

array [a · *ray*] *v.* align, place, parade, systematize, group.

arrears [a · *reerz*] *n.* unpaid debts, obligations, delinquency, overdue payments ("arrears in alimony").

arrest [a · *rest*] *n.* apprehension, captivity, capture, confinement, detention, incarceration; stoppage, suspension, halt, cessation ("His arrest was of indefinite duration").

arrest [a · *rest*] *v.* apprehend, catch, capture, block, seize ("The thief was arrested"); stop, block, foil, obstruct, hinder ("arrested development").

arrogate [*ar* · o · gate] *v.* appropriate, assume, encroach, confiscate ("Under the Constitution, the president cannot arrogate to himself the power to declare war").

arson [*ar* · sen] *n.* pyromania, setting a fire, torching.

art *n.* skill, aptitude, craft, cunning, trade.

article [*ar* · tikl] *n.* item, commodity, substance; column, editorial, essay; division, part, title.

articulate [ar · *tik* · yoo · late] *v.* enunciate, speak, state, vocalize, fit together ("The speaker articulated perfectly").

articulate [ar · *tik* · yoo · let] *adj.* clear, coherent, eloquent, fluent, lucid ("the articulate argument").

artificial [ar · ti · *fi* · shel] *adj.* manmade, synthetic, manufactured ("an artificial condition"); contrived, sham, spurious, specious ("an artificial argument").

ascendant [a · *send* · ent] *n.* ancestor, forefather, forebearer, sire; superior, dominant, eminent ("an ascendant position in the company").

ascertain [as · *cer* · tane] *v.* conclude, deduce, find out, prove, verify, determine, discover.

asportation [ass · por · *tay* · shen] *n.* carrying away, moving, transfer, transmission.

assailant [a · *say* · lent] *n.* attacker, aggressor, enemy, foe, hit man.

assassination [as · *sas* · sin · a · shun] *n.* murder, killing, destruction, slaying.

assault [a · *salt*] *n.* attack, advance, strike, violation ("The assault was aggressive").

assault [a · *salt*] *v.* abuse, advance, assail, jump, set upon, bash, violate, storm ("The pedestrian assaulted the child").

assay [*ass* · ay] *n.* analysis, assessment, examination, test ("The doctor's assay wasn't promising").

assay [*ass* · ay] *v.* appraise, evaluate, weigh ("He assayed the property").

assembly [a · *sem* · blee] *n.* congregation, accumulation, band, conference, gathering, group; attachment, joining, manufacture, construction.

assent [a · *sent*] *n.* acceptance, accession, approval, concord, compliance, affirmation, accord ("The assent was welcome").

assent [a · *sent*] *v.* accede, consent, defer, embrace, conform to ("He assented to the offer").

assert [a · *sert*] *v.* insist, advance, allege, attest, proclaim, contend, state, profess.

assess [a · *sess*] *v.* evaluate, determine, size up, estimate.

assessment [a · *sess* · ment] *n.* appraisal, determination, valuation, estimation, judgment, investigation.

assessor [a · *ses* · er] *n.* charger, estimator, collector, evaluator.

assets [*ass* · ets] *n.* resource, capital, reserve, possessions, funds, money ("partnership assets").

asseveration [a · sev · uh · *ray* · shen] *n.* averment, deposition, assurance, protestation, testimony, profession.

assign [a · *sine*] *v.* allot, allow, appoint, cast, delegate, empower.

assignable [a · *sine* · abl] *adj.* conveyable, transmittable, transferable.

assignee [a · sine · *ee*] *n.* grantee, recipient, transferee, donee.

assignment [a · *sine* · ment] *n.* responsibility, task, appointment, commission, authorization.

assist [a · *sist*] *v.* aid, promote, serve, foster, help, participate.

assistant [a · *sis* · tant] *n.* clerk, helper, aide, associate, partner, collaborator, paralegal.

associate [a · *so* · see · et] *n.* partner, collaborator, assistant, helper, aide.

associate [a · *so* · see · ayt] *v.* join, bring together, synthesize ("associate these seemingly unrelated ideas); attend, combine, keep company with ("He associated with criminals").

association [a · so · see · *ay* · shen] *n.* organization, partnership, coalition, cartel, league, union ("National Association for Trial Advocacy"); relationship, connection, bond, dealings, fraternization ("her unlikely association with the complaining witness").

assume [a · *syoom*] *v.* undertake, accept, adopt ("assume responsibility"); take over, put on ("assume a new identity"); presume, expect, suppose, accept ("to assume the truth of a statement").

assumption [a · *sump* · shen] *n.* acceptance, taking on, adoption ("assumption of the risk"); belief, inference, theory, conjecture ("his assumption concerning delivery terms"); appropriation, seizure, usurpation ("assumption of power").

assurance [a · *shoor* · ens] *n.* pledge, vow, commitment, guaranty, insurance; self-confidence, self-control.

assure [a · *shoor*] *v.* encourage, console, inspire, hearten; attest, vow, indemnify, pledge, endorse.

assured [a · *shoord*] *adj.* confirmed, ensured, guaranteed.

asylum [a · *sile* · em] *n.* cover, den, haven, refuge, retreat, sanctuary.

at large *adj.* loose, unrestrained, unconfined, free ("The prisoner escaped and is now at large").

atrocity [a · *tros* · ity] *n.* abomination, wickedness, savagery, infamy, iniquity.

attach [a · *tach*] *v.* staple, adhere, bind, accompany, combine, enlist; confiscate, seize, take ("to attach property"); attribute, ascribe, impute ("attach significance to the testimony").

attached [a · *tachd*] *adj.* confiscated, garnished, secured, sequestered, seized ("attached funds"); connected ("attached garage").

attachment [a · *tach* · ment] *n.* seizure, confiscation, garnishment, dispossession; affixation, appending, securing ("the attachment of the seal on the document"); addendum, supplement, ancillary materials, supporting materials ("the attachments to the brief"); fondness, affection, loyalty, connection, affinity ("her attachment to the vice president").

attack [a · *tak*] *n.* physical assault, blitz, advance, assault, foray ("The attack was brutal").

attack [a · *tak*] *v.* assail, raid, molest, mug, hurt, overwhelm, hit.

attain [a · *tane*] *v.* achieve, accomplish, realize, earn, procure, reap

attempt [a · *tempt*] *v.* try, make effort, endeavor ("The athlete attempted the jump").

attempt [a · *tempt*] *n.* effort, exertion, fling, shot, undertaking, try ("The attempt was feeble").

attest [a · *test*] *v.* adjure, announce, assert, aver, certify, swear, support, sustain.

attestation [a · tes · *tay* · shen] *n.* endorsement, affirmation, certification, testimony, evidence ("an attestation clause").

attorn [a · *tern*] *v.* transfer, deliver, assign, convey, grant, relinquish.

attorney [a · *tern* · ee] *n.* lawyer, counselor, advocate, legal advisor, barrister, counsel, legal eagle.

auction [*awk* · shen] *n.* bargain, jam, sell-off, sale.

audit [*aw* · dit] *v.* analyze, balance, investigate, examine, monitor, probe ("The accountant audited the books").

audit [*aw* · dit] *n.* analysis, review, scrutiny, verification ("The audit is complete").

auditor [*aw* · dit · er] *n.* accountant, bookkeeper, cashier, inspector.

auspices [*au* · spi · sez] *n.* sponsorship, backing, encouragement, tutelage, management, guidance.

authentic [aw · *then* · tik] *adj.* genuine, real, accurate, actual, true, unadulterated, credible, reliable, valid, verifiable.

authenticate [aw · *then* · ti · kate] *v.* accredit, attest, certify, confirm, corroborate, legitimate.

authentication [aw · then · ti · *kay* · shen] *n.* verification, legitimation, documentation, evidence, acknowledgment, attestation.

author [*aw* · ther] *n.* producer, maker, originator, biographer, inventor, creator, planner.

authority [aw · *thaw* · ri · tee] *n.* strength, prestige, charge, domination, esteem; power, right, ability ("She had actual authority").

authorize [*aw* · ther · ize] *v.* assent, advocate, recommend, bless, vouch for, empower, confirm, legalize, sanction.

A

autocracy [aw · *tok* · re · see] *n.* absolutism, oppression, tyranny.

autograph [*aw* · to · graf] *n.* endorsement, signature, inscription, seal ("The autograph was authentic").

autograph [*aw* · to · graf] *v.* endorse, engross, inscribe ("The author autographed my copy of the book").

autonomy [aw · *tawn* · e · mee] *n.* independence, freedom, liberty, sovereignty, self-rule.

autopsy [*aw* · top · see] *n.* dissection, necrosis, pathological examination.

auxiliary [awg · *zil* · yer · ee] *n.* helper, accessory, accomplice, companion, partner, subordinate.

auxiliary [awg · *zil* · yer · ee] *adj.* dependent, complementary, collateral, ancillary ("the auxiliary documents").

avail [a · *vale*] *v.* aid, assist, help, serve; accomplish, realize, produce, cause.

aver [a · *ver*] *v.* allege, plead, assert, state.

average [*av* · er · ej] *n.* normal, mean, middle, midpoint ("The average was two"); typical, normal, commonplace, unexceptional ("an average closing statement").

average [*av* · er · ej] *v.* balance, even out, obtain the numerical mean, score, tally.

averment [a · *ver* · ment] *n.* positive statement, allegation, assertion.

avert [a · *vert*] *v.* divert, deflect, parry, prevent.

avoid [a · *voyd*] *v.* cancel, vacate; elude, shun, avert, forbear.

avoidance [a · *voy* · dense] *n.* eluding, evasion, deviation, escape, bypass, resistance, eschewal.

avouch [a · *vouch*] *v.* acknowledge, affirm, proclaim, declare.

avow [a · *vow*] *v.* state, profess, confess, claim, declare, maintain, grant.

avowal [a · *vow* · el] *n.* statement, admission, proclamation, protestation, confession.

avulsion [a · *vul* · shen] *n.* tearing away, separation by force, ripping, splitting.

award [a · *ward*] *v.* confer, grant, give, determine, donate, allot, settle, conclude ("The student was awarded a scholarship").

award [a · *ward*] *n.* decision, decree, judgment, verdict ("The award is $500").

awry [uh · *rye*] *adj.* amiss, askance, astray, off course, wrong, bad.

ax *v.* fire, discharge, terminate, remove.

axiom [*ak* · see · um] *v.* principle, belief, maxim, fundamental belief, postulate.

axiomatic [aks · ee · uh · *mat* · ik] *adj.* definite, decisive, unambiguous, doubtless, certain, sure, aphoristic.

babble [bab · bil] *n.* gibberish, gossip, jabber, muttering, drivel, ranting.

babble [bab · bil] *v.* blab, chat, gibber, gossip, yak, run on, prate, rant, rave.

back *v.* abet, advocate, endorse, finance, sustain, uphold ("If the bank requires someone to back your loan, I'll be your cosigner").

back *adj.* reverse, final, following, rear, former, overdue, past ("back pay").

bad *adj.* defective, inferior, inadequate, below standard, poor ("bad design"); evil, depraved, immoral ("bad intentions"); incorrect, faulty, questionable ("a bad move"); severe, harsh, cruel, tragic ("a bad winter").

bad faith *n.* abjection, deceit, conspiracy, treachery, deception, dishonesty, fraud, perfidy.

bail *n.* bond, guarantee, security, warrant, collateral.

bailee [bay · lif] *n.* manager, overseer, supervisor, attendant, deputy.

balance [bal · ense] *v.* make equal, neutralize, parallel ("The scales balanced").

balance [bal · ense] *n.* self-control, proportion, stability ("There was balance in the community").

ballot [bal · et] *n.* choice, lineup, tally, poll.

ban *n.* boycott, embargo, censorship, prohibition ("a ban on imports").

ban *v.* banish, bar, disallow, halt, eliminate, outlaw ("the movement to ban the manufacture of firearms").

banishment [ban · ish · ment] *n.* discharge, ostracism, segregation, dismissal, expulsion.

bank *n.* financial institution, credit union, repository, exchequer, coffer, safe, vault; hill, mound, dune, ridge.

bankrupt [bank · rupt] *adj.* insolvent, indigent, wiped out, penniless, destitute, broke, out of business.

bankruptcy [bank · rupt · see] *n.* insolvency, failure, disaster, defaulting. *Ant.* solvency.

banning [ban · ing] *n.* prohibiting, outlawing, excluding.

bar *v.* prevent, block, exclude, hinder, secure.

bar *n.* barrier, snag, restraint, blockage ("a bar was placed in the doorway"); court, fend, tribunal, judiciary ("case at bar"); defense, plea ("a bar to his action").

bare *adj.* naked, open, bald ("the bare truth").

bare *v.* reveal, divulge, disclose, publish, unveil ("The witness bared all").

B

bargain [*bar* · gen] *n.* treaty, pact, settlement, deal, agreement, transaction, contract, covenant, stipulation.

barratry [*bar* · a · tree] *n.* troublemaking, champerty, litigiousness.

barren [*bahr* · en] *adj.* bare, empty, sparse, infertile, sterile, desolate, void.

barter [*bahr* · ter] *v.* exchange, swap, trade, haggle, negotiate ("It is customary to barter for goods in some countries").

base *n.* basis, foot, key, fundamental part, foundation.

base *adj.* vulgar, corrupt, foul, vile, immoral ("base motives"); impure, adulterated, inferior ("base metal").

baseless [*base* · less] *adj.* unfounded, groundless.

basis [*bay* · siss] *n.* foundation, authority, principle, premise ("basis for the argument"); cost ("the tax basis of the property").

bastard [*bas* · terd] *n.* illegitimate child, adulterine, colt.

battery [*bat* · er · ee] *n.* beating, mugging, flogging, hitting, assault, thrashing, injury ("commit a battery"); batch, cluster, array ("a battery of elements").

bear *v.* fund, provide, yield, produce, generate ("I want to put my money in an account that bears interest"); abide, stand, undergo, tolerate ("I cannot bear his presence"); bolster, uphold, prop, fortify, support ("bear weight").

bearer [*bare* · er] *n.* carrier, recipient, courier, possessor, holder, payee.

beat *v.* defeat, surmount, surpass, defeat; abuse, batter, hit, punch, pummel.

before [be · *for*] *adj.* ahead, afore, former, formerly, previous.

before [be · *for*] *prep.* ahead of, in front of, preceding ("the case before the court").

behalf [be · *haf*] *n.* defense, help, profit, service, benefit, benevolence.

belief [be · *leef*] *n.* canon, creed, theory, persuasion, faith, doctrine; confidence, opinion, assurance, conviction.

believable [be · *leev* · uh · bul] *adj.* credible, plausible, trustworthy, tenable, convincing, reliable, conceivable.

belligerent [be · *lij* · e · rent] *adj.* threatening, hostile, quarrelsome, combative, pugilistic.

below [be · *loh*] *adv.* beneath, down, underneath; inferior, under ("a rank below sergeant").

bench *n.* bank, counter, board, worktable; judges, justices, chamber, tribunal, court.

beneficial [ben · e · *fish* · el] *adj.* favoring, gainful, serviceable, useful, valuable.

beneficiary [ben · e · *fish* · ee · air · ee] *n.* heir, recipient, successor, legatee, assignee.

benefit [*ben* · e · fit] *n.* aid, asset, exhibition ("a benefit for the homeless"); advantage, profit, gain, utility, return ("the benefit of success").

benefit [*ben* · e · fit] *v.* help, build, aid, assist ("The concert benefited the children's home").

benevolent [ben · *ev* · e · lent] *adj.* caring, considerate, humane, kind-hearted, charitable, philanthropic.

bequeath [be · *kweeth*] *v.* grant, give, assign, remit, leave, provide.

bequest [be · *kwest*] *n.* gift, devise, endowment, heritage, legacy.

best *adj.* choice, greatest, paramount, select, supreme, exemplary, superior, optimal, unrivaled.

bestow [be · *stoh*] *v.* grant, give, devote, favor, lavish.

bet *v.* gamble, speculate, venture ("to bet money").

bet *n.* action, pledge, risk, lottery ("The bet was off").

betray [be · *tray*] *v.* divulge, declare, reveal, inform, disclose; cheat, defraud, dupe, violate, swindle.

betterment [*bet* · er · ment] *n.* advancement, upgrading, progress.

biannual [by · *an* · yoo · el] *adj.* biennial, semiannual.

bias [*by* · es] *n.* prejudice, preconception, partiality, leaning, inclination, proclivity, penchant, predilection.

bias [*by* · es] *v.* skew, sway, prejudice ("that evidence could bias the jury").

bid *v.* demand, ask for, charge, greet, invite; submit, tender, propose, present; attempt, try, essay.

bid *n.* try, proposal, suggestion, approach, price, offer, submission ("All bids were open").

bifurcate [*by* · fer · kayt] *v.* divide, partition, split, separate, dichotomize, halve, sunder.

bigot [*big* · ut] *n.* dogmatist, fanatic, persecutor, zealot, redneck.

bill *v.* record, render, solicit, figure, charge money for goods ("to bill a customer").

bill *n.* proposed law, draft, resolution ("the bill before Congress"); invoice, account, fee, record, expenses, debit, cost ("the bill for legal services").

bind *n.* predicament, quandary, tight spot ("The commissioner was in a bind").

bind *v.* obligate, require, compel; restrict, hinder, restrain, yoke, detain.

binder [*bine* · der] *n.* deposit, pledge, stake, collateral, escrow, security ("a binder on the deal").

binding [*bine* · ding] *n.* cover, adhesive, fastener.

binding [*bine* · ding] *adj.* compulsory, conclusive, obligatory, mandatory, necessary ("a binding agreement").

bipartisan [by · *par* · ti · zen] *adj.* dual, two-sided, duplicated, conciliatory.

blacklist [*blak* · list] *v.* ban, bar, boycott, censure.

blackmail [*blak* · male] *v.* threaten, coerce, compel, demand, force, shake, squeeze.

blackmail [*blak* · male] *n.* ransom, extortion, exaction, payoff, hush money, bribery.

blame *v.* accuse, fault, implicate, rebuke, reproach, condemn, execrate.

blame *n.* accusation, criticism, denunciation, reproof, reprobation, castigation ("I'll take the blame"); accountability, attribution, assignment ("allocation of blame").

blank *n.* void, opening, gap, chasm, hollowness ("fill in the blank").

blank *adj.* bare, clean, empty, unfilled, unused ("a blank slate"); dull, expressionless, vacuous, impassive, noncommittal ("a blank expression"); complete, absolute, utter, complete, total, thorough ("the blank truth").

blanket [*blang* · ket] *adj.* complete, total, all-encompassing ("a blanket power of attorney").

blanket [*blang* · ket] *v.* surround, envelop, overspread ("blanket the area"); cover, cloak, obscure, eclipse ("blanket the view").

blasé [bla · *zay*] *adj.* nonchalant, indifferent, unmoved, bored; knowing, worldly, sophisticated.

blasphemy [*blass* · fe · mee] *n.* irreverence, swearing, indignity.

blatant [*blay* · tent] *adj.* clear, manifest, noticeable, obvious, patent, plain.

B

blind *adj.* unexposed, inconspicuous, private, sheltered; heedless, indiscriminate, undiscerning, inattentive, indifferent; visionless, groping, visually impaired.

blindness [*blind* · ness] *n.* sightlessness, defect, darkness.

bloodline [*blood* · line] *n.* ancestry, parentage, family, descent, genealogy.

blotter [*blot* · er] *n.* booking, rough minutes, wastebook.

board *v.* embark, enter, mount, climb ("board the bus").

board *n.* committee, trustees, directors, management, bureau, cabinet, commissionary ("the board of the Red Cross").

body [*bod* · ee] *n.* bones, being, creature, crowd, text; board, commission ("the governing body"); main part, corpus, substance ("Paragraph 3 is the body of the contract").

bogus [*boh* · gus] *adj.* counterfeit, phony, fake, false, sham ("a bogus check").

bona fide [*bone* · ah fide] *adj.* real, honest, true, sincere, legitimate, genuine, honorable, just.

bond *n.* bargain, contract, obligation, relationship, affiliation, affinity; binding, manacle, handcuff, chain.

bond *v.* fasten, fix, connect, fuse, bind ("to bond together").

bonded [*bon* · ded] *adv.* secured, obligated, guaranteed.

bondsman [*bondz* · man] *n.* surety, guarantor, voucher.

bonus [*bone* · us] *n.* fringe benefit, perquisite, additional compensation, tip, gratuity.

book *n.* album, record, register, manuscript, manual, tract, publication.

book *v.* arrange for, order, organize ("book a band for the dance"); accuse, arrest, indict ("book the assailant"); procure, slate, engage ("book the reservation").

bookkeeper [*book* · keep · er] *n.* accountant, clerk, examiner, inspector.

bookkeeping [*book* · kee · ping] *n.* accounting, recording.

bookmaker [*book* · maik · er] *n.* gambler, bookie.

boom *n.* gain, growth, expansion, upsurge, spread, development, escalation; prosperity, expansion, advancement,

boot *v.* kick, oust, terminate ("to boot out of the club").

booty [*boo* · tee] *n.* spoils, plunder, king's loot.

borough [*bur* · oh] *n.* geographical territory, area, division, zone ("the borough of Manhattan").

boycott [*boy* · kot] *n.* ban, embargo, exclusion, strike, rejection.

boycott [*boy* · kot] *v.* spurn, reject, ignore, exclude, picket, rebuff.

branch *n.* part, division, department, office, chapter, unit ("the Decatur branch"); offshoot, subordinate, subsidiary.

branch *v.* split, divide, elaborate.

brand *n.* mark, sign, trademark, insignia, symbol ("A well-known brand"); type, style, kind, variety ("his brand of humor").

brand *v.* mark, engrave, identify, label; stigmatize, defame, expose, defile, malign, deprecate.

brandish [*bran* · dish] *v.* show, display, dangle, wield, flaunt, swing, display.

bravado [bra · *va* · do] *n.* valor, pretense, arrogance, bluster, bombast, grandiosity, self-glorification.

B

brave *adj.* courageous, dauntless, undismayed, resolute, valiant, fearless.

brave *v.* endure, bear, confront, suffer ("brave the cold weather").

brawl *n.* fight, altercation, riot, uproar, disturbance, commotion, mêlée, row, fracas.

brawl *v.* fight, scrap, wrangle, bicker, clamor, quarrel, altercate.

breach *n.* evasion, neglect, dereliction, inobservance, default, nonadherence, repudiation ("breach of contract"); split, crack, crevice, schism, fissure, opening, gap ("a breach in the wall").

break *v.* breach, annul, violate, defy, disregard ("break an agreement"); fracture, sever, crack, snap, chip ("break the lamp").

break *n.* breach, tear, separation, opening, rupture ("a break in the vertebra"); recess, respite, interval, breather, lull, hiatus, interlude ("a break in the conversation"); opportunity, chance, opening, occasion ("give him a break").

bribe *n.* payoff, offering, illegal money, graft, kickback, lure, inducement, hush money, payola, blackmail.

bribe *v.* buy, buy off, lure, influence, seduce, tamper, tempt.

bribery [*bri* · ber · ee] *n.* corruption, perfidy, allurement, cajolery, inveiglement, connivance, venality, opportunism.

brief *adj.* short, concise, succinct, pithy, curt, terse, hasty ("a brief review of the facts"); quick, fast, swift, hasty ("a brief visit").

brief *n.* legal argument; summary, abstract, digest, outline, synopsis, review, abridgement, restatement.

brief *v.* advise, prepare, orient, inform, apprise, update ("Please brief me on this situation").

brink *n.* border, verge, boundary, edge, periphery, threshold.

broad *adj.* wide, extensive, far-reaching, universal, large, unlimited, widespread ("broad appeal"); clear, apparent, evident, glaring, pronounced ("a broad hint").

broker [*bro* · ker] *n.* agent, middleman, proxy, representative, emissary, mediator, intermediary.

brothel [*broth* · el] *n.* house of prostitution, whorehouse, bordello, parlor house, house of ill repute.

browbeat [*brow* · beet] *v.* badger, bully, intimidate, harass, humiliate, tyrannize, domineer, oppress.

browse *v.* scan, peruse, skim, survey, read, glance at.

brutal [*brew* · tul] *adj.* cruel, harsh, heartless, rough, uncivil, savage, vicious, severe, violent, ruthless.

brutality [*brew* · *tal* · i · tee] *n.* cruelty, inhumanity, violence, truculence, savagery, fierceness, ferocity, sadism, atrocity.

budget [*bud* · jet] *n.* allotment, share, quota, account, statement, blueprint, allocation, allowance, reserve.

budget [*bud* · jet] *v.* allocate, apportion, distribute, estimate.

bug *n.* disease, germ, infection, virus; insect, pest, vermin; craze, obsession, mania, enthusiasm, rage; surveillance, monitor, device.

bug *v.* wiretap, monitor, spy, snoop, eavesdrop; bother, annoy, irk, irritate, disturb, pester.

buggery [*bug* · ger · ee] *n.* sodomy, bestiality.

B

build *v.* increase, accelerate, expand, enlarge, develop ("build a medical practice"); construct, engineer, produce, form, make, erect, create ("build a bridge").

builder [*bild* · er] *n.* developer, owner, maker, manufacturer, architect, fabricator, crafter.

building [*bild* · ing] *n.* structure, dwelling, construction, premises, edifice, home, house ("a beautiful building").

bulk *n.* size, mass, volume, substance ("a great amount of bulk"); majority, most, best, preponderance, lion's share ("I did the bulk of the work").

bulletin [*bull* · ih · tin] *n.* announcement, dispatch, notification, statement, report, information, publication, release, news flash.

bundle [*bun* · dil] *n.* collection, cluster, group, pile, assortment, array; package, box, parcel.

burden [*bur* · den] *n.* duty, obligation, responsibility, charge, requirement ("the burden of proof"); stress, hardship, strain, weight, grievance, difficulty, concern, worry ("a heavy burden").

burden [*bur* · den] *v.* encumber, strain, saddle with, afflict, oppress, impede, make responsible for.

bureau [*byoor* · oh] *n.* division, branch, office, department, ministry, board, authority ("the Bureau of Indian Affairs").

bureaucracy [byoor · *ok* · ra · see] *n.* administration, management, system; red tape, rules, regulations, forms.

burglar [*berg* · lir] *n.* robber, thief, prowler, looter, felon, trespasser, marauder, criminal, pilferer.

burglary [*berg* · lar · ee] *v.* robbery, larceny, breaking and entering, housebreaking, looting, crime, forcible entry, raiding, marauding.

burial [*ber* · i · al] *n.* internment, funeral, sepulcher, entombment; hiding, shrouding, cover-up, concealment.

burn *v.* incinerate, kindle, ignite, inflame, consume.

bury *n.* conceal, cloak, hide, cover, shroud, stash; entomb, inter, inhume, lay to rest, embalm.

business [*biz* · ness] *n.* trade, occupation, calling, activity, profession, field ("the cosmetology business"); concern, affair, responsibility, duty, interest, matter ("It's not your business"); commerce, manufacture, industry, intercourse, dealings ("doing business").

buttress [*but* · ress] *v.* support, bolster, carry, uphold, strengthen, sustain, brace, shore up.

buy *n.* acquisition, deal, purchase, bargain ("a good buy").

buy *v.* purchase, obtain, procure, secure, acquire; bribe, corrupt, fix, palm, hire, pay off.

buyer [*bi* · er] *n.* pruchaser, customer, client, consumer, user, vendee, patron, investor. *Ant.* seller.

bylaw [*bi* · law] *n.* rule, regulation, ordinance, order, canon, standard.

bystander [*bi* · stand · er] *n.* spectator, observer, witness, passer-by, eyewitness, nonparticipant, viewer, attestant, onlooker.

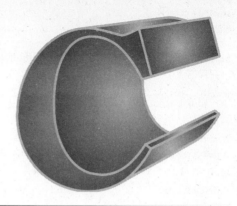

cabinet [*kab* · ih · net] *n.* council, assembly, panel; closet, depository.

cache [kash] *n.* shelter, refuge, confinement; safe, repository, storehouse, warehouse.

calamity [ka · *lam* · itee] *n.* disaster, cataclysm, misfortune, adversity.

calendar [*kal* · en · der] *n.* diary, journal, register, schedule, lineup, program, chronology.

caliber [*kal* · i · ber] *n.* quality, status, capability, eminence; ability, faculty, competence, acumen.

call *v.* command, order, invite, require, summon ("call to court for an appearance"); name, label, identify, designate, term ("call his speech defamation").

call *n.* address, plea, bid, cry, entreaty ("the call for help was clear"); option, choice, alternative ("the right of put and call").

callable [*kol* · abl] *adj.* redeemable, retrievable, reclaimable ("a callable bond").

calumny [*kal* · um · nee] *n.* slander, defamation, libel, vituperation, opprobrium, debasement.

cambist [*kam* · bist] *n.* dealer, broker.

camouflage [*kam* · uh · flazh] *v.* conceal, cover up, embellish, obfuscate, disguise.

cancel [*kan* · sel] *v.* call off, rub out, repeal, overthrow, annul, set aside, abrogate, rescind, quash, drop.

cancellation [kan · sel · *ay* · shen] *n.* abandonment, reversal, recall, nullification, erasure, revocation, termination, withdrawal, rescission ("cancellation of the ethics committee meetings").

candid [*kan* · did] *adj.* open, sincere, honest, straightforward, ingenuous.

candidate [*kan* · di · date] *n.* bidder, suitor, seeker, job-hunter, nominee, contender.

canon [*kan* · uhn] *n.* law, rule, statute, act, code, order; standard, criterion, measure, ethic, norm, test.

canvass [*kan* · vess] *v.* solicit, survey, petition ("canvass the neighborhood"); examine, review, scrutinize, audit, probe, dissect ("canvass the ballots").

capable [*kape* · uh · bul] *adj.* effective, qualified, skilled, able, proficient, accomplished, efficient.

capacity [ke · *pass* · i · tee] *n.* competency, ability, capability, license, right ("capacity to contract"); skill, talent, ability, caliber, stature, capability ("a debater of great capacity"); position, duty, responsibility, job ("her capacity as warden").

capita [*ka* · pi · tuh] *n.* head, each.

C

capital [*kap* · i · tel] *n.* cash, stock, wealth, holdings, financial assets, funds, resources, principal.

capital [*kap* · i · tel] *adj.* basic, outstanding, prime, vital, chief, primary, principal, cardinal, leading, controlling.

capitalism [*kap* · i · tel · izm] *n.* free market economy, private enterprise, democracy, competition.

capitalize [*kap* · i · ta · lize] *v.* exploit, gain, take advantage of, profit from, obtain.

capitol [*kap* · i · tel] *n.* statehouse, dome, center.

capricious [ka · *prish* · ess] *adj.* careless, impulsive, moody, arbitrary, whimsical, unreasonable, frivolous, flighty.

caption [*kap* · shen] *n.* heading, title, inscription ("the caption of the case").

captive [*kap* · tiv] *n.* hostage, pawn, prisoner, convict, subject.

captivity [*kap* · tiv · i · tee] *n.* bondage, custody, confinement, imprisonment, impoundment, internment.

cardinal [*kar* · dih · nul] *adj.* basic, central, main, material, vital, rudimentary; dominant, outstanding, leading, prime, supreme, unparalleled, paramount, predominant.

care *n.* custody, safekeeping, interest, regard, attention, awareness, caution.

care *v.* beware, be cautious, guard; foster, nurture, watch, support, supervise.

careless [*kare* · less] *adj.* unthinking, oblivious, unwary, heedless, unattentive, lax, casual.

caretaker [*kare* · tay · ker] *n.* attendant, guardian, curator, warden; officeholder, administrator, superintendent.

carnal [*kar* · nel] *adj.* erotic, vulgar, worldly, sensual, lustful, fleshly, wanton.

carriage [*kar* · ij] *n.* posture, pace, demeanor, appearance, deportment ("her confident carriage"); transport, transportation, portage, shipment ("the carriage of goods").

carrier [*kah* · ree · er] *n.* runner, transporter, bearer, messenger ("a carrier for hire"); transmitter, possessor ("a carrier of tuberculosis").

carry [*kah* · ree] *v.* achieve, attain, gain, prevail ("carry the day"); transport, move, haul, bring ("carry the packages").

carte blanche [kart *blonsh*] *n.* freedom, unlimited authority, permit, sanction, free rein, power, discretion.

cartel [*kar* · *tel*] *n.* syndicate, coalition, association, consortium, block ("the oil cartel"); agreement, accord, bargain, deal ("the cartel with neighboring countries").

case *n.* action, lawsuit, litigation, controversy, dispute, proceeding ("the case of *Roe v. Wade*"); example, instance, paradigm, illustration ("a case of mistaken identity"); thesis, reasoning, position, side, evidence, hypothesis ("We stated our case well").

cash *n.* coin, money, funds, currency, notes, legal tender.

cash *v.* make change, pay, draw, liquidate, redeem ("to cash a check").

castigate [*kas* · tih · gayt] *v.* admonish, reprimand, chastise, criticize, thrash, excoriate, rebuke, upbraid.

castration [kas · *tray* · shen] *n.* emasculation, asexualization, removal, sterilization, severing.

casual [*kazh* · yoo · el] *adj.* uncertain, unplanned, accidental, unexpected, spontaneous ("our casual encounter"); irregular, erratic, occasional, intermittent ("casual employment"); informal, relaxed ("casual dress").

casualty [*kazh* · yoo · ul · tee] *n.* disaster, accident, calamity, catastrophe, tragedy, misfortune.

catalyst [*kat* · a · list] *n.* inspiration, force, motivation, instigator, impetus.

caucus [*kaw* · kus] *n.* group, convention, gathering, conclave, session, assembly, meeting, council.

causation [kaw · *zay* · shen] *n.* production, origination, root, spawning, formation.

cause *n.* stimulus, inducement, derivation, source, motive, agent ("the cause of the accident"); belief, conviction, faith, issue, purpose ("a charitable cause"); lawsuit, trial, case, legal proceeding ("cause of action").

cause *v.* bring into being, generate, create, sire, provoke, compel, launch, effectuate ("His bankruptcy caused his depression").

caution [*kaw* · shen] *n.* warning, advice, vigilance, prudence, watchfulness, circumspection.

caution [*kaw* · shen] *v.* warn, tip off, alert, inform, forewarn, apprise, admonish.

caveat [*ka* · vee · at] *n.* warning, caution, sign, alarm.

cease *v.* stop, desist, adjourn, quit, quell, suspend, terminate.

cede [seed] *v.* abandon, yield, give up, forsake, release, relinquish ("A nation transfers territory by ceding it").

cedent [*see* · dent] *n.* grantor, assignor.

celebrate [*sel* · e · brate] *v.* proclaim, rejoice, enjoy, eulogize, glorify, exalt, extol ("celebrate a victory"); observe, perform, conduct ("celebrate holiday rituals").

celebrity [see · *leb* · ri · tee] *n.* star, hero, famous person, luminary, big shot; fame, notoriety, prestige, repute, prominence.

cell *n.* cage, confinement, jail, prison, compartment, hole, nook, retreat, chamber.

censor [*sen* · ser] *v.* forbid, restrict, suppress, withhold, examine, delete, expurgate, bowdlerize, abridge, amend, proscribe.

censor [*sen* · ser] *n.* examiner, reviewer, critic, inspector.

censorship [*sen* · ser · ship] *n.* forbiddance, banning, control, restriction, suppression, prohibition, stifling, purification, blockage, elimination.

censure [*sen* · shoor] *n.* disapproval, rebuke, reproach, reprimand, criticism, condemnation, denunciation, disapproval, castigation.

censure [*sen* · shoor] *v.* condemn, criticize, scold, reprimand, admonish, reprove, decry, assail, chastise, denigrate.

census [*sen* · sus] *n.* tally, tabulation, measurement, enumeration.

center [*sen* · ter] *n.* focus, midpoint, focal point, middle; essence, nucleus, heart, pith, gravamen, main point.

central [*sen* · tral] *adj.* basic, essential, pivotal, primary, principal, dominant, elemental ("a central idea"); center, middle, medial, halfway ("central filing").

certain [*ser* · ten] *adj.* definite, specific, ascertained, clear, explicit ("The price was certain"); confident, secure, assured ("Her demeanor was certain"); doubtless, conclusive, irrefutable, unquestionable, irrevocable ("certain defeat").

certainty [*ser* · ten · tee] *n.* inevitability, sure thing, reality, verity, foregone conclusion ("It is a certainty that our client will be convicted"); confidence, assertiveness, assurance, credence, conviction ("The witness answered with certainty").

C

certificate [ser · *tif* · i · ket] *n.* pass, authorizing document, permit, ticket, affidavit, diploma, voucher, endorsement, assurance, credential.

certification [ser · ti · fi · *kay* · shen] *n.* assertion, substantiation, validation, endorsement, authentication, verification, license, declaration.

certified [*ser* · ti · fide] *adj.* confirmed, guaranteed, approved, authenticated, validated, verified, authorized, licensed, established ("a certified legal assistant").

certitude [*ser* · ti · tyood] *n.* certainty, irrefutability, undeniability, sureness.

cession [*sesh* · en] *n.* surrender, yielding, relinquishment, ceding, transfer, conveyance, release.

chain *n.* succession, series, order, progression, sequence ("chain of custody").

chain *v.* bind, attach, hold, fasten, restrict ("chain the prisoner").

chairman [*chare* · man] *n.* leader, head, director, presider, presiding officer.

challenge [*chal* · enj] *v.* confront, dare, defy, contradict, impeach, dispute, question ("challenge the witness"); invite, summon, call, arouse ("challenge all comers").

challenge [*chal* · enj] *n.* objection, rejection, protest ("a challenge to juror 12"); test, contest, match, confrontation, adventure ("Winning this case will be a real challenge").

chamber [*chame* · ber] *n.* panel, assembly, bench, committee, forum; compartment, box, cell, alcove, hall, parlor.

champerty [*cham* · per · tee] barratry, intermeddling, illegal bargain.

chance *n.* luck, good fortune, fortuitousness; possibility, contingency, likelihood, prospect.

chance *v.* attempt, risk, try, gamble.

change *n.* alteration, modification, conversion, transition, addition, deviation, innovation, variation, refinement, amendment.

change *v.* make different, substitute, reverse, alter, redo, shift, modify, deviate, transform, reconstruct, reconfigure, amend, revise ("change the venue in the interest of fairness").

chapter [*chap* · ter] *n.* section, part, article, clause, portion ("Chapter 7 bankruptcy").

character [*kar* · ak · ter] *n.* individuality, integrity, attribute, disposition, personality, nature, kind; reputation, standing.

charge *v.* encumber, entrust, delegate, assign ("charge the jury"); accuse, blame, indict, implicate, inculpate, incriminate ("charge the accused with theft").

charge *n.* price, cost, fee, tariff, assessment, payment, debt, quotation ("The charge is 10 dollars"); indictment, accusation, complaint, arraignment, gravamen, citation, summons ("The charge against him was child molestation"); instruction, command, advice ("the charge to the jury").

charisma [ka · *riz* · ma] *n.* allure, magnetism, charm, appeal.

charitable [*char* · ih · tuh · bul] *adj.* benevolent, eleemosynary, philanthropic, altruistic, giving, generous, magnanimous, humane ("charitable contribution"); forgiving, lenient, obliging, merciful, agreeable ("a charitable review").

charity [*char* · i · tee] *n.* altruism, benevolence, donation, generosity, philanthropy.

charter [*char* · ter] *v.* reserve, borrow, rent, hire, lease, let, engage.

charter [*char* · ter] *n.* treaty, document, privilege, decree, pact, conveyance, agreement, entitlement.

chattel [*chat* · el] *n.* property, possessions, assets, belongings, tangibles, effects.

check *n.* draft, note, negotiable instrument, banknote; inspection, examination, review, audit, analysis; obstruction, restraint, control, limitation, cessation.

check *v.* inspect, examine, verify, assess, scrutinize, probe, question ("check the murder scene"); restrain, balance, curb, inhibit, constrain, harness ("check his power").

chicanery [chi · *kane* · e · ree] *n.* deception, double dealing, dishonesty, trickery, subterfuge, treachery, machination.

chief *adj.* dominant, leading, preeminent, foremost, ranking, paramount.

child *n.* kid, adolescent, minor, youth, juvenile, youngster.

chilling [*chil* · ing] *adj.* inhibiting, dampening, restricting, curbing, restraining, impeding ("a chilling effect").

choate [*ko* · ate] *adj.* complete, completely formed, perfect, whole, ready, perfected ("a choate lien").

choice *n.* option, selection, pick, alternative; decision, outcome, selection, judgment.

choose *v.* select, prefer, opt for, decide, embrace, resolve, settle.

chronic [*kron* · ik] *adj.* habitual, unremitting, continuous, lingering, persistent, unyielding.

circuit [*ser* · kit] *n.* district, area, section, jurisdiction, territory, division ("circuit court").

circumstantial [ser · kum · *stan* · shel] *adj.* indirect, inferential, deduced, conjectural, implicative ("circumstantial evidence").

citation [sy · *tay* · shen] *n.* writ, notice, order, bidding, notification, warrant, summons ("The driver received a citation"); reference, source, credit, attribution, documentation ("the citation for the case").

cite *v.* summon, notify, name, inform, implicate, incriminate ("to cite for speeding"); refer to, adduce, indicate, establish, specify, document ("cite adverse authority").

citizen [*sit* · i · zen] *n.* denizen, resident, subject, inhabitant, taxpayer, voter.

city [*sit* · ee] *n.* large town, urban place, downtown, metropolis, village, municipality.

civic [*siv* · ik] *adj.* common, community, governmental, official, public, municipal ("civic duty").

civil [*siv* · el] *adj.* community, civic, social, public, societal; noncriminal ("a civil case"); courteous, obliging, civilized, diplomatic, deferential, gracious, refined ("Civil behavior is required in the courtroom").

civilian [sih · *vil* · yen] *n.* nonmilitary person, citizen, commoner, subject.

civilian [sih · *vil* · yen] *adj.* nonmilitary, private, lay, secular, mundane.

claim *n.* assertion, contention, declaration, advocacy, insistence ("her claim of innocence"); accusation, plea, complaint, presentment, suit, cause of action ("a claim against the manufacturer").

claimant [*klay* · ment] *n.* petitioner, challenger, plaintiff, appellant, litigant, party, pleader.

clarify [*klar* · ih · fy] *v.* explain, interpret, refine, illuminate, explicate.

class *n.* group, type, category, variety ("a constitutionally protected class"); style, standing, status.

class *v.* group, classify, specify, separate ("The law classes this as a misdemeanor").

classification [klas · i · fi · *kay* · shen] *n.* allocation, allotment, analysis, arrangement, hierarchy, distribution, grouping, placement.

clause *n.* provision, section, part, passage, stipulation, condition.

C

clean *adj.* blameless, chaste, faultless, precise, uncluttered.

clear *v.* clean, purify, refine, unclog, erase; exonerate, emancipate, acquit, liberate, discharge; make, net, realize, profit, acquire, earn.

clear *adj.* understandable, open, apparent, sharp, unhindered, absolute, certain, decided, definite; absolved, discharged, innocent, dismissed.

clearing [*kleer* · ing] *n.* allowance, clearance, open space, empty space, margin ("See the clearing ahead").

clearinghouse [*kleer* · ing hows] *n.* central location, exchange, distribution center.

clearly [*kleer* · lee] *adv.* distinctly, openly, overtly, surely, unmistakably, lucidly, undoubtedly.

clemency [*klem* · en · see] *n.* forgiveness, compassion, fairness, lenience, charity, absolution, mercy, grace.

clerical [*kler* · i · kel] *adj.* secretarial, routine, clerkly, office ("clerical work"); churchly, holy, pastoral, sacred ("clerical robes").

clerk *n.* assistant, salesperson, secretary, teller, recordkeeper, researcher, scribe, administrator ("clerk of the court").

clerkship [*klerk* · ship] *n.* internship, employment.

client [*klie* · ent] *n.* customer, consumer, patron, purchaser, shopper, patronizer. *Ant.* seller.

clinical [*klin* · i · kal] *adj.* dispassionate, detached, impersonal, objective, scientific ("a clinical opinion").

close [kloze] *v.* complete, finish, agree to, seal, confirm ("close the deal"); terminate, conclude, suspend, cease ("close the account"). *Ant.* open; start.

close [kloze] *n.* conclusion, ending, completion, termination; premises.

close [klose] *adj.* near, tight, crowded, dense ("close quarters"); intimate, allied, devoted, confidential ("a close relationship").

closed [klozed] *adj.* finished, over, resolved, settled, shut, terminated, sealed. *Ant.* unsettled; open.

closing [*kloze* · ing] *adj.* final, summing-up, completing ("closing argument"). *Ant.* beginning.

closing [*kloze* · ing] *n.* summation, ending, completion ("The closing was scheduled for 6:00 p.m.").

coaching [*koh* · ching] *v.* instructing, educating, training, teaching ("coaching the witness").

coalesce [ko · uh · *less*] *v.* combine, unite, fuse, solidify, consolidate, join, intermingle.

coalition [ko · a · *lish* · un] *n.* alliance, league, society, partnership, union, party, mixture, association.

coax *v.* attract, bait, lure, prod, suggest, urge, cajole.

cocaine [koh · *kane*] *n.* drug, controlled substance, crack, nose candy, snow, blow, white lady.

coconspirator [koh · kun · *spir* · e · ter] *n.* abettor, collaborator, partner in crime, schemer, confederate, accomplice. *Ant.* bystander.

code *n.* rule, statute, ethics, canon, constitution, law, precedent ("code of professional responsibility"); secret, guidelines, cryptograph, cipher ("They wrote in code").

codicil [*kod* · i · sil] *n.* addition, supplement, appendix, accessory, addendum, attachment, extension ("codicil to a will").

C

codification [kod · if · i · kay · shen] *n.* categorization, arrangement, classification, compilation, collection.

codify [kod · i · fy] *v.* create, collect, arrange, systematize, assemble.

coerce [ko · erse] *v.* force, dictate, intimidate, dominate, compel, press, bully, drive, terrorize.

coercion [ko · er · shen] *n.* compulsion, pressure, duress, force, intimidation ("confession obtained by coercion"). *Ant.* volition.

cogent [ko · gent] *adj.* forceful, logical, solid, sound, convincing, effective ("a cogent argument").

cognizable [kog · ni · zih · bul] *adj.* accountable, justiciable, triable, proper, clear ("The offense was cognizable before the superior court").

cognizance [kog · ni · zense] *n.* dominion, judicial notice ("The court has cognizance over maritime cases"); understanding, apprehension, attention, awareness ("The judge took cognizance of the objection").

cohabitation [ko · ha · bi · tay · shen] *n.* living together, common-law marriage, alliance, union, residing together. *Ant.* separation.

coherent [ko · here · ent] *adj.* logical, explanatory, cogent, unambiguous, understandable, concise, reasoned.

cohort [ko · hort] *n.* ally, associate, abettor, colleague, friend, partner.

coif [koyf] *n.* hat, cap.

coincide [ko · in · side] *v.* agree, approve, concur, endorse; correspond, coexist, match, confirm, synchronize, acquiesce.

coincidence [ko · in · si · dents] *n.* agreement, accord, correlation, concurrence; accident, fortuity, fluke, happening.

cold *adj.* frozen, iced, chilly, nippy, glacial, shivery; aloof, passionless, reserved, unresponsive, distant, unemotional, frigid, phlegmatic.

cold-blooded *adj.* cruel, savage, merciless, ruthless, inhumane, callous.

collaborate [ko · lab · uh · rait] *v.* collude, team up, cooperate, work together with, join with, coact.

collaborator [ko · lab · uh · ray · tor] *n.* associate, partner, colleague, assistant, helper.

collapse [ke · laps] *v.* cave in, fold, give in, disintegrate ("The building collapsed"); fail, go under, falter ("The business collapsed").

collapse [ke · laps] *n.* downfall, failure, bankruptcy, destruction, disintegration.

collateral [ko · lat · er · el] *n.* deposit, security, endorsement, pledge, promise.

collateral [ko · lat · er · el] *adj.* indirect, secondary, accessory, related, additional, auxiliary, ancillary, subordinate, corresponding, side ("a collateral issue").

collation [ko · lay · shen] *n.* comparison, blend, confirmation, matching, checking ("the collation of property"); assembling, organizing ("collation of pages"). *Ant.* separation.

collect [ko · lekt] *v.* amass, gather, incorporate, unite, accumulate, muster, congregate, flock, convene; acquire, secure, raise, dig up. *Ant.* disburse, pay out.

collection [ko · lek · shen] *n.* compilation, accumulation, digest, pile, gathering, contribution, group, clump. *Ant.* disbursement.

collective [ko · lek · tiv] *adj.* common, unified, consolidated, relating, assembled ("the law team's collective efforts").

collective [ko · lek · tiv] *n.* organization, association, work team ("the farming collective").

collide [ko · lide] v. clash, conflict, dissent, disagree, oppose; crash, bump, smash, strike, converge.

colloquim [ko · loh · kwee · um] n. conference, group discussion, session, round table, seminar ("the colloquim on leadership").

collude [ke · lood] v. conspire, plot, scheme, band together, unite, contrive. *Ant.* divide.

collusion [ke · loo · zhen] n. agreement for fraud, conspiracy, secret agreement, scheming, trickery, perfidy, plotting, contrivance.

color [kuhl · er] n. deception, facade, falsification, misrepresentation, influence ("color of law"); pigment, color, dye, shade ("a lovely color"); complexion, description, features, likeness ("she has lost her color").

color [kuhl · er] v. taint, prejudice, affect, influence ("His military background colored his perception of the case").

colorable [kuhl · er · abl] adj. deceptive, fraudulent, specious, bogus ("a colorable transaction"); plausible, credible, conceivable ("She possessed colorable authority").

coma [ko · ma] n. unconsciousness, sleep, stupor, torpor, trance.

comaker [koh · may · ker] n. cosigner, originator.

combination [kom · bi · nay · shen] n. alliance, association, coalition, consortium, union ("an illegal combination in restraint of trade").

combine [kom · bine] v. integrate, connect, merge, mix, link ("combine our resources"). *Ant.* sever, separate.

comity [koe · mih · tee] n. recognition, willingness, accommodation, consideration, goodwill, reciprocity ("the comity of nations"). *Ant.* hostility.

comment [kom · ent] n. remark, note, notation, observation, assertion, explication, exposition.

comment [kom · ent] v. remark, declare, explicate, expound, interject, discuss, opine.

commerce [kom · erss] n. exchange, marketing, commercialism, business, trade, interchange, industry.

commercial [ke · mer · shel] adj. monetary, wholesale, retail, bartering, for-profit; pecuniary, crass, exploitative.

commingling [ko · ming · gling] n. combining, intermixing, merging, uniting, blending, marshaling ("commingling of funds").

commission [ke · mish · en] n. authority, duty, role, office, power ("her commission to enforce fair labor practices"); group, agency, board, council, panel, cabinet ("the tax commission").

commissioner [ke · mish · e · ner] n. administrator, manager, representative, delegate.

commit [ke · mit] v. enact, complete, perform, fulfill, achieve ("She committed the crime"); deliver, allocate, arrest, impound, incarcerate, imprison ("The person was committed to jail"); entrust, engage, invest, empower, convey ("commit funds").

commitment [ke · mit · ment] n. confinement, imprisonment, detention, restraint ("Because he was insane, his commitment was legal"); promise, assurance, obligation, vow, duty ("I had her commitment to pay the loan"); allegiance, duty, engagement, involvement ("commitment to the cause").

committee [ke · mit · ee] n. group, board, body, task force, council.

commodity [ke · mod · i · tee] n. merchandise, possession, product, stock, material.

common [*kom* · en] *adj.* accepted, constant, mutual, prevailing, customary, established ("The way I do it is common practice"); shared, public, communal ("This is common property"); vulgar, low, second-rate, inferior, cheap ("Her manners were so common"). *Ant.* unusual; refined.

commonwealth [*kom* · en · welth] *n.* public citizens, society, democracy, federation, community. *Ant.* individual.

communicate [ko · *mune* · i · kate] *v.* say, relate, give, notice, broadcast, narrate, utter, publicize, inform.

communication [ko · *mune* · i · kay · shun] *n.* discourse, dialogue, conversation, correspondence, interlocution; announcement, message, news, information, report.

communism [*kom* · yoo · niz · um] *n.* collectivism, socialism, state ownership, common property, Marxism. *Ant.* capitalism.

community [ko · *mune* · i · tee] *n.* locality, society, neighborhood, town, colony, district, hamlet.

community [ko · *mune* · i · tee] *adj.* shared, common, public.

commutation [kom · yoo · *tay* · shen] *n.* change, alteration, abatement, modification, adjustment, lessening ("the commutation of his sentence").

compact [*kom* · pakt] *n.* contract, alliance, deal, pact, treaty ("We had a compact for peace").

compact [*kom* · pakt] *adj.* condensed, pressed, solid, hard, firm, thick, tight, small.

company [*kum* · pe · nee] *n.* group, association, partnership, corporation, business group, enterprise, force ("John and Mary formed a company to sell shoes"); companionship, fellowship, friendship, camaraderie ("I like Jonathan's company"). *Ant.* individual, isolation.

comparable [*kom* · per · uh · bul] *adj.* similar, equivalent, corresponding, commensurate, equal.

comparative [kem · *par* · i · tiv] *adj.* comparable, relative, proportionate, allocated ("the doctrine of comparative negligence"). *Ant.* absolute.

compare [kom · *pare*] *v.* measure, liken, juxtapose, analogize, differentiate.

compel [kom · *pell*] *v.* coerce, impel, force, impose, oblige, require, threaten, decree.

compelling [kom · *pel* · ing] *adj.* powerful, strong, significant, emphatic, commanding, persuasive.

compensate [*kom* · pen · sate] *v.* counterbalance, equilibrate, offset, stabilize; pay, reimburse, remunerate, satisfy.

compensation [kom · pen · *say* · shen] *n.* payment, reimbursement, payoff, consideration, settlement; balancing, counterbalancing, redress, canceling out.

compensatory [kom · *pen* · se · to · ree] *adj.* remunerative, actual, repaying, atoning, redemptive, reimbursing, providing restitution ("compensatory damages").

competency [*kom* · pe · ten · see] *n.* adequacy, capability, expertise, capacity.

competent [*kom* · pe · tent] *adj.* eligible, qualified, capable, fit, polished, efficient, responsible, able. *Ant.* uncapable.

competition [kom · *pe* · tish · un] *n.* contest, rivalry, test, opposition, engagement, vying, encounter.

competitive [kom · *pet* · i · tiv] *adj.* combative, opposing, rivaling, contending, contentious; public, unclosed, accessible, unrestricted ("competitive bidding").

compilation [kom · pih · *lay* · shen] *n.* gathering, arrangements, accumulation, selection.

C

compile [kom · *pile*] *v.* gather, group, accumulate, prepare, select, arrange, cumulate.

complain [kom · *plane*] *v.* disapprove, disparage, contravene, blame, protest, cavil, find fault with, deprecate, castigate ("complain about conditions"); charge, accuse, prosecute, arraign, sue, challenge, file a claim ("complain of a criminal act").

complainant [kom · *play* · nent] *n.* plaintiff, claimant, petitioner, litigant. *Ant.* defendant.

complaint [kom · *playnt*] *n.* petition, charge, pleading, indictment, accusation ("Susan was served with a complaint"); objection, criticism, rebuke, protest, grievance ("Michael's complaint was justified").

complete [*kom* · pleet] *adj.* full, absolute, inclusive, unimpaired, unrestricted, plenary, thorough, entire, blanket, unconditional ("complete liquidation"); closed, concluded, executed, done, terminated ("The deal is complete").

complex [kom · *plecks*] *adj.* difficult, involved, abstruse, entangled, perplexing, complicated ("a complex case").

complex [kom · *plecks*] *n.* development, compound, organization, structure, network; entanglement, maze, difficulty, complication.

compliance [kom · *ply* · ants] *n.* assent, accommodation, concurrence, submission, yielding, agreement, cooperation.

comply [kom · *ply*] *v.* concur, consent, obey, accommodate, defer to, satisfy.

component [kom · *pone* · ent] *n.* part, section, segment, sector, unit, ingredients, aspect.

composite [kom · *poz* · it] *n.* aggregate, medley, fusing, gathering, assembly, conjoining.

composite [kom · *poz* · it] *adj.* fused, aggregated, assembled, joined, gathered.

composition [kom · po · *zish* · un] *n.* agreement, compact, concession, release, settlement ("composition in bankruptcy"); makeup, organization, structure, constitution, nature ("the composition of the team").

compound [kom · *pound*] *v.* blend, mix, combine, unite, merge ("To make a cake, you must compound proper ingredients"); intensify, aggravate, widen, worsen, complicate ("compound the situation").

compound [*kom* · pound] *n.* mixture, conglomeration, merger, blend; complex, site, campus ("held hostage at the compound").

comprehend [*com* · pree · hend] *v.* understand, grasp, know, discern, fathom; cognize, apprehend.

comprehensive [*kom* · pree · hen · siv] *adj.* all-inclusive, all-embracing, consummate, total, unconditional, extensive.

compromise [*kom* · pre · mize] *n.* agreement, bargain, concession, settlement, deal ("Our compromise brought peace").

compromise [*kom* · pre · mize] *v.* expose, jeopardize, embarrass, imperil, weaken, discredit ("He compromised his values").

comptroller [kon · *trole* · er] *n.* officer, accountant, registrar, inspector, examiner.

compulsion [kom · *pul* · shun] *n.* coercion, force, oppression, urgency, obsession, craze, fetish, fixation, mania, infatuation, preoccupation.

compulsory [kem · *pul* · se · ree] *adj.* obligatory, required, mandatory, involuntary, necessary ("Compulsory arbitration was required by statute").

con *n.* in opposition, against, dissenting ("We argued the point thoroughly, both pro and con").

conceal [*kon* · seal] *v.* hide, cloak, shield, obscure, shroud, protect, screen, seclude.

concealment [*kon* · seal · ment] *n.* hiding, disguise, evasion, obfuscation, furtiveness, camouflage, cover.

concede [kon · *seed*] *v.* assent, accept, submit, yield, settle, consent, endorse.

conceive [kon · *seeve*] *v.* grasp, perceive, know, apprehend, realize; create, generate, originate, give birth to.

concentrate [*kon* · sin · trate] *v.* accumulate, compress, congregate, focus, consolidate; contemplate, consider, scrutinize, think deeply, focus attention on, mediate, be engrossed in.

concept [*kon* · sept] *n.* idea, thought, theory, opinion, postulate, assumption, presumption, tenet.

conception [ken · *sep* · shen] *n.* fertilization, inception, formulation, beginning, invention.

concerted [ken · *ser* · ted] *adj.* coordinated, mutual, planned, premediated, united, consensual, conjoined, collaborative.

conciliation [kon · sil · ee · *ay* · shen] *n.* mediation, compromise, agreement, mitigation.

conclude [kon · *klude*] *v.* end, terminate, rule, decide, declare, find, hold, deem, deduce.

conclusion [ken · *kloo* · zhen] *n.* termination, end, completion, closure, payoff ("conclusion of the trial"). *Ant.* beginning.

conclusive [ken · *kloo* · siv] *adj.* absolute, final, clear, compelling, indisputable ("conclusive evidence"); settled, completed, decided. *Ant.* contestable, arguable.

concur [kon · *ker*] *v.* agree, approve, come together, consent, support, condone, uphold; coincide, accompany, occur simultaneously.

concurrent [kon · *ker* · ent] *adj.* coupled, accompanying, linked, merged, allied ("Concurrent powers may be exercised by both the federal and state governments"). *Ant.* incompatible, independent.

condemn [ken · *dem*] *v.* convict, punish, damn, adjudicate, blame, appropriate.

condemnation [kon · dem · *nay* · shen] *n.* conviction, accusation, disproof, doom, damnation, taking.

condition [ken · *dish* · en] *v.* prepare, adapt, accustom, teach, warm up, inure, train, ready, modify.

condition [ken · *dish* · en] *n.* requirement, limitation, provision ("It's a condition of the contract"); contingency provision, prerequisite, specificiation ("I said I'd prepare dinner on the condition that she would mow the lawn"); happening, position, posture, quality ("The condition of his hair was awful").

conditional [ken · *dish* · en · el] *adj.* contingent, incidental, dependent, qualified, provisional. *Ant.* absolute.

condominium [kon · de · *min* · um] *n.* home, multiunit dwelling, separate ownership.

condonation [kon · do · *nay* · shen] *n.* forgiveness, pardon, overlooking, clemency, discharge, acquittal.

condone [kon · *dohn*] *v.* allow, tolerate, accept, bear with, permit, relent, yield.

conduct [*kon* · dukt] *n.* actions, behavior, performance, operation, style, way, code, method, comportment ("good conduct").

conduct [kon · *dukt*] *v.* handle, operate, administer, direct, discharge, oversee, regulate.

conduit [kon · *doo* · it] *n.* channel, means, medium, method, path; agent, delegate, envoy, representative, middleman, intermediary.

confederacy [kon · *fed* · e · ra · see] *n.* conspiracy, plot, scheme, collusion, alliance; affiliation, consolidation, combination, compact, combine, union. *Ant.* individual.

C

confederation [kon · fed · e · *ray* · shen] *n.* agreement, compact, league, group.

confess [*kon* · fess] *v.* admit, inculpate, reveal, declare, confirm, own up, acknowledge, concede.

confession [ken · *fesh* · en] *n.* admission, acknowledgement, declaration, disclosure, revelation. *Ant.* denial.

confide [con · *fide*] *v.* disclose, divulge, share, reveal; entrust, rely on, believe in, have faith in.

confidence [*kon* · fi · dense] *n.* belief, assurance, faith, self-possession, trust ("She has confidence in me"); secret, intimate information ("I will keep Mary's confidence about her child's father"). *Ant.* mistrust, public knowledge.

confidence man *n.* swindler, trickster, bunco artist.

confidential [kon · fih · *den* · shel] *adj.* secret, classified, privileged, intimate.

confine [ken · *fine*] *v.* enclose, limit, bind, cage, detain, imprison, restrain, restrict. *Ant.* release, liberate.

confinement [ken · *fine* · ment] *n.* detention, jail, imprisonment, restriction, constraint. *Ant.* freedom.

confirm [kon · *ferm*] *v.* corroborate, prove, attest, authenticate, ratify, verify.

confirmation [kon · fer · *may* · shen] *n.* approval, authorization, endorsement, acknowledgment, verification ("confirmation of sale").

confiscate [*kon* · fis · kate] *v.* steal, seize, grab, impound, take. *Ant.* restore.

conflict [*kon* · flikt] *n.* clash, dispute, opposition, dissent, difference, controversy, hostility, resistence, rivalry.

conflict [kon · *flikt*] *v.* contrast, contradict, vary, oppose, dissent, diverge, contend, refute.

conform [ken · *form*] *v.* comply with, obey, observe, follow ("conform to the company's policy"); match, suit, follow, reconcile ("conform to the specifications").

confrontation [kon · fron · *tay* · shen] *n.* conflict, argument, altercation, struggle, collision, strife, opposition, discord, hostility. *Ant.* harmony, peace.

confuse [ken · *fyooz*] *v.* puzzle, frustrate, mislead, fluster, bewilder, muddle, befuddle, mix up. *Ant.* clarify.

confusion [ken · *fyoo* · zhen] *n.* disorder, unrest, disorientation, jumble, mess, tumult, commotion; ambiguity, incertitude, vagueness, enigma, dilemma.

conglomerate [kon · *glom* · er · et] *n.* corporation, monopoly, firm, giant, group. *Ant.* individual.

conglomerate [ken · *glom* · e · rate] *v.* mix, blend, mingle, join, associate.

congress [*kong* · gress] *n.* delegation, assembly, association, conference, gathering, convention.

congressman [*kong* · gress · man] *n.* representative, delegate, lawmaker, congresswoman.

conjecture [kon · *jek* · sure] *n.* guess, presumption, supposition, surmise, speculation.

conjoint [kon · *joint*] *adj.* combined, paired, associated, coupled ("a conjoint theft").

conjugal [*kon* · je · gul] *adj.* matrimonial, spousal, paired, united, wedded. *Ant.* single.

connect [ko · *nekt*] *v.* blend, fuse, join, match, unite, intertwine; interrelate, associate, link, cohere.

connivance [ke · *nye* · vens] *n.* secret, conspiracy, concert, collusion, consent, overlooking, condoning, contrivance.

connubial [ke · *noo* · bee · el] *adj.* conjugal, married, nuptial, wedded, spousal.

C

consanguinity [kon · san · *gwin* · i · tee] *n.* affiliation, blood relationship, brotherhood, kindred, kinship. *Ant.* unrelated.

conscience [*kon* · shense] *n.* principles, scruples, duty, inner voice, standards, ethics, moral sense.

conscientious [kon · shee · *en* · shes] *adj.* meticulous, fastidious, diligent, responsible ("The new paralegal was highly conscientious").

conscious [*kon* · shus] *adj.* awake, alert, alive, living; aware, attentive, heedful, mindful, understanding.

consent [ken · *sent*] *v.* agree, accept, allow, approve, concede, yield, comply, sanction, ratify.

consent [ken · *sent*] *n.* agreement, approval, acquiescence, concession, allowance, permission, accord, affirmance, concordance.

consequence [*kon* · se · kwense] *n.* result, outcome, effect, repercussion, reaction ("a consequence of drinking and driving"); significance, importance, influence, value, meaning ("A female president would be of great consequence").

conservation [*kon* · ser · vey · shun] *n.* preservation, protection, saving, fostering, maintenance.

conservator [ken · *ser* · ve · tore] *n.* guardian, protector, manager, preserver, overseer, caretaker.

consideration [ken · sid · e · *ray* · shen] *n.* value, incentive, recompense, inducement, reward, benefit ("Consideration is an essential element of a valid and enforceable contract"); kindness, respect, courtesy, thoughtfulness ("She had a lot of consideration for her mother"); thought, advisement, rumination ("Take it under consideration").

consign [kon · *sine*] *v.* deliver, entrust, send, ship, transfer, authorize.

consignee [ken · sine · *ee*] *n.* receiver, salesperson, representative, seller. *Ant.* consignor.

consignment [ken · *sine* · ment] *n.* entrusting, distribution, committal, transmittal.

consignor [ken · sine · *or*] *n.* shipper, sender. *Ant.* consignee.

consist [kon · *sist*] *v.* be made up of, be composed of, contain, constitute, involve, entail, encompass.

consistent [kon · *sis* · tent] *adj.* uniform, consonant, regular, equal, equitable, logical, regular, dependable, unchanging, true, agreeing, compatible.

consolidate [ken · *sol* · i · date] *v.* unify, combine, connect, integrate, bind ("The county's four school districts have been consolidated into a single district"). *Ant.* sever, disconnect, weaken.

consolidation [ken · sol · i · *day* · shen] *n.* combination, alliance, fusion, incorporation, merger. *Ant.* separation.

consortium [kon · *sore* · shum] *n.* conjugal fellowship, affection, intimacy, companionship ("She lost her husband's consortium because of his accident"); alliance, union, trust, pool, consolidation ("The cable company formed a consortium to keep prices high").

conspicuous [ken · *spik* · yoo · us] *adj.* clear, pronounced, well-marked, manifest, obvious, observable, visible, noticeable, distinct. *Ant.* concealed, hidden.

conspiracy [ken · *spi* · re · see] *n.* connivance, counterplot, frame, plot, scheme, trickery.

conspire [ken · *spire*] *v.* agree, plan, plot, unite, abet, coact.

constable [*kon* · ste · bul] *n.* peace officer, police officer, processor.

constant [kon · stent] *adj.* continuous, invariable, dependable, incessant, sustained, stable, certain, unswerving.

constant [kon · stent] *n.* standard, usual practice, regularity, pattern, form.

constitute [kon · sti · toot] *v.* set up, establish, form, comprise, institute, create ("We constituted an apartment alliance").

constitution [kon · sti · too · shen] *n.* charter, code, formation, written law, supreme law.

constitutional [kon · sti · too · shen · el] *adj.* approved, chartered, lawful, democratic, enforceable. *Ant.* unconstitutional.

constrain [kon · strane] *v.* bind, confine, detain, restrict, restrain; prevent, prohibit.

construction [ken · struk · shen] *n.* definition, inference, translation, version, clarification ("strict construction of the Bill of Rights"); assembly, building, arrangement, origination, erection ("the construction of a house").

constructive [ken · struk · tiv] *adj.* effective, positive, practical, helpful, beneficial ("constructive criticism"); inferred, implied, presumed ("constructive eviction").

construe [kon · strew] *v.* interpret, restate, explain, clarify, convey, decode, decipher, infer, deduce.

consul [kon · sul] *n.* delegate, emissary, envoy, representative, ambassador.

consult [kon · sult] *v.* discuss, seek, advice, confer with, refer to; meet, discuss, exchange views, deliberate, confer.

consume [kon · soom] *v.* eat, employ, empty, exhaust, deplete, use, utilize, spend, waste ("consume energy"); destroy, annihilate, demolish, level, devastate ("consumed by fire").

consumer [kon · soom · er] *n.* buyer, client, patron, purchaser, vendee, customer.

consummate [kon · sum · mate] *v.* realize, achieve, accomplish, effectuate, fulfill, perfect.

consummation [kon · sum · may · shun] *n.* completion, perfection, realization, achievement, fulfillment.

consumption [kon · sump · shun] *n.* use, utilization, assimilation, depletion, waste, loss, destruction, exhaustion. *Ant.* conservation.

contact [kon · takt] *n.* touching, connection, meeting, impact, nexus, junction, joining ("offensive contact"); lead, referral, connection, tie, reference ("a business contact").

contact [kon · takt] *v.* communicate with, reach, call, notify, correspond, inform, signal; touch, connect, join, overlap, abut, connect, attach, border.

contagious [kon · tay · jus] *adj.* communicable, infectious, spreadable, transmittable, transferrable, transmissible, infective.

contain [kon · tane] *v.* hold, include, embrace, be composed of, subsist of; restrain, bind, check, restrict, inhibit, jail, constrain, lock up, hold back.

contaminate [kon · tam · i · nate] *v.* spoil, poison, pervert, corrupt, degrade, defile, ruin.

contemplate [kon · tem · plate] *v.* ponder, deliberate, ruminate, cogitate, study, examine ("contemplate the risks"); anticipate, envision, foresee, expect, intend ("I do not contemplate calling any witnesses").

contemplation [kon · tem · play · shun] *n.* deliberation, rumination, pondering, consideration, thought, reverie; anticipation, intention, purpose, forethought, goal.

contemporaneous [kon · tem · per · ay · nee · us] *adj.* concurrent, simultaneous, coexistent, contemporary, synchronous ("contemporaneous transaction").

contemporary [kon · tem · po · ra · ree] *n.* peer, equal, colleague, friend.

contemporary [kon · *tem* · po · ra · ree] *adj.* simultaneous, concurrent, related, coincident, attendant, linked; modern, recent, state-of-the-art, chic, avant-garde, fashionable, current, topical.

contempt [kon · *tempt*] *n.* disregard, defiance, disrespect, violation, disobedience ("contempt of court"); disdain, scorn, hatred, abhorrence, opprobrium, loathing, condescension, scoffing, arrogance ("contempt for criminals").

contemptible [kon · *temp* · ti · bul] *adj.* abhorrent, vile, evil, hateful, wicked, perfidious, despicable, depraved, base, deplorable.

contemptuous [kon · *temp* · choo · us] *adj.* scornful, derogatory, disparaging, disdainful, hateful, rude, haughty, pompous, arrogant, condescending.

contend [kon · *tend*] *v.* vie, disagree, compete, dispute, contradict, dissent; maintain, argue, advance, assert, hold, insist, state, attest.

content [*kon* · tent] *n.* subject matter, thought, substance, meaning, nature, purpose, motif, thesis, essence, gist; form, structure, composition, framework.

content [kon · *tent*] *adj.* satisfied, pleased, happy, agreeable, appeased, willing, complacent.

contention [kon · *ten* · shun] *n.* position, claim, viewpoint, issue, ground, point, proposition; quarrel, opposition, friction, disaccord, antagonism, hostility, debate, dissent.

contents [*kon* · tents] *n.* substance, essence, text, topics, scope, components, subject, sense.

contest [*kon* · test] *n.* competition, struggle, battle, war, fight, engagement, disagreement, variance; game, sweepstakes, lottery.

contest [kon · *test*] *v.* oppose, dispute, challenge, question, counter, object to, fight, resist.

context [*kon* · tekst] *n.* background, surroundings, environment, setting; meaning, tenor, purport, sense, scope.

contiguous [kon · *tig* · yoo · us] *adj.* abutting, adjacent, adjoining, against, beside, bordering, near, close, proximate, touching.

contingency [kon · *tin* · jen · see] *n.* possibility, circumstance, likelihood, happening, chance, conditional event.

contingent [kon · *tin* · jent] *adj.* possible, dependent, conditioned, subordinate, provisional, subject to ("contingent claim").

continual [kon · *tin* · yoo · ul] *adj.* perpetual, unending, everlasting, constant, persistent, endless, uninterrupted.

continuance [kon · *tin* · yoo · ants] *n.* adjournment, stay, postponement, cessation; prolongation, protraction, extension, lengthening, repetition.

continuation [kon · *tin* · yoo · *ay* · shun] *n.* resumption, reestablishment, reversion, reinstatement, recommencement, reopening ("continuation of a suit"); lengthening, protraction, addition, extension ("a continuation of the lien").

continue [kon · *tin* · yoo] *v.* persist, persevere, pursue, prevail, forge ahead, progress ("continue to the end"); adjourn, delay, postpone, suspend, hold over, table, shelve ("continue the case"); remain, endure, stay, maintain ("continue as attorney of record").

continuing [kon · *tin* · yoo · ing] *adj.* ongoing, constant, enduring, subsisting, present.

continuity [kon · ti · *new* · i · tee] *adj.* coherence, consistency, connection, constancy, succession, flow.

continuous [kon · *tin* · yoo · us] *adj.* uninterrupted, unbroken, whole, sustained, ceaseless, constant, unceasing ("continuous adverse possession").

C

contort [*kon* · tort] *v.* distort, bend, deform, twist, convolute, pervert, disfigure.

contour [*kon* · toor] *n.* outline, figure, form, profile, picture, silhouette; shape, frame, structure.

contra [*kon* · tra] *adv.* against, opposite, adverse to, confronting, opposed to.

contraband [*kon* · tra · band] *n.* illegal goods, bootlegged items, plunder, prohibited articles, smuggled goods.

contract [*kon* · trakt] *n.* agreement, understanding, bargain, compact, mutual promise, covenant, accord, arrangement, promise, assurance.

contract [*kon* · *trakt*] *v.* agree, promise, engage, undertake, covenant, bargain, obligate, pledge; condense, shrink, recede, lessen.

contractual [*kon* · *trak* · choo · el] *adj.* binding, obligatory, promised, settled, consensual, pledged, stipulated ("a contractual obligation").

contradict [kon · tra · *dikt*] *v.* deny, refute, controvert, rebut, gainsay, contrast, argue, conflict, differ, dissent, counter.

contradiction [kon · tra · *dik* · shun] *n.* discrepancy, disagreement, incongruity, inconsistency, variance, controversion, rebuttal, negation.

contradictory [kon · tra · *dik* · tuh · ree] *adj.* inconsistent, clashing, irreconcilable, contrary, opposed, discrepant, negating, nullifying ("a contradictory statement").

contrary [*kon* · trair · ree] *adj.* counter, adverse, against, opposite, irreconcilable, at variance, contradictory, denying ("contrary to law").

contrast [*kon* · trast] *n.* difference, distinction, disparity, differentiation, antithesis, polarity.

contrast [kun · *trast*] *v.* differentiate, oppose, compare, distinguish.

contravene [*kon* · tra · veen] *v.* go against, violate, foil, thwart, disobey, frustrate, oppose, disregard, conflict with, nullify.

contribute [kon · *trib* · yoot] *v.* give, assist, donate, furnish, provide, aid ("contribute to charity"); help produce, participate, influence, help cause, advance ("contribute to his own injury"); indemnify, restore, return, reimburse, make restitution.

contribution [*kon* · tri · byoo · shun] *n.* donation, gift, charity, assistance, grant; collaboration, cooperation, help, interest, complicity, indemnification, restitution, reparation, repayment, satisfaction.

contrite [kon · *trite*] *adj.* remorseful, penitent, apologetic, humble, sorrowful, regretful.

contrivance [kon · *trive* · ants] *n.* plot, plan, mechanism, method, artifice, deception, fabrication, connivance.

contrive [kon · *trive*] *v.* scheme, conspire, collude, plot, organize; conceive, imagine, invent, create, fashion, improvise, develop.

control [*kon* · *troll*] *n.* power, authority, jurisdiction, dominion, mastery, supervision, regulation, care, charge, dominance; restraint, moderation, deterrence, inhibition.

control [kon · *troll*] *v.* arrest, confine, constrain, restrain, prohibit; regulate, direct, govern, rule, oversee, command, supervise.

controller [kon · *troll* · er] *n.* comptroller, accountant, inspector, auditor, bookkeeper, bursar.

controversial [kon · tro · *ver* · shul] *adj.* provocative, debatable, arguable, widely discussed; at issue, contestable, in dispute, contended, litigious.

controversy [*kon* · tro · ver · see] *n.* lawsuit, case, legal action, legal proceeding; debate, altercation, dispute, squabble, disharmony, dissention, discord.

controvert [kon · tro · vert] v. dispute, oppose, contest, counter, negate, rebut, refute, disprove, contravene, deny.

convene [kon · veen] v. assemble, collect, mobilize, gather, summon, amass, round up, consolidate.

convenience [kon · veen · yence] n. accommodation, benefit, comfort, relief, support, avail, assistance ("the convenience of a second bathroom"); chance, freedom, opportunity, leisure, spare moment ("at your convenience").

convenient [kon · veen · yent] adj. suitable, advantageous, accessible, easy, useful, carefree, nearby, available, commodious.

convention [kon · ven · shun] n. meeting, gathering, forum, conclave, assembly; custom, protocol, tradition.

conventional [kon · ven · shun · ul] adj. standard, accepted, normal, regular, routine, approved, orthodox, established, familiar, usual, typical.

converge [kon · verj] v. unite, combine, approach, coalesce, merge, gather, congregate, convene.

conversation [kon · ver · say · shun] n. discourse, dialogue, discussion, colloquy, exchange, interchange, conference, rap.

conversion [kon · ver · zhen] n. change, transformation, shift, metamorphosis, transmutation; theft, larceny, misappropriation, deprivation, embezzlement.

convertible [kon · vert · uh · bul] adj. exchangeable, transformable, interchangeable, permutable, adaptable, adjustable.

convince [kon · vince] v. persuade, sway, entice, convert, win over, coax, influence, allure, enlist.

convincing [kon · vin · sing] adj. persuasive, compelling, credible, strong, plausible, substantial, powerful ("a convincing argument").

convoy [kon · voy] n. escort, guard, fleet, contingent, group.

cooperate [ko · op · er · ate] v. collaborate, collude, participate, unite, ally, act jointly, work together.

cooperation [ko · op · er · ay · shun] n. participation, assistance, concert, collaboration, complicity, reciprocity, solidarity, agreement.

cooperative [ko · op · er · a · tiv] n. alliance, collective, association, federation, partnership, coalition.

cooperative [ko · op · er · a · tiv] adj. helpful, assisting, obliging, accommodating, harmonious, easy, synergistic.

co-opt [ko · opt] v. preempt, assume, usurp, absorb.

coordinate [ko · or · din · ate] v. adjust, arrange, harmonize, combine, balance, synchronize, mesh, integrate, equalize.

copious [kope · ee · us] adj. ample, full, abundant, prolific, profuse, replete, generous, voluminous, bountiful.

copy [kah · pee] v. reproduce, duplicate, trace, print, transcribe; forge, cheat, plagarize, mimic, ape, falsify, infringe, impersonate.

copy [kah · pee] n. reproduction, transcript, duplicate, facsimile, likeness, image, impression; forgery, fake, imitation.

copyright [kah · pee · rite] n. authority, grant, license, permit, privilege, authorization.

corollary [kore · o · lair · ee] n. consequence, outcome, effect, conclusion, offshoot, outgrowth, addition, correlation.

C

corporation [kore · per · *ay* · shun] *n.* business, company, enterprise, organization, association, establishment, firm.

corporal [*kore* · per · ul] *adj.* bodily, physical, fleshly ("corporal punishment").

corporeal [kore · *poe* · ree · ul] *adj.* tangible, bodily, actual, real, fleshly, physical, palpable ("corporeal punishment").

corpse *n.* body, remains, victim, deceased, cadaver, dead body, stiff.

corpus [*kor* · puss] *n.* aggregate, bulk, quantity, sum, total, body, substance ("corpus of a trust").

correct [ko · *rekt*] *v.* alter, modify, remedy, fix, adjust, amend; punish, reprimand, censure, chastize.

correct [ko · *rekt*] *adj.* proper, actual, true, exact, factual, careful, valid ("a correct statement of the law").

correction [ko · *rek* · shun] *n.* alteration, modification, change, amendment, remedy, adjustment; improvement, reform, remediation, rehabilitation; penalty, discipline, reprimand, retribution, scolding.

correlate [*kor* · re · late] *v.* connect, relate, coordinate, affiliate, match, parallel.

correspond [kor · ess · *pond*] *v.* communicate, notify, write, reply, contact; relate, fit, equal, approximate, correlate, harmonize, cohere, match.

correspondence [kore · ess · *pon* · dents] *n.* communication, mail, letters, writing; similarity, equivalence, resemblance, agreement, congruity, uniformity, parity.

corroborate [ko · *rob* · er · ate] *v.* substantiate, confirm, affirm, verify, attest, validate, endorse, strengthen ("corroborate an alibi").

corrupt [ko · *rupt*] *adj.* tainted, dishonorable, unprincipled, debased, wicked, perfidious, insincere, venal.

corrupt [ko · *rupt*] *v.* adulterate, spoil, pollute, subvert, pervert, defraud.

corruption [ko · *rup* · shun] *n.* deception, disloyalty, graft, perfidy, villainy, dishonesty, injustice, abuse of trust, knavery.

cosign [ko · sine] *v.* endorse, certify, assure, insure, validate, underwrite, comake.

cosignee [ko · sy · nee] *n.* comaker, guarantor, surety.

cost *n.* price, rate, charge, worth, value, bill, fee ("the cost of a new car"); sacrifice, injury, consequence, loss, suffering ("the cost of war").

coterie [ko · te · ree] *n.* circle, club, clique, group, clan, alliance, society.

council [*koun* · sil] *n.* board, committee, advisors, cabinet, convention, caucus.

counsel [*koun* · sel] *n.* attorney, lawyer, counselor, advocate, legal advisor; advice, guidance, opinion, warning, instruction.

counsel [*koun* · sel] *v.* advise, recommend, caution, urge, propose, instruct, direct.

count *n.* claim, charge, allegation, declaration, cause of action, listing, enumeration.

counter [*koun* · ter] *v.* oppose, offset, rebut, resist, contradict, defy.

counterfeit [*kown* · ter · fit] *adj.* false, imitation, sham, phony, fraudulent, bogus, forged. *Ant.* true, real, original.

countermand [kown · ter · *mand*] *v.* revoke, withdraw, change, cancel, annul, abolish.

countermand [kown · ter · *mand*] *n.* offer, counterproposal, different proposal, compromise. *Ant.* offer.

countersignature [kown · ter · *sig* · ne · choor] *n.* signature, cosignee, witness, underwriter.

country [*kun* · tree] *n.* nation, land, state, territory, citizenry.

county [*kown* · tee] *n.* subdivision, district, parish, region, municipal, corporation, province.

coupon [*koo* · pon] *n.* certificate, share, interest, dividend, voucher, ticket, token, credit.

course *n.* path, direction, route, passage, development, order, plan.

court *n.* unit of government, forum, chamber, panel, bench, bar, justice, judge, session.

covenant [*kov* · e · nent] *n.* agreement, promise, pledge, vow, bond, compact, commitment ("covenant not to sue").

cover [*kuv* · er] *v.* protect, wrap, hide, conceal, safeguard, camouflage. *Ant.* reveal.

cover [*kuv* · er] *n.* replacement, exchange, alternate, buyer's right.

coverage [*kuv* · er · ej] *n.* reimbursement, premium, protection, warranty, guarantee.

covert [koe · *vert*] *adj.* undercover, hidden, clandestine, secret, mysterious, unseen.

coverture [*kuv* · er · cher] *n.* marriage, nuptial bond, married state. *Ant.* single.

crack *n.* cocaine; break, solve ("crack the case").

create [*cree* · ate] *v.* develop, form, launch, originate, make, construct, cause.

credence [*cree* · dense] *n.* believability, certainty, trust, acceptance, faith.

credentials [kre · *den* · shelz] *n.* authorization, recommendations, endorsement, qualifications, references.

credibility [kred · ih · *bil* · uh · tee] *n.* believability, integrity, trustworthiness, reliability, soundness.

credible [kred · ih · bul] *adj.* believable, conceivable, creditable, honest, plausible, likely, worthy ("His testimony isn't credible"). *Ant.* dubious, unlikely.

credit [*kred* · it] *v.* accredit, accept, acknowledge, attribute to.

credit [*kred* · it] *n.* rating, trust, standing, authority, loan, mortgage ("He has good credit").

creditor [*kred* · it · er] *n.* lender, assignee.

crime *n.* felony, misdemeanor, criminal act, misconduct, delinquency, corruption, offense, lawlessness.

criminal [*krim* · i · nul] *n.* felon, culprit, violator, offender, delinquent, transgressor.

criminal [*krim* · i · nul] *adj.* unlawful, felonious, illegal, notorious, blameworthy, noncivil ("criminal intent").

criterion [kry · *teer* · ee · on] *n.* basis, standard, test, yardstick, guide, measure, model.

critical [*krit* · i · kul] *adj.* crucial, decisive, major, vital, grave ("the critical vote"); blaming, judgmental, carping, rebuking, disapproving ("critical mother").

criticize [*krit* · i · size] *v.* disparage, impugn, reprove, condemn, decry; adjudge, assess, appraise, rate, value.

cross *v.* blend, mingle, pollinate; betray, hinder, impede, interfere, obstruct, foil, frustrate; converge, intersect, meet, divide.

cross *adj.* angry, annoyed, crabby, grouchy, petulant, irritable.

crossing [*kross* · ing] *n.* passage, exchange, interchange, traverse, pathway.

crucial [*kroosh* · al] *adj.* critical, determining, pivotal, vital, supreme, essential, decisive.

cruel [krool] *adj.* brutal, malevolent, savage, heartless, malicious, inhumane, oppressive.

cruelty [*kroo* · ul · tee] *n.* brutality, harshness, spitefulness, viciousness, torture, violence ("cruelty to animals"). *Ant.* sympathy, kindness.

cry *v.* notify, advertise, proclaim, pronounce, broadcast; weep, lament, whimper, moan, grieve.

C

cudgel [*kud* · jell] *n.* bat, club, cane, stick, ferrule, weapon.

culpable [*kulp* · uh · bul] *adj.* blameworthy, blamable, responsible, chargeable, punishable, answerable. *Ant.* innocent.

cumulative [*kyoo* · myoo · lah · tiv] *adj.* accruing, additive, advancing, amassed, increasing, totaling ("cumulative effect").

curative [*kyoo* · re · tiv] *adj.* remedial, mending, correcting, healing ("curative legislation").

curator [*kyoo* · ray · ter] *n.* guardian, conservator, manager, caretaker ("curator of the museum").

cure *n.* recovery, improvement, remedy, restoration, correction, palliative, panacea, antidote, elixir.

curfew [*ker* · few] *n.* limitation, restriction, prohibition.

currency [*ker* · en · see] *n.* money, legal tender, cash, bills, funds, dollars.

current [*ker* · ent] *adj.* immediate, prevailing, contemporary, actual, customary. *Ant.* past, uncommon.

cursory [*kurr* · suh · ree] *adj.* brief, hasty, indifferent, shallow, unmindful, harried, lax, perfunctory ("a cursory reading"). *Ant.* careful, thorough.

curtail [kur · *tale*] *v.* diminish, lessen, abate, reduce, cut short, abridge.

curtilage [*ker* · tih · lidj] *n.* enclosure, yard, grounds.

custodial [kuss · *toe* · dee · ul] *adj.* confined, detained, supervised.

custodian [kuss · *toe* · dee · en] *n.* caretaker, overseer, governor, curator, maintainer, protector, watchman, conservator, janitor.

custody [*kuss* · te · dee] *n.* care, control, protection, possession, management, preservation, restraint, impoundment, charge.

custom [*kuss* · tem] *n.* habit, practice, convention, routine, established, precedent, procedure.

customary [*kuss* · te · meh · ree] *adj.* accepted, expected, regular, frequent, popular, ordinary, established, habitual, commonplace.

customer [*kus* · te · mer] *n.* buyer, client, user, purchaser, shopper, patron, consumer.

customs [*kuss* · temz] *n.* duty, tax, tariff, toll, assessment ("The customs on my Dior dress was high").

cut *n.* incision, gash, nick, cleavage, laceration; reduction, diminution, decrease; share, slice, part, portion, allotment, percentage.

cut *v.* sever, split, clip, nick, slash; shorten, lessen, lower, reduce, curtail; dilute, weaken, thin, adulterate.

cutback *n.* reduction, decrease, lessening, curtailment ("a cutback in spending").

cycle [*sigh* · kul] *n.* era, phase, period, age; chain, rhythm, succession, series.

cynical [*sin* · i · kul] *adj.* sarcastic, sardonic, pessimistic, scornful, contemptuous, ironic, wry.

dab *n.* bit, speck, spot, dollop, smidgen, drop.

dab *v.* daub, swab, pat.

dactylography [dak · ti · *log* · re · fee] *n.* fingerprint analysis, scientific analysis.

dally [*dah* · lee] *v.* dawdle, procrastinate, putter, linger, loiter, tarry.

damage [*dam* · ej] *n.* loss, hurt, harm, destruction, impairment. *Ant.* benefit.

damages [*dam* · eh · jez] *n.* restoration, compensation, restitution, repayment, recovery, reparation, expenses, expiation.

danger [*dane* · jer] *n.* peril, risk, crisis, hazard, uncertainty, emergency.

dangerous [*dane* · jer · ess] *adj.* hazardous, precarious, unsafe, harmful, destructive, injurious.

dangle [*dang* · gul] *v.* hang, suspend, swing, entice, tempt.

dark *n.* night, shade, doom, dusk, twilight ("meet you at dark"); ignorance, secrecy, seclusion, mystery ("kept in the dark").

dark *adj.* dull, dim, indistinct, gloomy, faint, deep, mystical, mysterious, hidden, secret; evil, bad, satanic, corrupt, nefarious, wicked.

dash *n.* bit, drop, hint, sprinkling, touch, taste, smidgen, suggestion; sprint, run, race; style, flair, energy, esprit, vigor, vivacity, panache.

dash *v.* hasten, run, race, rush, bolt, scurry ("dash to the bank"); foil, dampen, discourage, frustrate, ruin, spoil ("dash his hopes").

dashing [*dash* · ing] *adj.* gallant, dapper, debonair, stylish, flamboyant.

data [*day* · tah] *n.* facts, information, documentation, evidence, compilations, statistics.

day in court *n.* due process of law, hearing, opportunity, right to be heard.

daze *n.* shock, trance, coma, bewilderment.

daze *v.* confuse, shock, astonish, mystify, perplex, stun.

de facto [day *fak* · toe] *adj.* in fact, in reality, existing. *Ant.* de jure.

de jure [day *zhoor*] *adj.* rightful, authorized, lawful, sanctioned. *Ant.* de facto.

de minimis [day *min* · ih · mis] *adj.* minimal, insignificant, trivial, unimportant.

dead *adj.* lifeless, deceased, obsolete, useless, departed, expired, extinct. *Ant.* living, alive, vital.

deadlock [*ded* · lok] *n.* blockage, impasse, standstill, stoppage.

D

deadly [ded · lee] *adj.* dangerous, destructive, lethal, fatal, hazardous, grave, murderous, perfidious.

dealer [deel · er] *n.* wholesaler, merchant, broker, retailer, representative, vendor, middleman. *Ant.* consumer.

death *n.* end of life, expiration, annihilation, extinction, end, destruction. *Ant.* life, resurrection.

debar [dee · bar] *v.* exclude, bar, shut out ("debar the unethical lawyer").

debase [dee · base] *v.* adulterate, cheapen, belittle, reduce, dishonor, pollute, contaminate. *Ant.* upgrade, encourage.

debatable [dee · bate · uh · bul] *adj.* arguable, in question, open to doubt, unresolved, disputable, suspect, dubious, conjectural.

debate [de · bate] *v.* discuss, altercate, controvert, wrangle, confute, consider, ponder.

debauchery [de · baw · che · ree] *n.* self-indulgence, lust, excesses, seduction, vice, overindulgence.

debenture [de · ben · cher] *n.* unsecured bond, unsecured note.

debilitate [de · bill · ih · tayt] *v.* cripple, enervate, weaken, eviscerate, exhaust, devitalize.

debit [deb · it] *v.* charge, list, post.

debit [deb · it] *n.* debt, indebtedness, obligation, arrears, liability. *Ant.* credit.

debt *n.* obligation, liability, debit, dues, commitment, encumbrance.

debtee [det · ee] *n.* creditor, lender.

debtor [det · er] *n.* borrower, buyer, deadbeat.

deceased [de · seessd] *n.* dead person, departed, decedent.

decedent [de · see · dent] *n.* deceased, testator, intestate, dead individual, departed.

deceit [de · seet] *n.* fraud, misrepresentation, cheating, dishonesty, trickery, duplication, falsification.

deceive [de · seev] *v.* delude, mislead, swindle, scam, defraud, dupe, hoodwink, screw, trick, victimize.

decent [dee · sent] *adj.* proper, suitable, ethical, honorable, prudent, respectable, courteous, kind, thoughtful, obliging.

deception [de · cep · shun] *n.* fraud, betrayal, trickery, pretense, duplicity, cunning, insincerity.

decide [de · side] *v.* adjudge, conclude, hold, find, decree, determine, establish, resolve, rule.

decision [de · sizh · en] *n.* conclusion, resolution, agreement, judgment, adjudication, outcome, ruling.

declarant [de · clare · ent] *n.* speaker, affirmant, informer, deponent, witness.

declaration [dek · la · ray · shun] *n.* affirmation, statement, admission, profession, expression, proclamation, revelation.

declaratory [de · klar · uh · toh · ree] *adj.* elucidating, explanatory, clarifying, assertive ("declaratory judgment"). *Ant.* confusing.

declare [de · klare] *v.* allege, admit, convey, attest, feel, disclose, assert, state.

decline [de · cline] *v.* reject, renounce, repudiate, veto, spurn, repel ("decline representation"); fall, decay, drop, ebb, wane ("prices decline").

decrease [de · kreese] *v.* diminish, subside, curtail, abate, deduct, recede, taper, quell.

decrease [*dee* · kreese] *n.* fall, reduction, diminution, dwindling, loss, declination, attenuation.

decree [de · *kree*] *v.* order, dictate, ordain, enact, announce, command.

decree [de · *kree*] *n.* mandate, commandment, directive, ordinance, statute, decision, ruling.

decry [de · *kry*] *v.* criticize, blame, vilify, disparage, traduce, condemn, defame, denounce.

dedicate [*ded* · i · kate] *v.* pledge, commit, devote, endow, convey, apportion.

dedication [ded · i · *kay* · shen] *n.* setting aside, donation, endowment, conveyance, presentation, honor, celebration.

deductible [de · *duk* · tih · bul] *adj.* removable, allowable, discountable.

deduction [de · *duk* · shen] *n.* subtraction, withdrawal, removal, exemption, allowance ("the home office deduction"); conclusion, assumption, understanding, inference, answer ("Holmes's deduction was accurate").

deed *v.* transfer, convey, grant.

deed *n.* instrument, release, assignment, conveyance, contract ("warranty deed"); achievement, action, accomplishment, performance ("good deed").

deeded [*deed* · ed] *adj., adv.* conveyed, granted, given, transferred.

deem *v.* consider, believe, determine, perceive, regard, conceive.

deface [dee · *fayss*] *v.* destroy, blemish, injure, disfigure, tarnish, mar, mutilate, vandalize.

defalcation [dee · fal · *kay* · shen] *n.* misappropriation, embezzlement, fraud, misuse; reduction, setoff, counterclaim, recoupment.

defamation [def · e · *may* · shen] *n.* libel, slander, defamatory statement, deprecation, belittlement, slur, vilification, traducement, opprobrium, calumny. *Ant.* praise.

defamatory [de · *fam* · e · toh · ree] *adj.* abusive, shameful, slanderous, injurious, detracting, derogatory, insulting. *Ant.* laudatory.

default [de · *fawlt*] *v.* defraud, neglect, evade, dishonor, omit, shirk, fail ("He defaulted on his loan").

default [de · *fawlt*] *n.* nonperformance, breach, neglect, negligence, evasion; fault, neglect, omission. *Ant.* compliance, performance.

defeasance [dee · *fee* · zens] *n.* cancellation, annulment ("a clause covering defeasance").

defeasible [dee · *feez* · ibl] *adj.* voidable, revocable, dissoluble, removable. *Ant.* unalterable.

defect [de · *fekt*] *v.* abandon, depart, desert, reject, renounce, revolt ("defect to another country").

defect [*dee* · fekt] *n.* imperfection, shortcoming, deformity, insufficiency, impairment, error, fault, flaw ("a latent defect").

defective [de · *fek* · tiv] *adj.* imperfect, impaired, flawed, abnormal, inadequate, unsound, nonmarketable, broken. *Ant.* sound, sufficient.

defend [de · *fend*] *v.* represent, advocate, vindicate, assert, protect, secure, watch, save, nourish, plead, prove a case, counter, argue for, propound. *Ant.* attack.

defendant [de · *fen* · dent] *n.* accused, respondent, responding litigant, the party charged. *Ant.* plaintiff.

defender [de · *fen* · der] *n.* attorney, advocate, counsel, pleader.

D

defense [de · *fense*] *n.* explanation, rebuttal, vindication, justification, plea, rationalization ("a winning defense"); protection, preservation ("the defense of freedom of speech"). *Ant.* offense.

defer [de · *fer*] *v.* delay, detain, postpone, suspend, set aside. *Ant.* hasten.

deficiency [de · *fish* · en · see] *n.* insufficiency, lack, shortage, inadequacy, absence, scantiness, want. *Ant.* adequacy.

deficit [*def* · ih · sit] *n.* deficiency, arrears, lack, default.

define [de · *fine*] *v.* describe, formulate, name, establish, label, explain, limit.

definite [*def* · ih · nit] *adj.* conclusive, sure, certain, fixed, ascertained, precise, positive, true, exact.

definition [def · ih · *nish* · un] *n.* description, meaning, clarification, identification, denotation, signification.

definitive [de · *fin* · e · tiv] *adj.* conclusive, complete, absolute, decisive, perfect, ultimate, final, clear ("Because the court's final judgment is definitive, and no appeal has been taken, the lawsuit is ended").

defraud [de · *frawd*] *v.* cheat, deceive, bamboozle, burn, delude.

defunct [de · *funkt*] *adj.* dead, expired, inoperative, invalid, obsolete, void, inactive, nonexistent. *Ant.* functioning, working.

defy [de · *fie*] *v.* disregard, disobey, resist, oppose, flout, battle, repulse, challenge, frustrate.

degradation [deg · ra · *day* · shun] *n.* debasement, humiliation, ignominy, shame, odium, abjection.

degree [de · *gree*] *n.* magnitude, intensity, extent, range, caliber, level, rank.

dehors [dee · *hohrz*] *prep.* beyond, unconnected, foreign to ("dehors the record").

delay [de · *lay*] *n.* detainment, pause, stall, wait, interruption, suspension, postponement ("a delay in the proceedings").

delay [de · *lay*] *v.* arrest, block, retard, slacken, detain, hold up, postpone, prolong.

delegate [*del* · e · gate] *v.* authorize, appoint, commission, assign ("to delegate authority").

delegate [*del* · e · get] *n.* agent, appointee, consul, representative, proxy, spokesperson ("Her delegate attended the conference").

delegation [del · e · *gay* · shen] *n.* appointment, authorization, commissioning, assignment ("the delegation of authority from one person to another"); representatives, commission, organization, gathering ("She was appointed a member of the Georgia state delegation").

delete [de · *leet*] *v.* cancel, erase, omit, remove, obliterate, excise, expel, efface.

deliberate [dee · *lib* · e · rate] *v.* ponder, consider, think, contemplate, brood, ruminant, reflect, speculate ("The jury deliberated for three days before reaching a verdict").

deliberate [dee · *lib* · e · ret] *adj.* conscious, calculated, considered, willfully, intended, knowingly ("a deliberate mistake").

deliberation [de · lib · e · *ray* · shen] *n.* examination, consideration, forethought, reflection, attention.

delinquency [de · *link* · wen · see] *n.* carelessness, failure, negligence, default, nonobservance, neglect ("delinquency in loan payments"); corruption, wrongdoing, misbehavior ("juvenile delinquency"). *Ant.* performance; good behavior.

delinquent [de · *link* · went] *adj.* outstanding, unpaid, tardy ("delinquent payments"); criminal, neglectful, immoral, scandalous ("a delinquent minor"). *Ant.* honest, innocent.

D

delinquent [de · *link* · went] *n.* offender, wrongdoer, lawbreaker, undesirable, derelict, felon, hoodlum, miscreant, young offender.

deliver [de · *liv* · er] *v.* convey, carry, remit, transfer, transport, turn over, send, forward; free, liberate, emancipate; announce, declare, express.

delivery [de · *liv* · e · ree] *n.* conveyance, passage, relinquishment, commitment, transferral, consignment; birth, childbirth, labor, bearing, birthing; speech, presentation, elocution.

delude [de · *lood*] *v.* misstate, misrepresent, deceive, cheat, swindle, misguide, misinform.

delve *v.* inquire into, investigate, probe, peer, search, penetrate, unearth, ferret out.

demand [de · *mand*] *v.* require, insist, assert, order, plead, summon, ask, request, necessitate.

demand [de · *mand*] *n.* requirement, order, ultimatum, claim, request ("make a demand for satisfaction of payment").

demarcate [de · *mar* · kate] *v.* mark, separate, border, demark, zone, delimit, limit.

demean [de · *meen*] *v.* debase, belittle, humiliate, shame, deprecate, disparage; appear, resemble, comport.

demeanor [de · *meen* · er] *n.* presence, conduct, attitude, manner, style, bearing, conduct ("The demeanor of that witness, particularly the fact that he wouldn't make eye contact, makes me question his credibility").

demise [de · *mize*] *v.* lease, bequeath, transmit, confer, endow.

demise [de · *mize*] *n.* lease, conveyance, transfer ("the demise of an estate"); decease, passing, fall, collapse, extermination ("High levels of crime led to the demise of the community").

democracy [de · *mok* · re · see] *n.* commonwealth, equalitarianism, freedom, justice, representative government.

demonstrate [*dem* · un · strait] *v.* show, establish, indicate, determine, prove; explain, illustrate, describe, express; march, strike, protest, rally.

demonstrative [de · *mahn* · stre · tiv] *adj.* illustrative, clarifying, elucidating, supportive ("demonstrative evidence"); expressive, passionate, effusive, emotional ("a demonstrative witness").

demur [de · *mer*] *v.* challenge, protest, dissent, refute, balk, disagree, object to, take exception to.

demure [de · *myoor*] *adj.* modest, retiring, bashful, coy, prudent, shy. *Ant.* brash.

denial [de · *ny* · el] *n.* renunciation, rebuttal, contradiction, challenge, dissent, disowning ("denial of allegations"); rejection, refusal, turndown, veto ("The trial proceeded after the judge's denial of a directed verdict"). *Ant.* acknowledgment; granting.

denigrate [*den* · i · grayt] *v.* degrade, humiliate, belittle, smear, vilify, denounce, defame, vituperate, divide, dishonor.

denizen [*den* · i · zen] *n.* citizen, resident, occupant, inhabitant.

denote [de · *note*] *v.* mean, symbolize, signify, express, designate.

denunciation [de · *nontz* · ee · ay · shun] *n.* tirade, calumny, aspersion, invective, vilification, vituperation, incrimination, deprecation, recrimination.

deny [dee · *nie*] *v.* disagree, controvert, disbelieve, negate, oppose, refute. *Ant.* concede, grant.

department [de · *part* · ment] *n.* branch, section, office, agency, bureau, unit, division.

departure [de · *par* · choor] *n.* exit, retreat, removal, withdrawal ("His departure was scheduled for noon"); divergence, change, digression ("a departure from the norm").

dependency [dee · *pen* · den · see] *n.* attachment, helplessness, contingency, connection, need. *Ant.* self-sufficiency, independence.

dependent [dee · *pen* · dent] *n.* minor, charge, ward.

dependent [dee · *pen* · dent] *adj.* clinging, reliant, helpless, under control of, parasitic ("A child is dependent on its parent"); contingent, ancillary, corollary ("dependent counterclaim"). *Ant.* autonomous; unconditional.

depict [de · *pikt*] *v.* characterize, exemplify, personify, render, sketch, typify, portray.

deplete [de · *pleet*] *v.* dissipate, decrease, reduce, waste, exhaust, drain.

depletion [de · *plee* · shen] *n.* emptying, exhausting, diminishment, draining, drying up, reduction, deduction.

deplore [de · *plohr*] *v.* regret, lament, mourn; hate, condemn, abhor, censure.

deponent [de · *pone* · ent] *n.* witness, attester, informant, testifier.

deport [de · *port*] *v.* banish, bar, exile, expel, oust, remove, evict, eject ("deport the alien"); carry, behave, comport ("deport oneself professionally").

deportation [dee · por · *tay* · shen] *n.* banishment, exile, eviction, removal, extradition.

depose [dee · *poze*] *v.* attest, state, testify, give sworn testimony ("depose the witness"); impeach, discharge, usurp, dismiss ("The monarchy was deposed").

deposit [de · *pah* · zit] *v.* entrust, save, store, locate, amass, bank, hoard ("She deposits all her money into Swiss bank accounts").

deposit [de · *pah* · zit] *n.* retainer, security, installment, pledge ("Miguel made a deposit on a new car"); accumulation, sediment, alluvium ("The flood created a large deposit of soil").

deposition [dep · e · *zish* · en] *n.* testimony, sworn testimony, testimony under oath, affidavit, declaration.

depositor [de · *pah* · zit · er] *n.* customer, creditor, bailor.

depository [de · *pah* · zit · or · ee] *n.* safe, vault, warehouse, treasury, archives.

depot [*de* · poe] *n.* station, terminal, repository, warehouse, storehouse.

depreciation [de · pree · shee · *ay* · shen] *n.* devaluation, reduction, deflation, depression, deterioration, erosion. *Ant.* appreciation.

depression [de · *pres* · shun] *n.* despondency, abjection, sorrow, melancholy, gloom, sadness; economic decline, recession, downturn, inflation, crisis, slump.

deprive [de · *prive*] *v.* dispossess, divest, seize, wrest, expropriate.

deputy [*dep* · yoo · tee] *n.* subordinate, assistant, delegate, substitute, appointee, surrogate, agent ("deputy clerk of court").

deraign [dee · *rane*] *v.* prove, vindicate.

deranged [de · *raingd*] *adj.* demented, confused, incompetent, mad, unbalanced, delusional, frenzied.

deregulate [dee · *reg* · yoo · late] *v.* decontrol, liberate, disencumber.

derelict [*der* · e · likt] *n.* outcast, tramp, wanderer, drifter.

derelict [*der* · e · likt] *adj.* forsaken, discarded, neglected, unwanted, abandoned, dilapidated.

dereliction [der · e · *lik* · shen] *n.* carelessness, evasion, delinquency, omission, neglect, default. *Ant.* accountability.

deride [de · *ride*] *v.* disparage, scorn, taunt, mock, ridicule.

derivation [der · i · *vay* · shun] *n.* root, source, origin, ancestry, inception.

derivative [de · *riv* · e · tiv] *adj.* secondary, subordinate, consequential, ensuing, resulting, caused, attributable. *Ant.* primary.

derive [de · *rive*] *v.* deduce, draw, infer, formulate, conclude, develop, determine.

derogation [der · e · *gay* · shen] *n.* repeal, annulment, abolishment.

descend [de · *send*] *v.* endow, give, bequeath, bestow, pass down.

descendant [dee · *sen* · dent] *n.* offspring, family, progeny, heir, lineage, kin. *Ant.* ascendant.

descent [de · *sent*] *n.* lineage, ancestry, bloodline, heritage, heirs, kin, pedigree, origin; declination, sinking, settlement.

describe [de · *skribe*] *v.* explain, express, narrate, recount, specify, relate, impart, state.

description [des · *krip* · shen] *n.* representation, identification, illustration, classification, portrayal, characterization ("a legal description"); narration, telling.

desecration [des · e · *kray* · shen] *n.* defilement, debasement, blasphemy, profanation, sacrilege. *Ant.* adoration, righteousness.

desegregate [de · *seg* · ruh · gayt] *v.* integrate, unify, mix, coalesce, intermingle, merge, assimilate.

desertion [de · *zer* · shen] *n.* abandonment, forsaking, renunciation, relinquishment, departure, abdication.

design [de · *zine*] *n.* purpose, intention, objective, aspiration, hope, aim, goal; sketch, blueprint, pattern, plan, preparation.

design [de · *zine*] *v.* craft, create, structure, devise, conceive, plan, invent, construct, arrange.

designated [*dez* · ig · nay · ted] *adj.* appointed, selected, chosen, assigned, denoted.

designation [*dez* · ig · nay · shun] *n.* choosing, appointment, identification, denomination, indication; symbol, mark, token, sign, emblem, name.

desire [de · *zire*] *v.* wish, want, request, hunger, need, covet, crave, solicit, pursue.

desire [de · *zire*] *n.* ambition, aspiration, wish, hunger, passion, yen, fondness, fancy, craving, lust, urge.

destination [des · tih · *nay* · shen] *n.* goal, object, plan, aim, ambition, design, intention.

destitute [*des* · te · toot] *adj.* impoverished, needy, indigent, bereft, helpless, exhausted, poverty-stricken. *Ant.* affluent.

destruction [dis · *truk* · shen] *n.* defeat, rescission, elimination, liquidation, ruination, abolition; loss, ruin, annihilation, demolition. *Ant.* creation.

desuetude [de · *sway* · tude] *n.* disuse, inaction, stoppage, suspension, nonuse, discontinuance.

detach [de · *tatch*] *v.* sever, remove, disentangle, disengage.

detail [de · *tale*] *v.* explain, illuminate, particularize, elucidate, depict, delineate, narrate, tell ("detail your experience"); assign, allocate, order, impose, relegate.

detail [*dee* · tale] *n.* aspect, part, item, component, ingredient, section, fragment.

detain [de · *tane*] *v.* restrain, stop, inhibit, obstruct, stall, constrain, hold, arrest, suppress.

detainer [de · *tane* · er] *n.* holding, detention, impoundment.

detention [de · *ten* · shen] *n.* confinement, detainment, custody, captivity, incarceration, imprisonment.

D

D

deter [de · *turr*] *v.* dissuade, divert, deflect, block, thwart, ward off, repel, discourage.

deteriorate [de · *teer* · ee · oh · rayt] *v.* decline, depreciate, degrade, devalue, worsen, decay, retrogress.

determinable [de · *ter* · min · uh · bul] *adj.* ascertainable, compatible, measurable, knowable, discoverable.

determinant [de · *ter* · mih · nent] *n.* cause, factor, influence, essential element, driving force.

determinate [de · *ter* · min · et] *adj.* fixed, set, established, definite ("a determinate sentence").

determination [de · ter · min · *ay* · shen] *n.* judgment, conclusion, resolution, opinion, solution, declaration, recommendation ("The court's determination was in favor of the plaintiff"); resoluteness, strength, motive, purpose, tenacity ("As the attorney for the defendant, Ileana was filled with determination").

determine [de · *ter* · min] *v.* decide, define, settle, elect, establish, direct, impel, find, hold.

detraction [de · *trak* · shen] *n.* removal, diversion, diminishment, abuse, defamation, aspersion, discrediting, disparagement, disrespect.

detriment [*det* · ri · ment] *n.* drawback, limitation, hindrance, impairment, affliction, liability, misfortune, harm, disadvantage ("I relied upon his promise, to my detriment"). *Ant.* benefit.

develop [de · *vel* · ip] *v.* cultivate, grow, progress, unfold, improve, mature, proceed.

developer [de · *vel* · e · per] *n.* entrepreneur, promoter, planner, designer, organizer, contractor.

development [de · *vel* · ep · ment] *n.* advancement, progression, evolution, growth, improvement, expansion ("the development of modern technology"); circumstance, phenomenon, episode, happening, occurrence ("a new development in the case").

deviation [dee · vee · *ay* · shen] *n.* variance, variation, discrepancy, diversion, disparity, digression.

device [de · *vise*] *n.* instrument, mechanism, contraption, invention, construction, apparatus ("an eating device"); scheme, plot, design, fraud, hoax ("a clever device to overthrow the government").

devious [*dee* · vee · us] *adj.* crafty, cunning, sneaking, scheming, wily, insidious, deceitful, underhanded.

devise [de · *vize*] *v.* confer, bequeath, convey, endow ("She devised her business operation to her daughter"); plan, formulate, arrange, concoct, construct ("He devised a way to attract attention").

devise [de · *vize*] *n.* inheritance, legacy, transfer, conveyance ("the devise of the family jewels").

devoid [de · *voyd*] *adj.* barren, wanting, lacking, desolate, uninhabited, deprived of, unsupplied.

devolution [de · voh · *loo* · shen] *n.* assignment, transference, delegation, transmission.

devolve [dee · *volv*] *v.* pass, transmit, grant, transfer, bequeath.

devote [de · *voht*] *v.* dedicate, assign, apply, heed, consecrate, pledge, consign.

diabolic [di · uh · *bol* · ik] *adj.* demonic, evil, wicked, satanic, fiendish, horrible, monstrous, profane.

diagnose [*di* · ag · noce] *v.* analyze, classify, estimate, specify, evaluate.

diatribe [*di* · uh · tribe] *n.* accusation, outburst, denunciation, upbraiding, attack, castigation, harangue.

dicker [*dik* · er] *v.* barter, hassle, negotiate, trade, deal, haggle ("dicker about terms").

dictate [*dik* · tayt] *v.* command, compel, demand, prescribe, require ("dictate terms"); read, speak, say, record, transmit, utter ("dictate a report").

dictator [*dik* · tay · ter] *n.* tyrant, ruler, authoritarian, autocrat.

dictum [*dik* · tum] *n.* assertion, statement, comment, remark, observation, pronouncement ("judicial dictum").

die *v.* expire, decease, perish, pass on; wither, recede, deteriorate, decay, decline.

differ [*dif* · er] *v.* disagree, oppose, take exception to, take issue, repudiate; vary, dissent, digress, disaccord.

different [*dif* · uh · rent] *adj.* diverse, unusual, dissimilar, atypical, varied, various, idiosyncratic, novel.

difficult [*dif* · ih · kult] *adj.* complex, hard, problematic, perplexing, troublesome, obscure, arduous, complicated.

diffident [*dif* · ih · dent] *adj.* cautious, demure, timid, unassuming, unsure, unpretentious, reserved, retiring, self-effacing.

diffuse [dih · *fyoos*] *adj.* dispersed, scattered, extended, prevalent; wordy, rambling, prolix, lengthy.

digest [*die* · jest] *n.* summary, abstract, synopsis, restatement, review.

digest [dih · *jest*] *v.* understand, consider, analyze, summarize.

digression [dih · *gres* · shun] *n.* deviation, aside, straying, detour, variation, wandering.

dilatory [*dil* · e · tor · ee] *adj.* tardy, languid, neglectful, late, dawdling, forestalling, delaying, deferring ("a dilatory motion").

dilemma [de · *lem* · uh] *n.* predicament, quandary, confusion, puzzle, perplexity.

diligence [*dil* · ih · jens] *n.* perseverance, determination, assiduity, constancy, zeal, resolution, care, due care. *Ant.* laziness.

diligent [*dil* · ih · jent] *adj.* persistent, conscientious, hardworking, careful, industrious, assiduous.

dilute [*dih* · loot] *v.* weaken, adulterate, moderate, alter, attenuate.

diminish [de · *min* · ish] *v.* shorten, lower, decline, abate, narrow, wither, lessen, assuage, temper, reduce, mitigate.

diminution [dim · in · *yoo* · shen] *n.* reduction, alleviation, abatement, minimizing, cutback ("diminution of damages").

dingy [*din* · gee] *adj.* shabby, seedy, gloomy, drab, dull, rundown.

diplomatic [dip · le · *mat* · ik] *adj.* cautious, prudent, discreet, tactful, civil.

dire *adj.* terrible, catastrophic, extreme, dismal, dreaded, grim, horrible, drastic, pressing, fearful ("dire circumstances").

direct [de · *rekt*] *v.* point, show, indicate, steer ("I can direct you to the D.A.'s office"); govern, regulate, control.

direct [de · *rekt*] *adj.* unbroken, continuous, immediate, uninterrupted, proximate; candid, blunt, forthright, plain, sincere, straightforward.

direction [de · *rek* · shen] *n.* instruction, regulation, prescription, charge, rule, injunction, command, order; control, management, supervision.

D

director [de · *rek* · ter] *n.* supervisor, boss, chief administrative officer, leader, chairperson, manager, president.

directory [de · *rek* · te · ree] *n.* catalogue, schedule, docket, register, index, record.

directory [de · *rek* · te · ree] *adj.* advisory, instructive, nonbinding.

disability [dis · e · *bil* · ih · tee] *n.* incapacity, unfitness, incompetence, inability ("His disability as a witness was detrimental to the case"); handicap, affliction, weakness, defect, disorder, impairment ("She suffered a permanent disability from the car accident"). *Ant.* advantage, strength.

D

disadvantage [dis · ad · *van* · taj] *n.* drawback, hindrance, disability, restriction, handicap, difficulty, obstacle.

disaffirm [dis · uh · *ferm*] *v.* disavow, recant, negate, veto, rescind, renege, renounce, deny, repudiate. *Ant.* affirm.

disagree [dis · uh · *gree*] *v.* differ, controvert, oppose, deny, diverge.

disagreement [dis · uh · *gree* · ment] *n.* argument, contradiction, difference, feud, controversy, discrepancy, strife.

disallow [dis · uh · *louw*] *v.* overrule, reject, deny, veto, forbid, repudiate, rebuff, spurn, abrogate. *Ant.* grant.

disarm [dis · *arm*] *v.* cripple, debilitate, weaken, disable, enervate; placate, mollify, pacify, assure, assuage.

disaster [dis · *as* · tur] *n.* devastation, calamity, misery, ruin, fiasco, affliction, casualty.

disbar [dis · *bar*] *v.* disqualify, suspend, remove, rescind, expel.

disbarment [dis · *bar* · ment] *n.* banishment, debarment, discharge, dismissal, ejection, eviction, removal.

disbursement [dis · *bers* · ment] *n.* payment, outlay, expense, remittance, fees. *Ant.* receipt.

discharge [dis · *charj*] *v.* perform, execute, effect, accomplish, comply, implement ("You must discharge your duty before taking on more work"); pay off ("discharge a debt"); extricate, absolve, acquit, liberate, emancipate ("She received an honorable discharge from the military"); fire, release, terminate, remove, sack, dismiss ("We discharged him for cause").

discharge [*dis* · charj] *n.* release, dismissal, termination, removal ("I received a discharge from the obligations of the contract"); accomplishment, fulfillment, execution, achievement ("discharge of duty").

discipline [*dis* · ih · plihn] *v.* administer, command, supervise; castigate, penalize, reprove, punish; train, accustom, coach, condition, instruct.

disclaim [dis · *klame*] *v.* renounce, rescind, spurn, deny, cancel, disavow, annul.

disclaimer [dis · *klame* · er] *n.* relinquishment, renunciation, retraction, disowning, revocation, disavowal. *Ant.* acceptance.

disclosure [dis · *kloh* · zher] *n.* exposure, uncovering, acknowledgment, admission, publication, revelation. *Ant.* concealment.

discontinuance [dis · ken · *tin* · yoo · ense] *n.* termination, cancellation, suspension, dismissal, cessation, abandonment.

discontinuous [dis · ken · *tin* · yoo · us] *adj.* infrequent, irregular.

discount [*dis* · kownt] *n.* reduction, markdown, rebate, break, cutback, deduction. *Ant.* increase.

discount [dis · *kownt*] *v.* reduce, belittle, ignore ("discount his contribution to the project").

discourage [dis · *kur* · adj] *v.* dissuade, dampen, caution, divert, daunt, warn, demoralize.

discover [dis · *kuv* · er] *v.* learn, uncover, unearth, deduce, determine, ascertain.

discovery [dis · *kuv* · eh · ree] *n.* identification, exposure, uncovering, disclosure, investigation, finding, breakthrough, pretrial device.

discredit [dis · *kred* · it] *v.* tarnish, downgrade, demean, disgrace, puncture, impeach, malign, disparage. *Ant.* support.

discreet [dis · *kreet*] *adj.* guarded, judicious, sensitive, cautious, careful, subtle, diplomatic.

discretion [dis · *kresh* · en] *n.* will, choice, decision, selection, calculation, consideration, precaution; tact, prudence.

discretionary [dis · *kresh* · en · air · ee] *adj.* optional, nonobligatory, elective, open, unrestricted ("discretionary power"). *Ant.* mandatory.

discriminate [dis · *krim* · ih · nayt] *v.* differentiate, separate, classify, compare, contrast, characterize ("discriminate between fine art and kitsch"); disfavor, reject, shun, hate, victimize ("discriminate against women").

discrimination [dis · krim · in · *ay* · shen] *n.* bigotry, prejudice, partiality, injustice, unfairness, favoritism, hatred; acumen, keenness, taste, judgment, distinction, perspicacity.

disease [*de* · zees] *n.* illness, sickness, affliction, disorder, condition, infirmity.

disenfranchise [dis · en · *fran* · chize] *v.* withhold, disinherit, disqualify, deprive, dispossess, disfranchise.

disfavor [dis · *faiv* · ur] *n.* unpopularity, shame, dislike, disregard, mistrust, disgrace.

disgrace [dis · *grase*] *n.* humiliation, abasement, indignity, blemish, dishonor.

disgrace [dis · *grase*] *v.* dishonor, humiliate, shame, abase, demean, ridicule, deride.

disguise [dis · *gise*] *n.* façade, front, mask, pretense, covering, masquerade, deception.

disguise [dis · *gise*] *v.* conceal, deceive, mask, simulate, hide, alter, becloud.

dishonest [dis · *on* · est] *adj.* lying, insincere, spurious, deceiving, deceptive, disreputable, nefarious, corrupt, unethical.

dishonor [dis · *on* · er] *v.* discredit, humiliate, disgrace, blemish, disrepute, abase, shame, degrade, defile; reject. *Ant.* respect; accept.

dishonor [dis · *on* · er] *n.* shame, disgrace, scorn, indignity, aspersion, opprobrium.

disingenuous [dis · in · *gen* · yoo · us] *adj.* deceptive, artificial, misleading, dishonest, wily, unethical, insincere.

disinherit [dis · in · *herr* · it] *v.* cut off, withhold, renounce, deprive, disclaim, forsake.

disinheritance [dis · in · *herr* · i · tense] *n.* abandonment, repudiation, renouncement, deprivation. *Ant.* bestowal.

disinter [dis · in · *turr*] *v.* exhume, disentomb, resurrect, unearth.

disinterested [dis · *in* · ter · es · ted] *adj.* impartial, unbiased, uninvolved, fair, nonpartisan, neutral ("disinterested witness"); indifferent, detached, remote ("disinterested demeanor"). *Ant.* biased; involved.

dismiss [dis · *miss*] *v.* suspend, eject, oust, remove, expel, fire, adjourn, disregard, ignore, refuse. *Ant.* convene, embrace.

dismissal [dis · *miss* · el] *n.* termination, discharge, removal, elimination, discontinuance, disposal.

disorderly [dis · *or* · der · lee] *adj.* unruly, riotous, boisterous, uncivil, undisciplined, rebellious, unmanageable.

D

disparage [dis · *pa* · rej] *v.* smear, belittle, ridicule, discredit, detract, dishonor, condemn, demean, downgrade, criticize. *Ant.* acclaim.

disparate [*dis* · pur · it] *adj.* different, unlike, divergent, distinct, separate, unequal.

disparity [dis · *par* · ih · tee] *n.* discrepancy, difference, incongruity, variation, imbalance, divergency ("disparity between his testimony today and his earlier statement").

dispatch [*dis* · patch] *n.* communiqué, news flash; haste.

dispatch [dis · *patch*] *v.* send, rush, remit, expedite, transmit, hasten; complete, conclude, execute.

dispel [dis · *pell*] *v.* dismiss, remove, release, diffuse ("dispel an inference").

dispensation [dis · pen · *say* · shen] *n.* permission, authorization, clearance, relinquishment, pardon, allowance.

dispense [dis · *pents*] *v.* provide, apportion, dole out, do, assign, bestow, tender; operate, execute, manage, administer; absolve, discharge, release, exonerate.

displace [dis · *plase*] *v.* dislocate, dismiss, oust, evict ("The worker was displaced"); replace, substitute, supplant.

dispose [dis · *pose*] *v.* relinquish, sell, convey, bestow, discard, allocate; adapt, adjust, make willing, prepare, motivate.

disposition [dis · pe · *zish* · en] *n.* conveyance, transfer, relinquishment, disposal ("The will allowed for the proper disposition of property"); attitude, temperament, character, mood, humor, personality ("She has a lovely disposition").

dispositive [dis · *pahz* · e · tiv] *adj.* controlling, conclusive, disposing.

dispossess [dis · poe · *zess*] *v.* expel, oust, eject, evict. *Ant.* install.

dispossession [dis · poe · *zesh* · en] *n.* eviction, exile, foreclosure, usurpation, ejectment, displacement.

disprove [dis · *proov*] *v.* nullify, confute, prove false, negate, controvert.

dispute [dis · *pyoot*] *v.* contest, doubt, take exception, challenge, deny, contradict ("dispute the testimony"); debate, disagree, argue.

dispute [dis · *pyoot*] *n.* conflict, altercation, commotion, controversy, disturbance, feud, quarrel. *Ant.* agreement.

disqualification [dis · kwall · ih · fih · *kay* · shen] *n.* elimination, expulsion, exclusion, removal, denial, rejection; defect, disability, shortcoming.

disqualified [dis · *kwall* · ih · fide] *adv.* ineligible, rejected, incompetent, subject to challenge.

disqualify [dis · *kwall* · ih · fy] *v.* bar, expel, eliminate, exclude, disable.

dissect [dih · *sekt*] *v.* cut up, dismember, section, take apart; analyze, inspect, scrutinize, investigate, examine.

dissent [di · *sent*] *n.* nonagreement, objection, opposition, variance, noncompliance, protest, nonconcurrence.

dissent [dis · *sent*] *v.* disagree, dispute, challenge, contradict, argue, repudiate, refuse, decline.

dissolution [diz · eh · *loo* · shen] *n.* termination, cessation, finish, nullification, discontinuance, liquidation, disintegration, dissipation. *Ant.* establishment.

distinct [dis · *tinkt*] *adj.* clear, evident, pronounced, well-defined, explicit; different, special, discrete, unique.

distinctive [dis · *tink* · tiv] *adj.* characteristic, distinguishing, particular, uncommon, idiosyncratic, salient.

distinguish [dis · *ting* · wish] *v.* separate, differentiate, classify, divide, categorize, characterize.

distort [dis · *tort*] *v.* bend, color, slant, change, falsify, misconstrue ("distort the truth").

distrain [dis · *train*] *v.* seize, impound, attach, sequester, appropriate.

distress [dis · *tress*] *n.* confiscation, impoundment, dispossession, attachment ("distress for payment"); suffering, agony, torment, pain, despair ("Jennifer suffered much distress after the accident").

distribute [dis · *trib* · yoot] *v.* apportion, allot, classify, allocate, deliver, disseminate, divide, organize. *Ant.* collect.

distributee [dis · trih · byoo · *tee*] *n.* recipient, beneficiary, heir, donee.

distribution [dis · trih · *byoo* · shen] *n.* allocation, assignment, organization, grouping, allotment, transference, arrangement. *Ant.* accumulation.

district [*dis* · trikt] *n.* region, unit, zone, section, province, domain, community.

district attorney *n.* prosecutor, prosecution, state's attorney, accuser.

disturbance [dis · *terb* · ants] *n.* unrest, confusion, disorder, revolt, tumult, affray.

diverse [die · *verse*] *adj.* different, mixed, varied, heterogeneous, sundry, various, unlike.

diversion [dih · *ver* · zhen] *n.* detour, digression, distraction, deflection ("The defendant's trick created a menacing diversion for the jury"); hobby, pastime, recreation, entertainment ("Sailing can be a wonderful diversion").

diversity [die · *ver* · sih · tee] *n.* variety, multiplicity, assortment, variation.

divest [die · *vest*] *v.* forfeit, displace, strip, discharge, remove, deprive. *Ant.* confer.

dividend [*div* · ih · dend] *n.* profit, benefit, reward, share, allowance, bonus.

divisible [di · *viz* · uh · bul] *adj.* severable, detachable, breakable, separable.

divorce [di · *vorss*] *n.* separation, division, break, breakup, parting, rupture, disunion.

divorce [di · *vorss*] *v.* rescind, dismiss, annul, cease, dissolve.

divulge [di · *vulge*] *v.* reveal, confess, communicate, admit, proclaim, expose, impart.

dock *v.* deduct, abridge, decrease, reduce, subtract ("dock his pay").

dock *n.* pier, harbor, wharf, landing.

docket [*dok* · et] *n.* register, agenda, program, diary, plan, calendar, record.

doctrine [*dok* · trin] *n.* dogma, theory, philosophy, belief, rule, principle, tradition.

document [*dok* · yoo · ment] *n.* report, publication, paper, instrument, certificate, form, record.

domain [doh · *main*] *n.* kingdom, holding, territory, estate, province ("your personal domain"); jurisdiction, authority, command ("The government has domain over this piece of land").

domestic [de · *mes* · tik] *adj.* local, native, household, indigenous, national. *Ant.* foreign.

domicile [*dom* · ih · sile] *n.* residence, abode, establishment, home ("She claimed Tampa, Florida, as her permanent domicile").

domicile [*dom* · ih · sile] *v.* locate, occupy, dwell, abide ("Because the defendant was domiciled there, the complaint was filed in Clayton County").

domiciliary [dom · ih · *sil* · ee · er · ee] *n.* citizen, native, dweller, inhabitant, resident ("He is a domiciliary of the state of Alabama").

dominant [*dom* · ih · nent] *adj.* commanding, primary, supreme, chief, superior, principal.

dominion [de · *min* · yen] *n.* jurisdiction, power, domination, supremacy.

donate [*doh* · nayt] *v.* award, bequeath, bestow, grant, pledge. *Ant.* receive.

donation [doh · *nay* · shen] *n.* offering, grant, gift, contribution, handout.

donee [doh · *nee*] *n.* transferee, heir, recipient, beneficiary, grantee. *Ant.* donor.

donor [*doh* · nor] *n.* giver, contributor, donator, grantor. *Ant.* recipient.

doomed *adj.* condemned, predestined, ruined, undone, destroyed, sentenced, sunk.

dope *n.* idiot, dunce, fool, dolt; news, information, lowdown, scoop; drug, narcotic.

dormant [*dor* · ment] *adj.* inactive, inert, passive, latent, quiescent, abeyant, inoperative, suspended, static, silent.

double [*duh* · bl] *adj.* twofold, dual, paired, duplicate, twin. *Ant.* single.

doubt *v.* suspect, dispute, question, distrust, challenge.

doubt *n.* uncertainty, suspicion, concern, hesitation, indecision, ambivalence, insecurity.

doubtful [*dowt* · ful] *adj.* dubious, hesitant, uncertain, ambivalent ("the juror's doubtful veracity"); questionable, unconvincing, speculative ("The report was of doubtful accuracy").

dowry [*dow* · ree] *n.* portion, allotment, settlement.

draconian [dra · *kone* · ee · en] *adj.* ruthless, rigid, austere, stringent, uncompromising, strict, brutal ("This calls for draconian measures"). *Ant.* mild.

draft *v.* frame, draw, prepare, compose ("You must draft your will").

draft *n.* money order, check, banknote, negotiable paper ("a bank draft"); version, attempt ("first draft of my brief").

draftsman [*drafts* · mun] *n.* creator, designer, inventor, maker, planner.

drastic [*dras* · tik] *adj.* extreme, radical, desperate, severe, strong ("drastic measures").

draw *v.* draft, prepare, make, compose ("draw up the papers"); extract, deplete, exhaust, withdraw ("Do you wish to draw on your savings account?"). *Ant.* deposit.

draw *n.* extraction, withdrawal, depletion, advance ("I made a draw on my checking account").

drawback [*draw* · bak] *n.* disadvantage, shortcoming, weakness, flaw, hitch, lack, obstacle.

dress *v.* clothe, adorn, bedeck, wear, don; adjust, align, straighten, trim; bandage, treat, sterilize, cover, cleanse.

dress *n.* clothing, attire, uniform, costume, apparel, appearance, garb.

drivel [*drihv* · ul] *n.* nonsense, babble, foolishness, gibberish, rubbish.

drop *v.* abandon, desert, quit, relinquish, reject, forsake, cancel; drip, dribble, ooze, trickle.

drug *n.* medication, compound, remedy, prescription, medicine, dope, pill, pharmaceutical.

drunk *adj.* intoxicated, inebriated, under the influence, saturated, sotted.

drunk *n.* alcoholic, inebriate, dipsomaniac, lush, boozer, drunkard.

drunkenness [*drunk* · en · ness] *n.* inebriation, intoxication, being under the influence.

dry *adj.* bare, barren, depleted, dull, boring, monotonous, plain, simple, tedious; sober.

due *adj.* outstanding, unpaid, collectable ("The loan payment is due"); proper, reasonable, lawful, appropriate, rightful, ready ("Juan is just about due for a promotion").

duly [*dew* · lee] *adv.* fittingly, properly, rightly, correctly, regularly.

dumb *adj.* mum, mute, impaired, voiceless; stupid, dense, moronic, idiotic, foolish.

dummy [*dum* · ee] *n.* stand in, double, duplicate, counterfeit, copy ("dummy corporation"). *Ant.* principal.

dun *v.* urge, press, insist, importune, besiege.

dupe *v.* deceive, defraud, overreach, outwit, fool, hoodwink, con, rip off.

duplicate [*dew* · pli · kayt] *v.* reproduce, replicate, copy, clone.

duplicate [*dew* · pli · ket] *n.* replica, twin, copy, facsimile, reproduction. *Ant.* original.

durable [*dew* · ruh · bull] *adj.* lasting, enduring, ongoing, permanent, sturdy, strong, hardy, sound, tough.

duration [dew · *ray* · shen] *n.* extent, tenure, span, term, course, while, phase.

duress [dew · *ress*] *n.* oppression, force, subjection, constraint, coercion, pressure, compulsion. *Ant.* free will.

duty [*dew* · tee] *n.* responsibility, requirement, role, assignment, charge, mandatory act, pledge, obligation; tax, import tax.

dwell *v.* reside, remain, inhabit, live, stay, occupy; prolong, linger, continue, brood over.

dwelling [*dwel* · ing] *n.* residence, home, habitation, shelter, quarters, abode.

dying [*die* · ing] *adj.* expiring, passing, deteriorating, declining, waning, receding, obsolete ("a dying doctrine").

D

eager [*eeg* · ur] *adj.* willing, interested, aspiring, excited, ready, passionate, pushy, desirous, voracious, enthusiastic.

earmark [*eer* · mark] *n.* feature, label, mark, symbol, sign, trademark, identification, stamp, attribute.

earn *v.* gain, draw, win, acquire ("earn wages"); deserve, merit, rate ("earn the promotion").

earnest [*ur* · nest] *adj.* sincere, diligent, serious, resolute, conscientious, intent, purposeful.

earnest money [*ur* · nest *mun* · ee] *n.* deposit, installment, downpayment, retainer, pledge.

earnings [*ur* · ningz] *n.* salary, profits, wages, revenue, proceeds. *Ant.* losses.

easement [*eez* · ment] *n.* privilege, liberty, servitude, advantage, right of way.

economic [ek · e · *nom* · ik] *adj.* financial, monetary, pecuniary, fiscal.

edge *n.* benefit, lead, advantage, odds ("He has an edge over his opponent"); border, fringe, rim, boundary, limit, bounds ("the edge of his property").

edict [*ee* · dikt] *n.* order, regulation, ordinance, mandate, injunction, pronouncement, dictate, judgment, law. *Ant.* suggestion.

educate [*ed* · joo · kate] *v.* instruct, prepare, teach, guide, direct, inform, train, tutor.

education [ed · joo · *kay* · shun] *n.* knowledge, learning, preparation, schooling, training, erudition.

effect [e · *fekt*] *v.* cause, enforce, execute, produce, create, initiate.

effect [e · *fekt*] *n.* outcome, result, consequence, aftermath, impression. *Ant.* cause.

effective [e · *fek* · tif] *adj.* useful, practical, accomplished, productive, adequate, proficient, functional, pragmatic.

effects [e · *fekts*] *n.* belongings, possessions, holdings, personalty, goods, assets, resources.

efficient [e · *fish* · ent] *adj.* competent, productive, capable, effective, timesaving. *Ant.* ineffective, unproductive.

effort [*ef* · urt] *n.* energy, exertion, vigor, work, assiduity, arduousness.

egress [*ee* · gress] *n.* exit, escape, way out, outlet.

eject [ee · *jekt*] *v.* remove, throw out, dislodge, displace; oust, expel, jettison, discard.

elder [*el* · dur] *n.* senior, veteran, chief, superior, leader.

elect [e · *lekt*] *v.* choose, accept, decide, conclude, determine, opt for. *Ant.* reject.

election [e · *lek* · shen] *n.* selection, designation, choice, nomination. *Ant.* rejection.

elective [e · *lek* · tiv] *adj.* optional, discretionary, nonobligatory, voluntary, facilitative. *Ant.* mandatory.

elector [e · *lek* · ter] *n.* voter, representative, proxy, stand-in, delegate.

eleemosynary [el · ee · e · *moss* · en · er · ee] *adj.* nonprofit, generous, charitable, altruistic, humanitarian. *Ant.* commercial.

elegant [el · e · *gant*] *adj.* formal, beautiful, cultivated, classy, dignified.

element [*el* · e · ment] *n.* part, portion, section, substance, segment, member, feature, ingredient ("an element needed to prove negligence").

elementary [el · e · *men* · tree] *adj.* basic, simple, primary, easy, foundational, obvious, rudimentary ("Elementary, my dear Watson!").

elevation [el · e · *vay* · shun] *n.* rise, altitude, steepness; advancement, stature, coronation, sanctification, eminence.

eligibility [el · e · je · *bil* · e · tee] *n.* suitability, acceptability, worthiness, preference. *Ant.* unacceptability.

eligible [*el* · e · jih · bul] *adj.* fit, proper, qualified, acceptable, suitable, worthy, satisfactory.

eliminate [e · *lim* · i · nayt] *v.* disallow, prohibit, exempt, expel, disregard, disqualify, oust; eradicate, demolish, stamp out, exterminate, expurgate, obliterate.

elite [e · *leet*] *adj.* select, noble, privileged.

elite [e · *leet*] *n.* select group, upper class, aristocracy, gentry, nobility, high society, privileged class.

elude [e · *lood*] *v.* evade, escape, flee, outwit, avoid ("elude the police").

emancipation [e · man · si · *pay* · shen] *n.* liberation, discharge, release, unletting, unbridling. *Ant.* subjugation.

embargo [em · *bar* · goe] *n.* restriction, prohibition, stoppage, detention, blockade.

embarrass [em · *barr* · as] *v.* fluster, upset, disquiet, mortify, humiliate, shame, abash, annoy, disconcert.

embassy [*em* · be · see] *n.* delegation, consulate, legation, commission, committee.

embezzlement [em · *bez* · ul · ment] *n.* abstraction, misappropriation, misuse, theft, larceny, defalcation, peculation, pilferage.

emblements [*em* · bul · ments] *n.* crop, output, production, produce, yield.

embody [em · *bod* · ee] *v.* include, incorporate, blend, assimilate, contain; represent, personify, epitomize, show, symbolize, typify.

embrace [em · *brays*] *v.* adopt, endorse, sanction, comprehend; caress, hold, hug.

emend [ee · *mend*] *v.* correct, improve, edit, amend.

emergency [e · *mer* · jen · see] *n.* urgency, extremity, jam, predicament, distress, plight, squeeze, exigency.

eminent domain [*em* · ih · nent doh · *main*] *n.* condemnation, expropriation, compulsory acquisition.

emission [ee · *mish* · en] *n.* discharge, exhalation, issue, transmission, venting, leakage, expulsion. *Ant.* reception.

emoluments [e · *moll* · yoo · ments] *n.* wages, benefits, gain, reward, earnings, allowance.

empirical [em · *pih* · ih · kul] *adj.* experimental, sensed, verified, concrete, scientific. *Ant.* speculative, theoretical.

E

employee [em · *ploy* · ee] *n.* servant, worker, agent, laborer, helper, personnel, jobholder.

employer [em · *ploy* · er] *n.* master, contractor, director, boss, chief. *Ant.* employee.

employment [em · *ploy* · ment] *n.* livelihood, service, business, trade, vocation, occupation, job, profession, work.

enable [en · *ay* · bul] *v.* empower, facilitate, endow, legalize, capacitate.

enact [en · *akt*] *v.* codify, decree, command, establish, dictate, proclaim, execute. *Ant.* repeal.

enactment [en · *akt* · ment] *n.* legislation, law, act, rule, ordinance, measure, statute.

encourage [en · *kerr* · ej] *v.* advocate, approve, assist, boost, enliven, excite. *Ant.* deter.

encroachment [en · *kroach* · ment] *n.* invasion, wrong, violation, infringement.

encumber [en · *kum* · ber] *v.* burden, hinder, block, cramp, hamper, retard. *Ant.* unburden.

encumbrance [en · *kum* · brenss] *n.* lien, charge, liability, impediment, claim, easement.

end *n.* aim, idea, target, goal, intent ("the ends of justice"); close, termination, fulfillment, conclusion, consummation, finish ("the end of my questions for this witness").

endangered [en · *dane* · jerd] *adj.* imperiled, jeopardized, threatened, unprotected.

endorse [en · *dorss*] *v.* advocate, affirm, approve, certify, confirm, guarantee.

endorsement [en · *dorss* · ment] *n.* affirmation, approval, favor, qualification, recommendation, advocacy.

endowment [en · *dow* · ment] *n.* award, benefit, bequest, donation, grant, property, funding.

enforce [en · *forss*] *v.* administer, apply, dictate, execute, fortify. *Ant.* disregard.

enforceable [en · *forss* · uh · bul] *adj.* binding, lawful, effective. *Ant.* unenforceable.

enforcement [en · *forss* · ment] *n.* execution, administration, fulfillment, management, obligation. *Ant.* waiver.

enfranchise [en · *fran* · chize] *v.* liberate, entitle, authorize. *Ant.* encumber.

engage [en · *gayj*] *v.* undertake, involve, participate, entertain ("to engage in a particular activity"); hire, appoint, obtain, secure ("They engaged the services of a maid to help with the party"); fight, combat, compete, contest ("The combatants engaged one another fiercely during the competition").

enhanced [en · *hanst*] *adj.* strengthened, intensified, augmented, enlarged. *Ant.* depreciated.

enigma [un · *nig* · muh] *n.* puzzle, mystery, paradox, confusion, problem, perplexity, riddle, conundrum.

enjoin [en · *joyn*] *v.* command, direct, charge, decree, ordain, exact, forestall, frustrate.

enjoyment [en · *joy* · ment] *n.* satisfaction, amusement, gratification, fun, diversion, use, tenancy, usage. *Ant.* loathing.

enlargement [en · *larj* · ment] *n.* appreciation, growth, increase, augmentation, amplification, extension, exaggeration.

enroll [en · *role*] *v.* impanel, engage, inscribe, catalogue, chronicle, list.

ensue [en · *soo*] *v.* result, develop, happen, transpire, proceed.

entail [en · *tayl*] *v.* demand, obligate, necessitate, impose, involve, require, encompass ("The trial of a lawsuit entails a great deal of preparation").

entanglement [en · *tang* · gul · ment] *n.* dilemma, predicament, problem, strait; confusion, disorder, chaos, tumult, disarray.

enter [en · ter] *v.* go into, board, insert, set foot, arrive, penetrate, infiltrate ("She entered into a binding agreement"); post, list, enroll, docket, document, calendar ("The clerk entered the defendant's appearance on the docket").

enterprise [en · tur · prize] *n.* activity, plan, campaign, scheme, engagement, undertaking; business, corporation, industry.

entice [en · *tice*] *v.* lure, tempt, seduce, invite.

entire [en · *tire*] *adj.* complete, full, comprehensive, undivided ("entire interest").

entirety [en · *tire* · tee] *n.* whole, aggregate, completeness, totality, gross. *Ant.* part.

entitle [en · *ty* · tel] *v.* authorize, warrant, permit, empower, charter, qualify. *Ant.* disqualify.

entitlement [en · *ty* · tel · ment] *n.* right, claim, birthright, interest.

entity [*en* · tih · tee] *n.* body, unit, existence, individual, object, being, item. *Ant.* illusion.

entrapment [en · *trap* · ment] *n.* temptation, deception, beguilement, ensnarement.

entry [*en* · tree] *n.* penetration, intrusion, infiltration, insertion, arrival ("The burglar's entry onto the estate immediately set off the alarm"); report, account, chronicle, document ("entry of judgment").

enumerate [e · *nyoo* · mur · ayt] *v.* list, record, itemize, specify, detail, count ("The powers that the Constitution expressly gives to the president are enumerated in Article I").

environment [en · *vy* · ren · ment] *n.* surroundings, environs, habitat, atmosphere, conditions, milieu, ecosystem.

envoy [*en* · voy] *n.* consul, legate, agent, delegate, emissary.

ephemeral [e · *fem* · e · ral] *adj.* fleeting, brief, evanescent, passing, transient, transitory, momentary, elusive.

epitome [e · *pit* · e · mee] *n.* embodiment, essence, model, representative ("the epitome of sleaze").

equal [*ee* · kwel] *adj.* alike, uniform, just, unbiased, impartial, balanced, even ("equal opportunity"); identical, same, coequal ("equal partners").

equalization [ee · kwall · ih · *zay* · shen] *n.* standardization, regulation, leveling, accommodation, balancing.

equitable [*ek* · wi · teh · bul] *adj.* just, fair, impartial, proper, honest, objective, rightful. *Ant.* biased.

equity [*ek* · wi · tee] *n.* fairness, justice, rightness, ethics, uprightness, propriety ("the equity of the situation"); interest, security, stake, claim ("my equity in my house").

equivalent [ee · *kwiv* · e · lent] *adj.* commensurate, corresponding, comparable, parallel, like, exact. *Ant.* dissimilar.

equivalent [ee · *kwiv* · e · lent] *n.* correspondent, match, parallel, peer, substitute, twin. *Ant.* opposite.

equivocal [e · *kwiv* · uh · kul] *adj.* ambiguous, nebulous, vague, imprecise, recondite, puzzling, unresolved, uncertain.

equivocate [e · *kwiv* · uh · kayt] *v.* dodge, elude, evade, avoid, hedge, prevaricate, misstate, deceive.

eradicate [e · *rad* · ih · kayt] *v.* demolish, obliterate, purge, eliminate, expurgate, destroy, remove.

erasure [e · *ray* · sher] *n.* elimination, cancellation, removal, effacement, annulment, expungement. *Ant.* insertion.

ergo [*ur* · goe] *adv.* therefore, accordingly, consequently.

erode [ee · *rode*] *v.* decay, recede, wear away, deteriorate, abrade, weaken.

error [*err* · er] *n.* mistake, misinterpretation, fault, defect, flaw, miscalculation, misapprehension, aberration, deviation.

escape [es · *kayp*] *v.* flee, dodge, vanish, disappear, evade, break out. *Ant.* capture.

escheat [es · *cheet*] *n.* reversion, forfeiture, seizure, appropriation.

escrow [*es* · kroh] *adj.* separate, designated, specified ("Keep the money in an escrow account").

espionage [*es* · pee · en · ahzh] *n.* spying, treason, betrayal, mutiny, eavesdropping.

essence [*ess* · enss] *n.* core, heart, nature, lifeblood, marrow, soul, backbone. *Ant.* periphery.

essential [e · *sen* · shul] *adj.* important, required, needed, primary, requisite, mandatory; inherent, intrinsic, fundamental.

establish [es · *tab* · lish] *v.* prove, convince, demonstrate, show, validate, confirm, substantiate ("It has been established that the couple will no longer reside together"); form, build, start, initiate, launch, commission ("She established the business 10 years ago").

estate [es · *tate*] *n.* assets, wealth, property, fortune, personalty, effects.

estimated [*est* · ih · may · ted] *adj.* approximated, calculated, speculated, surmised ("estimated tax").

estop [es · *top*] *v.* impede, restrict, hinder, thwart, block, restrain, preclude. *Ant.* authorize.

estoppel [es · *top* · el] *n.* impediment, prohibition, restraint, ban, bar, obstruction. *Ant.* allowance.

estovers [es · *toh* · verz] *n.* support, alimony.

et cetera [et *set* · e · ra] and others, and so on, and so forth.

ethical [*eth* · ih · kul] *adj.* good, honest, principled, professional, moral, uncorrupted, honorable, virtuous, upright.

ethics [*eth* · iks] *n.* principles, values, morals, mores, criteria, canon, rules.

evasion [ee · *vay* · zhen] *n.* avoidance, dodging, fabrication, escape, shunning. *Ant.* confrontation.

evasive [ee · *vay* · siv] *adj.* misleading, vague, ambivalent, covert. *Ant.* forthright.

event [e · *vent*] *n.* happening, transaction, affair, incident, episode, development.

evict [ee · *vikt*] *v.* displace, oust, expel, dispossess, turn out, eject, kick out, uproot.

eviction [ee · *vik* · shen] *n.* expulsion, ouster, ejection, dislodgement, removal, dispossession.

evidence [*ev* · i · denss] *n.* verification, substantiation, authentication, certification, corroboration, testimony, confirmation, proof ("based on the evidence").

evidence [*ev* · i · denss] *v.* certify, attest, reveal, display, demonstrate, prove, establish, suggest ("proof evidencing a crime").

evident [*ev* · i · dent] *adj.* plain, clear, obvious, apparent, discernible, noticeable, visible, unhidden, ostensible.

evoke [ee · *voke*] *v.* elicit, produce, arouse, generate, summon, stimulate ("evoke a response").

E

E

exact [eg · *zact*] *adj.* precise, literal, accurate, particular, strict, express ("the exact wording").

examination [eg · zam · i · *nay* · shen] *n.* investigation, inquiry, research, analysis, observation, questioning, search, inspection.

examine [eg · *zam* · in] *v.* inspect, analyze, scrutinize, study, monitor, observe; question, interview, interrogate.

examiner [eg · *zam* · in · er] *n.* investigator, researcher, inspector, reviewer, questioner.

except [ek · *sept*] *v.* pass, reject, delete, excuse, remove, disallow, ignore ("As a student she was excepted from jury duty"). *Ant.* incorporate.

except [ek · *sept*] *prep.* other than, excluding, saving, apart from ("Except for his inability to type, he was an excellent secretary").

exception [ek · *sep* · shen] *n.* protest, complaint ("The exception will be taken into consideration"); separation, departure, segregation, omission ("an exception to the rule").

excess [*ek* · sess] *adj.* extra, surplus, overflow, spare, excessive. *Ant.* scarce.

excessive [ek · *sess* · iv] *adj.* disproportionate, extreme, exorbitant, superfluous, exaggerated ("excessive damages"). *Ant.* modest.

exchange [eks · *chaynj*] *v.* transfer, swap, trade, transpose, substitute ("to exchange an item of clothing for a different size").

exchange [eks · *chaynj*] *n.* trade, deal, transfer, replacement, substitution ("He asked for 50 dollars in exchange for his cleaning services"); market, commission ("stock exchange").

excise [ek · *size*] *v.* cut, remove, extract, take out; tax, charge, collect, demand, exact.

excited [ek · *site* · ed] *adj.* active, emotional, ardent, strong, aroused.

exclusion [eks · *kloo* · zhen] *n.* rejection, omission, dismissal, elimination, disallowance, nonacceptance, repudiation.

exclusive [eks · *kloo* · siv] *adj.* restricted, private, limited, unique, not shared.

exculpate [*eks* · kul · pate] *v.* vindicate, justify, dissolve, clear, pardon. *Ant.* convict.

excusable [eks · *kyoo* · zuh · bul] *adj.* pardonable, forgivable, permissible ("excusable negligence").

excuse [eks · *kyooz*] *v.* pardon, vindicate, exculpate, forbear; absolve, liberate ("excuse from duty").

excuse [eks · *kyooss*] *n.* explanation, vindication, defense, rationalization ("a lame excuse").

execute [*ek* · se · kyoot] *v.* accomplish, perform, achieve, administer, complete ("She was quick to execute her obligations under the contract"); eliminate, finish, liquidate, condemn, assassinate ("The prisoner was scheduled to be executed at 9 a.m.").

executed [*ek* · se · kyoot · ed] *adj.* cut, signed, killed, terminated, destroyed.

execution [ek · se · *kyoo* · shen] *n.* fulfillment, achievement, performance, conclusion ("the execution of a contract"); capital punishment, death, elimination, condemnation ("The execution was administered by electric chair").

executive [eg · *zek* · yoo · tiv] *n.* chief, supervisor, boss, director, chairperson, president ("a corporate executive").

executive [eg · *zek* · yoo · tiv] *adj.* managerial, presidential, official, administrative.

executor [eg · *zek* · yoo · tor] *n.* administrator, fiduciary, custodian, personal representative.

executory [eg · *zek* · yoo · tor · ee] *adj.* incomplete, unfulfilled, contingent, deficient, partial, unexecuted. *Ant.* executed, completed.

exemplar [eg · zem · plur] *n.* example, sample, specimen.

exemplification [eg · zem · plih · fih · *kay* · shen] *n.* authentication, certification, verification.

exempt [eg · *zemt*] *v.* waive, excuse, absolve, clear, discharge ("I was exempted from the written examination"). *Ant.* obligate.

exempt [eg · *zemt*] *adj.* immune, privileged, freed, favored, excused ("The company was exempt from investigation"). *Ant.* accountable.

exemption [eg · *zemp* · shen] *n.* immunity, liberty, absolution, dispensation. *Ant.* obligation.

exercise [*eks* · er · size] *n.* use, utilization; drill, practice; physical labor.

exercise [*eks* · er · size] *v.* utilize, employ, apply, practice, administer. *Ant.* disregard.

exhaustion [eg · *zaws* · chen] *n.* fatigue, weariness, debility, enervation, draining.

exhibit [eg · *zib* · it] *n.* attachment, document, display, illustration, transcript ("Please refer to exhibit A").

exhibit [eg · *zib* · it] *v.* show, display, reveal, uncover, illustrate.

exhumation [eg · zyoo · *may* · shen] *n.* removal, unearthing, disentombment, resurrection. *Ant.* burial.

exigence [*ek* · zi · jenss] *n.* urgency, necessity, exigency.

exigency [*ek* · zi · jenss] *n.* imperativeness, flight, crisis.

exigent [*eggs* · ih · jent] *adj.* pressing, urgent, vital, crucial, grave, essential ("Exigent circumstances").

exist [eg · *zist*] *v.* endure, continue, remain, survive, last.

exoneration [eg · zon · e · *ray* · shen] *n.* dismissal, clearance, release, acquittal, exculpation.

expatriation [eks · pay · tree · *ay* · shen] *n.* migration, withdrawal, renouncement, relegation. *Ant.* immigration.

expect [eks · *pekt*] *v.* await, anticipate, look forward to; assume, predict, suppose, infer, surmise.

expectancy [eks · *pek* · ten · see] *n.* contingency, likelihood, probability, presumption.

expectant [eks · *pek* · tent] *adj.* hopeful, anticipating, readying, prospective.

expectation [eks · pek · *tay* · shun] *n.* anticipation, contemplation, prospect, expectancy, hope, preconception, promise.

expedite [*eks* · pe · dite] *v.* speed, facilitate, accelerate, quicken, encourage, dispatch, push forward.

expense [ex · *pents*] *n.* cost, charge, rate, payment, price, value, debit, sacrifice, surrender, loss, forfeit.

experience [eks · *peer* · ee · ense] *n.* skill, training, proficiency, exposure, competence, expertise ("experience in litigation"); event, occasion, adventure, occurrence, situation ("a scary experience").

expert [*eks* · pert] *n.* authority, professional, specialist, virtuoso, scholar, veteran, master. *Ant.* layperson.

expert [*eks* · pert] *adj.* skilled, qualified, competent, accomplished, proficient.

explain [eks · *plane*] *v.* clarify, elucidate, unravel, define, illuminate, solve, untangle.

E

explicit [eks · *pliss* · iht] *adj.* clear, definite, exact, obvious, manifest, unambiguous, lucid, stated, expressed, understandable.

exploit [eks · *ployt*] *v.* abuse, victimize, oppress, persecute, take advantage of; use, operate, apply, avail, utilize.

export [eks · *port*] *v.* convey, transport, converge, send out ("to export goods").

export [*eks* · port] *n.* trade goods, wares, articles ("musical export").

exportation [eks · por · *tay* · shen] *n.* sending, transporting. *Ant.* importation.

exports [*eks* · ports] *n.* goods, trade goods, shipments, shipped wares.

exposure [eks · *poh* · zher] *n.* uncovering, acknowledgment, display, openness, publicity.

express [eks · *press*] *v.* put into words, verbalize, indicate, communicate, state, declare, articulate ("He expressed his concerns").

express [eks · *press*] *adj.* stated, declared, clear, explicit, precise, unmistakable ("an express duty").

expression [ex · *press* · shun] *n.* manifestation, exhibition, indication, sign ("an expression of his intent"); assertion, communication, remark, declaration ("the expression of his idea").

expropriate [eks · *pro* · pree · ayt] *v.* seize, assume, impound, confiscate, foreclose ("The land was expropriated for state use").

expropriation [eks · pro · pree · *ay* · shen] *n.* appropriation, taking, assumption, seizure, condemnation.

expulsion [eks · *pul* · shen] *n.* banishment, discharge, dismissal, ban, rejection, ousting ("expulsion from school").

expungement [eks · *punj* · ment] *n.* abolition, obliteration, extermination, annihilation ("the expungement of the monarchy").

extant [eks · *tent*] *adj.* alive, existing, surviving, living. *Ant.* extinct.

extend [eks · *tend*] *v.* broaden, widen, add, augment, enlarge, lengthen, continue ("extend the porch"); offer, proffer, put forth, present, hold out, give ("extend my thanks").

extension [eks · *ten* · shen] *n.* enlargement, continuation, prolongation, addition, elongation, stretching ("I was given an extension of time for my paper").

extenuating [eks · *ten* · yoo · ay · ting] *adj.* mitigating, alleviating, diminishing, explanatory, exculpating.

extenuation [eks · ten · yoo · *ay* · shen] *n.* mitigation, moderation, reduction, justification ("an extenuation of the sentence").

extinguishment [eks · *ting* · wish · ment] *n.* elimination, discharge, destruction, termination, cancellation, suffocation ("extinguishment of the debt").

extort [eks · *tort*] *v.* extract, cheat, blackmail, demand, wrest, coerce ("They extorted money from the government").

extortion [eks · *tor* · shen] *n.* coercion, intimidation, fraud, stealing, oppression ("the criminal extortion of funds").

extra [*eks* · tra] *adv.* particularly, extremely, especially.

extra [*eks* · tra] *adj.* excess, additional, spare, ancillary ("an extra pair of glasses").

extra [*eks* · tra] *n.* addition, complement, bonus, supplement ("The free air conditioning was an added extra for buying the car").

extradition [eks · tra · *dish* · en] *n.* surrendering, deportation, transfer.

extrajudicial [eks · tra · joo · *dish* · el] *adj.* private, separate, independent, out-of-court.

extralegal [eks · tra · *leeg* · el] *adj.* out of reach, unattainable, beyond, out-of-court, nonlegal.

extraneous [eks · *tray* · nee · us] *adj.* irrelevant, unneeded, impertinent, inadmissible, inessential, foreign ("extraneous evidence").

extraordinary [eks · *trore* · dih · nair · ee] *adj.* bizarre, inconceivable, outstanding, rare, individual, unusual, remarkable, uncommon ("extraordinary diligence").

extreme [esk · *treem*] *adj.* intense, extensive, excessive, drastic, harsh, egregious, outrageous; last, furthest, final, outermost, ultimate.

extrinsic [eks · *trin* · sik] *adj.* foreign, extraneous, imported, outside, irrelevant, unrelated, peripheral, contingent.

eyewitness [eye · *wit* · ness] *n.* bystander, observer, onlooker, corroborator, identifier, spectator.

E

fabricate [*fab* · rih · kayt] *v.* falsify, defraud, concoct, produce ("She gave fabricated testimony"); construct, manufacture, compose, create ("fabricate the product").

face *n.* appearance, disguise, display, visage.

face *v.* confront, encounter, challenge, meet, defy.

facilitate [fe · *sil* · e · tayt] *v.* aid, assist, advance, enable, speed up, foster, expedite, simplify, make possible.

facilitation [fe · sil · e · *tay* · shen] *n.* furthurance, promotion, expedition.

facility [fe · *sil* · ih · tee] *n.* ease, efficiency, aptitude; accommodation, network, resource, training place.

facsimile [fak · *sim* · uh · lee] *n.* reproduction, copy, replica, simulation, likeness.

fact *n.* verifiable truth, experience, actuality, reality, occurrence, certainty, matter.

factor [*fak* · ter] *n.* ingredient, determinant, consideration, instrumentality, point; bailee, consignee, commission, merchant.

factual [*fak* · tyoo · ul] *adj.* accurate, undistorted, faithful, unbiased, undisputed, authentic, realistic, verifiable, objective, true.

faculty [*fak* · ul · tee] *n.* ability, proficiency, talent, aptitude, capacity, competency ("his faculty at math"); instructors, professors, lecturers ("a fine faculty").

fail *v.* refuse, abort, abandon, desert, forsake; decline, deteriorate, fall, miscarry.

failing [*fayl* · ing] *n.* defect, deficiency, fault, flaw, achilles heel.

failure [*fayl* · yer] *n.* inability, inadequacy, nonperformance, nonsuccess, defeat ("failure to reach your quota"); defaulter, deadbeat, loafer, nonperformer, underachiever ("He was considered a failure by his peers").

faint *adj.* weak, light-headed; ambiguous, obscure, dark.

fair *adj.* impartial, unprejudiced, nonpartisan, unbiased, detached ("a fair trial"); mediocre, intermediate, medium, moderate, reasonable ("a fair ball player").

fairness [*fayr* · nus] *n.* justice, equity, honesty, rectitude, equality, uprightness, integrity, open-mindedness.

faith *n.* trust, assurance, dependence, loyalty, allegiance, certitude, belief, hope, conviction.

fake *n.* forgery, copy, imitation, reproduction, hoax, replica, fabrication.

fake *v.* deceive, pretend, simulate, dupe, feign.

fallacy [*fal* · uh · see] *n.* mistake, misinterpretation, deception, distortion, illusion, delusion.

false *adj.* untrue, concocted, deceiving, fallacious, distorted; dishonest, hypocritical, perjured, malicious; adulterated, counterfeit, fake, simulated.

falsify [*fal* · sih · fie] *v.* alter, lie, misrepresent, misreport, doctor, misstate, tamper with, twist ("falsify the records").

family [*fam* · ih · lee] *n.* classification, progeny, descendants, paternity, genealogy; brood, household, family unit, issue.

fascism [*fash* · izm] *n.* regimentation, bureaucracy, racism, absolutism.

fatal [*fay* · tel] *adj.* deadly, lethal, destructive, calamitous ("fatal injury"); critical, crucial, decisive, determining ("fatal error").

fault *n.* negligence, blame, frailty, malfeasance, oversight, inadequacy, flaw, imperfection, weakness.

fault *v.* criticize, chastise, condemn, censure ("She faulted the board of directors for making the wrong decision").

faulty [*fall* · tee] *adj.* flawed, inferior, inadequate, improper, defective, blemished, imperfect, substandard, aberrant ("faulty wiring").

favor [*fayv* · er] *n.* encouragement, endorsement, support ("win his favor"); partiality, disposition, liking, inclination, favoritism, fondness ("the candidate of favor"); kindness, good deed, courtesy ("Do me a favor").

favor [*fayv* · er] *v.* prefer, support, promote, champion, advance, endorse, back, boost.

favoritism [*fav* · ur · ih · tizm] *n.* partiality, bias, prejudice, fondness, discrimination, proneness, one-sidedness. *Ant.* impartiality.

fear *n.* fright, trepidation, worry, anxiety, apprehension, concern, dread, terror.

fear *v.* apprehend, dread, fret, be afraid of, be concerned about, be terrified of.

feasible [*fee* · zih · bul] *adj.* doable, workable, viable, conceivable, manageable.

feature [*feet* · chur] *n.* characteristic, mark, trait, point, quality; specialty, lead, item, main attraction.

federal [*fed* · er · ul] *adj.* United States, national, central, constitutional, associated, merged.

federation [fe · de · *ray* · shen] *n.* coalition, alliance, syndicate, union, association.

fee *n.* compensation, wage, payment, commission, charge ("fixed fee"); estate, property, inheritance, holding ("absolute fee").

feigned [faynd] *adj.* pretended, specious, spurious, fraudulent, fake, bogus.

felon [*fel* · en] *n.* criminal, wrongdoer, offender, convict, miscreant.

felonious [fe · *lone* · ee · us] *adj.* villainous, criminal, illegal, heinous, malignant, unlawful, wrongful.

felony [*fel* · uh · nee] *n.* gross offense, serious offense, transgression, wrongdoing, crime.

fence *n.* railing, barrier, hedge, enclosure; thief, burglar, receiver.

fiat [*fee* · aht] *n.* proclamation, decree, ordinance, pronouncement, mandate.

fictitious [fik · *tish* · es] *adj.* imaginary, counterfeit, false, pretend, untrue, deceptive, misrepresented, simulated.

fidelity [fih · *del* · ih · tee] *n.* loyalty, good faith, devotion, fealty, allegiance, honor, dedication; accuracy, adherence, precision.

fiduciary [fi · *doo* · she · air · ee] *n.* trustee, guardian, executor, custodian, caretaker.

fiduciary [fi · *doo* · she · air · ee] *adj.* trustworthy, reliable, confidential ("fiduciary duty").

file *v.* deliver, register, enter, submit ("We filed the documents with the proper authorities"); categorize, organize, collate, arrange, index ("They filed our names in alphabetical order").

file *n.* archives, portfolio, census, information, record ("The file was under lock and key").

final [*fine* · ul] *adj.* concluding, ultimate, terminal, ending ("final adjudication"); absolute, decisive, irrefutable, unappealable ("final offer").

finance [*fine* · anse] *v.* capitalize, promote, subsidize, underwrite, invest ("The investor financed the endeavor").

finance [fin · *anse*] *n.* commerce, investment, economics, revenue, fiscal matters ("The bank was involved in high finance").

financial [fin · *an* · shel] *adj.* pecuniary, monetary, budgetary, economic, banking ("the financial situation").

find *v.* achieve, acquire, attain, procure, gain; discover, locate, detect, ascertain, decipher, uncover, expose ("Scientists will find a cure"); determine, establish, decree, decide, conclude, adjudge ("the jury finds").

finder [*fine* · der] *n.* locater, agent, broker, investigator.

finding [*fine* · ding] *n.* decision, recommendation, verdict, ascertainment, pronouncement, deduction ("The court's finding is for the plaintiff").

fine *n.* assessment, damages, punishment, reparation, penalty.

fine *v.* charge, impose, confiscate, levy, penalize, tax.

fine *adj.* splendid, excellent, masterly, exquisite ("a fine painting"); clear, dry, sunny ("a fine day").

fingerprints [*fin* · gur · prints] *n.* prints, marks, identification, impression, trademark, characteristic.

firearm [*fire* · arm] *n.* weapon, gun, pistol, shotgun, revolver, munitions.

firm *n.* enterprise, establishment, partnership, organization, office, conglomerate, institution.

firm *adj.* definite, secured, abiding, unalterable ("firm offer").

first *adj.* initial, paramount, premiere, introductory, prime, champion, dominant, ruling.

first *adv.* beforehand, initially, originally, to start with.

fiscal [*fis* · kul] *adj.* monetary, treasury, capital, commercial.

fitness [*fit* · ness] *n.* suitability, aptness, value, usefulness, utility ("fitness for a particular purpose").

fix *v.* adjust, arrange, regulate, coordinate, establish ("fix prices"); affirm, set, secure, confirm ("fix your salary"); repair, heal, improve, rectify, refurbish, recondition, service ("fix the stove"); settle, determine, establish, resolve ("fix the meeting time").

fixed *adj.* permanent, established, situated, steady, entrenched; undeviating, unfaltering, enduring, persistent.

fixture [*fiks* · cher] *n.* attachment, permanent addition, immovable object.

flaw *n.* defect, weakness, blemish, shortcoming, imperfection, deficiency.

flee *v.* abscond, evade, abandon, depart.

flight *n.* fleeing, exfiltration, retreat, departure, escape.

flim-flam [*flim* · flam] *n.* confidence game, fraud, sham, deception, bunco.

F

float *v.* launch, activate, initiate, start up ("The company must float stock to pay for land it is purchasing"); drift, glide, fly ("float through the air").

floating [*flote* · ing] *adj.* ongoing, fluctuating, uncommitted; drifting, gliding, flying.

flood *n.* torrent, deluge, downpour, inundation.

flood *v.* inundate, overwhelm.

floor *n.* base, bottom, minimum, minimum level ("The minimum wage acts set a floor for wages").

flow *n.* movement, discharge, circulation.

flow *v.* move, drain, discharge, emit.

follow [*foll* · oh] *v.* displace, ensue, supervene, succeed; trail, pursue, persecute, escort; accord, emulate, harmonize, reflect; appreciate, apprehend, realize.

for *prep.* concerning, notwithstanding, supposing, pro, toward.

force *n.* coercion, duress, stimulus, potential; gumption, determination, obligation, persuasiveness.

force *v.* compel, obtrude, demand, impose, coerce, oblige, constrain.

forcible [*for* · sih · bul] *adj.* aggressive, potent, vehement, vigorous; effective, convincing.

forebearance [for · *bare* · ense] *n.* resisting, refraining, endurance, patience, temperance, holding back.

foreclose [for · *kloze*] *v.* block, confiscate, forfeit, bar.

foreclosure [for · *kloh* · zher] *n.* blockage, obstruction, confiscation, prohibition, removal, dispossession, removal, eviction.

forego [for · *goe*] *v.* go before, precede.

foregoing [for · *goh* · ing] *adj.* antecedent, precedent, prior, above.

foreign [*forr* · en] *adj.* alienated, borrowed, extraneous, inaccessible; irrelevant, impertinent, inconsistent.

foreman [*for* · men] *n.* spokesperson, supervisor, leader.

forensic [fo · *ren* · sik] *adj.* judicial, legal, argumentative, controversial, disputable, contestable, litigious, juristic ("forensic medicine").

foreseeable [for · *see* · uh · bul] *adj.* imminent, prospective, forthcoming.

forfeit [*for* · fit] *v.* abandon, relinquish, renounce, sacrifice, surrender, escheat, repudiate, shun, eschew, forsake, spurn, waive.

forfeiture [*for* · fit · sher] *n.* dispossession, confiscation, seizure, punishment ("The drug dealer's car is subject to forfeiture").

forge *v.* counterfeit, design, duplicate, imitate, reproduce; construct, invent, build, manufacture.

forgery [*for* · jer · ee] *n.* falsification, fraudulence, misrepresentation, manipulation.

forgo [for · *goe*] *v.* do without, pass up.

form *n.* datasheet, paper, application, chart; ceremony, behavior, fashion, method, style; arrangement, appearance, conformation, formation.

formal [*for* · mel] *adj.* certain, fixed, firm, set, explicit, traditional. *Ant.* informed.

formalize [*for* · mel · ize] *v.* legalize, legitimate, validate, make official, legitimize ("to formalize an agreement").

former [*for* · mer] *adj.* prior, previous.

fornication [for · ni · *kay* · shen] *n.* copulation, seduction, coition, intercourse.

forswear [for · *sware*] *v.* perjure, deceive, lie, equivocate.

forthwith [forth · *with*] *adv.* immediately, directly, instantly, promptly, abruptly.

fortuitous [for · *too* · ih · tus] *adj.* unexpected, accidental, surprise, unintended, unexpected, chance, haphazard ("a fortuitous event").

forum [*for* · em] *n.* tribunal, bench, judiciary, court, assembly, platform, panel, arena, space.

forward [*for* · wurd] *v.* aid, expedite, cultivate, foster; consign, send, remit, transport.

forward [*for* · wurd] *adj.* advanced, accelerated; rude, offensive, harsh, aggressive.

foster [*foss* · ter] *v.* promote, support, encourage, protect, cherish, nourish, accommodate, stimulate; harbor, help, oblige, sustain.

foster [*foss* · ter] *adj.* substitute, replacement ("foster parents").

found *v.* begin, initiate, create, introduce, commence, ("to found a company"); erect, base, support, raise ("to found an argument on fact").

foundation [foun · *day* · shen] *n.* endowment, charity, institute, society; authority, rationale, purpose, justification; base, basis, support, underpinning.

founded [*found* · ed] *adv.* grounded, supported, established ("Her motion is well-founded").

fracas [*fray* · cus] *n.* battle, brawl, scuffle, fight, fuss, fray, disturbance.

fractional [*frak* · shen · ul] *adj.* partial, divided, incomplete, segmented ("a fractional share of corporate stock").

frame *v.* conceive, contrive, invent, formulate, prepare ("frame an argument"); draft, write ("frame a statute"); set up, entrap ("frame the suspect").

franchise [*fran* · chize] *n.* license, authorization, privilege, exemption.

frank *adj.* direct, unembellished, forthright, honest; abrasive, rude.

fraternal [fre · *ter* · nul] *adj.* related, shared, common, mutual, brotherly, friendly, intimate, kind.

fraud *n.* misrepresentation, dishonesty, collusion, beguilement, deception, guile, deceit, chicanery, trickery.

fraudulent [*frawd* · je · lent] *adj.* deceptive, devious, phony, bogus, dishonorable, deceitful, dishonest, spurious, crooked.

free *v.* discharge, liberate, release; acquit, pardon, exonerate.

free *adj.* unconstrained, unimpeded, emancipated, unencumbered ("a free man"); cleared, exonerated, spared, disencumbered, excused ("free and clear").

freedom [*free* · dum] *n.* liberty, autonomy, deregulation, authorization, independence, abolition, emancipation, salvation, immunity.

freeze *v.* stop, suspend, inhibit, dishearten, preserve.

freight *n.* conveyance, encumbrance, burden, fare, tonnage.

fresh *adj.* prompt, immediate, current, timely ("fresh pursuit"); young, dewy, new.

friend *n.* confidant, companion, cohort, compatriot, ally, partner, comrade.

friendly [*frend* · lee] *adj.* receptive, sympathetic, amicable, amiable, courteous, civil, accessible, auspicious.

frisk *v.* inspect, scan, explore, investigate, search, probe, scrutinize.

frivolous [*friv* · uh · lus] *adj.* trivial, impractical, superficial, senseless, volatile, insufficient, trifling ("a frivolous appeal").

F

frolic [*froll* · ik] *n.* antic, spree, fun, amusement; mischief, caprice.

from *prep.* separating, against, taken away.

front *n.* forward, beginning, façade, foreground; aspect, demeanor, disguise, manner.

front *adj.* advanced, first, frontal, headfirst, preliminary ("front money").

front *v.* confront, border, overlay, meet.

frozen [*froh* · zen] *adj.* immobilized, restricted, unavailable, inaccessible ("His assets were frozen").

fruit *n.* benefit, consequence, return, ware, accrual, product, return ("Profit is the fruit of property").

frustrate [*frus* · trait] *v.* foil, hinder, obstruct, prevent, cancel, check, confound.

frustration [frus · *tray* · shen] *n.* dissatisfaction, annoyance, nuisance, circumvention.

fugitive [*few* · je · tiv] *n.* deserter, runaway, outlaw, outcast, refugee, escapee.

full *adj.* complete, adequate, plenteous, plentiful, ample, sated.

function [*funk* · shun] *n.* task, role, responsibility, duty, purpose, utility.

fund *v.* capitalize, endow, finance, subsidize, underwrite, contribute, donate.

fund *n.* endowment, reserve, stock, treasury, accumulation, reservoir, pool.

fundamental [*fun* · da · men · tal] *adj.* integral, requisite, substantive, elemental, basic, essential, underlying, primary.

fungible [*fun* · jih · bul] *adj.* replaceable, interchangeable ("Wheat is a fungible commodity").

furnish [*fer* · nish] *v.* give, accommodate, invest, prepare, bestow, transfer, distribute.

further [*fer* · thur] *v.* advance, encourage, promote, assist, facilitate, help, aid.

further [*fer* · thur] *adv.* additionally, distant, again.

further [*fer* · thur] *adj.* added, extra, more, farther.

furtherance [*fer* · thur · ense] *n.* advancement, advocacy, progression, elevation, backing.

future [*few* · cher] *n.* eternity, outlook, prospect, afterward.

future [*few* · cher] *adj.* approaching, destined, imminent, yet to come, succeeding ("future damages").

fuzzy *adj.* ambiguous, unclear, indefinite.

F

gain *n.* acquisition, profit, appreciation, enhancement.

gain *v.* accomplish, attain, procure, consummate.

gainful [*gain* · ful] *adj.* beneficial, lucrative, profitable, advantageous, rewarding ("gainful employment").

gamble [*gam* · bul] *v.* bet, jeopardize, risk, imperil, challenge.

game *n.* entertainment, festivity, amusement, recreation.

game *adj.* courageous, gallant, spirited, unafraid.

garnish [*gar* · nish] *v.* attach, impound, seize, levy, sequester; decorate, adorn, beautify, grace.

garnishment [*gar* · nish · ment] *n.* attachment, levy, appropriation, collection.

general [*jen* · ih · rul] *adj.* common, ordinary, generic, prevalent, routine, extensive, average, popular.

generation [jen · e · *ray* · shen] *n.* production, evolution, causation, origination; era, age, epoch, span.

generic [jen · *err* · ik] *adj.* common, all-inclusive, universal, collective, broad, nonspecific, nonexclusive.

gentrification [jen · tri · fi · *kay* · shen] *n.* redevelopment, restoration, repair, upgrading.

genuine [*jen* · yoo · in] *adj.* authentic, accurate, legitimate, unquestionable ("a genuine instrument").

germane [jer · *main*] *adj.* appropriate, connected, suitable, relative, pertinent, relevant, apropos.

gestation [jes · *tay* · shen] *n.* evolution, growth, incubation, ripening.

gift *n.* endowment, benefaction, allowance, donation ("a gift to the hospital"); talent, attribute, flair, capacity ("the gift of gab").

gist *n.* essence, basis, substance, main point, reason, gravamen, keystone ("the gist of an argument").

give *v.* contribute, bequeath, convey, donate, provide, grant.

go *v.* advance, proceed, depart, progress, move, pass.

goal *n.* target, aim, ambition, purpose, object, objective, mission, intention.

going [*goh* · ing] *adj.* forward, onward, ongoing, existing, functioning ("a going concern").

good *adj.* admirable, commendable, exceptional, reputable, stupendous; honorable, innocent, irreproachable, respectable; legitimate, reliable, worthy, valid.

goods *n.* belongings, chattels, encumbrances, property; merchandise, vendibles, wares, materials.

govern [*guv* · ern] *v.* control, administer, conduct, dictate, regulate, manage, oversee ("govern a state"); influence, incline, guide, regulate ("Judicial opinions are governed by precedent").

government [*guv* · ern · ment] *n.* management, supervision, guidance, leadership, administration, bureaucracy.

governmental [guv · ern · *men* · tel] *adj.* administrative, bureaucratic, regulatory, municipal.

governor [*guv* · er · ner] *n.* chief executive, head, leader, director, administrator, manager, official.

grace *n.* indulgence, favor, mercy, clemency, forgiveness, leniency, pardon.

grade *n.* incline, rank, degree, step, stage.

grade *v.* evaluate, mark, rank ("grade his presentation"); flatten, level, even ("grade the road").

graduated [*grad* · joo · ay · ted] *adj.* measured, progressive, increasing, continuous, regular, perceptible ("a graduated tax").

graft *n.* corruption, kickback, bribery, blackmail, profiteering, illegal profit.

grand *adj.* elevated, great, outstanding; formal, pompous, ceremonial.

grant *v.* authorize, allow, relinquish; award, donate, assign, allot; consent, yield, agree, acknowledge.

grant *n.* allocation, gift, contribution, privilege, endowment, donation.

gratis [*gra* · tiss] *adj.* free, without charge, pro bono, complimentary, unrecompensed, expenseless.

gratuitous [*gre* · *too* · it · ess] *adj.* indefensible, unessential, unjustified, unprovoked; complimentary, charitable, voluntary, free, donated ("Pro bono legal representation is gratuitous"); unsolicited, unsought ("He gives a lot of gratuitous advice").

gratuity [*gre* · *too* · i · tee] *n.* gift, contribution, bonus, dividend, tip, honorarium; graft, kickback, hush money.

gravamen [*grah* · va · men] *n.* substance, core, foundation, nucleus, focal point, thrust, essence, gist, cornerstone.

gravity [*grav* · i · tee] *n.* acuteness, severity, urgency, momentousness, consequence; pressure, weight, heaviness, force.

great *adj.* extraordinary, large, prodigious, extreme, outrageous ("great bodily harm"); outstanding, influential, significant, noteworthy, superior ("a great oration").

grievance [*gree* · venss] *n.* affliction, hardship, injustice, injury, complaint, protest, allegation, accusation, objection.

grievous [*gree* · vus] *adj.* severe, painful, disturbing, offensive, unbearable ("grievous bodily harm").

gross *adj.* obvious, apparent, flagrant, exorbitant, unmitigated; large, obese, portly, corpulent; callous, lewd, obscene, coarse; whole, entire, all, aggregate, total, sum.

ground *n.* basis, premise, pretext, rationale, foundation ("My attorney says I have insufficient ground for a lawsuit"); earth, soil, land ("on hallowed ground").

group *n.* accumulation, congregation, conglomerate, formation, body.

G

group *v.* assemble, arrange, classify, associate.

growth *n.* development, ripening, unfolding, maturation; increase, expansion, accumulation, aggrandizement, inflation.

guarantee [gair · en · *tee*] *v.* pledge, promise, assure, endorse.

guarantee [gair · en · *tee*] *n.* attestation, certification, commitment, oath, warranty.

guaranteed [gair · en · *teed*] *adj.* approved, affirmed, vested, confirmed, definite, attested, secure.

guaranty [*gair* · en · tee] *n.* engagement, pledge, promise, covenant, indemnity, security.

guardian [*garr* · dee · en] *n.* protector, custodian, sponsor, curator, champion.

guest *n.* patron, invitee, confidante, recipient, caller.

guilt *n.* misconduct, turpitude, dishonesty, delinquency; dishonor, blame, liability, remorse, regret.

guilty [*gill* · tee] *adj.* culpable, accountable, condemned, incriminated, blameworthy, responsible, culpable.

gun *n.* firearm, rifle, pistol, weapon, shotgun, arms.

G

habit [*hab* · it] *n.* custom, inclination, course of conduct, practice, pattern, procedure, routine, repetition.

habitable [*hab* · i · tuh · bull] *adj.* livable, fit, acceptable, occupiable, tenantable. *Ant.* uninhabitable.

habitation [hab · ih · *tay* · shen] *n.* domicile, abode, residence, dwelling, home; occupation, possession, residence, tenancy.

habitual [hab · *it* · shoo · el] *adj.* constant, customary, hardened, accustomed, usual, common, ordinary, regular, routine, recurrent ("habitual intoxication").

habitually [hab · *it* · shoo · e · lee] *adv.* customarily, regularly, traditionally.

had *v.* brought, commenced, maintained ("Can an action be had in this situation?").

haggle [*hag* · gull] *v.* argue, bargain, negotiate, quibble, wrangle, deal, dicker.

halt *v.* stop, block, curb, deter, restrict, restrain, discontinue, interrupt, arrest.

halt *n.* stop, pause, respite, cessation, delay, stoppage, truce, lapse, lull.

hand down *v.* decide, judge, opine ("The court handed down its decision yesterday").

handcuff *n.* shackle, chain, harness, collar, pinion.

handcuff *v.* shackle, tie, fasten, manacle, lash, leash.

handicap [*han* · dee · kap] *v.* hinder, interfere, obstruct, frustrate.

handicap [*han* · dee · kap] *n.* obstruction, blockade, disadvantage, liability, deficiency, impairment.

handicapped [*han* · dee · kapt] *adj.* disabled, physically challenged, impaired.

handle [*han* · dul] *v.* regulate, supervise, guide, administer, oversee, direct, have charge of.

handwriting [*hand* · rite · ing] *n.* script, penmanship, writing, hand, longhand, autography.

happening [*hap* · pen · ing] *n.* event, occurrence, action, incident, matter, phenomenon.

harass [huh · *rass*] *v.* annoy, hound, molest, intimidate, persecute, badger.

harassment [huh · *rass* · ment] *n.* annoyance, badgering, irritation, disturbance, aggravation, intimidation.

hard labor [hard *lay* · ber] *n.* compulsory labor, bondage, servitude.

harm *v.* hurt, cripple, abuse, inflict, damage, injure, impair.

harm *n.* injury, misfortune, damage, detriment, aggravation, evil, disservice.

harmful [*harm* · ful] *adj.* destructive, dangerous, injurious, detrimental, deleterious, harmful, evil.

harmonize [*harr* · mun · ize] *v.* bring into accord, adapt, accommodate, reconcile, integrate.

harry [*har* · ree] *v.* harass, badger, heckle, tease, pester, bully, bother, hound, offend, provoke.

haste *n.* hurry, eagerness, rush, frenzy, flurry ("In his haste, he forgot the chart").

have *v.* possess, hold ("Do I have a cause of action in this situation?").

havoc [*hav* · uk] *n.* chaos, disorder, shambles, ruin, devastation.

hazard [*haz* · erd] *n.* peril, threat, crisis, danger, menace, uncertainty.

hazard [*haz* · erd] *v.* venture, risk, gamble ("hazard a guess").

hazardous [*haz* · er · dus] *adj.* dangerous, harmful, unsafe, risky, perilous.

head *n.* leader, chief, person in charge, authority, principal person ("head of household"); brain, intellect, instinct, sense, intuition ("a good head for business").

health *n.* well-being, fitness, soundness, strength, vitality.

hear *v.* try, hold court, adjudicate ("hear a case"); understand, heed, submit, listen, note, notice ("hear his point").

hearing [*heer* · ing] *n.* trial, inquiry, litigation, adjudication, review, legal proceedings.

hearsay [*heer* · say] *n.* secondhand information, gossip, report, indirect evidence, grapevine, rumor ("hearsay testimony").

heat *n.* passion, insanity, emotion; warmth. *Ant.* premeditation; chill.

hedge *v.* evade, avoid, dodge, equivocate, prevaricate, sidestep.

heed *v.* follow, obey, comply with, be guided by, hear, notice.

heighten [*hite* · en] *v.* augment, intensify, enhance, enlarge, magnify; raise, uplift, build up.

heinous [*hay* · nuss] *adj.* hateful, dreadful, diabolic, mean, despicable, shameful, villainous ("a heinous crime").

heir *n.* successor, descendant, inheritor, recipient, beneficiary, donee ("my heirs and assigns").

held *v.* decided, asserted, adjudicated ("The court held that privity was not required"); conducted ("held court"); possessed, owned ("held title").

help *v.* aid, assist, avail, accommodate, benefit, improve, remedy, facilitate.

help *n.* aid, assistance, favor, succor, support, backing, guidance.

helpless [*help* · less] *adj.* unarmed, unprotected, exposed, vulnerable; impotent, powerless, weak, feeble, dependent, debilitated.

henceforth [*henss* · forth] *adv.* from now on, following, succeeding.

hereafter [heer · *aft* · er] *adv.* after now, at some future time, later, afterwards.

hereditaments [herr · eh · *dit* · a · ments] *n.* land, real property, personal property, inheritance.

hereditary [herr · *ed* · ih · terr · ee] *adj.* biological, genetic, inherited, innate, instinctive, inborn, native, lineal, constitutional, congenital.

heretofore [*heer* · to · for] *adv.* previously, until now, before the present, formerly ("The fact that the gun was not loaded was heretofore unknown to this court").

heroic [he · *row* · ik] *adj.* brave, bold, noble, valiant, courageous, dauntless, stalwart, resolute.

H

hesitant [*hez* · i · tant] *adj.* reluctant, timid, undecided, tentative, wavering, cautious, doubting.

hesitate [*hez* · i · tait] *v.* dally, delay, wait, waver, pause, falter, demur.

heterogeneous [het · er · oh · *geen* · ee · us] *adj.* mixed, different, varied, dissimilar, diverse, assorted.

hidden [*hid* · en] *adj.* latent, concealed, masked, veiled, submerged, undisclosed ("a hidden defect").

hide *v.* conceal, shroud, suppress, veil, obscure, harbor, envelop, deceive.

high *adj.* elevated, important, significant ("The high court of this state"); tall, lofty ("a high structure").

highest [*hy* · est] *adj.* supreme, major, paramount, foremost, top, best ("the highest and best use for this piece of property").

highway [*hy* · way] *n.* road, roadway, street, freeway, expressway, avenue, interstate.

hijack [*hy* · jak] *v.* abduct, seize, take, intercept, capture, snatch, take captive.

hijacking [*hy* · jak · ing] *n.* robbery, kidnapping, abduction, capturing, commandeering, air piracy.

hinder [*hin* · der] *v.* obstruct, block, impede, frustrate, restrain.

hint *v.* suggest, intimate, imply, indicate, refer, connote ("hint at the answer").

hint *n.* clue, suggestion, indication, allusion, insinuation.

hire *v.* employ, enlist, retain, contract ("Their company won't hire ex-convicts").

hire *n.* payment, charge, fee ("We could not afford her hire").

historic [*hiss* · *tor* · ik] *adj.* of major importance, famous, well-known, significant, crucial.

hitherto [*hith* · ur · too] *adv.* previously, once, until now, formerly.

hoard *v.* accrue, accumulate, store, store away, keep in reserve, collect, gather.

hoax *n.* ruse, scheme, deceit, sham, trick, fraud, chicanery, pretense, joke, dupery.

hold *v.* own, have title to ("To hold a negotiable instrument"); possess, occupy ("He holds a life estate in that property"); retain, control ("He holds that money in trust for his sister"); decide, rule, announce, decree, settle ("What did the court hold in this situation last year?"); conduct, administer, manage, oversee ("The agency will decide whether to hold a hearing ") occupy, maintain, direct, be in charge of ("to hold office"); grasp, grip ("hold my hand").

hold *n.* domination, power, control, sway, domination ("She's really got a hold on me").

hold up *v.* delay, impede, interrupt, halt, restrain ("hold up the proceedings"); rob, plunder, sack, take by theft ("hold up the bank").

holder [*hole* · der] *n.* owner, possessor, bearer, keeper, recipient.

holding [*hole* · ding] *n.* decision, conclusion, order, adjudication, bottom line ("the court's holding").

holdings [*hole* · dingz] *n.* property, belongings, assets, goods.

holiday [*hol* · ih · day] *n.* observance, celebration, day off, occasion, vacation.

holographic [hol · uh · *graf* · ik] *adj.* written, handwritten, penned, printed, scripted, inscribed ("holographic will").

homage [*hom* · aj] *n.* honor, regard, reverence, allegiance, exaltation, veneration.

home *n.* residence, domicile, house, abode, domain; native land, birthplace, motherland, fatherland.

H

H

homestead [*home* · sted] *n.* dwelling, domicile, home residence.

homicide [*hom* · ih · side] *n.* murder, manslaughter, slaying, assassination, killing, slaughter, felony, elimination, termination of life, extermination.

honest [*on* · est] *adj.* genuine, sincere, frank, ethical, moral, true, just, decent, trustworthy.

honesty [*on* · es · tee] *n.* candor, openness, truthfulness, fairness, candor, integrity, sincerity.

honor [*on* · er] *v.* credit, redeem, make good ("The store honors personal checks"); praise, acclaim, value, venerate, extol, revere, recognize, commemorate ("to honor the dead").

honor [*on* · er] *n.* honesty, integrity, principle, trustworthiness, virtue, veracity, credibility, dignity.

honorable [*on* · er · ebl] *adj.* honest, good, moral, right, meritorious.

honorarium [on · e · *rare* · ee · um] *n.* emolument, commission, payment, consideration, recompense, salary, compensation, stipend.

hoodlum [*hude* · lum] *n.* scoundrel, ruffian, juvenile delinquent, thief, villain, mobster, miscreant, rogue, peculator.

hoodwink [*hud* · wenk] *v.* fool, trick, deceive, outwit, beguile, dupe, cheat.

horizontal [horr · i · *zawn* · tel] *adj.* even, level, straight, parallel to the ground, lengthwise.

hornbook [*horn* · buk] *n.* digest, manual, abstract, study guide, treatise, commentary, exposition, outline, dissertation, capsule, elementary work, primer, elementary law ("The hornbook on torts").

hostage [*hoss* · tej] *n.* prisoner, captive, pawn, victim.

hostile [*hoss* · tel] *adj.* antagonistic, adverse, argumentative, warlike, bellicose, belligerent, combative ("a hostile demeanor"); uncooperative, opposed ("hostile witness").

hot *adj.* stolen, pilfered; furious, enraged, provoked, angry, excited, frenzied; warm, burning, scalding.

house *n.* abode, dwelling, domicile, residence; business, establishment, company.

housebreaking [*hows* · brake · ing] *n.* burglary, stealing, thievery, looting, raiding, plundering, filching.

household [*hows* · hold] *n.* family, residence, homestead, lodging.

household [*hows* · hold] *adj.* domestic, residential; everyday, common, routine.

humanitarian [hyoo · man · ih · *tare* · ee · en] *adj.* philanthropic, compassionate, benevolent, charitable, human, kind, humane.

humanity [hue · *man* · ih · tee] *n.* people, mankind, humankind, human beings.

humiliate [hue · *mill* · ee · ate] *v.* disgrace, shame, abase, embarrass, malign, put down, mock, ridicule.

hypothecate [hy · *poth* · e · kayt] *v.* pledge, mortgage.

hypothesis [hy · *poth* · e · sis] *n.* assumption, theory, supposition, postulate, presumption.

hypothesize [hy · *poth* · e · size] *v.* assume, suppose, presume, theorize.

hypothetical [hype · e · *thet* · ih · kal] *adj.* theoretical, assumed, imaginary, supposed.

hysterical [hiss · *terr* · ih · kul] *adj.* distraught, unmanageable, uncontrollable, overcome, irrational, possessed, crazy.

idea [eye · *dee* · uh] *n.* concept, thought, belief, proposal.

identical [eye · *dent* · ih · kul] *adj.* alike, matching, twin, uniform, indistinguishable, duplicate.

identification [eye · den · tih · fih · *kay* · shen] *n.* verification, authentication, ascertainment, recognition.

identify [eye · *dent* · ih · fie] *v.* specify, name, designate, determine, recognize ("identify the perpetrator").

identity [eye · *den* · tih · tee] *n.* sameness, resemblance, similarity; individuality, uniqueness. *Ant.* universality, dissimilarity.

idiocy [*id* · ee · e · see] *n.* mental retardation, lunacy, insanity, imbecility.

idle [*eye* · dul] *adj.* inactive, disengaged, inert, still; jobless, inoccupied, lazy, slothful, unemployed.

ignorance [*ig* · ner · ense] *n.* lack of knowledge, unenlightenment, unawareness, incomprehension, unfamiliarity, absence of knowledge. *Ant.* comprehension.

illegal [il · *lee* · gul] *adj.* unlawful, contrary to law, illicit, felonious, forbidden, improper, unauthorized, proscribed.

illegality [il · lee · *gal* · ih · tee] *n.* unlawfulness, wrongdoing, criminality, malfeasance, transgression.

illegitimate [il · le · *jit* · ih · met] *adj.* unlawful, impermissible; wrong, erroneous, improper, invalid; bastard.

illicit [il · *liss* · it] *adj.* unlawful, illegal, forbidden by law, not permitted, improper, banned, proscribed, unauthorized. *Ant.* authorized.

illusory [il · *looz* · e · ree] *adj.* imaginary, fictitious, unreal, false, misleading, delusive, spurious, sham, seeming.

illustrate [*il* · luss · trayt] *v.* explain, demonstrate, clarify, illuminate, show, expound.

illustration [*il* · luss · tray · shun] *n.* showing, example, depiction, explanation, demonstration, representation, case in point.

imbecility [im · be · *sil* · ih · tee] *n.* mental incapacity, mental deficiency, feeble-mindedness.

imbue [im · *bew*] *v.* instill, indoctrinate, permeate, drench, inculcate.

imitation [im · ih · *tay* · shen] *n.* forgery, fraud, reproduction, duplication, infringement.

immaterial [im · e · *teer* · ee · el] *adj.* not material, irrelevant, not pertinent, not important, of no consequence, insignificant, unessential, minor, beside the point. *Ant.* material, relevant.

immediate [ih · *mee* · dee · et] *adj.* close, near, direct, proximate; prompt, instant, speedy, timely; impending, upcoming.

immediately [ih · *mee* · dee · et · lee] *adv.* promptly, instantly, at once, directly. *Ant.* later.

immemorial [im · e · *more* · ee · el] *adj.* dateless, archaic, ancestral.

immigrant [*im* · ih · grent] *n.* foreigner, nonnative, alien, emigrant.

immigration [im · ih · *gray* · shen] *n.* migration, admission, expatriation, alien entry, ingress, transmigration.

imminent [*im* · ih · nent] *adj.* probable, impending, unavoidable, inevitable, close ("imminent danger").

immoral [im · *more* · el] *adj.* unethical, unscrupulous, corrupt, dishonest, depraved, deviant, wicked, evil. *Ant.* moral.

immorality [im · more · *al* · ih · tee] *n.* corruption, wrong, delinquency, debauchery.

immune [ih · *myoon*] *adj.* sheltered, screened, exempt, excused, unexposed, safe, protected ("immune from prosecution").

immunity [ih · *myoon* · ih · tee] *n.* exemption, privilege, indemnity, release, insusceptibility, guarantee, absolution, safety ("absolute immunity").

impact [*im* · pakt] *n.* effect, meaning, consequence ("What was the impact of his speech?"); crash, collision, contact, striking ("The impact of the cars").

impair [im · *pare*] *v.* hurt, hinder, stifle, taint, waste, weaken, deplete, devalue.

impairment [im · *pare* · ment] *n.* limitation, defect, error, flaw, obstruction, disability, handicap.

impanel [im · *pan* · el] *v.* list, enroll, enter, schedule, docket.

impartial [im · *par* · shel] *adj.* fair, unbiased, neutral, unprejudiced, objective.

impass [*im* · pass] *n.* cessation, stop, standstill, stalemate, dilemma, discontinuance, block.

impeach [im · *peech*] *v.* accuse, blame, censure, contradict, dispute, denounce, decry, castigate.

impeachment [im · *peech* · ment] *n.* indictment, complaint, charge, castigation, vilification, censure, disapproval, reproof, discrediting, removal.

impediment [im · *ped* · ih · ment] *n.* bar, disqualification, obstruction, obstacle, blockade, deterrent, barrier, hindrance.

impel [im · *pell*] *v.* start, urge, motivate, mobilize, incite, launch, instigate, prompt, propel.

imperative [im · *per* · ah · tiv] *adj.* mandatory, urgent, compulsory, obligatory, crucial, commanding.

imperfect [im · *per* · fekt] *adj.* incomplete, flawed, defective, deficient, faulty, lacking, tainted, impaired, unsatisfactory.

impermissible [im · per · *miss* · ih · bul] *adj.* illegal, wrongful, actionable, unsanctioned, proscribed, punishable.

impersonation [im · per · seh · *nay* · shen] *n.* imitation, copy, fraud, representation.

impetus [*im* · pe · tus] *n.* stimulus, incentive, boast, pressure, push, propellant, motive.

implausible [im · *plaus* · ih · bul] *adj.* unbelievable, incredible, unlikely, questionable, inconceivable ("an implausible alibi").

implead [*im* · pleed] *v.* join, bring in, sue.

implicate [*im* · plih · kayt] *v.* involve, accuse, associate, inculpate, incriminate, link, expose, entangle. *Ant.* dissociate.

implicated [*im* · plih · kay · ted] *adj.* involved, accused, incriminated, linked.

implication [im · plih · *kay* · shen] *n.* suggestion, innuendo, insinuation, hint; connection, involvement, complicity.

implicit [im · *pliss* · it] *adj.* unstated, tacit, implied, suggested, understood, unspoken.

implied [im · *plyd*] *adj.* implicit, suggested, inferred, assumed, insinuated, tacit, undeclared.

imply [im · *plie*] *v.* insinuate, indicate, hint, connote, denote, allude, suggest.

import [im · *port*] *v.* introduce, carry, transport, convey, ship.

import [*im* · port] *n.* importance, significance, meaning, seriousness.

important [im · *por* · tent] *adj.* momentous, noteworthy, powerful, outstanding, illustrious, major, grand; urgent, crucial, critical, vital, necessary.

impose [im · *poze*] *v.* burden, inflict, levy, order, enact ("Do you think the government will impose a new tax?"); intrude, interpose, interfere, transgress, force, infringe ("he always imposes himself").

imposition [im · po · *zish* · en] *n.* tax, impost, charge, duty, toll, levy; burden, constraint, encroachment, encumbrance, hindrance.

impossibility [im · poss · ih · *bil* · ih · tee] *n.* futility, insurmountability, infeasibility, unattainability, failure, unfeasibility, difficulty, failure.

impossible [im · *poss* · ih · bul] *adj.* unachievable, unworkable, absurd, unobtainable, inconceivable, preposterous, hopeless.

impost [*im* · post] *n.* tax, duty, levy.

impotence [*im* · pe · tenss] *n.* inability, incapacity, weakness, ineffectiveness, powerlessness, ineptitude, incapacity, sterility, barrenness.

impotent [*im* · pe · tent] *adj.* powerless, helpless, ineffective, sterile.

impound [im · *pownd*] *v.* take possession of, secure, seize, confiscate, sequester, appropriate.

impracticable [im · *prak* · tih · ke · bul] *adj.* unattainable, unfeasible, impossible, unrealizable, unmanageable, unwieldy, unviable. *Ant.* feasible.

impress [im · *press*] *v.* reach, touch, affect, influence, inspire, stir; seize, impound, acquire, levy, take, sequester.

imprisonment [im · *priz* · en · ment] *n.* detention, restraint, confinement, detainment, incarceration.

improper [im · *prop* · er] *adj.* incorrect, indecent, unallowable, unsuitable, forbidden, erroneous, unsound, immoral ("improper advances").

impropriety [im · pro · *pry* · eh · tee] *n.* imprudence, indiscretion, misbehavior, incorrectness; tactlessness, bad taste, indecorum, indecency, indelicacy.

improve [im · *proov*] *v.* make better, upgrade, enhance, enrich, fix, renovate.

improvement [im · *proov* · ment] *n.* bettering, enhancement, advancement, enrichment, renovation.

impugn [im · *pyoon*] *v.* assail, criticize, discredit, denounce, contest, disbelieve, raise questions about, oppose.

impulse [*im* · puls] *n.* desire, inclination, drive, force, stimulant ("an uncontrollable impulse").

I

impulsive [im · *pul* · siv] *adj.* bold, rash, unthinking, spontaneous, hasty, risky, sudden, unadvised, unconsidered. *Ant.* planned.

impunity [im · *pyoon* · ih · tee] *n.* exemption, absolution, freedom, immunity, protection, privilege ("act with impunity").

impute [im · *pyoot*] *v.* ascribe, attribute, credit, assign, attach.

imputed [im · *pyoo* · ted] *adj.* attributed, blamed, implicated, ascribed, charged ("The paralegal's neglect is the attorney's imputed neglect").

in lieu of *prep.* in place of, for, instead of, in substitution for ("Will you allow me to pay in Canadian money in lieu of U.S. funds?").

inability [in · uh · *bil* · ih · tee] *n.* inadequacy, helplessness, failure, ineptness, incompetency, incapability, powerlessness.

inactive [*in* · act · iv] *adj.* idle, inert, inoperative; deficient, lacking, incapable, unsatisfactory; feeble, helpless, disabled.

inadequate [in · *ad* · e · kwet] *adj.* incomplete, wanting, lacking, defective, substandard.

inadmissible [in · ad · *mis* · ih · bul] *adj.* objectionable, not allowed, banned, disallowed, unacceptable, excludable, barred, improper.

inalienable [in · ale · *yen* · uh · bul] *adj.* nontransferable, absolute, permanent, inherent, unforfeitable ("inalienable rights").

inapplicable [in · ap · *lik* · uh · bul] *adj.* inappropriate, improper, irrelevant, extraneous, immaterial.

inauguration [in · awg · yer · *ay* · shen] *n.* beginning, putting into effect, induction, consecration, swearing in.

incapacity [in · ke · *pass* · ih · tee] *n.* feebleness, dotage, incompetence, inability, infirmity, weakness, helplessness, lack of fitness.

incarcerate [in · *kar* · ser · ayt] *v.* jail, confine, imprison, hold captive, restrain.

incendiary [in · *sen* · dee · e · ree] *n.* arsonist, houseburner, pyromaniac.

incentive [in · *sen* · tiv] *n.* motivation, inducement, impulse, cause, catalyst, motive, allure, attraction.

inception [in · *sep* · shen] *n.* initial stage, starting point, birth, genesis, initiation; beginning, commencement, start.

inchoate [in · *koh* · ayt] *adj.* imperfect, inadequate, not completely formed, partial, developing, undeveloped, beginning, rudimentary ("inchoate interest"). *Ant.* perfected.

incident [*in* · si · dent] *n.* event, occasion, happening, occurrence, experience.

incident [*in* · si · dent] *adj.* following, related to, relative to, associated, implicated.

incidental [in · si · *den* · tel] *adj.* secondary, subordinate, minor, additional, dependent, linked, contingent.

incite [in · *site*] *v.* arouse, stir up, encourage, goad, inflame, instigate, set in motion, awaken, energize.

inclusive [in · *cloos* · iv] *adj.* all-embracing, comprehensive, extensive, exhaustive, full, sweeping, broad.

income [*in* · kum] *n.* wages, salary, earning, profit, livelihood.

incommunicado [in · kum · yoo · nih · *kah* · doh] *adj./adv.* isolated, cutoff, sequestered, separate ("The police held her incommunicado for eight hours after her arrest").

incompatible [in · kum · *pat* · ih · bul] *adj.* antagonistic, discordant, disagreeing, uncongenial, hostile; contradictory, conflicting, antithetical.

incompetence [in · *kom* · pe · tense] *n.* incompetency, neglect, inability, inadequacy, ineptness.

incompetent [in · *kom* · pe · tent] *adj.* invalid, unqualified, incapable, inept, inefficient, bungling, inadequate, deficient, insufficient. *Ant.* competent, skilled.

incomprehensible [in · kom · pre · hen · sih · bul] *adj.* unfathomable, puzzling, inconceivable, inexplicable, unimaginable.

inconclusive [in · kon · *kloo* · siv] *adj.* unproven, unpersuasive, weak, unconvincing, indefinite, unsubstantiated, uncorroborated.

inconsequential [in · kon · sih · *kwen* · shul] *adj.* unimportant, trifling, minor, trivial, immaterial, irrelevant ("an inconsequential detail").

inconsistency [in · kun · *sis* · ten · see] *n.* contradiction, variance, difference, disparity, divergence, inconsonance ("an inconsistency in his testimony").

inconsistent [in · kun · *sis* · tent] *adj.* incompatible, contradictory, conflicting, discordant, opposing.

inconspicuous [in · kon · *spik* · yoo · us] *adj.* unnoticed, unobtrusive, unseen, unperceivable, indistinct, hidden, blurred.

incontestable [in · kon · *test* · ih · bul] *adj.* clear, conclusive, irrefutable, unassailable, undeniable, unambiguous.

incontrovertible [in · kon · tre · *ver* · tih · bul] *adj.* incontestable, definitive, conclusive, certain, noncontestable.

inconvenience [in · kun · *vee* · nee · enss] *n.* annoyance, nuisance, bother, burden, hardship, hindrance, hassle.

incorporate [in · *kore* · per · ayt] *v.* combine, include, merge, weave, fuse, mix ("incorporate graphs into the presentation").

incorporeal [in · kore · *pore* · ee · el] *adj.* intangible, bodiless, nonphysical, nonmaterial, spiritual.

incorrect [in · ko · *rekt*] *adj.* mistaken, wrong, unfactual, inaccurate, false, amiss, erroneous.

incorrigible [in · *korr* · ih · jih · bul] *adj.* unmanageable, disobedient, uncontrollable, unruly, unreformable, unsalvageable, wicked, unrepentant.

increase [*in* · kreese] *n.* addition, gain, hike, boost, enlargement, growth, rise, accrual.

increase [in · *kreese*] *v.* enlarge, proliferate, expand, extend, supplement, raise, surge.

incredible [in · *kred* · ih · bul] *adj.* fabulous, wonderful, awesome, amazing; absurd, impossible, ridiculous, preposterous, unthinkable, suspect, suspicious.

increment [*in* · kre · ment] *n.* increase, addition, advancement, raise.

incriminate [in · *krim* · ih · nayt] *v.* implicate, involve, impeach, connect, indict, charge.

incrimination [in · krim · ih · *nay* · shen] *n.* accusation, indictment, blame, decrial, impeachment.

inculcate [*in* · kul · kayt] *v.* instill, inspire, indoctrinate, educate, propagandize, impress, imbue, preach.

inculpate [*in* · kul · payt] *v.* incriminate, accuse, charge, impute, blame, denounce.

inculpatory [in · *kul* · pe · tore · ee] *adj.* incriminating, damning, damaging, blaming, accusatory, impugning ("I think the defendant will be convicted because his own testimony was inculpatory").

incumbent [in · *kum* · bent] *n.* officeholder, occupant, official, bureaucrat. *Ant.* candidate.

incur [in · *kerr*] *v.* undertake, assume, acquire, become responsible, bring on ("incur a penalty by late payment of taxes").

indebted [in · *det* · ed] *adj.* accountable, bound, liable, obligated, answerable for, beholden, encumbered.

indebtedness [in · *det* · ed · ness] *n.* liability, debts, responsibility; appreciation, gratitude.

indecent [in · *dee* · sent] *adj.* vulgar, lewd, lascivious, obscene, immoral, unseemly.

indefeasible [in · de · *fee* · zih · bul] *adj.* inalienable, incontrovertible, immutable, incontestable, irreversible, confirmed, binding, settled.

indefinite [in · *def* · ih · nit] *adj.* temporary, uncertain, vague, ill-defined, boundless, open, open-ended, indeterminate, unclear.

indemnification [in · dem · nih · fih · *kay* · shen] *n.* restitution, amends, compensation, insurance, payment, reparation.

indemnify [in · *dem* · nih · fie] *v.* compensate, reimburse, secure, make amends, guarantee, restore, repay, redeem.

indemnity [in · *dem* · nih · tee] *n.* repayment, security, restitution, assurance, restoration.

independent [in · de · *pen* · dent] *adj.* unrestricted, separate, autonomous, sovereign, nonpartisan, free, unbound, unassociated, self-reliant.

indestructible [in · de · *struk* · tih · bul] *adj.* endless, indefeasible, perpetual, permanent, enduring, unbreakable.

indeterminate [in · de · *ter* · mih · net] *adj.* open, vague, imprecise, unclear, amorphous, nebulous, unspecified, unresolved.

index [*in* · deks] *n.* list, inventory; indication, basis, rule.

index [*in* · deks] *v.* list, classify, codify, inventory.

indicate [*in* · dih · kayt] *v.* imply, signify, suggest, allude to, evidence, intimate, hint.

indication [in · dih · *kay* · shun] *n.* hint, suggestion, forewarning, evidence, mention, sign, warning, symptom, omen, indicator.

indicia [in · *dish* · a] *n.* indicators, indications, signs, evidence, expressions, tokens ("The sale of his business for almost nothing, and the fact that he concealed his assets, are indicia of fraud").

indict [in · *dite*] *v.* charge, arraign, implicate, prosecute, blame, accuse.

indictable [in · *dite* · uh · bul] *adj.* prohibited, illegal, impermissible, punishable.

indicted [in · *dite* · ed] *adj.* formally charged, blamed, accused.

indictment [in · *dite* · ment] *n.* complaint, denunciation, allegation, charge, incrimination.

indifferent [in · *dif* · rent] *adj.* neutral, disinterested, impartial, aloof, reserved, passive, detached, unemotional.

indigent [*in* · dih · jent] *adj.* poor, needy, deprived, poverty-stricken, penniless.

indignity [in · *dig* · ne · tee] *n.* insult, humiliation, cruelty, disrespect, degrading conduct.

indirect [in · dih · *rekt*] *adj.* not direct, roundabout, circuitous, deviating, ancillary, oblique, inferential, collateral. *Ant.* direct.

indiscretion [in · dis · *kress* · shun] *n.* mistake, poor judgment, imprudence, injudiciousness, thoughtlessness, misdeed, misconduct.

indispensable [in · dis · *pen* · suh · bul] *adj.* essential, vital, mandatory, crucial, required, necessary, cardinal, imperative.

individual [in · de · *vid* · joo · el] *n.* person, autonomous entity, distinct person, body, party, character, human being.

individual [in · de · *vid* · yoo · el] *adj.* personal, separate, single, particular, unique, specific.

indivisible [in · dih · *viz* · ih · bul] *adj.* entire, inseverable, united, inseparable, unsunderable.

indorse [in · *dorss*] *v.* support, back, finance, recommend, authorize, authenticate, sign, ratify, validate.

indorsement [in · *dorss* · ment] *n.* sanction, consent, permission, support, backing, encouragement, confirmation.

induce [in · *dooss*] *v.* lead on, influence, cause, persuade, pressure, motivate, precipitate, actuate.

inducement [in · *dooss* · ment] *n.* motivation, motive, impulse, catalyst, cause, attraction, stimulant.

induction [in · *duk* · shen] *n.* inauguration, installation, ordination, selection.

industrial [in · *dus* · tree · ul] *adj.* commercial, mass-produced, mechanized, manufactured, technological, standardized.

industry [*in* · dus · tree] *n.* field, business, enterprise, profession, production, work; diligence, drive, zeal, persistence, activity, determination.

inebriation [in · *ee* · bree · ay · shun] *n.* drunkenness, insobriety, intemperance, intoxication.

ineffective [in · e · *fek* · tiv] *adj.* unproductive, fruitless, useless, invalid, futile, ineffectual, powerless, nugatory.

ineligible [in · *el* · ih · jih · bul] *adj.* disqualified, unsuitable, disallowed, unentitled, inapplicable. *Ant.* eligible.

inept [in · *ept*] *adj.* unqualified, unfit, inefficient, clumsy, unable, awkward, incompetent, bungling, inappropriate.

inequality [in · e · *kwal* · ih · tee] *n.* prejudice, partiality, imbalance, discrepancy, injustice, inconsistency, bias, disproportion.

inevitable [in · *ev* · ih · tuh · bul] *adj.* unalterable, ineluctable, certain, sure, destined, definite, imminent. *Ant.* uncertain.

inexact [in · eggs · *act*] *adj.* estimated, unclear, rough, unspecified, imperfect, imprecise, hazy ("an inexact science").

inexcusable [in · eks · *kyooz* · ih · bul] *adj.* unforgivable, indefensible, reprehensible, unpardonable, heinous, cruel, unjustifiable.

inexplicable [in · eks · *plik* · uh · bul] *adj.* mysterious, puzzling, undecipherable, incomprehensible, baffling, enigmatic.

infamous [*in* · fem · us] *adj.* notorious, ill-famed, despicable, villainous, disreputable, profligate, perfidious, heinous.

infamy [*in* · fuh · mee] *n.* disgrace, discredit, disrespect, shame, notoriety, aspersion, opprobrium.

infancy [*in* · fen · see] *n.* childhood; inception, start, conception, genesis.

infant [*in* · fent] *n.* child, minor, juvenile, toddler, tot, youngster.

infect [in · *fekt*] *v.* contaminate, impair, taint, sully, stain, pollute, debase.

infer [in · *fer*] *v.* reason, conclude, deduce, construe, assume.

inference [*in* · fe · rense] *n.* belief, assumption, deduction, conclusion, conjecture ("a likely inference").

inferior [in · *feer* · ee · er] *adj.* of lower rank, secondary, lesser, under, junior, subordinate, subsidiary, minor; faulty, poor, shoddy, imperfect, second-rate, unacceptable, defective.

inferred [in · *ferd*] *adj.* concluded, deduced, reasoned, presumed, constructed.

infidelity [in · fih · *del* · ih · tee] *n.* unfaithfulness, betrayal, cheating, adultery, disloyalty, deceit.

infirm [in · *ferm*] *adj.* defective, weak, purposeless ("Your legal argument is infirm"); sickly, feeble, powerless ("I am feeling infirm").

infirmative [in · *fer* · me · tiv] *adj.* exculpatory, invalidating ("infirmative testimony").

infirmity [in · *fer* · mih · tee] *n.* defect, disability, disease, weakness, frailty, debility, incapacity.

inflated [in · *flay* · ted] *adj.* enlarged, swollen, dilated, air-filled, distended ("an inflated balloon"); amplified, embellished, overpriced, overvalued, excessive ("inflated worth"); vain, boastful, immodest, overdone, pompous, conceited ("inflated sense of self").

inflation [in · *flay* · shun] *n.* extension, enlargement, upsurge, distension, aggrandizement; currency devaluation, price increase.

inflict [in · *flikt*] *v.* impose, mete out, apply, wound, punish, force, hurt, harm.

influence [*in* · flew · ense] *v.* alter, move, sway, affect, direct, guide.

influence [*in* · flew · ense] *n.* power, authority, pressure, manipulation, force, leadership, leverage.

inform [in · *form*] *v.* notify, advise, explain, relate, proclaim, publish ("inform the attorney"); divulge, betray, inculpate, reveal, disclose ("inform on a friend").

informal [in · *form* · el] *adj.* unofficial, common, unauthorized, casual, ordinary, relaxed, perfunctory, spontaneous, unconventional.

informant [in · *form* · ant] *n.* source, spy, stool pigeon, tipster; adviser, envoy, communicator.

information [in · fer · *may* · shen] *n.* knowledge, facts, material, news; wisdom, enlightenment; charge, accusation, complaint, allegation ("felony information").

informed [in · *formd*] *adj.* knowledgeable, conscious, aware, forewarned, prepared, notified, apprised. *Ant.* unaware.

informer [in · *fore* · mer] *n.* informant, divulger, spy, source, tipster, tattler, reporter, notifier, messenger.

infraction [in · *frak* · shen] *n.* violation, breach, infringement, transgression, lawbreaking, noncompliance, contravention. *Ant.* compliance.

infringement [in · *frinj* · ment] *n.* violation, misfeasance, invasion, encroachment, interference, breach ("infringement of patent").

infuse [in · *fyooz*] *v.* instill, implant, ingrain, imbue, inculcate, introduce.

ingredient [in · *greed* · ee · ent] *n.* component, part, element, section, unit, aspect, factor.

inhabitant [in · *hab* · ih · tent] *n.* resident, citizen, native, dweller, tenant, occupant.

inherent [in · *here* · ent] *adj.* intrinsic, innate, ingrained, integral, inseparable, natural, essential. *Ant.* incidental.

inherit [in · *herr* · it] *v.* take by succession, be left, be the heir of, acquire, receive, obtain, succeed, take over.

inheritance [in · *herr* · ih · tense] *n.* legacy, devise, bequest, endowment, birthright, share, dispensation.

inhibit [in · *hib* · it] *v.* restrain, restrict, arrest, prohibit, hinder, suppress, prevent.

initial [ih · *nish* · ul] *adj.* beginning, first, introductory, maiden, incipient, original, early ("initial meeting"). *Ant.* terminal.

initiation [ih · nish · ee · *ay* · shen] *n.* introduction, admission, indoctrination, induction, baptism.

initiative [ih · *nish* · ye · tiv] *n.* first step, first move, beginning; determination, drive, aggressiveness, enthusiasm, leadership.

inject [in · jekt] *v.* infuse, saturate, drive in, instill, introduce, imbue.

injudicious [in · joo · *dish* · us] *adj.* unsound, unreasoned, hasty, inexpedient, reckless, incautious, unwise.

injunction [in · *junk* · shen] *n.* ban, stay, order, enjoinder, interdiction, restraint, mandate, prohibition.

injure [in · *jer*] *v.* harm, damage, misuse, mistreat, abuse, violate, tarnish, hurt, wound.

injury [in · jer · ee] *n.* wrong, damage, loss, detriment, harm, offense. *Ant.* benefit.

injustice [in · *juss* · tiss] *n.* injury, wrong, unfairness, inequality, inequity, prejudice, transgression, bias, abuse, partiality. *Ant.* fairness.

inland [in · land] *adj.* internal, domestic, heartland.

inmate [in · mayt] *n.* prisoner, convict, captive; roomer, dweller, occupier.

innate [in · ayt] *v.* inborn, hereditary, fundamental, basic, natural, essential, congenital, native.

innocence [in · e · sense] *n.* blamelessness, sinlessness, naiveté, purity, inexperience. *Ant.* guilt, cunning.

innocent [in · e · sent] *adj.* faultless, blameless, not guilty; pure, trustful, naive. *Ant.* guilty.

innovation [in · uh · *vay* · shun] *n.* change, departure, modification, revision, modernization, alteration.

inoperative [in · *op* · e · re · tiv] *adj.* not in effect, ineffective, worthless, deficient, broken, inadequate, imperfect.

inquire [in · *kwire*] *v.* ask, probe, investigate, examine, explore, look into, quiz.

inquiry [in · *kwy* · ree or in · kwih · ree] *n.* inquest, investigation, examination, hearing; question, query, interrogatory.

insane [in · *sain*] *adj.* unsound, deranged, demented, absurd, bizarre, mad.

insanity [in · *san* · ih · tee] *n.* madness, lunacy, derangement, mental illness, disorientation, dementia.

inscription [in · *skrip* · shen] *n.* registration, recording, engraving, dedication, notation, caption, autograph, legend.

insecure [in · se · *kyoor*] *adj.* uncertain, vulnerable, frail, unconfident; risky, unreliable, unprotected, unassured, precarious.

inseparable [in · *sep* · er · uh · bul] *adj.* indivisible, joined, consolidated, fused, intertwined; intimate, devoted ("The twins were inseparable").

insertion [in · *ser* · shun] *n.* addition, interjection, addendum, supplement, penetration.

insider [in · *sy* · der] *n.* officer, director, member, intimate, associate.

insider [in · *sy* · der] *adj.* private, protected, nonpublic, undisclosed ("insider information").

insight [*in* · site] *n.* intuition, cognizance, perception, realization, keenness, acuteness, acumen, understanding.

insignificance [in · sig · *nif* · ih · kants] *n.* unimportance, immateriality, irrelevance, triviality, insubstantiality.

insist [in · *sist*] *v.* stress, urge, demand, dictate, command, require, emphasize, impose.

insolvency [in · *sol* · ven · see] *n.* bankruptcy, destitution, indebtedness, default, ruin, failure. *Ant.* financial stability, solvency.

insolvent [in · *sol* · vent] *adj.* bankrupt, indigent, destitute, broke, impecunious, ruined.

inspection [in · *spek* · shen] *n.* examination, investigation, evaluation, observation, checking.

inspire [in · *spire*] *v.* stimulate, influence, prompt, urge, encourage, stir, induce, incite.

install [in · *stall*] *v.* induct, place, set up, position, affix, connect, hook up. *Ant.* remove.

installment [in · *stall* · ment] *n.* partial payment, allotment, segment, portion, parcel, section.

instance [*in* · stenss] *n.* urging, request ("At the instance of the judge, he concluded his argument quickly"); example, case in point, situation ("in this instance").

instant [*in* · stent] *adj.* present, current, at hand ("the instant case"); quick, immediate, fast, sudden ("the instant appearance of the witness").

instant [*in* · stent] *n.* moment, blink of an eye, flash.

instantaneous [in · sten · *tay* · nee · us] *adj.* immediate, direct, spontaneous, simultaneous, speedy, prompt, quick.

instanter [in · *stan* · ter] *adv.* instantly, at once, immediately.

instigate [*in* · stih · gayt] *v.* incite, stir up, induce, generate, provoke, rouse. *Ant.* hamper.

institute [*in* · stih · toot] *v.* start, establish, commence, begin, launch ("I'm going to institute an action").

institute [*in* · stih · toot] *n.* organization, foundation, academy, college, university, association, institution, school ("the American Law Institute").

institution [*in* · sti · *too* · shen] *n.* establishment, organization, alliance, center, association, academy, school ("a fine institution"); custom, norm, code, law, tradition ("the institution of slavery").

instruct [in · *strukt*] *v.* direct, order, give instructions, guide, teach, advise, tutor.

instrument [*in* · struh · ment] *n.* record, legal document, writing, contract; tool, device, apparatus, equipment, machinery.

instrumentality [in · struh · men · *tal* · ih · tee] *n.* means, method, agency; operation, device, tool, vehicle, resource.

insubordination [in · sub · or · dih · *nay* · shen] *n.* disobedience, noncompliance, impudence, unruliness, defiance. *Ant.* submissiveness.

insufficient [*in* · se · fish · ent] *adj.* lacking, deficient, meager, sparse, depleted, wanting, paltry, slight.

insurance [in · *shoor* · ense] *n.* indemnification, assurance, coverage, policy, warranty, covenant, security, guarantee, indemnity against contingencies, precaution, safeguard.

insure [in · *shoor*] *v.* obtain insurance, secure against loss, underwrite, guard, safeguard, shield, back, check, warrant, arrange, provide, assure, reassure.

insurer [in · *shoor* · er] *n.* indemnitor, indemnifier, guarantor, assurer, surety, underwriter.

I

insurgent [in · *ser* · jent] *n.* rebel, rioter, revolutionary, agitater, mutineer, traitor, insurrectionist, reformer, dissident, guerrilla, resister. *Ant.* loyalist, obedient, jingoist.

insurrection [in · ser · *rek* · shen] *n.* uprising, riot, coup d'état, insurgence, revolution, subversion, coup, anarchy, sedition, outbreak, disturbance, revolt.

intangible [in · *tan* · jih · bul] *adj.* nonphysical, abstract, imperceptible, impalpable, transcendental, nonmaterial, metaphysical, disembodied, soulful, intellectual, philosophical, theoretical, psychic.

integration [in · te · *gray* · shen] *n.* desegregation, assimilation, union, harmonization, coexistence. *Ant.* separation.

intemperance [in · *tem* · per · ense] *n.* excess, self-indulgence, abandon, extravagance, exaggeration, insatiability, unreasonableness, self-gratification, gluttony, debauchery, insobriety, drunkenness, alcoholism. *Ant.* restraint.

intend [in · *tend*] *v.* mean, plan, aim, calculate, premeditate, propose, scheme, resolve.

intent [in · *tent*] *n.* determination, scheme, plan, resolve, view, goal, contemplation, will, leaning, premeditation, end, mark, resolution, target, aim, ambition, destination, object, objective, idea ("intent of Congress"); drift, implication, connotation, essence, indication, signification, message, significance ("Your intent is clear").

intention [in · *ten* · shen] *n.* course, proclivity, purpose, route, propensity, purpose, plan, object, aim, goal ("the intention of the parties"); penchant, bias, leaning, impetus, current.

intentional [in · *ten* · shen · ul] *adj.* preplanned, calculated, plotted, intended, considered; contemplated, resolved, purposeful, schemed, designed, contrived, willed, prearranged, voluntary. *Ant.* fortuitous.

inter [in · *terr*] *v.* entomb, inurn, sepulcher, bury.

interest [*in* · trest] *n.* stake, holding, portion, property, part, ownership, possession, investment, stock, percentage ("an interest in the company"); premium, profit, gain, return, increase; accrual, dividend; benefit, enrichment, boon, advantage; solicitude, attention, concern, heed, notice, regard, anxiety, conscientiousness, wariness; thoughtfulness, preoccupation, enthusiasm, mindfulness ("an interest in the child's welfare"); pursuit, avocation, engrossment, pastime ("diverse interests").

interested [*in* · tres · ted] *adj.* influenced, biased, concerned, prejudiced, undetached, jaundiced, affected, connected, engaged, involved ("an interested party"). *Ant.* detached.

interference [in · ter · *feer* · ense] *n.* obstruction, interruption, interloping ("interference with contract").

interim [*in* · ter · im] *adj.* temporary, makeshift ("an interim appointment").

interim [*in* · ter · im] *n.* intermission, recess, pause, interlude, meantime, interregnum, break. *Ant.* future, permanent.

interlineation [in · ter · lin · ee · *ay* · shen] *n.* insertion, interjection, placement, sliding in, infusion, interpolation, supplement, inset.

interlocutory [in · ter · *lok* · yoo · tore · ee] *adj.* provisional, tentative, intermediary, interim ("an interlocutory appeal"); transient, intervening. *Ant.* permanent.

interloper [*in* · ter · loh · per] *n.* intermeddler, trespasser, busybody, infiltrater, encroacher, raider, crasher.

intermeddle [in · ter · *med* · ul] *v.* invade, trespass, intrude, infringe, interrupt, intercept, hinder, inhibit, thwart. *Ant.* ignore.

intermediary [in · ter · *mee* · dee · air · ee] *n.* mediator, arbitrator, broker, middleman, go-between, moderator, medium, emissary.

intermediate [in · ter · *mee* · dee · et] *adj.* halfway, in-between, median, intermediary, central, mid, equidistant, intervening, transitional, interposed. *Ant.* terminal.

intermingling [in · ter · *ming* · gling] *n.* mixing, commingling, confusing.

intern [in · *tern*] *v.* confine, restrict, detain.

intern [*in* · tern] *n.* journeyman, novice, apprentice, trainee, neophyte, graduate, assistant.

internal [in · *tur* · nul] *adj.* inner, innermost, inmost, home, in-house, civil, municipal, state, national ("internal audit"); inborn, congenital, intrinsic, basic, fundamental ("internal quality").

international [in · ter · *nash* · e · nul] *adj.* foreign, worldwide, global, universal, cosmopolitan. *Ant.* domestic.

internment [in · *tern* · ment] *n.* detention, confinement.

interpolation [in · ter · pe · *lay* · shen] *n.* injection, introduction, change, rewriting.

interpretation [in · ter · pre · *tay* · shen] *n.* construction, clarification, definition, analysis, understanding.

interpreter [in · *ter* · pre · ter] *n.* translator, assistant, explicator.

interrogation [in · terr · e · *gay* · shen] *n.* grilling, inquisition, catechizing, cross-examination, scrutiny, testing, questioning ("He waived his *Miranda* rights prior to the interrogation").

interrogatories [in · te · *raw* · ge · toh · reez] *n.* questions, inquiries.

interrupt [*in* · ter · rupt] *v.* meddle, intrude, disturb, stop, suspend, break in, delay.

interruption [in · te · *rup* · shen] *n.* interference, severance, suspension, stoppage, intermission, disturbance, pause, hiatus, standstill, cessation, recess, interlude. *Ant.* continuation.

intersection [in · ter · *sek* · shun] *n.* crossing, juncture, junction, connection, meeting point.

interspousal [in · ter · *spouw* · zel] *adj.* marital, conjugal, matrimonial, connubial, nuptial, paired, hymeneal, wedded, uxorial ("the doctrine of interspousal immunity").

intervening [in · ter · *veen* · ing] *adj.* intruding, interfering, obtrusive, parenthetical, infringing, interrupting, breaking in, intercepting.

intervention [in · ter · *ven* · shen] *n.* intrusion, interference, intermeddling, encroachment, interruption, obstruction, overstepping, incursion, insertion, interjection ("intervention in the case"); arbitration, ministry, intercession, negotiation ("intervention by the referee").

interview [*in* · ter · vyoo] *n.* meeting, audition, consultation, examination, evaluation, conference.

interview [*in* · ter · vyoo] *v.* examine, question, interrogate, quiz, sound out, consult.

intimate [*in* · tih · mit] *adj.* friendly, guarded, confidential, personal, private, secret.

intimidation [in · tim · ih · *day* · shun] *n.* coercion, duress, extortion, undue influence.

into [*in* · too] *adv.* within, inside of.

intolerance [in · *tol* · er · ants] *n.* partiality, narrow-mindedness, bias, prejudice, racism, aversion, dislike, hatred, bigotry, repulsion.

intoxicant [in · *tok* · sih · kent] *n.* controlled substance, drug.

intoxicated [in · *tok* · sih · kay · ted] *adj.* drunk, drunken, inebriated, plastered, loaded, high, dazed, befuddled, alcoholic. *Ant.* sober.

intoxication [in · tok · sih · *kay* · shen] *n.* inebriation, drunkenness, dipsomania, incompetence, intemperance, insobriety, alcoholism. *Ant.* sobriety.

intrinsic [in · *trin* · zik] *adj.* internal, fundamental, natural, indwelling, permanent, authentic, real, inner, basic, indigenous, innate, constitutional, substantial, congenital, underlying. *Ant.* incidental.

introduce [in · tro · dooss] *v.* enter, offer, submit, present, put forward.

intruder [in · *troo* · der] *n.* trespasser, aggressor, invader, infiltrator, raider, encroacher, unlawful entrant. *Ant.* guest.

invalid [in · *val* · id] *adj.* unfounded, faulty, inoperative, untrue, ineffective, illegal.

invalid [in · ve · lid] *n.* shut-in, convalescent, cripple, amputee, victim, patient, stricken person, paraplegic.

invalidate [in · *val* · ih · dayt] *v.* overrule, cancel, reverse, abolish ("I'm certain the court will invalidate this contract").

invasion [in · *vay* · zhen] *n.* intrusion, incursion, interference, trespass, overstepping, intermeddling, inroad, breach, penetration, assault. *Ant.* respect.

invent [in · *vent*] *v.* formulate, develop, author, fashion, originate, devise, conceive, hatch, imagine, produce, patent, envisage, dream up ("invent a new design"); pretend, distort, fabricate, concoct, fake, make up ("invent an alibi").

invention [in · *ven* · shen] *n.* finding, discovery, creation, improvisation, concoction, composition, innovation, fabrication.

inventor [in · *ven* · tor] *n.* author, maker, creator, deviser, pioneer, improviser.

inventory [in · ven · tore · ee] *n.* itemized list, menu, checklist, stocklist, catalog, index, accounting, roster, register, account, enumeration, statement, tally.

inverse [in · *verss*] *adj.* opposite, backward, contrary, transposed, inverted, converse.

invest [in · *vest*] *v.* speculate, lay out, put out capital, sink money into, support, venture ("invest in a fund"); endow, vest, license, confer, appoint, commission, entrust, mandate, delegate, ordain, authorize, sanction, grant, enable ("invest with authority").

investigate [in · *ves* · tih · gate] *v.* inspect, look into, seek evidence, track, inquire into, probe, observe, examine, analyze, scrutinize, dissect, explore.

investigation [in · ves · tih · *gay* · shen] *n.* inquiry, examination, inspection, research, exploration, scrutiny, search, study.

investment [in · *vest* · ment] *n.* financing, venture, capital, speculation, stock, portfolio, holding, securities.

invidious [in · *vid* · ee · us] *adj.* hostile, offensive, malicious, overt ("invidious discrimination").

invitation [in · vih · *tay* · shen] *n.* enticement, attraction, allurement, petition, offer, solicitation, overture, inducement, provocation, stimulus. *Ant.* rejection.

invitee [in · vy · *tee*] *n.* guest, patron, customer.

invoice [in · voiss] *n.* written account, statement, bill, account; inventory, reckoning, enumeration.

involuntary [in · *vol* · en · tair · ee] *adj.* forced, unwilling, coercive, obligatory, mandatory, imperative, unintentional, automatic. *Ant.* voluntary.

involve [in · *volv*] *v.* implicate, accuse, incriminate, inculpate, draw in, charge ("involve a codefendant"); relate, support, participate, enter into, collude, collaborate, connect, act in concert.

iota [*eye* · oh · tuh] *n.* fragment, morsel, scintilla, bit, drop, dab, shred, trace, grain.

ironclad [*eye* · urn · klad] *adj.* definite, firm, final, certain, strict.

irrational [ir · *rash* · uh · nul] *adj.* unsensible, unreasonable, ridiculous, illogical, injudicious, ludicrous.

irrebuttable [ir · re · *but* · eh · bul] *adj.* conclusive, incontestable, definite.

irreconcilable [ir · rek · en · *sy* · luh · bul] *adj.* irretrievable, irremedial.

irrecusable [ir · re · *kyoo* · zih · bul] *adj.* imposed, mandated.

irrefutable [ir · ree · *fyoot* · ih · bul] *adj.* firm, positive, proven, indisputable, certain, sure ("irrefutable proof").

irregular [ir · *reg* · yoo · ler] *adj.* abnormal, out of order, nonconforming, erratic, inconsistent, variable, improper, flawed, aberrant, intermittent.

irregularity [ir · reg · yoo · *lar* · ih · tee] *n.* deviation, nonconformity, divergence, aberration, abnormality.

irrelevant [ir · *rel* · e · vent] *adj.* not relevant, impertinent, unconnected, extraneous, immaterial, unrelated, inapplicable, beside the point, foreign, not germane, inappropriate ("irrevelant evidence"). *Ant.* pertinent.

irreparable [irr · *rep* · ruh · bul] *adj.* irreversible, beyond repair, irremediable, irrevocable, beyond correction, hopeless, lost, remediless, incurable, unfixable, unsalvageable. *Ant.* salvageable.

irresistible [ir · re · *zis* · tih · bul] *adj.* overwhelming, unavoidable, compelling, overpowering, inexorable, formidable, omnipotent, vigorous, invincible. *Ant.* resistible.

irreversible [ir · re · *ver* · sih · bul] *adj.* persistent, irrevocable, lost, final, perpetual ("an irreversible coma").

irrevocable [ir · *rev* · e · ke · bul] *adj.* irreversible, final, unmodifiable, inextinguishable, unalterable, immovable, indissoluble, immutable, fixed ("an irrevocable offer"). *Ant.* revocable.

issue [*ish* · yoo] *v.* print, disseminate, publish, announce, distribute, reveal, enunciate, circulate, release.

issue [*ish* · yoo] *n.* issuance, dissemination, publication, presentation, exhibition, emergence, disclosure, dispensation, granting ("a stock issue"); question, cause, problem, dispute, contention, topic, subject, affair, theme, disputed, matter ("an issue in this case"); heirs, progeny, children, grandchildren, decendants, posterity, family, lineage, seed, line, young ("die without issue").

item [*eye* · tum] *n.* entry, piece, particular, object, feature, aspect, circumstance, thing, subject, point, detail, sample, ingredient, member.

itemize [*eye* · tem · eyz] *v.* individualize, catalog, particularize, rank, inventory, tabulate, designate, register one-by-one, enumerate ("itemize tax deductions").

itinerant [eye · *tin* · e · rent] *adj.* traveling, moving, peripatetic, nomadic, migrant, journeying ("an itinerant salesperson").

jactitation [jak · ti · *tay* · shen] *n.* false claims, boast, brag, vanity, pretension, swagger, puffery.

jail *n.* house of detention, gaol, correctional institution, lockup, brig, prison, pen, penitentiary, penal institution, reformatory, cell.

jail *v.* lock up, restrain, restrict, imprison, isolate, take into custody, incarcerate.

jealous [*jel* · us] *adj.* envious, covetous, possessive, suspicious, insecure, doubting, distrustful.

jeopardize [*jep* · er · dize] *v.* imperil, threaten, endanger, risk, stake, gamble.

jeopardy [*jep* · er · dee] *n.* exposure, threat, peril, insecurity, danger, precariousness, venture, uncertainty, endangerment, instability.

jettison [*jet* · ih · sun] *v.* throw away, cast, cast aside, discharge, expel, dismiss, eject, eliminate, drop, reject.

jobber [*job* · bur] *n.* middleman, supplier, representative, salesperson, broker, wholesaler, cosigner, operator.

joinder [*join* · der] *n.* uniting, joining, merger, consolidation.

joint *adj.* mutual, collaborative, combined, concerted, common, allied, united, merged, collective, unified, consolidated, communal, undivided, inseparable.

joint *n.* jail, pen, house, rack, slammer; marijuana cigarette, doobie, hooter, spliff, blunt.

jointly [*joint* · lee] *adv.* unitedly, in concert, in conjunction, in combination, collectively, in common, mutually, conjointly. *Ant.* individually.

journal [*jer* · nel] *n.* chronicle, register, log, registry, ledger, notebook, diary, periodical, calendar, magazine.

journalist [*jer* · nel · ist] *n.* writer, commentator, correspondent, newsperson, reporter.

journeyman [*jer* · nee · man] *n.* worker, artisan, employee.

judge *n.* justice, adjudicator, surrogate, magistrate, arbitrator, chancellor, jurist, decider, arbiter.

judge *v.* consider, conclude, reckon, settle, referee, try, pronounce, decree, find, opine, hold.

judgment [*juj* · ment] *n.* decree, holding, ruling, conclusion, opinion, award, sentence, finding, adjudication, verdict, arbitration ("the judgement of the court"); understanding, perception, acumen, insight, reasoning, discrimination, discernment ("a woman of judgment").

judicature [*joo* · dih · kuh · cher] *n.* administration, judiciary; jurisdiction, power.

judicial [joo · *dish* · el] *adj.* juristic, legal, judiciary ("a judicial act"); discriminating, wise, sagacious, prudent, just, fair, magisterial, perspicacious ("a judicial demeanor").

judiciary [joo · *dish* · ee · ehr · ee] *n.* courts, bench, system of justice.

judicious [joo · *dish* · ess] *adj.* wise, well-considered, prudent, astute, rational, logical ("a judicious prosecutor").

jump *v.* leap, vault, spring; escape, avoid, neglect; attack, mug.

junior [*joo* · nyer] *adj.* younger, subordinate, second, secondary, lesser ("A junior mortgage is one filed after the first mortgage"). *Ant.* senior.

junket [*jung* · kit] *n.* trip, excursion, frolic, tour.

juridical [joo · *rid* · i · kel] *adj.* legal, judicious, judicial.

jurisdiction [joo · ris · *dik* · shen] *n.* capacity, authority, authorization, right, charter, judicature, license, sovereignty; territory, region, domain, district, circuit, state, quarter, field, province ("The matter has not been decided in this jurisdiction").

jurisprudence [joor · is · *proo* · dense] *n.* philosophy, theory, legal foundation, philosophy of law, system of laws.

jurist [*joor* · ist] *n.* learned counsel, law professor, legal authority, legal expert.

juror [*joor* · er] *n.* factfinder, trier of fact, appraiser, arbiter.

jury [*joor* · ee] *n.* factfinder, trier of fact, reviewers, panel, veniremen, array, arbiters.

just *adj.* rightful, equitable, principled, honest, merited, due, fair, reasonable, rational, unbiased, fitting, appropriate, authentic, justifiable, constitutional, judicious, bona fide, factual. *Ant.* inequitable.

justice [*juss* · tis] *n.* fairness, equity, even-handedness, fair play, legality, impartiality, uprightness, integrity, probity, rectitude.

justiciable [jus · *tish* · uh · bul] *adj.* litigable, prepared for court action, actionable, ready, suitable ("a justiciable controversy"). *Ant.* premature, moot.

justifiable [jus · tih · *fy* · uh · bul] *adj.* rightful, merited, defensible, acceptable, reasonable, allowable, vindicable, valid, proper. *Ant.* unwarranted.

justification [jus · tih · fih · *kay* · shen] *n.* explanation, rationalization, vindication, apology, basis, foundation, alibi.

juvenile [*joo* · ve · nile] *n.* infant, youth, youngster, minor, teenager, stripling, kid, ward, teen.

juvenile [joo · ve · nile] *adj.* childish, inexperienced, puerile, sophomore, irresponsible, infantile, unwise, adolescent. *Ant.* adult.

juxtapose [*jux* · ta · pose] *v.* border, abut, adjoin, connect, neighbor.

J

kangaroo court [kang · guh · *roo* kort] *n.* lynching, lynch mob, mob justice.

keen *adj.* enthusiastic, interested, impassioned; sharp, incisive, acute, cutting; astute, shrewd, wise, perceptive, intelligent.

keep *v.* maintain, carry on, conduct, manage, hold; tend, nurture, feed, subsidize, support; prevent, detain, deter, inhibit, stop, restrain.

keeper [*keep* · er] *n.* custodian, caretaker, warden, guard, protector.

keeping [*keep* · ing] *n.* maintaining, conducting, managing, caring for ("keeping a gaming house"); accordance, agreement ("in keeping with the contract").

kidnap [*kid* · nap] *v.* abduct, seize, snatch.

kidnapping [*kid* · nap · ing] *n.* abduction, child stealing, seizure, hijacking.

kill *v.* defeat, destroy, crush, nullify, invalidate ("kill the bill"); murder, injure, slay, assassinate.

kin *n.* relatives, relations, family.

kind *n.* type, category, class, sort, variety, grouping, classification.

kind *adj.* gentle, considerate, giving, altruistic, loving, good, generous, benevolent.

kinship [*kin* · ship] *n.* ancestry, family; friendship, brotherhood, sisterhood.

knowingly [*noh* · ing · lee] *adv.* with knowledge, deliberately, consciously, intentionally, purposely, willfully.

knowledge [*naw* · ledj] *n.* cognizance, awareness, perception, recognition, information; wisdom, erudition, learning, intelligence.

known *adj.* famous, familiar, recognized, popular, noted, celebrated.

kook *n.* nut, crackpot, crank, lunatic, flake, fruitcake.

kowtow [*kow* · tow] *v.* grovel, stoop, fawn, cower, pander.

kudos [*koo* · doze] *n.* praise, acclaim, glory, honor, distinction, esteem.

label [*lay* · bul] *v.* classify, denominate, brand, identify, designate.

label [*lay* · bul] *n.* tag, identification, brand, mark, description.

labor [*lay* · ber] *n.* work, occupation, undertaking, toil, enterprise, task, responsibility; energy, exertion, effort.

labor [*lay* · ber] *v.* work, agonize, struggle, toil, slave, travail, strain.

laborer [*lay* · ber · er] *n.* worker, employee, help, toiler.

laches [*lash* · ez] *n.* delay, nonfeasance, laxity, procrastination, laggardliness, inattention, remissness.

land *n.* real estate, property, earth, terrain, soil, ground, nation, realty, territory, acreage.

land *v.* earn, win, achieve, acquire ("to land a contract").

landlord [*land* · lord] *n.* lessor, landowner, possessor, proprietor. *Ant.* lessee.

landmark [*land* · mark] *n.* monument, marker, stake, feature.

landmark [*land* · mark] *adj.* significant, precedential, decisive, key ("a landmark decision").

landowner [*land* · oh · nur] *n.* landlord, owner, proprietor, possessor, title holder.

lapse *n.* termination, extinguishment, forfeiture; break, pause, recess.

lapse *v.* cease, expire, terminate, discontinue, abate.

lapsed *adj.* terminated, extinguished, expired, elapsed, outdated ("a lapsed devise").

larcenous [*lar* · sen · ess] *adj.* thieving, criminal, predatory, felonious, rapacious ("She took it with larcenous intent").

larceny [*lar* · sen · ee] *n.* theft, embezzlement, burglary, pilferage, misappropriation, stealing.

lascivious [le · *siv* · ee · ess] *adj.* lewd, lustful, erotic, licentious, indecent, bawdy, improper, promiscuous.

last *adj.* final, ultimate, concluding, definitive, newest, latest, lowest, worst, above, foregoing, former.

last *v.* endure, survive, continue, persevere, remain, withstand ("built to last a lifetime").

late *adj.* dead, departed, deceased; tardy, dilatory, lagging, delayed, unpunctual.

latent [*lay* · tent] *adj.* hidden, concealed, not discoverable, submerged, veiled, passive, inactive, lurking ("latent defect").

lateral [*lat* · e · rel] *adj.* sideways, from the side, flanked.

laundering [*lawn · der · ing*] *n.* fraud, deception, illegal passing.

law *n.* rules of conduct, mandate, code, constitution, statute, ordinance, regulation, judicial decision, command, act, precedent, authority, canon, holding.

lawful [*law · ful*] *adj.* legal, legitimate, permitted, permissible, sanctioned, warranted, proper, legalized, licit ("lawful arrest").

lawless [*law · less*] *adj.* illegal, wrongful, criminal, disobedient; chaotic, violent, disorganized, anarchistic, uncontrolled.

lawsuit [*law · soot*] *n.* action, proceeding, suit, case, cause of action, cause.

lawyer [*loy · er*] *n.* attorney, barrister, counselor, solicitor, legal advocate, counsel.

lay *adj.* nonexpert, nonprofessional, amateur ("a lay witness"); nonclerical ("a lay deacon").

laying [*lay · ing*] *v.* establishing, creating, making, constructing ("laying a foundation").

layoff [*lay · off*] *n.* discharge, suspension, firing, unemployment, removal, termination.

layperson [*lay · per · sen*] *n.* nonprofessional, amateur, nonexpert ("He is not a physician; he is a layperson").

lax *adj.* slack, careless, casual, remiss, negligent, indifferent, sloppy.

leading [*lee · ding*] *adj.* primary, most important, predominant, foremost, chief ("a leading case"); guiding, directing, suggestive ("a leading question").

learned [*ler · ned*] *adj.* knowledgeable, educated, accomplished, wise, judicious.

lease *v.* let, rent, convey, grant, charter, hire.

lease *n.* contract, agreement, grant, instrument.

leave *v.* dispose of, give, grant, deposit, abandon, discard; depart, retreat, embark.

leave *n.* permission, authorization, license, sanction; absence, parting, break, removal, pause ("take leave").

ledger [*lej · er*] *n.* book of account, register, diary, journal, accounts, logbook, passbook, record.

legacy [*leg · e · see*] *n.* grant, bequest, endowment, present; tradition, history, meaning ("the legacy of Thurgood Marshall").

legal [*lee · gul*] *adj.* authorized, permitted, sanctioned, proper, constitutional, legitimate, formal, statutory, allowable.

legality [*le · gal · ih · tee*] *n.* conformity with the law, lawfulness, permissibility, constitutionality, rightfulness, sanction.

legalization [*lee · gul · ih · zay · shen*] *n.* legitimation, validation, legalizing, authorization, sanction, ratification, approval.

legalize [*lee · gul · ize*] *v.* make legal, legitimate, approve, authorize, sanction, validate, legislate.

legally [*lee · gul · ee*] *adv.* according to law, properly, appropriately, formally.

legatee [*leg · e · tee*] *n.* recipient, devisee, beneficiary, donee, legal heir.

legation [*le · gay · shen*] *n.* diplomatic representative, ambassador, consulate, delegation, envoy; embassy, headquarters.

legislate [*lej · is · layt*] *v.* codify, prescribe, ordain, enact, establish, formulate, rule.

legislation [*lej · is · lay · shen*] *n.* law, regulation, statute, ordinance, ruling, measure, act.

legislative [*lej · is · lay · tiv*] *adj.* congressional, statutory, parliamentary, codified, statutory.

legislator [*lej* · is · lay · ter] *n.* council member, senator, lawmaker, delegate, representative, congressperson.

legislature [*lej* · is · lay · choor] *n.* house, chamber, assembly, parliament, senate, council.

legitimacy *n.* lawfulness, genuineness, validity, correctness, authenticity.

legitimate [le · *jit* · ih · mit] *adj.* lawful, genuine, valid, correct, right.

legitimate [le · *jit* · ih · mayt] *v.* make lawful, certify, validate, legalize, license.

lend *v.* supply, furnish, lease, let, loan, provide, advance.

lender [*len* · der] *n.* creditor, seller, bank, supplier, loaner.

lessee [less · *ee*] *n.* renter, possessor, leaseholder, boarder, tenant.

lessor [less · *or*] *n.* lender, creditor, owner, landlord.

let *v.* allow, authorize, permit, endorse ("let the decision stand"); lease, sublet, convey, lend ("Did she let her apartment?").

let *n.* obstruction, hindrance, impediment ("Grantee shall have the right to use this easement without let or hindrance").

lethal [*lee* · thul] *adj.* deadly, mortal, fatal, murderous, devastating ("a lethal weapon").

letter [*let* · er] *n.* document, written communication, missive, message, note, memo.

letting [*let* · ing] *v.* awarding, granting ("letting a contract"); leasing, renting ("letting a studio").

levy [*lev* · ee] *v.* assess, impose, require, demand, exact, inflict; seize, attach, confiscate, declare, instigate, originate.

levy [*lev* · ee] *n.* tax, toll, duty, fine, charge; seizure, attachment, arrogation, appropriation ("a levy of execution").

lewd [lood] *adj.* lascivious, lustful, wanton, indecent, obscene, gross, prurient.

lewdness [*lood* · nes] *n.* indecency, obscenity, wantonness, debauchery.

liability [ly · e · *bil* · ih · tee] *n.* responsibility, debt, obligation, indebtedness, encumbrance; handicap, disadvantage, shortcoming.

liable [*lie* · uh · bul] *adj.* responsible, accountable, answerable, obligated ("The law holds people liable for breach of contract"); likely to happen, subject, susceptible, prone ("The hurricane is liable to hit any moment").

libel [*lie* · bul] *n.* defamation, slander, malice, denunciation, accusation, aspersion, calumny, vilification.

libelant [*lie* · bel · unt] *n.* plaintiff, complainant.

libelee [*lie* · bel · ee] *n.* defendant, answerable party.

libelous [*lie* · bel · us] *adj.* defamatory, damaging, maligning, injurious, slanderous, vilifying, scandalous, disparaging.

liberal [*lib* · e · rul] *adj.* broad, generous, flexible, extended ("liberal interpretation"); generous, bountiful, unsparing, magnanimous, lavish; tolerant, unbiased, neutral, impartial; flexible, progressive ("liberal in his thinking").

liberty [*lib* · er · tee] *n.* freedom, independence, privilege, right, emancipation, choice, autonomy.

license [*ly* · sense] *n.* privilege, authorization, sanction, permission, entitlement.

license [*ly* · sense] *v.* authorize, legitimize, sanction, approve, validate.

licentiousness [ly · *sen* · shes · ness] *n.* obscenity, immorality, lasciviousness; lawlessness, recklessness, wantonness.

L

licit [*liss* · it] *adj.* legal, lawful, legitimate, admissible, allowed; *Ant.* unlawful, illegitimate.

lie *v.* be maintainable, subsist, be available, be warranted, stand ("An action for damages will not lie unless there has been injury"); beguile, con, deceive, falsify, pervert, fabricate ("The suspect lied"); be, sit, exist, occupy, reach, remain ("to lie in bed").

lie *n.* perjury, deception, deceit, forgery, slander, tale, fraud.

lien [*leen*] *n.* debt, obligation, mortgage, interest ("The mortgage is a lien on the house").

life *n.* endurance, survival, subsistance, animation, cycle, span, duration, course, endurance, period ("for the life of the car"); vitality, animation, vivacity, esprit, soul, vigor ("the life of the party").

light *n.* illumination, shining, glow, aurora, beacon, lamp ("light up ahead"); angle, approach, insight, slant, view, interpretation ("to see in a new light").

light *adj.* carefree, chipper, merry, perky, sunny, up, weightless ("She was in a light mood").

light *v.* animate, brighten, illuminate, ignite, shine, highlight, turn on ("to light the lamp").

limit [*lim* · it] *n.* extreme, edge, border, perimeter, bounds, compass, confines, edge, end ("the city limits"); bar, cap, check, obstacle, limitation, blockade ("the limit of our involvement").

limit [*lim* · it] *v.* restrict, suppress, hinder, bar, block, obstruct, control ("to limit access"). *Ant.* facilitate.

limitation [lim · ih · *tay* · shen] *n.* impediment, drawback, constraint, hindrance, cramp, condition ("The system has limitations"). *Ant.* expansion.

limited [*lim* · ih · ted] *adj.* confined, bounded, prescribed, checked, curbed, fixed ("Our options are limited"); dull, narrow, simple, slow, unimaginative ("He is of limited mind").

line *n.* rim, edge, border, perimeter, limit, boundary, cutoff ("property line").

lineage [*lin* · ee · ej] *n.* race, family, descendants, ancestry, heritage.

lineal [*lin* · ee · ul] *adj.* hereditary, ancestral, uninterrupted, continuous, undeviating ("lineal progression").

lineup [*line* · up] *n.* group, array, arrangement, formation, showing, inspection, row ("the police lineup").

liquid [*lik* · wid] *adj.* convertible, interchangeable, fluid, free, negotiable, quick ("The bonds are very liquid and may be cashed in at any time"). *Ant.* frozen.

liquidate [*lik* · wi · dayt] *v.* discharge, clear, cancel, honor, pay off, quit ("liquidate my debts"); cash, convert, exchange, realize ("liquidate the bonds"); abolish, annihilate, eliminate, kill, remove, wipe out ("liquidate the company"). *Ant.* incur; create.

liquidated [*lik* · wi · day · ted] *adj.* ascertained, determined, declared ("a liquidated amount of the mortgage").

liquidation [*lik* · wi · day · shen] *n.* elimination, abolition, rescission.

liquor [*lik* · er] *n.* spirits, inebriant, drink, alcohol, intoxicant, extract, elixir ("They drank liquor on New Year's Eve").

list *v.* itemize, docket, enroll, calendar, log, chart ("list the home for sale").

list *n.* account, agenda, inventory, manifest, poll, record, contents, schedule, roster, outline ("the jury list").

L

literacy [*lit* · e · see] *n.* ability to read, intelligence, learning, education, background, cultivation ("The state has a low literacy rate").

literal [*lit* · e · rel] *adj.* strict, verbatim, correct, actual, true, plain ("a literal interpretation of the Constitution"). *Ant.* loose, creative, virtual.

literary [*lit* · e · rair · ee] *adj.* published, poetic, artistic, educated, bookish, classical, formal, well-spoken ("The professor seemed very literary").

litigant [*lit* · ih · gent] *n.* litigator, disputant, contender, challenger, adversary, opponent, party ("The litigants in the case were both injured in the accident").

litigate [*lit* · ih · gate] *v.* dispute, contest at law, file, sue, prosecute, appeal ("She will not litigate that cause of action").

litigation [lit · ih · *gay* · shen] *n.* judicial contest, prosecution, action, lawsuit, case, cause ("Massive amounts of litigation have backlogged the courts").

litigious [lih · *tij* · ess] *adj.* argumentative, combative, pugnacious, militant, belligerent, bellicose.

littoral [*lit* · oh · rel] *adj.* coastal, waterfront, beach.

live [lyve] *adj.* living, breathing, animate, aware, conscious ("a live cat"); active, alert, brisk, current, dynamic, hot, vital ("The crowd is live tonight").

live [liv] *v.* dwell, room, being, abide, bide, bunk, nest ("I live upstairs"); breathe, persist, prevail, persevere, continue ("He will live only for a few more days").

living [*liv* · ing] *n.* surviving, being, existing, ongoing, continuing ("The tree is still living").

loading [*loh* · ding] *n.* stacking, putting, inserting, packing, heaping, burdening, lading ("She is loading the trunk").

loan *v.* allow, credit, lend, provide, stake, touch.

loan *n.* financing, advance, credit, allowance, mortgage, floater ("a loan on the house").

loanshark [*lone* · shark] *n.* usurer, extortionist.

lobbyist [*lob* · ee · ist] *n.* advocate, espouser, representative, ally, supporter.

local [*loh* · kel] *adj.* localized, native, home, regional, narrow, restricted ("local government"). *Ant.* national, general.

locate [*loh* · kayt] *v.* establish, move to, reside, camp, stay, take, root, dig in ("The company chose to locate in Delaware").

location [*loh* · kay · shun] *n.* spot, area, residence, locale, neck of the woods, region ("pinpoint the ship's location").

lockout [*lok* · owt] *n.* work stoppage, labor dispute, close-out.

lockup [*lok* · up] *n.* place of detention, jail, facility, prison.

locus [*loh* · kus] *n.* place, point, locality ("the locus of the burglary").

lodger [*lod* · jer] *n.* roomer, guest, boarder, tenant, dweller, lessee.

lodging house [*lod* · jing] *n.* abode, domicile, hotel, inn, quarters, boarding house, bed and breakfast.

logical [*loj* · ih · kul] *adj.* consistent, reasonable, sound, coherent, lucid.

logrolling [*log* · rol · ing] *n.* trading favors, playing politics.

loiter [*loy* · ter] *v.* linger, wander, dally, loaf, tarry, lag, halt, pause, get not place fast, put off, idle ("Don't loiter in the hall").

loitering [*loy* · ter · ing] *n.* idling, dallying, hanging around, lingering.

long *adj.* deep, expanded, far-reaching, extended, widespread, considerable ("Alaska is a long way away"). *Ant.* confined, short.

look out [look owt] *v.* beware, watch for, be alert, be wary, have a care, heads up, notice, pay attention ("Look out for children playing in the street").

lookout [*look* · owt] *n.* guard, sentinel, scout, watcher ("The lookout watched for the police").

loophole [*loop* · hole] *n.* ambiguity, vagueness, omission, windfall, opening, opportunity ("The new tax law has several loopholes").

lose *v.* misplace, miss, mislay, vanish, be deprived of ("to lose a book"); forfeit, fail, abort, fall short, suffer defeat, succumb ("to lose the Superbowl").

loss *n.* damage, deprivation, depletion, casualty, mishap, grief, detriment, ruin ("Her loss wasn't as great as she thought").

lost *adj.* misplaced, missing, mislaid, gone, disappeared; ("the lost treasure map"); distroyed, vanquished, defeated, demolished ("lost in battle"); confused, unclear, bewildered, mystified ("The new clerk was lost").

lottery [*lot* · e · ree] *n.* game of chance, bet, gamble, scheme, sweepstake, draw, raffle, wager ("the Florida lottery").

loyalty [*loy* · ul · tee] *n.* allegiance, fealty, devotion, bond, faith, support ("He has shown great loyalty to his country").

lucid [*loo* · sid] *adj.* clear, coherent, understandable, rational, sane.

lucrative [*loo* · kre · tiv] *adj.* profitable, worthwhile, money-making, fruitful, productive, advantageous.

lunacy [*loon* · e · see] *n.* insanity, mania, foolishness, abnormality, madness, dementia.

lynch law *n.* lawlessness, mob rule, terrorism, anarchy, mobocracy.

L

mad *adj.* crazy, insane, demented, unstable, unbalanced, psychotic; angry, infuriated, incensed, livid, furious; impassioned, keen, wild, ardent, enthusiastic.

made *adj.* constructed, formed, designed, assembled, fabricated, created, built ("a man-made object").

magisterial [maj · ih · *steer* · ee · ul] *adj.* important, formal, elevated, pompous, arrogant, prodigal.

magistrate [*maj* · ih · strayt] *n.* judge, judicial officer, official, arbiter.

maim *v.* cripple, maul, incapacitate, break, disable, mar.

main *adj.* principal, leading, chief, cardinal, major, fundamental.

maintain [mane · *tane*] *v.* prosecute, pursue, persevere, keep on, continue, preserve, conserve, uphold ("She is determined to maintain her lawsuit"); service, save, preserve, protect, overhaul ("maintain the car"); sustain, care for, finance, nourish, shelter, nurture ("He maintains both of his parents as well as his children"); advocate, affirm, fight for, insist, profess, state ("Even though she was convicted, she continues to maintain that she is innocent"). *Ant.* damage, abandon, deny, discontinue.

maintenance [*mane* · teh · nense] *n.* upkeep, conservation, preservation, care, repair, protection ("Bring the car in for scheduled maintenance"); help, aid, finances, alimony, subsistence, livelihood ("maintenance for her health").

major [*may* · jer] *adj.* greater, larger, more powerful, main, leading, principal, preeminent, outstanding, notable, significant.

majority [ma · *jaw* · rih · tee] *n.* legal age, full age, age of responsibility, drinking age, estate, manhood ("He has now reached the age of majority"); plurality, bulk, mass, lion's share, most, preponderance ("She has a majority of the shares of stock").

make *v.* fabricate, create, originate, manufacture, cast, erect ("to make a law"); execute, draft, prepare ("I'll make a check to your order"); induce, compel, coerce, cause, require ("make me do it").

maker [*may* · ker] *n.* author, producer, fabricator, creator.

malefactor [mal · uh · *fak* · ter] *n.* criminal, offender, felon, villain, outlaw, perpetrator ("The malefactor was sentenced to 10 years").

malfeasance [mal · *feez* · ens] *n.* dereliction, wrongful conduct, mismanagement, misdeed, negligence, carelessness, transgression.

malice [*mal* · iss] *n.* willfulness, animosity, callousness, hate, bad blood, evil, grudge, intent.

malicious [mel · *ish* · ess] *adj.* malevolent, wicked, evil, nasty, spiteful, vicious, callous ("malicious abuse of process").

malingerer [mel · *ing* · ger · er] *n.* loafer, dodger, evader, shirker.

malpractice [mal · *prak* · tiss] *n.* misconduct, incompetence, negligence, carelessness, dereliction, misdeed, violation, transgression ("malpractice insurance").

management [*man* · ej · ment] *n.* leaders, directors, administrators, authority, board, front office ("The management laid the employee off"); government, control, handling, administration, direction, rule ("poor management of the company").

manager [*man* · e · jer] *n.* administrator, director, supervisor, boss, conductor, overseer.

mandate [*man* · dayt] *n.* direction, edict, decree, charge, command, fiat ("the mandate of the people").

mandate [*man* · dayt] *v.* require, order, command ("The court mandated desegregation").

mandatory [*man* · de · tore · ee] *adj.* obligatory, imperative, required, binding, forced, imperious ("a mandatory provision").

manifest [*man* · ih · fest] *adj.* open, obvious, not hidden, apparent, bold, clear-cut ("The reasoning was manifest").

manifest [*man* · ih · *fest*] *v.* show, reveal, demonstrate, display, declare, expose, express. *Ant.* conceal.

manifesto [*man* · ih · *fes* · toh] *n.* announcement, proclamation, broadcast, credo, affirmation, edict.

manner [*man* · ur] *n.* behavior, conduct, bearing, look, tone; method, approach, style, habit, custom.

manual [*man* · yoo · ul] *adj.* hand-operated, physical, menial, arduous, standard ("Peter grew tired from the manual labor"). *Ant.* automatic.

manual [*man* · yoo · ul] *n.* primer, guidebook, handbook, bible, compendium ("The manual contained the assembly instructions"). *Ant.* scholarly treatise.

manufacture [man · yoo · *fak* · cher] *v.* build, assemble, fashion, form, cast, frame ("The company manufactured cars").

manufacture [man · yoo · *fak* · cher] *n.* construction, production, assembling, creation, casting, completion.

manumission [man · yoo · *mish* · en] *n.* liberation, enfranchisement. *Ant.* slavery.

margin [*mar* · jin] *n.* rim, fringe, confine, skirt, bound, edge, brim ("the margin of the page").

marine [ma · *reen*] *adj.* aquatic, oceanic, naval, pelagic, coastal, maritime ("marine life"). *Ant.* terrestrial.

marital [*mehr* · ih · tul] *adj.* spousal, matrimonial, conjugal, nuptial, wedded ("marital status").

maritime [*mehr* · ih · tym] *adj.* naval, oceanic, aquatic, seafaring, riparian, pelagic. *Ant.* terrestrial.

mark *n.* indicator, signal, trademark, identification, symbol, initials, indicator ("A bill of sale is a mark of ownership"); line, border ("low water mark"); criterion, standard, norm, measure ("a mark of excellence").

market [*mar* · kit] *n.* trade center, exchange, marketplace, bazaar, mart, shop ("Get me some bread from the market"); region, section ("Our company is trying to break into the Asian market"); consumer demand, want, vogue, call, need, interest ("There is an active market for gold").

marketable [*mar* · ket · uh · bul] *adj.* saleable, merchantable, commercial, in vogue, vendable, tradable ("marketable title").

markup [*mark* · up] *n.* increase, profit, margin.

marriage [*mehr* · ej] *n.* matrimony, wedlock, nuptial state, nuptials, sacrament, espousal ("to be joined in marriage"). *Ant.* divorce.

marshal [*mar* · shel] *v.* gather, shepherd, allocate, regiment, array, direct, lead, order ("marshal the payroll").

marshaling [*mar* · shel · ing] *n.* collecting, commingling, arranging, prioritizing.

marvelous [*mar* · ve · lus] *adj.* amazing, astounding, incredible, extraordinary, fantastic, unbelievable ("Otis's marvelous catch"); great, fantastic, splendid, spectacular, divine, magnificent ("Darling, you look marvelous").

mask *n.* cover, façade, veil, visor; pretense, pretext, simulation, semblance.

mask *v.* hide, cover, dissemble, pretend.

mass *n.* carload, bundle, block, accumulation, mob, gob, bunch ("a mass of people").

master [*mass* · tur] *n.* officer, official, employer, boss, director, leader, commandant, head ("office master"); artisan, expert, professional ("a master at karate").

master [*mass* · tur] *adj.* first, paramount, dominant, principal, main, controlling ("the master agreement").

master [*mass* · tur] *v.* become proficient, learn, study, excel.

material [ma · *teer* · ee · ul] *adj.* important, relevant, significant, influential, consequential, applicable, primary, substantial ("material witness"). *Ant.* insignificant.

material [ma · *teer* · ee · ul] *n.* supplies, goods, fabric, bolt, cloth, stock ("We didn't have enough material for the dress"); data, evidence, facts, information, notes ("material to support the thesis").

maternal [muh · *ter* · nul] *adj.* motherly, protective, nourishing, sensitive, caring.

mathematical [math · e · *mat* · ih · kul] *adj.* accurate, scientific, exact, statistical, computed, meticulous.

matrimonial [mat · rih · *moh* · nee · ul] *adj.* betrothed, conjugal, engaged, marital, nuptial, wedded.

matter [*mat* · ur] *n.* issue, topic, question, problem, case, proposition ("the matter in question"); amount, body, material, object, stuff, thing ("gray matter").

mature [ma · *choor*] *adj.* experienced, ripe, dependable, adult, grown up, wise, seasoned, of age ("The boy seemed mature for his age").

mature [ma · *choor*] *v.* ripen, come of age, perfect, age, maturate, evolve ("When does this promissory note mature?").

matured [ma · *choord*] *adj.* ripened, come due, due, finished ("The bond has matured").

maturity [ma · *choor* · ih · tee] *n.* development, readiness, perfection, prime, reliability, dependability, advancement, cultivation, completion.

maxim [*mak* · sim] *n.* precept, canon, teaching, adage, dictum, rule.

mayhem [*may* · hem] *n.* anarchy, commotion, disorder, pandemonium, trouble, violence.

mean *n.* average, midpoint, medium, balance, center, par.

meander [me · *an* · der] *v.* twist, snake, wander, change, drift, roam.

meaning [*meen* · ing] *n.* message, significance, content, interpretation.

M

means *n.* assets, backing, bankroll, budget, income, stake ("the means to support the family"); aid, equipment, instrumentality, medium, organ, mode ("the means to an end").

measure [*mezh* · er] *n.* criterion, standard, gauge, scale, yardstick, test ("What is the measure for ocean depth?"); act, enactment, statute, regulation, bill, rule ("the price-supports measure").

mediate [*mee* · dee · it] *adj.* secondary, subordinate, indirect ("mediate descent").

mediate [*mee* · dee · ayt] *v.* negotiate, settle, judge, intercede, moderate, referee, arbitrate.

mediation [mee · dee · *ay* · shen] *n.* intervention, conciliation, negotiation, interposition, arbitration, intercession.

mediator [*mee* · dee · ay · tor] *n.* go-between, intermediary, referee, liaison, advocate, medium, umpire, conciliator.

meet *v.* connect, join, abut, link; face, greet, come across, assemble, rally, convene, gather.

meeting [*meet* · ing] *n.* assembly, convocation, caucus, gathering, congregation, session, rally ("Stockholder's meeting").

member [*mem* · ber] *n.* associate, fellow, teammate, enrollee, initiate ("fraternity member"); arm, component, element, limb, organ, piece ("to maim or lose a member").

memorandum [mem · uh · *ran* · dum] *n.* memo, notation, recapitulation, dispatch, letter, summary, precis, message ("The memorandum concerned safety precautions").

memorial [mem · *or* · ee · ul] *adj.* commemorative, monumental, ceremonial, dedicatory, celebrative ("memorial statue").

memorialize [mem · *or* · ee · ul · eyz] *v.* honor, dedicate, observe, conserve ("memorialized in solid gold").

memory [*mem* · e · ree] *n.* remembrance, recall, recreation, recollection, subconsciousness, thought ("The witness's memory isn't as good as it used to be").

mental [*men* · tel] *adj.* psychic, rational, thinking, brainy, cerebral, thoughtful.

mention [*men* · shun] *v.* inform, state, tell, notify, remark, assert, declare.

mention [*men* · shun] *n.* acclaim, honor, accolade, respect, tribute, laudation, praise.

merchandise [*mer* · chen · dize] *n.* commodity, effects, material, wares, stock, moveables ("The store's merchandise").

merchandise [*mer* · chen · dize] *v.* advertise, buy and sell, promote, trade, traffic, handle ("They merchandise the event of Christmas").

merchant [*mer* · chent] *n.* dealer, seller, buyer, broker, trader, vendor ("The merchant sold us the lamp").

merchantable [*mer* · chen · tuh · bul] *adj.* fit, saleable, marketable ("merchantable quality").

mere *adj.* pure, simple, bald, plain, utter, unmixed, minimum, bare.

meretricious [mehr · re · *trish* · us] *adj.* immoral, obscene, lewd, cheap; blatant, showy, trashy, superficial, sham, hollow, plastic, bogus, deceptive, lying, misleading.

merger [*mer* · jer] *n.* federation, union, consolidation, alliance, fusion, tie-in.

merit [*mehr* · it] *n.* value, worth, quality, stature, goodness, superiority ("The case was decided on its merits").

merit [*mehr* · it] *v.* rate, invite, qualify for, be worthy of, prompt, deserve, earn ("It did not merit my attention").

M

meritorious [mehr · ih · *toh* · ree · us] *adj.* sound, praiseworthy, commendable, choice, excellent, noble.

metropolitan [met · re · *pol* · ih · tun] *adj.* municipal, urban, populated, sophisticated, city, modern, urbane ("metropolitan area").

middleman [*mid* · ul · man] *n.* go-between, broker, liaison, intermediary, factor, attorney, envoy ("The attorney was the middleman in the adoption").

mileage [*my* · lej] *n.* reimbursement, payment, allotment, compensation, levy, rate ("We were given mileage for the trip to and from the courthouse"); distance traveled.

military [*mil* · ih · teh · ree] *n.* army, navy, air force, marine corps, troops, legions, divisions, militia ("the military advanced on the enemy"); spartan, warlike, combative, armed, aggressive, gladiatorial ("The vehicle had a military design").

militia [mi · *lish* · uh] *n.* volunteers, minutemen, reserves, standbys.

mind *n.* intelligence, faculties, judgment, reasoning, psyche, intellect.

minimum [*min* · ih · mum] *n.* margin, bottom line, smallest amount, dab, least, slightest ("minimum contacts test").

minister [*min* · ih · ster] *v.* cater to, wait on, accommodate, pander, nurse, tend ("I will minister to his cuts").

minister [*min* · ih · ster] *n.* secretary, commissioner, chief, consul, delegate, prime minister ("the minister of defense"); pastor, clergyman, father, parson, preacher, lecturer ("married by a minister").

ministerial [min · ih · *steer* · ee · ul] *adj.* implemental, administrative, subsidiary, ancillary, clear, fixed ("He has ministerial authority").

minor [*my* · ner] *adj.* inferior, trivial, secondary, slight, insignificant, small.

minor [*my* · ner] *n.* adolescent, baby, youngster, infant, juvenile, child.

minority [my · *naw* · rih · tee] *n.* nonage, childhood, infancy, juvenility, youth ("The children still are in their minority"); outvoted number, less than half, secondary group, lesser proportion, handful ("a minority position").

minutes [*min* · ets] *n.* notes, summary, outline, transcript, memorandum ("the minutes of the meeting").

misadventure [mis · ad · *ven* · cher] *n.* setback, mishap, casualty, debacle, failure, lapse.

misapplication [mis · ap · li · *kay* · shen] *n.* misuse, abuse, misappropriation, squandering, illegal handling, corrupt use.

misappropriate [mis · uh · *pro* · pree · ayt] *v.* take, swindle, rob, defalcate, defraud ("misappropriate funds").

miscarriage [mis · *kehr* · ej] *n.* stillbirth, spontaneous abortion ("to have a miscarriage"); defeat, error, misadventure, miss, nonsuccess, perversion ("miscarriage of justice").

miscellaneous [mis · sel · *ane* · ee · us] *adj.* varied, mixed, collected, unclassified, jumbled, diversified.

mischief [*mis* · chif] *n.* wrongfulness, wrongdoing, annoyance, misconduct, prank.

misconduct [mis · *kon* · dukt] *n.* dereliction, misdeed, offense, impropriety, naughtiness, transgression.

misconstrue [mis · kon · *strew*] *v.* misinterpret, confuse, mistake, misunderstand, misconceive, misread.

miscue [*mis* · kew] *n.* mistake, error, blunder, slip, fumble.

M

misdemeanor [mis · de · *meen* · er] *n.* offense, transgression, wrong, misdeed, violation, trespass, impropriety.

misfeasance [mis · *fee* · zense] *n.* dereliction, negligence, transgression, wrongfulness, peccadillo, breach.

mishandle [*mis* · han · dul] *v.* misuse, squander, waste, misdirect ("mishandle funds").

mislead [mis · *leed*] *v.* deceive, betray, misrepresent.

mismanage [mis · *man* · aj] *v.* misuse, maladminister, mishandle, administer inefficiently, bungle.

misnomer [mis · *no* · mer] *n.* slip, misusage, misnaming, malapropism.

misrepresent [mis · rep · re · *zent*] *v.* fabricate, distort, lie, deceive, falsify, prevaricate.

misrepresentation [mis · rep · ree · zen · *tay* · shen] *n.* fraud, deception, deceit, distortion, fabrication, exaggeration.

mistake [mis · *tayk*] *n.* misconception, inaccuracy, lapse, slip, confusion, erratum ("a mistake of identity").

mitigating [*mit* · ih · gay · ting] *adj.* exonerative, modifying, cushioning, softening, alleviating, relieving ("mitigating circumstances") .

mitigation [mit · ih · *gay* · shen] *n.* reduction, abatement, moderation, softening, extenuation, lessening ("mitigation of damages").

mixed *adj.* blended, merged, composite, brewed, kneaded, united.

mob *n.* throng, horde, mass, assemblage, gang, pack.

model [*mod* · ul] *n.* plan, archetype, mold, prototype, image, facsimile ("model jury instructions").

modification [mod · ih · fih · *kay* · shen] *n.* qualification, deviation, limitation, inflection, variation, amendment, refinement, change, alteration.

modify [*mod* · ih · fie] *v.* adjust, alter, revamp, revise, amend, refine, change, improve.

molestation [mo · les · *tay* · shen] *n.* abuse, mischief, annoyance, malice, affliction, persecution, interference.

mollify [*mol* · ih · fie] *v.* assuage, pacify, quiet, subdue, calm.

monetary [*mon* · e · ter · ee] *adj.* budgetary, capital, financial, fiscal, pecuniary.

money [*mun* · ee] *n.* capital, cash, revenue, greenback, coin, specie, legal tender; assets, wealth, affluence, fortune, wherewithal, treasure.

M

monopoly [muh · *nop* · uh · lee] *n.* domination, corner, oligopoly ("The company has a monopoly on the business"); cartel, trust, amalgamation, consortium, holding ("The company is a monopoly").

monument [*mon* · yoo · ment] *n.* footstone, memorial, headstone, tombstone, pillar, gravestone ("The monument marked his resting place"); reminder, shrine, landmark, marker, tribute ("The monument commemorated the battle").

moot *adj.* academic, theoretical, abstract, speculative, of no practical importance, hypothetical, debatable, unsettled.

moral [*mor* · el] *adj.* ethical, honest, above-board, principled, honorable, worthy ("a moral person").

moral [*mor* · el] *n.* lesson, principle, honesty, point, teaching, proverb ("the moral of the story").

morality [more · *al* · ih · tee] *n.* virtue, integrity, honor, ethics, honesty.

morals [*more* · elz] *n.* personal principles, standards, behavior, conduct, scruples, ideas.

moratorium [more · e · *toh* · ree · um] *n.* postponement, pause, freeze, discontinuance, stoppage, abeyance, stay, respite.

mortal [*more* · tel] *adj.* deadly, fatal, lethal, dire, extreme ("a mortal wound").

mortal [*more* · tel] *n.* animal, being, body, human, soul, person.

mortality [more · *tal* · ih · tee] *n.* human race, humanity, mankind, vulnerability, frailty, evanescence, mortals ("limited by one's mortality").

mortgage [*more* · gej] *v.* hypothecate, obligate, encumber, stake, post, hock ("They mortgaged the farm").

mortgage [*more* · gej] *n.* encumbrance, indebtedness, debt, obligation, security, pledge ("mortgage on the property").

motion [*moh* · shen] *n.* request, petition, proposition, plan, demand, offering ("motion to dismiss").

motive [*moh* · tiv] *n.* inducement, rationale, stimulus, drive, spur, passion, provocation, purpose, causation.

movable [*move* · uh · bul] *adj.* transportable, adaptable, not fastened, removable, mobile, conveyable.

movables [*move* · uh · bulz] *n.* chattels, personal property, personalty, goods, possessions.

move *v.* petition, demand, request, propose, propound, urge ("He moved for a new trial").

mug *v.* accost, assault, attack, rob ("to be mugged in the park").

mulct *v.* fine, penalize, punish, cheat, defraud, deceive, swindle.

mulct *n.* fine, penalty, punishment.

multiple [*mul* · tih · pul] *adj.* several, plural, divergent, assorted, many, mixed.

municipal [myoo · *niss* · ih · pel] *adj.* urban, community, neighborhood, city, civic, town, metropolitan ("municipal ordinance").

municipality [myoo · niss · ih · *pal* · ih · tee] *n.* metropolis, town, country, village, township, parish.

murder [*mer* · der] *n.* liquidation, slaughter, killing, slaying, homicide, execution, unlawful killing.

must *n.* charge, imperative, requirement, compulsory, mandatory, obligatory.

mute *adj.* soundless, dumb, taciturn, wordless, reserved, silent, quiescent.

mutilation [myoo · tih · *lay* · shen] *n.* confusion, injury, maiming, hurt, destruction.

mutiny [*myoo* · tih · nee] *n.* disobedience, insurrection, revolt, riot, strike ("a shipwide mutiny").

mutiny [*myoo* · tih · nee] *v.* disobey, insurrect, rebel, resist, rise up ("The crew was ready to mutiny at the slightest excuse"). *Ant.* submission.

mutual [*myoo* · choo · el] *adj.* bilateral, interchanged, related, leagued, collaborative, connected.

mutuality [myoo · choo · *al* · ih · tee] *n.* reciprocity, interchange, correspondence, interdependence, correlation, exchange.

mystery [*mis* · te · ree] *n.* puzzle, riddle, enigma, obscurity.

myth *n.* fable, fantasy, legend, folklore, tradition, fiction, falsehood.

M

naive [*ni · eev*] *adj.* innocent, credulous, simple, trusting, unschooled, unworldly, plain, unaffected.

naked [*nay · ked*] *adj.* plain, bare, nude, defenseless, conspicuous, noticeable, observable, overt, evident, perceptible.

named *adj.* articulated, designated, appointed.

narcotic [*nar · kot · ik*] *n.* dope, anesthetic, analgesic, painkiller, drug, contraband, opiate, sedative, controlled substance.

narrative [*nehr · e · tiv*] *n.* story, telling, tale, description, communication, rendition, depiction.

narrow [*nehr · oh*] *adj.* restricted, tight, constricted, strict; intolerant, closed-minded, partisan, bigoted.

nation [*nay · shen*] *n.* republic, sovereignty, union, community, democracy, commonwealth.

national [*nash · en · el*] *adj.* civil, domestic, federal, governmental, political, widespread, nationwide ("the national government").

nationality [*nash · en · al · ih · tee*] *n.* native land, origin, citizenship, allegiance, community, country.

nationalization [*nash · en · e · lih · zay · shen*] *n.* seizing, taking over, socialization, appropriation.

natural [*nat · sher · el*] *adj.* normal, everyday, accustomed, customary, typical; spontaneous; foreseeable; innate, inherent, untaught, fundamental, genetic ("his natural talent for oratory").

naturalization [*nat · sher · e · lih · zay · shen*] *n.* acceptance, admission, enfranchisement.

navigable [*nav · ih · guh · bul*] *adj.* transversable, passable, unobstructed, negotiable ("navigable waters").

navigate [*nav · ih · gayt*] *v.* travel, steer, guide, maneuver, traverse, journey.

necessaries [*ness · e · sair · eez*] *n.* essentials, needs, requirements, prerequisites, necessities, fundamentals.

necessary [*ness · e · sair · ee*] *adj.* essential, indispensable, required, imperative ("a necessary party"); appropriate, convenient, useful; unalterable, irrevocable, settled, certain ("necessary damages"). *Ant.* optional.

necessitous [*ne · sess · ih · tuss*] *adj.* destitute, impoverished, needy, indigent, disadvantaged ("necessitous circumstances"). *Ant.* wealthy.

necessity [ne · *sess* · ih · tee] *n.* essential, imperative, need, fundamental requirement, prerequisite ("a necessity for survival"); power, impulse, coercion, motivation ("public necessity").

need *n.* demand, precondition, obligation, requirement, necessity ("the need for complete honesty"); absence, scarcity, deprivation, paucity, shortage ("to be in need").

need *v.* require, demand, want, yearn, crave.

negative [*neg* · e · tiv] *n.* denial, refusal, refutation, disavowal.

negative [*neg* · e · tiv] *v.* deny, veto, reject, refuse, consent.

negative [*neg* · e · tiv] *adj.* disapproving, dissenting, opposing, objecting, adverse.

neglect [neg · *lekt*] *n.* delinquency, disdain, disregard, inconsideration, indifference.

neglect [neg · *lekt*] *v.* overlook, abandon, procrastinate, discount, omit, ignore.

negligence [*neg* · lih · jense] *n.* thoughtlessness, default, breach of duty, oversight, delinquency, irresponsibility, carelessness, dereliction, recklessness, inattentiveness ("The doctor's negligence caused the tumor to go undetected").

negligent [*neg* · lih · jent] *adj.* careless, heedless, inattentive, lax, reckless, irresponsible.

negotiable [ne · *go* · she · bul] *adj.* transferable, assignable, alienable; open, undetermined, malleable, bargainable ("Her fee was negotiable"). *Ant.* nonnegotiable, fixed.

negotiable instrument [ne · *go* · she · bul *in* · stroo · ment] *n.* draft, check, bond, note, money order, instrument.

negotiate [ne · *go* · shee · ayt] *v.* deal, mediate ("negotiate a compromise"); bargain, arrange, discuss.

negotiation [ne · go · shee · *ay* · shen] *n.* agreement, compromise, mediation, discussion.

nepotism [*nep* · e · tizm] *n.* partiality, injustice, unfairness, partisanship, cronyism, preferential treatment.

net *n.* cloth, netting, fabric; gain, profit, return, accumulation, taxes.

net *adj.* remaining, residual, surplus, unspent ("net profits").

neurosis [new · *roh* · sis] *n.* disorder, insanity, abnormality, affliction, derangement.

new *adj.* original, novel, fresh, mint, recent, unexplored, different.

next *adj.* adjoining, consequent, following, adjacent, proximate.

next friend *n.* guardian, appointee.

nighttime [*nite* · time] *n.* twilight, dusk, dark, nightfall.

nil *n.* nothing, zero, naught.

no *n.* none, zero; denial, rejection.

nominal [*nom* · ih · nel] *adj.* minimal, inconsequential, insubstantial, insignificant, simple.

nominate [*nom* · ih · nayt] *v.* designate, select, choose, draft, recommend.

nomination [nom · ih · *nay* · shen] *n.* choice, designation, recommendation, appointment.

nominee [nom · ih · *nee*] *n.* aspirant, candidate, entrant, bidder.

nonage [*noh* · nij] *n.* infancy, minor, minority.

nonappearance [non · e · *peer* · ense] *n.* default, truancy, nonattendance, absenteeism, nonpresence.

nonconforming [non · ken · *for* · ming] *adj.* contrary, noncompliant, dissenting, differing, defiant, deviant.

noncontestable [non · ken · *tes* · te · bul] *adj.* incontrovertible, undeniable, nonchallengeable, nondebatable.

nondisclosure [non · dis · *kloh* · zher] *n.* concealment, silence, withholding.

nonfeasance [non · *fee* · zense] *n.* disregard, omission, dereliction, failure, avoidance.

nonnegotiable [non · ne · *goh* · she · bul] *adj.* nontransferable, non-assignable; closed, set, established, not bargainable ("My fee is $100 an hour, firm—it is nonnegotiable").

nonpayment [non · *pay* · ment] *n.* delinquency, evasion, arrearage, remissness, repudiation.

nonperformance [non · per · *form* · ense] *n.* dereliction, omission, evasion, infringement, noncompliance. *Ant.* compliance.

nonprofit [non · *prof* · it] *adj.* altruistic, philanthropic, unselfish, magnanimous, benevolent, eleemosynary.

nonresident [non · *rez* · ih · dent] *n.* nonoccupant, nondomiciliary, noncitizen, alien, foreigner, visitor, interloper.

nonsuit [*non* · soot] *n.* default, dismissal, directed verdict.

nonuse [non · *yooss*] *n.* forbearance, abstinence, disuse.

norm *n.* standard, custom, average, rule, generality, habit.

note *n.* commentary, observation; voucher, draft ("bank note"); significance, importance, distinction ("person of note").

note *v.* observe, regard, realize, witness, notice; record, register, docket, document, enter, mark down.

notice [*noh* · tiss] *n.* communication, information, announcement, release, statement; awareness, intelligence, knowledge; heed, consideration, watchfulness, care, caution; warning, admonition, caveat.

notice [*noh* · tiss] *v.* apprise, inform, impart, publish, reveal, proclaim ("notice a hearing"); observe, perceive, witness, note, see, view ("to notice what the perpetrator was wearing").

notify [*noh* · tih · fie] *v.* contact, communicate, inform, proclaim, state, tell, divulge, announce.

notorious [no · *tore* · ee · us] *adj.* disreputable, scandalous, infamous, well-known, prominent, preeminent.

notwithstanding [not · with · *stan* · ding] *adv.* nonetheless, although, despite.

novation [no · *vay* · shen] *n.* replacement, extinguishment, substitution.

novel [*nov* · el] *adj.* new, original, unique, atypical, creative, unorthodox, singular, unusual, uncommon.

novelty [*nov* · el · tee] *n.* innovation, rarity, mutation, specialty.

nude *adj.* bare, mere; naked, unclothed, exposed, garmentless.

nugatory [*noo* · ge · tore · ee] *adj.* invalid, futile, worthless, unenforceable, ineffective ("His will was nugatory because he never executed it").

nuisance [*noo* · sense] *n.* annoyance, inconvenience, bother, intrusion, aggravation, devilment, hindrance, problem. *Ant.* benefit.

null *adj.* nonexistent, valueless, absent, ineffective, invalid ("If you deface that check it will be null and void").

nullification [null · ih · fih · *kay* · shen] *n.* cancellation, voiding, revocation, suspension, discontinuance.

N

nullify [*null* · ih · fy] *v.* cancel, annul, rescind, void, vacate.

nullity [*null* · ih · tee] *n.* erasure, naught, nihilism, nonreality, futility, invalidity.

number [*num* · ber] *n.* character, numeral, digit, figure.

nuncupative [nun · *kyoo* · pah · tiv] *adj.* oral, spoken, unwritten, declared, voiced, parole.

nuptial [*nup* · chew · al] *adj.* marital, matrimonial, spousal, conjugal, connubial.

N

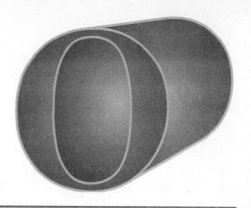

oath *n.* promise, affidavit, affirmation, avowal, pledge, attestation ("oath of allegiance").

obedient [o · *beed* · ee · ent] *adj.* compliant, dedicated, dutiful, faithful, pliant, behaved, submissive, tractable.

obey [oh · *bay*] *v.* submit, succumb, comply, conform, follow, serve, perform.

obfuscate [*ob* · fuss · skayt] *v.* confuse, muddle; stupefy, befuddle. *Ant.* clarify.

object [ob · *jekt*] *v.* oppose, attack, controvert, protest, dispute, except, disapprove.

object [*ob* · jekt] *n.* aim, article, idea, motive, point, purpose, goal ("the object of a statute").

objection [ob · *jek* · shen] *n.* censure, challenge, disapproval, grievance, opposition, protest.

objectionable [ob · *jek* · shun · uh · bul] *adj.* unappealing, obnoxious, displeasing, disgraceful, unsavory, repulsive, vile ("his objectionable manner"); improper, unsuitable ("objectionable evidence").

obligation [ob · lih · *gay* · shen] *n.* commitment, contract, assignment, promise, accountability, duty, responsibility.

obliteration [ob · lih · te · *ray* · shen] *n.* repeal, removal, murder, abolition, abatement, elimination, erasure.

obscene [ob · *seen*] *adj.* offensive, atrocious, improper, loathsome, lustful, suggestive, pornographic, wanton, vulgar.

obscenity [ob · *sen* · ih · tee] *n.* indecency, immorality, abomination, impropriety, vulgarity, smut, pornography.

obscure [ob · *skyoor*] *adj.* complex, profound, deep, hidden, egoteric, abstruse; remote, isolated, private, foreign.

obscure [ob · *skure*] *v.* mislead, veil, becloud, obfuscate, suppress, blur.

obsess [ob · *sess*] *v.* dominate, compel, craze, dement, possess, torment, bedevil.

obsession [ob · *sess* · shun] *n.* compulsion, fanaticism, mania, passion, preoccupation.

obsolete [ob · se · *lete*] *adj.* ancient, antiquated, disused, outmoded, unfashionable.

obstruct [ob · *strukt*] *v.* prevent, impede, hinder, barricade, curb, suppress.

obstruction [ob · *struk* · shun] *n.* barrier, hindrance, limitation, restriction, constraint, prevention, preclusion.

obvious [*ob* · vee · us] *adj.* apparent, conspicuous, evident, noticeable, distinct, unmistakable, overt, explicit.

occupancy [*ok* · yoo · pen · see] *n.* control, possession, tenancy, tenure, residency. *Ant.* relinquishment.

occupant [*ok* · yoo · pent] *n.* dweller, inhabitant, inmate, tenant, resident.

occupation [ok · yoo · *pay* · shen] *n.* livelihood, trade, avocation; use, possession, domination, influence.

occupy [*ok* · yoo · pie] *v.* absorb, engage, fascinate, engross, excite ("occupy the mind"); own, possess, inhabit, reside in ("occupy a house").

occur [oh · *kur*] *v.* happen, transpire, materialize, proceed, arise.

odd *adj.* peculiar, strange, unconventional, weird, eccentric; uneven, irregular; varied, various, sundry, miscellaneous.

offend [uh · *fend*] *v.* insult, affront, provoke, snub; disobey, transgress, infringe.

offender [uh · *fen* · der] *n.* violator, lawbreaker, transgressor, felon, wrongdoer.

offense [uh · *fense*] *n.* infraction, malfeasance, transgression, wrongdoing; hurt, wrong, misdeed.

offensive [uh · *fen* · siv] *adj.* noxious, abhorrent, detestable, objectionable, reprehensible; noxious, unsanitary, unsightly; aggressive, forward.

offer [*off* · ur] *v.* present, advance, propose, provide, award, suggest.

offer [*off* · ur] *n.* proposal, suggestion, endeavor, proposition, submission, bid.

offering [*off* · er · ing] *n.* donation, contribution, gift, benefaction, bequest, subsidy, alms ("an offering at church"); sale, issue, distribution ("a stock offering").

office [*off* · iss] *n.* business, appointment; occupation, employment, charge, responsibility; department, division, branch ("the home office").

officer [*off* · ih · ser] *n.* commander, administrator, agent, official, representative.

official [uh · *fish* · ul] *n.* administrator, manager, executive, bureaucrat.

official [uh · *fish* · ul] *adj.* accredited, approved, valid, licensed, recognized, formal.

officiate [uh · *fish* · ee · ayt] *v.* oversee, manage, administer, conduct, direct.

officious [uh · *fish* · us] *adj.* meddlesome, dictatorial, obtrusive, interfering, domineering ("an officious intermeddler").

offset [off · *set*] *v.* counterbalance, compensate, equalize, countervail, neutralize.

offset [*off* · set] *n.* counterclaim, recoupment, setoff, deduction.

old *adj.* used, elderly, worn, matured, declining, decayed, rundown.

ombudsman [*om* · budz · mun] *n.* referee, agent, moderator, representative.

omission [oh · *mish* · en] *n.* breach, neglect, cancellation, disregard, exclusion, oversight, repudiation.

omit [oh · *mit*] *v.* bypass, pass over, leave out, exclude, delete, neglect.

on *prep.* about, above, forward, adjacent, near.

one *adj.* alone, individual, lone, odd, only, single ("Just one vote shy").

one *pron.* person, individual ("One is free to do as one wishes").

onerous [*ohn* · e · ress] *adj.* burdensome, oppressive, demanding, cumbersome, fatiguing, overwhelming.

one-sided *adj.* unfair, unjust, slanted, prejudiced, interested, uneven ("a one-sided deal").

onset [*on* · set] *n.* beginning, inception, outbreak, coming, dawn; advance, assault, charge.

onus [*own* · us] *n.* burden, duty, responsibility, affliction; accusation, charge, fault; blemish, dishonor, infamy, degradation.

open [*oh* · pen] *v.* begin, expose, breach, display, initiate, originate ("open a file").

open [*oh* · pen] *adj.* receptive, unprejudiced ("open to suggestion"); apparent, manifest ("open defiance"); equivocal, available, undecided ("an open question"); candid, honest, exposed; uncensored, obvious; unrestricted, unobstructed, free, public ("open admission").

operate [*op* · e · rayt] *v.* perform, run, execute, accomplish, function, engage.

operative [*op* · e · re · tiv] *adj.* accessible, functional, efficacious, practicable, service-able, capable, efficient.

opinion [*oh* · *pin* · yen] *n.* judgment, conclusion, decree, ruling, position, order ("opinion of the court"); persuasion, conviction, viewpoint, belief, outlook.

opportunity [*op* · ur · *tune* · ih · tee] *n.* chance, luck, occasion, propitiousness, time, turn ("opportunity to be heard").

oppose [uh · *poze*] *v.* counter, contend, rebut, protest, fight, debate, disagree ("oppose a motion").

oppression [oh · *presh* · en] *n.* abuse, hardship, persecution, injustice, domination, torment, cruelty.

option [*op* · shen] *n.* advantage, offer, choice, preference, prerogative ("option to purchase").

oral [*ohr* · el] *adj.* spoken, articulate, narrated, voiced, uttered, unwritten.

ordain [or · *dane*] *v.* establish, anoint, designate, install, nominate; decree, order, man-date, command.

ordeal [or · *deal*] *n.* tribulation, affliction, torment, adversity, calamity.

order [*or* · der] *v.* dictate, require, rule, demand, ordain, prescribe.

order [*or* · der] *n.* decree, command, mandate, demand, judgment ("order of the court"); arrangement, grouping, layout, pattern, placement, rotation ("order of creditors").

ordinance [*or* · dih · nense] *n.* command, mandate, law, regulation, order, statute, rule.

ordinary [*or* · dih · ner · ee] *adj.* usual, normal, common, reoccurring, routine, traditional, conventional, reasonable.

organic [or · *gan* · ik] *adj.* fundamental, basic, structural, inherent, biological.

organization [or · ge · nih · *zay* · shen] *n.* group, alliance, league, coalition, affiliation, consortium, federation.

origin [*or* · ih · jin] *n.* beginning, cause, birth, genesis, foundation; descent, heritage, lineage, bloodline.

original [uh · *rij* · ih · nel] *n.* standard, archetype, paradigm, precursor, model, first.

original [o · *rij* · ih · nel] *adj.* innovative, introductory, unique, clever, basic, formative, fundamental, earliest, first, primary.

ostensible [oh · *sten* · sih · bul] *adj.* alleged, presumable, assumed, purported, plausible, apparent, seeming.

oust *v.* banish, repudiate, discharge, expulse, remove, eject.

ouster [*owst* · ur] *n.* deportation, banishment, deprivation, ejection, expulsion.

out *adj.* absent, expired, finished, extinguished.

outcome [*owt* · kum] *n.* result, decision, resolution, finding, ruling, culmination, conse-quence, aftermath.

O

outcry [*owt* · krie] *n.* clamor, outburst, protest, uproar, complaint, accusation, disapproval, castigation.

outdated [owt · *day* · ted] *adj.* archaic, obsolete, primitive, old-fashioned, passé.

outlaw [*owt* · law] *n.* criminal, fugitive, crook, desperado, hoodlum, recidivist, bandit, robber, felon.

outlaw [*owt* · law] *v.* ban, condemn, exclude, forbid, illegalize.

outlay [*owt* · lay] *n.* expense, cost, disbursement, charge, expenditure.

outlet [*owt* · let] *n.* opening, gate, vent, egress, access.

outmoded [owt · *moad* · ed] *adj.* outdated, obsolete, out-of-fashion, anachronistic, passé, dated ("an outmoded style of dress").

output [*owt* · put] *n.* proceeds, product, return, result, yield, harvest, crop.

outrage [*owt* · rayj] *n.* injustice, violation, abomination, transgression, violence.

outrage [*owt* · rayj] *v.* exasperate, provoke, infuriate, discombobulate, affront.
   Ant. benefit, pacify.

outrageous [owt · *ray* · jus] *adj.* shocking, wild, unwarranted, atrocious, excessive, despicable, intolerable ("outrageous behavior").

outright [*owt* · rite] *adj.* complete, absolute, direct, thorough, unequivocal ("outright gift").

outstanding [owt · *stan* · ding] *adj.* uncollected ("outstanding debt"); unresolved, in arrears, existing, remaining ("an outstanding charge"); distinctive, excellent, memorable, extraordinary, distinguished ("outstanding performance").

over [*oh* · ver] *adj.* closed, completed, concluded, ended, finished, settled.

over [*oh* · ver] *adv.* beyond, exceeding, transcending, surpassing; on top of, above.

overcharge [*oh* · ver · charj] *v.* deceive, cheat, fleece.

overcome [*oh* · ver · *kum*] *v.* surmount, transcend, rise above, prevail, triumph; overwhelm, stun, bowl over, daze, crush.

overdue [oh · ver · *dew*] *adj.* late, delinquent, outstanding, unsettled, belated.

overestimate [oh · ver · *ess* · tih · mate] *v.* exceed, enlarge, magnify, overstate, misjudge, maximize.

overhang [*oh* · ver · hang] *n.* projection, eave, awning, protuberance.

overhang [*oh* · ver · *hang*] *v.* bulge, jut, loom, portend, protrude, extend, project.

overhead [*oh* · ver · hed] *n.* budget, cost, expenses, outlay, upkeep.

overlook [oh · ver · *look*] *v.* excuse, forgive, pardon, disregard ("overlook this transgression"); guide, oversee, govern, administer, steer, command ("overlook the project").

overreach [oh · ver · *reech*] *v.* abolish, obliterate, overturn, disrupt, remove, topple, surmount; exceed, go beyond; deceive, intimidate, take advantage of.

overreaching [oh · ver · *ree* · ching] *n.* misconduct, trickery, circumvention, misleading, undermining.

override [oh · ver · *ride*] *v.* nullify, counteract, void, supersede, defeat, dominate.

overrule [oh · ver · *rool*] *v.* void, abrogate, invalidate, disallow, override, reverse, quash, veto, annul, nullify.

overt [oh · *vurt*] *adj.* open, exposed, conspicuous, noticeable, perceptible, observable.

overthrow [oh · ver · *throh*] *v.* abolish, obliterate, overturn, disrupt, remove, topple, surmount.

O

overture [*oh* · ver · tchyoor] *n.* beginning, advance, approach, proposal, invitation, proposition.

owe *v.* be behind, be in arrears, be bound, be obligated, be indebted.

owing [*oh* · wing] *adj.* due, unpaid, attributable, outstanding, payable.

own *v.* control, dominate, hold, occupy, retain.

own *adj.* inherent, intrinsic, personal, private, particular.

owner [*oh* · ner] *n.* buyer, landlord, possessor, proprietor.

ownership [*oh* · ner · ship] *n.* claim, occupancy, possessorship, tenancy, dominion, control, seisin, title, tenure.

O

pacify [*pass* · ih · fy] *v.* appease, settle, soothe, please, placate, relieve, harmonize, mollify, calm. *Ant.* antagonize.

pack *n.* assemblage, bundle, collection, lot, mass.

pack *v.* arrange, load, collect, charge, arrange.

package [*pak* · ej] *n.* bundle, batch, container, amalgamation, baggage, parcel.

pact *n.* alliance, arrangement, treaty, transaction, concord.

paid *adj.* satisfied, remunerated, resolved.

pain *n.* discomfort, anguish, suffering, torment, affliction, misery, ordeal.

palatable [*pal* · uh · tih · bul] *adj.* acceptable, agreeable, satisfactory, unobjectionable; tasty, savory, appetizing, delicious.

palliate [*pal* · ee · ayt] *v.* ease, abate, curb, curtail, pacify, reduce; excuse, absolve, release, exonerate, clear, forgive.

paltry [*pol* · tree] *adj.* insignificant, small, minute, scanty, negligible, piddling, trivial ("a paltry amount").

panacea [pan · uh · *see* · uh] *n.* cure-all, remedy, solution, answer, balm, cure.

pandering [*pan* · dur · ing] *n.* soliciting, pimping, hustling.

panel [*pan* · ul] *n.* forum, body, committee, board, assembly, jurors, triers of fact, jury.

paper [*pay* · per] *n.* certificate, instrument, record, document; composition, essay, report.

par *n.* equivalence, correspondence, unity, equilibrium, balance; average, norm, expectations ("His recent work has been below par").

paradigm [*par* · uh · dime] *n.* model, archetype, guide, standard, pattern.

paralegal [*pehr* · e · lee · gul] *n.* legal assistant, paraprofessional, aide, lay advocate, legal technician.

paramount [*pehr* · e · mount] *adj.* superior, unsurpassed, dominant, prevailing, supreme.

paraphernalia [pehr · e · fer · *nayl* · ya] *n.* gear, property, furnishings, accessories, supplies, equipment, accessories, articles.

parasite [*par* · ih · site] *n.* scavenger, leech, borrower, sycophant, sponge.

parcel [*par* · sel] *v.* apportion, partition, distribute, allow, prorate.

parcel [*par* · sel] *n.* package, lot, tract, plot, enclosure.

pardon [*par* · den] *n.* release, forgiveness, exoneration, clemency, vindication.

pardon [*par* · den] *v.* excuse, exonerate, vindicate, acquit, release.

parent [*pair* · ent] *n.* procreater, antecedent, ancestor, mother, father, predecessor, progenitor, begetter.

parental [pa · *ren* · tel] *adj.* maternal, paternal, motherly, fatherly.

parish [*pehr* · ish] *n.* territory, archdiocese, community, church, subdivision.

parity [*pehr* · ih · tee] *n.* uniformity, equilibrium, semblance, balance, subsidy.

parlance [*par* · lens] *n.* speech, vocabulary, manner, terminology ("in contemporary parlance").

parliamentary [par · le · *men* · te · ree] *adj.* legislative, deliberative, orderly.

parochial [pe · *roh* · kee · el] *adj.* narrow, provincial, regional, sectional, confined, insular, bigoted ("parochial consideration").

parol [*par* · ul] *adj.* oral, unwritten, nuncupative, voiced, uttered ("parol evidence").

parole [pa · *roll*] *n.* release, freedom, emancipation, conditional release.

parole [pa · *roll*] *v.* discharge, release, liberate, let out, disimprison, unchain, unfetter.

part *n.* portion, section, allocation, measure, chunk, division, piece ("the major part of the estate"); role, performance, representation, character, portrayal ("playing the part").

part *v.* leave, depart, escape, withdraw, remove; separate, disentangle, divide, sunder, subdivide.

partial [*par* · shel] *adj.* fragmentary, fractional, limited ("partial payment"); biased, prejudiced, unobjective ("The judge recused himself as being partial to the defendant").

participate [par · *tiss* · ih · pate] *v.* share, join, partake, contribute, encourage, experience.

participation [par · tiss · ih · *pay* · shen] *n.* involvement, engagement, cooperation, partaking.

particular [par · *tik* · yoo · ler] *adj.* definite, distinguished, individual, specific, distinct.

particularity [par · tik · you · *lehr* · ih · tee] *n.* precision, fastidiousness, meticulousness, detail, care, carefulness.

particulars [par · *tik* · yoo · lerz] *n.* specifications, details, features, niceties, articles, specifics.

partisan [*part* · ih · zan] *adj.* partial, predisposed, clannish, factional, party.

partition [par · *tish* · en] *n.* division, splitting, apportionment, allotment, segmentation; wall, fence, divider.

partition [par · *tish* · en] *v.* separate, section, parcel out, divide.

partner [*part* · nur] *n.* participant, associate, confrere, collaborator, confederate, member, teammate, aid, ally.

partnership [*part* · nur · ship] *n.* federation, alliance, league, association, collaboration, business, enterprise, undertaking.

party [*par* · tee] *n.* adversary, participant, litigant, disputant, claimant, conspirator, collaborator, partner, partaker; political organization, coalition, league, group, caucus.

pass *n.* license, authorization, sanction, legalization, validation; route, way, opening, pathway.

pass *v.* ratify, approve, adopt ("pass a bill"); succeed, accomplish, achieve ("pass the course"); declare, render, decide, announce ("pass sentence"); transfer, give, grant, deed ("pass title").

P

passage [*pass* · ej] *n.* authorization, endorsement, confirmation, validation, acceptance ("passage of the bill"); route, channel, conduct, path ("Northwest Passage"); segment, piece, selection, excerpt, segment ("a passage from the text").

passenger [*pass* · en · jer] *n.* guest, traveler, commuter, client, patron.

passion [*pash* · en] *n.* anger, excitement, emotion, fervor, rapture, ire, fire, zeal.

passive [*pass* · iv] *adj.* inactive, dormant, submissive, docile, obliging.

past *adj.* former, previous, prior, obsolete, old.

patent [*pay* · tent] *adj.* obvious, visible, noticeable, apparent, evident, unmistakable, tangible, definite, indubitable.

patent [*pat* · ent] *n.* permit, license, certificate, trademark, right, legal right.

paternity [pa · *ter* · nih · tee] *n.* fatherhood, derivation, ancestry, lineage, descent.

pathological [path · e · *loj* · ih · kul] *adj.* demented, deranged, unbalanced, abject.

patient [*pay* · shent] *n.* victim, convalescent, sufferer, invalid, sick person, client.

patient [*pay* · shent] *adj.* diligent, sympathetic, unperturbed, balanced, determined, indefatigable, relentless, steadfast, persistent, unflappable.

patronage [*pay* · tren · ej] *n.* sponsorship, advocacy, guardianship, auspices, sustenance.

pattern [*pat* · ern] *n.* standard, classification, repetition, method, outline; model, example, prototype.

paucity [*paws* · ih · tee] *n.* lack, dearth, shortage, scarcity, inadequacy, lack.

pauper [*paw* · per] *n.* indigent, beggar, insolvent, mendicant, debtor.

pause *n.* break, delay, stoppage, respite, stay, interval, intermission, hesitation.

pause *v.* stop, suspend, deliberate, wait, hold back, consider, dwell, discontinue.

pawn *n.* collateral, instrument, medium, vehicle.

pawn *v.* mortgage, stake, obligate, post, deposit, encumber, pledge.

pay *n.* compensation, consideration, income, wage.

pay *v.* expend, remit, honor, settle, disburse.

payable [*pay* · e · bul] *adj.* mature, owed, in arrears, due, redeemable, collectable.

payment [*pay* · munt] *n.* satisfaction, defrayal, subsidy, reimbursement, remittance, amortization, outlay.

peace *n.* quiet, order, tranquility, harmony, concord, security, goodwill, serenity, unanimity, cooperation.

peaceable [*peess* · e · bul] *adj.* peaceful, gentle, calm, amicable, unbellicose.

peaceful [*peess* · ful] *adj.* nonaggressive, nonviolent, passive, patient.

peculation [pek · yoo · *lay* · shen] *n.* embezzlement, deception, cheating, misappropriation.

pecuniary [pe · *kyoo* · nee · e · ree] *adj.* monetary, financial, fiscal, budgetary.

pedestrian [ped · *ess* · tree · en] *n.* stroller, walker, bystander.

pedestrian [ped · *ess* · tree · en] *adj.* unimaginative, mediocre, commonplace ("a pedestrian performance").

peer *n.* associate, colleague, equal, equivalent, match, mate.

penal [*peen* · el] *adj.* punitive, disciplinary, castigatory, retributive, corrective.

penalize [*pen* · uhl · eyz] *v.* punish, cost, fine, mulct, confiscate, forfeit.

penalty [*pen* · ul · tee] *n.* sanction, sentence, forfeiture, castigation, retribution, punishment, consequence, reprisal.

P

pendency [*pen · den · see*] *n.* duration, continuance, interval, interim.

pendent [*pen · dent*] *adj.* supplemental, adjunct, connecting, allied, undecided.

pending [*pen · ding*] *adj.* not concluded, undecided, inconclusive, unresolved, approaching, prospective ("pending action").

penetration [pen · e · *tray* · shen] *n.* entering, invasion, encroachment, insertion.

penitentiary [pen · ih · *ten* · sher · ee] *n.* prison, jail, detention, cage, lock-up, joint, slammer.

pension [*pen* · shen] *n.* benefits, annuity, compensation, social security, support, reward ("A vested pension").

pensive [*pen* · sive] *adj.* thoughtful, reflective, rapt, deliberative, musing, absorbed, engrossed, dreamy.

penumbra [pee · *num* · bra] *n.* margin, shadow, shade, border, boundary, reflection.

peonage [*pee* · en · ej] *n.* slavery, servitude ("Many African-Americans have had to serve in peonage").

people [*pee* · pul] *n.* citizens, population, mankind, community, general public ("We, the people").

per *adv.* by, through, in, by means of, in accordance with, according to, under ("I will deliver the goods by July 1, per our contract").

perceive [pur · *ceev*] *v.* see, observe, apprehend, become aware of, note, notice, witness, understand.

percentage [pur · *sen* · tej] *n.* portion, share, commission, ratio, dividend. *Ant.* entirety.

percolating [*pur* · ke · lay · ting] *adj.* filtering, draining, seeping, oozing.

peremptory [pur · *emp* · ter · ee] *adj.* unconditional, absolute, irreversible, binding, positive, unequivocal, axiomatic, total, unalterable; assertive, firm, necessary, obligatory, compulsory, authoritative, inflexible.

perfect [*pur* · fikt] *adj.* complete, incontestable, finished, whole, consummate, demonstrable, real; flawless, ideal, correct, precise, exact, excellent, superb, masterful.

perfect [pur · *fekt*] *v.* finish, complete, consummate, execute, perform, fulfill, conclude, close ("to perfect title").

perfected [pur · *fek* · ted] *adj.* finished, completed, executed, performed, finalized ("The will had to be perfected").

perfection [pur · *fek* · shen] *n.* realization, accomplishment, attainment, flawlessness ("I strive for perfection"); completion, consummation, fulfillment, attainment ("perfection of title").

perform [pur · *form*] *v.* execute, fulfill, transact, accomplish, finish, do ("I will perform my duties to the best of my abilities"); enact, enforce, observe, respect ("perform a contract").

performance [pur · *form* · ense] *n.* fulfillment, effort, production, work, skill, accomplishment, satisfaction, conclusion, achievement ("Her job performance was excellent"); presentation, showing, entertainment, exhibition ("Our dance performance brought the audience to its feet!").

peril [*pehr* · il] *n.* risk, threat, menace, hazard, danger, pitfall. *Ant.* safety, security.

period [*peer* · ee · ed] *n.* span, interval, season, term, duration, cycle ("His period of tenure was 10 years").

periodic [peer · ee · *odd* · ik] *adj.* intermittent, recurrent, systematic, cyclic, routine ("We have periodic job reviews"). *Ant.* constant.

P

periodical [peer · ee · *odd* · ih · kul] *n.* magazine, publication, journal, newspaper, press.

perishable [*pehr* · ish · uh · bul] *adj.* decayable, decomposing, disappearing, destructible, unstable ("a perishable commodity").

perjure [*pur* · jer] *v.* lie, misrepresent, deceive, trick ("Fear of the mob caused him to perjure himself"). *Ant.* confess, confirm.

perjury [*pur* · jer · ee] *n.* mispresentation, deceit, misstatement, dishonesty, false testimony, distortion ("The judge knew she was guilty of perjury").

perks *n.* perquisites, benefits, advantages, extras, pluses ("the perks make some mediocre jobs more tempting").

permanent [*pur* · men · ent] *adj.* enduring, irrevocable, fixed, unending, constant, lasting ("permanent disability"). *Ant.* temporary, transient.

permission [pur · *mish* · en] *n.* leave, license, sufferance, authority, approval, consent, acceptance ("He has my permission to come in"). *Ant.* prohibition.

permissive [pur · *miss* · iv] *adj.* permitted, allowed, tolerated ("a permissive counterclaim").

permit [pur · *mit*] *v.* admit, allow, authorize, endorse, concede ("Will you permit me to post this sign?"). *Ant.* deny.

permit [*pur* · mit] *n.* permission, license, authorization, concession, privilege ("Serving alcohol requires a permit"). *Ant.* prohibition.

perpetrate [*pur* · pe · trayt] *v.* commit, perform, cause, administer, execute, enact ("the person who perpetrates a homicide is guilty of murder"). *Ant.* avoidance.

perpetration [pur · pe · *tray* · shen] *n.* commission, enactment, doing, performance.

perpetrator [*per* · pe · tray · ter] *n.* offender, criminal, felon, wrongdoer, lawbreaker ("The rapist was the perpetrator"). *Ant.* bystander, law-abiding citizen.

perpetual [pur · *pet* · shoo · el] *adj.* continuous, everlasting, constant, ceaseless, recurrent ("perpetual succession"). *Ant.* temporary.

perpetuity [pur · pe · *tyoo* · ih · tee] *n.* eternity, continuation, indefiniteness, forever.

perquisites [*pur* · kwe · zits] *n.* privileges, benefits, extras, perks, rewards, bonuses ("A company car is a perquisite of my job"). *Ant.* burden.

persist [pur · *sist*] *v.* endure, persevere, prevail, linger, plug away, hold on, remain.

person [*pur* · sen] *n.* human, individual, customer, mortal ("Each man and woman is considered a person first"); corporation, party, association, partnership ("Legally, IBM is considered a person with certain rights").

personal [*pur* · sen · ul] *adj.* intimate, private, confidential, special, individual ("Religious beliefs are personal"). *Ant.* public.

personality [pur · sen · *al* · ih · tee] *n.* identity, character, makeup, uniqueness, nature, being, selfness.

personalty [*pur* · sen · ul · tee] *n.* property, assets, effects, holdings, investments, resources.

persuade [pur · *swayd*] *v.* influence, motivate, induce, sway, urge, coax, cajole, compel, convert, exhort.

persuasive [pur · *sway* · siv] *adj.* convincing, compelling, cogent, effective, irresistible ("a persuasive argument").

pertinent [*pur* · tin · ent] *adj.* relevant, pertaining, applicable, material, associated, suitable ("a pertinent objection"). *Ant.* irrelevant.

P

peruse [pe · *ruze*] *v.* browse, scan, review, look over, explore, examine, inspect, study, peer into.

pessimism [*pess* · ih · mizm] *n.* hopelessness, dejection, cynicism, glumness, disconsolation, despondence, despair.

petit [pe · *teet*] *adj.* small, petty, little. *Ant.* large, grand.

petition [pe · *tish* · en] *n.* appeal, request, plea, prayer, motion, application, demand ("The tenants circulated a petition demanding new carpeting").

petition [pe · *tish* · en] *v.* plead, seek, solicit, ask, urge, entreat, apply for ("We petitioned the court for mercy").

petitioner [pe · *tish* · en · er] *n.* pleader, litigant, applicant, asker, supplicant ("The petitioner asked for relief"). *Ant.* respondent.

pettifogger [*pet* · ee · fog · er] *n.* wrongdoer, shyster, charlatan, cheater.

petty [*pet* · ee] *adj.* small, minor, lower, subordinate, worthless, spiteful, bigoted.

peyote [pay · *oh* · tee] *n.* cactus, drug, mescaline, hallucinogen.

phase *n.* facet, feature, part; period, term, tenure, span, state, epoch.

phobia [*fo* · bee · uh] *n.* fear, dread, abhorrence, terror, aversion, horror, loathing.

physical [*fiz* · ih · kul] *adj.* tangible, material, real, concrete ("physical evidence"); bodily, earthly, fleshly, personal, nonspiritual ("My physical condition is excellent"). *Ant.* intangible, mental.

picket [*pik* · et] *v.* patrol, march, protest, rally ("We picketed the erring employer's plant").

picket [*pik* · et] *n.* demonstrator, protestor, striker, signholder, guard ("Mary was a picket in last week's strike").

pickpocket [*pik* · pok · et] *n.* thief, wrongdoer, sneak.

piercing [*peerse* · ing] *adj.* biting, offensive, malicious, noisy ("The sound was piercing"). *Ant.* gentle.

pilfer [*pil* · fur] *v.* steal, take, rob, snatch, deprive of ("He pilfered the gold"). *Ant.* restore.

pilferage [*pil* · fer · ej] *n.* stealing, larceny, robbery, embezzlement ("The pilferage of the house was extensive").

pillage [*pil* · ej] *n.* piracy, plunder, robbery, thievery ("The pillage of the town by the gangsters was awful"). *Ant.* replacement, restoration.

pillage [*pil* · ej] *v.* destroy, devastate, ransack, ravage ("The bear pillaged our campsite").

pimp *n.* panderer, purveyor, procurer, madam, runner ("Prostitutes are often controlled by a pimp").

pimp *v.* pander, hustle ("His job was to pimp for my sister").

pimping [*pimp* · ing] *n.* pandering, hustling, procuring.

pinnacle [*pin* · uh · kul] *n.* peak, acme, apex, zenith, summit, top, culmination, apogee, tip.

pioneer [*py* · e · neer] *n.* developer, explorer, inventor, harbinger.

piracy [*py* · re · see] *n.* robbery, stealing, plundering, larceny, pillage, plagiarism, infringement, appropriation ("Printing an article without the author's permission is piracy").

pirate [*py* · ret] *n.* thief, wrongdoer, privateer, robber.

pirate [*py* · ret] *v.* sack, seize, steal, plunder, despoil, loot, pillage.

P

place *n.* location, vicinity, area, territory, locale ("I told him the place to meet"); rank, position, status, standing, grade ("His place was beneath the Queen"); habitat, location, residence, house, home; appointment, occupation, office, work, position.

place *v.* locate, situate, spot, install; order, arrange, delegate, appoint, designate, name; identify, recognize, finger, peg, know.

plagiarism [*play* · jer · izm] *n.* counterfeiting, falsification, fraud, copying, forgery, piracy.

plain *adj.* apparent, clear, blatant, visible ("His handicap was plain"); common, commonplace, ordinary, usual ("She was so plain that no one noticed her in the crowd"); frank, clear, honest ("He made his opinions plain"). *Ant.* unclear, beautiful, cryptic.

plaintiff [*playn* · tif] *n.* complainant, accuser, suitor, petitioner, opponent, litigant.

plan *n.* strategy, course, agenda, method, pattern, system, intention, arrangement, design, projection.

plan *v.* arrange, design, orchestrate, concoct, manage; intend, consider, contemplate, propose.

plat *n.* map, plan, chart, sketch, diagram ("We needed to see the plat of the city").

plea *n.* appeal, petition, request, prayer ("Her plea was based on her innocence"); excuse, defense, argument, claim ("Joe's plea was insanity").

plead *v.* prosecute, allege, argue, present ("to plead one's case in court"); ask, appeal, request, implore ("I plead for quiet from the children but seldom get it").

pleading [*plee* · ding] *n.* allegation, answer, claim, complaint, statement, accusation, defense, denial.

plebiscite [*pleb* · ih · site] *n.* vote, election, ballot, referendum, choice.

pledge *n.* commitment, assurance, contract, promise, vow, deposit, bailment, pact, oath, guarantee. *Ant.* denial.

pledge *v.* guarantee, warrant, promise, assure, swear ("He pledged undying love to me").

plenary [*plen* · e · ree] *adj.* full, complete, entire, total, whole ("plenary jurisdiction").

plenipotentiary [plen · ih · poh · *ten* · shee · air · ee] *n.* agent, consul, delegate, emissary, spokesman, deputy, ambassador.

plight *n.* adversity, difficulty, trouble, problem, predicament, position ("The plight of the elderly").

plot *n.* field, land, area; plan, scheme, conspiracy, trick, deception; story, design, events, scene, scenario ("Agatha Christie's plots are fun to read").

plot *v.* design, prepare, plan, scheme, outline, conspire ("She plotted her actions very carefully").

plunder [*plun* · der] *v.* pillage, loot, seize, pilfer, ruin, steal ("plunder the abandoned house").

plunder [*plun* · der] *n.* loot, treasure, haul, spoils, booty ("The pirates' plunder was extensive").

plural [*ploo* · rel] *adj.* more than one, many, several, mass, multiple. *Ant.* singular, one.

plurality [ploo · *ral* · ih · tee] *n.* majority, preponderancy, bulk, multitude.

poaching [*poh* · ching] *v.* trespassing, encroaching, hunting illegally, intruding, plundering ("He was poaching on my land").

pocket veto [*pok* · et *vee* · toh] *n.* nullification, inaction, veto.

P

point *n.* detail, thought, part, subject ("She made her point quite clearly"); dividend, fee, charge ("The buyer did not have to pay the points on the house").

point *v.* aim, direct, lead, guide, head ("Joe's dog pointed him in the right direction").

poison [*poy* · zen] *n.* venom, contagion, harm, contaminant, toxicant ("She unknowingly drank the poison").

poison [*poy* · zen] *v.* contaminate, pollute, destroy, infect.

police [po · *leess*] *n.* officer, detective, cop, law enforcement authority.

police [po · *leess*] *v.* guard, patrol, watch, secure, oversee ("We depend on others to police our property").

policy [*pol* · ih · see] *n.* guidelines, goals, system, custom, plan, form ("public policy"); insurance; lottery, gambling, numbers.

politic [*pol* · ih · tik] *adj.* clever, artful, shrewd, calculating, continued; prudent, thoughtful, cautious, sagacious.

political [po · *lit* · ih · kul] *adj.* civic, official, governmental, partisan.

poll *n.* list, register, census, figures, returns, questionnaire, referendum, vote, count.

poll *v.* ask, question, inquire, tabulate, count.

pollute [po · *loot*] *v.* contaminate, adulterate, defile, tarnish, violate, taint, poison, stain.

pollution [po · *loo* · shen] *n.* poisoning, violation, corruption, deterioration. *Ant.* purification, cleanliness.

polyandry [*pol* · ee · an · dree] *n.* polygamy, plurality, bigamy. *Ant.* monogamy.

polygraph [*pol* · ee · graf] *n.* examination, inspection, lie detector machine.

ponder [*pon* · der] *v.* consider, cogitate, weigh, reason, mull over, evaluate, digest.

pool *n.* combination, agreement, monopoly, union, coalition ("Honest trade prevents illegal pools"); purse, reserve, jackpot ("the betting pool totaled $100").

pool *v.* unite, merge, blend, unify, ally ("Let's pool our resources").

poor *adj.* destitute, indigent, insolvent, bankrupt; inadequate, inferior, dismal, pitiful, paltry, defective, low quality.

popular [*pop* · yoo · ler] *adj.* familiar, common, standard, ordinary, public, prevailing, fashionable, current, general, well-known, favorite, likeable, lovable, prominent. *Ant.* unconventional; personal.

pornographic [por · noh · *graf* · ik] *adj.* graphic, carnal, lascivious, obscene, lewd, off-color. *Ant.* pure, innocent.

pornography [por · *nog* · re · fee] *n.* debauchery, lust, graphic portrayal, erotica, smut, indecency, obscenity, vulgarity.

port *n.* harbor, dock, landing, boatyard, dockyard.

portend [por · *tend*] *v.* forecast, predict, forewarn, herald, indicate, augur, announce.

portfolio [port · *foh* · lee · oh] *n.* investment, securities, funds, bonds ("I wish my portfolio was more diverse"); case, folder, briefcase ("the artist's portfolio").

portray [por · *tray*] *v.* characterize, represent, reproduce, depict, convey, picture.

position [po · *sih* · shun] *n.* outlook, attitude, posture, bias, predilection ("his position on new taxes"); circumstance, plight, state, predicament ("in a difficult position"); job, duty, occupation, role, work, career ("the position of district attorney").

positive [*paw* · zi · tiv] *adj.* definite, absolute, conclusive, certain ("She was positive about his guilt"); ordained, adopted, decreed, prescribed, legislated ("This law is positive, effective tomorrow"); happy, optimistic ("What a positive person!").

P

possess [poh · *zess*] *v.* occupy, acquire, gain, retain, obtain ("He wants to possess my land").

possessed [poh · *zest*] *v.* demented, deranged, overtaken, crazed, obsessed, mad ("Mary thought he was possessed").

possession [poh · *zesh* · en] *n.* dominion, proprietorship, ownership, holding, guardianship, keeping ("I have possession of my family's land"); goods, assets, valuables, belongings ("The thief had my possessions").

possessor [poh · *zess* · er] *n.* occupier, tenant, resident, dweller. *Ant.* nonresident.

possibility [poss · ih · *bil* · ih · tee] *n.* potential, hope, expectation, contingency, prospect, likelihood. *Ant.* certainty.

possible [*poss* · ih · bul] *adj.* thinkable, plausible, viable, conceivable, believable, achievable.

post *v.* publish, announce, broadcast, report ("The school posts job offers"); advise, inform, brief, clue, notify ("The lookout will post us on strangers approaching").

post *n.* camp, base, headquarters, lookout, position ("His post was at the front door"); support, column, doorpost, stake, brace ("The post under our treehouse fell down").

posterity [*pawss* · terr · ih · tee] *n.* future, family, heirs, breed, lineage, successors, succeeding generations.

posthumous [*poss* · choo · muss] *adj.* after death, delayed, late, post-orbit ("His book was posthumously published"). *Ant.* contemporary, present.

postpone [post · *pone*] *v.* delay, defer, interrupt, wait, hesitate, suspend, shelve, reserve ("I wanted to postpone the meeting"); subordinate, downgrade ("The payback was postponed until the first debt was paid").

postponement [post · *pone* · ment] *n.* delay, continuance, interruption, abeyance, stay, subordination.

potential [po · *ten* · shul] *adj.* anticipated, expected, possible, probable, apparent, imminent ("potential interest").

potential [po · *ten* · shel] *n.* capacity, potentiality, expectation, gift ("This woman's potential for excellence was obvious"). *Ant.* deficiency, lack.

poverty [*pov* · ur · tee] *n.* indigence, need, destitution, impoverishment, scarcity, lack.

power [*pow* · er] *n.* authority, potency, competency, potential, strength, might, force, endowment, brawn, muscle. *Ant.* incompetency, weakness.

powwow *n.* meeting, discussion, conference, get-together.

practice [*prak* · tiss] *n.* manner, method, rule, system, way, routine ("Night court was a general practice for Talbot City"); exercise, application, action, homework, training ("He needed more practice to be an expert in karate"); calling, business, vocation, employment, discipline, conduct ("practice of law").

practice [*prak* · tiss] *v.* repeat, exercise, polish, hone ("practice his skills"); undertake, execute, perform, pursue ("We practice abstinence").

practitioner [prak · *tish* · e · ner] *n.* worker, doer, performer, craftsperson, employer, laborer ("She was a practitioner of the law").

pragmatic [prag · *mat* · ik] *adj.* reasonable, utilitarian, useful, practical ("a pragmatic solution").

prayer [*pray* · er] *n.* petition, plea, motion, beseechment, appeal ("prayer for relief"); devotion, benediction, worship, adoration, thanksgiving ("prayer to God").

P

preamble [*pree* · am · bul] *n.* preface, introduction, opening, prologue ("preamble to the state constitution").

precarious [pre · *kare* · ee · us] *adj.* uncertain, unstable, insecure, dangerous, revocable ("precarious situation").

precatory [*prek* · uh · tore · ee] *adj.* suggestive, pleading, appealing, beseeching, imploring, wishing, prayerful, asking ("precatory language"). *Ant.* ordering.

precedence [*press* · e · dense] *n.* priority, seniority, preference, lead, advantage.

precedent [*press* · e · dent] *n.* guide, model, standard, foundation ("*Roe v. Wade* is a precedent in abortion law").

precedent [pre · *see* · dent] *adj.* prior, earlier, previous, preexistent ("A precedent condition to getting a credit card is having good credit").

precept [*pree* · sept] *n.* warrant, writ, order ("Sheriff Gomez ordered a precept"); code, rule, principle, doctrine, axiom, action ("One of the precepts in court is respectful behavior").

precinct [*pree* · sinkt] *n.* ward, section, province, parish, area, community, district.

precise [pre · *sise*] *adj* exact, accurate, literal, distinct, unerring, express, truthful.

preclusion [pree · *kloo* · zhen] *n.* prevention, ban, forbidding, constrainment. *Ant.* facilitation.

precognition [pree · kog · *nish* · en] *n.* examination, deposition, discovery; clairvoyance, foresight.

predatory [*pred* · e · tore · ee] *adj.* predative, preying, ravaging, thieving, hunting ("predatory animal").

predecessor [*pred* · e · sess · er] *n.* ancestor, forebear, forerunner, previous, prototype ("Seaboard Coastline is the predecessor of CSX Transportation").

predicament [pre · *dik* · a · mint] *n.* situation, circumstance, position, state, difficulty, crisis.

predict [pre · *dikt*] *v.* forecast, portend, envision, foresee, promise, bode, prognosticate.

predilection [*pred* · ih · lek · shun] *n.* penchant, leaning, proclivity, tendency, liking, proneness, partiality, bent, bias.

predisposition [pree · dis · pe · *zish* · en] *n.* willingness, inclination, proclivity, bias, leaning, proneness, tendency.

preempt [pree · *empt*] *v.* assume, capture, occupy, preclude, usurp.

preemption [pree · *emp* · shen] *n.* appropriation, substitution, usurpation, replacement, annexation ("preemption doctrine").

prefer [pree · *fer*] *v.* like, choose, fancy, pick, espouse, advance, elevate, favor.

preference [*pref* · e · rense] *n.* partiality, election, advantage; priority, prejudice, promotion, upgrading, precedence. *Ant.* even-handedness, equality.

preferential [pref · e · *ren* · shel] *adj.* favored, select, better, special, privileged, choice, first-rate ("preferential treatment"). *Ant.* inferior.

preferred [pre · *ferd*] *adj.* favorite, chosen, elected, picked, singled-out ("a preferred creditor").

prejudge [*pre* · judj] *v.* predetermine, presuppose, assume, presume, jump to a conclusion.

prejudice [*prej* · e · diss] *v.* bias, sway, influence, predispose, spoil ("He tried to prejudice the jury"); injure, impair, harm, hurt, weaken, damage, destroy ("That admission really prejudiced his case").

prejudicial [prej · e · *dish* · el] *adj.* harmful, bigoted, bad, damaging, hurtful; reversible ("prejudicial error"). *Ant.* beneficial.

preliminary [pre · *lim* · ih · ner · ee] *adj.* preceding, initial, beginning, previous ("preliminary investigation").

premeditate [pree · *med* · ih · tayt] *v.* prearrange, think out, scheme, plan, intend, contrive.

premeditated [pree · *med* · ih · tay · ted] *adj.* advised, careful, planned, contemplated, calculated, deliberate, intentional, malicious ("premeditated murder"). *Ant.* spontaneous, thoughtless.

premeditation [pree · med · ih · *tay* · shen] *n.* forethought, care, deliberation, malice, consideration ("A crime of passion usually isn't one of premeditation"). *Ant.* spontaneity.

premise [*prem* · iss] *n.* statement, belief, proposition, assumption, assertion.

premises [*prem* · iss · ez] *n.* grounds, property, dwelling, boundaries ("Protesters were dragged off the premises").

premium [*pree* · mee · yum] *n.* reward, gift, compensation; consideration, payment ("The premium on the car insurance is due").

premium [*pree* · mee · yum] *adj.* popular, scarce, choice, excellent ("premium bond").

preparation [prep · uh · *ray* · shun] *n.* groundwork, readiness, readying, planning, provision, preliminary work.

preponderance [pre · *pon* · dur · ants] *n.* majority, dominance, prevalence, plurality.

prerequisite [pree · *rek* · wiz · it] *adj.* precondition, requirement, necessity, essential, condition, must, qualification.

prerogative [pre · *rog* · e · tiv] *n.* right, privilege, option, advantage, choice.

prescribe [pre · *skribe*] *v.* appoint, assign, choose, define, ordain, dictate.

prescription [pre · *skrip* · shen] *n.* claim, interest, right, license, permit, convention, custom, usage; charge, command, ordinance, rule.

prescriptive [pre · *skrip* · tiv] *adj.* customary, settled, fixed, time-honored, accepted, recognized, traditional.

presence [*prez* · ense] *n.* being, occupancy, existence, attendance ("His presence gave me the chills"); appearance, demeanor, aura, air, behavior ("Her stately presence was intimidating"); closeness, nearness, proximity, vicinity ("The pit bull's presence was too close for comfort").

present [*prez* · ent] *n.* gift, gratuity, endowment, donation; existing time, here-and-now.

present [pre · *zent*] *v.* introduce, demonstrate, acquaint, submit ("The man presented his argument to me"); give, award, bestow, confer ("present the award"); accuse, incriminate, charge, cite ("present the indictment").

present [*prez* · ent] *adj.* current, existing, contemporary, immediate, recent ("present danger"); in view, in attendance.

presented [pre · *zent* · ed] *v.* submitted, given, done, accomplished ("I've presented my point of view").

presenter [pre · *zen* · ter] *n.* demonstrator, giver, donor, communicator, submittor.

presentment [pre · *zent* · ment] *n.* accusation, presentation, production ("The grand jury gave a presentment to the defendant").

presents [*prez* · ents] *n.* instrument, document ("Know all men by these presents").

preservation [prez · er · *vay* · shun] *n.* care, perpetuation, upkeep, protection, defense, guarding, saving, maintenance, shielding, conservation.

P

preserve [pre · *zerv*] *v.* conserve, secure, nourish, maintain, aid, keep, uphold.

preside [pree · *zide*] *v.* direct, control, oversee, chair, supervise, manage. *Ant.* follow.

president [*prez* · ih · dent] *n.* chief, officer, head, director, official, title.

press *n.* media, journalists, reporters, correspondents, news writers.

pressure [*preh* · shur] *v.* compel, coerce, force, prod, plead, coax, cajole, beseech, push, solicit.

pressure [*preh* · shur] *n.* tension, anxiety, intensity; need, obligation, crisis, urgency.

presume [pree · *zoom*] *v.* assume, suppose, deduce, infer, believe ("We presumed that the innocent-looking young woman was the victim"); encroach, infringe, intrude, impose ("Because I was friendly to him, he presumed to touch me").

presumption [pree · *zump* · shen] *n.* inference, probability, deduction, assumption, supposition; boldness, aggressiveness.

presumptive [pree · *zump* · tiv] *adj.* inferred, assumed, apparent, likely, presumed, conjectured, probable ("presumptive evidence"). *Ant.* unassumed.

pretend [pree · *tend*] *v.* affect, assume, fake, mislead, purport, imagine, feign, misrepresent.

pretext [*pree* · tekts] *n.* claim, purpose, lie, justification, obfuscation, false motive, pretense, excuse, evasion, misrepresentation, fraud ("The policy was a pretext for discrimination").

prevail [pree · *vale*] *v.* dominate, overcome, beat, succeed, persist; govern, control, exist, abound; persuade, inspire, motivate, woo, lure.

prevailing [pree · *vay* · ling] *adj.* overcoming, victorious, winning, dominant ("prevailing argument"); universal, majority, popular, fashionable, widespread, current ("prevailing opinion").

prevalent [*prev* · uh · lent] *adj.* accepted, accustomed, general, ordinary, customary, pandemic, prevailing.

prevent [pree · *vent*] *v.* stop, avert, arrest, restrain, ward off, deter, halt, limit, restrict.

preventive [pree · *ven* · tiv] *adj.* precautionary, watchful, deterrent, restrictive, protective ("preventive measures").

price *n.* consideration, value, compensation, fare, bill ("The price of the course is reasonable"); consequence, sacrifice, toll, penalty ("Sometimes freedom carries a high price").

prima facie *adj.* adequate, satisfactory, legally sufficient; seemingly, ostensibly, presumable, on its face, apparently.

primary [*pry* · mer · ee] *adj.* best, principal, excellent, world-class ("His primary motive was love"); original, first, initial, earliest ("Her primary step in bettering herself was enrolling in school").

prime *adj.* major, first, primary ("prime suspect in the case"); best, choice, highest, mature, peak ("a prime cut").

prime *n.* height, maturity, peak ("in his prime").

prime *v.* educate, teach, brief, guide ("prime the witness").

primogeniture [pree · moh · *jen* · e · cher] *n.* priority, firstborn, superior, heir, inheritance.

primordial [prih · *mor* · dee · ul] *adj.* basic, elementary, fundamental, primeval, aboriginal, rudimentary.

principal [*prin* · sih · pul] *n.* investment, debt, assets, capital ("principal borrowed from Donald was $1,000"); administrator, chief, boss, director ("school principal"); party, accomplice, accessory, actor ("principals in the crime").

principal [*prin* · sih · pul] *adj.* chief, prime, first, strongest, key ("the principal contractor").

principle [*prin* · sih · pul] *n.* law, truth, standard, doctrine, axiom, rule ("Due process is a fundamental principle of American constitutional law").

prior [*pry* · er] *adj.* preceding, earlier, previous, former, past ("Her prior criminal record was complicated"); primary, predominant, superior ("Mary's prior debts come before her new car debt").

priority [pry · *aw* · rih · tee] *n.* lead, order, superiority, primacy, preference, precedence, right, seniority, rank.

prison [*priz* · en] *n.* penitentiary, confinement, jail, house of detention, reformatory, guardhouse, pen, cell, facility.

prisoner [*priz* · en · er] *n.* convict, jailbird, detainee, felon, captive, wrongdoer, inmate, hostage.

privacy [*pry* · ve · see] *n.* confidentiality, noninfringement, secrecy, solitude, concealment.

private [*pry* · vet] *n.* GI, infantry, soldier, enlisted person.

private [*pry* · vet] *adj.* personal, subjective, privileged, confidential ("private information"); hidden, exclusive, restricted, discreet, concealed ("private getaway").
Ant. open; nonexclusive.

privilege [*priv* · ih · lej] *n.* right, due, allowance, advantage, immunity; liberty, license, entitlement, power, authorization.

privileged [*priv* · ih · lejd] *adj.* protected, excused, immune, exempt, elite ("a privileged class"); confidential, secret, exceptional, top-secret ("privileged records").

privity [*priv* · ih · tee] *n.* connection, relationship, link, tie, closeness ("privity of contract").

privy [*priv* · ee] *adj.* secret, buried, concealed, confidential ("privy council").

prize *n.* reward, winnings, premium, purse.

prize *v.* value, esteem, treasure, revere.

probability [prob · e · *bil* · ih · tee] *n.* likelihood, chance, conceivability, prospect, odds, outlook, possibility, promise.

probable [*prob* · e · bul] *adj.* likely, apparent, expected, credible, conceivable, reasonable.
Ant. implausible, unexpected.

probate [*proh* · bayt] *v.* validate, authenticate, certify, establish, substantiate ("The court must probate this will").

probate [*proh* · bayt] *n.* validation, adjudication, verification, confirmation.

probation [pro · *bay* · shen] *n.* conditional release, test period, trial period, parole, furlough, exemption.

probative [*pro* · be · tiv] *adj.* evidentiary, demonstrative, probatory, empirical, contributing ("probative evidence").

problem [*prob* · lum] *n.* concern, difficulty, trouble, obstacle, case, dilemma, enigma, quandary.

procedural [pro · *seed* · jer · el] *adj.* methodical, administrative, technical, mechanical.
Ant. substantive.

procedure [pro · *seed* · jer] *n.* process, system, method, policy, routine, action, operation ("federal rules of civil procedure").

P

proceeding [pro · *seed* · ing] *n.* undertaking, course, happening ("The divorce proceeding took longer than I thought"); records, minutes, report, account, transactions ("The proceedings from GALA are kept in a file").

proceeds [pro · seedz] *n.* earnings, gains, profit, results, revenue.

process [*pross* · ess] *n.* method, sequence, procedure, proceeding, routine, strategy ("The legal process can be complicated"); subpoena, writ, citation, command.

process [*pross* · ess] *v.* alter, dispose, fulfill, handle, complete, prepare ("I will process the paperwork").

proclamation [prok · le · *may* · shen] *n.* broadcast, announcement, decree, notification, publication, declaration ("A proclamation went out to all the world").

procrastinate [pro · *krass* · tih · nayt] *v.* prolong, tarry, neglect, dally, dawdle, be neglectful, be dilatory, loaf, hesitate.

proctor [*prok* · ter] *n.* supervisor, proxy, delegate, monitor, representative, advocate, agent, vicar.

proctor [*prok* · ter] *v.* oversee, administer, direct.

procure [pro · *kyoor*] *v.* instigate, effect, induce, initiate, pander, pimp; acquire, obtain, get, purchase.

procurement [pro · *kyoor* · ment] *n.* acquisition, buying, appropriation, gaining.

procurer [pro · *kyoor* · er] *n.* panderer, pimp, parasite ("A prostitute sometimes uses a procurer").

prod *v.* encourage, incite, push, induce, goad, urge, entice.

prodigal [*prod* · ih · gul] *adj.* extravagant, careless, squandering, wasteful, thriftless, lavish, improvident, profligate.

produce [*pro* · dewss] *n.* crop, harvest, yield, emblements, staples, fruit, vegetables.

produce [pro · *dewss*] *v.* exhibit, disclose, present, show ("produce witnesses"); concoct, create, build, manufacture, construct, materialize ("He produced great diagrams").

product [*prod* · ukt] *n.* result, item, article, merchandise; handiwork, outcome, accomplishment, returns.

production [pro · *duk* · shen] *n.* creation, construction, preparation, formation, execution; performance, presentation, spectacle, parade, extravaganza.

profanity [pro · *fan* · ih · tee] *n.* desecration, immorality, cursing, blasphemy, irreverence, vituperation, vulgarity.

profession [pro · *fesh* · en] *n.* trade, avocation, business, career, occupation ("profession of medicine"); declaration, assertion, claim, allegation, testimony ("profession of faith").

professional [pro · *fesh* · en · el] *n.* specialist, authority, pro, superstar, practitioner, expert, master.

professional [pro · *fesh* · en · el] *adj.* skilled, trained, unique, specialized, ethical, learned, adept.

proffer [*prof* · er] *v.* offer, bid, tender, suggest, adduce, advance, submit, propose ("He proffered proof of his heritage").

proficient [pro · *fish* · int] *adj.* capable, skilled, able, accomplished, competent, qualified, trained, talented, experienced ("a proficient trial attorney").

profit [*prof* · it] *v.* gain, capitalize, benefit, realize ("to profit from mistakes"). *Ant.* lose.

profit [*prof* · it] *n.* accumulation, acquisition, proceeds, gain, earnings ("the profit from the sale"). *Ant.* loss.

P

profitable [*prof* · it · e · bul] *adj.* money-making, fruitful, viable, valuable, advantageous, remunerative, paying, lucrative, worthwhile, favorable.

profiteering [prof · ih · *teer* · ing] *n.* graft, manipulation, racketeering ("Some oil companies have been guilty of profiteering").

profligate [*prof* · lih · git] *adj.* corrupt, evil, wicked, depraved, immoral, base, nefarious, vile, foul.

profound [pro · *fownd*] *adj.* deep, perceptive, philosophical, erudite, learned, thoughtful, astute, sagacious.

progeny [*proj* · e · nee] *n.* children, descendants, offspring, lineage, family.

prognosis [prog · *no* · sis] *n.* forecast, estimate, outlook, conjecture, guess, belief, presumption.

program [*pro* · gram] *n.* plan, outline, schedule, system, agenda, strategy, curriculum ("the program for the evening"); software, design, code ("a computer program").

program [*pro* · gram] *v.* arrange, schedule, docket, direct, design, outline, organize.

progress [*prog* · ress] *n.* development, achievement, growth, success, improvement, movement, betterment.

progress [pro · *gress*] *v.* move, press on, advance, climb, forge ahead, make headway, proceed.

progressive [pro · *gress* · iv] *adj.* liberal, forward-thinking, advanced, corrective, modern.

prohibit [pro · *hib* · it] *v.* prevent, forbid, restrain, constrain, inhibit ("intended to prohibit certain behavior").

prohibited [pro · *hib* · ih · ted] *adj.* forbidden, banned, barred, illegal, taboo ("Incest is prohibited behavior").

prohibition [pro · hi · *bish* · en] *n.* prevention, suppression, outlawing, ban, barrier. *Ant.* legalization.

project [*proj* · ekt] *n.* task, undertaking, pursuit, venture, deal, assignment.

project [pro · *jekt*] *v.* extend, protrude, jut, stick out; propel, thrust, eject, emit, impel; forecast, guess, estimate.

prolix [pro · *lix*] *adj.* boring, protracted, tedious, wordy, rambling, discursive, verbose.

promiscuous [pro · *miss* · kyoo · us] *adj.* immodest, carnal, wild, unchaste, free, casual, indiscriminate.

promise [*prom* · iss] *v.* affirm, warrant, bargain, swear, vow, pledge, covenant, vouch ("I promise I will do this for you").

promise [*prom* · iss] *n.* oath, declaration, affirmation, vow, pledge, assurance, endorsement, covenant, hope, warrant ("I have her promise of loyalty").

promote [pro · *mote*] *v.* support, endorse, advertise, aid, advocate, foster.

promoter [pro · *mote* · er] *n.* organizer, incorporator, planner; backer, patron, sponsor, advancer, supporter.

prompt *adj.* punctual, expeditious, timely, speedy, immediate ("prompt service"). *Ant.* slow, late, delayed.

P

prompt *v.* advise, cue, evoke, help, guide ("He prompted me on my lines").

promptly [*prompt* · lee] *adv.* punctually, expeditiously, timely, fast, rapidly.

promulgate [*pro* · mul · gayt] *v.* publish, announce, proclaim, broadcast, circulate, communicate ("The Labor Department will promulgate a regulation on this subject shortly").

promulgation [pro · mul · *gay* · shen] *n.* declaration, rule, proclamation, announcement, communication, decision, mandate.

prone *adj.* apt, inclined, partial, tending, disposed, compliant, willing; flat, horizontal.

pronounce [pro · *nownss*] *v.* pass, rule, decide, declare, announce, articulate, judge ("the judge will pronounce sentence on him"); speak, say, articulate, recite, deliver ("pronounce the word correctly").

proof *n.* establishment, certification, confirmation, evidence, authentication, verification, assurance ("Mario has proof of the crime").

propensity [pro · *pen* · sih · tee] *n.* inclination, tendency, flair, leaning, penchant, proclivity.

proper [*prop* · er] *adj.* appropriate, fitting, suitable, correct ("proper attire"); right, valid, dignified, respectable, formal ("He is a proper person"). *Ant.* inappropriate.

property [*prop* · er · tee] *n.* possessions, investments, holdings, capital ("his property at death"); characteristic, quality, attribute, trait ("a property of water"); land, real estate, realty, territory, acreage ("a beautiful piece of property").

prophylactic [pro · fil · *ak* · tik] *adj.* preventive, protective, salutary ("a prophylactic measure").

propinquity [pro · *ping* · kwih · tee] *n.* affiliation, kinship, relationship, connection, consanguinity; closeness, nearness, juxtaposition.

proponent [pro · *pone* · ent] *n.* advocate, backer, champion, supporter, defender, friend.

proportion [pro · *pore* · shen] *n.* apportionment, measure, share, balance, relationship.

proposal [pro · *poze* · el] *n.* offer, suggestion, idea, motion, outline, report, analysis, commentary.

proposition [prop · e · *zish* · en] *n.* suggestion, scheme, invitation, plan, tender; theory, premise, assumption.

propound [pro · *pownd*] *v.* propose, offer, advance, explain, declaim.

proprietary [pro · *pry* · e · ter · ee] *adj.* exclusive, private, landed, restrictive.

proprietor [pro · *pry* · e · ter] *n.* owner, holder, possessor, manager, keeper, administrator.

prorate [*pro* · rate] *v.* divide, shave, assess, distribute, allocate ("The property taxes will be prorated").

proscribed [pro · *skribd*] *adj.* forbidden, prohibited, censured, denounced, excluded ("The proscribed behavior is clearly specified"). *Ant.* welcome, allowed.

prosecute [*pross* · e · kyoot] *v.* indict, litigate, sue, arraign ("She will prosecute this case"); persevere, conduct, direct, execute, manage ("Leslie understands it's up to her to prosecute her own interests").

prosecution [pross · e · *kyoo* · shen] *n.* litigation, trial, suit, proceedings, action; district attorney, state's attorney, government, state, people.

prosecutor [*pross* · e · kyoo · ter] *n.* public officer, district attorney, prosecuting attorney.

prospect [*pros* · pekt] *n.* outlook, forecast, chance, likelihood ("the prospects for success"); recruit, candidate, client ("a highly regarded prospect").

prospective [pro · *spek* · tiv] *adj.* anticipated, potential, expected, future, intended ("a prospective client").

prospectus [pro · *spek* · tus] *n.* details, design, list, program, synopsis, statement, résumé ("CSX's prospectus is impressive").

prostitute [*pross* · tih · toot] *n.* whore, hooker, harlot, tart, call girl.

prostitute [*pross* · tih · toot] *v.* degrade, belittle, demean, taint, desecrate.

protagonist [pro · *tag* · uh · nist] *n.* hero, principal character, leading agent.

protect [pro · *tekt*] *v.* secure, look after, take care of, preserve, safeguard, shield, conserve, immunize, support, guard.

protection [pro · *tek* · shun] *n.* custody, preservation, support, cover ("I needed his protection"); money, bribe, racketeering ("Vera demanded protection from the shop owner if he didn't want the windows broken").

protective [pro · *tek* · tiv] *adj.* guarding, securing, careful, safeguarding, watchful ("protective custody").

protest [*pro* · test] *n.* objection, resistance, revolt, demonstration, exception, defiance.

protest [pro · *test*] *v.* dissent, oppose, complain, object, challenge, dispute; affirm, assert, proclaim.

prothonotary [pro · *thon* · noh · ter · ee] *n.* clerk, official, officer ("Jim was a prothonotary of Cobb County Court").

protocol [*pro* · tuh · koll] *n.* agreement, code, compact; custom, decorum, etiquette, courtesy.

provable [*proov* · uh · bul] *adj.* incontestable, confirmable, indisputable, verifiable ("a provable claim").

prove *v.* establish, affirm, ascertain, attest, certify.

proven [*proo* · ven] *adj.* authentic, certified, established, settled, tested ("The test has been proven to be accurate").

proverbial [pro · *verb* · ee · el] *adj.* well-known, familiar, commonplace, legendary, traditional.

provide [pro · *vide*] *v.* supply, deliver, furnish, equip, feed, stock, sustain ("provide materials"); plan, prepare, organize, ready ("provide for their arrival").

provident [*prov* · ih · dent] *adj.* frugal, careful, prudent, thrifty; circumspect, discerning, thoughtful, vigilant.

province [*prov* · inss] *n.* district, county, division, zone, subdivision ("Nova Scotia is a province of Canada"); duty, function, expertise, authority, responsibility ("Surgery is not within the province of a psychologist").

provincial [pro · *vinch* · ul] *adj.* narrow, limited, illiberal, insular, parochial.

provision [pro · *vizh* · en] *n.* supplies, arrangement, foundation, stockpile ("He had provisions set up for the flood"); condition, clause, term, article, qualification ("per the provision in the will").

provisional [pro · *vizh* · en · el] *adj.* contingent, tentative, conditional, limited ("the provisional government").

proviso [pro · *vy* · zoh] *n.* clause, provision, condition, stipulation.

provocation [prov · e · *kay* · shen] *n.* incitement, stimulus, prompt, instigation, agitation, enragement, causation, incentive ("His provocation started the fight").

provocative [pro · *vok* · a · tiv] *adj.* alluring, titillating, arresting, ravishing, seductive, exciting; interesting, intriguing, influential, persuasive, thought-provoking.

provoke [pro · *voke*] *v.* incite, arouse, cause, prompt, goad, force ("Mike provoked the attack"). *Ant.* stop, block; calm.

proximate [*prok* · sih · met] *adj.* near, nearest, close, immediate, expected, following, connected. *Ant.* remote, distant.

P

proxy [*prox* · ee] *n.* representative, delegate, emissary, agent, broker ("Joe was my proxy at the meeting"); authorization, power ("I gave her my proxy").

prudence [*proo* · dens] *n.* precaution, planning, diligence, wisdom. *Ant.* sloppiness, negligence.

prudent [*proo* · dent] *adj.* sensible, cautious, reasonable, careful, sound, guarded. *Ant.* careless, reckless.

prurient [*proo* · ree · ent] erotic, sexual, obscene, lewd, vulgar, carnal, ribald, lustful ("an appeal to prurient interests").

psychosis [sy · *koh* · sis] *n.* mental disorder, illness, disease, insanity.

public [*pub* · lik] *n.* people, community, citizenry.

public [*pub* · lik] *adj.* unrestricted, accessible, common, communal, available, national ("U.S. parks are public areas").

publication [pub · lih · *kay* · shen] *n.* presentation, circulation, publishing, announcement; disclosure, discovery, notification, revelation ("publication in the newspaper").

publish [*pub* · lish] *v.* issue, distribute, disseminate, circulate; communicate, announce, advertise, spread ("publish an opinion"). *Ant.* suppress.

puffing [*puf* · ing] *v.* exaggerating, augmenting, boosting, hyping, pushing.

punishable [*pun* · ish · e · bul] *adj.* indictable, chargeable, impeachable, culpable ("Her crime was punishable").

punishment [*pun* · ish · ment] *n.* fine, penalty, chastisement, sentence, correction, infliction.

punitive [*pyoon* · ih · tiv] *adj.* correctional, disciplinary, punishing, avenging, retributive ("Strong punitive measures will be sought").

purchase [*per* · ches] *n.* acquisition, procurement, investment, property ("My purchase was a valuable piece of art").

pure *adj.* untainted, unadulterated, unquestionable, definite, clean, fresh, honest, uncontaminated ("pure water").

purge *v.* free, abolish, clarify, dismiss ("purge of guilt"); cleanse, excrete, unload, rid ("He purged the poison from his system").

purport [*per* · port] *n.* meaning, intention, significance, bearing, rationale ("purport of the lease").

purport [per · *port*] *v.* claim, allege, pretend, pose ("He purports to be an expert").

purpose [*per* · pes] *n.* plan, intent, target, vision, goal, aim, objective ("The purpose of the course was education"); determination, will, persistence, tenacity ("She has a strong purpose in life").

purposely [*per* · pes · lee] *adv.* intentionally, knowingly, willfully, deliberately.

purpresture [per · *pres* · cher] *n.* obstruction, encroachment.

purse *n.* prize, kitty, gift, award, reward, contest ("The race's purse was substantial"); handbag, tote, bag, carry-all ("The thief snatched her purse").

purser [*per* · ser] *n.* officer, bursar.

pursue [per · *soo*] *v.* track, follow, search, trail ("pursue the criminal"); strive, aspire, work, struggle ("pursue success").

pursuit [per · *soot*] *n.* quest, chase, campaign, struggle ("pursuit of happiness").

purview [*per* · vyoo] *n.* boundary, limit, jurisdiction, design, scope, range ("Interrogatories have to stay within a certain purview").

P

pusillanimous [pew · sil · *an* · ih · mus] *adj.* cowardly, dastardly, craven, recreant, poltroonish.

put *v.* place, deposit, position, establish.

putative [*pyoo* · te · tiv] *adj.* accepted, assumed, presumed, acknowledged, recognized ("putative father").

P

quack *n.* phony, incompetent, pretender, faker, sham, con man ("The doctor was a quack").

qualification [kwah · lih · fih · *kay* · shen] *n.* standard, requisite, eligibility, ability, competence, capacity ("qualification to be president"); limitation, caveat, condition, restriction, stipulation, exception ("estate with a qualification").

qualified [*kwah* · lih · fide] *adj.* eligible, capable, worthy, proper, certified, knowledgeable ("qualified voter"); reserved, defined, narrowed, temporary ("qualified right of remitter"). *Ant.* unqualified; absolute.

qualify [*kwah* · lih · fie] *v.* authorize, certify, accredit, permit, prepare; restrict, limit, confine, control.

qualifying [*kwah* · lih · fie · ing] *adj.* limiting, extenuating, conditional.

quality [*kwal* · ih · tee] *n.* excellence, superiority, merit, ability, value, worth ("a person of quality"); attribute, characteristic, trait, feature ("She has an unusual quality"); nature, condition, endowment ("inferior quality of the material").

quandary [*kwan* · duh · ree] *n.* dilemma, predicament, difficult situation, plight, problem, quagmire.

quantity [*kwan* · tih · tee] *n.* amount, number, totality, multitude, aggregate.

quarantine [*kwar* · en · teen] *n.* sequestration, confinement, seclusion, cordon, detachment, separation, division *Ant.* release.

quarter [*kwor* · ter] *n.* division, farthing, fourth, semester, part, portion ("quarter of an hour"); zone, district, locality, point, precinct ("What quarter of town?"); clemency, favor, grace, leniency, mercy, pity ("to give quarter").

quarter [*kwor* · ter] *v.* accommodate, board, billet, shelter, domiciliate, canton ("to quarter the soldiers"); cleave, cut, dismember, cut up ("draw and quarter").

quash *v.* suppress, abate, void, annul ("a motion to quash the indictment"). *Ant.* sanction.

quasi [*kway* · zye or *kwah* · zee] *adj.* apparent, semi, near, virtual, partly nominal, resembling ("quasi-judicial").

quell *v.* crush, suppress, subdue, stifle, quash. *Ant.* foment.

query [*kweer* · ee] *n.* concern, doubt, dubiety, skepticism, problem, uncertainty ("a query as to how the funds were spent").

query [*kweer* · ee] *v.* ask, cross-examine, audit, search, investigate, impugn, challenge ("to query the witness's trustworthiness").

Q

question [*kwes* · chen] *n.* point, proposal, theme, topic, hypothesis ("the question at hand"); query, inquiry, quiz, request, scrutiny ("answer the question"); doubt, controversy, uncertainty, misgiving, mystery, confusion, probability ("There was a question as to whether he told the truth").

question [*kwes* · chen] *v.* scrutinize, test, enquire, inquire, interrogate, petition, solicit ("to question the witness").

quick *adj.* fast, speedy, fleet, express ("a quick runner"); smart, adept, clever, competent, intelligent, perceptive, shrewd ("a quick study").

quiet [*kwy* · et] *adj.* collected, inactive, placid, sedate, sequestered, undisturbed ("to be quiet"); unmolested, pacific, tranquil, peaceful, untroubled ("quiet enjoyment"); low, muffled, reticent, taciturn, unspeaking, quiescent ("a quiet audience").

quiet [*kwy* · et] *v.* allay, mollify, squelch, pacify, make tranquil, calm.

quirk *n.* oddity, peculiarity, habit, eccentricity, mannerism.

quit *v.* leave, retreat, vacate, abandon, evacuate, withdraw ("He quit the lease"); cease, end, resign, secede, discontinue, desist ("He quit painting").

quittance [*kwit* · ense] *n.* release, leaving, departure.

quixotic [kwik · *zot* · ic] *adj.* visionary, fanciful, impractical, fantastic, chimerical. *Ant.* practical.

quota [*kwoh* · tuh] *n.* percentage, share, quotient, allocation, ration, parcel, proportion.

quotation [kwo · *tay* · shen] *n.* quote, repetition, excerpt, report, citation, extract, selection.

quote [kwote] *v.* cite, repeat, reiterate, reference, verify, restate, give word-for-word, adduce.

race *n.* ancestry, ethnic group, people, culture, parentage.

race *v.* hurry, dash, speed, sprint, tear, hustle, accelerate.

racism [*ray* · sizm] *n.* apartheid, bigotry, sectarianism, prejudice, bias.

racketeer [rak · e · *teer*] *n.* gangster, criminal, extortionist, miscreant, malefactor, pirate.

radical [*rad* · ih · kal] *adj.* extreme, total, whole, thorough ("Radical changes are needed"); militant, free-thinking, ultra-liberal, rebellious, uncompromising ("a radical idea").

raffle [*raf* · uhl] *n.* sweepstakes, drawing, lottery, disposition, wager, gaming.

raid *n.* attack, takeover, strike.

raid *v.* attack, pillage, plunder, assault, rape, take over.

railroad [*rail* · rode] *v.* push, goad, urge, intimidate, accelerate, speed, hasten, shove, press.

raise *v.* activate, prompt, launch, evoke, kindle, instigate ("raise a presumption"); accede, hike, augment, increment, add, jump ("raise her salary"); rear, bring up ("raise children").

ransom [*ran* · sem] *n.* liberation, redemption, emancipation, deliverance, expiation ("$100,000 ransom").

rape *v.* molest, sexually assault, debauch, defile, ravish ("The woman was raped"); raid, sack, loot, pillage, ravage, desecrate, maltreat ("rape the museum's holdings").

rape *n.* violation, assault, sexual assault, nonconsensual sex, defilement, seduction, abuse, defloration, despoilation.

rapport [ra · *por*] *n.* accord, agreement, relationship, harmony, understanding, empathy, connection, intimacy.

rare *adj.* uncommon, unique, precious, unusual, scarce, priceless, singular, noteworthy, special.

rasure [*ray* · zher] *n.* erasure, obliteration.

rate *v.* rank, appraise, quantify, prioritize, gauge ("rate the value of the house"); be accepted, be favorable, be worthy, deserve, merit, prosper ("to rate well").

rate *n.* cost, payment, tariff, rent, assessment, quotation ("rate of payment"); clip, dash, measure, spurt, velocity, pace ("rate of speed").

ratification [rat · ih · fih · *kay* · shen] *n.* endorsement, certification, sanction, vindication, confirmation, corroboration, approbation. *Ant.* repudiation.

R

ratify [*rat* · ih · fy] *v.* sanction, embrace, confirm, acquiesce, countersign, agree, affirm, authorize. *Ant.* repudiate.

ration [*ra* · shun] *n.* portion, allotment, part, share, quota, provision, dispensation.

rational [*rash* · en · el] *adj.* sensible, logical, cognitive, efficacious, pragmatic, common-sensical, reasonable.

rationale [rash · en · *aal*] *n.* reason, cause, basis, justification, excuse, philosophy, motive.

ravish [*rav* · ish] *v.* abuse, defile, force, rape, violate, outrage ("He ravished the woman"); allure, captivate, enthrall, mesmerize, please, overjoy ("He was ravished by the colorful lights").

reaction [re · *ak* · shun] *n.* response, rejoinder, reply; opposition, resistance, disagreement.

ready [*red* · ee] *adj.* prepared, completed, finished, available, primed, waiting.

reaffirm [re · uh · *firm*] *v.* repeat, restate, reiterate, accentuate, emphasize, insist.

real *adj.* authentic, genuine, substantive, demonstrable, intrinsic, perceptible. *Ant.* spurious, fake.

realize [*ree* · uh · lize] *v.* gain, earn, receive, make, acquire, obtain, win ("to realize a profit"); comprehend, perceive, fathom, discern, assimilate, grasp ("I realize my mistake").

realtor [*real* · ter] *n.* agent, broker.

realty [*real* · tee] *n.* property, real estate, land.

reapportionment [re · a · *por* · shen · ment] *n.* reallotment, reclassification, rearrangement, redistribution, equalization.

reason [*ree* · zen] *n.* insight, intelligence, comprehension, lucidity, perception ("to lose one's reason"); notion, motive, excuse ("For what reason?").

reason [*ree* · zen] *v.* discuss, deliberate, think, explain, cogitate, deduce ("reason with him").

reasonable [*ree* · zen · e · bul] *adj.* fair, moderate, just, equitable, pragmatic, conscientious ("a reasonable amount of money"); intelligent, practical, cerebral, logical, level-headed, tenable, ratiocinative ("a reasonable decision").

rebate [*ree* · bayt] *n.* abatement, discount, reimbursement, decrease, payback, kickback, reduction, refund, inducement.

rebellion [ree · *bell* · yen] *n.* apostasy, heresy, dissent, revolution, uprising, strike, revolt. *Ant.* submission.

rebuff [ree · *buf*] *v.* ignore, slight, scorn, reprove, spurn, jilt, dismiss, insult.

rebut [ree · *but*] *v.* deny, refute, contravene, rebuff, negate, dispute, contradict, retort, counterclaim, parry ("It is more difficult to rebut some presumptions than others"). *Ant.* substantiate.

rebuttable [ree · *but* · e · bul] *adj.* negatable, refutable, inconclusive.

rebuttal [ree · *but* · el] *n.* retort, contradiction, counterargument, invalidation, upset, overthrow. *Ant.* confirmation.

recall [*ree* · koll] *n.* repudiation, rescission, withdrawal, dismissal, veto, reversal ("recall of the governor"). *Ant.* reinstatement.

recall [ree · *koll*] *v.* remember, retrace, reminisce, recreate, evoke, place ("recall your wedding day"). *Ant.* forget.

recant [ree · *kant*] *v.* abjure, apostulate, disown, retract, disclaim, retract, abrogate ("He recanted his earlier testimony because it was untruthful").

recaption [ree · *kap* · shen] *n.* reprisal, repossession.

recapture [ree · *kap* · cher] *v.* restore, regain, repossess, countermand, rescue, liberate, recover, retake ("recapture the glory of the past").

receipt [ree · *seet*] *n.* admission, memo, slip, release, stub, proof of purchase ("Your receipt is in the bag with your purchase"); reception, acceptance, custody, acquisition, arrival ("in receipt of delivery"); cash flow, earnings, gain, revenue, returns, stream.

receivable [ree · *seev* · uh · bul] *adj.* due, owing, unpaid, outstanding, payable ("accounts receivable").

receive [ree · *seev*] *v.* get, obtain, secure, acquire, procure, realize ("receive the goods"); allow, permit, accept, welcome, tolerate ("receive into evidence").

receiver [ree · *seev* · er] *n.* trustee, supervisor, administrator, depository, overseer, manager, collector.

recess [*ree* · sess] *n.* cessation, closure, hiatus, pause, rest, interregnum, respite, intermission. *Ant.* continuation.

recess [re · *sess*] *v.* adjourn, pause, suspend, rest, stop, postpone, halt.

recidivist [re · *sid* · ih · vist] *n.* habitual criminal, repeat offender, repeat criminal, incorrigible criminal, hardened criminal, outlaw, convict, reprobate.

reciprocal [ree · *sip* · re · kel] *adj.* mutual, bilateral, interdependent, corresponding, analogous, correlative. *Ant.* independent.

reciprocity [ress · ih · *pross* · ih · tee] *n.* cooperation, reciprocation, interchange, correspondence, quid pro quo, mutuality.

recital [ree · *site* · el] *n.* description, recitation, narration, summary, chronical, depiction ("the recitals of the will"); performance, concert ("The Sydeman recital received mixed reviews").

recite [ree · *site*] *v.* declaim, enumerate, recapitulate, soliloquize, communicate, list, repeat.

reckless [*rek* · less] *adj.* impulsive, unwary, careless, irresponsible, improvident, hasty, inattentive ("reckless driving"). *Ant.* circumspect, prudent.

recklessness [*rek* · less · ness] *n.* indifference, gross negligence, impulsiveness, negligence, precipitiousness, impetuousness, irresponsibility.

reclaim [ree · *clame*] *v.* recover, reacquire, repossess, replevin, reestablish, rebuild.

reclamation [rek · le · *may* · shen] *n.* retaking, repossession; restoration, reestablishment.

recognition [rek · eg · *nish* · en] *n.* perception, detection, remembrance, awareness, understanding, citation ("The phrase gained national recognition"); appreciation, honor, praise, approval, notice, credit, salute ("recognition for a job well done").

recognize [*rek* · eg · nize] *v.* identify, remember, comprehend, discover, discern, recollect ("recognize the man"); accept, embrace, realize, uphold, validate, own ("recognize his task").

recollection [rek · e · *lek* · shen] *n.* recognition, memory, recall, consciousness, reminiscence, reconstruction, impression.

recompense [*rek* · em · pense] *n.* reward, compensation, remuneration, amends, emolument, expiation.

reconciliation [rek · en · sil · ee · *ay* · shen] *n.* restoration, conciliation, rapprochement, concordance, propitiation, rapport, detente.

reconstruct [ree · kon · *strukt*] *v.* duplicate, redo, recreate; restore, renovate, regenerate, refurbish.

R

record [*rek* · erd] *n.* account, annals, documentation, register, transcript, minutes, dossier, muster, enumeration ("record of the proceedings"); accomplishment, performance, reign, resume, reputation ("president's foreign policy record").

record [ree · *kord*] *v.* make note, transcribe, docket, document, register, calendar, chronicle, tabulate.

recorder [ree · *kore* · der] *n.* archivist, registrar, stenographer, historian, scribe, clerk, court reporter.

recording [ree · *kore* · ding] *n.* copy, record, memorandum, transcript, tape.

recount [re · *kownt*] *v.* tell, narrate, impart, describe, detail, recapitulate, divulge, render ("recount the experience").

recoup [ree · *koop*] *v.* regain, get back, redeem, remunerate, requite, satisfy, replevin, atone.

recoupment [ree · *koop* · ment] *n.* reduction, rebate, mitigation, offsetting.

recourse [*ree* · korse] *n.* remedy, access, device, entreaty, asylum, option, refuge.

recover [ree · *kuv* · er] *v.* repossess, regain, reacquire, secure, replevy, collect ("to recover the lost treasure"); mend, revive, recuperate, rejuvenate, heal, rally ("to recover from battle wounds").

recovery [ree · *kuv* · er · ee] *n.* satisfaction, award, indemnification, restitution, redress, collection, repossession, reversion, procurement, retrieval, replevy; healing, convalescence, revival, restoration.

recrimination [ree · krim · ih · *nay* · shen] *n.* countercharge, retort, rejoinder, counterattack, reprisal, blame, retribution.

rectify [*rek* · ti · fy] *v.* cure, attune, correct, modify, amend, calibrate, enumerate, revise, improve, square.

recuse [ree · *kyooz*] *v.* disqualify, eliminate, challenge.

red tape *n.* bureaucracy, paperwork, procedures, protocol, nonsense, triviality.

redeem [ree · *deem*] *v.* make good, satisfy, discharge, fulfill, acquit, perform ("redeem the note"); deliver, liberate, free, unbind, unchain, manumit ("redeem the prisoner").

redemption [ree · *demp* · shun] *n.* restoration, repossession, indemnification, retrieval, discharge, rescue.

red-handed [red · *han* · ded] *adv.* in the act, during commission, actively engaged.

redlining [*red* · ly · ning] *n.* discrimination, prejudice; editing, correction.

redress [*ree* · dress] *n.* indemnification, amends, compensation, propitiation, appeasement, acquittal.

redress [ree · *dress*] *v.* adjust, amend, counter, check, mend, recompense, revise, rectify.

reduce [ree · *doose*] *v.* decrease, diminish, lessen, minimize, cut down, shorten, compress, attenuate.

reduction [ree · *duk* · shen] *n.* decrease, limitation, abridgement, abatement, diminution, attenuation, mitigation. *Ant.* increase, aggravation.

redundancy [ree · *dun* · den · see] *n.* superfluity, duplication, profusion, surfeit, tautology, pleonasm, reiteration, surplus, excess.

redundant [ree · *dun* · dent] *adj.* superflous, needless, frivolous, expendable, gratuitous, repetitive, repetitious, unrequired.

refer [ree · *fer*] *v.* accredit, allude, impute, interpolate, exemplify, cite, commit, consign, introduce, recommend, transfer, turn over.

R

referee [ref · e · *ree*] *n.* adjudicator, arbiter, conciliator, master, umpire, interceder.

reference [*ref* · er · ense] *n.* mention, referral, allusion, implication, quotation, note ("in reference to Mrs. Smith's Porsche"); endorsement, voucher, commendation, statement, declaration, affirmation ("a reference as to your good work").

referendum [ref · e · *ren* · dum] *n.* proposition, proposal, election, question, mandate, plebiscite.

reform [ree · *form*] *v.* cure, rectify, reconstitute, better, change, ameliorate, regenerate, rework, transform. *Ant.* deteriorate.

reform [ree · *form*] *n.* change, betterment, amelioration, melioration.

refresh [ree · *fresh*] *v.* revive, regenerate, strengthen, remind, prod ("refresh the witness's memory").

refund [ree · fund] *n.* acquittance, compensation, consolation, repayment, reimbursement, remuneration, retribution.

refund [ree · *fund*] *v.* return, redeem, recompense, indemnify, relinquish, remit, remunerate.

refusal [ree · *fyoo* · zel] *n.* abnegation, declension, rejection, disavowal, enjoinment, veto, repudiation, dissent.

refuse [ree · *fyooz*] *v.* object, decline, reject, abstain, deny, repudiate, renege, forbear ("I refuse to work for that man"). *Ant.* consent.

refuse [*ref* · yooss] *n.* debris, rejectamenta, sediment, rubbish, excrement, trash, garbage. *Ant.* valuables.

refute [ree · *fyoot*] *v.* abnegate, contravene, negate, rebut, contradict, counter, deny, disprove.

regime [re · *zheem*] *n.* rule, reign, administration, government, system.

register [*rej* · is · ter] *v.* enroll, enter, record, chronicle, schedule, inscribe ("to register for fall classes"); come home, get through, have an effect, impress, dawn, sink in, tell ("It finally registered what he was doing").

register [*rej* · is · ter] *n.* annals, archives, catalog, diary, ledger, roster, schedule ("Mark the date in the register").

registered [*rej* · is · terd] *adj.* enrolled, recorded, certified, official ("registered securities").

registrar [*rej* · is · trar] *n.* recorder, clerk, official.

registration [rej · is · *tray* · shen] *n.* recording, reservation, inscription, enrollment, filing, listing.

registry [*rej* · is · tree] *n.* list, book, office.

regress [ree · *gress*] *v.* deteriorate, wane, sink, return, relapse, retrogress.

regs *n.* regulations, rules, standards ("Your plan is illegal under the new regs issued by the Justice Department").

regular [*reg* · yoo · ler] *adj.* normal, established, prevalent, traditional, orthodox, sanctioned ("the regular way of doing things"); even, exact, methodical, patterned, periodic, regulated ("at regular intervals"). *Ant.* sporadic.

regularly [*reg* · yoo · ler · lee] *adv.* consistently, habitually, persistently, traditionally, customarily, usually. *Ant.* rarely.

regulate [*reg* · yoo · late] *v.* direct, establish, govern, systematize, superintend, monitor ("regulate interstate commerce").

R

regulation [reg · yoo · *lay* · shun] *n.* regimentation, conduct, arrangement, standardization, governance, modulation, coordination ("regulation of the fish's air flow"); canon, decree, directive, dictate, ordinance ("military regulations").

rehabilitate [ree · huh · *bil* · ih · tayt] *v.* renovate, reconstruct, furbish, reintegrate, reinvigorate, rebuild; heal, cure.

rehabilitation [ree · huh · *bil* · ih · tay · shun] *n.* correction, renewal, indoctrination, convalescence, rejuvenation, renascence, salvation.

reimburse [ree · im · *berss*] *v.* restore, repay, compensate, indemnify, requite, recompense.

reimbursement [ree · im · *berss* · ment] *n.* repayment, compensation, indemnification.

reinstate [ree · in · *stayt*] *v.* reconstitute, resuscitate, reinstall, reinvest, restore.

reinstatement [ree · in · *stayt* · ment] *n.* restoration, rehiring, readmittance.

reject [re · *jekt*] *v.* decline, despise, jettison, jilt, refuse, disaffirm, reprobate, rebuff ("to reject an appeal"). *Ant.* accept.

reject [*ree* · jekt] *n.* castaway, leftover, waste, castoff, outcast ("That auto part is a defective reject").

rejection [ree · *jek* · shun] *n.* abandonment, disallowance, denial, snub, slight, proscription, abnegation, contempt, eviction, refusal, waiver.

rejoinder [re · *joyn* · der] *n.* answer, response, defense, countercharge, reply.

relate [ree · *layt*] *v.* pertain, tie, interrelate, concern, correlate, affect, identify ("does it relate to the issue at hand?"); tell, impart, narrate, speak ("relate the story").

related [ree · *lay* · ted] *adj.* affiliated, cognate, connected, allied, consanguine, enmeshed, germane, leagued.

relation [ree · *lay* · shun] *n.* relationship, rapport, connection, relevance, nexus, liaison, mutuality ("That has no relation to our topic"); relative, kin, family member ("He is one of our relations").

relative [*rel* · e · tiv] *n.* agnate, cognate, clansman, relation, kin, kindred ("We are blood relatives").

relative [*rel* · e · tiv] *adj.* comparative, respective, dependent, analogous, reciprocal, referring, reliant ("That is relative to your point of view").

release [ree · *leess*] *n.* relinquishment, discharge, deliverance, indemnity, exoneration, amnesty ("sign a release"); freedom, liberation, discharge ("a release from prison").

release [ree · *leess*] *v.* discharge, let go, relinquish, emancipate, clear, deliver, exonerate, free, dismiss.

relevance [*rel* · e · vense] *n.* materiality, pertinence, importance, applicability, significance.

relevant [*rel* · e · vent] *adj.* pertinent, material, germane, on target, congruent, related, applicable, cognate ("relevant evidence"). *Ant.* irrelevant.

reliance [ree · *ly* · ense] *n.* trust, confidence, dependence, credence, credit, conviction.

relief [ree · *leef*] *n.* remedy, abatement, allayment, extrication, mollification, palliation, assuagement ("relief for damages inflicted"); welfare, aid, dole, handout, charity, care, ministry ("relief for the poor").

remainder [ree · *mane* · der] *n.* balance, residue, surplus, excess, remains; estate, interest, property.

remand [ree · *mand*] *n.* return, reassignment.

remand [ree · *mand*] *v.* return, recommit, reassign, send back.

R

remediable [re · *meed* · ee · e · bul] *adj.* salvageable, amenable, inalleable, fixable.

remedial [re · *meed* · ee · el] *adj.* corrective, medicinal, therapeutic, prophylatic, recuperative, beneficial, vulnery, healing, reformative.

remedy [*rem* · e · dee] *v.* alleviate, ameliorate, assuage, fix, heal, mollify, revive, mitigate ("to remedy the mistake"). *Ant.* exacerbate.

remedy [*rem* · e · dee] *n.* antidote, countermeasure, pharmaceutical, physic, restorative ("a home remedy"); reparation, remediation, restitution, solution, redress, counteraction ("a legal remedy").

remembrance [ree · *mem* · brants] *n.* recollection, memory, recall, reconstruction; commemoration, tribute, testimonial, keepsake, celebration, memento.

reminder [ree · *mine* · der] *n.* memo, note, cue, hint, tickler, suggestion, souvenir, memorial, keepsake.

remise [ree · *mize*] *v.* give up, surrender, release, quitclaim.

remission [ree · *mish* · en] *n.* absolution, amnesty, discharge, exoneration, indulgence, reprieve, pardon ("the remission of the charges"); abatement, abeyance, diminution, ebb, reduction, relaxation, respite ("The disease has gone into remission"). *Ant.* imposition; aggravation.

remit [ree · *mit*] *v.* transmit, forward, disburse, proffer, consign, dispatch; alleviate, exonerate, modulate, rescind, reprieve, mitigate. *Ant.* retain; impose.

remonstrance [ree · *mons* · trens] *n.* protest, objection, disapproval, admonishment, warning, reprobation, castigation, criticism, exception.

remorse [ree · *morse*] *n.* grief, regret, anguish, concern, sorrow, contrition.

remote [ree · *mote*] *adj.* distant, sequestered, segregated, foreign, inaccessable ("remote reaches of the galaxy"); improbable, meager, imperceptible, small, inconsequential, negligible ("a remote chance"). *Ant.* neighboring; substantial.

removal [ree · *move* · ul] *n.* relocation, transplantation, transference ("requires the removal of the jury"); elimination, eradication, extermination, excavation, abstraction ("removal of the stain"). *Ant.* installation; preservation.

remove [ree · *move*] *v.* eliminate, expunge, abolish, liquidate, eliminate, take away, exclude ("remove the trash"); transfer, change venue, relocate, switch, send, shift ("remove a case to federal court").

remuneration [ree · myoo · ne · *ray* · shen] *n.* compensation, pay, salary, reward.

render [*ren* · der] *v.* state, deliver, convey, impute, proffer, administer ("render a decision"); cede, distribute, exchange, relinquish, tender ("render payment"); construe, paraphrase, transcribe, transliterate, ("render intelligible").

rendezvous [*ron* · day · voo] *n.* appointment, meeting, encounter, engagement, get-together ("My rendezvous with MSH").

rendezvous [ron · day · *voo*] *v.* meet, gather, get together, convene, assemble.

rendition [ren · *dish* · en] *n.* arrangement, construction, transcription, interpretation, rendering, version.

renege [ree · *neg*] *v.* quit, reverse, revoke, vacate, contradict, go back on, invalidate ("to renege on the deal").

renew [ree · *new*] *v.* regenerate, recommence, revitalize, resuscitate, redress, revive, redeem. *Ant.* cancel.

renewal [ree · *new* · el] *n.* enhancement, continuation, salvage, salvation, reclamation, modernization. *Ant.* deterioration.

R

renounce [ree · *nownss*] *v.* repudiate, disclaim, abdicate, deny, recant, disavow, waive, abjure.

rent *v.* lease, let, charter, farm out, engage, contract.

rent *n.* hire, lease, payment, rental, tariff ("Rent is $250 per month"); breach, discord, dissension, perforation, schism ("a large rent left between buyer and seller").

renunciation [ree · nun · see · *ay* · shun] *n.* abandonment, rejection, abdication, disavowal, disclaimer, forbearance ("the renunciation of the throne"). *Ant.* retention.

reorganization [ree · or · ge · nih · *zay* · shun] *n.* restructuring, overhaul, restoration, reconstitution, revision, conversion.

repair [ree · *pare*] *v.* fix, recondition, renovate, rejuvenate, rectify ("to repair a leaky faucet"); leave, retire, proceed, recur, refer, withdraw ("repair to bed").

repair [ree · *pare*] *n.* adjustment, improvement, reconstruction, substitution, replacement, overhaul ("a major repair").

reparation [rep · e · *ray* · shun] *n.* adjustment, atonement, propitiation, expiation, indemnification, quittance.

repay [ree · *pay*] *v.* accord, balance, compensate, indemnify, recompense, restore ("repay a debt"); avenge, vindicate, reciprocate, revenge, punish ("repay her evil deeds").

repeal [ree · *peel*] *v.* abrogate, abolish, rescind, annul, recall, revoke.

repeal [re · *peel*] *n.* abrogation, annulment, cancellation, nullification, rescindment, rescission, withdrawal.

replace [ree · *plaiss*] *v.* compensate, reconstitute, duplicate, reinstate, supplant, supersede, subrogate, switch, swap, supplant.

replacement [ree · *plaiss* · ment] *n.* equivalent, duplicate, reconstitution, replica, reconstruction, refund, reorganization.

replevin [ree · *plev* · in] *n.* acquisition, repossession, recovery, retrieval.

reply [ree · *ply*] *n.* rejoinder, replication, retort, refutation, retaliation, response, answer.

reply [ree · *ply*] *v.* answer, counter, acknowledge, react, return.

report [ree · *port*] *v.* inform, circulate, disseminate, apprise, notify, divulge ("report your findings").

report [re · *port*] *n.* article, narration, chronicle, story, communiqué, tidings ("a report on the ozone hole"); rumor, suggestion, gossip, insinuation, hearsay, hint ("Reports tell us that the governor will run for president").

reporter [ree · *port* · er] *n.* announcer, journalist, newscaster, correspondent, writer, interviewer.

repossession [ree · po · *zesh* · en] *n.* recapture, restoration, retrieval, seizure, reacquisition, recovery.

represent [rep · re · *zent*] *v.* evoke, portray, exemplify, imitate, indicate, signify, symbolize ("The sun in the painting represents God"); depict, delineate, outline, illustrate, narrate ("to represent the seriousness of the problem"); speak for, act for, replace, factor, act as attorney for ("to represent a client").

representative [rep · re · *zen* · tuh · tiv] *n.* assemblyman, commissioner, congressperson, deputy, councilor, delegate, proxy ("our representative in Washington"); archetype, embodiment, epitome, exemplar, personification, specimen ("a representative of the group").

representative [rep · re · *zen* · tuh · tiv] *adj.* adumbrative, delineative, depictive, typical, typifying, evocative, exemplary, prototypical, indicative, symbolic ("a representative sample").

reprieve [ree · *preev*] *n.* abatement, abeyance, clemency, deferment, mitigation, palliation, remission.

reprimand [rep · rih · mand] *n.* admonishment, castigation, censure, reprehension, chiding, lecture, warning, reproval.

reprimand [*rep* · rih · mand] *v.* chastise, rebuke, reprove, admonish, castigate, deprecate.

reprisal [ree · *pry* · zel] *n.* revenge, counterblow, requital, retribution, vengeance.

reproduce [ree · pro · *dooss*] *v.* copy, mimic, imitate; produce, beget, make, generate, proliferate, sire, spawn, breed.

repudiation [ree · pyoo · dee · *ay* · shun] *n.* denial, rejection, renunciation, repeal, retraction, nullification, spurning, disaffirmation.

repugnancy [ree · *pug* · nen · see] *n.* incompatibility, contradiction; unpleasantness, repulsiveness, obscenity, undesirability.

repugnant [ree · *pug* · nent] *adj.* disgusting, foul, horrid, odious, noisome, hateful, contemptible, revolting.

reputation [rep · yoo · *tay* · shun] *n.* acceptability, fame, infamy, notoriety, position, prominence, acclaim, distinction, standing, status, repute.

repute [ree · *pyoot*] *v.* deem, assume, presume, suppose, judge, reckon, estimate.

reputed [ree · *pyoot* · ed] *adj.* assumed, estimated, alleged, supposed ("the reputed gangster").

request [ree · *kwest*] *n.* appeal, application, entreaty, inquiry, solicitation, requisition.

request [ree · *kwest*] *v.* ask, desire, appeal, petition, plead, summon, urge, want, solicit, importune.

require [ree · *kwire*] *v.* order, command, compel, necessitate, obligate ("to require an appearance before the court"); need, crave, lack ("to require a great deal of attention").

requirement [ree · *kwire* · ment] *n.* obligation, prerequisite, rule, regulation, commandment, fiat, provision, directive.

requisition [rek · wi · *zish* · en] *n.* appropriation, order, commandeering, request, summons, demand, application, petition, injunction.

rescind [ree · *sind*] *v.* avoid, invalidate, reject, take back, abrogate, renege, counterorder, undo, disavow, annul.

rescission [ree · *sizh* · en] *n.* unmaking, termination, withdrawal, vitiation, voidance, extricating.

rescript [ree · *skript*] *n.* directive, order, statement.

rescue [*ress* · kyoo] *n.* deliverance, emancipation, succor, redemption, ransom, relief; recaption, reprisal, repossession. *Ant.* abandonment.

rescue [*ress* · kyoo] *v.* save, redeem, ransom, deliver.

research [*ree* · surch] *n.* investigation, scrutiny, study, inquiry, examination.

research [*ree* · surch] *v.* analyze, examine, probe, study, inspect, pursue.

reservation [rez · er · *vay* · shun] *n.* circumscription, hesitancy, provision, restriction, proviso ("have a reservation about attending the meeting"); bespeaking, limitation, restriction, retainment, booking ("reservation for a future date"); enclave, preserve, reserve, sanctuary, territory, tract ("Indian reservation").

reserve [ree · *zerv*] *v.* retain, withhold, preserve, amass, conserve, accrue ("reserve some funds").

reserve [ree · *zerv*] *n.* supply, funds, accumulation, stock, resource, cache ("reserves to last a week"); detachment, rigidity, composure, condescension, inhibition, diffidence, reticence ("a cool reserve").

reserved [ree · *zervd*] *adj.* retained, withheld, engaged, appropriated, preempted, restricted, taken ("this seat is reserved"); diffident, demure, misanthropic, sedate, shy, taciturn ("a reserved person").

reside [ree · *zide*] *v.* abide, dwell, be intrinsic to, endure, occupy, tenant, populate, live.

residence [*rez* · ih · dense] *n.* abode, address, domicile, inhabitancy, household, headquarters, home.

resident [*rez* · ih · dent] *n.* citizen, denizen, dweller, squatter, suburbanite, native, domiciliary.

resident [*rez* · ih · dent] *adj.* remaining, stationary, fixed, present, settled.

residual [rec · *zid* · joo · el] *adj.* surplus, remaining, excess, residue, spare.

residuary [ree · *zid* · joo · e · ree] *adj.* surplus, spare, remaining, leftover, outstanding, excess ("a residuary bequest").

residue [*rez* · ih · dew] *n.* debris, dregs, excess, leavings, remnants, residuum, slag, remainder.

resignation [rez · ig · *nay* · shun] *n.* abandonment, abdication, quitting, termination, yielding, divestment ("I received her resignation"); acquiescence, compliance, deference, docility, forbearing, fortitude ("resignation to the job he was assigned").

resist [ree · *zist*] *v.* oppose, contest, disregard, retaliate, frustrate, dissent, obstruct.

resistance [ree · *zist* · ants] *n.* protest, noncompliance, rebellion, defiance, opposition, contravention.

resolution [rez · e · *loo* · shun] *n.* determination, dedication, perseverance, purpose, sincerity, tenacity ("to have tremendous resolution to do a task"); declaration, exposition, presentation, settlement, solution, verdict ("the council's resolution").

resort [ree · *zort*] *v.* address, devote, recur, utilize, exercise, employ.

resort [ree · *zort*] *n.* camp, haven, holiday spot, spa, haunt, rendezvous, retreat, asylum ("vacation resort").

resources [ree · *sore* · sez] *n.* wealth, property, possession, income, capital; ability, capacity, capability, facility.

respect [ree · *spekt*] *n.* regard, recognition, esteem, favor, reverence, tribute.

respect [ree · *spekt*] *v.* regard, abide by, recognize, comply with.

respond [ree · *spond*] *v.* answer, reply, plead, discuss, explain, counterclaim, parry.

respondent [ree · *spon* · dent] *n.* defendant, appellee, accused, responding litigant. *Ant.* petitioner.

responsive [ree · *spon* · siv] *adj.* reciprocal, reactive, sympathetic, receptive, sensitive, understanding. *Ant.* unresponsive.

rest *n.* cessation, intermission, interval, leisure, pause, quiescence, respite ("rest from the day's work"); balance, dregs, heel, remnant, residuum, superfluity ("Eat the rest of your food").

rest *v.* breathe, compose, relax, slumber, unwind ("rest your eyes"); end, finish, conclude ("The prosecution rests").

restatement [ree · *stayt* · ment] *n.* review, summary, recapitulation, recital, iteration, abstract ("Restatement of Torts").

restitution [res · tih · *tew* · shen] *n.* compensation, repayment, amends, dues, recompense, reparation, squaring, remitter, redress.

restrain [ree · *strayn*] *v.* arrest, circumscribe, constrain, fetter, govern, imprison, pinion, repress, bridle, curb, check.

restraint [ree · *straynt*] *n.* abstemiousness, coercion, curtailment, moderation, suppression, abridgement, limitation, prohibition, self-control.

restrict [ree · *strikt*] *v.* constrict, delimit, demarcate, modify, regulate, restrain, limit.

restriction [ree · *strik* · shun] *n.* constriction, impediment, curb, contraction, obstruction, demarcation, reservation, stipulation, limitation.

restrictive [ree · *strik* · tiv] *adj.* restraining, prohibitive, obstructive, qualifying, controlled, exclusive.

result [ree · *zult*] *n.* upshot, decision, denouement, aftermath, eventuality, development, consequence, judgment. *Ant.* cause.

resulting [ree · *zult* · ing] *adj.* concluding, emerging, consequent, emanating, ensuing, issuing.

resurrect [*rez* · er · ekt] *v.* rejuvenate, revitalize, revive, bring back, recondition.

retailer [*ree* · tale · er] *n.* businessperson, merchant, seller, dealer, entrepreneur.

retain [ree · *tane*] *v.* employ, hire, secure, commission, recruit, consult ("retain the lawyer's services"); maintain, secure, restrain, clutch, memorize, clench, absorb ("retain its freshness").

retainer [ree · *tane* · er] *n.* fee, contract, engagement fee, compensation, remuneration.

retaliation [ree · tal · ee · *ay* · shun] *n.* revenge, reprisal, recrimination, vengeance, requital, reciprocation.

retire [ree · *tire*] *v.* terminate, withdraw, quit, abdicate; redeem, reclaim; isolate, remove, seclude, retreat.

retraction [ree · *trak* · shen] *n.* withdrawal, repudiation, abjuration, disavowal, denial.

retreat [ree · *treet*] *n.* departure, ebb, evacuation, retirement, withdrawal ("a steady retreat from the field"); cloister, habitat, refuge, resort ("summer retreat").

retreat [ree · *treet*] *v.* withdraw, disengage, pull back, reverse, flee, evacuate.

retroactive [reh · tro · *ak* · tiv] *adj.* retrospective, ex post facto.

return [ree · *tern*] *v.* replace, reinstate, deliver, reset, reinstall, reposition ("return it to its original position"); repeat, come back, resurrect, reoccur ("I have returned"); reciprocate, retaliate, requite, retort, refund, redress ("the fund returned a nice amount"); render, adjudicate, pronounce, hand down, publish, impart ("return a decision").

return [ree · *tern*] *n.* profit, yield, inflation, appreciation, harvest, compensation ("a good return on investment").

reveal [ree · *veel*] *v.* confess, unearth, display, announce, affirm, disclose, uncover, publish.

revenue [*rev* · e · new] *n.* receipts, gross, proceeds, income, dividends, emolument, stipend.

reversal [ree · *vur* · sul] *n.* annulment, voiding, retraction, nullification, countermandment, invalidation, overturning.

R

reverse [ree · *vurse*] *v.* overthrow, vacate, annul, nullify, transpose, disaffirm. *Ant.* affirm.

reverse [ree · *vurse*] *adj.* opposite, contrary ("reverse discrimination").

reversed [ree · *vursd*] *adv.* set aside, vacated, repealed, annulled, undone ("The trial court's ruling was reversed").

reversion [ree · *vur* · zhen] *n.* remainder, future interest, residue, estate, interest; return, throwback, retrogression, regression, turnaround.

revert [ree · *vurt*] *v.* retreat, resume, deteriorate, relapse, retrogress, decay ("revert to old habits"); come back, return ("After Bill dies, the life estate which Sam granted Bill will revert to Sam").

review [ree · *vyoo*] *n.* analysis, inspection, reassessment, revision, scrutiny, retrospective, critique ("a review of the material").

review [ree · *vyoo*] *v.* consider, examine, contemplate, study, analyze, investigate, deliberate ("review a decision").

revise [ree · *vize*] *v.* improve, rearrange, amend, alter, change, recalibrate, scrutinize, modify, update.

revision [ree · *vizh* · en] *n.* alteration, modification, change, redraft, amendment, reappraisal.

revival [ree · *vy* · vel] *n.* restoration, resurrection, revitalization, rebirth, awakening, invigoration.

revive [ree · *vive*] *v.* animate, rekindle, invigorate, reanimate, resuscitate, reactivate, enliven, renew, restore, resurrect, revitalize.

revocable [*rev* · e · ke · bul] *adj.* reversible, retractible, voidable, cancellable.

revocation [rev · e · *kay* · shen] *n.* termination, elimination, disavowal, abrogation, defeasance, dissolution. *Ant.* confirmation.

revoke [ree · *voke*] *v.* recall, annul, repudiate, ban, abrogate, expunge.

revolution [rev · e · *loo* · shen] *n.* anarchy, destruction, innovation, insubordination, metamorphosis, reformation, tumult ("American revolution"); circumviolation, gyration, cycle, rotation, whirl, pirouette ("revolution around the sun").

reward [ree · *ward*] *n.* accolade, bonus, remuneration, award, prize, recompense, emolument, gratuity.

rider [*ry* · der] *n.* attachment, extension, insertion, supplement, addendum, codicil ("a rider to the bill").

right *adj.* righteous, honorable, de jure, licit, sanctioned, punctilious ("do the right thing"); appropriate, accurate, precise, perfect, infallible, wholesome ("the right way to go").

right *n.* claim, license, entitlement, liberty, heritage, certification ("right of remitter"); virtue, merit, righteousness, principle, probity, fidelity ("It is right to protect the innocent").

rightful [*right* · ful] *adj.* legal, legitimate, deserving, statutory, proper, just, lawful, true ("the rightful heir").

rigid [*rij* · id] *adj.* stiff, inflexible, taut, tense, harsh, inelastic, precise, unbending, unalterable.

riot [*ry* · et] *n.* fight, brawl, fracus, donnybrook, affray, anarchism, brannigan, distemper ("A riot started over the voting policy").

riot [*ry* · et] *v.* fight, brawl, resist, oppose, rebel, pillage.

ripe *adj.* advanced, provident, complete, consummate, opportune, inclined, fully matured, ready, fully developed, mellow ("ripe fruit"); favorable, auspicious, ideal, suitable ("The conditions were ripe").

risk *n.* speculation, vulnerability, exposure, susceptibility, insecurity, gamble, peril ("Investing in that stock now is a big risk").

risk *v.* jeopardize, speculate, threaten, imperil, compromise, wager ("to risk it all").

road *n.* artery, way, asphalt, highway, boulevard, expressway, pavement, thoroughfare.

rob *v.* abscond, bereave, defalcate, divest, pillage, steal.

robbery [rob · e · ree] *n.* theft, holdup, piracy, commandeering, embezzlement, expropriation, abduction.

role *n.* part, assignment, job, mission, position, work.

roll *v.* bowl, circle, circumduct, elapse, furl, swathe, undulate; bombinate, drum.

roll *n.* annals, census, chronicle, master register, table, record ("the tax rolls"); cannonade, echo, ruffle.

roomer [room · er] *n.* boarder, tenant, occupant, lodger.

rooming house [room · ing hows] *n.* boarding house, home, lodging, inn.

root *n.* foundation, cause, reason, essence ("the root of the problem").

routine [roo · teen] *n.* procedure, pattern, habit, technique, practice, formula.

routine [roo · teen] *adj.* habitual, established, customary, everyday, typical, standard, normal, repeated, ritual.

royalty [roy · el · tee] *n.* consideration, compensation, pay, payments; nobility, aristocracy, monarchy.

rule *v.* manage, administer, officiate, domineer, resolve, adjudicate, adjudge, establish, arbitrate, conclude ("rule on the issue"); manipulate, predominate, direct, command, oversee, preside over ("rule the country");

rule *n.* ordinance, legislation, statute, code, norm, principle, decree, mandate, dictate, imperative ("rule of the game"); sovereignty, dominion, administration, leadership, authority, management ("rule of the king").

ruling [roo · ling] *n.* decree, mandate, adjudication, order, pronouncement, resolution, verdict ("the judge's ruling").

ruling [roo · ling] *adj.* cardinal, central, controlling, dominant, guiding, reigning, sovereign ("the ruling class").

running [run · ing] *adj.* continuous, executing, incessant, perpetual, unbroken, unceasing.

running [run · ing] *n.* administration, coordination, functioning, maintenance, oversight, superintendency ("the running of the store"); passing, elapsing ("running of the statute of limitations").

ruthless [rooth · les] *adj.* cruel, focused, draconian, treacherous, cold-blooded, merciless, ferocious, vicious.

R

sabotage [*sab · e · tahzh*] *n.* demolition, impairment, subversion, treachery, treason, wrecking.

sadism [*say · dizm*] *n.* cruelty, debauchery, deviation.

safe *adj.* guarded, secure, covered, innocuous, impregnable, unassailable, protected, inpenetrable ("a safe place"); modest, cautious, responsible, circumspect, timid ("a safe investor").

safe *n.* chest, strongbox, depository, trunk, case, locker.

safekeeping [*safe · keep · ing*] *n.* custody, conservation, supervision, shelter, guardianship, auspices, trust, protective custody.

salable [*sale · e · bul*] *adj.* merchantable, acceptable, needed, fashionable, staple, desirable.

salary [*sal · e · ree*] *n.* earnings, emolument, recompense, remuneration, stipend, wage, pay.

sale *n.* exchange, trade, transaction, barter, vendition, reduction.

salesperson [*saylz · per · sen*] *n.* clerk, seller, vendor, merchant, agent.

salient [*sail · ee · ant*] *adj.* outstanding, noticeable, prominent, conspicuous.

salvage [*sal · vej*] *n.* remains, junk, debris, surplus, flotsam, residuum, salvation ("salvage from the crash").

salvage [*sal · vej*] *v.* recapture, save, retrieve, restore, rehabilitate, regenerate, ransom ("to salvage the ship").

same *adj.* aforementioned, alike, comparable, compatible, equivalent, indistinguishable, likewise; changeless, consistent, invariable, perpetual, unaltered, uniform.

sample [*sam · pul*] *n.* constituent, element, exemplification, example, fragment, typification, specimen ("a fine sample of our product").

sanction [*sank · shen*] *v.* concur, agree, authorize, support, validate, indorse, endorse, countenance ("The match was sanctioned by the IBF"); punish, ban, boycott ("The bar sanctioned the erring attorney").

sanction [*sank · shen*] *n.* acquiescence, allowance, endorsement, countenance, encouragement, ratification, sufferance ("the official sanction of Major League Baseball"); ban, boycott, decree, injunction, penalty, sentence, punishment ("unimposed sanctions").

sanctuary [*sank · choo · er · ee*] *n.* altar, chancel, sanctum, holy place ("The service was held in the sanctuary"); asylum, cover, harborage, oasis, retreat, shelter ("sanctuary from the authorities"); asylum, preserve, park, refuge, reserve, shelter ("wildlife sanctuary").

S

sane *adj.* balanced, composed, judicious, moderate, competent, sagacious, sober.

sanitary [san · ih · tare · ee] *adj.* healthful, hygienic, purified, salubrious, sanitive, sterile.

sanity [san · ih · tee] *n.* acumen, comprehension, judiciousness, lucidity, sagacity, saneness, soundness.

satisfaction [sat · is · *fak* · shen] *n.* payment, compensation, settlement, amends, atonement, indemnification ("satisfaction of a debt"); fulfillment, pleasure, contentment, felicity, gratification, realization ("satisfaction from helping others").

satisfactory [sat · is · *fak* · ter · ee] *adj.* adequate, sufficient, delighting, gratifying, competent, average.

satisfied [sat · is · fide] *adj.* paid, compensated; content, pleased, gratified.

satisfy [sat · is · fy] *v.* repay, reimburse, requite, fulfill, compensate, settle, annul ("satisfy a debt"); satiate, appease, gratify, assuage, indulge, amuse ("satisfy her every need"); convince, persuade, assure, reassure, answer ("satisfy the jury").

save *v.* rescue, salvage, preserve, safeguard, ransom, help, aid, shield, cover ("save from harm"); economize, retrench, accumulate, shelve, reserve, hoard ("save money").

saving [save · ing] *adj.* exempting, excluding, reserving, excepting ("a saving clause"); conserving, accumulating ("a saving account").

savings [say · vingz] *n.* resources, funds, capital, money, accumulations.

scam *n.* fraud, deception, trick, artifice, hoax.

scandal [skan · del] *n.* aspersion, belittlement, calumny, defamation, depreciation, ignominy, opprobrium, reproach, gossip, slander; outrage, outcry, fuss, furor, commotion.

scandalous [skan · del · ess] *adj.* offensive, shocking, infamous, disgraceful, odious, impertinent.

scarce *adj.* scant, deficient, wanting, rare, limited, insufficient, unavailable.

scarcity *n.* paucity, dearth, lack, inadequacy, want, need.

scene *n.* locality, location, place, surroundings, site, episode, act, setting.

schedule [sked · jool] *n.* agenda, appointments, calendar, itinerary, registry, timetable ("the schedule for today").

schedule [sked · jool] *v.* organize, register, record; arrange, book, card, catalog ("to schedule an appointment").

scheme *n.* arrangement, plan, blueprint, codification, contrivance, presentation, strategy, tactics, theory, notion.

scheme *v.* plan, arrange, plot, conspire, connive, machinate, design, devise.

schism [skiz · im] *n.* break, rift, rupture, falling-out, difference, dissent, nonconformity, separation, division. *Ant.* union.

school *n.* academy, college, department, discipline, faculty, institute ("school of fine arts"); adherents, circle, class, clique, devotees, disciples ("school of followers"); belief, creed, faith, persuasion, outlook ("the old school").

school *v.* advance, teach, coach, cultivate, indoctrinate, educate, discipline, prime ("school him in martial arts").

scienter [see · *en* · ter] *n.* knowledge, guilty knowledge, intent, purpose.

scintilla [sin · *til* · a] *n.* trifle, spark, trace, smidgen, modicum, fleck, atom, grain ("a scintilla of evidence").

scope *n.* range, breadth, latitude, ambit, purview, extension, zone, extent ("scope of authority").

scrawl *v.* doodle, inscribe, scrabble, scratch, scribble, squiggle, mark.

script *n.* calligraphy, chirography, penmanship, longhand, characters ("Write the certificate in a nice script"); article, dialogue, lines, manuscript, scenario, text, typescript ("Stick to the lines in the script").

scrivener [*skri* · ve · ner] *n.* writer, scribe, reporter, drafter.

scrutiny [*skroo* · tih · nee] *n.* analysis, review, inquiry, examination, probe ("strict scrutiny").

scrutinize [*skroo* · tih · nize] *v.* examine, analyze, investigate, probe, review.

seal *n.* emblem, logo, imprint, imprimatur, certification, authentication, trademark ("seal of the school").

seal *v.* close, cork, isolate, quarantine, segregate, plug ("seal the opening"); assure, authenticate, clinch, conclude, consummate, establish, ratify ("Seal the deal").

sealed *adj.* closed, hidden, private, secured, occluded ("a sealed bid").

search *n.* prying, probe, inspection, scrutiny, pursuit, examination, perusal, inquisition, reconnaissance ("a search for stolen goods").

search *v.* pry, probe, investigate, chase, scrutinize, examine, peruse, rummage.

season [*see* · zen] *n.* division, interval, junction, occasion, opportunity, term ("season for football").

season [*see* · zen] *v.* acclimate, accustom, anneal, inure, mature, temper, qualify ("seasoned with age"); color, enliven, lace, leaven, spice, add zest ("season the food").

seasonable [*see* · zen · e · bul] *adj.* timely, propitious, opportune, apposite, serviceable, felicitous, fortunate.

seat *n.* chair, place, chesterfield, davenport, recliner, settee, stall ("There's a seat for you at the head of the table"); abode, axis, capital, cradle, polestar, source ("seat of government"); base, foundation, jitney, groundwork, seating, support ("seat of the building"); backside, breech, derriere, posterior, rear, behind, butt ("shot in the seat").

second [*sek* · end] *adj.* runner-up, next, alternate, consequent, resultant, subsequent ("second in line").

second [*sek* · end] *n.* flash, instant, moment, split second ("just a second"); assistant, backer, double, exponent, supporter ("a second in the duel").

second [*sek* · end] *v.* aid, approve, assist, encourage, support, endorse, promote ("second the motion").

secondary [*sek* · en · dare · ee] *adj.* auxiliary, consequential, subservient ("of secondary importance"); derivative, borrowed, consequent, eventual, proximate, resultant, subsidiary ("a secondary matter").

secret [*see* · kret] *adj.* hidden, clandestine, covert, private, abstruse, conspiratorial, disguised ("a secret matter").

secret [*see* · kret] *n.* confidence, private affair, mystery, classified facts, privileged information ("It's a secret").

secrete [se · *kreet*] *v.* bury, cache, finesse, screen, hide, cover, seclude, veil ("secrete the information"); discharge, emit, emanate, extricate, extrude, perspire ("secrete sweat").

section [*sek* · shen] *n.* part, segment, component, subdivision ("a section of the class"); area, part, sector, neighborhood, locale, precinct, parcel ("this section of town"); classification, component, moiety.

S

section [*sek* · shen] *v.* divide, partition, allocate, sector, segment.

secular [*sek* · yoo · ler] *adj.* nonreligious, lay, mundane, materialistic, worldly.

secure [sek · *yoor*] *adj.* safe, defended, guarded, immune, protected, riskless, unassailable.

secure [se · *kyoor*] *v.* assure, cover, defend, ensure, guarantee, screen, shield ("secure the debt"); adjust, anchor, bind, bolt, cement, fasten, moor, pinion, rivet ("secure the sail").

secured [se · *kyoord*] *adj.* guaranteed, protected, insured, sheltered ("a secured debt").

securities [se · *kyoor* · ih · teez] *n.* stocks, convertible debentures, negotiables, coupons, bills, warranties.

security [se · *kyoor* · ih · tee] *n.* warranty, bail, surety, escrow, collateral, debenture, assurance ("security for the mortgage"); safety, defense, strength, bulwark, fortification, stability, preservation, impregnability, immunity ("personal security").

sedition [se · *dish* · en] *n.* defiance, rebellion, mutiny, insubordination, apostasy, treachery, treason, infidelity.

seduce [se · *douss*] *v.* lure, bewitch, tempt, allure, cajole; violate, abuse, defile, corrupt.

sedulous [*sed* · yoo · lus] *adj.* diligent, industrious, hardworking, persevering, assiduous.

segregation [seg · re · *gay* · shen] *n.* classification, isolation, grouping, detachment, allocation, differentiation; bigotry, discrimination, prejudice, racial prejudice, ostracism, apartheid.

seisin [*see* · zin] *n.* possession, control, occupation, ownership, title ("equitable seisin").

seize *v.* sequester, sequestrate, capture, snatch, confiscate, mulct, pillage, plunder, appropriate, take.

seizure [*see* · zher] *n.* capture, confiscation, impoundment, annexation, expropriation, dispossession ("seizure of the money"); fit, paroxysms, stroke, attack, throe, spasm, visitation, crisis, spell ("convulsive seizure").

select [se · *lekt*] *v.* pick, cull, adopt, specify, choose, delimit, determine, discriminate, differentiate, except ("select a jury").

select [se · *lekt*] *adj.* excellent, elite, preferable, superior, culled, delicate, exquisite ("a select wine").

selective [se · *lek* · tiv] *adj.* particular, precise, discriminating, differentiating.

self *n.* individual, person, being.

sell *v.* peddle, vend, auction, trade, wholesale, traffic in, furnish, exchange, deal.

seller [*sel* · ur] *n.* agent, businessperson, retailer, merchant, dealer, peddler, shopkeeper, trader.

semblance [*sem* · blents] *n.* closeness, similarity, likeness; air, appearance, identity, guise, look.

senator [*sen* · et · er] *n.* representative, legislator, lawmaker.

send *v.* mail, post, transfer, transmit, freight; discharge, give, cast, convey, issue.

senior [*seen* · yer] *n.* ancient, dean, doyen, doyenne, elder, matriarch, patriarch, pensioner, superior ("seniors of the group").

senior [*seen* · yer] *adj.* superior, older, prior ("a senior interest"). *Ant.* junior.

seniority [see · *nyor* · ih · tee] *n.* tenure, longevity, longer service, station, rank, standing.

sense *n.* intelligence, judgment, comprehension, prudence, reason, wisdom ("common sense"); instinct, perception, awareness, impression, apprehension, notion ("a sense of forbidding").

sensitive [*sen · si · tiv*] *adj.* critical, mindful, discerning, perceptive, perspicacious, alert; susceptible, vulnerable, easily affected, touchy, impressionable.

sentence [*sen · tense*] *v.* penalize, commit, punish, fine, imprison, condemn, denounce ("sentence the prisoner").

sentence [*sen · tense*] *n.* penalty, censure, condemnation, decision, dictum, pronouncement ("The sentence was severe").

sentencing [*sen · ten · sing*] *n.* punishment, adjudication, penalty.

separable [*sep · e · re · bul*] *adj.* severable, divisible, detachable.

separate [*sep · e · rayt*] *v.* break, divide, cleave, distinguish, dichotomize, detach, disentangle, sort, disjoint, dissever ("separate the copies").

separate [*sep · ret*] *adj.* abstracted, apart, apportioned, disassociated, discrete, different, distinct, unconnected, isolated, severed ("a separate consideration").

separation [*sep · e · ray · shen*] *n.* detachment, embarkation, disrelation, disassociation, partition, parting, sorting, rupture, uncompiling, disunion, alienation, cleavage.

sequester [*se · kwest · er*] *v.* cloister, confine, separate, insulate, secrete, segregate, withdraw, isolate ("sequester the jury"); attach, arrogate, confiscate, impound ("sequester assets").

sequestration [*se · kwes · tray · shen*] *n.* attachment, appropriation, seizure ("the sequestration of property"); isolation, insulation, quarantine ("the sequestration of witnesses").

serial [*seer · ee · el*] *adj.* continuous, periodical, successive, tabulated, scheduled, recurring ("serial killer"); sequential, consecutive.

series [*seer · eez*] *n.* cycle, regimen, progression, train, suit, circuit, routine, sequence, succession.

serious [*seer · ee · us*] *adj.* genuine, earnest, definite, real, heartfelt, fervent; precarious, grim, grave, onerous, troublesome, alarming, critical.

servant [*ser · vent*] *n.* assistant, attendant, domestic, drudge, hireling, menial, minion, retainer.

serve *v.* arrange, assist, deal, deliver, work, distribute, oblige, present, provision, succor ("serve in the military").

service [*ser · viss*] *n.* ceremony, formality, liturgy, observance, ritual ("Sunday service"); action, active duty, combat duty, fighting ("military time in service"); labor, employment, work ("community service"); notice, notification ("service by mail").

service [*ser · viss*] *v.* fix, check, inspect, repair, tune ("service the car").

servitude [*ser · ve · tewd*] *n.* slavery, subjugation, oppression, serfdom, enthrallment, obedience, submission, vassalage.

session [*sesh · en*] *n.* affair, assembly, concourse, discussion, hearing, huddle, conference, term.

set *adj.* agreed, appointed, concluded, stipulated ("a set price"); intended, inveterate, fixed, obstinate, immovable, rigid, situate ("set in her ways").

set *v.* affix, anchor, arrange, bestow, ensconce, lay, level ("set in stone"); allocate, allot, designate, stipulate, dictate, establish, impose, ordain ("set a price"); abet, begin, commence, foment, initiate, instigate, provoke ("set in motion").

S

set *n.* array, assemblage, class, clique, compendium, coterie, gaggle, organization, series, group.

setoff [*set* · off] *n.* reduction, mitigation, adjustment, offset.

settle [*set* · uhl] *v.* resolve, accommodate, work out, mediate, reconcile, rectify, unravel ("settle the dispute"); allay, assure, pacify, quell, quieten, reassure, sedate, calm ("settle the children down"); abide, colonize, dwell, establish, reside, squat ("settle out West").

settlement [*set* · ul · ment] *n.* decision, adjustment, compensation, disposition, liquidation, remuneration, resolution, termination ("to reach a settlement"); colony, outpost, residence, reservation, hamlet, refuge.

sever [*sev* · er] *v.* bisect, carve, cleave, detach, disjoin, disunite, rend, slice, sunder ("sever a limb"); abandon, disjoin, dissolve, divide, separate, terminate ("sever ties").

severable [*sev* · er · e · bul] *adj.* separable, divisible, apportionable, fissile, fissionable, detachable.

several [*sev* · rel] *adj.* certain, considerable, disparate, individual, numerous, proportionate ("several books on the subject"); separate, distinct, severable.

severally [*sev* · rel · ee] *adv.* distinctly, separately, personally, apart from others ("severally liable").

severance [*sev* · rense] *n.* separation, termination, partition, division.

sex *n.* intercourse, lust, reproduction, attraction; gender, masculinity, femininity.

sexism [*sek* · sizm] *n.* bias, discrimination, chauvinism.

sexual [*sek* · shoo · el] *adj.* prurient, erotic, carnal, indecent.

sham *adj.* artificial, counterfeit, adulterated, fictitious, substitute, feigned, false, pretended.

sham *n.* burlesque, caricature, façade, deceit, fake, imitation, fraud, pretext.

share *v.* parcel out, partition, apportion, partake, divide, measure, mete, allot, assign ("to share the profits").

share *n.* portion, allotment, contribution, ratio, percentage, quantum, pittance, need ("share of the business"); stock, security, asset ("corporate shares").

shareholder [*share* · hole · der] *n.* stockholder, owner, investor.

shave *v.* oppress, overreach, cut away, skim, reduce, cheat.

shelter [*shel* · ter] *n.* sanctuary, care, cover, asylum, support, lodging ("shelter from the storm"); benefit, advantage, hedge, gain ("tax shelter").

sheriff [*sherr* · if] *n.* police, official, marshal.

shifting [*shif* · ting] *adj.* varying, wavering, vacillating, alternating, drifting, changing.

ship *n.* boat, freighter, vessel, yacht.

ship *v.* address, consign, direct, dispatch, embark, freight, transfer, deliver ("ship these goods").

shipment [*ship* · ment] *n.* delivery, cargo, goods, property.

shipper [*ship* · er] *n.* carrier, transporter, consignor.

shirk *v.* evade, neglect, avoid, shun, dodge, duck, ignore.

shoplifting [*shop* · lif · ting] *n.* larceny, theft, stealing.

shore *n.* waterside, border, brim, littoral, margin, shingle, embankment ("down by the shore").

S

shore *v.* beef up, bolster, bulwark, buttress, strengthen, sustain, underpin, upbear ("shore up").

short *adj.* succinct, laconic, terse, concise, scanty, abridged ("short story"); small, truncated, stunted, dwarfish, diminutive, minuscule, bantam ("short person"); deficient, exiguous, inadequate, meager, needy, lacking, wanting ("short on funds").

show *v.* brandish, demonstrate, exhibit, flaunt, proffer, showcase ("to show the goods"); appear, demonstrate, evince, manifest, proclaim, reveal ("show remorse").

show *n.* burlesque, carnival, entertainment, pageant, performance, presentation, spectacle ("to go to a show"); affectation, air, display, guise, illusion, ostentation, semblance ("to put on a show of happiness").

shyster [*shy* · ster] *n.* con man, charlatan, cheat, ripoff artist.

sick *adj.* unhealthy, unsound, miserable, distressed, perverted, infirm.

sight *n.* afterimage, appearance, perception, eyesight, ken, seeing ("to lose one's sight"); spectacle, display, exhibit, pageant, scene, show ("what a sight!").

sign *n.* indication, assurance, augury, divination, omen, foretoken, portent, presager ("sign of things to come"); board, billboard, placard, poster, bulletin, beacon, guidepost ("street sign").

sign *v.* acknowledge, authorize, autograph, initial, inscribe, subscribe, witness ("sign on the dotted line"); beckon, express, flag, gesticulate, signalize, signify ("sign to him to walk this way").

signature [*sig* · ne · cher] *n.* autograph, endorsement, John Hancock, holograph.

significance [sig · *nif* · ih · kants] *n.* import, importance, value, relevance, weight, substance, note, momentousness.

silence [*sy* · lense] *n.* quiet, muteness, speechlessness, quietude, reticence, timidity ("Silence is required in the library").

silence [*sy* · lense] *v.* still, hush, muzzle, nullify, quell, allay, diminish, curb ("silence the crowd").

silent [*sy* · lent] *adj.* quiet, reticent, reserved, uncommunicative, uninformative ("The officer remained silent"); undeclared, nonpublic, implied, hidden, concealed ("a silent partner").

similar [*sim* · ih · ler] *adj.* like, cognate, analogous, collateral, correlative, homogeneous, identical, kindred. *Ant.* antithetic.

simple [*sim* · pul] *adj.* single, plain, ordinary, basic, fundamental, unembellished, unmixed ("a simple book of instructions"); uncomplicated, straightforward, uninvolved, manageable, unsophisticated, transparent ("a simple solution"); amateur, honest, trusting, naive, unpretentious, unsophisticated ("a simple person").

simulated [*sim* · yoo · lay · ted] *adj.* imitated, pretended, practice, counterfeited, feigned ("a simulated journey").

simultaneous [sy · mul · *tay* · nee · yes] *adj.* contemporaneous, concurrent, synchronic, accompanying, contemporary.

single [*sing* · gul] *adj.* distinguished, especial, exclusive, original, private, unique, unitary ("single most important issue"); bachelor, celibate, unmarried, mateless, unattached, companionless, unfetched ("singles bar").

singular [*sing* · gyoo · lur] *adj.* different, distinct, exclusive, odd, eccentric, uncommon, unique, particular, unusual.

sit *v.* assemble, hold court, gather, convene, officiate, congregate, deliberate, reign ("A circuit court sits every day"); ensconce, install, lie, relax, remain, rest ("sit down").

skeptical [*skep* · tih · kul] *adj.* doubting, mistrusting, incredulous, suspicious. *Ant.* credulous.

skill *n.* aptitude, talent, expertise, intelligence, facility, proficiency, ability.

skilled *adj.* expert, qualified, talented, adept, able.

slander [*slan* · der] *n.* defamation, slur, aspersion, calumny, vilification, denigration, vituperation ("slander of character").

slander [*slan* · der] *v.* discredit, impugn, belittle, defame, anathematize, denigrate, malign, degrade ("slander one's name"). *Ant.* praise.

slanderous [*slan* · der · us] *adj.* defamatory, derogatory, vilifying, denigrating.

slavery [*slay* · ver · ee] *n.* exploitation, captivity, enslavement, duress, subjugation, conquest, shackles, serfdom.

slight *n.* insult, disrespect, affront, discourtesy, disdain, indifference, neglect, rebuff ("a slight against someone").

slight *adv.* insignificant, insubstantial, meager, minor, negligible, paltry, superficial ("a slight difference").

small *adj.* little, tiny, short, minimal, diminutive ("a small amount"); petty, bigoted, parochial ("a small person").

smuggling [*smug* · ling] *v.* bootlegging, exporting, pirating, pushing, running.

sober [*so* · bur] *adj.* rational, reasonable, moderate; somber, grave, serious.

social [*so* · shel] *adj.* societal, sociological, collective, communal, interdependent, common, human, civil.

society [*so* · *sy* · e · tee] *n.* association, group, civilization, commonwealth, fellowship, humanity ("today's society in America"); alliance, brotherhood, clique, coterie, fraternity, institute, league ("society of professional engineers"); aristocracy, elite, gentry, haut monde, quality, patriciate ("high society").

sodomy [*sod* · e · mee] *n.* bestiality, perversion, deviation, depravity, degeneration, anal intercourse.

sole *adj.* singular, single, unattached, alone, exclusive, solitary, particular, unconditional ("the sole heir").

solemn [*saw* · lem] *adj.* austere, deliberate, dignified, grave, serious, earnest, funereal, pensive, portentous ("solemn occasion"); ceremonial, devotional, dignified, hallowed, majestic, momentous, ostentatious ("solemn oath").

solicit [*so* · *liss* · it] *v.* accost, canvass, implore, inquire, postulate, request, query; pander, pimp, procure.

solicitation [so · liss · ih · *tay* · shen] *n.* petition, requisition, entreaty, demand, proposal, adjuration, plea.

solicitor [so · *liss* · ih · ter] lawyer, attorney, counsel, public attorney.

solution [so · *loo* · shun] *n.* answer, explanation, resolution; substance, compound, mixture, solvent.

solve *v.* resolve, untangle, answer, explain, fathom, understand, penetrate, unlock, decipher ("solve the mystery").

solvent [*sol* · vent] *adj.* sound, financially stable, reliable, creditworthy, responsible, solid.

sound *v.* signal, babble, burst, chatter, crack, murmur, resound, reverberate ("sound the call").

S

sound *adj.* accurate, advisable, consequent, judicious, profound, sensible; authoritative, canonical, dependable, legal, solid, solvent, valid ("sound advice"); whole, healthy, sane ("sound mind").

sound *n.* noise, din, clamor; tone, vibration, intonation, music.

source *n.* root, foundation, cause, origin, initiator; informer, informant, stool pigeon.

sovereign [*sov · ren*] *adj.* governing, absolute, imperial, authorized, independent, autonomous, dominant ("sovereign body").

sovereign [*sov · ren*] *n.* monarch, queen, king, ruler, tyrant, head, czar, autocrat ("sovereign of the country").

sovereignty [*sov · ren · ty*] *n.* self-rule, dominion, jurisdiction, autonomy, primacy, loyalty.

space *n.* distance, room, latitude; area, acreage, territory, footage, range.

special [*spe · shul*] *adj.* unique, limited, specific, noteworthy, extraordinary, idiosyncratic, distinct, distinctive, personal, generous, atypical, particular; favored, select, unusual, extraordinary.

specialist [*speh · shul · ist*] *n.* master, expert, authority, skilled practitioner, scholar, virtuoso.

specific [spe · *sif* · ik] *adj.* explicit, definite, distinctive, categorical, pertinent, relevant, circumscribed, particular, limited.

specification [spess · ih · fih · *kay* · shen] *n.* enumeration, designation, stipulation, termization, description, recital.

specificity [spess · ih · *fiss* · ih · tee] *n.* detail, particularity, precision.

speculation [spek · yoo · *lay* · shen] *n.* belief, cerebration, contemplation, deliberation, guesswork, opinion ("speculation as to where the attack will be"); gamble, backing, flutter, hazard, plunge, venture, trading ("speculation on the market"); contemplation, meditation, reflection.

speculative [*spek* · yoo · le · tiv] *adj.* theoretical, hypothetical, unproven, unconfirmed, suppositional, tentative, indefinite.

speech *n.* articulation, communication, diction, dialogue, enunciation, expression, idiom ("strange speech pattern"); address, debate, disquisition, harangue, panegyric, parlance ("a long speech").

spendthrift [*spend* · thrift] *n.* improvident, prodigal, profligate, wastrel.

spirit [*spir* · it] *n.* soul, character, energy, vigor, zeal, vitality, intent, psyche.

split *n.* opening, breach, chasm, cleavage, cleft, cut, bisection, separation ("a split in one's pants"); division, alienation, discord, dissension, divergence, estrangement, fissure ("a split in the justices' opinions").

split *v.* bifurcate, burst, dichotomize, dissever, isolate, sever ("to split up").

spoil *v.* impair, harm, hurt, mutilate, ruin, wreck, botch, mess up ("spoil the party"); decay, decompose, sour, turn ("The fruit will spoil"); plunder, loot, despoil, ransack ("spoil the town").

spoils *n.* takings, booty, haul, loot, prize, winnings.

spokesman [*spokes* · man] *n.* voice, speaker, agent, delegate, messenger, mouthpiece, go-between.

spoliation [spo · lee · *ay* · shen] *n.* alteration, destruction; plundering, pillaging.

sponsor [*spon* · ser] *n.* patron, benefactor, backer, supporter, promoter, advocate.

sponsor [*spon* · ser] *v.* endorse, finance, support, patronize, underwrite, back, promote.

S

spontaneous [spon · *tane* · ee · us] *adj.* casual, extemporaneous, impromptu, instinctive, irresistible, unavoidable, unpremeditated ("a spontaneous exclamation").

spouse *n.* wife, husband, mate, companion, partner.

spurious [*spyoor* · ee · es] *adj.* apocryphal, contrived, sham, bogus, deceitful, feigned, illegitimate, simulated, false, fake, counterfeit, unauthentic.

spy *n.* informant, investigator, agent, sleuth, snoop, secret agent.

spy *v.* observe, detect, view, watch, see, pry, eavesdrop, snoop.

staff *n.* assistants, workers, associates, faculty, crew, clerical staff, personnel.

stake *n.* pale, paling, picket, post, spike, stone ("tent stake"); ante, chance, hazard, peril, pledge, risk ("What are the stakes?"); claim, concern, interest, involvement, prize, purse ("stake in a company").

stake *v.* bankroll, capitalize, finance, grubstake, imperil, jeopardize ("to stake everything").

stale *adj.* unasserted, wasted, effete, withered, faded, untimely, stagnant ("stale claim").

stamp *n.* seal, certification, endorsement, attestation, sign, authentication, identification.

stand *n.* angle, attitude, carriage, determination, bent, bias, view, slant, standpoint ("stand on an issue"); board, booth, box, bracket, platform, station, post ("take the stand").

stand *v.* cock, dispose, erect, locate, mount, place, poise ("stand up"); be valid, continue, endure, fill, halt, hold, prevail, stay ("the decision stands").

standard [*stan* · derd] *n.* archetype, axiom, barometer, exemplar, gauge, median, principle ("standard for others"); banner, colors, emblem, ensign, figure, insignia, pennant ("The standard is always present at a military parade").

standard [*stan* · derd] *adj.* regular, accepted, classic, customary, orthodox, regulation, normal, established ("standard deduction").

standing [*stan* · ding] *n.* position, cachet, consequence, dignity, eminence, repute ("The colonel's standing with the president").

standing [*stan* · ding] *adj.* continuing, permanent, existing, perpetual, regular, repeated ("standing army").

staple [*stay* · pul] *adj.* necessary, basic, essential, fundamental, important, predominant, standard.

start *n.* origin, beginning, outset, opening, genesis, derivation.

stash *v.* hide, store, hoard, cache, conceal, put.

state *n.* accompaniment, capacity, character, circumstance, contingency, essential ("a state of flux"); cachet, ceremony, consequence, display, majesty, prestige; commonwealth, community, federation, kingdom, nation, republic, sovereignty ("controlled by the state").

stated [*stay* · ted] *adj.* decided, ordained, defined, ascertained, stipulated, mandated, declared, expressed; agreed, settled, official.

statement [*state* · ment] *n.* acknowledgement, affidavit, allegation, description, dictum, manifesto, testimony, deposition, proclamation, utterance, vocalization ("statement on the record"); affidavit, audit, bill, budget, charge, invoice, reckoning ("monthly bank statement").

status [*stat* · iss] *n.* rank, cachet, position, dignity, merit, mode, prominence.

statute [*stat* · shoot] *n.* law, bill, act, canon, edict, ordinance, precept, mandate, enactment.

statutory [*sta · tyoo · tore · ee*] *adj.* legal, lawful, sanctioned, authorized, legislative.

stay *v.* abide, continue, dally, linger, loiter, sojourn, remain, hover ("stay here"); adjourn, arrest, hinder, postpone, intermit, obstruct, suspend ("stay the execution").

stay *n.* deferment, halt, remission, reprieve, standstill, suspension ("stay of execution"); brace, underpinning, buttress, reinforcement, truss, stanchion ("a supporting stay").

steal *v.* abduct, appropriate, cozen, divert, pillage, purloin ("to steal money"); creep, flit, glide, insinuate, skulk, slip ("to steal a bunt").

stealthy *adj.* covert, clandestine, secretive, shifty, sly, underhanded.

stellar [*stel · lur*] *adj.* eminent, main, outstanding, principal, paramount, distinguished; astral, starry, sidereal, starlike.

step *n.* advance, achievement, move, procedure, degree, rung, progression, act, action.

sterile [*ste · ril*] *adj.* barren, bare, fallow; clean, hygenic, sanitary, germ-free.

stipulate [*stip · yoo · layt*] *v.* agree, covenant, designate, particularize, specificate, mandate, require, impose ("If you are hired, I will stipulate the terms of your employment").

stipulation [*stip · yoo · lay · shen*] *n.* agreement, circumscription, designation, precondition, engagement, requirement, reservation, admission, concession; mandate, requirement, condition.

stock *n.* merchandise, array, assets, cache, commodities, reservoir, store, supply ("large stock"); animals, beasts, domestic animals, flock, fowl, horses, livestock ("Our stock is at 20 head"); background, breed, clan, extraction, forebears, parentage, pedigree ("from good stock"); assets, blue chips, bonds, capital, convertible paper, share ("stock in the company").

stock *adj.* commonplace, banal, conventional, customary, boilerplate, overused, traditional ("a stock answer").

stock *v.* accumulate, amass, equip, furnish, gather, provision ("to stock up").

stockbroker [*stok · bro · ker*] *n.* broker, securities broker, agent.

stop *v.* cease, close, desist, discontinue, finish, pause, end, tarry ("stop working"); arrest, bar, congest, hinder, restrain, repress, stall, suspend ("stop and frisk").

stop *n.* barricade, block, check, control, cutoff, stoppage, layoff ("work stop"); destination, sojourn, station, termination ("reach one's stop on the train route").

stoppage [*stop · ej*] *n.* abeyance, blockage, check, closure, cutoff, deduction, hindrance, interruption.

storage [*store · ej*] *n.* accumulation, storing, saving, collection, stockpiling.

store *v.* accumulate, amass, hoard, stockpile, treasure ("store for later use").

store *n.* arsenal, bank, cache, conservatory, depository, depot, pantry ("take supplies to the store").

story [*stor · ee*] *n.* lie, deceit, fabrication, concoction, distortion, fantasy, myth, prevarication; narrative, recounting, account, tale, article, report.

straight *adj.* genuine, reliable; direct, frank, bold; uncurved, linear, level; heterosexual, normal, non-gay.

stranger [*strane · jer*] *n.* foreigner, newcomer, disinterested party, bystander, immigrant, interloper.

strategy [*strat · e · gee*] *n.* approach, plan, course, tactics, means, system, method, proposed action.

street *n.* artery, road, avenue, boulevard, byway, passage, terrace, thoroughfare.

S

stress *n.* strain, exertion, anxiety, burden, pressure, tension, demand; emphasis, importance, accent, weight.

strict *adj.* austere, dictatorial, despotic, exacting, stringent, puritanical, adamant ("strict parents"); complete, faithful, meticulous, precise, restrictive, scrupulous, utter, veracious ("strict regimen"); literal, narrow ("strict construction").

strike *v.* hit, bang, beat, chastise, clobber, impel, pummel, punch ("To strike one's spouse"); achieve, attain, come across, effect, encounter, seize, take ("to strike gold"); arbitrate, mediate, mutiny, resist, revolt, slow down ("to strike from work"); be plausible, carry, have semblance, impress, influence, inspire ("to strike someone as being smart"); eliminate, disqualify, dismiss ("to strike a juror").

strike *n.* stoppage, revolt, walkout, dispute, boycott.

striking [*strike* · ing] *adj.* arresting, astonishing, compelling, dazzling, forcible, impressive.

study [*stuh* · dee] *v.* review, read, reflect on, learn, investigate, observe, explore, analyze.

style *v.* address, caption, heading, call, denominate, designate ("How is the case styled?").

style *n.* appearance, bearing, behavior, carriage, genre, idiosyncrasy, trend ("today's style").

subdivision [*sub* · dih · vizh · en] *n.* class, community, area, development, group, sub-class, subsidiary.

subdue [*sub* · *doo*] *v.* beat, conquer, suppress, quell, quiet, silence, tame, curb, calm, humble.

subject [*sub* · jekt] *n.* topic, affair, discussion, material, proposal, problem, question ("stay on the subject"); case, client, customer, dependent, liege, patient, vassal ("the king's subject").

subject [*sub* · jekt] *adj.* accountable, captive, dependent, collateral, contingent, exposed, vulnerable, obedient, prone.

submission [sub · *mish* · en] *n.* compliance, acquiescence, defeat, humility, pliability, tractability, surrender.

submit [sub · *mit*] *v.* abide, surrender, accede, acquiesce, capitulate, indulge, succumb, tolerate, refer, present, propose, suggest ("submit issues for your consideration").

subordinate [sub · *or* · din · et] *n.* aide, assistant, attendant, inferior, junior, second ("to be a subordinate to one's boss").

subordinate [sub · *or* · din · et] *adj.* auxiliary, ancillary, secondary, subalternate, subsidiary, unequal ("The captain is a subordinate officer to the general").

subordination [sub · or · dih · *nay* · shen] *n.* submission, subservience, surrender ("a subordination agreement").

subpoena [sub · *peen* · uh] *v.* order, command, summon, beckon, demand.

subpoena [sub · *peen* · uh] *n.* order, command, mandate, citation, summons, writ, call, directive.

subrogation [sub · ro · *gay* · shen] *n.* displacement, substitution, transfer, transference, exchange, switch, supplanting.

subscribe [sub · *skribe*] *v.* buy, endorse, enroll, register, ("subscribe to the magazine"); accede, adhere, advocate, consent, endorse, favor, sanction, sign ("to subscribe to a school of thought").

subscribed [sub · *skribed*] *adv.* signed, approved of, sanctioned.

subscription [sub · *skrip* · shun] *n.* enrollment, acceptance, registration; endorsement, confirmation, signature.

subsequent [*sub* · se · kwent] *adj.* succeeding, ensuing, sequential, trailing, eventual, proximate. *Ant.* prior.

subsidiary [sub · *sid* · ee · er · ee] *adj.* secondary, subordinate, auxiliary, adjurant, collateral, tributory.

subsidize [*sub* · sih · dize] *v.* bankroll, contribute, endow, finance, promote, sponsor, support, underwrite.

subsidy [*sub* · sih · dee] *n.* grant, alimony, bequest, allowance, gift, gratuity, indemnity, pension, subsidization.

subsist [sub · *sist*] *v.* continue, endure, persist, survive, last, live.

subsistence [sub · *sis* · tense] *n.* affluence, competence, income, livelihood, necessities, provision, ration, support, allowance.

substance [*sub* · stense] *n.* actuality, concreteness, reality, corpus, fabric, person, staple ("analyze an unknown substance"); effect, essentiality, focus, import, innards, marrow, quintessence ("the substance of an argument"); wealth, affluence, assets, estate, fortune, means, resources ("a person of substance").

substantial [sub · *stan* · shel] *adj.* abundant, consequential, durable, extraordinary, heavyweight, plentiful ("a substantial supply"); actual, concrete, existent, physical, righteous, sensible, tangible ("substantial problem"); affluent, comfortable, easy, opulent, prosperous, solvent.

substantiate [sub · *stan* · chee · ayt] *v.* corroborate, prove, verify, attest, affirm, uphold, validate.

substantive [*sub* · sten · tiv] real, essential, fundamental, elemental, vital, meritorious. *Ant.* procedural.

substitute [*sub* · stih · tewt] *n.* alternate, auxiliary, backup, delegate, expedient.

subversive [sub · *ver* · siv] *n.* insurgent, revolutionary, radical, defiant.

subversive [sub · *ver* · siv] *adj.* revolutionary, radical, undermining.

subvert [sub · *vert*] *v.* defeat, undo, topple, disestablish, dismantle, extinguish, extirpate.

succeed [suk · *seed*] *v.* accomplish, achieve, acquire, earn, conquer, master ("succeed in finishing the race"); accede, assume, ensue, follow, postdate, inherit, replace ("succeed to the throne").

successor [suk · *sess* · er] *n.* heir, substitute, recipient, donee, grantee, beneficiary.

succinct [*suk* · sinkt] *adj.* brief, concise, terse, laconic, compact, pithy, curt. *Ant.* verbose.

sudden [*sud* · en] *adj.* instant, immediate, unexpected, unanticipated, unplanned, abrupt.

sue *v.* accuse, appeal, beseech, litigate, plead, prosecute, claim.

suffer [*suf* · er] *v.* ache, agonize, brave, deteriorate, droop, hurt, languish, sicken, writhe ("suffer great pain"); abide, accept, acquiesce, countenance, indulge, sustain ("suffer the consequences").

suffering [*suf* · er · ing] *n.* adversity, anguish, affliction, discomfort, dolor, martyrdom.

sufficient [suh · *fish* · ent] *adj.* enough, acceptable, ample, aplenty, commensurable, competent, copious, adequate.

suit *n.* case, cause, litigation, proceeding, trial ("a suit in court").

suit *v.* accord, agree, befit, beseem, conform, correspond, match ("It suits me just fine").

S

sum *n.* aggregate, amount, body, bulk, entirety, integral, total, synopsis.

summarily [sum · *ehr* · ih · ly] *adv.* arbitrarily, expeditiously, forthwith, immediately, peremptorily, promptly, quickly.

summary [*sum* · e · ree] *n.* abbreviation, abridgment, abstract, compendium, epitome, essence, headnote, precise, prospectus, sketch ("a summary of the speech").

summary [*sum* · e · ree] *adj.* short, concise, brief, cursory, laconic, succinct.

summation [sum · *ay* · shen] *n.* summary, recapitulation, closing argument, final argument, summing-up.

summon [*sum* · en] *v.* arouse, call, assemble, beckon, cite, petition, mobilize, muster.

summons [*sum* · enz] *n.* citation, mandate, process, notification, command, direction.

supercilious [soo · per · *sil* · ee · us] *adj.* arrogant, haughty, patronizing, lofty, disdainful, pompous, prideful.

superficial [soo · per · *fish* · al] *adj.* cursory, hasty, surface, perfunctory ("a superficial examination of the room"); shallow, unthinking, depthless, empty ("a superficial person").

superfluous [su · *per* · flew · us] *adj.* excessive, unnecessary, irrelevant. *Ant.* essential.

superior [soo · *peer* · ee · er] *n.* director, senior, principal, commander, master, leader, foreman ("my superior at work").

superior [soo · *peer* · ee · er] *adj.* excellent, better, sterling, eminent, marvelous, nonpareil, distinguished, inimitable ("superior quality"); sanctimonious, snobby, lordly, arrogant, vainglorious, patronizing ("a superior attitude").

supersede [soo · per · *seed*] *v.* supplant, abandon, annul, desert, replace, discard, outmode, suspend, void.

supervening [soo · per · *veen* · ing] *adj.* additional, subsequent, new, independent.

supervision [soo · per · *viz* · en] *n.* guidance, control, care, administration, management, charge.

supervisor [*soo* · per · vy · zer] *n.* administrator, caretaker, boss, curator, superintendent, inspector, director.

supplant [suh · *plant*] *v.* replace, displace, dismiss, supersede, eject, drive out, substitute, take the place of.

supplemental [sup · le · *men* · tel] *adj.* supplementary, additional, incidental, extraneous, further.

supply [suh · *ply*] *v.* equip, provide, stock, deliver, bestow, endow, furnish.

supply [suh · *ply*] *n.* amount, hoard, cache, provisions.

support [sup · *ort*] *v.* bolster, buttress, embed, reinforce, undergird ("The beam supports the ceiling"); bankroll, encourage, maintain, nourish, stiffen, underwrite ("His parents still support him"); abet, assist, countenance, justify, substantiate, uphold, verify ("support her claim").

support [sup · *ort*] *n.* abutment, backing, collar, flotation, fulcrum, pillar, reinforcement ("Good supports hold the building up"); aid, assistance, encouragement, succor, patronage, sustenance, loyalty ("to give support to an upset person"); alienation, alimony, maintenance, provision, responsibility, sustenance ("child support").

suppress [suh · *press*] *v.* annihilate, censor, muffle, overthrow, quench, spike ("to suppress rebellion"); restrain, conceal, exclude ("suppress the evidence").

suppression [suh · *presh* · en] *n.* control, concealment, inhibition, restraint.

supra [*soo* · pra] *adv.* above-mentioned, foregoing.

supremacy [soo · *prem* · e · see] *n.* mastery, leadership, superiority, preeminence, excellence, dominance.

surcharge [*ser* · charj] *n.* surtax, fee, penalty.

surety [*shoor* · e · tee] *n.* sponsor, backer, indemnitor, insurer, cosigner, bondsman, signatory, voucher.

surface [*ser* · fiss] *n.* covering, expanse, exterior, periphery, superficiality, superficies, veneer ("the surface of the space shuttle").

surface [*ser* · fiss] *adj.* apparent, covering, depthless, exterior, shallow, superficial ("surface paint").

surface [*ser* · fiss] *v.* appear, arise, emerge, materialize, transpire ("The body surfaced in the lake").

surfeit [*sur* · fit] *n.* excess, abundance, profusion, oversupply, surplus, glut.

surname [*ser* · name] *n.* last name, family name.

surpass [ser · *pass*] *v.* beat, exceed, outrank, prevail, outshine.

surplus [*ser* · plus] *n.* balance, overage, overflow, plethora, residue, surfeit ("The grocery store has a surplus of meat products").

surplus [*ser* · plus] *adj.* superfluent, supernumery, extra, unused, excess, spare ("surplus material").

surplusage [*ser* · plus · ej] *n.* surplus, redundancy, irrelevance, immateriality, verbosity, extravenous material.

surprise [ser · *prize*] *n.* amazement, bewilderment, fortune, precipitance, wonder, marvel, awe.

surprise [ser · *prize*] *v.* amaze, astound, discomfit, discover, flabbergast, petrify, stagger ("to surprise someone").

surrender [ser · *en* · der] *v.* abandon, capitulate, give up, consign, knuckle under, relinquish, renounce ("to surrender the army").

surrender [ser · *en* · der] *n.* abandonment, abdication, acquiescence, capitulation, sedition, relenting ("the army's surrender").

surreptitious [sur · ep · *tish* · us] *adj.* secret, furtive, covert, stealthy, sly, clandestine, underhand.

surrogate [*ser* · e · get] *n.* alternate, substitute, agent, vicarious, actor, delegate, recourse, proxy, stand-in ("surrogate mother").

surveillance [ser · *vale* · ense] *n.* observation, bugging, control, direction, examination, scrutiny, supervision, vigil, eavesdropping, wiretapping.

survey [ser · *vey*] *v.* appraise, assay, canvass, measure, prospect, reconnoiter, scrutinize, superintend ("to survey the land").

survey [*ser* · vey] *n.* analysis, study, audit, outline, scan, review, précis, syllabus ("a survey of the history of western civilization").

survival [ser · *vy* · vel] *n.* sustenance, staying, lasting, leftover, durability, vestige, relic.

survive [ser · *vyve*] *v.* last, live, hang on, endure.

survivor [ser · *vy* · ver] *n.* widow, widower, orphan, descendant, heir, beneficiary.

suspect [sus · *pekt*] *v.* distrust, conceive, disbelieve, mistrust, presume, speculate, surmise ("to suspect someone of murder").

suspect [*sus* · pekt] *n.* accused, alleged criminal, defendant.

suspect [*sus* · pekt] *adj.* doubtable, dubious, incredible, questionable, suspicious, unclear ("suspect origins").

suspend [sus · *pend*] *v.* append, dangle, sling, swing, attach, hang down ("to suspend a banner from the ceiling"); adjourn, discontinue, intermit, put off, procrastinate, retard, postpone, eliminate ("The committee has suspended its deliberations"); withdraw, revoke ("suspend his license").

suspended [sus · *pen* · ded] *adj.* tabled, discontinued, deferred, shelved, withheld, delayed, put off ("a suspended sentence").

suspense [sus · *pense*] *n.* anxiety, uncertainty, dilemma, expectation, impatience, perplexity, tension.

suspension [sus · *pen* · shen] *n.* delay, abeyance, adjournment, cessation, deferment, intermission, latency, interruption; removal, withdrawal.

suspicion [sus · *pish* · en] *n.* cynicism, incredulity, qualm, belief, surmise, wariness ("on suspicion of murder").

sustain [sus · *tane*] *v.* approve, bolster, continue, uphold, nourish, nurse, prolong ("sustain the statute"); endure, abide, brook, digest, encounter, tolerate, undergo ("sustain one's faith through the experience").

swear *v.* affirm, attest, vow, avow, depose, maintain, testify ("swear to tell the truth"); bedamn, blaspheme, curse, cuss, execrate, imprecate ("Swearing is very crude").

swindle [*swin* · dul] *v.* cheat, defraud, misrepresent, con, deceive, exploit.

sworn *adj.* verified, stated under oath, certified ("a sworn statement").

syllabus [*sil* · e · bus] *n.* headnote, outline, brief, abstract, summary.

symbol [*sim* · bul] *n.* mark, note, indication, trademark, emblem, manifestation, sign.

symbolic [sim · *bahl* · ik] *adj.* suggestive, illustrative, denotative, figurative, constructive. *Ant.* actual.

syndicate [*sin* · dik · et] *n.* association, board, cartel, chamber, committee, conglomerate, organization.

synopsis [sin · *op* · sis] *n.* review, summation, brief, outline, summary, abstract.

synthesize [*sin* · thih · size] *v.* integrate, harmonize, coordinate, combine.

system [*sis* · tem] *n.* program, strategy, technique, means, method, design, procedure.

systematic [sis · te · *mat* · ik] *adj.* regular, deliberate, organized, careful, precise, efficient.

tabloid [*tab · loyd*] *n.* newspaper, journal, press.

tacit [*tass · it*] *adj.* silent, implied, allusive, assumed, inarticulate, inferred, undeclared, unstated.

taciturn [*tass · ih · turn*] *adj.* reserved, untalkative, reticent, laconic, quiet, restrained, brusque.

taint *v.* poison, pollute, spoil, blemish, adulterate, befoul; pervert, tarnish, debase, defile.

take *n.* cut, gate, proceeds, receipts, revenue ("the take from the robbery").

take *v.* abduct, arrest, attain, clutch, entrap, overtake, seize ("to take an item"); abduct, approach, annex, rob, confiscate, purloin, seize ("to take jewelry from a store"); accept, accommodate, bear, suffer, weather, undergo ("take the pain"); devour, feed, drink, inhale, ingest, eat ("take the medicine").

taking [*tay · king*] *n.* dispossession, seizure, appropriation.

tamper [*tam · per*] *v.* interfere, alter, diversify, interpose, interlope, manipulate; corrupt, fix, influence, lubricate, manipulate, rig,

tampering [*tam · per · ing*] *n.* altering, meddling, adulteration, interference.

tangible [*tan · jih · bul*] *adj.* appreciable, corporeal, touchable, material, detectable, discernable, incarnate, manifest.

target [*tar · get*] *n.* ambition, destination, function, intention, objective, goal, purpose ("deficit targets"); byword, game, prey, quarry, victim ("target of our jokes").

tariff [*tahr · if*] *n.* assessment, tax, duty, fee, charge, excise, impost, rate, toll.

tawdry [*taw · dree*] *adj.* cheap, common, crass, crude, shoddy, shabby, sleazy, vulgar, gaudy, tacky, inelegant.

tax *n.* levy, assessment, tribute, impost, exaction, imposition, capitulation, tithe ("a graduated tax").

tax *v.* assess, levy, exact, collect, require; burden, oppress, overload, deplete, enervate, wear down, encumber, weigh, task ("to tax my patience"); arraign, censure, criminate, impeach, impute, inculpate, reproach ("to tax one's credibility").

taxable [*tak · se · bul*] *adj.* liable to taxation, assessible, chargeable, exactable ("a taxable gift").

teacher [*tee · cher*] *n.* instructor, professor, educator, master, mentor, academician, guide.

T

technical [*tek* · nih · kul] *adj.* skilled, specialized, scientific, vocational, technological, particularized, esoteric, abstruse ("a technical field"); immaterial, clerical, insubstantial, without prejudice ("a technical error").

technicality [tek · nih · *kal* · ih · tee] *n.* detail, minor point, trifle, triviality, fine point.

temporary [*tem* · pe · rer · ee] *adj.* fading, limited, provisional, momentary, evanescent, ephemeral, elusive, pro tempore.

tenancy [*ten* · en · see] *n.* holding, leasing, occupancy, residence, rental.

tenant [*ten* · ent] *n.* lessee, occupier, renter, boarder, leaseholder, inhabitant, roomer.

tender [*ten* · der] *adj.* caring, affectionate, benevolent; delicate, fragile, weak, vulnerable; painful, sore, aching, inflamed; young, inexperienced, youthful.

tender [*ten* · der] *n.* payment, offer.

tender [*ten* · der] *v.* advance, offer, give, pay, submit.

tenement [*ten* · e · ment] *n.* slum housing, rental housing, apartment building, dwelling.

tenet [*ten* · et] *n.* doctrine, belief, principle, creed, presumption, rule, canon.

tenor [*ten* · er] *n.* meaning, current, direction, terms, evolution, inclination, substance, purport, tendency ("the tenor of a note or deed").

tentative [*ten* · tuh · tiv] *adj.* provisional, conditional, negotiable, exploratory; cautious, doubtful, hesitant, wavering.

tenure [*ten* · yer] *n.* administration, term, incumbency, occupancy, proprietorship, residence.

term *n.* interval, tenure, session, incumbency, semester, cycle ("the president's term in office"); appellation, article, caption, nomenclature, terminology, vocable ("term of art"); limit, boundary, culmination, fruition, limitation, confine.

terminable [*term* · in · e · bul] *adj.* defeasible, limitable, finite, conditional ("a terminable interest").

termination [term · ih · *nay* · shen] *n.* abortion, ending, consequence, cessation, desistance, finale, outcome, terminus, cancellation ("the termination of a contract").

terminus [*ter* · me · nus] *n.* boundary, limit, ending point.

terms *n.* conditions, provisions, details ("terms of the deed").

territory [*tehr* · ih · tore · ee] *n.* area, boundary, nation, commonwealth, mandate, neighborhood, province.

terrorism [*tare* · or · iz · em] *n.* coercion, duress, cruelty, inhumanity.

test *n.* examination, assessment, confirmation, elimination, evaluation, check, inspection, trial, investigation.

test *v.* examine, analyze, experiment, investigate, evaluate, question, appraise, inquire ("to test one's knowledge").

testament [*tes* · te · ment] *n.* attestation, colloquy, covenant, demonstration, statement, exemplification, testimonial, will, last will.

testify [*tes* · tih · fy] *v.* affirm, announce, corroborate, depose, evince, swear, warrant, declare, attest.

testimony [*tes* · tih · moh · nee] *n.* affidavit, attestation, corroboration, demonstration, evidence, substantiation, assertion, deposition.

theft *n.* stealing, annexation, deprivation, embezzlement, peculation, pilferage, purloining, rapacity, larceny, seizure.

theory [*theer* · ee] *n.* hypothesis, approach, assumption, codification, guesswork, philosophy, postulate, principle.

thereafter [thair · *af* · ter] *adv.* afterward, thereby, somewhat, generally, nigh, roughly.

thereby [*thair* · by] *adv.* by reason of, by virtue of, because of.

thief *n.* pirate, robber, embezzler, defrauder, pilferer, purloiner, kleptomaniac, criminal, peculator, outlaw, lawbreaker.

thing *n.* apparatus, commodity, corporeality, instrument, phenomenon, substance ("What is that thing?"); accomplishment, deed, episode, obligation, occasion, phenomenon, proceeding ("to do the thing"); attitude, craze, fad, fetish, fixation, crush, mania ("to have a thing for someone").

third degree [thurd de · *gree*] *n.* interrogation, examination, inquiry, inquest, prolonged questioning.

threat *n.* warning, rattling, intimidation, imminence, fulmination, impendence, menace, blackmail, omen.

through *adv.* complete, concluded, over, terminated, done ("to be through with something").

through *adj.* constant, nonstop, opened, rapid, regular, unbroken ("through street").

through *prep.* by the agency of, via, on account of, as a consequence of, in the name of, as the agent of ("through the power invested in me"); about, clear, in and out, into, throughout, past, around, straight ("through the door").

thwart *v.* defeat, stifle, stop, impede, interrupt, obstruct, avert.

ticket [*tik* · et] *n.* admission, badge, board, card, pass, credential, document, license, receipt.

tide *n.* course, direction, ebb, flow, flux, torrent, vortex, wave.

time *n.* age, allotment, day, duration, interval, juncture, tempo ("time of day"); break, chance, occasion, peak, shot, show ("Now is the time").

timely [*time* · lee] *adj.* appropriate, auspicious, convenient, opportune, propitious, toward.

title [*ty* · tel] *n.* appellation, banner, caption, headline, description, rubric ("title of a book"); brand, cognomen, epithet, decoration, honorific, pseudonym ("title of honor"); authority, claim, commission, holding, entitlement ("clear title to the land").

title [*ty* · tel] *v.* baptize, christen, denominate, designate, dub, entitle, label, style, term ("to title the book").

token [*toh* · ken] *n.* badge, clue, symbol, mark, indicia, keepsake, manifestation, memento, sample.

tolerance [*tol* · er · ents] *n.* patience, compassion, understanding, abiding, endurance, capacity, freedom from prejudice, ability to withstand, fortitude.

tolerate [*tol* · er · ayt] *v.* accept, endure, forbear, allow, abide, suffer, submit to, stand, indulge.

toll *v.* announce, ring, chime, knell, peal, signal ("Toll the good news"); interrupt, suspend ("Toll the statute of limitations").

toll *n.* assessment, charge, customs, duty, exaction, impost, levy ("pay the toll"); casualties, cost, expense, inroad, losses, penalty ("the hurricane's death toll").

tort *n.* wrong, civil wrong, violation, breach of duty.

torture [*tore* · cher] *n.* agony, distress, dolor, excruciation, impalement, martyrdom.

torture [*tore* · cher] *v.* hurt, maim, agonize, excruciate, inflict pain, punish.

total [*toh* · tel] *n.* aggregate, all, budget, entirety, gross, quantum, sum ("the sum total").

total [*toh* · tel] *adj.* absolute, comprehensive, consummate, integral, plenary, totalitarian ("the total amount").

total [*toh* · tel] *v.* add, calculate, comprise, number, reckon, summate, totalize, tote ("total the invoice").

totalitarianism [to · tal · ih · *tair* · e · en · izm] *n.* oppression, coercion, tyranny, control.

town *n.* city, community, borough, hamlet, metropolis, village, municipality, township.

toxic [*tok* · sik] *adj.* poison, polluted, hazardous, infectious, poisonous.

tract *n.* lot, district, expanse, extent, parcel, spread, stretch; leaflet, pamphlet.

trade *n.* barter, commerce, enterprise, interchange, merchantry, transaction, truck ("world trade"); art, avocation, business, employment, handicraft, pursuit ("business trade").

trade *v.* exchange, buy, barter, deal, sell, transact, traffic, do business.

trademark [*trade* · mark] *n.* logo, brand, identification, mark, design, initials, logotype, stamp.

trading [*tray* · ding] *adj.* commercial, mercantile, business ("a trading company").

traditional [tra · *dish* · ih · nal] *adj.* usual, customary, common, accepted, long-standing, conventional, fixed.

traffic [*traf* · ik] *n.* movement, freight, gridlock, passengers, flow, vehicles ("heavy traffic on the roads"); barter, communion, familiarity, intimacy, intercourse, merchantry ("business traffic"); passing, transfer, dealings, sale, exchange ("traffic of goods").

traffic [*traf* · ik] *v.* barter, contact, deal, interact, sell, buy, interface, network ("to traffic drugs").

traitor [*tray* · ter] *n.* betrayer, informer, turncoat, deserter, conspirator, Judas, apostate.

transaction [tranz · *ak* · shen] *n.* action, activity, convention, negotiation, occurrence, purchase, business, dealing.

transcend [tran · *send*] *v.* exceed, go beyond, surmount, prevail, outrank, outshine.

transcript [*tran* · skript] *n.* copy, record, writing.

transfer [tranz · *fer*] *v.* assign, delegate, express, carry, relegate, tote ("to transfer title to someone").

transfer [*tranz* · fer] *n.* alteration, convention, deportation, relegation, passing, transference ("The transfer of power is complete").

transferable [tranz · *fer* · e · bul] *adj.* negotiable, assignable, transmissible.

transform [tranz · *form*] *v.* convert, reconstruct, alter, modify, redo, restyle, revamp, revolutionize.

transgression [tranz · *gress* · shun] *n.* crime, breach, wrong, wrongdoing, misconduct, misbehavior, infringement, violation.

transit [*tran* · zit] *n.* carriage, conveyance, infiltration, permeation, transference, passing ("goods in transit").

transition [tran · *zih* · shun] *n.* movement, passing, break, change, conversion, shift.

transitory [*tran* · zih · tore · ee] *adj.* fleeting, ephemeral, passing, evanescent.

transmit [trans · *mit*] *v.* deliver, dispatch, send, ship, communicate, transport.

trauma [*trawm* · uh] *n.* agony, anguish, collapse, derangement, upheaval, upset, injury.

traverse [tra · *vurs*] *v.* bisect, cross, negotiate, peregrinate, ply, range, transverse ("traverse the desert"); balk, contest, contravene, disaffirm, frustrate, gainsay ("traverse the lower court's opinion").

traverse [*trav* · ers] *adj.* denying, contradicting, crossing.

treason [*tree* · zen] *n.* crime, deceit, duplicity, faithlessness, perfidy, sedition.

treasurer [*trezh* · er · er] *n.* corporate officer, officer, controller, accountant.

treasury [*trezh* · er · ee] *n.* archive, bursar, cache, coffer, repository, vault.

treatise [*tree* · tis] *n.* argument, commentary, disquisition, dissertation, pamphlet, tractate, work, book.

treatment [*treet* · ment] *n.* cure, therapy, medication, regimen.

treaty [*tree* · tee] *n.* accord, alliance, concordance, entente, negotiation, settlement, understanding.

trespass [*tress* · pas] *n.* breach, contravention, entry, encroachment, iniquity, misdemeanor, obtrusion, poaching.

trial [*try* · el] *n.* analysis, audition, endeavor, probation, struggle, venture ("a trial of my abilities"); action, citation, hearing, litigation, prosecution, suit ("trial by jury"); adversity, affliction, bane, irritance, plague, rigor, tribulation ("trial in my life").

trial [*try* · el] *adj.* exploratory, pilot, test, preliminary, provisional, tentative ("a trial run").

tribe *n.* association, caste, division, horde, society, race, group, family.

tribunal [try · *byoon* · el] *n.* court, board, commission, panel, committee, bench, chancery, judiciary.

trick *n.* ambush, artifice, circumvention, distortion, imposition, scheme, intrigue, maneuver ("a magic trick"); accomplishment, frolic, gamble, lark, sport, stunt ("a nasty trick"); ability, command, craft, key, device, facility, gift ("the trick to something").

trite *adj.* ordinary, common, overused, banal, hackneyed, prosaic, stale, platitudinous, stock, commonplace.

trivial [*triv* · ee · ul] *adj.* unimportant, meaningless, petty, small, inconsequential, negligible, nugatory, trifling.

trouble [*trub* · el] *n.* hardship, difficulty, adversity, distress, catastrophe, misfortune, trial, tribulation, problem, affliction.

trover [*tro* · vur] *n.* return, reparation, compensation, redress, requital, recoupment, satisfaction, recompense.

true *adj.* accurate, appropriate, authentic, indubitable, legitimate, undeniable, unfeigned ("A true Picasso"); allegiant, conscientious, devoted, dutiful, liege, loyal, staunch ("a true friend").

true *adv.* correctly, perfectly, precisely, unerring, veraciously, veritable ("The shot was true").

trust *n.* assurance, certainty, certitude, dependence, positiveness, reliance ("the trust you have in your parents"); account, charge, duty, guardianship, liability, obligation ("in trust for"); bunch, cartel, combine, conglomerate, crowd, multinational, outfit, syndicate ("a corporate trust").

trust *v.* advance, aid, command, consign, delegate, store, transfer ("to trust a keepsake to someone"); have faith in, place reliance on, lean on, rely on, confide in, count on ("Trust your friend").

trustee [trust · *ee*] *n.* guardian, fiduciary, custodian.

truth *n.* accuracy, certainty, factualism, legitimacy, rectitude, truism ("a known truth"); authenticity, candor, dedication, dutifulness, openness, verity ("truth in advertising").

try *v.* aspire, contend, essay, go after, propose, speculate, venture ("to try to play"); appraise, check, evaluate, sample, scrutinize, taste ("Try some broccoli"); agonize, crucify, imitate, martyr, plague, test, tax, torture ("try one's patience"); adjudge, arbitrate, examine, hear, judge, referee ("to try in court").

turpitude [*terp* · ih · tewd] *n.* corruption, depravity, wrong, delinquency.

typical [*tip* · ih · kal] *adj.* common, prevailing, popular, usual, stereotyped, regular, recurrent, model, conforming, prosaic, customary.

T

ubiquitous [yoo · *bik* · kwih · tus] *adj.* omnipresent, pervasive, universal.

ulterior [ul · *teer* · ee · ur] *adj.* hidden, veiled, unseen, undisclosed, undivulged, obscure, secret ("ulterior motives").

ultimate [*ul* · tih · met] *adj.* capping, conclusive, decisive, last, farthest, furthermost, ("the ultimate try"); maximum, paramount, preeminent, superlative, surpassing, transcendent, unequalable ("the ultimate sacrifice"); absolute, categorical, elemental, empyreal, empyrean, transcendental ("the ultimate rule").

ultra [*ul* · tra] *adj.* beyond, outside of, more than, in excess of ("an ultra vires act").

umpire [*um* · pyre] *n.* adjudicator, arbitrator, assessor, compromiser, mediator, negotiator, proprietor, referee.

unadjusted [un · uh · *just* · ed] *adj.* uncertain, unsettled, pending ("an unadjusted claim").

unadulterated [un · uh · *dul* · ter · ay · ted] *adj.* pure, genuine, unmixed, uncorrupted, undiluted.

unaffected [un · uh · *fek* · ted] *adj.* sincere, frank, honest, open, straightforward, natural, unpretentious ("an unaffected manner"); unaltered, unstirred, indifferent, untouched, unmoved, unchanged ("unaffected by his plea").

unambiguous [un · am · *big* · yoo · us] *adj.* clear, lucid, obvious, precise, articulate, explicit, evident, sure, certain.

unanimous [yoo · *nan* · ih · mus] *adj.* accepted, collective, communal, complete, undisputed, unified.

unauthorized [un · *aw* · ther · izd] *adj.* illegal, illegitimate, unapproved, unofficial, unwarranted, wrongful.

unavoidable [un · e · *void* · e · bul] *adj.* certain, compulsory, inductable, inevasible, obligatory, necessary, inevitable.

unbelievable [un · bee · *leev* · uh · bul] *adj.* incredible, inconceivable, staggering, unthinkable, awesome; dubious, distrusted, questionable, unlikely.

unbiased [un · *bi* · assed] *adj.* fair, impartial, open, neutral, just, detached, independent, nonpartisan, nonprejudiced, unslanted, objective.

uncertain [un · *sert* · in] *adj.* disputable, contestable, obscure, indeterminate, vague; tentative, unconfirmed, suspect, untrustworthy, precarious.

unconditional [un · ken · *dish* · en · el] *adj.* actual, decisive, genuine, indubitable, unconstrained, unequivocal, absolute.

U

unconscionable [un · *kon* · shen · e · bul] *adj.* excessive, preposterous, exorbitant, unscrupulous, inexcusable, unequal, grossly unfair.

unconstitutional [un · kon · sti · *too* · shen · el] *adj.* illegal, impermissible, unenforceable.

uncontested [un · ken · *test* · ed] *adj.* not disputed, unopposed, consensual, accepted, admitted, unchallenged.

undecided [un · dee · *side* · ed] *adj.* open, pending, unsettled; dubious, doubting, tentative, indefinite, vacillating, wavering.

undeniable [un · dee · *ny* · uh · bul] *adj.* certain, clear, compelling, proven, established, unquestionable, uncontrovertable, evident, firm ("an undeniable truth").

under [*un* · der] *adv./prep.* beneath, concealed by, down, inferior, nether, amenable, belonging, collateral, governed, obeying, subsequent, subservient.

undersigned [*un* · der · sined] *n.* signatory, subscriber, signer, attestant.

understand [un · der · *stand*] *v.* comprehend, grasp, glean, cognize, know, absorb, digest.

understanding [un · der · *stan* · ding] *n.* acumen, apperception, decipherment, penetration, perspicacity, savvy ("the students' understanding of the material"); acceptance, conception, estimation, judgment, perception, significancy, viewpoint ("Her understanding is that she will be paid"); accord, agreement, concord, deal, harmony ("an understanding for the purchase of the house").

understanding [un · der · *stan* · ding] *adj.* compassionate, discerning, empathetic, generous, sensitive, perceptive ("an understanding woman").

undertaking [un · der · *tay* · king] *n.* adventure, business, engagement, outfit, operation.

underwrite [*un* · der · rite] *v.* accede, approve, guarantee, countersign, initial, sanction, subsidize.

undisclosed [un · dis · *klozed*] *adj.* unrevealed, hidden, clandestine, deceptive.

undisputed [un · dis · *pyoo* · ted] *adj.* unquestioned, absolute, accepted, undoubted, positive.

undivided [un · di · *vy* · ded] *adj.* absorbed, circumspect, concentrated, engrossed, minute, unanimous, united, vigilant, wholehearted ("undivided attention").

undue [*un* · dew] *adj.* excess, exorbitant, disproportionate, inappropriate, extreme ("undue burden").

unearned [un · *ernd*] *adj.* gratuitous, unprovoked, excessive, groundless, arbitrary, unfair, undeserved, unmerited.

unemployed [un · em · *ployd*] *adj.* jobless, idle, inactive.

unequal [un · *e* · kwal] *adj.* biased, partial, unfair, prejudiced, one-sided.

unequivocal [un · ee · *kwiv* · e · kul] *adj.* absolute, categorical, incontestible, indubitable, manifest, palpable, certain, clear, unambiguous.

unessential [un · e · *sen* · shul] *adj.* needless, secondary, irrelevant, superfluous, incidental.

unethical [un · *eth* · ih · kul] *adj.* corrupt, disreputable, immoral, unprofessional, prohibited, mercenary, underhanded, unprincipled, unscrupulous.

unfair [un · *fare*] *adj.* arbitrary, bigoted, biased, discriminatory, illegal, immoral, iniquitous, partisan, unreasonable, unethical.

unfavorable [un · *fave* · er · uh · bul] *adj.* adverse, hostile, inopportune, bad, ominous.

uniform [*yoon* · ih · form] *n.* attire, costume, dress, garb, habit, khaki, livery, regalia ("nurse's uniform").

uniform [*yoon* · ih · form] *adj.* consistent, compatible, habitual, homogeneous, equal, even, identical, constant, undeviating, conventional ("Uniform Code of Military Justice").

unilateral [yoon · ih · *lat* · er · el] *adj.* lone, singular, independent, one-sided, unaided, single.

union [*yoon* · yen] *n.* abutment, centralization, merger, conciliation, intercourse, melding, unison ("the union of two railroads"); alliance, brotherhood, coalition, guild, federation, syndicate ("trade union").

unit [*yoon* · it] *n.* assemblage, bunch, complement, detachment, entirety, system ("the entire unit"); block, part, item, compound, constituent, fraction, integer, sequent ("the refrigerator's cooling unit").

unite [yoo · *nite*] *v.* join, link, connect, blend, concur, coalesce, combine, cement.

united [yoo · *ny* · ted] *adj.* joint, cooperative, conjoint, affiliated, associated.

unity [*yoon* · ih · tee] *n.* alliance, coadunation, confederation, consensus, homogeneity, rapport, solidarity.

universal [yoo · nih · *ver* · sel] *adj.* accepted, worldwide, global, catholic, empyrean, mundane, planetary, ubiquitous, total, usual.

unjust [un · *just*] *adj.* biased, inequitable, partisan, undeserved, unmerited, unrighteous, unfair ("unjust enrichment").

unlawful [un · *law* · ful] *adj.* actionable, banned, illegal, illicit, nefarious, taboo.

unliquidated [un · *lik* · wih · day · ted] *adj.* unpaid, not satisfied, not discharged; unsettled, uncertain.

unmarried [un · *mehr* · eed] *adj.* celibate, eligible, single, uncoupled.

unnatural [un · *nat* · sher · el] *adj.* aberrant, concocted, synthetic, contrived, imitation, perverted, theatrical, unorthodox.

unnecessary [un · *ness* · e · ser · ee] *adj.* gratuitous, unneeded, unearned, immaterial.

unprecedented [un · *press* · e · den · ted] *adj.* aberrant, anomalous, eccentric, outlandish, unique, unusual, new, original.

unprofessional [un · pro · *fesh* · en · el] *adj.* amateurish, unethical, dishonest, immoral, illegal.

unreasonable [un · *reez* · en · e · bul] *adj.* absurd, biased, headstrong, invalid, quirky, senseless, unreasoned ("an unreasonable boss"); absonant, exorbitant, inordinate, unconscionable, unrightful, unwarranted, wrongful ("unreasonable punishment").

unresponsive [un · ree · *spon* · siv] *adj.* evasive, aloof, passive, taciturn, phlegmatic.

unrestricted [un · ree · *strik* · ted] *adj.* unlimited, open, limitless, comprehensive, boundless, uncontrolled.

unruly [un · *rule* · ee] *adj.* wild, uncontrolled, disobedient, contrary, irrepressible, obstinate.

unsatisfactory [un · sat · iss · *fak* · tuh · ree] *adj.* deficient, poor, insufficient, unfit, unacceptable, disapproved, inadequate, inferior ("in unsatisfactory condition").

unsettled [un · *set* · uld] *adj.* open, uncertain, changeable ("unsettled terms"); nervous, agitated, unsteady, upset, disturbed ("unsettled stomach").

unsolicited [un · so · *liss* · ih · ted] *adj.* free, offered, uninvited, unwelcome, gratuitous, unwanted, unrequested.

unsound [*un* · sownd] *adj.* fallacious, erroneous, deficient; frail, sick, infirm.

untenantable [un · *ten* · ent · e · bul] *adj.* unfit, uninhabitable.

until [un · *til*] *prep.* before, continuously, prior to, up to, up till.

untrue [un · *troo*] *adj.* apocryphal, counterfactual, wrong, deceitful, delusive, false, inaccurate, erroneous, prevaricating.

unusual [un · *yoozh* · oo · ul] *adj.* notable, different, unorthodox, alien, original, atypical, striking, bizarre, distinctive.

unveil [un · *vale*] *v.* divulge, bare, uncloak, show, present, display, expose.

unwritten [un · *rit* · en] *adj.* oral, implied, customary, nuncupative, traditional, parol ("unwritten law").

uphold [up · *hold*] *v.* affirm, sustain, endorse, corroborate, bolster, support, stand by.

upkeep [*up* · keep] *n.* budget, conservation, expenditure, preservation, sustenance, subsistence, maintenance.

upset [up · *set*] *v.* disturb, fluster, bother, agitate, enrage; reverse, quash, overturn.

urban [*er* · ben] *adj.* city, citified, civil, municipal, nonrural.

urge *v.* beg, persuade, prompt, propel, coax, beseech, rouse, impel, instigate.

usage [*yoo* · sej] *n.* acceptance, convention, habitude, mode, routine, custom, practice.

use [*yooss*] *n.* adoption, applicability, convenience, exertion, mileage, relevance; benefit, profit, right.

use [*yooz*] *v.* accept, exercise, handle, practice, relate, run, utilize.

useful [*yooss* · ful] *adj.* advantageous, commodious, functional, pragmatic, salutary, utile, beneficial, serviceable.

user [*yoo* · zer] *n.* party, person; addict.

usual [*yoo* · zhoo · el] *adj.* chronic, current, familiar, material, prevalent, accustomed, ordinary, typical.

usurious [yoo · *zhoor* · ee · us] *adj.* excessive, predatory, exorbitant, avaricious, greedy, stingy.

usurpation [yoo · zer · *pay* · shen] *n.* seizure, preemption, assumption, intrusion, deprivation.

usury [yoo · *zher* · ee] *n.* excessive interest, overcharge, cheating.

utility [yoo · *til* · i · tee] *n.* adequacy, usefulness, benefit, practicality, relevance, service.

utter [*ut* · er] *adj.* complete, absolute, outright, thorough, total, unmitigated, unqualified ("the utter truth").

utter [*ut* · er] *v.* affirm, announce, chime, exclaim, put forth, modulate, pronounce ("to utter a noise"); forge, counterfeit.

vacancy [*vay* · ken · see] *n.* void, opening, space; position, situation, opportunity, job; room, lodging.

vacant [*vay* · kant] *adj.* empty, unoccupied, available, untaken, deserted, uninhabited; blank, foolish, vapid, vacuous, silly, stupid, inane.

vacate [*vay* · kate] *v.* abrogate, quash, rescind, reverse, revoke ("vacate a judgement"); quit, depart, leave ("vacate the premises").

vacation [vay · *kay* · shen] *n.* break, holiday, intermission, layoff, recess, respite, sabbatical.

vagrancy [*vay* · gren · see] *n.* drifting, wayfaring, roaming, gallivanting, hoboism, roving, homelessness, vagabondage.

vagrant [*vay* · grent] *n.* wanderer, nomad, tramp, vagabond, hobo, homeless person.

vague *adj.* unclear, obscure, ambiguous, indefinite, imprecise, indistinct, undefined.

vagueness [*vayg* · nes] *n.* obscurity, fuzziness, obfuscation, dimness, dubiousness, inexactness, opaqueness, inconstancy.

valid [*val* · id] *adj.* attested, authentic, compelling, irrefutable, proven, substantial ("a valid transcript"); effective, legal, lawful ("valid contract"); convincing, powerful, well-founded ("a valid argument").

validate [*val* · ih · date] *v.* authenticate, corroborate, endorse, justify, legalize, sanction, permit, approve, confirm.

validity [vuh · *lid* · ih · tee] *n.* genuineness, cogency, efficacy, grounds, legality, potency.

valuable [*val* · yoo · bul] *adj.* esteemed, meritorious, fine, treasured, select, deserving ("a valuable addition"); sufficient, adequate ("valuable consideration").

valuation [val · yoo · *ay* · shen] *n.* price, worth, value.

value [*val* · yoo] *n.* worth, appraisal, assessment, equivalent, price, expense, rate ("the value of the house"); bearing, connotation, denotation, esteem, importance, merit ("the value of doing it this way").

vandalism [*van* · del · izm] *n.* destruction, mischief, ruination.

variable [*vair* · ee · uh · bul] *adj.* capricious, fickle, changeable, fluctuating, protean, temperamental, vacillating. *Ant.* fixed.

variance [*vair* · ee · ense] *n.* inconsistency, conflict, discord, disunity, fluctuation, mutation.

vehicle [vee · *ik* · ul] *n.* car, carrier, transportation, auto, automobile; agency, instrumentality, method, means.

veil *n.* screen, shelter, mask, shroud, camouflage, concealment.

vendor [*ven* · der] *n.* businessperson, dealer, hawker, merchant, seller, peddler.

venture [*ven* · cher] *n.* gamble, adventure, endeavor, essay, hazard, jeopardy, stake ("a risky venture").

venture [*ven* · cher] *v.* assay, grope, attempt, operate, speculate, defy, endanger ("to venture out").

venue [*ven* · yoo] *n.* county, district, zone, area, neighborhood, place of jurisdiction.

veracity [ve · *rass* · i · tee] *n.* actuality, exactitude, genuineness, impartiality, precision, rectitude, truthfulness.

verbal [*ver* · bel] *adj.* spoken, expressed, lingual, oral, rhetorical, stated, unwritten.

verbatim [ver · *bay* · tim] *adj.* accurately, directly, literally, precisely ("a verbatim transcript").

verdict [*ver* · dikt] *n.* adjudication, arbitration, conclusion, decision, decree.

verification [vehr · ih · fi · *kay* · shen] *n.* confirmation, proof, evidence, corroboration.

verified [*vehr* · ih · fide] *adj.* sworn, sworn to, authenticated.

verify [*vehr* · i · fy] *v.* attest, authenticate, confirm, debunk, document, justify, establish, certify; swear, declare, state, avow.

verisimilitude [*ver* · ih · sih · mil · ih · tyood] *n.* likeness, similarity, semblance; authenticity, credibility, plausibility.

vertical [*ver* · ti · kul] *adj.* upright, cocked, erect, perpendicular, plumb, sheer, upward.

very [*vehr* · ee] *adv.* extremely, greatly, unusually, uncommonly, exceptionally.

vest *v.* authorize, bestow, confer, empower, endow, pertain.

vested [*vest* · ed] *adj.* accrued, absolute, irrevocable, inalienable, immutable, inviolable, unconditional, definite, established, fixed ("a vested estate").

veteran [*vet* · ren] *n.* expert, past master, professional, trooper, master ("trial court veteran").

veteran [*vet* · ren] *adj.* adept, disciplined, exercised, expert, hardened, inured ("veteran ballplayer").

veto [*vee* · toh] *n.* ban, declination, denial, interdiction, nonconsent, prohibition ("the president's veto").

veto [*vee* · toh] *v.* ban, decline, deny, discountenance, forbid, interdict ("to veto the idea").

vexatious [vek · *say* · shes] *adj.* afflicting, disturbing, pesky, provoking, troublesome; annoying, harassing ("vexatious litigation").

viable [*vy* · eh · bul] *adj.* applicable, doable, feasible, operable, usable, workable.

vicarious [vy · *kehr* · ee · us] *adj.* commissioned, delegated, deputed, empathetic, surrogate, pretended, indirect, second-hand ("vicarious liability").

vice *n.* carnality, debasement, debauchery, iniquity, licentiousness, malignance ("Smoking is a vice"); blemish, demerit, fault, foible, imperfection, shortcoming ("Working too hard is my vice").

vicinity [vih · *sin* · ih · tee] *n.* district, environs, locality, nearness, precinct, propinquity, purloins.

vicious [*vish* · es] *adj.* dangerous, bad, corrupt, cruel.

victim [*vik* · tem] *n.* target, complainant, aggrieved, prey, sufferer, injured party.

view *n.* appearance, aspect, glimpse, illustration, vista, prospect, spectacle, stretch ("The view from the window was wonderful"); analysis, audit, contemplation, display, inspection, scrutiny; attitude, concept, deduction, judgment, notion, opinion, persuasion ("to have a view on abortion").

view *v.* consider, descry, discern, spy, explore, beam, canvass ("View this picture through the glass").

viewer [*vyoo* · er] *n.* witness, eyewitness, bystander, observer, watcher.

village [*vil* · ej] *n.* center, crossroads, hamlet, town, suburb, community.

vindicate [*vin* · di · kate] *v.* absolve, exculpate, acquit, release, justify, pardon, excuse, clear.

violate [*vy* · uh · late] *v.* breach, disobey, encroach, resist ("violate the law"); abuse, befoul, defile, deflower, desecrate, invade, profane ("to violate the sanctity of marriage").

violation [*vy* · uh · *lay* · shen] *n.* abuse, contravention, illegality, misdemeanor, transgression ("a violation of the law"); assault, defacement, destruction, dishonor, pollution, profanation, rapine, ruin, sacrilege ("a violation of the sanctity of marriage").

violence [*vy* · uh · lens] *n.* brutality, constraint, fierceness, sharpness, storminess, terrorism, aggressiveness, savagery, assault, fury, eruption.

violent [*vy* · o · lent] *adj.* savage, brutal, coercive, berserk, demonic, hysterical, murderous, potent ("a violent crime"); acute, devastating, immoderate, outrageous, painful, terrible ("a violent seizure").

virtual [*ver* · choo · el] *adj.* constructive, essential, implicit, implied, indirect, potential.

virtue [*ver* · choo] *n.* character, ethicality, innocence, morality, respectability, uprightness; effect, power, efficacy.

visible [*viz* · ih · bul] *adj.* perceptible, clear, apparent, noticeable, blatant.

visitor [*viz* · ih · ter] *n.* caller, guest, habitué, inspector, invitee, transient, visitant.

vital [*vy* · tel] *adj.* essential, basic, principal, material, significant; living, breathing.

vitiate [*vish* · ee · ate] *v.* invalidate, nullify, void.

vocation [*vo* · *kay* · shen] *n.* career, employment, métier, occupation, trade, profession, pursuit, work.

void [voyd] *adj.* abandoned, barren, bereft, deprived, empty, tenantless ("a void area in space"); nullified, avoided, fruitless, ineffectual, unenforceable, unnotified ("a void check").

void [voyd] *v.* clear, discharge, dispose, evacuate, relieve, vacate ("to void a container"); abnegate, annul, invalidate, launder, sanitize, trim, vacate ("to void a check").

void [voyd] *n.* blank, cavity, hollow, nihility, nullity, space, vacuity ("a void in space").

voidable [*void* · uh · bul] *adj.* avoidable, reversible, revokable, nullifiable ("a voidable contract").

voluntary [*vol* · un · tayr · ee] *adj.* uncoerced, elective, gratuitous, unimpelled, volitional, chosen.

volunteer [vol · un · *teer*] *n.* unpaid worker, charity worker, gratuitous worker, good samaritan ("a Red Cross volunteer").

volunteer [vol · un · *teer*] *v.* step forward, present oneself, submit, put forward, donate, supply ("to volunteer for the mission").

V

vote *n.* ballot, preference, suffrage, franchise, say, plebiscite, election ("the presidential vote").

vote *v.* choose, confer, declare, determine, enact, judge, opt, pronounce ("to vote for the governor").

vouch *v.* substantiate, certify, authenticate, warrant, underwrite, document, affirm.

voucher [*vowch* · er] *n.* receipt, release, acknowledgment.

vow *n.* promise, word, affirmation, convenant, pledge, oath.

vow *v.* declare, promise, pledge, swear, testify, covenant.

voyeur [vwa · *yer*] *n.* peeping tom, snooper, eavesdropper, visual rapist.

vulnerable [*vul* · ner · uh · bul] *adj.* dependent, defenseless, unprotected, accessible, emotional.

V

waffle [*waf · *ful] *v.* hedge, flounder, bobble, grope.

wage *n.* allowance, compensation, emolument, payment, salary, stipend ("daily wage").

wage *v.* carry out, conduct, do, fulfill, make, prosecute, pursue ("to wage a war").

wager [*way · *jer] *n.* action, challenge, gamble, bet, parlay, stake, venture ("a wager on the game").

wager [*way · *jer] *v.* bet, chance, hazard, lay, pledge, risk ("to wager on the football game").

waive *v.* abandon, cede, defer, forgo, postpone, prorogue, resign, suspend.

waiver [*way · *ver] *n.* abandonment, abdication, forgoing, refusal, relinquishment, renunciation.

walkout [*wawk · *out] *n.* strike, protest, work stoppage, picket.

want *n.* desire, appetite, craving, fancy, hankering, necessity ("the want of food"); absence, dearth, lack, exigency, impoverishment, paucity ("for want of water").

want *v.* ache, aspire, choose, covet, desire, lust ("to want a new car"); be deficient, be insufficient, be without, miss, require, starve ("to want for water in the desert").

wanton [*want · *en] *adj.* extravagant, lustful, dissipated, promiscuous, unconscionable, unprincipled ("wanton need"); cruel, malicious, gratuitous, groundless, malevolent, perverse ("wanton misconduct"); capricious, fanciful, heedless, intemperate, lavish, reckless, volatile, whimsical ("wanton disregard for human life").

wanton [*want · *en] *n.* debauchee, libertine, pampered person, prostitute, rake, spoiled person.

war *n.* combat, battle, conflict, hostility, fight, feud.

ward *n.* district, canton, diocese, division, parish, quarter ("city ward"); charge, client, dependent, godchild, guardianship, minor, orphan ("The bachelor supports his young ward").

warden [*ward · *en] *n.* administrator, caretaker, curator, deacon, guardian, skipper, superintendent.

warehouse [*ware · *hows] *n.* depository, distribution center, establishment, storehouse, stockroom, store.

warning [*worn · *ing] *n.* notice, alert, foreboding, admonition, caution.

warrant [*war · *ent] *v.* guarantee, authorize, affirm, empower, endorse, permit, assure, promise, stipulate ("to warrant that delivery will be made on time").

warrant [*war · ent*] *n.* authorization, authentication, permit, license, shingle, subpoena ("a warrant for his arrest").

warranty [*war · en · tee*] *n.* assurance, bail, bond, certificate, covenant, guarantee, pledge, assurance, obligation.

waste *n.* decay, desolation, disuse, improvidence, misapplication, squandering ("a waste of time"); badlands, barrens, brush, jungle, solitude, tundra ("a waste of desert land"); debris, dregs, excess, leavings, leftovers, rummage, scrap ("the pile of waste").

waste *v.* atrophy, corrode, debilitate, decline, emaciate, gnaw, misemploy, prodigalize, thin ("to waste away"); depreciate, desolate, despoil, pillage, rape ("to waste a good canvas").

watch *v.* observe, witness, see, discern, notice, glimpse, behold.

way *n.* action, approach, method, contrivance, expedient, manners, modus, scheme ("Which way will we do this?"); access, admittance, alternative, boulevard, entrance, path ("the way to the back room"); aspect, behavior, custom, detail, fashion, fettle, proxis ("That's just her way").

ways *n.* manner, method, means.

weapon [*wep · en*] *n.* arms, armament, artillery, firearm, cudgel, explosive.

wedlock [*wed · lok*] *n.* marriage, matrimony, connubiality, union.

weight *n.* adiposity, mass, ballast, density, gross, ponderosity ("to be beyond one's ideal weight"); anchor, ballast, counterpoise, pendulum, plumb, sandbag ("The scale's weight was too light"); access, authority, clout, credit, efficacy, force ("to give weight to a pressing matter"); burden, duty, encumbrance, incubus, onus, oppression ("to carry emotional weight").

welfare [*wel · fair*] *n.* prosperity, happiness, success, benefit, profit, felicity, affluence, relief, assistance, financial aid. *Ant.* destitution.

whole *n.* aggregate, assemblage, complex, integral, quantum, supply ("the group as a whole").

whole *adj.* accomplished, consummate, exhaustive, integral, plenary, unabbreviated ("the whole pizza"); cured, fit, healed, hearty, recovered, robust, sound ("to be a whole person again").

wholesale [*hole · sale*] *adj.* bulk, complete, extensive, general, indiscriminate, sweeping ("wholesale changes").

wholly [*hole · ee*] *adv.* altogether, comprehensively, outright, perfectly, quite, roundly, utterly ("wholly committed").

will *n.* aim, appetite, decisiveness, liking, purpose, temperament ("free will"); bequest, bestowal, declaration, disposition, estate, legacy ("last will and testament").

will *v.* authorize, bid, command, decree, effect, enjoin, request ("to will that something occur"); bequest, confer, devise, legate, probate ("to will an estate to someone").

willful [*wil · ful*] *adj.* adamant, bullheaded, contumacious, factional, intransigent, refractory, conscious, deliberate, designed, planned, intentional, premeditated, studied ("willful violation of the law").

wish *v.* aspire, entreat, hanker, prefer, request, solicit ("to wish for a new car").

wish *n.* ambition, inclination, invocation, preference, urge, yearning ("a wish for the future").

withdrawal [*with · draw · ul*] *n.* abandonment, abdication, abjuration, exodus, relinquishment, rescission, secession, drawing back ("withdrawal from conspiracy").

withhold [*with · hold*] *v.* retain, keep, suppress, repress, deny, limit, impede.

within [with · *in*] *adv.* in, indoors, inner, interior, not beyond, not over.

without [with · *out*] *adv.* after, beyond, externally, out, outdoors, outwardly; lacking.

witness [*wit* · nes] *v.* attend, behold, be present, look on, make note, perceive ("to witness a will"); testify, authenticate, affirm, corroborate, indicate, observe.

witness [*wit* · nes] *n.* attestant, attestor, eyewitness, signatory, testifier, viewer ("a witness to the murder").

word *n.* chat, colloquy, confabulation, conversation, discussion, talk ("to have a word with someone"); account, adage, directive, declaration, hearsay, proverb, remark ("the word from the White House"); concept, morpheme, phrase, term, usage, utterance, vocable ("our word in the English language"); behest, charge, decree, dictate, injunction, mandate ("give the word"); affirmation, assertion, engagement, guarantee, promise, parole, plight ("to give one's word").

work *v.* toil, sweat, practice, endeavor, drudge, slave.

work *n.* manual labor ("sweatshop work"); endeavor, pursuit, attempt, discipline, métier ("a person's choice of work"); creation, composition, deed, feat, fruit, invention, handiwork ("work of art").

worker [*wer* · ker] *n.* artisan, breadwinner, employee, laborer, toiler, trader.

working [*wer* · king] *adj.* active, occupied, alive, dynamic, engaged, laboring, moving.

works *n.* factory, mill, foundry, workshop, plant, assembly.

world *n.* planet, globe, earth, microcosm, nature, sphere, terrain ("in the entire world"); class, division, everybody, group, humankind, man, race, realm ("The whole world comes together"); ambience, atmosphere, business, domain, kingdom, memory ("in his own little world").

worth *n.* assistance, avail, caliber, desirability, merit, significance, value, importance.

worthless [*werth* · les] *adj.* abandoned, barren, bogus, despicable, mediocre, unessential, unimportant, valueless.

wreck *v.* batter, decimate, devastate, founder, impair, ravage, sabotage ("to wreck the car").

wreck *n.* collapse, debacle, debris, derelict, founder, litter, relic ("The 50-year-old car is a wreck").

writ *n.* command, decree, document, replevin, subpoena, summons, warrant.

writing [*rite* · ing] *n.* autograph, calligraphy, handwriting, hieroglyphics, print, scribble ("His writing is difficult to read"); article, discourse, dissertation, document, literature, opus ("His writing on disease prevention is informative").

wrong *n.* blunder, immorality, omission, trespass, abuse, malfeasance, infringement ("to commit a wrong against society").

wrong *adj.* lawless, corrupt, detestable, delinquent, illegitimate, vicious ("a wrong act towards another"); incorrect, false, mistaken, imprecise, erroneous, fallacious ("a wrong assumption").

wrongdoer [*rong* · doo · er] *n.* lawbreaker, tortfeasor, transgressor, offender, convict, villain, criminal.

wrongful [*rong* · ful] *adj.* evil, blameworthy, dishonest, improper, unethical, unlawful, illegal, harmful, damaging, unfair, inequitable, immoral.

wrongfully [*rong* · ful · lee] *adv.* unlawfully, illegally, harmfully, unfairly, immorally.

W

X

x-ray *n.* radiograph, picture, skiagraph, fluoroscope, encephalogram.

Y

yard *n.* lawn, garden, courtyard, grounds, enclosure.

yarn *n.* fiber, thread, wool; story, tall tale, narrative, anecdote.

year *n.* period, cycle, span, epoch, age.

yearn *v.* dream, long, thirst, want, chafe, ache, hunger.

yield *v.* accrue, allow, discharge, tender, give, turn out ("The fields will yield crops"); abandon, break, capitulate, cede, relax, relent ("to yield to demands"); accede, surrender, acquiesce, admit, concede ("to yield in battle").

yield *n.* crop, earnings, harvest, revenue, takings, turnout ("The year's yield was good").

youngster [*yung* · stir] *n.* youth, minor, child, juvenile.

youth *n.* child, minor, youngster; childhood, innocence, salad days, minority, inexperience.

youthful [*yooth* · ful] *adj.* juvenile, adolescent, inexperienced, childlike.

Z

zeal *n.* vigor, determination, passion, conviction, purpose, enthusiasm.

zealous [*zell* · es] diligent, earnest, active, ardent, committed, impassioned.

zenith [*zee* · nith] *n.* apex, top, pinnacle, peak, acme, crest. *Ant.* nadir.

zone *n.* area, belt, circuit, district, realm, territory, tract, sector.

zoom *v.* dart, dash, speed, tear, rip, hurtle.

APPENDIX A

The Constitution of the United States of America

We the People of the United States, in Order to form a more perfect Union, establish Justice, insure domestic Tranquility, provide for the common defence, promote the general Welfare, and secure the Blessings of Liberty to ourselves and our Posterity, do ordain and establish this Constitution for the United States of America.

ARTICLE I

Section 1 All legislative Powers herein granted shall be vested in a Congress of the United States, which shall consist of a Senate and House of Representatives.

Section 2 (1) The House of Representatives shall be composed of Members chosen every second Year by the People of the several States, and the Electors in each State shall have the Qualifications requisite for Electors of the most numerous Branch of the State Legislature.

(2) No Person shall be a Representative who shall not have attained to the age of twenty-five Years, and been seven Years a Citizen of the United States, and who shall not, when elected, be an Inhabitant of that State in which he shall be chosen.

(3) Representatives and direct Taxes shall be apportioned among the several States which may be included within this Union, according to their respective Numbers, which shall be determined by adding to the whole Number of free Persons, including those bound to Service for a Term of Years, and excluding Indians not taxed, three fifths of all other Persons. The actual Enumeration shall be made within three Years after the first Meeting of the Congress of the United States, and within every subsequent Term of ten Years, in such Manner as they shall by Law direct. The Number of Representatives shall not exceed one for every thirty Thousand, but each State shall have at Least one Representative; and until such enumeration shall be made, the State of New Hampshire shall be entitled to chuse three, Massachusetts eight, Rhode Island and Providence Plantations one, Connecticut five, New York six, New Jersey four, Pennsylvania eight, Delaware one, Maryland six, Virginia ten, North Carolina five, South Carolina five, and Georgia three.

(4) When vacancies happen in the Representation from any State, the Executive Authority thereof shall issue Writs of Election to fill such Vacancies.

(5) The House of Representatives shall chuse their Speaker and other Officers; and shall have the sole Power of Impeachment.

Section 3 (1) The Senate of the United States shall be composed of two Senators from each State, chosen by the Legislature thereof, for six Years; and each Senator shall have one Vote.

(2) Immediately after they shall be assembled in Consequence of the first Election, they shall be divided as equally as may be into three Classes. The Seats of the Senators of the first Class shall be vacated at the Expiration of the second Year, of the second Class at the Expiration of the fourth Year, and of the third Class at the Expiration of the sixth Year, so that one third may be chosen every second Year; and if Vacancies happen by Resignation, or otherwise, during the Recess of the Legislature of any State,

the Executive thereof may make temporary Appointments until the next Meeting of the Legislature, which shall then fill such Vacancies.

(3) No Person shall be a Senator who shall not have attained to the Age of thirty Years, and been nine Years a Citizen of the United States, and who shall not, when elected, be an Inhabitant of that State for which he shall be chosen.

(4) The Vice President of the United States shall be President of the Senate, but shall have no Vote, unless they be equally divided.

(5) The Senate shall chuse their other Officers, and also a President pro tempore, in the Absence of the Vice President, or when he shall exercise the Office of the President of the United States.

(6) The Senate shall have the sole Power to try all Impeachments. When sitting for that Purpose, they shall be on Oath or Affirmation. When the President of the United States is tried, the Chief Justice shall preside: And no Person shall be convicted without the Concurrence of two thirds of the Members present.

(7) Judgment in Cases of Impeachment shall not extend further than to removal from Office, and disqualification to hold and enjoy any Office of honor, Trust or Profit under the United States: but the Party convicted shall nevertheless be liable and subject to Indictment, Trial, Judgment and Punishment, according to Law.

Section 4 (1) The Times, Places and Manner of holding Elections for Senators and Representatives, shall be prescribed in each State by the Legislature thereof; but the Congress may at any time by Law make or alter such Regulations, except as to the Places of chusing Senators.

(2) The Congress shall assemble at least once in every Year, and such Meeting shall be on the first Monday in December, unless they shall by Law appoint a different Day

Section 5 (1) Each House shall be the Judge of the Elections, Returns and Qualifications of its own Members, and a Majority of each shall constitute a Quorum to do Business; but a smaller Number may adjourn from day to day, and may be authorized to compel the Attendance of absent Members,

in such Manner, and under such Penalties as each House may provide.

(2) Each House may determine the Rules of its Proceedings, punish its Members for disorderly Behaviour, and, with the Concurrence of two thirds, expel a Member.

(3) Each House shall keep a Journal of its Proceedings, and from time to time publish the same, excepting such Parts as may in their Judgment require Secrecy; and the Yeas and Nays of the Members of either House on any question shall, at the Desire of one fifth of those Present, be entered on the Journal.

(4) Neither House, during the Session of Congress, shall, without the Consent of the other, adjourn for more than three days, nor to any other Place than that in which the two Houses shall be sitting.

Section 6 (1) The Senators and Representatives shall receive a Compensation for their Services, to be ascertained by Law, and paid out of the Treasury of the United States. They shall in all Cases, except Treason, Felony and Breach of the Peace, be privileged from Arrest during their Attendance at the Session of their respective Houses, and in going to and returning from the same; and for any Speech or Debate in either House, they shall not be questioned in any other Place.

(2) No Senator or Representative shall, during the Time for which he was elected, be appointed to any civil Office under the authority of the United States, which shall have been created, or the Emoluments whereof shall have been encreased during such time; and no Person holding any Office under the United States, shall be a Member of either House during his Continuance in Office.

Section 7 (1) All Bills for raising Revenue shall originate in the House of Representatives; but the Senate may propose or concur with Amendments as on other Bills.

(2) Every Bill which shall have passed the House of Representatives and the Senate, shall, before it become a Law, be presented to the President of the United States; If he approve he shall sign it, but if not he shall return it, with his Objections to that House in which it shall have originated, who shall enter the Objections at large on their Journal, and proceed to reconsider it. If after such Reconsideration two thirds of that House shall

agree to pass the Bill, it shall be sent, together with the Objections, to the other House, by which it shall likewise be reconsidered, and if approved by two thirds of that House, it shall become a law. But in all such Cases the Votes of both Houses shall be determined by Yeas and Nays, and the Names of the Persons voting for and against the Bill shall be entered on the Journal of each House respectively. If any Bill shall not be returned by the President within ten Days (Sunday excepted) after it shall have been presented to him, the Same shall be a Law, in like Manner as if he had signed it, unless the Congress by their Adjournment prevent its Return, in which Case it shall not be a Law.

(3) Every Order, Resolution, or Vote to which the Concurrence of the Senate and House of Representatives may be necessary (except on a question of Adjournment) shall be presented to the President of the United States; and before the Same shall take Effect, shall be approved by him, or being disapproved by him, shall be repassed by two thirds of the Senate and House of Representatives, according to the Rules and Limitations prescribed in the Case of a Bill.

Section 8   (1) The Congress shall have Power To lay and collect Taxes, Duties, Imposts and Excises, to pay the Debts and provide for the common Defence and general Welfare of the United States; but all Duties, Imposts and Excises shall be uniform throughout the United States;

(2) To borrow Money on the credit of the United States;

(3) To regulate Commerce with foreign Nations, and among the several States, and with the Indian Tribes;

(4) To establish an uniform Rule of Naturalization, and uniform Laws on the subject of Bankruptcies throughout the United States;

(5) To coin Money, regulate the Value thereof, and of foreign Coin, and to fix the Standard of Weights and Measures;

(6) To provide for the Punishment of counterfeiting the Securities and current Coin of the United States;

(7) To establish Post Offices and post Roads;

(8) To promote the Progress of Science and useful Arts, by securing for limited Times to Authors and Inventors the exclusive Right to their respective Writings and Discoveries;

(9) To constitute Tribunals inferior to the supreme Court;

(10) To define and punish Piracies and Felonies committed on the high Seas, and Offenses against the Law of Nations;

(11) To declare War, grant Letters of Marque and Reprisal, and make Rules concerning Captures on Land and Water;

(12) To raise and support Armies, but no Appropriation of Money to that Use shall be for a longer Term than two Years;

(13) To provide and maintain a Navy;

(14) To make Rules for the Government and Regulation of the land and naval Forces;

(15) To provide for calling forth the Militia to execute the Laws of the Union, suppress Insurrections and repel Invasions;

(16) To provide for organizing, arming, and disciplining, the Militia, and for governing such Part of them as may be employed in the Service of the United States, reserving to the States respectively, the Appointment of the Officers, and the Authority of training the Militia according to the discipline prescribed by Congress;

(17) To exercise exclusive Legislation in all Cases whatsoever, over such District (not exceeding ten Miles square) as may, by Cession of particular States, and the Acceptance of Congress, become the Seat of the Government of the United States, and to exercise like Authority over all Places purchased by the Consent of the Legislature of the State in which the Same shall be, for the Erection of Forts, Magazines, Arsenals, dock-Yards, and other needful Buildings;—And

(18) To make all Laws which shall be necessary and proper for carrying into Execution the foregoing Powers, and all other Powers vested by this Constitution in the Government of the United States, or in any Department or Officer thereof.

Section 9   (1) The Migration or Importation of such Persons as any of the States now existing shall think proper to admit, shall not be prohibited by the Congress prior to the Year one thousand eight hundred and eight, but a Tax or Duty may be imposed on such Importation, not exceeding ten dollars for each Person.

(2) The Privilege of the Writ of Habeas Corpus shall not be suspended unless when in Cases of Rebellion or Invasion the public Safety may require it.

(3) No Bill of Attainder or ex post facto Law shall be passed.

(4) No Capitation, or other direct, Tax shall be laid, unless in Proportion to the Census or Enumeration herein before directed to be taken.

(5) No Tax or Duty shall be laid on Articles exported from any State.

(6) No Preference shall be given by any Regulation of Commerce or Revenue to the Ports of one State over those of another; nor shall Vessels bound to, or from, one State, be obliged to enter, clear or pay Duties in another.

(7) No Money shall be drawn from the Treasury, but in Consequence of Appropriations made by Law; and a regular Statement and Account of the Receipts and Expenditures of all public Money shall be published from time to time.

(8) No Title of Nobility shall be granted by the United States: And no Person holding any Office of Profit or Trust under them, shall, without the Consent of the Congress, accept of any present, Emolument, Office, or Title, of any kind whatever, from any King, Prince or foreign State.

Section 10 (1) No State shall enter into any Treaty, Alliance, or Confederation; grant Letters of Marque and Reprisal; coin Money; emit Bills of Credit; make any Thing but gold and silver Coin a Tender in Payment of Debts; pass any Bill of Attainder, ex post facto Law, or Law impairing the Obligation of Contracts, or grant any Title of Nobility.

(2) No State shall, without the Consent of Congress, lay any Imposts or Duties on Imports or Exports, except what may be absolutely necessary for executing its inspection Laws: and the net Produce of all Duties and Imposts, laid by any State on Imports or Exports, shall be for the Use of the Treasury of the United States; and all such Laws shall be subject to the Revision and Controul of the Congress.

(3) No State shall, without the Consent of Congress, lay any Duty of Tonnage, keep Troops, or Ships of War in time of Peace, enter into any Agreement or Compact with another State, or with a foreign Power, or

engage in War, unless actually invaded, or in such imminent Danger as will not admit of Delay.

ARTICLE II

Section 1 (1) The executive Power shall be vested in a President of the United States of America. He shall hold his Office during the Term of four Years, and, together with the Vice President, chosen for the same Term, be elected, as follows:

(2) Each State shall appoint, in such Manner as the Legislature thereof may direct, a Number of Electors, equal to the whole Number of Senators and Representatives to which the State may be entitled in the Congress: but no Senator or Representative, or Person holding an Office of Trust or Profit under the United States, shall be appointed an Elector.

The Electors shall meet in their respective States, and vote by Ballot for two Persons, of whom one at least shall not be an Inhabitant of the same State with themselves. And they shall make a List of all the Persons voted for, and of the Number of Votes for each; which List they shall sign and certify, and transmit sealed to the Seat of the Government of the United States, directed to the President of the Senate. The President of the Senate shall, in the presence of the Senate and House of Representatives, open all the Certificates, and the Votes shall then be counted. The Person having the greatest Number of Votes shall be the President, if such Number be a Majority of the whole Number of Electors appointed; and if there be more than one who have such Majority, and have an equal Number of Votes, then the House of Representatives shall immediately chuse by Ballot one of them for President; and if no Person have a Majority, then from the five highest on the List the said House shall in like Manner chuse the President. But in chusing the President, the Votes shall be taken by States, the Representation from each State having one Vote; a quorum for this Purpose shall consist of a Member or Members from two thirds of the States, and a Majority of all the States shall be necessary to a Choice. In every Case, after the Choice of the President, the Person having the greatest Number of Votes of the Electors shall be the Vice

President. But if there should remain two or more who have equal Votes, the Senate shall chuse from them by Ballot the Vice President.

(3) The Congress may determine the Time of chusing the Electors, and the Day on which they shall give their Votes; which Day shall be the same throughout the United States.

(4) No Person except a natural born Citizen, or a Citizen of the United States, at the time of the Adoption of this Constitution, shall be eligible to the Office of President; neither shall any Person be eligible to that Office who shall not have attained to the Age of thirty five Years, and been fourteen Years a Resident within the United States.

(5) In Case of the Removal of the President from Office, or of his Death, Resignation, or Inability to discharge the Powers and Duties of the said Office, the Same shall devolve on the Vice President, and the Congress may by Law provide for the Case of Removal, Death, Resignation or Inability, both of the President and Vice President, declaring what Officer shall then act as President, and such Officer shall act accordingly, until the Disability be removed, or a President shall be elected.

(6) The President shall, at stated Times, receive for his Services, a Compensation, which shall neither be increased nor diminished during the Period for which he shall have been elected, and he shall not receive within that Period any other Emolument from the United States, or any of them.

(7) Before he enter on the Execution of his Office, he shall take the following Oath or Affirmation:—"I do solemnly swear (or affirm) that I will faithfully execute the Office of President of the United States, and will to the best of my Ability, preserve, protect and defend the Constitution of the United States."

Section 2 (1) The President shall be Commander in Chief of the Army and Navy of the United States, and of the Militia of the several States, when called into the actual Service of the United States; he may require the Opinion, in writing, of the principal Officer in each of the executive Departments, upon any Subject relating to the Duties of their respective Offices, and he shall have Power to grant Reprieves and Pardons for Offenses against the United States, except in Cases of Impeachment.

(2) He shall have Power, by and with the Advice and Consent of the Senate, to make Treaties, provided two thirds of the Senators present concur; and he shall nominate, and by and with the Advice and Consent of the Senate, shall appoint Ambassadors, other public Ministers and Consuls, Judges of the supreme Court, and all other Officers of the United States, whose Appointments are not herein otherwise provided for, and which shall be established by Law: but the Congress may by Law vest the Appointment of such inferior Officers, as they think proper, in the President alone, in the Courts of Law, or in the Heads of Departments.

(3) The President shall have Power to fill up all Vacancies that may happen during the Recess of the Senate, by granting Commissions which shall expire at the End of their next Session.

Section 3 He shall from time to time give to the Congress Information of the State of the Union, and recommend to their Consideration such Measures as he shall judge necessary and expedient; he may, on extraordinary Occasions, convene both Houses, or either of them, and in Case of Disagreement between them, with Respect to the Time of Adjournment, he may adjourn them to such Time as he shall think proper; he shall receive Ambassadors and other public Ministers; he shall take Care that the Laws be faithfully executed, and shall Commission all the Officers of the United States.

Section 4 The President, Vice President and all Civil Officers of the United States, shall be removed from Office on Impeachment for, and Conviction of, Treason, Bribery, or other high Crimes and Misdemeanors.

ARTICLE III

Section 1 The judicial Power of the United States, shall be vested in one supreme Court, and in such inferior Courts as the Congress may from time to time ordain and establish. The Judges, both of the supreme and inferior Courts, shall hold their Offices during good Behaviour, and shall, at stated Times, receive for their Services, a Compensation, which shall not be diminished during their Continuance in Office.

Section 2 (1) The judicial Power shall extend to all Cases, in Law and Equity, arising under this Constitution, the Laws of the United States, and Treaties made, or which shall be made, under their Authority;—to all Cases affecting Ambassadors, other public Ministers and Consuls;—to all Cases of admiralty and maritime Jurisdiction;—to Controversies to which the United States shall be a party;—to Controversies between two or more States;—between a State and Citizens of another State;—between Citizens of different States;—between Citizens of the same State claiming Lands under Grants of different States, and between a State, or the Citizens thereof, and foreign States, Citizens or Subjects.

(2) In all Cases affecting Ambassadors, other public Ministers and Consuls, and those in which a State shall be Party, the supreme Court shall have original Jurisdiction. In all the other Cases before mentioned, the supreme Court shall have appellate Jurisdiction, both as to Law and Fact, with such Exceptions, and under such Regulations as the Congress shall make.

(3) The Trial of all Crimes, except in Cases of Impeachment, shall be by Jury; and such Trial shall be held in the State where the said Crimes shall have been committed; but when not committed within any State, the Trial shall be at such Place or Places as the Congress may by Law have directed.

Section 3 (1) Treason against the United States, shall consist only in levying War against them, or in adhering to their Enemies, giving them Aid and Comfort. No Person shall be convicted of Treason unless on the Testimony of two Witnesses to the same overt Act, or on Confession in open Court.

(2) The Congress shall have Power to declare the Punishment of Treason, but no Attainder of Treason shall work Corruption of Blood, or Forfeiture except during the Life of the Person attainted.

ARTICLE IV

Section 1 Full Faith and Credit shall be given in each State to the public Acts, Records, and judicial Proceedings of every other State. And the Congress may by general Laws prescribe the Manner in which such Acts, Records and Proceedings shall be proved, and the Effect thereof.

Section 2 (1) The Citizens of each State shall be entitled to all privileges and Immunities of Citizens in the several States.

(2) A Person charged in any State with Treason, Felony, or other Crime, who shall flee from Justice, and be found in another State, shall on Demand of the executive Authority of the State from which he fled, be delivered up, to be removed to the State having Jurisdiction of the Crime.

(3) No Person held to Service of Labour in one State, under the Laws thereof, escaping into another, shall, in Consequence of any Law or Regulation therein, be discharged from such Service or Labour, but shall be delivered up on Claim of the Party to whom such Service or Labour may be due.

Section 3 (1) New States may be admitted by the Congress into this Union; but no new State shall be formed or erected within the Jurisdiction of any other State; nor any State be formed by the Junction of two or more States, or Parts of States, without the Consent of the Legislatures of the States concerned as well as of the Congress.

(2) The Congress shall have power to dispose of and make all needful Rules and Regulations respecting the Territory or other Property belonging to the United States; and nothing in this Constitution shall be so construed as to Prejudice any Claims of the United States, or of any particular State.

Section 4 The United States shall guarantee to every State in this Union a Republican Form of Government, and shall protect each of them against Invasion; and on Application of the Legislature, or of the Executive (when the Legislature cannot be convened) against domestic Violence.

ARTICLE V

The Congress, whenever two thirds of both Houses shall deem it necessary, shall propose Amendments to this Constitution, or, on the Application of the Legislatures of two thirds of the several States, shall call a Convention for proposing Amendments, which, in either Case, shall be valid to all Intents and Purposes, as Part of this Constitution, when ratified by the Legislatures of three fourths of the several States, or by Conventions in three fourths thereof, as the one or the other Mode of Ratification may be proposed by the Congress; Provided that no

Amendment which may be made prior to the Year One thousand eight hundred and eight shall in any Manner affect the first and fourth Clauses in the Ninth Section of the first Article; and that no State, without its Consent, shall be deprived of its equal Suffrage in the Senate.

ARTICLE VI

(1) All Debts contracted and Engagements entered into, before the Adoption of this Constitution, shall be as valid against the United States under this Constitution, as under the Confederation.

(2) This Constitution, and the Laws of the United States which shall be made in Pursuance thereof; and all Treaties made, or which shall be made, under the Authority of the United States, shall be the supreme Law of the Land; and the Judges in every State shall be bound thereby, any Thing in the Constitution or Laws of any State to the Contrary notwithstanding.

(3) The Senators and Representatives before mentioned, and the Members of the several State Legislatures, and all executive and judicial Officers, both of the United States and of the several States, shall be bound by Oath or Affirmation, to support this Constitution; but no religious Test shall ever be required as a Qualification to any Office or public Trust under the United States.

ARTICLE VII

The Ratification of the Conventions of nine States, shall be sufficient for the Establishment of this Constitution between the States so ratifying the Same.

ARTICLES IN ADDITION TO, AND AMENDMENT OF, THE CONSTITUTION OF THE UNITED STATES OF AMERICA, PROPOSED BY CONGRESS, AND RATIFIED BY THE SEVERAL STATES, PURSUANT TO THE FIFTH ARTICLE OF THE ORIGINAL CONSTITUTION

AMENDMENT I (1791)

Congress shall make no law respecting an establishment of religion, or prohibiting the free exercise thereof; or abridging the freedom of speech, or of the press; or the right of the people peaceably to assemble, and to petition the Government for a redress of grievances.

AMENDMENT II (1791)

A well regulated Militia, being necessary to the security of a free state, the right of the people to keep and bear Arms, shall not be infringed.

AMENDMENT III (1791)

No Soldier shall, in time of peace be quartered in any house, without the consent of the Owner, nor in time of war, but in a manner to be prescribed by law.

AMENDMENT IV (1791)

The right of the people to be secure in their persons, houses, papers, and effects, against unreasonable searches and seizures, shall not be violated, and no Warrants shall issue, but upon probable cause, supported by Oath or affirmation, and particularly describing the place to be searched, and the persons or things to be seized.

AMENDMENT V (1791)

No person shall be held to answer for a capital, or otherwise infamous crime, unless on a presentment or indictment of a Grand Jury, except in cases arising in the land or naval forces, or in the Militia, when in actual service in time of War or public danger; nor shall any person be subject for the same offence to be twice put in jeopardy of life or limb; nor shall be compelled in any criminal case to be a witness against himself, nor be deprived of life, liberty, or property, without due process of law; nor shall private property be taken for public use, without just compensation.

AMENDMENT VI (1791)

In all criminal prosecutions, the accused shall enjoy the right to a speedy and public trial, by an impartial jury of the State and district wherein the crime shall have been committed, which district shall have been previously ascertained by law, and to be informed of the nature and cause of the accusation; to be confronted with the witnesses against him; to have compulsory process for obtaining witnesses in his favor, and to have the Assistance of Counsel for his defence.

AMENDMENT VII (1791)

In Suits at common law, where the value in controversy shall exceed twenty dollars, the right of trial by jury shall be preserved, and no fact tried by a jury, shall be otherwise re-examined in any Court of the United States, than according to the rules of the common law.

AMENDMENT VIII (1791)

Excessive bail shall not be required, nor excessive fines imposed, nor cruel and unusual punishments inflicted.

AMENDMENT IX (1791)

The enumeration in the Constitution, of certain rights, shall not be construed to deny or disparage others retained by the people.

AMENDMENT X (1791)

The powers not delegated to the United States by the Constitution, nor prohibited by it to the States, are reserved to the States respectively, or to the people.

AMENDMENT XI (1798)

The Judicial power of the United States shall not be construed to extend to any suit in law or equity, commenced or prosecuted against one of the United States by Citizens of another State, or by Citizens or Subjects of any Foreign State.

AMENDMENT XII (1804)

The Electors shall meet in their respective states and vote by ballot for President and Vice-President, one of whom, at least, shall not be an inhabitant of the same state with themselves; they shall name in their ballots the person voted for as President, and in distinct ballots the person voted for as Vice-President, and they shall make distinct lists of all persons voted for as President, and of all persons voted for as Vice-President, and of the number of votes for each, which lists they shall sign and certify, and transmit sealed to the seat of the government of the United States, directed to the President of the Senate;—The President of the Senate shall, in the presence of the Senate and House of Representatives, open all the certificates and the votes shall then be counted;—The person having the greatest number of votes for President, shall be the President, if such number be a majority of the whole number of Electors appointed; and if no person have such majority, then from the persons having the highest numbers not exceeding three on the list of those voted for as President, the House of Representatives shall choose immediately, by ballot, the President. But in choosing the President, the votes shall be taken by states, the representation from each state having one vote; a quorum for this purpose shall consist of a member or members from two-thirds of the states, and a majority of all the states shall be necessary to a choice. And if the House of Representatives shall not choose a President whenever the right of choice shall devolve upon them, before the fourth day of March next following, then the Vice-President shall act as President, as in the case of the death or other constitutional disability of the President—The person having the greatest number of votes as Vice-President, shall be the Vice-President, if such number be a majority of the whole number of Electors appointed, and if no person have a majority, then from the two highest numbers on the list, the Senate shall choose the Vice-President; A quorum for the purpose shall consist of two-thirds of the whole number of Senators, and a majority of the whole number shall be necessary to a choice. But no person constitutionally ineligible to the office of President shall be eligible to that of Vice-President of the United States.

AMENDMENT XIII (1865)

Section 1 Neither slavery nor involuntary servitude, except as a punishment for crime whereof the party shall have been duly convicted, shall exist within the United States, or any place subject to their jurisdiction.

Section 2 Congress shall have power to enforce this article by appropriate legislation.

AMENDMENT XIV (1868)

Section 1 All persons born or naturalized in the United States and subject to the jurisdiction thereof, are citizens of the United States and of the State wherein they reside. No State shall make or enforce any law which shall abridge the privileges or immunities of citizens of the United States; nor shall any State deprive any person of life, liberty, or property, without due process of law; nor deny to any person within its jurisdiction the equal protection of the laws.

Section 2 Representatives shall be apportioned among the several States according to their respective numbers, counting the whole number of persons in each State, excluding Indians not taxed. But when the right to vote at any election for the choice of electors for President and Vice-President of the United States, Representatives in Congress, the Executive and Judicial officers of a State, or the members of the Legislature thereof, is denied to any of the male inhabitants of such State, being twenty-one years of age, and citizens of the United States, or in any way abridged, except for participation in rebellion, or other crime, the basis of representation therein shall be reduced in the proportion which the number of such male citizens shall bear to the whole number of male citizens twenty-one years of age in such State.

Section 3 No person shall be a Senator or Representative in Congress, or elector of President and Vice-President, or hold any office, civil or military, under the United States, or under any State, who, having previously taken an oath, as a member of Congress, or as an officer of the United States, or as a member of any State legislature, or as an executive or judicial officer of any State, to support the Constitution of the United States, shall have engaged in insurrection or rebellion against the same, or given aid or comfort to the enemies thereof. But Congress may by a vote of two-thirds of each House, remove such disability.

Section 4 The validity of the public debt of the United States, authorized by law, including debts incurred for payment of pensions and bounties for services in suppressing insurrection or rebellion, shall not be questioned. But neither the United States nor any State shall assume or pay any debt or obligation incurred in aid of insurrection or rebellion against the United States, or any claim for the loss or emancipation of any slave; but all such debts, obligations and claims shall be held illegal and void.

Section 5 The Congress shall have power to enforce, by appropriate legislation, the provisions of this article.

AMENDMENT XV (1870)

Section 1 The right of citizens of the United States to vote shall not be denied or abridged by the United States or by any State on account of race, color, or previous condition of servitude.

Section 2 The Congress shall have power to enforce this article by appropriate legislation.

AMENDMENT XVI (1913)

The Congress shall have power to lay and collect taxes on incomes, from whatever source derived, without apportionment among the several States, and without regard to any census or enumeration.

AMENDMENT XVII (1913)

The Senate of the United States shall be composed of two Senators from each State, elected by the people thereof, for six years; and each Senator shall have one vote. The electors in each State shall have the qualifications requisite for electors of the most numerous branch of the State legislatures.

When vacancies happen in the representation of any State in the Senate, the executive authority of such State shall issue writs of election to fill such vacancies: *Provided,* That the legislature of any State may empower the executive thereof to make temporary appointments until the people fill the vacancies by election as the legislature may direct.

This amendment shall not be so construed as to affect the election or term of any Senator chosen before it becomes valid as part of the Constitution.

AMENDMENT XVIII (1919)

Section 1 After one year from the ratification of this article the manufacture, sale, or transportation of intoxicating liquors within, the importation thereof into, or the exportation thereof from the United States and all territory subject to the jurisdiction thereof for beverage purposes is hereby prohibited.

Section 2 The Congress and the several States shall have concurrent power to enforce this article by appropriate legislation.

Section 3 This article shall be inoperative unless it shall have been ratified as an amendment to the Constitution by the legislatures of the several States, as provided in the Constitution, within seven years from the date of the submission hereof to the States by the Congress.

AMENDMENT XIX (1920)

The right of citizens of the United States to vote shall not be denied or abridged by the United States or by any State on account of sex.

Congress shall have power to enforce this article by appropriate legislation.

AMENDMENT XX (1933)

Section 1 The terms of the President and Vice President shall end at noon on the 20th day of January, and the terms of Senators and Representatives at noon on the 3d day of January, of the years in which such terms would have ended if this article had not been ratified; and the terms of their successors shall then begin.

Section 2 The Congress shall assemble at least once in every year, and such meeting shall begin at noon on the 3d day of January, unless they shall by law appoint a different day.

Section 3 If, at the time fixed for the beginning of the term of the President, the President elect shall have died, the Vice President elect shall become President. If a President shall not have been chosen before the time fixed for the beginning of his term, or if the President elect shall have failed to qualify, then the Vice President elect shall act as President until a President shall have qualified; and the Congress may by law provide for the case wherein neither a President elect nor a Vice President elect shall have qualified, declaring who shall then act as President, or the manner in which one who is to act shall be selected, and such person shall act accordingly until a President or Vice President shall have qualified.

Section 4 The Congress may by law provide for the case of the death of any of the persons from whom the House of Representatives may choose a President whenever the right of choice shall have devolved upon them, and for the case of the death of any of the persons from whom the Senate may choose a Vice President whenever the right of choice shall have devolved upon them.

Section 5 Sections 1 and 2 shall take effect on the 15th day of October following the ratification of this article.

Section 6 This article shall be inoperative unless it shall have been ratified as an amendment to the Constitution by the legislatures of three-fourths of the several States within seven years from the date of its submission.

AMENDMENT XXI (1933)

Section 1 The eighteenth article of amendment to the Constitution of the United States is hereby repealed.

Section 2 The transportation or importation into any State, Territory or possession of the United States for delivery or use therein of intoxicating liquors, in violation of the laws thereof, is hereby prohibited.

Section 3 This article shall be inoperative unless it shall have been ratified as an amendment to the Constitution by conventions in the several States, as provided in the Constitution, within seven years from the date of the submission hereof to the States by the Congress.

AMENDMENT XXII (1951)

Section 1 No person shall be elected to the office of the President more than twice, and no person who has held the office of President, or acted as President, for more than two years of a term to which some other person was elected President shall be elected to the office of the President more than once. But this Article shall not apply to any person holding the office of President when this Article was proposed by the Congress, and shall not prevent any person who may be holding the office of President, or acting as President, during the term within which this Article becomes operative from holding the office of President or acting as President during the remainder of such term.

Section 2 This Article shall be inoperative unless it shall have been ratified as an amendment to the Constitution by the legislatures of three-fourths of the several States within seven years from the date of its submission to the States by the Congress.

AMENDMENT XXIII (1961)

Section 1 The District constituting the seat of Government of the United States shall appoint in such manner as the Congress may direct:

A number of electors of President and Vice President equal to the whole number of Senators and Representatives in Congress to which the District would be entitled if it were a State, but in no event more than the least populous State; they shall be in addition to those appointed by the States, but they shall be considered, for the purposes of the election of President and Vice President, to be electors appointed by a State; and they shall meet in the District and perform such duties as provided by the twelfth article of amendment.

Section 2   The Congress shall have power to enforce this article by appropriate legislation.

AMENDMENT XXIV (1964)

Section 1   The right of citizens of the United States to vote in any primary or other election for President or Vice President, for electors for President or Vice President, or for Senator or Representative in Congress, shall not be denied or abridged by the United States or any State by reason of failure to pay any poll tax or other tax.

Section 2   The Congress shall have power to enforce this article by appropriate legislation.

AMENDMENT XXV (1967)

Section 1   In case of the removal of the President from office or of his death or resignation, the Vice President shall become President.

Section 2   Whenever there is a vacancy in the office of the Vice President, the President shall nominate a Vice President who shall take office upon confirmation by a majority vote of both Houses of Congress.

Section 3   Whenever the President transmits to the President pro tempore of the Senate and the Speaker of the House of Representatives his written declaration that he is unable to discharge the powers and duties of his office, and until he transmits to them a written declaration to the contrary, such powers and duties shall be discharged by the Vice President as Acting President.

Section 4   Whenever the Vice President and a majority of either the principal officers of the executive departments or of such other body as Congress may by law provide, transmit to the President pro tempore of the Senate and the Speaker of the House of Representatives their written declaration that the President is unable to discharge the powers and duties of his office, the Vice President shall immediately assume the powers and duties of the office as Acting President.

Thereafter, when the President transmits to the President pro tempore of the Senate and the Speaker of the House of Representatives his written declaration that no inability exists, he shall resume the powers and duties of his office unless the Vice President and a majority of either the principal officers of the executive department or of such other body as Congress may by law provide, transmit within four days to the President pro tempore of the Senate and the Speaker of the House of Representatives their written declaration that the President is unable to discharge the powers and duties of his office. Thereupon Congress shall decide the issue, assembling within forty-eight hours for that purpose if not in session. If the Congress, within twenty-one days after receipt of the latter written declaration, or, if Congress is not in session, within twenty-one days after Congress is required to assemble, determines by two-thirds vote of both Houses that the President is unable to discharge the powers and duties of his office, the Vice President shall continue to discharge the same as Acting President; otherwise, the President shall resume the powers and duties of his office.

AMENDMENT XXVI (1971)

Section 1   The right of citizens of the United States, who are eighteen years of age or older, to vote shall not be denied or abridged by the United States or by any State on account of age.

Section 2   The Congress shall have power to enforce this article by appropriate legislation.

AMENDMENT XXVII (1992)

No law varying the compensation for the services of the senators and representatives shall take effect, until an election of representatives shall have intervened.

APPENDIX B

Legal Research

One of the things you may be called upon to do as a paralegal is legal research. This appendix is not intended to teach you how to do legal research, but rather is an overview of the resources you will be using when doing legal research. You have already had or will have a special class in legal research in your paralegal education. This chapter will help you fit legal research into the context of working as a paralegal in a law office.

Before you can begin to do effective research, it is important to understand why legal research is necessary and how it fits into the legal process. Legal research is the process by which legal professionals determine what the law is. To determine what the law is, you should primarily look at two sources: statutes and case law. Statutes are the "laws," and case law is interpretations by various courts of how the "laws" apply in specific situations. To determine what the "law" is, one must look to both statutes and case law.

The following hypothetical situation should help you understand how legal research fits into the legal process:

Mr. Cheny comes into your firm's offices one day to discuss the death of his wife. According to Mr. Cheny, Mrs. Cheny drank heavily and was drunk at the time she had the head-on collision that killed her. The bartender at the bar where Mrs. Cheny was drinking prior to her death knew Mrs. Cheny and knew about her alcoholism. Mr. Cheny wants to sue the bar and/or bartender for the wrongful death of his wife.

The attorney working with you advises you that he needs to determine whether any new laws have been enacted concerning bartender or bar liability. This information is needed so that the attorney can determine if Mr. Cheny has a case against the bar or bartender or whether there is some law precluding recovery in situations such as what occurred in the death of his wife.

As you can see from the above hypothetical situation, legal research is an integral tool in the legal process. Research is necessary for the legal professional to determine 1) whether a client has any legal rights or liabilities in a particular situation, 2) what course of action to take in a particular situation, 3) what procedures a client must follow in order to conform his or her actions to the law.

Fundamentally, legal research provides the framework in which a legal professional works. Without knowing what the law is, it is difficult to advise a client what course of action to take or not to take.

SOURCES OF LEGAL INFORMATION

Before you can begin to do legal research, it is essential to understand what books the law library contains and how they fit into the scheme of legal research. At first glance, you will probably be overwhelmed and not know what book to pull first or, at worst, in what corner of the room to begin. To understand where to begin, you need to learn the types of law books and how each of the various types of books fits into the whole.

Statutes

Statutes, or codes, from various legislative bodies comprise the foundation for legal

research. Statutes are laws passed by legislative bodies. Legislative bodies include the United States Congress and state legislatures, such as the Georgia General Assembly. The laws codified by the United States Congress are contained in the United States Code, which is designated as U.S.C. The annotated version of the code is U.S.C.A. An annotated version includes cases decided by various courts interpreting what the statutes mean after each statute is listed.

The statutes of various states are contained in the state codes. Each state, from Alabama to Wyoming, has its own code. These codes list the laws passed by each state's legislative body. When beginning legal research, it is essential to look at the codes to determine whether there are any applicable laws on the books designating what the law is for a specific situation.

Case Law

Case law is legal opinions written by various courts. The books containing case law are known as reporters. It is important to remember that government in the United States is divided into state and federal levels. The courts in the federal level that report their decisions are as follows:

United States District Courts—Opinions are contained in the reporters known as the *Federal Supplements.*

United States Circuit Courts of Appeal—Opinions are contained in the reporters known as the *Federal Reporters.*

United States Supreme Court—Opinions are contained in the *U.S. Reporter,* the *Supreme Court Reporter,* and the lawyers' editions of these reporters. The official reporter for the United States Supreme Court is the *U.S. Reporter.* Both the *Supreme Court Reporter* and *Lawyers' Editions* contain supplemental information, which is added to assist the reader in understanding the opinion.

Reporters known as regional reporters contain the opinions of several states' courts. They are designated as the *Southern Reporter, Southwestern Reporter, Southeastern Reporter, Pacific Reporter, Northeastern Reporter, Atlantic Reporter, Northwestern Reporter,* and one set each for California and New York. The states within each area have their decisions published in that particular reporter.

Digests

Digests are the keys to locating the laws in the reporters. Items are listed by topic, and then cases are cited that stand for a particular proposition. For example, digests have categories for contracts, torts, civil procedure, criminal procedure, landlord/tenant, etc. If, for example, you are researching the issue of bartender liability for Mr. Cheny, you might first go to the state digest section on torts or negligence and look for a subcategory of "bartender liability." By determining what area of the law you need, you will go to that section of the digest and look for cases that relate to the subject you are researching.

Shepard's

This is the book that paralegals most often use. It is a key to determine if a particular case has been overruled or reversed and also gives a good starting point to locate other cases on a particular point. To use Shepard's, you locate the book and page number of the case in a particular reporter and find that same book and page number in Shepard's. The initials beside the entries will indicate whether or not the case has been reversed and will give you other relevant information.

Martindale-Hubbell Law Directory

This set of books is also used frequently by paralegals. Martindales lists attorneys by states and cities, giving biographical data on each attorney. Usually firms list their names in the directory with names of partners and associates under the firm name. The book lists any firm specialties as well as representative clients. This information becomes imperative if it is necessary to associate counsel in another jurisdiction. There are several other features of Martindale-Hubbell that are helpful to the paralegal. First, in each state's section, attorneys are listed in alphabetical order, a list of private investigators and court reporters is provided, and a list of colleges and universities in the state is also contained in the book. Second, a separate volume of Martindale contains a summary of the general laws of each jurisdiction. This volume is especially helpful when you need to have a general idea of what the law is in another jurisdiction. For example, if you

need to domesticate a judgment from state A, which has enacted the Uniform Enforcement of Foreign Judgments in state B, prior to doing so you must determine if state B recognizes this act. By looking at the summary in Martindale, you can easily ascertain whether state B recognizes a judgment from another jurisdiction under this act.

Martindale-Hubbell has recently come out with a compact disc version of their law directory, which can be used on systems which use CD-ROM technology.

COMPUTER-ASSISTED LEGAL RESEARCH

Computer-assisted legal research is different from legal research through digests and reporters. Computer research is "literal." Literal research means that you do not have to determine the area of the law that you are researching to begin. For example, in our hypothetical Cheny case, you would not look under torts first, but would type in the words "bartender liability." The search will pull up any cases that have the words "bartender liability" in the opinions.

There are three major systems for computer-assisted legal research. These systems are Lexis, a service provided by Mead Data Central; Westlaw, a service provided by West Publishing Company; and Veralex, a service provided by Lawyers' Co-op. All of the systems are essentially the same in that they are literal research mechanisms.

Computer-assisted legal research has other capabilities that are almost impossible to accomplish using traditional research methods. By inputting the name of a judge or an attorney, you can make the systems print out all cases in which that judge or attorney has been involved. This function can be especially beneficial in particular types of cases, such as a patent case in front of a particular judge, when you would like to see how the judge has ruled on similar cases. It can also give you an idea of the types of cases opposing counsel has worked on or whether the opposing party has been previously sued in a similar cause of action.

With a computer terminal in the office, a law firm literally has all of the sources it could possibly need within its reach. Law review articles, periodicals, statutes from other jurisdictions, census information,

congressional records, the Federal Register, and legislative history are other types of information available in computer-assisted research. The Westlaw system also has *Black's Law Dictionary* on-line. Mead Data Central also offers a library called Nexis, which contains the full texts of many general and news publications, including the major wire services. Thus, if your client were recently mentioned in the *Wall Street Journal,* you could instantly obtain that article without having a hard copy of the newspaper in front of you. Lexis also has the latest edition of the *Encyclopedia Britannica* on-line, as well as the annual reports of corporations listed on the American and New York stock exchanges. Similar to Lexis, Westlaw has on-line additional sources of information, such as the Accountant's Index; Disclosure, which has extracts from the S.E.C. filings of over 10,000 companies; *Wall Street Journal; Dow Jones News Service; Barron's National Business and Financial Weekly;* as well as price quotations for over 6,000 stocks and securities. Both Westlaw and Lexis have directories listing consultants and experts available in a wide variety of topics.

Services on these programs include Shepard's and instant case retrieval systems. In the Lexis system, cases can be easily retrieved by typing in the cite on the Autocite service. This same capability is available on Westlaw in the Insta-Cite service.

All of these services continue to expand and add new services. To determine the latest data basis for each system, check the latest newsletter from the service or contact the service representative. With the new age of computer-assisted research, the well-trained paralegal must be trained on at least one computer-assisted research system, but preferably on all systems. Larger firms usually provide training to new paralegals; however, it is a good idea to know at least the basic skills before graduating from paralegal school.

Information America

Another type of "legal research program" available in many areas and one used primarily by paralegals is the Information America system. This system permits the user to obtain documents from the secretary of states' offices, court dockets, real property listings, tax liens, trade names registrations,

plaintiff/defendant indices, and real property title information. One can also utilize the system to hold a name for a corporation at the secretary of state's office. It also assists in skip tracing and obtaining financial information on companies, available from Dunn & Bradstreet. Although this system is not available nationwide, it continues to grow and expand both geographically and in terms of the information available on the data bases.

The next section discusses specific tools of legal research as provided by Lawyers Cooperative Publishing.

APPENDIX C

The Living Law

THE
LIVING LAW

A GUIDE TO MODERN
LEGAL RESEARCH

1992-1993

Table of Contents

Introduction

Successful legal research requires no magic, only common sense and a little background knowledge. This booklet will give the user more knowledge than he or she may want for a particular assignment—but that knowledge will be increasingly valuable in future research projects.

In order to simplify the material in this booklet, and to streamline your research habits, the following thought is offered: Every legal research project requires a minimum of three steps. The researcher who short cuts or skips any step will take more time and be far less effective than the one who calmly goes through steps 1, 2, and 3 in regular order.

Step 1:
GO TO A LAW FINDER: That is, go to a law service which will direct you to the place where your answer is found. The most widely used Law Finders are:
Indexes
Tables
Digests
Citators
Auto-Cite
Cross References
Words and Phrases
Classification Schemes (or Tables of Contents)

Step 2:
GO TO THE LAW: Go to where your answer is found—it may not always be where you thought it would be, but a cross-reference will no doubt direct you to the proper place. This is the book which contains the statement of law. The statement may be a case, a statute, a regulation, or ruling of an administrative agency. The statement may be of primary or secondary authority: the point is that *it states what the law is* on your subject. In this large group of books and services are found:
Statutes (Annotated and Unannotated)
Reports

Administrative Rulings and Regulations
Annotations in ALR, ALR Fed, and Lawyers
   Edition of U. S. Reports
Textbooks
Encyclopedias
Restatements and Commentaries
Loose Leaf Services
Handbooks and Manuals
Articles in Periodicals

Step 3:
SUPPLEMENT IT: Bring the statement of law up to date! Assure yourself that the statement is the latest utterance on the subject. Supplements are issued in different forms and at various intervals. Typical supplements are:
Cumulative Pocket Parts
Bound Supplements
Replacement Volumes
Continuation Volumes
Later Editions
Later Series
Advance Opinions
Legislative Services
Slip Laws
Loose Leaf Releases

Recognizing that every legal research project involves a minimum of 3 separate steps, law publishers have designed editorial devices according to those steps. The user is cautioned, therefore, to use the services for the purpose for which they were designed. By the same token, one should not rely on a service which is used in Step 1 to do the job of a service for Step 2, or Step 3, and vice versa. The books and services discussed in this booklet can be easily classified according to whether they should be used in Step 1 or Step 2 or Step 3. Your understanding of when to use a particular book will not only speed up your research, but it will also make it infinitely more effective.

The Need for a Modern Approach to Legal Research

One of the most striking features of the American legal system today is sheer bulk. Congress and the administrative agencies generate tens of thousands of enactments and rulings each year. The nation's high courts add some 35,000 opinions annually. And the individual states contribute enough statutes and regulations to turn the tide into a flood.

It is essential that the legal profession begin to develop new systems to control and apply this immense flow of information. Meanwhile, it remains the practicing lawyer's responsibility to locate, dissect, analyze, reconstruct, and apply this information to meet the individual needs of his or her clients

In a lifetime of legal work, much of your energy will necessarily be committed to this process of legal research on behalf of your clients—a process involving an enormous amount of information, and perhaps too much of your time.

The purpose of The Living Law, is to help you achieve a modern, systematic approach to legal research; an approach that will save you time without sacrificing thoroughness, thus releasing you for the more creative and remunerative phases of your practice.

This systematic approach to legal research provides the professional with all the tools necessary to find the law, keep it up-to-date and then be referenced to the forms, procedure or practical sources to get the job done. This referencing is called The Total Client-Service Library.

The Total Client-Service Library

A Modern Legal Information System

A thoroughly modern and coordinated legal research system called the Total Client-Service Library (TCSL) has been created by Lawyers Cooperative Publishing and the Bancroft-Whitney Company. The TCSL represents the first successful attempt in over a century to develop a new system of legal research that is specifically designed to meet the needs of the modern lawyer. The various units of national scope in this coordinated system, pictured here by representative volumes, are described in the pages which follow. They are:
(1) Am Jur 2d; (2) Am Jur Legal Forms 2d;
(3) Am Jur Pleading and Practice Forms, Revised;
(4) Am Jur Proof of Facts 1st, 2d and 3d Series;
(5) Am Jur Trials; (6) the ALR System (ALR 1st, 2d, 3d,4th and 5th Series, ALR Federal);
(7) United States Code Service (USCS);
(8) United States Supreme Court Reports, Lawyers' Edition 2d (L Ed); (9) Federal Procedure, L Ed; (10) Federal Procedural Forms, L Ed; (11) Federal Rules Service;
and (12) Federal Rules of Evidence Service.

Each of the TCSL publications may be used independently. But legal problems are seldom one-dimensional. Rarely will you find a case which can be considered "just a tort problem" or "simply a matter involving contracts or trial practice." However, under the pressure of the legal curriculum, many students tend to think in these terms and approach the matter at hand by the first aspect which presents itself—an approach that could prove disastrous if the other aspects of the problem were not investigated.

The unique strength of the TCSL is the way it functions as an integrated system. No matter how you approach your legal research—no matter which handle of the problem you grasp first—the other facets of the problem are automatically brought to your attention. The TCSL allows you to pursue each avenue of research to whatever degree adequately meets your needs.

So, for example, when you go to Am Jur 2d for background information on that "tort problem," you'll find a variety of signposts at your disposal, directing you to other units in the TCSL: to ALR annotations for in-depth examinations of the law in point; to ALR Federal annotations for a similar in-depth treatment of the federal matters involved; to USCS and L Ed for coverage of federal statutes and Supreme Court Reports; and to Federal Procedure, L Ed, and the other "how-to-do-it" units of the TCSL for practical suggestions and examples of litigation techniques and forms as these apply to your problem. Thus, when you use any of the standard units of the TCSL, you will find not only what that particular set has to offer, but you'll also gain the added support and strength of the other units.

Thus, the TCSL is designed to aid the modern lawyer in serving his or her clients more effectively. As a coordinated system, the TCSL frees you from the time-consuming drudgery of ferreting out each aspect of an individual problem.

TOTAL CLIENT-SERVICE LIBRARY

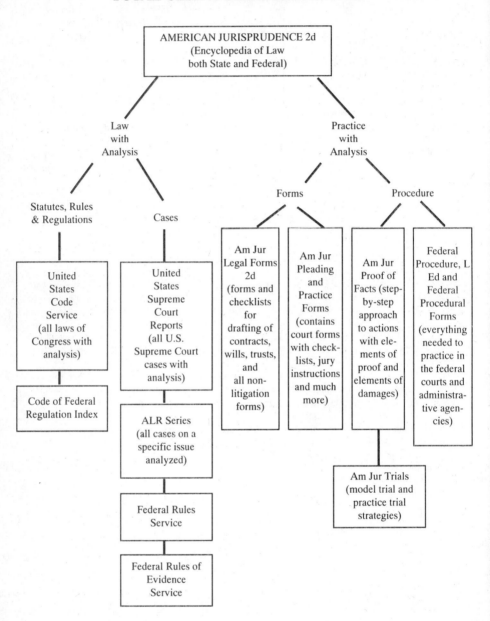

In addition to the major national TCSL units mentioned above, there are numerous state TCSL units, as well as many other local publications that work effectively with the TCSL. For more information on your specific needs call (800) LCP-0430.

American Jurisprudence 2d

principles of law which can be readily understood and applied. Knowing this, the lawyer-editors of Am Jur 2d search, sift, and analyze an immense amount of legal information to create each Am Jur 2d article. At the same time, the broad principles of law are explained and developed in concert with the way they must be applied by the lawyer and the courts. This selective editorial process weeds out the obsolete and the redundant, leaving the law that relates to the point, supported by the controlling cases that interpret and construe that law.

The Law in Breadth
American Jurisprudence 2d (Am Jur 2d) is a comprehensive legal encyclopedia containing expository statements of law, alphabetically arranged under more than 430 subjects, or titles. It provides an unparalleled breadth of coverage of all fields of American law—state and federal, civil and criminal, substantive and procedural. Noncritical in its approach, Am Jur 2d not only provides you with the objective background necessary to begin your research on any point, but it also serves as a case finder and statute locator.

Encyclopedic Coverage
No student or lawyer can ever hope to become an authority on all the law. Initially, however, it is desirable to obtain as *broad* a perspective as possible on the problem at hand. You must begin by understanding the principles of law which underlie the problem. The *guiding* principles for any point of law are relatively few, but often widely scattered throughout a multitude of sources. By the same token, there may be more facets to the problem than you can perceive at the initial stage of your analysis. This is why so many lawyers begin their search with Am Jur 2d, for it provides organized and disciplined statements of law, in logical sequence, that alert you to the entire range of diverse arguments and authority available.

Editorial Acumen
Obviously, a profusion of citations to reported cases is of little value to the researcher unless the cases are collected, examined, and summarized as

Always Up-to-Date
Am Jur 2d keeps pace with the tremendous growth and change in the law by means of a three-pronged approach:

(1) Each volume is kept up-to-date by means of annual cumulative pocket supplements.

(2) The Am Jur 2d New Topic Service discusses newly emerging areas of the law.

(3) When major changes in the law require a major re-evaluation of or new approach to a topic, replacement volumes are issued.

Federal Coverage
Am Jur 2d keeps pace with the growth and increasing importance of federal law. Major articles are devoted to such topics as Aliens and Citizens (Immigration Law), Copyright, Federal Practice and Procedure, and Social Security and Medicare. The discussion in these articles is supported not only by the case law but also by references to the United States Code Service and appropriate Federal Rules. Three volumes are devoted entirely to federal tax law, and because this area of the law is constantly in flux, these volumes are rewritten and replaced annually.

TCSL Referencing
Finally, Am Jur 2d is thoroughly referenced to the other elements of the Total Client-Service Library, enabling you to examine each facet of your problem within the framework of a completely modern and systematic approach to legal research.

In all, Am Jur 2d has been designed to be the most useful and current legal encyclopedia available today . . . and tomorrow.

The Elements of Am Jur 2d

The Desk Book   A handy legal almanac containing historical and legal documents, facts, tables, charts, and statistics of special interest to anyone working in the field of law. Sample contents include the Constitution, Magna Carta, Gettysburg Address, Code of Professional Responsibility, Organization of the Courts, Weights and Measures, etc. The Desk Book also has a complete listing of the titles in Am Jur 2d.

The General Index   The pamphlet General Indexes provide easy access to Am Jur 2d.

The Text Volumes   Here is the heart of Am Jur 2d, which consists of easy to read and understand volumes of text.

The Federal Tax Volume   The purpose of these volumes is to highlight potential tax problems and suggest how to capitalize on benefits and avoid pitfalls. Volumes 33, 34 and 34A cover Federal Taxation and provide current coverage of federal tax law—including income, estate, gift, generation-skipping, and excise tax. These volumes are entirely rewritten and republished annually, with pocket supplements issued during the year as changes in the law occur.

The Federal Topic Service   The New Topic Service extends Am Jur 2d to give comprehensive coverage to new titles of law as they emerge, and to those existing titles that are undergoing dramatic changes. The New Topic Service is one of the many ways that Am Jur 2d is constantly kept up-to-date.

The Tables Volume   This separate volume provides another means of access to the text volumes by showing where they have cited the United States Code Service, the Federal Rules of Practice, Procedure, and Evidence, and the Uniform Laws.

Finding the law in Am Jur 2d

Once the facts of the case have been analyzed, most legal research requires three steps:
• Finding the Law
• Reading the Law
• Updating, or supplementing the Law
To illustrate this process as it applies to Am Jur 2d, consider the steps one would take to conduct research for a client interested in the dissolution of a limited partnership, and specifically, the grounds for such a dissolution.

The Topical Approach

In many instances, a legal researcher can quickly find the treatment of a client's problem in Am Jur 2d simply by thinking of which topic is most likely to treat the problem, pulling that volume off the library shelf, and searching the analytical outline found in the front of the article. To assist in finding the volume, Am Jur 2d volumes have the first and last titles of topics contained in the volume stamped on the spine of the book.

When the subject matter is unfamiliar to you or potential topics do not come immediately to mind, you may look to a comprehensive list of titles found in the Desk Book at Item 133, or use the Index Pamphlets.

In our example, one might naturally expect that issues relating to limited partnerships would be treated under the topic Partnership, found in volume 59A of the Am Jur 2d set.

You can quickly check your intuition by referring to several useful features found at the front of Am Jur 2d articles. The first features encountered are three paragraphs designed to provide orientation to the treatment found in the article:
• Scope of topic: Tells you exactly what is and is not covered within the topic.
• Federal aspects: Alerts you to any federal matters involved.
• Treated elsewhere: Brings to your attention other places in Am Jur 2d where related topics are treated in full.

A check of the "Scope of topic" paragraph confirms that limited partnerships and dissolution are discussed in the article. If the client was interested in dissolution because of economic hardship, the "Federal aspects" paragraph quickly identifies where partnership bankruptcy is discussed. The client might also be interested in material identified in the "Treated elsewhere" paragraph such as appointment of a receiver in proceedings for partnership dissolution. The Research References feature also provides the researcher with a guide for finding other text and practice works in the TCSL.

PARTNERSHIP

by
Lonnie E. Griffith, Jr., J.D.; Robert R. Crane, J.D.

Scope of topic: This article discusses the law of partnership, including general partnerships, limited partnerships, and partnership associations, treating their formation, powers, dissolution, accounting, winding up, and termination. It includes a discussion of the partners' rights, powers, liabilities, property, and interests among themselves and in relation to third parties; the admission of new partners; the retirement, withdrawal, or expulsion of partners; the death of partners; arbitration of partnership disputes; civil actions by and against partnerships and among partners; and partners' criminal liability.

Federal aspects: Partnership bankruptcy is treated in 9 and 9A Am Jur 2d, BANK-RUPTCY. Partnership aspects of federal securities regulation are discussed in 69 Am Jur 2d, SECURITIES REGULATION-FEDERAL, and coverage of partnership labor and labor relations is found in 48 and 48A Am Jur 2d, LABOR AND LABOR RELATIONS. Federal practice and procedure in actions involving partnerships is discussed in 32, 32A, and 32B Am Jur 2d, FEDERAL PRACTICE AND PROCEDURE. As to federal taxation of partnerships, see "Tax References," infra.

Treated elsewhere:

Assignment of partnership assets for the benefit of creditors (see 6 Am Jur 2d, ASSIGNMENTS FOR BENEFIT OF CREDITORS §§ 12-14)

Associations and clubs (see 6 Am Jur 2d, ASSOCIATIONS AND CLUBS)

Bills or negotiable instruments, partners' rights to execute (see 11 Am Jur 2d, BILLS AND NOTES § 560)

Business trusts (see 13 Am Jur 2d, BUSINESS TRUSTS)

Corporations (see 18, 18A, 18B, 19 Am Jur 2d, CORPORATIONS)

Crop or agricultural lease on shares, partnership between sharecropper and landlord by agreement to share crops produced, as opposed to agreement to share profits (see 21A Am Jur 2d, CROPS § 40)

Dower or curtesy in specific partnership property (see 25 Am Jur 2d, DOWER AND CURTESY § 58)

Embezzlement by partner of partnership funds or property (see 26 Am Jur 2d, EMBEZZLEMENT § 28)

Exemption of partnership property from claims of creditors (see 31 Am Jur 2d, EXEMPTIONS §§ 104-108)

False pretenses of partner for obtaining partnership [ ] Jur 2d, FALSE PRETENSES §§ 7, 39)

Fraternal orders and lodges (see 36 Am Jur 2d, [ ] SOCIETIES)

Infants or minors as partners (see 42 Am Jur 2d, INF[ ]

Inheritance or estate tax liability of partners on par[ ] 2d, INHERITANCE, ESTATE AND GIFT TAXES § 147)

Insurable interests of partnership or partners in the [ ] 2d, INSURANCE § 989), and in partnership propert[ ] § 966), and the distribution of insurance proceeds [ ] INSURANCE §§ 1758, 1759)

Joint-stock companies (see 46 Am Jur 2d, JOINT STO[ ]

Joint ventures, generally (see 46 Am Jur 2d, JOINT V[ ] Am Jur 2d, JOINT VENTURES §§ 3, 4)

Larceny of partner with respect to partnership fund[ ] LARCENY § 84)

A BRIEF DESCRIPTION OF THE SUBJECT TELLS EXACTLY WHAT IS COVERED

ALERTS YOU TO FEDERAL MATTERS

LEADS YOU TO RELATED SUBJECTS

GUIDES YOU TO OTHER TEXTS AND PRACTICE WORKS IN THE TCSL

PARTNERSHIP   59A Am Jur 2d

Research References

Text References:

Uniform Commercial Code § 1-103
Uniform Fraudulent Conveyance Act § 8
UPA §§ 1 et seq.
ULPA §§ 1 et seq.
RULPA (1976, and as amended 1985) §§ 1 et seq.
Restatement, Agency 2d, §§ 14A, Comment a; 479, Comment c
Restatement, Conflict of Laws, §§ 342, 345
Restatement, Judgments 2d, § 60 (1) and (2)
Am Jur 2d Desk Book, Item 124

Annotation References:

ALR Digest to 3d, 4th, and Federal: Partnership
Index to Annotations: Arbitration and Award; Partnership

Practice References:

1 Am Jur Pl & Pr Forms (Rev), Abatement, Revival, and Stay, Forms 190, 213; 2 Am Jur Pl & Pr Forms (Rev), Assumpsit, Form 38; 5 Am Jur Pl & Pr Forms (Rev), Bills and Notes, Form 62.1 (Supp); 5 Am Jur Pl & Pr Forms (Rev), Captions, Prayers, and Formal Parts, Forms 62, 63, 152, 182, 351, 565, 719; 7 Am Jur Pl & Pr Forms (Rev), Conspiracy, Form 32; 7 Am Jur Pl & Pr Forms (Rev), Contribution, Forms 41-44; 9A Am Jur Pl & Pr Forms (Rev), Executors and Administrators, Form 682; 12 Am Jur Pl & Pr Forms (Rev), Good Will, Form 7; 14 Am Jur Pl & Pr Forms (Rev), Indemnity, Forms 32, 33; 14A Am Jur Pl & Pr Forms (Rev), Insurance, Form 515; 19 Am Jur Pl & Pr Forms (Rev), Partnership, Forms 1 et seq.; 20 Am Jur Pl & Pr Forms (Rev), Process, Form 348; 21 Am Jur Pl & Pr Forms (Rev), Replevin, Form 22

1 Am Jur Legal Forms 2d, Accounts and Accounting § 6:46; 1 Am Jur Legal Forms 2d, Agency § 14:31; 2 Am Jur Legal Forms 2d, Arbitration and Award § 23:125; 5 Am Jur Legal Forms 2d, Contracts § 68:125; 9 Am Jur Legal Forms 2d, Good Will §§ 131:31-131:40; 10 Am Jur Legal Forms 2d, Investment Companies and Advisers §§ 152:2, 152:20, 152:56, 152:57; 10A Am Jur Legal Forms 2d, Judges § 156:35; 13 Am Jur Legal Forms 2d, Name §§ 182:17, 182:21; 14 Am Jur Legal Forms 2d, Partnership §§ 194:1 et seq.; 15 Am Jur Legal Forms 2d, Real Estate Investment Trusts and Syndications §§ 218:81 et seq.; 16 Am Jur Legal Forms 2d, Sale of Business §§ 226:171-226:176; 18 Am Jur Legal Forms 2d, Uniform Commercial Code § 253:1939

4 Am Jur POF2d 355, Status as Partner   24 Am Jur POF2d 455, Misconduct Warranting Judicial Dissolution of Partner[ ]

178

The Topical Approach (continued)
The next step in the Topical Approach to finding the law is to scan the analytical outlines found following the introductory features. The analytical outline consists of two distinct sections: (1) a skeleton outline for rapid orientation, arranged in logical divisions and subdivisions according to principles of law, and (2) an expanded outline showing every section of the article. In our

example, a check of the skeleton outline shows that limited partnerships are treated in Part Two of the article, and that dissolution matters are treated in Division XXXIII. A check of the expanded outline shows that grounds for dissolution are discussed in § 1404.

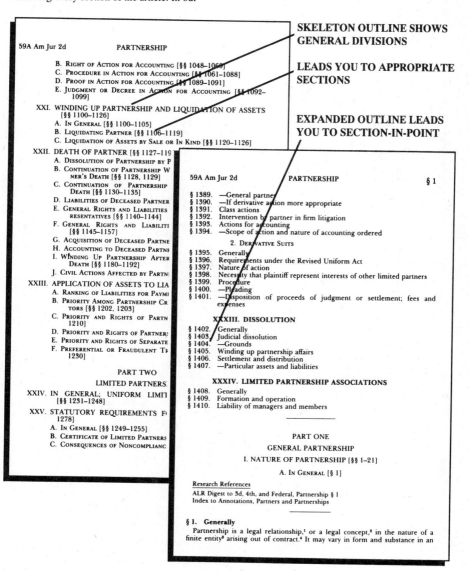

SKELETON OUTLINE SHOWS GENERAL DIVISIONS

LEADS YOU TO APPROPRIATE SECTIONS

EXPANDED OUTLINE LEADS YOU TO SECTION-IN-POINT

59A Am Jur 2d   PARTNERSHIP

B. Right of Action for Accounting [§§ 1048–1060]
C. Procedure in Action for Accounting [§§ 1061–1088]
D. Proof in Action for Accounting [§§ 1089–1091]
E. Judgment or Decree in Action for Accounting [§§ 1092–1099]

XXI. WINDING UP PARTNERSHIP AND LIQUIDATION OF ASSETS [§§ 1100–1126]
A. In General [§§ 1100–1105]
B. Liquidating Partner [§§ 1106–1119]
C. Liquidation of Assets by Sale or In Kind [§§ 1120–1126]

XXII. DEATH OF PARTNER [§§ 1127–119
A. Dissolution of Partnership by P
B. Continuation of Partnership W ner's Death [§§ 1128, 1129]
C. Continuation of Partnership Death [§§ 1130–1135]
D. Liabilities of Deceased Partner
E. General Rights and Liabilities resentatives [§§ 1140–1144]
F. General Rights and Liabiliti [§§ 1145–1157]
G. Acquisition of Deceased Partne
H. Accounting to Deceased Partne
I. Winding Up Partnership After Death [§§ 1180–1192]
J. Civil Actions Affected by Partn

XXIII. APPLICATION OF ASSETS TO LIA
A. Ranking of Liabilities for Paymi
B. Priority Among Partnership Cr tors [§§ 1202, 1203]
C. Priority and Rights of Partn 1210]
D. Priority and Rights of Partner:
E. Priority and Rights of Separate
F. Preferential or Fraudulent Ti 1230]

PART TWO

LIMITED PARTNERS

XXIV. IN GENERAL; UNIFORM LIMIT [§§ 1231–1248]

XXV. STATUTORY REQUIREMENTS F 1278]
A. In General [§§ 1249–1255]
B. Certificate of Limited Partners
C. Consequences of Noncomplianc

59A Am Jur 2d   PARTNERSHIP   § 1

§ 1389.   —General partne
§ 1390.   —If derivative action more appropriate
§ 1391.   Class actions
§ 1392.   Intervention by partner in firm litigation
§ 1393.   Actions for accounting
§ 1394.   —Scope of action and nature of accounting ordered

2. Derivative Suits

§ 1395.   Generally
§ 1396.   Requirements under the Revised Uniform Act
§ 1397.   Nature of action
§ 1398.   Necessity that plaintiff represent interests of other limited partners
§ 1399.   Procedure
§ 1400.   —Pleading
§ 1401.   —Disposition of proceeds of judgment or settlement; fees and expenses

XXXIII. DISSOLUTION

§ 1402.   Generally
§ 1403.   Judicial dissolution
§ 1404.   —Grounds
§ 1405.   Winding up partnership affairs
§ 1406.   Settlement and distribution
§ 1407.   —Particular assets and liabilities

XXXIV. LIMITED PARTNERSHIP ASSOCIATIONS

§ 1408.   Generally
§ 1409.   Formation and operation
§ 1410.   Liability of managers and members

PART ONE

GENERAL PARTNERSHIP

I. NATURE OF PARTNERSHIP [§§ 1–21]

A. In General [§ 1]

Research References

ALR Digest to 3d, 4th, and Federal, Partnership § 1
Index to Annotations, Partners and Partnerships

§ 1.   Generally

Partnership is a legal relationship,[1] or a legal concept,[2] in the nature of a finite entity[3] arising out of contract.[4] It may vary in form and substance in an

The Fact/Word Approach

An alternative to the Topical Approach is a Fact/Word Approach that utilizes Am Jur 2d's extensive indexes. Again, you can either go directly to the volume where you think the problem would most likely be treated, or you can consult the index pamphlets. Both the volume indexes and the index pamphlets extend the Fact/Word Approach to coverage in Am Jur 2d. In the volume indexes each topic contained within the volume is indexed separately. Simply look for descriptive words that suggest the Thing, Act,

Person, or Place (the TAPP-rule) involved in your problem. The alphabetical arrangement of words and concepts allows you to use the index in much the same way as you would use a dictionary. In our example, looking under the words "limited partnership" leads to a subgroup "dissolution of partnership" in which we can pinpoint the section on "grounds for judicial dissolution" as § 1404.

THOROUGH VOLUME INDEXING LEADS YOU TO THE SPECIFIC SECTIONS-IN-POINT

INDEX

PARTNERSHIP—Cont'd
Limited partnership—Cont'd
- corporations—Cont'd
- - preferred stock order, nature of limited partner as, § 1406
- - relationship between general and limited partners, § 1307
- - service of process on corporate general partner as service on limited partnership, § 1383
- - shareholder, limited partner in nature of, § 1344
- costs and expenses
- - derivative suits, costs and expenses of, § 1401
- - fees, infra this group
- counterclaim, crossclaim, and setoff
- - distribution of assets, § 1407
- - general and limited partners, actions between, § 1382
- - individual partner and limited partnership, actions between, § 1380
- crossclaim. Counterclaim, crossclaim, and setoff, supra
- damage actions, §§ 1318, 1379
- death of partner
- - amendment of certificate of limited partnership, § 1270
- - dissolution of partnership, §§ 1299, 1302
- - "events of withdrawal" which terminate general partner status, § 1304
- - executor or administrator as succeeding to rights of deceased limited partner, §§ 1242, 1243, 1299
- - general partner, § 1302
- - limited partner associations, effect of death of member of, § 1408
- - limited partners, § 1299
- - restrictions on carrying on of business on death of general partner, § 1326
- debtors and creditors
- - corporate general partner, liability of those controlling, § 1313
- - distribution, status or rights of partner entitled to, § 1316
- - general partner, liability for debts of firm, § 1332

PARTNERSHIP—Cont'd
Limited partnership—Cont'd
- debtors and creditors—Cont'd
- - unpaid contributions, creditors as parties who may enforce payment of, § 1359
- decrees. Judgments, decrees, and orders, infra this group
- defective limited partnership as applicable to one erroneously believing himself a limited partner, § 1352
- definitions, generally, §§ 1237-1239
- degree and standard of conduct by general partners, §§ 1335-1338
- demand as condition precedent to accounting action, § 1393
- derivative actions
- - generally, §§ 1390, 1395-1401
- - appropriateness of derivative action by individual partner, § 1390
- - class actions, propriety of, § 1391
- - corporation law, application of, § 1236
- - disposition of proceeds of judgment or settlement, § 1401
- - fees and expenses, § 1401
- - nature of action, § 1397
- - necessity that plaintiff represent interests of other limited partners, § 1398
- - pleadings, § 1400
- - procedure, §§ 1399-1401
- - requirements under Uniform Limited Partnership Act, § 1396
- discharge. Release or discharge, infra this group
- dissolution of partnership
- - generally, §§ 1402-1407
- - amendment of certificate of limited partnership, § 1270
- - application of Uniform Partnership Act, § 1235
- - associations, § 1410
- - bankruptcy or insolvency of general partner, § 1303
- - cancellation certificate, filing of, § 1273
- - certificate of limited partnership, effect of judicial act of ordering filing, § 1275
- - contract of partnership, provisions in, § 1286

Other Ways to Find the Law in Am Jur 2d
The TCSL: all units of the Total Client-Service
Library are referenced to each other. Am Jur 2d is
referenced extensively throughout the TCSL.

The Table of Statutes and Rules Cited Volume:
this volume shows you where provisions of the
United States Code Service, the Federal Rules
of Practice, Procedure, and Evidence, and the
Uniform Laws are cited in Am Jur 2d. Hence, you
can quickly find the sections in Am Jur 2d articles
in which a particular statute or rule is cited.

The Table of Statutes: a Table of Statues Cited
appears in the front of every volume of Am Jur 2d.
If you have a particular statute in mind and know
the topic treats the subject matter of the statute,
you can use the table to find where that statue is
cited in the article. In our example: if you had a
citation to the Uniform Limited Partnership Act
§ 16(4)(a), you could have gone to the Table of
Statutes at the front of Volume 59A and found the
reference to § 387.

TABLE OF STATUTES

UNIFORM LAWS—Continued

Am Jur 2d title and section	Am Jur 2d title and section
UNIFORM LIMITED PARTNERSHIP ACT— Cont'd	**UNIFORM MARRIAGE AND DIVORCE ACT** —Cont'd
16(1) .... PARTNERSHIP § 382	303(b)(6) .... DIVORCE AND SEPARATION § 274, 279
16(2) .... PARTNERSHIP § 382	
16(4)(a) .... PARTNERSHIP § 387	303(c) ... . DIVORCE AND SEPARATION § 263
16(4)(b) .... PARTNERSHIP § 387	303(d) ... . DIVORCE AND SEPARATION § 312
17(1) .... PARTNERSHIP § 378	303(e) ... DIVORCE AND SEPARATION § 166, 297
17(4) .... PARTNERSHIP § 382	303(f) ... . DIVORCE AND SEPARATION § 269
18 .... PARTNERSHIP § 380	304(a) ... . DIVORCE AND SEPARATION § 1055
19(1) .... PARTNERSHIP § 387	304(b) ... . DIVORCE AND SEPARATION § 328
19(2)-(4) .... PARTNERSHIP § 388	304(b)(1) .... DIVORCE AND SEPARATION § 960, 1055
19(7) .... PARTNERSHIP § 388	
20 .... PARTNERSHIP § 387	304(b)(2) .... DIVORCE AND SEPARATION § 326, 1055
21 .... PARTNERSHIP § 373	
22(1) .... PARTNERSHIP § 391	304(b)(3) .... DIVORCE AND SEPARATION § 326, 1055
22(2) .... PARTNERSHIP § 391	
23(1) .... PARTNERSHIP § 389	304(b)(4) .... DIVORCE AND SEPARATION § 327, 1055
23(2) .... PARTNERSHIP § 389	
24(1) .... PARTNERSHIP § 387	304(b)(5) .... DIVORCE AND SEPARATION § 325, 1055
24(2) .... PARTNERSHIP § 375	
25 .... PARTNERSHIP § 375	304(c) ... . DIVORCE AND SEPARATION § 328
26 .... PARTNERSHIP § 390	304(d) ... . DIVORCE AND SEPARATION § 328
28 .... PARTNERSHIP § 372	304(e) ... . DIVORCE AND SEPARATION § 325
29 .... PARTNERSHIP § 372	304(f)(1) .... DIVORCE AND SEPARATION § 329
101(11) .... CORPORATIONS § 2117	304(f)(2) .... DIVORCE AND SEPARATION § 329
	304(f)(3) .... DIVORCE AND SEPARATION § 329
UNIFORM MARRIAGE AND DIVORCE ACT	305 .... DIVORCE AND SEPARATION § 29
102(5) ...... DIVORCE AND SEPARATION § 1035, 1052	305(b)(1) ... DIVORCE AND SEPARATION § 339
	305(b)(2) ... DIVORCE AND SEPARATION § 339
301(a) ... DIVORCE AND SEPARATION § 231, 340	305(c) ... . DIVORCE AND SEPARATION § 339
301(b) ... . DIVORCE AND SEPARATION § 274	306(a) ... . DIVORCE AND SEPARATION § 817, 1038
301(c) ... . DIVORCE AND SEPARATION § 274, 296, 303	
	306(b) ... . DIVORCE AND SEPARATION § 842, 1038
301(d) ... . DIVORCE AND SEPARATION § 415	
301(e) ... . DIVORCE AND SEPARATION § 423	306(b)(2) ... DIVORCE AND SEPARATION § 1038
302 ...... DIVORCE AND SEPARATION § 263, 269	306(c) ... . DIVORCE AND SEPARATION § 842,
302(a)(1) .... DIVORCE AND SEPARATION § 242,	

The Table of Parallel References: Am Jur volumes are replaced when they become outdated. If you have a citation to an old version of the volume you can still find where the current treatment of the material is located by using the Table of Parallel References found in the front of every Am Jur 2d volume. In our example, if you had a cite to § 387 of the prior article, you could have used the Table of Parallel References to discover that the current treatment of that material is contained in §§ 1402-1405.

Court Opinions: Am Jur 2d is frequently cited as persuasive authority both in briefs of counsel and in court opinions.

Ballentine's Dictionary: As an adjunct to the TCSL, Ballentine's Law Dictionary is extensively referenced to Am Jur 2d. When looking up a definition, you will frequently be led to further treatment of the subject in Am Jur 2d.

Other Sources: Am Jur 2d is frequently referred to in law review articles, treatises, and other secondary sources.

---

xvi
TABLE OF PARALLEL REFERENCES
PARTNERSHIP—Continued

Am Jur 2d §§	Am Jur 2d (Rev) §§	Am Jur 2d §§	Am Jur 2d (Rev) §§	Am Jur 2d §§	Am Jur 2d (Rev) §§
367	548, 549	376	1249-1251, 1276, 1277	383	1311, 1312
368	577			384	1348-1352
369	587, 588, 614	377	1254, 1255	385	1308, 1309
370	1231, 1237-1239	378	1354, 1357, 1359	386	1314-1319
371	1232, 1240, 1241	378.5	1248	387	1402-1405
372	1234-1236	379	1320-1322, 1326-1328, 1333	388	1294-1298
373	1242-1244			389	1406, 1407
374	1256-1269	380	1345-1347	390	1379, 1381, 1388, 1392, 1395, 1396
375	1270, 1271, 1274, 1275, 1292	381	1353, 1365, 1366	391	1374, 1376
		382	1361	392	1408-1410

PARTY WALLS

Am Jur to Am Jur 2d

Am Jur §§	Am Jur 2d §§	Am Jur §§	Am Jur 2d §§	Am Jur §§	Am Jur 2d §§
1	Scope note	20	18	38	15, 24
2	1, 2	21	18, 20	39	13
3	3	22	19	40	13, 19, 21; Covenants, etc.
4	4	23	20	41	21; Covenants, etc.
5	9	24	21	42	13, 21
6	8	25	22	43	34
7	6	26	29	44	22, 34
8	7	27	30	45	35
9, 10	5	28	23	46	36
11	8	29	11	47	37
12	10	30	12	48	37, 38
13	14	31	2, 27	49	40
14	14, 15	32	28	50	39
15	15	33	26	51	41, 42
16	16	34	6, 8, 25, 26, 31, 33	52	43
17	4, 6	35	31	53	44
18	2	36	32		
19	17, 21, 44	37	14, 22, 25		

Am Jur 2d to Am Jur 2d Revised

Am Jur 2d §§	Am Jur 2d (Rev) §§	Am Jur 2d §§	Am Jur 2d (Rev) §§	Am Jur 2d §§	Am Jur 2d (Rev) §§
1	1	16	35	31	55
2	3-6	17	36, 42	32	56
3	20	18	37-40	33	57
4	7, 78, 79	19	41	34	68-71, 74, 76

TABLE OF STATUTES

UNIFORM LAWS—Continued

Am Jur 2d title and section	Am Jur 2d title and section
UNIFORM MARRIAGE AND DIVORCE ACT —Cont'd	UNIFORM MARRIAGE AND DIVORCE ACT —Cont'd
308(b)(3) .... DIVORCE AND SEPARATION § 666	407(b) ..... DIVORCE AND SEPARATION § 1010
308(b)(4) ... DIVORCE AND SEPARATION § 658	408(a) ...... DIVORCE AND SEPARATION § 991
308(b)(5) ... DIVORCE AND SEPARATION § 658	408(b) ...... DIVORCE AND SEPARATION § 987
308(b)(6) ... DIVORCE AND SEPARATION § 658	409(a) ...... DIVORCE AND SEPARATION § 1005
309........ DIVORCE AND SEPARATION § 1035	409(b) ...... DIVORCE AND SEPARATION § 1010
309(1) .... DIVORCE AND SEPARATION § 1043	409(c) ...... DIVORCE AND SEPARATION § 1010
309(2) .... DIVORCE AND SEPARATION § 1043	410..... DIVORCE AND SEPARATION § 996, 1008
309(3) .... DIVORCE AND SEPARATION § 1043	
309(4) .... DIVORCE AND SEPARATION § 1043	UNIFORM NARCOTIC DRUG ACT
309(5) .... DIVORCE AND SEPARATION § 1043	1(5) .. DRUGS, NARCOTICS, AND POISONS § 22
310..... DIVORCE AND SEPARATION § 231, 1062	1(6) .. DRUGS, NARCOTICS, AND POISONS § 22
311(a) ...... DIVORCE AND SEPARATION § 751, 1029	1(10) ... DRUGS, NARCOTICS, AND POISONS § 22
311(b) ...... DIVORCE AND SEPARATION § 751, 1029	1(11) ... DRUGS, NARCOTICS, AND POISONS § 19
	1(12) ... DRUGS, NARCOTICS, AND POISONS § 19
311(c) ...... DIVORCE AND SEPARATION § 751, 1029	1(13) ... DRUGS, NARCOTICS, AND POISONS § 19
	1(14) ... DRUGS, NARCOTICS, AND POISONS § 19
311(d) ...... DIVORCE AND SEPARATION § 799, 1065	1(16) ... DRUGS, NARCOTICS, AND POISONS § 22
311(e) ...... DIVORCE AND SEPARATION § 756, 799, 1056, 1065	2..... DRUGS, NARCOTICS, AND POISONS § 20,
311(f) ...... DIVORCE AND SEPARATION § 751, 1065	
312.... DIVORCE AND SEPARATION § 783, 1059	
313........ DIVORCE AND SEPARATION § 1061	
314(a) ...... DIVORCE AND SEPARATION § 420	
314(b) ...... DIVORCE AND SEPARATION § 427	
314(c)(1)... DIVORCE AND SEPARATION § 424	
314(c)(2)... DIVORCE AND SEPARATION § 424	
314(d) ...... DIVORCE AND SEPARATION § 419	
315..... DIVORCE AND SEPARATION § 751, 1075	
316(a) ...... DIVORCE AND SEPARATION § 711, 844, 958, 1081, 1083	
316(b) ...... DIVORCE AND SEPARATION § 671	
316(c) ...... DIVORCE AND SEPARATION § 1048, 1049	
401(a) ...... DIVORCE AND SEPARATION § 964	
401(d)(1)(i) .. DIVORCE AND SEPARATION § 983	
401(e) ...... DIVORCE AND SEPARATION § 982	
402........ DIVORCE AND SEPARATION § 974	
403(a) ...... DIVORCE AND SEPARATION § 996	
403(b) ...... DIVORCE AND SEPARATION § 996	
404(a) ...... DIVORCE AND SEPARATION § 985	
404(b) ...... DIVORCE AND SEPARATION § 984	
405(a) ...... DIVORCE AND SEPARATION § 984	
405(b) ...... DIVORCE AND SEPARATION § 984	
405(c) ...... DIVORCE AND SEPARATION § 984	
406(c) ... DIVORCE AND SEPARATION § 982, 984	
406(d) ...... DIVORCE AND SEPARATION § 984	
407(a) ...... DIVORCE AND SEPARATION § 999	

342

UNIFORM LAW CITATION LEADS TO SECTION-IN-POINT

CITATION TO OLD ARTICLE LEADS TO NEW TREATMENT

xii   TABLE OF PARALLEL REFERENCES

PARTNERSHIP—Continued

Am Jur §§	Am Jur 2d §§	Am Jur §§	Am Jur 2d §§	Am Jur §§	Am Jur 2d §§
114	101, 102, 104	188	159	263	229
115	102, 103, 109	189	160	264	191, 198
116	110	190	162, 163, 165	265	200
117	115	191	166	266	208, 209
118	116	192	167	267	201
119	117	193	168	268	204, 252
120	118-120	194	LIBEL & SLANDER	269	205
121	Deleted	195	MALICIOUS	270	202, 282
122, 123	120		PROSECUTION	271	203
124	121	196	169, 170, 195	272	204, 206
125, 126	120	197	171	273	218, 230
127	122	198	105, 107	274	218, 220
128	123, 124	199	106	275	218
129	125	200	107	276	221, 222
130	124	201	209	277	223, 231
131	369	202	210	278, 279	223
132	128	203	210, 225	280	223, 231
133	126	204-207	212	281	230
134	127	208, 209	214	282	230, 251
135	126	210	214, 215	283	231, 232
136	17, 129-131	211, 212	214	284	233
137	131	213, 214	216	285	234
138	132	215	215	286	235
139, 140	137	216, 217	216	287	236
141, 142	133	218	197, 214	288	237
143	129, 142	219	Deleted	289	258
144	142	220-225	217	290	239
145, 146	134	226-232	214-217	291	240
147	139	233	171	292	241
148	147	234	174	293	242
149	134	235	176	294	243
150	135	236	175	295	244
151	27, 32	237	186	296	248, 249
152	140	238	172, 187	297	250
153-155	141	239	188	298	251
156	144, 153	240	30, 173	299, 300	248
157	144	241	173	301-504	247
158	145, 146	242	175, 177, 178, 362	505	249
159, 160	142	243	182	506	257
161, 162	143	244	179	507	252, 258
163, 164	Deleted	245	191, 192	508	242, 292
165-170	BILLS AND NOTES	246	192, 193	509	253
		246.1	193	510	254
171	148	247	184, 191	511	255
172	149	248	191	512	256
173	150	249	191, 194	513, 514	245
174	151	250	197, 207	515	246
175	149	251	184	516	259
176, 177	152	252	190	517	260
178	153	253	189	518	261
179	136, 154, 155	254	196	519	262
180	154	255	185	520-522	263
181	137	256	186	523	264, 280
182	156	257	185	524	265
183	153	258	172, 224	525	265, 267
184	157	259	225	526	271, 272
185	157	260	226	527	271, 275
186	138	261	228	528	270
187	158	262	226, 227	529	266

Reading the law in Am Jur 2d

Once you have found the treatment of your problem in Am Jur 2d, you are ready to read the law. In our example, both the Topical Approach and the Fact/Word Approach have referred us to 59A Am Jur 2d, Partnership §§ 1402 to 1405 for treatment of dissolution of limited partnerships generally, and the grounds for such dissolution.

The illustration of the text found in those sections exhibits many of the features you will find in reading Am Jur 2d articles.

The text of an Am Jur 2d article is a distillation of pertinent case law and statutory material. It often states the majority view, the minority view, and cites the leading cases. In our example, the text details dissolution of limited partnerships material from an older Uniform law, from a modernized Uniform law, and from leading cases.

---

§ 1392   PARTNERSHIP   59A Am Jur 2d

‖‖‖‖ *Caution:* The court expressly disclaimed any opinion as to whether the limited partners, by so intervening, would be participating in management so as to become personally liable to creditors.[4]

§ 1393. Actions for accounting

Although the general partners are the managers of a limited partnership, a limited partner may compel them to account; as between them, he has the same rights as they and can be granted an accounting if the circumstances render it just and reasonable,[5] which they do when limited partners allege a breach of fiduciary duty, and an accounting may be granted even though the limited partners do not also pray for dissolution,[6] although a court may order dissolution, accounting, and termination all in a single action.[7]

To be entitled to an accounting, a limited partner must show a demand for an accounting and a failure or refusal to account by the partner who has the books, records, profits or other assets in his possession. This requirement is not met by a limited partner who has received monthly and annual financial statements prepared by the partnership's accounting firm, whose personal accountant was given access to the books, and who makes no claim of fraud or illegality nor any claim that generally accepted accounting practices were not followed, but only sets forth vague and conclusory allegations evincing dissatisfaction with the statements provided.[8] But a limited partner who shows that the general partners acted in contravention of the agreement or possessed partnership property, or assigned rights in specific partnership property, for other than partnership purposes, is entitled to an accounting.[9]

‖‖‖‖ *Observation:* When a limited partnership has been dissolved, a third party who asserts a claim against a partner's interest has no standing to demand a further accounting of the partnership, absent a showing of fraud or misrepresentation.[10]

A limited partnership agreement may validly contain an arbitration clause, and where the clause binds the parties to arbitrate all disputes without limitation, including any act or omission of a partner, it will be applied to the dispute which arises when a limited partner seeks dissolution and accounting for funds wrongfully appropriated by the general partner.[11] And a provision that the valuation of partnership interests will be conclusively determined, for all purposes, by the partnership's independent certified public accountants in accordance with generally accepted and sound accounting principles and

---

4. Personal liability of a limited partner, arising through participation in management, is discussed in §§ 1365 et seq.

5. Re Estate of Brandt (1st Dept) 81 App Div 2d 268, 440 NYS2d 189.

and had not asked to examine the books, and who did not contend the general partners had engaged in financial mismanagement, was not entitled to an accounting. Cafritz v Cafritz (Dist Col App) 347 A2d 267.

"Four-bar features" provide the reader with observations, practice guides, cautions, comments, form drafting guides, federal tax notes, checklists and other material meriting highlighting.

The footnote material provides: (1) citations to leading cases; (2) descriptive summaries of the citation to illustrative factual cases; (3) citations to Federal statutes, rules, and Uniform laws:

(4) references to annotations in ALR, ALR Fed, and L Ed; (5) Practice Aids leading to Am Jur Legal Forms 2d, Am Jur Pleading and Practice Forms (Rev), Am Jur Proof of Facts, Am Jur Trials, Federal Procedure, L Ed, and Federal Procedural Forms, L Ed; (6) citations to law review articles; and (7) citations to Restatements.

---

§ 1401   PARTNERSHIP   59A Am Jur 2d

expenses, including reasonable attorney's fees, but must direct him to remit the remainder of the proceeds to the partnership.[33]

XXXIII. DISSOLUTION [§§ 1402–1407]

Research References

UPA §§ 6(2), 32
ULPA §§ 10(1)(c), 16(4), 20, 23
RULPA §§ 801-804, 1104(6)
ALR Digest to 3d, 4th, and Federal, Partnership § 107
Index to Annotations, Partners and Partnerships
19 Am Jur Pl & Pr Forms (Rev), Partnership, Form 342
14 Am Jur Legal Forms 2d, Partnership §§ 194:1085, 194:1221 et seq.
16 Am Jur POF 651; 24 Am Jur POF2d 455

---

§ 1402.   Generally

The original (1916) Uniform Limited Partnership Act states that dissolution occurs on the retirement, death, or insanity of a general partner, unless the business is continued by the remaining general partners under a right to do so stated in the certificate of limited partnership, or with the consent of all members.[34]

The 1976 Revised Act provides that a limited partnership is dissolved, and its affairs must be wound up, when the first of the following occurs: either

—(1) the time specified in the certificate;
—(2) the occurrence of events specified in writing in the certificate;[35]
—(3) the written consent thereto of all partners;
—(4) an event of withdrawal of a general partner;[36] or
—(5) the entry of a decree of judicial dissolution.[37]

However, the 1976 statute also provides that an event of withdrawal does not cause dissolution if:

—(1) there is at least one other general partner and there is permission in

33. RULPA § 1004.

When a judgment has been rendered against the general partner for the amount of profit he made by selling property of the partnership, the amount recovered is a common fund for the benefit of the partnership, and the expense of legal services, including counsel fees, is a proper charge against that fund. Bassan v Investment Exchange Corp., 83 Wash 2d 922, 524 P2d 233 (decided at a time when the 1916 Act was in force and apparently referring to the legal expenses of the plaintiff limited partners, not those of the defendant general partner).

In a situation where, unless adjustments are made, any recovery to the partnership will benefit limited partners who are not entitled to damages because they have ratified the acts the suit aimed to redress, it is possible to apply an analogous rule of corporation law governing derivative actions, to the effect that, where the stockholders are few in number and are all

before the court, what amounts to a preferential dividend can be decreed, participation in which is restricted to the innocent. Phillips v Kula 200 II, 4 Hawaii App 350, 667 P2d 261.

34. ULPA § 20.

Practice Aids.—Form of agreement liquidating limited partnership. 14 Am Jur Legal Forms 2d, Partnership § 194:1232.

35. The 1985 amendments say events specified in writing in the partnership agreement.

36. "Event of withdrawal of a general partner" is a term of art in the 1976 Act. It covers death, incompetency, insolvency, and much else; see § 1304 for the full definition.

37. RULPA § 801.

Practice Aids.—Forms of provision in limited partnership agreement, regarding dissolution and winding up. 14 Am Jur Legal Forms 2d, Partnership §§ 194:1221 et seq.

950

RESEARCH REFERENCES

DESCRIPTIVE SUMMARIES OF LEADING CASES

LEADS TO PRACTICAL "HOW-TO-DO-IT" UNITS OF THE TCSL

Keeping the law up-to-date

Cumulative Annual Supplements:

After finding and reading the treatment of the law in Am Jur 2d, the law should be supplemented and updated by consulting the pocket part supplement found in the inside back cover of every volume of Am Jur 2d. The supplement provides references to later cases, annotations, practice aids, and other propositions supporting or illustrating the original Am Jur 2d text. New sections are added to the topics when appropriate.

New Topic Service:

The New Topic Service is a special binder volume included with the Am Jur 2d set. The New Topic Service, as the name suggests, provides coverage of (1) new topics of the law that have developed after publication of the volume in which they would have been placed alphabetically had they been in existence when the volume was published, and (2) important, new changes emerging within already published articles that warrant further in-depth treatment. Examples of new topics that have already appeared in the New Topic Service are:

Alternate Dispute Resolution, Consumer and Borrower Protection, Energy, and Real Estate Time-sharing.

Each article in the New Topic Service is separately bound and punched for insertion into the special binder. Additional pamphlets are issued as necessary. The articles in the New Topic Service binder are supplemented annually by a single pamphlet that fits into the binder. This single pamphlet provides update material for all the articles in the binder.

Replacement Volumes:

As the law grows and changes, Am Jur 2d volumes are replaced as necessary to provide you with up-to-date treatment of developing areas of the law. Recent replacement volumes include articles on such timely subjects as Corporations (volumes 18, 18A, and 19), Job Discrimination (volumes 45A and 45B), Pensions and Retirement Funds (volume 60A), Social Security and Medicare (volume 70A), Municipal, County, School, and State Tort Liability (volume 57), and Negligence (volumes 57A and 57B).

The ALR System

The ALR System may be thought of as a continuing series of up-to-date monographs that we now call annotations. These annotations are articles written by expert attorney-editors who have an exceptional ability to research, read, analyze and organize case law. The ALR annotation collects and analyzes every case decided on a particular point of law. And while each ALR annotation has a full report of a recent selected appellate case, the case is used to illustrate the point being annotated. Although there is a reported case, the annotation is the real value of the ALR and the annotation is what the researcher uses to find every case on a point of law.

Only ALR Has Every Case on Point

Each annotation collects, organizes, and evaluates, in meticulous detail, all of the case law relevant to a specific point of law or fact situation. The anno-tation shows explicitly and impartially which cases are controlling and why. Cases from every jurisdiction which has taken a position on the point are cited, and these cases are arranged according to jurisdiction to make it easy to find local authority. Word indexes, cross references, and other finding aids provide easy methods of entry. And finally, each annotation is kept up-to-date by separate supplementing services.

How Annotations Are Prepared

In preparing an annotation, the attorney-editors of ALR first identify a currently significant and practical point of law, as illustrated by a well-reasoned contemporary case. Then, after a careful and exhaustive search of all reported U.S. authority, they prepare an organized and disciplined treatise which analyzes the entire body of law on that particular point: its inception, development, and its present-day applicability. The rules which bear on the subject are clearly stated, along with the reasons for the rules and their application to specific fact situations. Definitions of relevant words and phrases are provided.

Depending upon the scope of the law under examination, an editor may spend several months of careful research and writing to prepare even a single annotation. Few attorneys or law students have this much time for their own research. Consequently, many lawyers and courts depend upon ALR for precise, thorough, and yet manageable legal information. In fact, ALR is the nation's most cited lawbook today.

The ALR Series

ALR has developed in six stages from 1919 to present. The resulting six series (not to be confused with editions) reflect the rapidly changing growth of American law and the development of increasingly sophisticated methods of legal research. All series are kept current with new case decisions.

The most recent series are:
1. ALR 5th, which was introduced in 1992, covers state topics and contains enhancements including citations to West digest topics and key numbers, as well as electronic search queries and statutory references. ALR 5th is compatible with all other methods of case law research. It is one of the best places to start a research project.
2. ALR 4th, which was introduced in 1980, in 90 volumes covers state topics only—no federal topics.
3. ALR 3d, published from 1965-1980 in 100 volumes. It presents both state and federal topics from 1965 to 1969, and only state topics from 1969 to 1980.
4. ALR Federal has presented only federal topics from 1969 to present. The introduction of ALR Federal was necessitated by the extraordinary growth in federal case law and its importance.

The two series that preceded ALR 3d, ALR 4th, and ALR Federal are:
5. ALR 2d, which was published from 1948-1965 in 100 volumes. Now available on microfiche, including all 100 volumes, Digest volumes 1-7, and the 3-volume Word Index.
6. ALR (First Series), which was published from 1919-1948 in 175 volumes. All available on microfiche, plus Permanent Digest volumes 1-12 and the 3-volume Word Index.

Various locating tools—described later in this booklet—provide complete access to ALR's annotations and case reports, and contain extensive cross-references. These enable you to find the very latest analysis and authority on your point of law.

ALR 2d and 1st, although dated, contain many annotations that are still relevant because the principles of law they cover are still fundamentally sound. One must remember, however, that in order to realize the full value from an annotation in any series of ALR, it should be updated with current case law. This has been accomplished either by supplementing services for these series, or through later annotations in the ALR System.

Reading the law in ALR

ALR's Features and What They Mean to You

On the following pages are illustrations demonstrating many features of a typical ALR annotation and its accompanying case report. Most of the illustrations are taken from a case and an annotation in 5 ALR 5th dealing with liability for defective heating equipment. This annotation contains all the law on this subject. It is a thorough collection, analysis, and discussion of all the cases from all the jurisdictions that have considered this situation.

You will find the illustrations and explanations on the following pages make it clear how the features of the ALR System can be important to you in your legal research. All of the features appear in both ALR 4th and ALR Federal.
They include:
* A contemporary case that illustrates the point of law under consideration. The case is only an example, as the real power of ALR is the annotation.
* Helpful TCSL references to other units of the Total Client-Service Library.
* A "scheme," or outline of how the annotation itself is organized.
* An alphabetical word index for the annotation.
* The Jurisdictional table of cited statutes and cases (in ALR 5th).
* A Table of Jurisdictions Represented (in ALR 4th) or a Table of Courts and Circuits in ALR Federal.
*The annotation itself, with its various important sections, such as the Scope, Related Matters, Summary, and Practice Pointers discussions, as well as the substantive sections of the discussion.

Later on in this pamphlet you will find separate discussions on the indexes and other finding aids that get you into the ALR System and on how the system is kept up-to-date.

The Reported Case

Treatment of a legal point or fact-situation in the ALR System contains, as an example, a reported case. This case is selected for reporting because it is a good illustration of the principles involved.

The report of the case includes a summary of the decision, the procedural evolution of the case, complete headnotes, and the complete opinion of the court.

A REPRESENTATIVE CASE PRECEDES
EACH ANNOTATION

A BRIEF SYNOPSIS OF THE CASE IS
PROVIDED

SUBJECT OF ANNOTATION

Beginning on page 1

Tort liability for pollution from underground storage tank

James CORNELL et al., Individually and as Guardians of
Joseph A. Leto et al., Infants, Respondents

v

EXXON CORPORATION et al., Appellants

Supreme Court, Appellate Division, Third
Department
June 28, 1990
162 App Div 2d 892, 558 NYS2d 647, 5 ALR5th 1053

SUMMARY OF DECISION

Property owners whose well water was contaminated by gasoline traced to leaking underground storage tanks at a gas station brought an action against the oil company which owned the tanks and the station owner, seeking recovery on the theories of negligence, trespass, and nuisance. The defendants cross-claimed against each other for indemnity. The trial court dismissed the plaintiffs' trespass claim, but denied the defendants' motions for summary judgment on all other counts.

The Supreme Court of New York, Appellate Division, Third Department, Mikoll, J., affirmed, ruling initially that the station owner was not entitled to dismissal of the negligence claim on the ground that it was barred by the applicable 3-year statute of limitations. Observing that a cause of action arising out of ingestion of a chemical substance accrues on the date of the last exposure to it, the court noted that the record contained evidence

**HEADNOTES SUMMARIZE THE
HOLDINGS OF THE COURT**

HEADNOTES

Classified to ALR Digests

**Limitation of Actions § 134 —
accrual of action — exposure
to chemical substance**

1. A cause of action arising out
of an injection, ingestion, or inha-
lation of a chemical substance accrues on the date of the last exposure to the substance.

**Limitation of Actions § 134 —
accrual of action — gasoline
pollution of well water**

2. A factual issue existed as to
the accrual date of a negligence
cause of action by property owners
whose well water was contaminated
by gasoline leaking from underground storage tanks at a gas station, where there was evidence in-

zene, toluene, and xylene as late as
December 1981, and the first clean
sample from the well was obtained
in September 1982, less than 3
years prior to commencement of
the action.

[Annotated]

**Environmental Management
§§ 48, 54; Waters § 66 — sufficiency of statement of claim
— injury from water pollution**

3. Property owners whose well
water was contaminated by gasoline leaking from underground
storage tanks at a gas station offered sufficient facts to state a
claim that their children suffered

**COURT OPINIONS ARE REPORTED
IN FULL**

OPINION OF THE COURT

MIKOLL, Justice.

Appeals (1) from that part of an order of the Supreme Court
(Smyk, J.), entered May 2, 1989 in Broome County, which partially
denied the motion of defendant Carmelina D. Chauncy for summary judgment dismissing the complaint and denied the cross
motion of defendant Exxon Corporation for summary judgment
dismissing the complaint, and (2) from that part of the judgment
entered thereon.

The primary questions presented on this appeal are whether (1)
Supreme Court properly ruled that a question of fact exists as to
when plaintiffs' negligence cause of action accrued, (2) plaintiffs'
conduct constituted an express assumption of risk barring their
negligence claim, (3) plaintiffs' sufficiently stated a cause of action
in negligence, and (4) Supreme Court correctly ruled that questions of fact exist with respect to the claim of defendant Exxon
Corporation for contractual indemnity from defendant Carmelina
D. Chauncy. We conclude that the answers to questions 1, 3 and 4
are in the affirmative while the answer to question 2 is in the
negative. The order and judgment of Supreme Court, insofar as

ALR's Research References, Scheme and Index
Every annotation has referenced a TCSL.
TCSL refers, of course, to the Total Client-Service Library. The annotation contains references to the other units of the TCSL that relate to the topic under consideration. These other units of the TCSL—and what they can do for you—are discussed elsewhere throughout this booklet.

The annotation continues with a scheme or outline by which the material in the annotation is organized. The scheme is thus one way to get into the body of the annotation.

Another way into the annotation is through the alphabetical word index that follows the scheme. Here you will find references to the many things, acts, persons, places, and legal concepts that are discussed in the annotation. Clear references help you locate your information quickly.

ANNOTATION FOLLOWS THE REPORTED CASE

STORAGE TANK POLLUTION   5 ALR5th
5 ALR5th 1

Table of Contents

Research References
Index
Jurisdictional Table of Cited Statutes and Cases

ARTICLE OUTLINE

I. PRELIMINARY MATTERS

§ 1. Introduction
   [a] Scope
   [b] Related annotations
§ 2. Summary and comment
   [a] Generally
   [b] Practice pointers

II. LIABILITY UNDER PARTICULAR THEORIES

A. NEGLIGENCE

1. ELEMENTS OF TORT

§ 3. Fault
   [a] Established or supportable
   [b] Not established
§ 4. Causation—causation in fact
§ 5. —Proximate cause
§ 6. Injury or damages
   [a] Established or supportable
   [b] Not established

2. DEFENSES

§ 7. Assumption of risk
   [a] Established or supportable
   [b] Not established

APPROPRIATE REFERENCES TO OTHER USEFUL UNITS IN THE TCSL

[a] Established or supportable
[b] Not established

Research References

TOTAL CLIENT-SERVICE LIBRARY® REFERENCES

The following references may be of related or collateral interest to a user of this annotation:

Annotations

See the related annotations listed in § 1[b].

Encyclopedias and Texts

1 Am Jur 2d, Adjoining Landowners § 11; 38 Am Jur 2d, Garages, and Filling and Parking Stations §§ 6, 137; 38 Am Jur 2d, Gas and Oil §§ 228-235; 61A Am Jur 2d, Pollution Control §§ 478, 479, 482, 575, 576; 63A Am Jur 2d, Products Liability §§ 798, 856; 75 Am Jur 2d, Trespass § 12

Practice Aids

11 Federal Procedure, L Ed, Environmental Protection §§ 32:665:21-32:671.1

18A Am Jur Pl & Pr Forms (Rev), Nuisances, Form 103; 20 Am Jur Pl & Pr Forms (Rev), Pollution Control, Form 67; 24A Am Jur Pl & Pr Forms (Rev), Waters, Form 172

3 Am Jur Proof of Facts 3d 517, Leaking Underground Gasoline Storage Tanks; 6 Am Jur Proof of Facts 2d 595, Contamination of Subterranean Water Supply by Sewage

18 Am Jur Trials 495, Subterranean Water Pollution

3

RESEARCH SOURCES

The following are the research sources that were found to be helpful in compiling this annotation:

Texts

BNA Environmental Reporter, Cases 711.01-711.30

ELI Environmental Law Reporter, Hazardous Waste—Common-law Liability; Torts

Restatement of Torts 2d §§ 519, 520, 832, 849

Speiser, American Law of Torts §§ 19:11, 20:37

Encyclopedias

1 Am Jur 2d, Adjoining Landowners § 11

38 Am Jur 2d, Garages, and Filling and Parking Stations §§ 6, 137; Gas and Oil §§ 228-235

61A Am Jur 2d, Pollution Control §§ 478, 479, 482, 575, 576

63A Am Jur 2d, Products Liability §§ 798, 856

75 Am Jur 2d, Trespass § 12

61A CJS, Motor Vehicles § 772, p 745 n 55

66 CJS, Nuisances §§ 50, 65; § 79, p 835 n 76

93 CJS, Waters § 97

Electronic Search Query

underground or subsurface or buried w/15 tank and pollut! or contamin! and nuisance or negligen! or trespass or strict liability or tort!

West Digest Key Numbers

Automobiles 395	Nuisance 43
Health and Environment 25.5(5), 25.5(5.5), 25.7(8), 28	Trespass 14
Negligence 22, 105	Waters and Water Courses 104, 107(1, 2, 3), 209

RESEARCH SOURCES INCLUDE REFERENCES TO TEXTS AND ENCYCLOPEDIAS (SUCH AS AM JUR 2d AND CJS FROM VARIOUS PUBLISHERS).

ELECTRONIC SEARCH QUERIES HAVE BEEN TESTED AND PROVEN PRODUCTIVE BY OUR ATTORNEYS IN PREPARING THE ARTICLE.

ALL WEST KEY NUMBERS WHICH YIELD ON-POINT CASES ARE CITED.

EACH ARTICLE HAS ITS OWN INDEX AND SCHEME.

COMPLETE WORD INDEX FOR THE ANNOTATION

INDEX

STORAGE TANK POLLUTION 5 ALR5th

5 ALR5th 1

Table of Contents

2

ANNOTATION TABLE OF CONTENTS SHOWS OVERALL SUBJECT ORGANIZATION

The Annotation: Jurisdiction Table, Scope, Related Matters Section, and Research Sources
ALR recognizes that readers may have a special interest in cases from a particular jurisdiction. To help you locate those cases at a glance, all schemed annotations have a Table of Jurisdictions Represented. This table lists by jurisdiction the section or sections in the annotation in which cases from each jurisdiction are discussed.

Each case in a section has its jurisdiction bold-faced to alert the reader to local precedent.

The body of the annotation begins with the Scope section, which defines the area explored by the annotation. The Scope is also used to tell you if earlier annotations are now superseded, and to define terms.

The next element in the annotation is the Related Matters section, which directs you to other annotations, and, in some instances, to law reviews and textbooks on closely related subjects.

ALR 5th contains a special section called Research Sources. Research Sources includes texts and encyclopedias from various publishers, suggested electronic search, and most digest topics and key numbers.

JURISDICTIONAL TABLES HELP YOU
LOCATE LOCAL AUTHORITY—BOTH
STATUTES AND CASES

---

5 ALR5th   STORAGE TANK POLLUTION

5 ALR5th 1

Jurisdictional Table of Cited Statutes and Cases*

ALABAMA

Pan American Petroleum Co. v Byars (1934) 228 Ala 372, 153 So 616—
§§ 8, 14, 16[a]

ARKANSAS

Southern Co. v Graham (1980) 271 Ark 223, 607 SW2d 677, CCH Prod
Liab Rep ¶ 8879—§§ 2[a, b], 13

GEORGIA

Ga Code § 105-1408. See § 3[a]

Citizens & Southern Trust Co. v Phillips Petroleum Co. (1989) 192 Ga
App 499, 385 SE2d 426—§§ 2[a], 9[b], 17[a]
North Georgia Petroleum Co. v Lewis (1973) 128 Ga App 653, 197 SE2d
437—§ 3[a]

SCOPE SECTION CLEARLY DELINEATES
SUBJECT OF ANNOTATION, AND
INDICATES ANY SUPERSESSION OF
EARLIER ANNOTATIONS

I. Preliminary Matters

§ 1. Introduction

[a] Scope

This annotation collects and analyzes the cases in which courts have discussed or decided the circumstances giving rise to tort liability for pollution from underground storage tanks. Included within the scope of this annotation are cases involving underground leakage from associated underground piping and pumps, as well as from the tanks themselves.

A number of jurisdictions may have rules, regulations, constitutional provisions, or legislative enactments directly bearing on this subject. These provisions are discussed herein only to the extent and in the form that they are reflected in the court opinions that fall within the scope of this annotation. The reader is consequently advised to consult the appropriate statutory or regualtory compilations to ascertain the current status of all statutes discussed herein, including those listed in the Jurisdic-

9

**RELATED MATTERS SECTION LEADS TO
OTHER ANNOTATIONS, LAW REVIEWS,
AND TEXTS**

tional Table of Cited Statutes and Cases.

[b] Related annotations

Measure and elements of damages for pollution of well or spring. 76 ALR4th 629.

Gasoline or other fuel storage tanks as nuisance. 50 ALR3d 209.

Pollution control: preliminary mandatory injunction to prevent, correct, or reduce effects of polluting practices. 49 ALR3d 1239.

Maintainability in state court of class action for relief against air or water pollution. 47 ALR3d 769.

Modern status of rules as to balance of convenience or social utility as affecting relief from nuisance. 40 ALR3d 601.

Landowner's right to relief against pollution of his water supply by industrial or commercial waste. 39 ALR3d 910.

Manufacturer's duty to test or inspect as affecting his liability for product-caused injury. 6 ALR3d 91.

Seller's duty to test or inspect as affecting his liability for product-caused injury. 6 ALR3d 12.

Status of gasoline and oil distributor or dealer as agent, employee, independent contractor, or independent dealer as regards responsibility for injury to person or damage to property. 83 ALR2d 1282.

fumes from premises. 54 ALR2d 764 (§ 7 superseded by "Recovery in trespass for injury to land caused by airborne pollutants," 2 ALR4th 1054).

Measure and elements of damages for pollution of a stream. 49 ALR2d 253.

Expense incurred by injured party in remedying temporary nuisance or in preventing injury as element of damages recoverable. 41 ALR2d 1064.

Liability for pollution of subterranean waters. 38 ALR2d 1265.

Liability for injury to property occasioned by oil, water, or the like flowing from well. 19 ALR2d 1025.

Damages for diminution of value of use of the property as recoverable for a permanent nuisance affecting real property. 10 ALR2d 669.

§ 2. Summary and comment

[a] Generally

By far the most common situation in which the issue of tort liability for leaking underground storage tanks has been raised has been the underground storage of fuel at filling stations. Typically, the oil company that owned the station and leased it to the operator has been the defendant, although sometimes tort actions have been

**IN THE SUMMARY AND COMMENT,
THE EXPERT WRITER OF THE ARTICLE
EXPRESSES ALL OF WHAT THEY HAVE
LEARNED IN THEIR ANALYSIS OF THE
ENTIRE LEGAL QUESTION OF THE
ARTICLE. THE EDITOR GIVES BACK-
GROUND NECESSARY TO SET THE
STAGE FOR THE SUBJECT PROVIDED**

Annotations contain a Practice Pointers section dealing with the practical and procedural aspects of the subject. Useful hints are given concerning how to handle a case within the scope of the annotation.

The most important part of the ALR annotation is the case law analysis. The text of ALR is an in-depth impartial analysis of all the law in point. All relevant cases are collected, organized, and cited. Each case is summarized, discussed, and interrelated to the others and to the principles of law involved. All rules are given and considered

as they apply to particular circumstances. The weight of authority is noted as well as the direction of emerging trends.

In sum, an ALR 1st, 2d, 3rd, 4th, 5th or ALR Federal annotation is an exhaustive legal synthesis. It collects and reconstructs all available authority on a given point. Nowhere else will you find the law presented more completely or more conveniently. And because of this, ALR is quoted and cited more often than any other source of secondary authority.

---

etor that creates a nuisance by causing harm to another person's interest in land or water is not the exercise of a riparian right.

[b] Practice pointers

Regardless of the tort theory chosen to establish liability for pollution from underground storage tanks, it is necessary to establish

24. For example, see South Cent. Bell Tel. Co. v Gaines Petroleum Co. (1986, La App 2d Cir) 499 So 2d 521.

25. For example, see Monroe "66" Oil Co. v Hightower (1965, La App 2d Cir) 180 So 2d 8.

26. Malone v Ware Oil Co. (1989, 4th Dist) 179 Ill App 3d 730, 128 Ill Dec 558, 534 NE2d 1003, corrected on other grounds (Ill App 4th Dist) 133 Ill Dec 665, 541 NE2d 876 and app den

been the testimony of a chemistry expert that the material in the underground storage tank matched samples at the site of contamination.[28]

Where underground storage tanks were located at filling stations, unexplained financial losses to the business have been important,[29] in addition to unexplained

without opinion 126 Ill 2d 560, 133 Ill Dec 669, 541 NE2d 1107.

27. Southern Co. v Graham (1980) 271 Ark 223, 607 SW2d 677. CCH Prod Liab Rep ¶ 8879.

28. Gaines 2d Cir)

29. Bell Te (1986,

---

5 ALR5th	Storage Tank Pollution	§ 16[a]
	5 ALR5th 1	

necessary to resolve whether a tenant was liable to a landlord for waste because of pollution from an underground storage tank.

In an action by a landlord to recover damages from a tenant who allegedly had leaked toxic waste from underground solvent storage tanks into the soil causing a diminution in the value of the leased property, the court, in PBN Associates v Xerox Corp. (1987) 136 Misc 2d 205, 517 NYS2d 1015, app dismd, mod, remanded on other grounds (2d Dept) 141 App Div 2d 807, 529 NYS2d 877, summary judgment gr, on reh on other grounds (App Div, 2d Dept) 575 NYS2d 451, denied the tenant's motion for summary judgment as to liability under a waste theory, where there was a dispute as to the existence of damage to the reversionary interest of the landlord. The court declared that a waste claim is improperly premised

edied prior to the expiration of the tenancy. According to the plaintiff, on the other hand, a proposed order or consent between the tenant and state department of environmental conservation required a remediation period in excess of the duration of the leasehold.

IV. Liability Under Undifferentiated[43] or Unspecified Theories

§ 16. Causation

[a] Established or supportable

Under the circumstances involved in the following cases in which the courts did not focus on a particular liability theory, the courts held that evidence of causation had been sufficiently shown or alleged to support liability, under multiple or unspecified theories, for pollution from leaking underground storage tanks.

Finding the law in the ALR System

As ALR annotations have been compiled and published over the years, so too have different finding tools evolved with each of the ALR series. Each of these finding methods is designed to accomplish a particular kind of research. Together, they provide a diversity of access to match the needs of many different research approaches.

I. The Index to Annotations Approach
A finding tool for the ALR system called Index to Annotations was published in 1986. This five-volume set provides complete and in-depth coverage for ALR 2d, ALR 3d, ALR 4th, ALR 5th, ALR Fed, and L Ed 2d. It integrates, improves, and replaces the ALR 2d Quick Index, the ALR 3d/4th Quick Index, the Federal Quick Index, and ALR Federal Tables Volume.

This new index is both easy and efficient to use. Now you need to look in only one index to find on-point annotations whether they appear in ALR 2d, 3d, 4th, 5th, Fed, or L Ed 2d. Coverage for these series is now in one comprehensive A-Z fact-word style index.

Index to Annotations has expanded depth of coverage. Applying the fact-word approach to indexing, more topic headings were created to provide more avenues of access to a given anno-

tation. Section references have been included in citations where appropriate to direct you to the specific point in the annotation which addresses your question.

Index entries on any point have been gathered in one place. Numerous, literally thousands, of topics and groups have been created in order to place entries under a variety of terms descriptive of specific things, acts, persons, and places. The descriptive word approach embraces both legal and factual terms and concepts. Collateral and interrelated material are tied together by the use of cross-references and legends to facilitate ready access to material within this index.

You need not search for the "perfect" term in order to locate an appropriate annotation. There are many places where the reference can be found. Shown here are sample pages from the Index to Annotations. Highlighted are references to an annotation involving defective heating equipment.

Index to Annotations has a pocket supplement located inside the front cover where you will find references to the most recent annotations from ALR 5th, ALR Fed, and L Ed 2d. Always consult this supplement in addition to the bound volume, to locate the most recent annotation on your point. These supplements are issued quarterly.

ANNOTATIONS APPEAR UNDER ALL
RELEVANT HEADINGS AND CITATIONS
TO PARTICULAR ANNOTATION
SECTIONS SAVE TIME

INDEX TO ANNOTATIONS

The *Annotation History Table* is an important feature of **Index to Annotations.** Located in Volume Five of the set, this table shows whether an annotation has been supplemented or superseded by a later annotation. References lead to the most recent treatment of your point.

The illustration shows how this table can speed your research. If you had located the earlier annotation before the later one, then this table would alert you to the more recent coverage.

TABLE LOCATES THE MOST RECENT ANNOTATIONS ON YOUR POINT

ANNOTATION HISTORY TABLE

55 ALR 361–369
Division V superseded 10 ALR Fed 881

55 ALR 380–385
Superseded 34 ALR2d 510

55 ALR 549–555
Superseded 37 ALR3d 337

55 ALR 750–768
Supplemented 62 ALR2d 298

55 ALR 779–781
Superseded 35 ALR2d 586

55 ALR 789–791
Superseded 19 ALR3d 1227

55 ALR 926–928
Superseded 51 ALR2d 697

55 ALR 997–1014
Supplemented 64 ALR2d 1375

55 ALR 1103–1108
Superseded 92 ALR2d 1298

55 ALR 1313–1319
Superseded 39 ALR2d 1055

56 ALR 247–249
Superseded 8 ALR2d 963

56 ALR 331–332
Superseded 1 ALR3d 677

56 ALR 390–392
Superseded 16 ALR3d 774

56 ALR 582–583
Superseded 11 ALR3d 1074

56 ALR 666–673
Superseded 70 ALR2d 1430

56 ALR 783
Superseded 41 ALR2d 905

56 ALR 1126–1127
Superseded 94 ALR3d 876

56 ALR 1155–1167
Superseded 61 ALR2d 711

56 ALR 1315–1320
Superseded 76 ALR2d 162

56 ALR 1340–1345
Superseded 20 ALR3d 599

56 ALR 1418–1550
Supplemented 4 ALR2d 761

57 ALR 7–17
Superseded 73 ALR2d 1378

57 ALR 33–38
Superseded 32 ALR3d 802

57 ALR 111–126
Superseded 58 ALR2d 10

57 ALR 136
Superseded 22 ALR2d 816

57 ALR 153–155
Superseded 13 ALR2d 168

57 ALR 244–253
Superseded 14 ALR2d 1376

57 ALR 268–275
Superseded 41 ALR2d 329

57 ALR 292–296
Superseded 73 ALR2d 1238

57 ALR 468–483
Superseded 90 ALR2d 501

57 ALR 504–506
Superseded 18 ALR2d 1287

57 ALR 535–541
Supplemented 13 ALR2d 1312

57 ALR 880–881
Superseded 14 ALR3d 1065

57 ALR 937–939
Superseded 27 ALR3d 1320

57 ALR 960–962
Superseded 6 ALR2d 391

57 ALR 972
Superseded 49 ALR3d 673

57 ALR 1180–1186
Superseded 5 ALR3d 715

58 ALR 151–152
Superseded 88 ALR2d 331

58 ALR 156–175
Superseded 62 ALR3d 918, 62 ALR3d 970, 62 ALR3d 1014

58 ALR 210–211
Superseded 13 ALR3d 404

58 ALR 326–327
Superseded 15 ALR3d 759

58 ALR 462
Superseded 25 ALR2d 928

58 ALR 639–645
Superseded 61 ALR3d 520 and 61 ALR3d 657

58 ALR 656–665
Superseded 93 ALR3d 643

58 ALR 737–744
Superseded 31 ALR2d 1078

58 ALR 751–757
Superseded 71 ALR2d 875

58 ALR 1031–1032
Superseded 9 ALR4th 695

Index to Annotations contains a *Table of Laws, Rules, and Regulations* which shows where federal statutes, regulations, court rules, uniform and model acts, restatements of law, and professional codes of ethics, are cited in annotations in ALR 3d, ALR 4th, ALR 5th, ALR Federal, and L Ed 2d.

THIS TABLE LISTS ANNOTATIONS WHICH DISCUSS PARTICULAR SECTIONS OF THE FEDERAL CODE, RULES, REGULATIONS, AND OTHER LAWS

UNITED STATES CODE SERVICE

Title and section	Vol. and page	Title and section	Vol. and page
42 USCS—Cont'd		**42 USCS—Cont'd**	
	ALR3d 6 § 1; 81 ALR3d 110 § 1; 90 ALR3d 1032 § 1; 94 ALR3d 552 § 1; 18 ALR4th 910; 31 ALR4th 11; 6 ALR Fed 76 § 1; 7 ALR Fed 9 § 1; 10 ALR Fed 903 § 1, 4; 14 ALR Fed 776 § 1; 23 ALR Fed 232 § 1; 31 ALR Fed 300 § 1, 2, 3, 4, 5, 6, 8, 9; 36 ALR Fed 166; 39 ALR Fed 182 § 1, 2, 6; 57 ALR Fed 942; 60 ALR Fed 796 § 1; 70 ALR Fed 781; 70 ALR Fed 941	416(h)(2)(B)	41 L Ed 2d 1228 § 6; 67 L Ed 2d 883 § 4
		416(h)(3)(B)	41 L Ed 2d 1228 § 6
		416(h)(3)(C)	36 ALR Fed 166
		416(h)(3)(C)(ii)	36 ALR Fed 166
		416(i)	22 ALR3d 440 § 1; 39 ALR Fed 182 § 1, 3, 5, 6
		416(i)	39 ALR Fed 182 § 5
		416(i)(1)	11 ALR3d 1134 § 1
416	11 ALR3d 1134 § 1; 22 ALR3d 440 § 1; 23 ALR3d 1034 § 1; 6 ALR4th 422 § 1; 7 ALR4th 799 § 1; 12 ALR4th 1158 § 1; 1 ALR Fed 644 § 1; 14 ALR Fed 776 § 1; 39 ALR Fed 182 § 2, 6; 60 ALR Fed 796 § 1; 61 ALR Fed 230 § 1; 70 ALR Fed 781	416(i)(1)(A)	7 ALR4th 799 § 1; 12 ALR4th 1158 § 1; 1 ALR Fed 644, 1; 7 ALR Fed 9 § 1; 10 ALR Fed 903 § 1; 14 ALR Fed 776 § 1, 8; 39 ALR Fed 182 § 1; 57 ALR Fed 942; 60 ALR Fed 796 § 1; 70 ALR Fed 427 § 1; 70 ALR Fed 781
		416(i)(2)(B)	1 ALR Fed 644 § 1
		416(i)(2)(D)	1 ALR Fed 644 § 1
416(b)(2)	36 ALR Fed 166	416(k)	68 ALR3d 1220 § 1; 75 ALR3d 1129 § 1; 10 ALR4th 767 § 1; 12 ALR4th 975; 1 ALR Fed 644 § 1; 7 ALR Fed 9 § 1; 23 ALR Fed 232 § 1; 31 ALR Fed 300 § 1; 36 ALR Fed 166; 39 ALR Fed 182 § 1; 54 ALR Fed 182 § 1; 57 ALR Fed 942; 70 ALR Fed 781
416(c)	31 ALR Fed 300 § 1, 3, 4; 70 ALR Fed 781		
416(c)(5)	63 L Ed 2d 832 § 8; 67 L Ed 2d 883 § 5; 31 ALR Fed 300 § 2; 70 ALR Fed 781		
416(e)	10 ALR Fed 903 § 2, 3, 4; 70 ALR Fed 781	416(k)(1)(A)	70 ALR Fed 781
416(e)(1)	36 ALR Fed 166	418	26, 37 ALR Fed 95 § 37
416(e)(2)	63 L Ed 2d 832 § 8	422(c)	39 ALR Fed 182 § 1
416(g)	70 ALR Fed 781	423	11 ALR3d 1134 § 1; 22 ALR3d 440 § 1; 23 ALR3d 1034 § 3, 8; 89 ALR3d 783 § 1; 1 ALR Fed 644 § 2; 7 ALR Fed 9 § 1; 10 ALR Fed 903 § 1; 14 ALR Fed 776 § 1; 39 ALR Fed 182 § 1-6; 47 ALR Fed 929; 60 ALR Fed
416(h)	31 ALR Fed 300 § 1, 2, 3, 4, 7, 8, 9		
416(h)(1)	31 ALR Fed 300 § 2, 6, 9		
416(h)(1)(A)	31 ALR Fed 300 § 2, 3, 5, 6, 7, 8, 9		

II. The Digest Approach

The theory of a digest, unlike that of an index, is that there is one logical place for each particular point of law to be referenced. The resulting method of search is often called the legal analysis or topical approach method. To use it, you first think of and locate the appropriate topic, then the proper topical division, and subdivision, and finally the specific section in the outline that covers your point. This section will contain references to the annotations that deal with the law in point.

The ALR Digests organize the law into more than 400 familiar legal topics. These are presented alphabetically. The Digest for ALR 3d, 4th, 5th and Federal contains nine volumes.

The ALR 2d Digest has seven volumes, arranged alphabetically, and covers all 100 volumes of ALR 2d. Volume seven contains the Table of Cases for ALR 2d. The Digest for ALR 1st is complete in 12 volumes, with a complete Table of Cases in volume 12. Each Table of Cases cites you to the digest topics and sections under which the issues of law are classified; thus you will be able to find all the pertinent law on your point.

THE DIGEST TAKES AN ANALYTICAL APPROACH

WASTE

Scope of Topic: This topic covers the spoliation, destruction, misuse, alteration, or neglect of premises by one lawfully in possession thereof, to the prejudice of the estate or interest therein of another.

Treated elsewhere are waste by tenants (see LANDLORD AND TENANT), cotenants (see COTENANCY AND JOINT OWNERSHIP), or life tenants (see LIFE TENANTS AND SUCCESSIVE BENEFICIARIES); waste as to mortgaged property (see MORTGAGE); opening of mines as waste (see MINES); protection of dower interests against waste (see DOWER); waste as a ground for the appointment of a receiver (see RECEIVERS); and environmental management (see ENVIRONMENTAL MANAGEMENT). Matters as to procedure and proof are treated in such topics as ACTION OR SUIT; DAMAGES; EVIDENCE; INJUNCTION; LIMITATION OF ACTIONS; PLEADING; etc.

§ 1 Generally
§ 2 By whom committed
§ 3 Actions for

§ 1 Generally

Text References:

51 Am Jur 2d, Life Tenants and Remaindermen §§ 2, 3; 55 Am Jur 2d, Mortgages §§ 990-995; 65 Am Jur 2d, Receivers § 35; 78 Am Jur 2d, Waste §§ 1-9

Practice References:

9 Am Jur Pl & Pr Forms (Rev), Estates, Form 51; 16 Am Jur Pl & Pr Forms (Rev), Life Tenants and Remaindermen, Forms 1, 2; 18 Am Jur Pl & Pr Forms (Rev), Mortgages, Forms 284, 289; 21 Am Jur Pl & Pr Forms (Rev), Receivers, Form 28; 24 Am Jur Pl & Pr Forms (Rev), Waste, Forms 1-10, 61

20 Am Jur Legal Forms 2d, Waste, §§ 259:1 et seq.

Annotations:

Right of contingent remainderman to maintain action for damages for waste, 56 ALR3d 677

What constitutes waste justifying appointment of receiver of mortgaged property, 55 ALR3d 1041

Forfeiture of life estate for waste, 16 ALR3d 1344

Auto-Cite®: Any case citation herein can be checked for form, parallel references, later his-tory, and annotation references through the Auto-Cite computer research system.

Forfeiture is not a remedy for waste in the absence of a permissible statute. *Worthington Motors v Crouse (1964) 80 Nev 147, 390 P2d 229, 16 ALR3d 1338.*

[Annotated]

REFERENCES TO ANNOTATIONS APPEAR UNDER APPROPRIATE DIGEST SECTIONS

WATERS

Consult pocket part for later cases

...ect on nonnavigable stream to file declaration of such intention. 40 ALR Fed 891

Authority of Secretary of Army to deny dredging and filling permit for ecological reasons under § 10 of Rivers and Harbors Act of 1899, 33 USCS § 403, 25 ALR Fed 706

Construction and application of Wilderness Act (16 USCS §§ 1131 et seq.) providing for national wilderness preservation system, 14 ALR Fed 508

§ 35 Dams generally

Text References:

78 Am Jur 2d, Waters § 200

Auto-Cite®: Any case citation herein can be checked for form, parallel references, later history and annotation references through the Auto-Cite computer research system.

The general purpose of statutes imposing on the owners of a dam the duties "to repair, operate, maintain, and control" their dam so that it does not become "a dam in disrepair," is to insure the supervision and control of the high and low water levels in the inland public waters of the state, and also of the instrumentalities by which these levels are affected. *Moulton v Groveton Papers Co. (1972) 112 NH 50, 289 A2d 68, 51 ALR3d 957.*

A statute imposing on the owners of a dam the duty to so maintain and repair it that it shall not become "a dam in disrepair" provides a standard of conduct on the part of the owners intended to protect against damage from the flooding of land of others by their dams. *Moulton v Groveton Papers Co. (1972) 112 NH 50, 289 A2d 68, 51 ALR3d 957.*

The plaintiffs whose land was damaged by the failure of the defendants' dam resulting in the discharge of a large amount of water downstream, were within the orbit of the risk of danger which would result from violation of a statute imposing a duty upon the owners to maintain and repair their dam. *Moulton v Groveton Papers Co. (1972) 112 NH 50, 289 A2d 68, 51 ALR3d 957.*

§ 36 Artificial conditions generally

Text References:

78 Am Jur 2d, Waters § 195

Practice References:

13 Federal Procedural Forms 1. Ed, Navigable Waters §§ 51:32, 51:41

1 Am Jur Pl & Pr Forms (Rev), Administrative Law, Forms 271-277

33 USCS § 1365(a)(2)

US L Ed Digest, Administrative Law §§ 205-207, 292-297; US L Ed Digest, Courts § 253; US L Ed Digest, Mandamus §§ 6, 9, 54; US L Ed Digest, Waters § 54

§ 37 —Raising or lowering level of waters

Text References:

78 Am Jur 2d, Waters § 205

CASE NOTES LEAD TO CASES REPORTED IN ALR

§ 41

§ 38 —Hastening or increasing flow

Text References:

78 Am Jur 2d, Waters § 13

§ 38.5 —Artificial accretion or reliction

Text References:

78 Am Jur 2d, Waters § 406-427

§ 40 Ponded or stored water; reservoirs

Text References:

26 Am Jur 2d, Eminent Domain §§ 56, 141, 165, 195; 27 Am Jur 2d, Eminent Domain § 350; 78 Am Jur 2d, Waters §§ 26-27, 32 et seq., 55, 79, 98 et seq., 200 et seq., 223 et seq., 359 et seq.

Practice References:

5 Am Jur Pl & Pr Forms (Rev), Canals, Forms 5, 7; 24 Am Jur Pl & Pr Forms (Rev), United States, Form 2; 24 Am Jur Pl & Pr Forms (Rev), Waters, Forms 351 et seq., 371 et seq.

4 Am Jur Legal Forms 2d, Canals §§ 52:11 et seq.; 18 Am Jur Legal Forms 2d, Waters §§ 260:111 et seq., 260:151 et seq.

1 Am Jur Proof of Facts 146, Act of God, Proof 1

2 Am Jur Trials 293, Locating Scientific and Technical Experts; 3 Am Jur Trials 377, Preparing and Using Models; 6 Am Jur Trials 555, Use of Engineers as Experts

US L Ed Digest, Eminent Domain §§ 15, 45, 79, 80; US L Ed Digest, Waters §§ 62-65, 67, 68

Annotations:

Res ipsa loquitur as applicable in actions for damage to property by the overflow or escape of water, 91 ALR3d 1065

Liability of governmental entity for issuance of permit for construction which caused or accelerated flooding, 62 ALR3d 514

Applicability of rule of strict or absolute liability to overflow or escape of water caused by dam failure, 51 ALR3d 965

Liability of water distributor for damage caused by water escaping from main, 20 ALR3d 1295

§ 41 —Seepage; percolation; discharge of impounded waters

Text References:

78 Am Jur 2d, Waters § 196

Annotations:

Applicability of rule of strict or absolute liability to overflow or escape of water caused by dam failure, 51 ALR3d 965

In an action by various plaintiffs for damages to their lands caused by the failure of the defendants' dam, resulting in the discharge of a large amount of water downstream, strict liability on the basis that the dam allegedly constituted an ultrahazardous activity, creating an undue risk of harm to other members of the

651

III. Citations for Annotations to Find the On-Point Annotation

A CASE CITATION LEADS TO AN ALR ARTICLE

NORTHEASTERN REPORTER, 2d SERIES **Vol. 74**

67A3944n
– 810 –
(330IIA598)
60A3937n
60A3950n
– 815 –
Case 1
(330IIA621)
49A3956n
– 823 –
(330IIA549)
93A3272n
– 837 –
(330IIA618)
7A3301n
– 853 –
(330IIA529)
61A3103n
64A3670n
– 858 –
(34Op251)
30A31155n
– 874 –
(321Mas90)
17A325n
17A346n
17A352n
– 920 –
(330IIA506)
90A3247n
– 925 –
(225Ind45)
8A3941n
– 927 –
(117InA294)
99A3416n

Vol. 72

– 1 –
(321Mas72)
15A295n
– 26 –
Case 1
(296NY839)
56A3132n
– 32 –
Case 2
(296NY852)
56A359n
– 34 –
Case 1
(296NY855)
22A3727n
22A3734n
– 35 –
Case 2
(296NY857)
(174AR401)
22A3269n
– 36 –
(296NY857)
30A31155n
30A31181n
– 46 –
(117InA296)
28A3758n
28A3768n
– 107 –
(47Abs234)
13A3892n
– 165 –
(296NY223)
50A4683n
– 172 –
(296NY236)
70A3956n
– 174 –
(296NY239)
17A3402n
– 210 –
(396Ill235)
42A4707n
– 238 –
(117InA357)
62A3331n
62A3351n
– 245 –
(147OS416)
(169AR668)
19A31023n
74A31057n
10A4582n
– 259 –
(147OS480)
48A3490n
– 266 –
Case 2
(148OS7)
35A31363n
– 267 –
(48Abs97)
(34Op295)
61A3674n
61A3684n
– 280 –
(79OA218)
2A3216n
15A31281n
– 286 –
(79OA255)
46A453n
– 293 –
(48Abs385)
14A329n
– 311 –
(396Ill554)
90A3427n
90A3448n
– 369 –
(147OS491)
26A3672n
49A3803n
– 378 –
(147OS437)
39A329n
39A380n
– 388 –
(47Abs344)
27A3689n
27A3757n
– 406 –
(321Mas110)
33A3946n
39A3680n
54A3472n
– 419 –
(321Mas174)
22A3385n
22A3415n
– 422 –
(321Mas170)
49A3348n
– 452 –
(331IIA110)
65A3183n
– 470 –
(34Op507)
51A31228n
4A4894n
– 477 –
(35Op234)
14A3911n
– 487 –
(79OA437)
38A31119n
38A31153n
– 511 –
(47Abs447)
10A3669n
– 518 –
(321Mas269)
21A4710n
– 528 –
(321Mas186)
17A322n
17A330n
17A3116n
– 536 –
(321Mas226)
(172AR1320)
18A3859n
– 538 –
(321Mas200)
(173AR497)
20A3327n
– 549 –
(321Mas240)
(174AR370)
80A3428n
– 580 –
(117InA504)
3A3431n
– 603 –
Case 2
(296NY860)
2A3586n
– 635 –
(331IIA129)
5A428n
– 662 –
(117InA379)
61A3700n
61A3724n
63A3104n
– 669 –
66A41149n
66A41181n
– 682 –
(81OA97)
36A3181n
– 697 –
(296NY249)
90A31362n
– 729 –
Case 2
(331IIA64)
65A3123n
65A3200n
– 744 –
(225Ind78)
9A4703n
– 789 –
(47Abs513)
50A3632n
86A344n
– 874 –
(331IIA207)
8A380n
8A3147n

Vol. 73

– 4 –
(331IIA192)
20A31322n
46A3810n
46A3848n
– 30 –
(296NY296)
(171AR759)
50A31326n
50A31393n
62A4358n
– 37 –
Case 1
(296NY915)
71A3290n
71A3400n
– 40 –
(296NY923)
39A31236n
39A31241n
39A31278n
– 41 –
Case 2
(296NY926)
27LE962n
56LE854n
88A3199n
88A3214n
30A41049n
37ARF707n
37ARF729n
– 44 –
Case 2
(296NY932)
41A380n
– 59 –
Case 1
(117InA455)
59A31345n
59A31352n
– 93 –
(34Op359)
55A3734n
– 113 –
(296NY308)
49A31286n
49A31301n
– 117 –
Case 1
(296NY936)
45A31376n
45A31413n
51A4280n
– 127 –
(331IIA405)
1A3106n
59A3176n
– 152 –
(331IIA412)
35A4553n
– 168 –
Case 2
(331IIA347)
– 181 –
(118InA292)
5A340n
5A379n
– 188 –
(117InA593)
49A3947n
– 192 –
(148OS82)
18A3514n
18A3517n
18A3539n
– 212 –
(80OA150)
31A330n
31A3110n
31A3188n
31A3254n
– 226 –
(48Abs310)
(35Op85)
55A41113n
– 261 –
Case 2
(296NY946)
49A3949n
– 262 –
(296NY948)
22A3270n
– 263 –
(296NY950)
33A3780n
36A3334n
36A3339n
36A3353n
38A3845n
38A3876n
– 272 –
(397Ill260)
37A3968n
37A3989n
– 378 –
(48Abs1)
65A348n
– 388 –
(49Abs29)
12A395n
– 441 –
(331IIA’95)
92A3997n
– 460 –
(321Mas316)
53A3670n
1A4589n
– 478 –
(225Ind169)
66A31003n
– 521 –
(47Abs488)
63A3616n
– 529 –
(296NY315)
23A4407n
23A4470n
– 536 –
(296NY330)
14ARF564n
– 543 –
(296NY342)
41A31030n
41A31046n
– 559 –
65A3237n
– 560 –
(296NY974)
34A4679n
– 581 –
Case 1
(296NY1007)
87A3965n
– 590 –
(321Mas387)
42A31259n
42A31294n
43A3934n
55A31268n
55A31273n
– 592 –
(321Mas390)
45A3811n
45A3854n
– 620 –
(331IIA591)
89A356n
– 624 –
(331IIA535)
29A3797n
29A3798n
– 647 –
Case 2
(331IIA552)
5A3317n
5A3344n
– 651 –
(331IIA410)
53A3686n
53A3697n
53A3715n
– 652 –
(331IIA418)
33A3566n
– 671 –
(331IIA610)
4A31404n
4A31433n
– 674 –
(225Ind176)
10A3780n
– 676 –
(225Ind195)
14A31350n
– 695 –
(117InA545)
78A3181n
– 731 –
(321Mas429)
2A3708n
53A3441n
– 737 –
(321Mas455)
22A3303n
28A3620n
28A3691n
– 740 –
(321Mas382)
95A334n
– 786 –
(331IIA585)
85A3435n
– 805 –
Case 1
(148OS139)
27A3689n
27A3757n
– 836 –
(321Mas423)
96A3460n
– 840 –
(321Mas507)
(173AR711)
14A3939n
14A3954n
– 898 –
(321Mas482)
55A3360n
– 902 –
(321Mas480)
27A4407n
– 916 –
Case 2
(296NY1053)
40A3362n
– 920 –
Case 2
(331IIA601)
18A341n

Vol. 74

– 22 –
(321Mas516)
65A3113n
– 97 –
Case 3
(49Abs65)
(36Op450)
59A343n
59A373n
– 119 –
(80OA245)
3A31195n
3A31217n
– 130 –
(79OA397)
61A3503n
– 141 –
(321Mas519)
21A31041n
– 162 –
(332IIA117)
6A3100n
6A3104n
6A3131n
– 174 –
(297NY460)
44A353n
44A363n
77A3375n
– 188 –
(297NY486)
12A3898n
12A3902n
– 192 –
Case 1
(297NY494)
44A3689n
63A3546n
63A3560n
– 195 –
(297NY500)
49A3565n
– 205 –
(79OA407)
38A31338n
38A31345n
– 242 –
(148OS221)
74A397n
– 246 –
(148OS242)
52A4366n
– 251 –
(148OS332)
59A31136n
– 261 –
(148OS342)
4A31097n
– 270 –
Case 3
(148OS410)
30A31217n
30A31232n
50A3632n
– 272 –
(48Abs229)
1A3185n
– 285 –
(35Op39)
31A3852n
– 319 –
(148OS306)
40A3265n
– 340 –
(148OS365)
52A4530n
53A4488n
– 411 –
(79OA432)
70A3937n
70A31042n
– 418 –
(80OA397)
63A3404n
– 468 –
Case 1
(297NY530)
49A31286n
49A31301n
– 477 –
Case 1
54A4678n
– 523 –
(397Ill305)
24A4321n
– 553 –
Case 3
(297NY579)
54A3582n
– 563 –
(80OA39)
2A3236n
– 648 –
65A4641n
– 671 –
(321Mas590)
33A3510n
– 685 –
(397Ill620)
8A31248n
– 735 –
Case 1
(332IIA281)
62A3792n

– 735 –
Case 2
(332IIA222)

IV. Other Ways to Find the Law in ALR

Along with each new volume of ALR 5th and ALR Federal, you will receive an Alert which facilitates your check for new annotations that may be on point for cases pending in your office. The Alert gives you a topical listing of annotations in both the current volume and the next scheduled volume, as well as highlighting selected annotations from both volumes through a brief text discussion.

Other publications also refer to the ALR System. Among these, of course, are the other standard units of the Total Client-Service Library, particu-larly American Jurisprudence 2d. Also, many of the definitions in Ballentine's Law Dictionary (3d Edition) will lead you to ALR. Finally, you will find that citations to ALR are common throughout the entire range of legal publications in America, including law reviews, treatises, encyclopedias, textbooks, legal briefs and memoranda, and thousands of reported court opinions. In fact, ALR is quoted and cited more often than any other source of secondary authority.

Keeping the law up-to-date

Each day our courts hand down new opinions that modify old rules of law or apply them to new circumstances. Your research is never complete until you have located the most recent authority on your problem. To make this easier for you, each ALR annotation is kept up-to-date by collecting all the cases on point decided after the annotation was written. These later cases are brought to you in the separate supplements to the various series of the ALR system. And, for even more current coverage, subsequent cases can be obtained by calling the toll free Latest Case Service number appearing on each supplement, (800) LCP-0430.

In the supplements, the later cases are listed under headings that correspond to the sections of the outline of the original annotation. New sections are added to the original outline for listing later cases that have expanded the annotation itself. The absence of any such section heading in the supplement means simply that there are no later cases affecting that section.

Where the effect of these later cases results in a significant departure from established precedents, or where other circumstances require, new annotations are written to supersede the earlier ones. The Annotation History Table, located in Volume 5 of the Index to Annotations, will lead directly to these new annotations, as will the ALR Blue Book of Supplemental Decisions and the ALR 2d Later Case Service, discussed later.

As they have been developed over the years, the supplemental services for the various series of ALR, though diverse in approach, have become increasingly more convenient and thorough. There are three basic methods of supplementation for the various series of ALR:

I. ALR 3d, ALR 4th, ALR 5th, and ALR Federal Supplements
To make your task as easy as possible, ALR 3d, ALR 4th, ALR 5th and ALR Federal are supplemented annually by new cumulative pocket supplements inserted in the back of each volume. When you have located an annotation, therefore, you will have all of the later cases for that annotation collected in the same volume.

II. ALR 2d Later Case Service

The ALR 2d Later Case Service is a separate set of books which supplement the annotations in ALR 2d. Labels on the spine of each volume indicate the volumes of ALR 2d which are supplemented therein. The supplementary material is arranged according to the page number of your ALR 2d annotation. Here are all of the relevant cases decided since the annotation was written.

The volumes of the Later Case Service themselves are supplemented annually by pocket parts inserted in the back of each volume. Consulting these supplements will complete your search for the most recent cases on any subject annotated in ALR 2d.

SECTION-BY-SECTION SUPPLEMENTATION WITH NEW SECTIONS ADDED WHEN APPROPRIATE

need for an in camera look at the records. Mehau v Gannett Pacific Corp. (1983) 66 Hawaii 134, 658 P2d 312, 9 Media L R 1337, 38 ALR4th 1088, later proceeding (Hawaii) 690 P2d 1304.

New York State Division of State Police would not be required to disclose all confidential investigative reports prepared by it "concerning the Newburgh police scandals which occurred approximately in 1972," where notwithstanding direction that names of confidential informants be redacted, speculation fueled by disclosure of the reports could subject sources to reprisals and imperil any future investigation of a similar nature. Public interest in right of a litigant to obtain evidence must, in such circumstances, give way to public interest in enabling government effectively to conduct sensitive investigations involving matters of demonstrably important public concerns. Brady v Ottaway Newspapers, Inc. (1983, 2d Dept) 97 App Div 2d 451, 467 NYS2d 417, 10 Media L R 1287, affd, ctfd ques ans 63 NY2d 1031, 484 NYS2d 798, 473 NE2d 1172, 11 Media L R 1149, later proceeding (App Div, 2d Dept) 487 NYS2d 367.

36 ALR2d 1323–1330

Education as element in allowance for benefit of child in decree of divorce or separation. 56 ALR2d 1207.

Adequacy of amount of money awarded as child support. 1 ALR3d 324.

extent of his reasonable ability to do so. Maclay v Maclay (1984, 3d Dept) 99 App Div 2d 629, 471 NYS2d 718.

In former wife's action seeking termination of trust and distribution of proceeds to herself and former husband, trust would not be terminated where it had been created by spouses on their divorce for purpose of children's education, where husband, as remainder beneficiary and cotrustee, resisted termination, where no child had yet graduated from college or attained age when most young people who aspire to advanced educations satisfy their aspirations, where trust provided for distribution of remainder only after children "terminated their advanced education," and where two of three children, who were 19½, 22½, and 24½ years old respectively, expressed strong aspirations for further higher education. Further, husband was entitled to reimbursement from trust for his attorney's fees where husband-trustee had fiduciary duty under state statute to defend trust from depletion of its assets by decree of termination. Sundquist v Sundquist (1981, **Utah**) 639 P2d 181.

36 ALR2d 1345–1355

§ 1 [36 ALR2d 1345]

Right of limited partner to maintain derivative action on behalf of partnership. 26 ALP⁴ᵗʰ ²⁶⁴

St
Act

SEPARATE VOLUMES WITH POCKET SUPPLEMENTATION

LATER CASE SERVICE   **36 ALR2d 548–563**

Fire & Marine Ins. Co. 142 **Conn** 669, 116 A2d 514, supra, § 10[b].

See Canal Ins. Co. v Howell, 248 **Miss** 678, 160 So 2d 218, supra § 5 (citing annotation).

§ 11. —Overturning, p. 527.

See Cagle v Home Ins. Co. 14 **Ariz** App 360, 483 P2d 592, supra § 2 (citing annotation).

Where only evidence was driver's incredible testimony that heavy machine fell off slowly turning trailer completely over 2-foot-high stakes, there was no showing that damage was caused by overturning or upset of truck or trailer, since insured was required to show at least a partial overturning or upsetting of trailer sufficient to spill machine onto the road. Crowley v New Hampshire Fire Ins. Co. (NH) 130 A2d 276 (citing annotation).

§ 14. —Theft or other dishonesty, p. 529.

Under policy protecting against theft of entire load, but not including pilferage, theft of 1,400 pounds of cotton from truck load of 8,000 or 9,000 pounds was not covered. New York Fire Ins. Co. v Ashley (**Tex** Civ App) 290 SW2d 954.

36 ALR2d 548–563

Excessiveness or inadequacy of damages for alienation of affections, criminal conversation, or seduction.

tion of affections of husband separated from wife but still having sexual relations with her; $7,500 punitive damages awarded by jury stricken because paramour did not show wanton indifference to wife's interest. McNelis v Bruce, 90 **Ariz** 261, 367 P2d 625.

—$12,500; defendant enticed plaintiff's husband by giving him gifts including automobile and so broke up marriage. Kuhn v Cooper (**W Va**) 87 SE2d 531.

—$10,000; to wife who suffered humiliation, mortification, disgrace, and shame engendered by sexual intercourse of husband with another. Vaughn v Blackburn (**Ky**) 431 SW2d 887.

[c] **Verdict held excessive.**

Where plaintiff and husband were not living in harmony, as evidenced by her frequent initiation of divorce proceedings and by the incidence of disputes involving physical violence between them, jury verdict of $15,000 was excessive in action for alienation of affections and criminal conversation. Alaimo v Schwanz, 56 **Wis** 2d 198, 201 NW2d 604.

§ 6. **Action against wife's paramour, p. 557.**

[a] **Late cases.**

Jury verdict for husband in unspecified amount was held not excessive for alienation of affections, where actions of paramour caused wife to leave husband and her 5 children. Copeland v Stewart (**Iowa**) 203 NW2d

How to Update an Annotation

Locate the most recent authority on your problem with—

- **Annual cumulative pocket supplements** inserted in the back of each ALR Federal volume—

    —all the relevant cases decided after the annotation was written are discussed under headings that correspond to the sections of the original annotation

    —new sections are added in the supplement as required by developing case law

    —later annotations and TCSL references relevant to the subject are also included

- **Latest Case Service Hotline.** Gives you the cites to cases decided since the last supplement, with one toll free phone call. See the front cover of any supplement for the phone number.

- **Auto-Cite® service** allows you to check any case citation from the annotation or supplement for form, parallel references, prior and later history, and other annotations that have discussed the case.

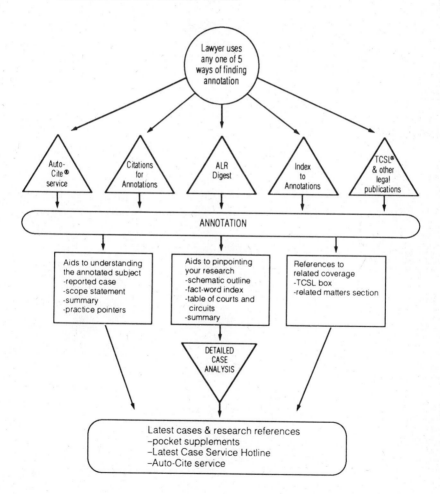

III. ALR 1st Blue Book of Supplemental Decisions

This is the supplementing service for ALR 1st. It too is a separate set of books, but it is arranged differently than the Later Case Service for ALR 2d, in that the supplementary material is compiled chronologically rather than cumulatively. There are six permanent Blue Book volumes and a seventh paper-bound volume that is updated annually. The first volume covers the period 1919-1946, the second volume covers 1946-1952, the third vol-ume covers 1952-1958, the fourth volume covers 1959-1967, the fifth volume covers 1968-1975, and the sixth volume covers 1976-1983. The seventh volume (paperback) covers 1984-present. While the Blue Book volumes are arranged chronologically, the material within each volume is arranged in the numerical order of the annotations, by volume and page. The Blue Book will also indicate whether an annotation in ALR 1st has been supplemented or superseded by a later annotation in the ALR System.

The Federal Law

The rapidly expanding growth and influence of federal law in recent years is a well-recognized phenomenon. Nowhere is this trend more evident than in the rising case load of the Federal District Courts. In 1970 those courts processed 87,000 cases; by 1980 the total had grown to 168,000—an increase of 93%. The 1990s promise an even larger increase.

Similarly, the case loads in the other two major parts of the federal adjudicatory system—the specialized courts and the administrative agencies—have reached all-time record highs. A single specialized court (Bankruptcy) handled 519,000 cases in 1981—far more than were filed in the Federal District Courts, the Courts of Appeals, and the Supreme Court combined. And, among hundreds of administrative agencies, one agency alone (NLRB) processed nearly 55,000 cases in 1980.

Concerning these agencies, the U.S. Comptroller said recently, "Federal executive departments and agencies process a larger case load than U.S. Courts, affect the rights of a larger number of citizens, and employ more than twice as many Administrative Law Judges as there are active judges in Federal trial courts."

The same period has witnessed a comparable growth in the number of new federal laws and regulations enacted by the legislative and executive branches of government. This trend is well-exemplified by the Federal Register, which filled more than 87,000 pages in 1980, up from 20,000 in 1970.

Inevitably, this aggregate growth has had an impact on the practice of law generally. Areas that were once viewed as exclusively "local" now have federal aspects that call for careful scrutiny. Real estate transactions, credit, pensions, social services, occupational safety, the environment, consumer protection, product safety, labor relations, urban development and job discrimination are just a few examples of these federally affected areas.

As a result of this influence, whether a practice is substantially "local" or federal, you have a need for our Total Client-Service Library. This cross-indexed, collateral-referenced research system covers all the fundamental areas of federal law in the publication of several major sets. Each set is designed to do its own particular job accurately and effectively and, at the same time, each set interrelates with the others.

The individual sets and their coverage include:
1. United States Code Service, offering complete and up-to-date coverage of the laws enacted by Congress.
2. Federal Procedure, Lawyers Edition, providing an encyclopedic text treatment of all aspects of federal procedure—civil, criminal, and administrative.
3. Federal Procedural Forms, Lawyers Edition, with step-by-step guidance for drafting instruments for proceedings in and for guidance through all federal courts and major federal agencies.
4. U.S. Supreme Court Reports, L Ed 2d, presents every reported decision of the U.S. Supreme Court, plus expert annotations on leading issues.
5. The U.S. Supreme Court Digest provides access to U.S. Supreme Court decisions since 1789.
6. ALR Federal, organizing, analyzing, summarizing, and evaluating all the federal law in depth. ALR Federal is treated with ALR.
7. Federal Rules Service and Federal Rules Digest provide text and access to all cases interpreting the Federal Rules of Civil Procedure and federal rules of appropriate procedure.
8. Federal Rules of Evidence Service and Federal Rules of Evidence Digest provide text and access to all cases interpreting the Federal Rules of Evidence.

Detailed descriptions of these sets (see earlier discussion of ALR for a description of ALR Federal), with illustrative instructions on how to use them, are on the following pages.

United States Code Service–USCS

Local law no longer stops at state boundaries. In fact, in many cases federal law—including case and statutory law as well as rulings and practices of federal administrative agencies—is even more pertinent to a client's circumstances than state law.

Such areas as Bankruptcy, Community Planning, Education, Housing, the Elderly, Veterans, Civil and Criminal Proceedings, Family and Estate Matters, Commerce and Trade, Federal Tax Matters, Real Estate, OSHA Compliances, and a mushrooming list of others all now have federal implications you must consider if you are to properly and effectively serve your clients.

In order to fill the federal information "gaps", today's attorneys depend more on federal statutes, their interpretations, and relationships to other reliable reference sources than ever before. Until USCS, no U.S. Code provided direct access to American Jurisprudence, ALR, ALR Federal, U.S. Supreme Court Reports, L Ed, Federal Procedure, Lawyers Edition, and Federal Procedural Forms, Lawyers Edition. And no U.S. Code prior to USCS systematically linked the laws enacted by Congress with the Code of Federal Regulations. So, most attorneys today consider the U.S. Code Service an essential element of their library.

A Summary of USCS Features

The United States Code Service represents the timely answer to the need for federal statute coverage that gives you what you require in today's practice context. Among its features, USCS provides:

1. The exact language of the Statutes at Large. USCS numbering corresponds directly to the titles and sections of the government's USC.
2. A complete history of each Code section with amendment notes.
3. Coverage of pertinent court and administrative rules.
4. Case notes drawn from cases decided by the courts and administrative agencies.
5. Comprehensive references to the Code of Federal Regulations (CFR), and a separate pamphlet containing an index and other finding aids to the CFR.
6. Annual pocket supplements.
7. Cumulative Later Case and Statutory Service published 3 times a year.
8. A monthly Advance Service covering the latest legislation, Presidential documents, and judicial and administrative rules of procedure.
9. Cross-linking references to the Total Client-Service Library (TCSL): American Jurisprudence 2d, Am Jur Legal Forms 2d, Am Jur Pleading and Practice Forms (Rev ed), Am Jur Proof of Facts, Am Jur Trials, Federal Procedure, L Ed, Federal Procedural Forms, L Ed, ALR, ALR Federal, and Supreme Court Reports, L Ed 2d; as well as to leading Law Reviews.
10. Easy access into the statutes and rules is provided by individual title indexes, and by a 6-volume Revised General Index which is kept current by a General Index Update Service binder.

Contents and Organization

The Titles of the U.S. Code numbers and names appear on the spines of the USCS volumes, enabling you to quickly scan the set and locate the volume you need. In addition to the Titles, USCS has volumes containing the Federal Rules of Evidence and the many court-promulgated rules, including the Federal Rules of Civil and Criminal Procedure, the Supreme Court Rules and Rules of Appellate Procedure, as well as rules for all major agencies (e.g., EEOC, FCC, FTC, ICC, IRS, NLRB, SEC, etc.)

Also provided in the Administrative Rules volumes are the major Conventions governing private international rights, including the Universal Copyright Convention and the Warsaw Convention. An additional volume containing notes to uncodified laws and treaties gives you access to material which is nowhere else readily available. Three Tables volumes, designed to aid the finding process, are also a part of the Service. A complete replacement for Title 26 volumes, necessitated by the enactment of the Internal Revenue Code of 1986, is also included. Five binders—two for statutory material and three for research references and interpretive notes and decisions—house several sequential pamphlets. The use of this format allows the annual replacement of pamphlets as needed, thereby providing the user with an up-to-date and integrated Title 26.

Replacement Volumes

Replacement of USCS volumes occurs when the flow of legislation and decided cases make the supplements bulky and difficult to use. On replacement, all the statutory amendments, case notes, CFR references, and other research aids appearing in the original volume, in its Supplement, and in the most recent Cumulative Later Case and Statutory Service, as well as in the latest Advance Service, are integrated in order to make research even easier and faster.

How to Find Your Material Quickly and Easily

Often, when a question with possible federal implications arises, you will know through the subject matter and your experience which Code Title the subject is treated under. For example, a problem involving consumer credit would be covered under Title 15, Commerce and Trade; tax problems fall under Title 26, Internal Revenue Code; Social Security under Title 42, Public Health and Welfare, and so on throughout the code. The examples used in this booklet are all taken from Title 5, Government Organization and Employees. Let's begin our entry into USCS by assuming you do not know which Title your subject is treated under. If this is the case, then go to the 6-volume Revised General Index. Using the TAPP-rule, simply think of the Thing, Act, Person or Place most closely associated with your question and pull the index volume where this fact/word would fall alphabetically.

Let's say we're searching for the federal statute on "freedom of information". Using the TAPP-rule, we begin our search by looking in the Revised General Index volume treating subjects beginning with "F" because "freedom" is the closest fact-word. In this instance, the appropriate volume is "E-H". Within that volume, on page 778, we find "Freedom of Information Act" which refers to Title 5, Government Organization and Employees, Section 552.

---

avoid, or recover fraudulent conveyances, 28 § 157

FRAUDULENT REPRESENTATION OR STATEMENTS
Fraud (this index)

FREDERICK LAW OLMSTEAD NATIONAL HISTORIC SITE
Establishment, 16 § 461 note

FREDERICKSBURG AND SPOTSYLVANIA COUNTY BATTLEFIELDS MEMORIAL
Appropriations, fund, deposit of moneys in Treasury account, 31 § 1321
Establishment, etc., 16 § 425 et seq.
Fund, deposit of moneys in Treasury account, appropriations, 31 § 1321

FRED LAWRENCE WHIPPLE OBSERVATORY
Land for, acquisition of, 20 § 50 note

FREEDMEN'S HOSPITAL
Repeal of laws applicable to, 20 § 124 note
Transfer
– funds for use in operation of teaching hospital facilities, 20 § 124 note
– hospital and functions to Federal Security Agency, 5 § 903 note, Reorg. Plan No. 4 of 1940, § 11
– to Howard University, all right, title, and interest of U.S., together with buildings, etc., 20 § 124

FREEDOM OF INFORMATION ACT
Generally, 5 § 552
Administrative Procedure (this index)
Federal Agencies and Instrumentalities (this index)
National security information and material
– classification on material after request made under, limitations on classification, 50 § 401 note, Ex. Ord. No. 12356, § 1.6
– classified or reclassified information, limitations on classification, request by, 50 § 401 note, Ex. Ord. No. 12356, § 1.6
– mandatory review for declassification of classified material, response to request for information, 50 § 401 note, Ex. Ord. No. 12356, § 3.4
– request for reclassification from public, mandatory review procedures for declassification, establishment of, 50 § 401 note, Ex. Ord. No. 12356, § 3.4
Old age, survivors, and disability insurance benefits, program information, 42 § 405
Presidential records. **Records** (this index)
Right of Privacy Act of 1974, conditions of disclosure of records, 5 § 552a(b)

FREE LIST
Customs Duties (this index)

FREE PUBLIC EDUCATION
See more specific topics

FREE TERRITORY OF DANZIG
Claims for loss, destruction, etc., of property during war
– **Foreign Claims Settlement Commission of the United States** (this index)
– **War Claims** (this index)

FREE TRADE UNION INSTITUTE
Grants to National Endowment for Democracy, use of, 22 § 4412

FREE TRADE ZONE ACT
Generally, 19 § 81a et seq.
Foreign Trade Zones (this index)

FREEZERS
Energy conservation program for consumer products. **Consumer Products** (this index)
Energy efficiency, State plans. **Energy Conservation** (this index)

FREIGHT
Aviation (this index)
Car Service (this index)
Embezzlement, larceny, etc., interstate or foreign shipments by carrier, 18 § 659
Inland Waters and Waterways (this index)
Insect pests and plant diseases inspection and disinfection of freight entering from Mexico, 7 § 149
Interstate Commerce Commission, emergency preparedness functions, domestic surface transportation and storage facilities, 50 Appx § 2251 note, Ex. Ord. No. 11490
Railroads
– Northeast and Midwest region, reorganization of. **Regional Rail Reorganization** (this index)
– **Railroads** (this index)
Service contract labor standards, exemption, carriage of, 41 § 356
Shipping (this index)
Transportation (this index)
United States Claims Court, jurisdiction, action to recover for price of freight and transportation, Government-aided railroads, 45 § 87

FREIGHT CARS
Car Service (this index)

FREIGHT FORWARDERS
Abandonment of service
– action by private person to enjoin, 49 § 11704

778   *References to the Code are to Title and Section*

FROM THE GENERAL INDEX VOLUME COVERING E-H

To assist you in locating your material, when you do know which Title covers the subject, go directly to the index in the back of the volume containing the Title. (If a Title is spread through more than one volume, the index is found at the back of the last volume.) The index for Title 5, Government Organization and Employees, will also refer you to Section 552.

FREEDMEN'S HOSPITAL

Transfer, hospital and functions to Federal Security Agency, 5 § 903 note, Reorg. Plan No. 4 of 1940, § 11

FREEDOM OF INFORMATION ACT

Generally, 5 § 552
Right of Privacy Act of 1974, conditions of disclosure of records, 5 § 552a(b)

If you know which Title covers your subject, there's still another method of locating your material. At the front of each volume there is an outline of the title chapters and, at the beginning of each chapter, there is an outline of the sections in that chapter. If you know that the Freedom of Information Act is part of the chapter on Administrative Procedure, the Title outline will direct you to Chapter 5, beginning at § 500.

Volume Outline

OF CONTENTS

TITLE 5 — GOVERNMENT ORGANIZATION AND EMPLOYEES

[Chapters 1-3, and §§ 500-553 of Chapter 5 are contained in this volume]

PART I. THE AGENCIES GENERALLY

PART II. CIVIL SERVICE FUNCTIONS AND RESPONSIBILITY

PART III. EMPLOY

Subpart A. General Pro

Subpart B. Employment and

Subpart C. Employee Perf

xv

Chapter Outline

Turning to Chapter 5 and scanning the analysis, we find "Public Information" at § 552.

CHAPTER 5. ADMINISTRATIVE PROCEDURE

SUBCHAPTER I. GENERAL PROVISIONS

SUBCHAPTER II. ADMINISTRATIVE PROCEDURE

Tables

Let's suppose you have a citation to a Public Law or a Statutes at Large. For example, a Court refers to a P.L. 93-502. How do you find the proper code title and section? A check of the "Tables" volume will take you from P.L. 93-502 to 5 USCS § 552. For an illustration of how this works, see the table below. (Instructions on how to use the individual tables are contained in the front of the parent Tables volumes.)

88 Stat			STATUTES AT LARGE				93d Cong	
Pub. L. Section	Stat. Page 1974 Oct	USCS Title Section —Cont'd	Status	Pub. L. Section 1974 Nov. 26	Stat. Page	USCS Title Section	Status	
93-499—Cont'd				93-503 1	1565	49 1601b nt		
2(b)	1550	26 613 nt	Added	2	1566	49 1601b		
3(a)	1550	26 4401		101	1566	49 1603		
3(b)	1550	26 4411		102	1566	49 1602		
3(c)(1)	1550	26 4424	Added	103(a)	1567	49 1604		
3(c)(2)	1551	26 prec 4421		103(b)	1571	49 1603		
3(d)(1)	1551	26 4401 nt	Added	104	1571	49 1602		
3(d)(2)	1551	26 4411 nt	Added	105	1572	42 3303		
93-500 1	1552	50		106	1572	49 1602		
2	1552 Appx.	50 2402 nt		107	1572	49 1604a 49 1604b	Rpld.	
3(a)	1552 Appx.	50 2402		108	1572	49 1604b		
3(b)	1552 Appx.	50 2403		109	1572	49 1602		
3(c), (d)	1553 Appx.	50 2409		110	1573	49 1602		
4(a)	1553 Appx.	50 2404		111	1573	49 1611		
4(b), (c)	1553 Appx.	50 2401		201-207	1574,			
5(a)	1553 Appx.	50 2402			1575	49 1605 nt		
5(b), (c)	1553 Appx.	50 2403		301, 302	1575	49 1605 nt		
5(d)	1554 Appx.	50 2404		1974 Nov. 29				
6	1554 Appx.	50 2409 nt		93-504	1575	36 1042		
7	1554 Appx.	50 2404		1974 Nov. 30				
8	1554 Appx.	50 2403		93-505 1	1576	47 303		
9, 10	1554 Appx. 1555,	50 2403a	Added	2	1576	47 310		
11	1556 Appx.	50 2403		93-506 1	1577	47 214		
12	1556 Appx.	50 2402		2	1577	47 222		
13	1557 Appx.	50 2403		93-507	1577	47 415		
14	1557 Appx.	50 2413		1974 Dec. 3				
93-501 101(a)	1557	42 2153 nt		93-508 1	1578	38 1501 nt	Added	
101(b)	1557	12 461		101(1)	1578	38 1501		
102(a)	1557	12 461 nt		101(2)	1578	38 1502		
102(b)	1558	12 1828		101(3)	1579	38 1504		
103	1558	12 1828 nt		102(1)	1579	38 1677		
201	1558	12 1425b		102(2)-(4)	1579	38 1682		
202	1558	12 85		102(5)	1580	38 1696		
203	1559	12 1831a	Added	103(1)-(3)	1580	38 1732		
204	1559	12 1730c	Added	103(4)	1580	38 1742		
205, 206	1559	12 687		104(1)	1580	38 1786		
301	1560	12 1831a nts		104(2),				
302	1560	12 371b-1	Added	(3)	1580	38 1787		
303	1560	12 1828		105	1581	38 1780 nt	Added	
304	1560	12 1425b		201	1581	38 1652		
	1561	12 371b-1 nt						
	1974 Nov. 21							
93-502 1-3	1561- 1564	5 552						
4	1564	5 552 nt	Added					

Another useful table, found in the "Tables" volume is "Table of Acts by Popular Name". Here, under "Freedom of Information Act", you will find another entry that will lead you to 5 USCS § 552.

POPULAR NAMES

Forest Transfer Act
Feb 1, 1905, ch 288, 33 Stat 628, 16 USCS §§ 472, 476, 495, 551, 554, 615b.

Forest Wildfire Emergency Pay Equity Act of 1988
Oct. 24, 1988, P. L. 100-523, 5 USCS §§ 5547 nt.

Forfeiture Act (Railroad Land Grants)
    See RAILROAD LAND GRANT
        FORFEITURE ACT

Former Presidents Act of 1958
Aug 25, 1958, P. L. 85-745, 72 Stat 838, 3 USCS § 102 note.
Sept 2, 1960, P. L. 86-682, 74 Stat 730, 3 USCS § 102 note.
Aug 14, 1964, P. L. 88-426, 78 Stat 412, 3 USCS § 102 note.
Sept 6, 1966, P. L. 89-554, 80 Stat 660, 3 USCS § 102 note.
Dec 16, 1967, P. L. 90-206, 81 Stat 642, 3 USCS § 102 note.
Jan 8, 1971, P. L. 91-658, 84 Stat 1963, 3 USCS § 102 note.

Fort Donelson National Battlefield Act
Sept 8, 1960, P. L. 86-738, 74 Stat 875, 16 USCS §§ 428k–428o.

Fort Hall Indian Reservation Act
June 6, 1900, ch 813, 31 Stat 672.

Fort Vancouver National Historic Site Act
June 19, 1948, ch 546, 62 Stat 532, 16 USCS §§ 450ff to 450ff-2.
June 30, 1961, P. L. 87-78, 75 Stat 196, 16 USCS §§ 450ff-3 to 450ff-6.

Fredericksburg and Spotsylvania County Battle-fields Memorial National Military Park Expansion Act of 1989
Dec. 11, 1989, P. L. 101-214, 16 USCS §§ 425k-425o.

Free Coinage of Gold Act
    See SPECIE PAYMENT RESUMPTION ACT

Freedman's Bureau Bills
March 3, 1865, ch 90, 13 Stat 507.
July 16, 1866, ch 200, 14 Stat 173.
July 6, 1868, ch 135, 15 Stat 83.

Freedman's Saving and Trust Company Acts
June 20, 1874, ch 349, 18 Stat 131.
Feb 13, 1877, ch 57, 19 Stat 231.
Feb 21, 1881, ch 64, 21 Stat 326.
Feb 17, 1883, ch 48, 22 Stat 420.
March 3, 1899, ch 440, 30 Stat 1353.

Freedom of Information Act
July 4, 1966, P. L. 89-487, 80 Stat 250 (See 5 USCS § 552).
June 5, 1967, P. L. 90-23, 81 Stat 54, 5 USCS § 552.
Nov 21, 1974, P. L. 93-502, 88 Stat 1561, 5 USCS § 552.

Freedom of Information Reform Act of 1986
Oct. 27, 1986, P. L. 99-570, 5 USCS § 552 nt.

Free Homestead Act
May 17, 1900, ch 479, 31 Stat 179, 43 USCS § 179.

Free Trade Zone Act
June 18, 1934, ch 590, 48 Stat 998, 19 USCS §§ 81a–81u.

USCS IS EQUIPPED WITH A FACT WORD INDEX TO THE CODE OF FEDERAL REGULATIONS, AS WELL AS EXTENDED CROSS REFERENCING FROM CFR TO USCS AND USCS TO CFR.

TABLE II—AUTHORITIES

CFR INDEX

Environmental Protection Agency—Cont'd
Solid wastes—Cont'd
- Land disposal guidelines, 40 CFR 241
- Lubricating oils containing re-refined oil, Federal procurement guidelines, 40 CFR 252
- Management, regions and agencies identification, 40 CFR 255
- Medical waste, standards for tracking and management, 40 CFR 259

Environmental Protection Agency—Cont'd
Toxic substances control—Cont'd
- Environmental effects testing guidelines, 40 CFR 797
- Fully halogenated chlorofluoroalkanes, 40 CFR 762
- General, fees, 40 CFR 700
- General practices and procedures, 40 CFR 702
- Good laboratory practice standards, 40 CFR 792

CFR TO USCS

CFR	USCS	CFR	USCS
9 Part 310	33 § 1254	9 Part 391	7 § 1624
9 Part 310	21 §§ 601—695	9 Part 391	7 § 1622
9 Part 310	7 § 450 et seq.	10 Parts 0-2	5 § 552
9 Part 310	7 § 1901 et seq.	10 Part 0	18 § 207
9 Parts 311-316	21 § 601 et seq.	10 Parts 0-2	5 § 553
9 Part 311	33 §§ 466—466k	10 Parts 0-2	42 § 5841
9 Parts 311-316	21 § 71 et seq.	10 Part 0	42 § 2035
9 Part 313	7 §§ 1901—1906	10 Parts 0-2	42 § 2201
9 Parts 314-317	33 §§ 466—466k	10 Part 1	42 § 2033
9 Part 316	21 § 621	10 Part 1	42 §§ 5843—5845
9 Part 317	21 §§ 601—695	10 Part 1	42 § 5849
9 Part 317	33 § 1171	10 Part 1	42 § 2039
9 Part 317	21 § 607	10 Part 1	42 § 10155
9 Part 317	21 § 457	10 Part 1	42 § 10152
9 Part 318	21 §§ 451—470	10 Part 1	42 § 2241
9 Part 318	21 §§ 601—695	10 Part 2	42 § 2241
9 Part 318	7 §§ 1901—1906	10 Part 2	42 § 10161
9 Part 318	7 § 450	10 Part 2	42 § 10155
9 Part 319	7 § 450 et seq.	10 Part 2	42 § 10154
9 Part 319	21 § 621	10 Part 2	42 § 2233
9 Parts 319-322	21 § 601 et seq.	10 Part 2	42 § 2282
9 Part 319	7 § 1901 et seq.	10 Part 2	42 § 2231

USCS TO CFR

USCS	CFR	USCS	CFR
42 USCS—Continued		42 USCS—Continued	
4321—4335	32 Part 214		40 Part 4
4321	7 Part 799		41 Parts 105-51, 114-50, 128-18
	14 Part 302		44 Part 25
	18 Part 1305		45 Part 15
	21 Part 25		49 Parts 24, 25
	36 Part 907	4626	23 Part 712
4331 et seq.	39 Part 775	4633	13 Part 310
	43 Parts 3160, 3590		23 Part 713
4331—4332	9 Part 94		41 Part 114-50
4331	7 Part 330		45 Part 15
	23 Part 772	4651—4655	23 Part 712
4332 et seq.	30 Parts 251, 280	4651	23 Part 713
4332	7 Parts 330, 650, 654	4728	5 Part 900
	10 Parts 2, 50, 51, 60, 72	4746	5 Part 410
	21 Parts 5, 25, 300, 500, 501, 505, 700, 801	4763	5 Part 900
	22 Part 216	4821—4846	24 Parts 35, 100, 200, 965
	23 Parts 770, 772	4831	21 Part 5
	24 Part 58	4901 et seq.	40 Part 32
	25 Part 225	4905	40 Parts 204-205
	34 Parts 75, 76	4907	40 Part 211
	41 Part 51-6	4909—4910	40 Parts 204, 205, 211
	46 Part 504	4910	40 Part 209
	49 Parts 520, 613, 623, 1105		

Thus, all means of access to
USCS bring you to the same
Code section dealing with
the Freedom of Information
Act. This is the section that
you are interested in.

§ 552.   Public information; agency rules, opinions, orders, records, and proceedings

(a) Each agency shall make available to the public information as follows:

(1) Each agency shall separately state and currently publish in the Federal Register for the guidance of the public—

(A) descriptions of its central and field organization and the established places at which, the employees (and in the case of a uniformed service, the members) from whom, and the methods whereby, the public may obtain information, make submittals or requests, or obtain decisions;

(B) statements of the general course and method by which its functions are channeled and determined, including the nature and requirements of all formal and informal procedures available;

(C) rules of procedure, descriptions of forms available or the places at which forms may be obtained, and instructions as to the scope and contents of all papers, reports, or examinations;

(D) substantive rules of general applicability adopted as authorized by law, and statements of general policy or interpretations of general applicability formulated and adopted by the agency; and

(E) each amendment, revision, or repeal of the foregoing.

Except to the extent that a person has actual and timely notice of the terms thereof, a person may not in any manner be required to resort to, or be adversely affected by, a matter required to be published in the Federal Register and not so published. For the purpose of this paragraph, matter reasonably available to the class of persons affected thereby is deemed published in the Federal Register when incorporated by reference therein with the approval of the Director of the Federal Register.

(2) Each agency, in accordance with published rules, shall make available for public inspection and copying—

(A) final opinions, including concurring and dissenting opinions, as well as orders, made in the adjudication of cases;

(B) those statements of policy and interpretations which have been adopted by the agency and are not published in the Federal Register; and

(C) administrative staff manuals and instructions to staff that affect a member of the public;

unless the materials are promptly published and copies offered for sale. To the extent required to prevent a clearly unwarranted invasion of personal privacy, an agency may delete identifying details when it makes available or publishes an opinion, statement of policy, interpretation, or staff manual or instruction. However, in each case the

Exact Language of the Statutes at Large

The exact language of the Statutes at large is explicitly followed throughout the set—an exclusive USCS feature. Wherever interpretations are necessary, bracketed words or references are inserted or explanatory notes written, but the language of the law is never reworded. Omissions or other changes that cannot be shown in brackets are explained in notes under the section.

For example: In United States v Bornstein (1976) 423 US 303, 46 L Ed 2d 514, 96 S Ct 523, the Supreme Court pointed out that "Since Title 31 has not been enacted into positive law, the official text of the statute is that which appears in the Revised Statutes." The Court further noted that the USC treatment differed from the Revised Statutes in some "important respects" and therefore found the codified version of the statute as it appeared in the USC to be unusable. Since the other annotated U.S. code follows the wording of the USC, only USCS properly represented the statute in the case.

Almost half of the Code titles have not been enacted into positive law; for these titles the exact wording of the Statutes at Large can be found only in USCS.

Brackets indicate words or references added for clarification.

---

tion, or staff manual or instruction that affects a member of the public may be relied on, used, or cited as precedent by an agency against a party other than an agency only if—

    (i) it has been indexed and either made available or published as provided by this paragraph; or

    (ii) the party has actual and timely notice of the terms thereof.

(3) Except with respect to the records made available under paragraphs (1) and (2) of this subsection, each agency, upon any request for records which (A) reasonably describes such records and (B) is made in accordance with published rules stating the time, place, fees (if any), and procedures to be followed, shall make the records promptly available to any person.

(4)(A)(i) In order to carry out the provisions of this section, each agency shall promulgate regulations, pursuant to notice and receipt of public comment, specifying the schedule of fees applicable to the processing of requests under this section and establishing procedures and guidelines for determining when such fees should be waived or reduced. Such schedule shall conform to the guidelines which shall be promulgated, pursuant to notice and receipt of public comment, by the Director of the Office of Management and Budget and which shall provide for a uniform schedule of fees for all agencies.

    (ii) Such agency regulations shall provide that—

        (I) fees shall be limited to reasonable standard charges for document search, duplication, and review, when records are requested for commercial use;

        (II) fees shall be limited to reasonable standard charges for document duplication when records are not sought for commercial use and the request is made by an educational or noncommercial scientific institution, whose purpose is scholarly or scientific research; or a representative of the news media; and

        (III) for any request not described in (I) or (II), fees shall be limited to reasonable standard charges for document search and duplication.

101

History; Ancillary Laws and Directives
Following each Code section, you'll find
"History; Ancillary Laws and Directives".
Wherever necessary, the material therein
explains references in the text, shows transfers
of function, gives a chronological listing of
amendments, and sets forth the effective dates.

HISTORY; ANCILLARY LAWS AND DIRECTIVES

Prior law and revision:

Derivation	U.S. Code	Revised Statutes and Statutes at Large
. . . .	5 USC § 1002	June 11, 1946, ch 324, § 3, 60 Stat. 238.

In subsec. (b)(3), the words "formulated and" are omitted as surplus-age. In the last sentence of subsec (b), the words "in any manner" are omitted as surplusage since the prohibition is all inclusive.

Standard changes are made to conform with the definitions applicable and the style of this title (5 USCS §§ 101 et seq.).

Explanatory notes:
A former 5 USC § 552 was transferred by Act Sept. 6, 1966, which enacted 5 USCS §§ 101 et seq., and now appears as 7 USCS § 2243.

Amendments:
1967. Act June 5, 1967 (effective 7/4/67, as provided by § 3 of such Act, which appears as a note to this section) substituted this section for one which read:

"§ 552. Publication of information, rules, opinions, orders, and public records
"(a) This section applies, according to the provisions thereof, except to the extent that there is involved—

"(1) a function of the United States requiring secrecy in the public interest; or

"(2) a matter relating solely to the internal management of an agency.

"(b) Each agency shall separately state and currently publish in the Federal Register—

"(1) descriptions of its central and field organizations, including delegations of final authority by the agency, and the established places at which, and methods whereby, the public may obtain information or make submittals or requests;

"(2) statements of the general course and method by which its functions are channeled and determined, including the nature and requirements of the formal or informal procedures available and forms and instructions as to the scope and contents of all papers, reports, or examinations; and

"(3) substantive rules adopted as authorized by law and statements of general policy or interpretations adopted by the agency for public guidance, except rules addressed to and served on named persons in accordance with law.

A person may not be required to resort to organization or procedure not so published.

107

The Code of Federal Regulations (CFR)
Recognizing the growing involvement of
attorneys with problems embracing federal
law, USCS systematically links the U.S. Code
with the Code of Federal Regulations. CFR
references lead you to the rules and regulations
of those governmental bodies that administer the
statutes. In addition, there is a separate pamphlet
which provides an index and other finding aids
for the CFR.

CODE OF FEDERAL REGULATIONS

Office of the Federal Register, incorporation by reference, 1 CFR Part 51.
Administrative Conference of the United States, organization and purpose, 1 CFR Part 301.
Administrative Conference of the United States, bylaws, 1 CFR Part 302.
Administrative Conference of the United States, public access to information, 1 CFR Part 304.
National Capital Planning Commission, Freedom of Information Act regulations, 1 CFR Part 456.
Cost Accounting Standards Board, public access to information, 4 CFR Part 303.
Office of Personnel Management, personnel records, 5 CFR Part 293.
Office of Personnel Management, availability of official records, 5 CFR Part 294.

Cross References
Under Cross References are listed (1) pertinent
related sections in the same and other Titles;
(2) Court and Administrative Rules which are
pertinent to the section; and (3) other sections in
which references to this section will be found.

CROSS REFERENCES

Keeping and examination of books and records relating to import or export of wheat, 7 USCS § 1642.
Examination of documentary material produced pursuant to civil investigative demand by Antitrust Division of Department of Justice, 15 USCS § 1313.
Confidentiality and disclosure of tax returns and return information, 26 USCS § 6103.
Unauthorized disclosure of tax returns and return information, 26 USCS § 7213.
Investigatory powers of National Labor Relations Board, 29 USCS § 161.
Disclosure of information in possession of agency, 42 USCS § 1306.
Federal Register Act, 44 USCS §§ 1502 et seq.
Preservation of presidential recordings and materials, 44 USCS § 2107.
Release of information obtained in confidence to other agencies, 44 USCS § 3508.

Research Guide

For an in-depth look at the question at hand, the Research Guide, following the Cross References, leads you to relevant material in other units of the Total Client-Service Library and to Law Reviews. The TCSL references are vital because they allow you to approach the problem from all angles—annotations, forms, proofs, trial techniques. The Law Reviews often explore and pinpoint the manner in which the law may be interpreted before the statute has actually been court-tested.

RESEARCH GUIDE

Federal Procedure L Ed:

2 Fed Proc, L Ed, Administrative Procedure, §§ 2:1–4.

6 Fed Proc, L Ed, Civil Rights, § 11:433.

8 Fed Proc, L Ed, Courts and Judicial System, § 20:342.

10 Fed Proc, L Ed, Economic Development and Stabilization, §§ 27:66, 97.

11 Fed Proc, L Ed, Environmental Protection, §§ 32:734, 804, 816, 828.

15 Fed Proc, L Ed, Freedom of Information, §§ 38:12, 16.

17 Fed Proc, L Ed, Health, Education, and Welfare, §§ 42:470, 988, 1019, 1052, 1053, 1064, 1892.

24 Fed Proc, L Ed, Natural and Marine Resources, § 56:1638.

25 Fed Proc, L Ed, Navigable Waters, §§ 57:136, 141, 146, 151, 353.

32 Fed Proc, L Ed, Transportation, §§ 76:556, 611.

Am Jur:

2 Am Jur 2d, Administrative Law §§ 229, 232.

15 Am Jur 2d, Civil Rights § 291.

18 Am Jur 2d, Copyright and Literary Property § 147.

45A Am Jur 2d, Job Discrimination § 1171.

61A Am Jur 2d, Pollution Control § 271.

63A Am Jur 2d, Public Funds § 50.

Law Review Articles:

Virden and Sutherland, Releasability Under the Freedom of Information Act of Documents Submitted by Government Contractors. 12 APLA QJ 50, Winter, 1984.

Drachsler, Freedom of Information Act and Right of Non-Disclosure. 28 Admin L Rev 1, Winter 1976.

Patten and Weinstein, Disclosure of Business Secrets under the Freedom of Information Act: Suggested Limitations. 29 Admin L Rev 193, Spring, 1977.

Belazis, The Government's Commercial Information Privilege: Technical Information and the FOIA's Exemption 5. 33 Admin L Rev 415, Fall, 1981.

Your Business, Your Trade Secrets and Your Government—A Seminar on Protecting and Obtaining Commercial Information From the Government. 34 Admin L Rev 107, Spring, 1982.

R. Stevenson, Protecting Business Secrets Under the Freedom of Information Act: Managing Exemption 4. 34 Admin L Rev 207.

Interpretive Notes and Decisions

To save you valuable research time, our USCS attorney-editors specifically tailor case notes to the U.S. Code. This service is designed to provide you with concisely written, specific notes for all cases which meaningfully construe or interpret the statutes. To locate these important cases, and then to compose notes relating what the courts have held, requires literally thousands of hours of editorial time. For you, this means there are no vague or marginal cases to wade through and weigh before getting to the heart of your problem.

Pertinent court decisions are analyzed and classified under the statutes affected. Included are the decisions of the U.S. Supreme Court, the Courts of Appeals, the District Courts and the many specialized federal courts (Tax Court, Court of International Trade, Court of Military Appeals, etc.), as well as pertinent state court decisions. An exclusive feature of USCS is the inclusion of administrative decisions of all important federal agencies and departments, such as the NLRB, Federal Labor Relations Council, Benefits Review Board, FTC, SEC, ICC, EPA, the various Boards of Contract Appeals, the Immigration and Naturalization Service, and many more. These court and administrative decisions are arranged in an easy-to-follow outline form.

INTERPRETIVE NOTES AND DECISIONS

I. IN GENERAL (notes 1–26)
II. PUBLICATION IN FEDERAL REGISTER
  A. In General (notes 27–29)
  B. Matters to be Published (notes 30–34)
  C. Effect of Failure to Publish (notes 35–41)
III. AVAILABILITY FOR PUBLIC INSPECTION AND COPYING
  A. In General (notes 42–54)
  B. Materials to be Made Available (notes 55–66)
  C. Persons to Whom Records Must be Made Available (notes 67–69)
  D. Request for Records Under 5 USCS § 552(a)(3) (notes 70–77)
  E. Compliance With Time Limits (notes 78–83)
  F. Fees (notes 84–91)
IV. STATUTORY EXEMPTIONS (5 USCS § 552(b))
  A. In General (notes 92–98)
  B. National Security or Foreign Policy Matters (5 USCS § 552(b)(1))
    1. In General (notes 99–103)
    2. Application to Particular Matters (notes 104–112)
  C. Internal Personnel Rules and Practices (5 USCS § 552(b)(2)) (notes 113–121)
  D. Matters Specifically Exempted From Disclosure By Statute (5 USCS § 552(b)(3))
    1. In General (notes 122–136)
    2. Information from Particular Agencies (notes 137–152)
  E. Trade Secrets and Commercial or Financial Information (5 USCS § 552(b)(4))
    1. In General (notes 153–162)
    2. Privilege and Confidentiality (notes 163–166)
    3. Particular Information (notes

    1. In General (notes 266–283)
    2. Grounds for Exemption (notes 284–310)
    3. Particular Records (notes 311–344)
    4. Review (notes 345–347)
  I. Regulation of Financial Institutions (5 USCS § 552(b)(8)) (notes 348, 349)
  J. Geological and Geographical Information (5 USCS § 552(b)(9)) (note 350)
V. ENFORCEMENT
  A. In General (notes 351–358)
  B. Jurisdiction and Venue (notes 359–375)
  C. Determination of Claim of Exemption
    1. In General (notes 376–402)
    2. Defenses (notes 403–406)
    3. Considerations in Sustaining Exemption (notes 407–414)
  D. Judgment and Relief (notes 415–429)
  E. Appellate Review (notes 430–432)
VI. ATTORNEY'S FEES AND COSTS
  A. In General (notes 433–440)
  B. Factors in Making Award
    1. In General (notes 441–447)
    2. Application in Particular Cases (notes 448–465)
  C. Amount of Award (notes 466–471)

I. IN GENERAL

1. Policy and purpose
2. —Disclosure of government information
3. —Balancing of interests
4. Construction
5. What constitutes agency within meaning of 5 USCS § 552
6. —Advisory committees
7. —Congress

USCS has unmatched administrative case coverage. This example shows six administrative decisions from USCS that would not be in the other annotated federal statutes.

Hunter Douglas, Inc. v Sheet Metal Workers International Asso. (1982, MD NC) 553 F Supp 324, affd (CA4 NC) 714 F2d 342, 114 BNA LRRM 2021, 98 CCH LC ¶ 10370.

Employer may not use fact that NLRB found union's picketing to be illegal secondary activity to obtain summary judgment in suit for damages caused by picketing, since issues are not identical. **Truck Transport, Inc. v International Allied Industries Workers (1982, ND Ill) 113 BNA LRRM 2313, 97 CCH LC ¶ 10142.**

Decision by administrative law judge in proceeding to determine discharged employee's right to unemployment benefits that employee was discharged for threatening supervisor does not preclude litigation of issue as to whether or not discharge was for just cause under collective bargaining agreement. **Munk v American Tel. & Tel. Co. (1982, SD NY) 96 CCH LC ¶ 14043.**

Employee is not precluded from bringing action under 29 USCS § 185 by state agency proceeding which was never judicially reviewed. Chatelain v Mt. Sinai Hospital (1984, SD NY) 580 F Supp 1414.

Res judicata and collateral estoppel bar general contractor's action to vacate arbitration award founded on argument that it is contrary to previous NLRB decision assigning work to union other than defendant union where court previously ruled that present dispute is arbitrable and that previous NLRB decision involved subcontractor not general contractor as employer. Associated General Contractors v Boston Dist. Council of Carpenters (1986, DC Mass) 642 F Supp 1435, 123 BNA LRRM 3308.

Court's denial of preliminary injunction and confirmation of arbitrator's award allowing employer to implement wage reductions in one city does not preclude arbitration regarding employer's authority under same bargaining agreement provision to implement wage reductions in other cities since arbitrator limited scope of decision to particular city and court's decision is limited to scope of discipline of particular grievants established that union accepted settlement rendering first award, concerning company's right to initiate program, final, binding and immune to challenge on statute of limitations grounds. **United Mine Workers v Jim Walter Resources, Inc., CV87-PT-0963-S (Sept 1, 1987, DC, ND Ala, Propost, J) LEXIS slip op, reconsideration den (ND Ala) LEXIS slip op.**

State unemployment compensation board's finding that employees were locked out during labor dispute and thus entitled to unemployment benefits does not prevent them from filing suit for breach of layoff provision in bargaining agreement since difference between layoff and lockout may not have been at issue in administrative proceeding and employees are thus not estopped from claiming layoff in federal court. **Montgomery v Stone Port Wentworth, Inc. (1988, SD Ga) 1988 US Dist LEXIS 6004.**

United States District Court order rescinding collective bargaining agreement in which employer recognized union as majority representative did not rebut presumption of union's majority status, arising from contract, since court order under 29 USCS § 185 does not supplant NLRB jurisdiction and since only NLRB has initial jurisdiction to determine whether employer violated 29 USCS § 158(a)(5). **Heyman (1975) 216 NLRB No. 154, 1974–75 CCH NLRB 15536.**

Res judicata bars action claiming union violated no-raid agreement since issue could have been previously litigated before state administrative body although prior hearing involved representation issue and current controversy is contract breach action. **Perry v International Longshoremen's Assoc., AFL-CIO (SD NY) No. 84 Civ. 4866 (RWS), 6/12/86.**

228. Appellate review

Coercive civil contempt order is analogous to criminal contempt order which must be obeyed in order to permit alleged contemnor to challenge

Interim supplementation

Later Case and Statutory Service pamphlets, issued three times a year (in June, September and January), serve as interim supplements between the annual, cumulative supplements. They contain a statement of new cases as well as all recent statutory amendments and pertinent Presidential documents. Each pamphlet is cumulative, so that it is necessary to look in only one place in these interim supplements. When the annual pocket supplements appear in May, the January pamphlets can be discarded. Index coverage of Later Case & Statutory Service material is found in the General Index Update Service binder, behind a tab which clearly identifies it.

Annual Pocket Supplements

USCS annual pocket supplements present new material researched since the issuance of the parent volumes, thus furnishing you with additions and changes to the statutes, Research Guide, and interpretive notes and decisions, as well as additional systematic references to the CFR. Supplement material is indexed in the General Index Update Service binder, behind a tab which clearly identifies it.

★ ★ ★ ★ UNITED STATES CODE SERVICE ★ ★ ★ ★
Lawyers Edition

July 1992

CUMULATIVE
LATER CASE
and
STATUTORY SERVICE

Public Laws 102-244 through 102-280

Constitution

TITLES 1-End

Court Rules

Administrative Rules of Procedure

Uncodified Laws and Treaties

Tables

Your shelf should contain the CLCSS pamphlet issued in July 1992.

Lawyers Cooperative Publishing
Aqueduct Building, Rochester, New York 14694

USCS Advance Service

Each month an Advance Service pamphlet is sent to every USCS subscriber. The pamphlet contains the newly enacted Public Laws, Presidential Proclamations, Executive Orders, other Presidential documents, Amendments to Court Rules, and selected Administrative Regulations.

The Public Laws are reprinted in the exact language of Congress. At the end of each Public Law you'll find the legislative history of the law which includes citations to the House and Senate Reports, Congressional Record, and Weekly Compilations of Presidential Documents. Each Advance Service pamphlet also contains a cumulative index, and various tables which pinpoint the sections of the U.S. Code that have been affected by recent legislative, Presidential, and regulatory activity.

In addition, new legislation received too late for presentation within the normal format of the pamphlet is referred to in a section entitled Late Items-Current Awareness Commentary. Here you'll also find summaries of recent U.S. Supreme Court decisions construing the U.S. Code and Constitution; and references to the most current annotations in ALR Federal and U.S. Supreme

Court Reports, L Ed 2d. Finally, other material of current interest, such as references to new federal court rules and procedures, is shown in the Late Items section.

You should always consult the Advance Service for the latest legislation, which may not yet have appeared in the pocket supplement or the Later Case Service.

In Summation

As does an X-ray, this discussion is designed to reveal the structural bones of USCS, but the flesh of the work remains yours to probe and put to use in the context of your own practice. For their part, the editors have striven not only to present the United States Code in its most easily understood and utilitarian form, but also to relate it to American law as a whole. Thus, USCS gives you the important federal aspects of a question, yet doesn't limit its coverage of your problem to the federal area. The Total Client-Service Library references, for instance, allow you to examine many more facets of the subject than Code coverage alone could provide. Hopefully, this brief discussion will serve as an instructive entry to USCS and help insure that you are able to make full and productive use of the vast store of material within the set.

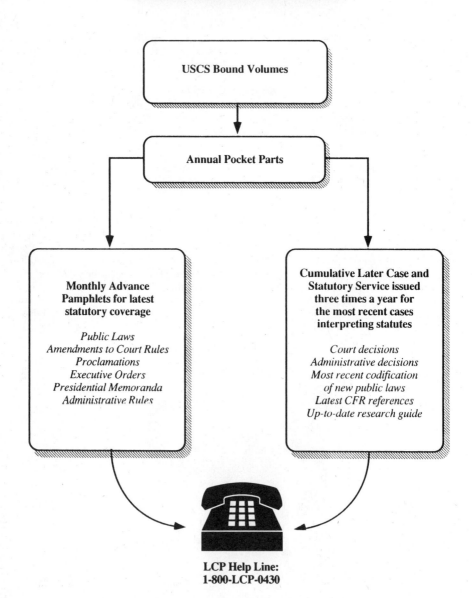

How USCS keeps you current...

USCS Bound Volumes

Annual Pocket Parts

Monthly Advance Pamphlets for latest statutory coverage

Public Laws
Amendments to Court Rules
Proclamations
Executive Orders
Presidential Memoranda
Administrative Rules

Cumulative Later Case and Statutory Service issued three times a year for the most recent cases interpreting statutes

Court decisions
Administrative decisions
Most recent codification of new public laws
Latest CFR references
Up-to-date research guide

LCP Help Line:
1-800-LCP-0430

Federal Procedure,
Lawyers Edition

Scope and Coverage of Federal Procedure,
L Ed

Federal Procedure, L Ed is the most comprehensive treatment of all federal procedure: in
the traditional courts, the specialized courts,
and the administrative agencies.

Traditional courts are the Federal District Courts,
the Courts of Appeals, and the U.S. Supreme
Court.

Specialized courts include such courts as the Tax
Court, the Court of International Trade, the Court
of Military Appeals, and the Bankruptcy Courts.

Administrative Agencies include such agencies as
the Environmental Protection Agency, the Federal
Trade Commission, the National Labor Relations
Board, the Social Security Administration, and the
Internal Revenue Service.

Federal Procedure, Lawyers Edition is unique
among practice works because it is the only set
which treats all three elements of the federal
adjudicatory system.

Organization of Federal Procedure, L Ed

Federal Procedure is practice-oriented, with 80 chapters organized alphabetically under familiar procedural and topical headings. This arrangement enables you to find all the materials related to a particular problem or lawsuit treated in a single place within the set. For example, if the matter at hand involves consumer product safety, you'll find all aspects of the question in chapter 16— rather than scattered throughout the set under whichever statute or rule may be applicable to a particular stage of the proceeding. On the other hand, if you prefer to conduct your research by statute or rule, you may use the extensive tables in the set to locate a text discussion of the statute or rule in question. The 80 chapters of Federal Procedure fall into two categories: core coverage chapters and topical chapters. Core coverage chapters discuss the general principles in the three leading courts of the federal adjudicatory system: the Federal District Courts, the Federal Courts of Appeals, and the Supreme Court. Examples of core coverage chapters are Access to District Courts, Class Actions, Discovery and Depositions, Pleadings and Motions, Process, Pretrial Procedure, Trial, and Witnesses. Topical chapters treat the application of general and specific procedural rules in a particular kind of action or proceeding. Examples are: Civil Rights; Environmental Protection; Food, Drugs and Cosmetics; Freedom of Information; Labor and Labor Relations; Securities Regulation; and Tort Claims Against U.S. The topical chapters of Federal Procedure cover all procedural matters, judicial and administrative.

FEDERAL PROCEDURE,
L ED LIST OF CHAPTERS

Chapter

1. Access to District Courts
2. Administrative Procedure
3. Appeal, Certiorari, and Review
4. Arbitration
5. Armed Forces, Civil Disturbances, and National Defense
6. Atomic Energy
7. Aviation and Space
8. Banking and Financing
9. Bankruptcy
10. Bonds, Civil Fines, and Forfeitures
11. Civil Rights
12. Class Actions
13. Commodity and Stock Exchanges
14. Condemnation of Property
15. Consumer Credit Protection
16. Consumer Product Safety
17. Contempt
18. Copyrights
19. Court of Claims (Claims Court)
20. Courts and Judicial System
21. Creditors' Provisional Remedies
22. Criminal Procedure
23. Declaratory Judgments
24. Deposits in Court
25. Derivative Actions by Shareholders
26. Discovery and Depositions
27. Economic Development and Stabilization
28. Elections and Elective Franchise
29. Employees' Compensation Acts
30. Employers' Liability Acts
31. Enforcement of Judgments
32. Environmental Protection
33. Evidence
34. Farms, Ranches, and Agricultural Products
35. Food, Drugs, and Cosmetics
36. Foreign Relations
37. Foreign Trade and Commerce
38. Freedom of Information
39. Government Contracts
40. Government Officers and Employees

Chapter

41. Habeas Corpus
42. Health, Education, and Welfare
43. Highways and Bridges
44. Housing and Urban Development
45. Immigration, Naturalization, and Nationality
46. Indians and Indian Affairs
47. Injunctions and Restraining Orders
48. Internal Revenue
49. Interpleader
50. Job Discrimination
51. Judgments and Orders
52. Labor and Labor Relations
53. Maritime Law and Procedure
54. Monopolies and Restraints of Trade
55. Multidistrict Litigation
56. Natural and Marine Resources
57. Navigable Waters
58. New Trial
59. Parties
60. Patents
61. Pensions and Retirement Systems
62. Pleadings and Motions
63. Postal Service
64. Pretrial Procedure
65. Process
66. Public Lands and Property
67. Railroads
68. References, Referees, and Masters
69. Removal of Actions
70. Securities Regulation
71. Social Security and Medicare
72. Telecommunications
73. Tort Claims Against United States
74. Trademarks
75. Trade Regulations and Unfair Trade Practices
76. Transportation
77. Trial
78. Unemployment Compensation
79. Veterans and Veterans' Affairs
80. Witnesses

Additional Features of Federal Procedure, L Ed

- *Scope of Topic* describes the federal statutes, court rules, and agency regulations covered in the chapter, referring to statutes by their popular name and USCS citation.
- State aspects offers an overview of the relationship between state and federal law and how they apply to procedural questions covered in the chapter.
- Collateral and General References, both at the beginning of each chapter and following the major divisions throughout the chapter, refer you to relevant material in other publications, including Federal Procedural Forms; ALR Federal; U.S. Supreme Court Reports, L Ed 2d; Am Jur 2d; ALR 2d, 3d, 4th and 5th.
- Controlling law is analyzed throughout by a careful examination of federal constitutional provisions, statutes, court rules, administrative regulations, court decisions, and decisions of administrative agencies. Extensive footnote citations support the textual analysis.
- Forms contained in Federal Procedural Forms, L Ed, the companion set to Federal Procedure, L Ed, are cited extensively.
- Practice Pointers, Observations, Cautions, and Comments call attention to opportunities and pitfalls relevant to the text.
- *Annotation references* are footnoted throughout, citing pertinent annotations in L Ed 2d, ALR Federal, and ALR 2d, 3d, 4th and 5th.
- *Law Review* commentaries synopsize pertinent articles in leading law reviews and direct you to those articles.
- *Trial Strategy* references direct you to relevant material in Am Jur Trials and Am Jur Proof of Facts.
- *Supreme Court Background* references direct you to relevant material in the U.S. Supreme Court Digest, Lawyers Edition.
- *Checklists* help you to choose from available remedies, determine effective strategies, and comply with requirements of federal procedural law.

- Tables at the front of individual volumes list the constitutional and statutory provisions, court rules, and administrative regulations and rules of practice cited in that volume. There is also a tables volume covering the entire set. These tables make it easy to locate text material related to particular constitutional provisions, statutes, rules, and regulations.
- Descriptive-word indexes are included at the back of each volume. There is also a three-volume general index for the entire set.
- Text of important statutes covered in Federal Procedure is set out in a separate volume.
- Federal Procedure Rules Service includes a national volume and 11 local volumes for the First through the Eleventh Circuits. In the national volume are the Federal Rules of Civil Procedure, Criminal Procedure, Evidence and Appellate Procedure; Rules for Trial of Misdemeanors Before Magistrates; Rules of Procedure of the Judicial Panel on Multi-district Litigation; Temporary Emergency Court of Appeals Rules; and Supreme Court Rules. Each of the 11 circuit volumes contains the text of rules for the Court of Appeals and District Courts within the circuit, and a comparator correlating the Federal Rules of Civil Procedure with state rule or statutory provisions governing civil procedure for those states within the particular circuit. Selected circuit volumes also include rules of the Court of Appeals for the District of Columbia, the Court of Appeals for the Federal Circuit, the Claims Court, and the Court of International Trade.
- Supplementation annually to keep you up-to-date.
- Federal Practice Advisory newsletter keeps you informed of the latest developments in federal procedural law. Issued six times a year, the newsletter highlights recent developments from the federal courts, Congress, and the federal agencies.

Chapter 38

Freedom of Information

Scope of topic:
This chapter discusses the Freedom of Information Act (5 USCS § 552); the Privacy Act (5 USCS § 552a); related statutes such as the Presidential Recordings and Materials Preservation Act (44 USCS § 2107 note), the Presidential Records Act of 1978 (44 USCS §§ 2201 et seq.), the Federal Advisory Committee Act (5 USCS Appx), and the Trade Secrets Act (18 USCS § 1905); and federal agency regulations implementing or interpreting such statutes. Specifically, the treatment includes the general provisions and interaction of such statutes; what agencies are subject thereto; the use as discovery devices of the Freedom of Information Act and the Privacy Act; what information is subject to or exempt from disclosure; proceedings before agencies for the release of information under the Freedom of Information Act; agency proceedings under the Privacy Act, both for securing access to records and amending them; judicial review of agency action under the Freedom of Information Act and the Privacy Act; and proceedings by private persons, organizations, or corporations to prevent governmental disclosure of information.

A BRIEF DESCRIPTION OF THE SUBJECT TELLS YOU EXACTLY WHAT IS COVERED

State aspects:
State agencies and instrumentalities are not subject to the FOIA, even if they are assisting in the administration of a federal program. Municipal corporations are not subject to the FOIA. Because the Privacy Act applies only to agencies of the United States Government, state or local officials who make unwarranted disclosures of statistical information are not subject to the Act. Even though the states are not subject to the Federal Freedom of Information Act, many states have enacted a state counterpart to the federal law. It is commonly observed that the state law was modeled on the federal law. Federal case law construing 5 USCS § 552 has been cited in state court cases involving the state freedom of information laws. Exemptions in some state freedom of information laws are similar to those in the federal FOIA.

29 states have a freedom of information law featuring a philosophy of disclosure, subject to a list of exemptions, plus an administrative procedure for requesting information, comparable to the federal Freedom of Information Act. 21 other states have an open records law that is not comparable to the federal Freedom of Information Act.

ALERTS YOU TO STATE MATTERS

FREEDOM OF INFORMATION

through the Auto-Cite® computer-assisted research service. Use Auto-Cite to check citations for form, parallel references, prior and later history, and annotation references.

Chapter Outline

I. OVERVIEW OF PUBLIC INFORMATION AVAILABILITY
- A. INTRODUCTION TO THE FREEDOM OF INFORMATION ACT AND PRIVACY ACT (§§ 38:1-38:16)
- B. RELATED LEGISLATION (§§ 38:17-38:25)

II. SCOPE OF INFORMATION AVAILABLE UNDER FOIA
- A. INFORMATION REQUIRED TO BE PUBLISHED (§§ 38:26-38:37)
- B. INFORMATION REQUIRED TO BE MADE AVAILABLE TO THE PUBLIC (§§ 38:38-38:55)
- C. EXEMPT INFORMATION GENERALLY (§§ 38:56-38:61)
- D. FIRST EXEMPTION: NATIONAL SECURITY OR FOREIGN POLICY MATTERS (§§ 38:62-38:76)
- E. SECOND EXEMPTION: AGENCY INTERNAL PERSONNEL RULES AND PRACTICES (§§ 38:77-38:85)
- F. THIRD EXEMPTION: STATUTORILY EXEMPT MATTERS (§§ 38:86-38:109)
- G. FOURTH EXEMPTION: TRADE SECRETS; PRIVILEGED OR CONFIDENTIAL COMMERCIAL OR FINANCIAL INFORMATION (§§ 38:110-38:135)
- H. FIFTH EXEMPTION: INTER-AGENCY OR INTRA-AGENCY MEMORANDUMS (§§ 38:136-38:165)
- I. SIXTH EXEMPTION: PERSONNEL, MEDICAL, AND SIMILAR PERSONAL FILES (§§ 38:166-38:190)
- J. SEVENTH EXEMPTION: LAW ENFORCEMENT INVESTIGATORY RECORDS (§§ 38:191-38:248)
- K. EIGHTH EXEMPTION: REPORTS BY FINANCIAL INSTITUTIONS (§§ 38:249-38:252)
- L. NINTH EXEMPTION: GEOLOGICAL OR GEOPHYSICAL INFORMATION CONCERNING WELLS (§§ 38:253-38:256)

III. SCOPE OF INFORMATION AVAILABLE UNDER PRIVACY ACT
- A. CONSTRUCTION OF STATUTORY TERMS (§§ 38:257-38:265)
- B. INDIVIDUAL'S RIGHT TO REVIEW OWN RECORDS (§§ 38:266-38:276)
- C. RESTRICTIONS ON GENERAL DISCLOSURE OF RECORDS (§§ 38:277-38:296)

15 Fed Proc, L Ed **3**

SKELETON OUTLINE SHOWS GENERAL DIVISIONS

LEADS YOU TO APPROPRIATE SECTIONS

6   15 Fed Proc, L Ed

**DETAILED
OUTLINE
LEADS YOU
TO SECTION-
ON-POINT**

§ 42:629   HEALTH, EDUCATION, AND WELFARE

Federal Quick Index: Child Nutrition Act; Food Stamps; Nutrition; Schools and School
  Districts
L Ed Index to Annotations: Child Nutrition Act of 1966; Food Stamp Act of 1964;
  Poor Persons; Schools
68 Am Jur 2d, Schools §§ 281–282
79 Am Jur 2d, Welfare Laws §§ 26–31
10 Fed Proc Forms, Health, Education, and Welfare §§ 37:1–37:70
Auto-Cite®—Any case citation herein can be checked for form, parallel references, later
  history, and annotation references through the Auto-Cite computer research system.

REFERS YOU TO MATERIAL IN OTHER TCSL PUBLICATIONS

A. NUTRITION PROGRAMS FOR CHILDREN

1. IN GENERAL

§ 42:629.   What programs are available

   Under the Child Nutrition Act of 1966,[18] the Department of Agriculture
conducts and supervises federal programs assisting schools in food service
programs for children,[19] and sponsors a special milk program,[20] a school
breakfast program,[21] a special supplemental food program for women, infants,
and children (WIC),[22] and nutrition education and training.[23] In addition,
under the National School Lunch Act,[24] the Department operates a school
lunch program,[25] a summer food service program,[26] a commodity supplemental
food program,[27] and a child care food program.[28]

llll *State aspects:* Money spent in the maintenance of a federal child nutrition
program, although derived from a federal fund, must be spent subject to the
provisions required by state fiscal laws.[29]

llll *Comment:* The Secretary of Agriculture has authority to determine the
amount of, settle, adjust, compromise, deny, or waive any claim arising under
either Act; however, this does not diminish the authority of the Attorney
General under 28 USCS § 516 to conduct litigation on behalf of the United
States.[30]

CONTROLLING LAW IS ANALYZED IN CLEAR, CONCISE TEXT

§ 42:630.   Who administers programs

   The Food and Nutrition Service (FNS) acts on behalf of the Department of
Agriculture in administering the nutrition programs for children.[31]

   Within the states, the state educational agency is generally responsible for

18. 42 USCS §§ 1771–1789.

19. 42 USCS § 1782.

20. 42 USCS § 1772.

21. 42 USCS § 1773.

22. 42 USCS § 1786.

23. 42 USCS § 1788.

Forms: School lunch and breakfast programs
generally. 10 Fed Proc Forms §§ 37:61–37:70.

Jurisprudence: 68 Am Jur 2d, Schools
§ 282.

79 Am Jur 2d, Welfare Laws § 31.

Annotations: Construction and application
of National School Lunch Act (42 USCS
§§ 1751 et seq.) and Child Nutrition Act of
1966 (42 USCS §§ 1771 et seq.). 14 ALR Fed
634.

Supreme Court background: US L Ed Digest, Poor and Poor Laws § 2.

24. 42 USCS §§ 1751–1769c.

25. 42 USCS § 1751.

26. 42 USCS § 1761.

27. 42 USCS § 1762a.

28. 42 USCS § 1766.

Jurisprudence: 68 Am Jur 2d, Schools
§ 281.

79 Am Jur 2d, Welfare Laws §§ 29–30.

29. Hunt v Allen (1948) 131 W Va 627, 53
SE2d 509.

30. 42 USCS § 1785(b); 7 CFR §§ 210.16(i),
215.12(h), 220.14(i), 225.22(h), 226.25(f).

31. 7 CFR §§ 210.3(a), 215.3(a), 220.3(a),
225.3(a), 226.3(a), 227.3(a), 246.3(a), 247.3(a).

DIRECTS YOU TO THE US L ED DIGEST FOR SUPREME COURT BACKGROUND

324   17 Fed Proc, L Ed

LEADS YOU TO PERTINENT ANNOTATIONS IN L ED 2d, ALR FEDERAL, AND ALR

IMPORTANT CASES—COURT DECISIONS AND AGENCY DECISIONS— ARE CITED

information, the courts have also held that Exemption 4 is to be narrowly[94] and strictly[95] construed.

§ 38:111.   Exemption as applied by federal agencies

Agency regulations frequently specify certain types of information, received by the agency, which are regarded as being within the fourth exemption. Such agencies include the Nuclear Regulatory Commission,[96] the Department of Energy,[97] the Federal Election Commission,[98] the Export-Import Bank,[99] the Commodity Futures Trading Commission,[1] the Securities and Exchange Commission,[2] the Pension Benefit Guaranty Corporation,[3] the Department of the Army,[4] the Department of the Air Force,[5] the Defense Logistics Agency,[6] the Pennsylvania Avenue Development Corporation,[7] the Federal Communications Commission,[8] and the Secretary of Transportation.[9]

§ 38:112.   Power of agency to disclose otherwise exempt information

The fourth exemption, like the other FOIA exemptions, merely limits the agency's obligation to disclose the specified information, and does not impose an affirmative duty on the agency to withhold information falling within the exemption.[10] In short, Exemption 4, like all the FOIA exemptions, is not a mandatory bar to disclosure.[11] But a submitter of confidential information may request confidentiality,[12] and agencies are required to give submitters of confidential commercial information advance notice of FOIA requests before making any disclosure.[13] The agency's discretion to release the information may be barred by a successful "reverse-FOIA" action brought by the submitter.[14]

▐▌▐▌ *Law review commentary:* One commentator has suggested that the Supreme Court's decision in the *Chrysler* case demonstrates the need for

CITES TO THE CFR HELP YOU CHECK AGENCY REGULATIONS

FORMS REFERENCES DIRECT YOU TO FEDERAL PROCEDURAL FORMS, L ED FOR SPECIFIC FORMS

94. Bristol-Myers Co. v Federal Trade Com. (1970) 138 App DC 22, 424 F2d 935, 1970 CCH Trade Cas ¶ 73120, cert den 400 US 824, 27 L Ed 2d 52, 91 S Ct 46; Shermco Industries, Inc. v Secretary of United States Air Force (1978, ND Tex) 452 F Supp 306, revd on other grounds (CA5) 613 F2d 1314.

95. Fisher v Renegotiation Board (1972) 153 App DC 398, 473 F2d 109.

Forms: Notice of appeal from denial of request for records under Freedom of Information Act. 1 Fed Proc Forms § 2:175.

Notice of appeal—From denial of request for records under Freedom of Information Act— Another form. 1 Fed Proc Forms § 2:175.5.

96. 10 CFR § 9.5(a)(4).

Forms: Request for information from Nuclear Regulatory Commission under Freedom of Information Act. 3 Fed Proc Forms § 6:218.

97. 10 CFR § 1004.11(f).

98. 11 CFR § 4.5(a)(4).

99. 12 CFR § 404.5(c).

1. 17 CFR § 145.5(d).

2. 17 CFR § 200.80(b)(4).

Forms: Request to CFTC or SEC for information or records under Freedom of Information Act. 14 Fed Proc Forms § 59:191.

3. 29 CFR § 2603.18.

4. 32 CFR § 518.33(d).

5. 32 CFR § 806.7(d).

6. 32 CFR § 1285.3(g)(4).

7. 36 CFR § 902.54.

8. 47 CFR § 0.457(d).

Forms: Request for information from FCC under the Freedom of Information Act. 15 Fed Proc Forms § 62:301.

9. 49 CFR § 7.69.

Forms: Request for information from DOT or DOT subagency under Freedom of Information Act. 16 Fed Proc Forms § 66:282.

10. Chrysler Corp. v Brown (1979) 441 US 281, 60 L Ed 2d 208, 99 S Ct 1705, 19 BNA FEP Cas 475, 19 CCH EPD ¶ 9121.

11. Chrysler Corp. v Brown (1979) 441 US 281, 60 L Ed 2d 208, 99 S Ct 1705, 19 BNA FEP Cas 475, 19 CCH EPD ¶ 9121.

12. § 38:120, infra.

13. Ex Or 12600, discussed in §§ 38:334–38:340, infra.

14. Reverse-FOIA actions are discussed in §§ 38:544–38:552, infra.

INDIVIDUAL VOLUME INDEXES
PLUS A GENERAL COMPREHENSIVE
PAMPHLET INDEX FOR THE ENTIRE
SET HELP YOU GAIN ENTRY TO THE SET

GENERAL INDEX

TABLES, COVERING BOTH INDIVIDUAL
VOLUMES AND THE ENTIRE SET,
HELP YOU LOCATE TEXT DISCUSSION
OF A PARTICULAR STATUTE, COURT
RULE, OR AGENCY REGULATION

Federal
Procedural Forms,
Lawyers Edition

Federal Procedural Forms, a companion set to Federal Procedure, L Ed, provides the tools for actions in all federal courts—civil and criminal—as well as for adversary and rulemaking proceedings before major administrative agencies. In addition, through its treatment of pertinent and timely federal decisions, statutes, court rules, and administrative rules and regulations, it is also a basic procedural guide to federal courts and agencies.

The set organizes these materials in 68 chapters, plus 2 volumes of General Index and Tables. The Tables include references to the statutory, court rule, administrative regulation, and constitutional provisions cited.

Overall, Federal Procedural Forms includes illustrative instruments for four broad general categories of procedures:

1. General procedural subjects, such as discovery, injunctions, references, new trial, and appeal;
2. Specific actions, such as tort claims, antitrust trademark infringement, and civil rights actions;
3. Special proceedings, such as arbitration and bankruptcy; and
4. Proceedings before major administrative agencies.

LIST OF CHAPTERS IN FEDERAL PROCEDURAL
FORMS, LAWYERS EDITION

Chapter

1. Actions in District Court
2. Administrative Procedure
3. Appeal, Certiorari, and Review
4. Arbitration
5. Armed Forces; Civil Disturbances and National Defense
6. Atomic Energy
7. Aviation and Space
8. Banking and Financing
9. Bankruptcy
10. Civil Rights
11. Class Actions
12. Commodity and Stock Exchanges
13. Condemnation of Property
14. Consumer Credit Protection
15. Consumer Product Safety
16. Contempt
17. Copyrights
18. Court of Claims
19. Creditors Provisional Remedies
20. Criminal Procedure
21. Declaratory Judgments
22. Derivative Actions by Shareholders
23. Discovery and Depositions
24. Economic Development and Stabilization
25. Elections and Elective Franchise
26. Employees' Compensation Acts
27. Employers' Liability Act
28. Enforcement of Judgments
29. Environmental Protection
30. Farms, Ranches, and Agricultural Products
31. Food, Drugs, and Cosmetics
32. Foreign Relations
33. Foreign Trade and Commerce
34. Government Contracts
35. Government Officers and Employees
36. Habeas Corpus
37. Health, Education, and Welfare
38. Highways and Bridges
39. Housing and Urban Development
40. Immigration, Naturalization, and Nationality
41. Indians and Indian Affairs
42. Injunctions and Restraining Orders
43. Internal Revenue
44. Interpleader
45. Job Discrimination
46. Labor and Labor Relations
47. Maritime Law and Procedure
48. Monopolies and Restraints of Trade
49. Multi-District Litigation
50. Natural and Marine Resources
51. Navigable Waters
52. Patents
53. Pensions and Retirement Systems
54. Postal Services
55. Public Lands and Property
56. Railroads
57. References, Referees, and Masters
58. Removal of Actions
59. Securities Regulation
60. Social Security and Medicare
61. States, Territories, and Possessions
62. Telecommunications
63. Tort Claims Against United States
64. Trademarks
65. Trade Regulations and Unfair Trade Practices
66. Transportation
67. Unemployment Compensation
68. Veterans and Veterans' Laws

Federal Procedural Forms is a practice-oriented set organized by chapter according to the needs of the user. Sixty-eight chapters presented in alphabetical sequence cover the key areas of modern federal practice and procedure.

There is a logical, step-by-step sequence in each chapter with scope notes describing the topic treated; research references to the Am Jur family, ALR system, and L Ed; references to Federal Procedure, Lawyers Edition; references to USCS; and references to practice aids in other sources.

In addition, each chapter contains a general or "skeleton" outline, followed by a more detailed outline listing each section in the chapter to assist in locating specific forms and other definitive material.

Chapter 8

Banking and Financing

STATEMENT OF SCOPE AND RELATED TOPICS

STATE ASPECTS

Scope of topic:
This chapter contains procedural forms and materials relating to federal banking agencies. Administrative and judicial proceedings relating to the Federal Reserve System, the Federal Deposit Insurance Corporation, the Office of the Comptroller of the Currency governing national banks, the Office of Thrift Supervision governing federal savings associations, international banks, farm credit, and public records under the Freedom of Information Act and Privacy Act are included.

Treated elsewhere:
Related subjects treated elsewhere include consumer credit protection (see Ch 14), foreign trade and commerce (see Ch 33), and domestic trade (see Ch 65). Also appearing elsewhere is general treatment of district court proceedings (see Ch 1), administrative proceedings (see Ch 2), and appeal and review (see Ch 3).

State aspects:
The contracts and dealings of national banks are subject to the operation of general and nondiscriminating state laws which do not conflict with the letter or general object of the federal banking legislation. No state is authorized to prohibit creation of new national banks. If a state bank is involved in a merger or consolidation, the appraisal of the shares of dissenting shareholders of the state bank is determined in a manner prescribed by state law, if such provision is found in the law of that state, and no such merger or consolidation is allowed in contravention of the law of the state under which such bank is incorporated. A consolidation of two national banks is in no way subject to state law. The opening of a new branch by a national bank is forbidden unless branching is expressly authorized for state banks by the law of the state where the national bank is operating, and the authorization must be affirmative and not merely by implication for the opening of a branch outside the locality where the national bank is operating. However, the opinions of state banking administrators on the advisability of a new branch bank are not binding on the Comptroller. Relocation across state lines is permitted, within the 30-mile limit, of the main office of a national bank, and a state law purporting to bar such a relocation is pre-empted by federal law.
General jurisdiction over actions by or against national banks is

3A Federal Forms 247

Chapter Outline

3A Federal Forms   249

**SKELETON OUTLINE OF
MAIN CHAPTER DIVISIONS**

**DETAILED OUTLINE OF
SECTIONS CONTAINING
FORMS AND OTHER
PERTINENT MATERIAL**

250   3A Federal Forms

LISTINGS OF APPLICABLE STATUTES, COURT RULES,
ADMINISTRATIVE REGULATIONS, AND RULES OF
PRACTICE AND PROCEDURE.

BANKING AND FINANCING §8:1

The General Index to the United States Code Service (USCS) should also
be checked.

Statutes:

5 USCS §§ 551 et seq. [Administrative Procedure Act].

12 USCS §§ 1 et seq. [Comptroller of the Currency].

12 USCS §§ 21 et seq. [National Banks].

12 USCS §§ 221 et seq. [Federal Reserve System].

12 USCS §§ 1421 et seq. [Federal Home Loan Banks].

12 USCS §§ 1461 et seq. [Federal Savings Associations].

12 USCS §§ 1701 et seq. [National Housing].

12 USCS §§ 1811 et seq. [Federal Deposit Insurance Corporation].

12 USCS §§ 1841 et seq. [Bank Holding Companies].

15 USCS §§ 1601 et seq. [Consumer Credit Cost Disclosure].

15 USCS §§ 1681 et seq. [Credit Reporting Agencies].

Court Rules:

Federal Rules of Appellate Procedure, Rules 15 et seq. [review or enforcement of
orders of administrative agencies], 16 [record on review or enforcement], 17 [filing of
record], 18 [stay pending review], 20 [applicability of other rules of FRAP (except
FRAP 3–14, 22, 23) to review or enforcement of agency orders].

Reminder: Always check the advance sheets to the United States Code Service (USCS)
for latest court rule changes.

Administrative Rules of Practice: [91]

Rules of practice and procedure in proceedings before the Comptroller of the Currency, 12 CFR §§ 19.3(a)(2) [notice of appearance by counsel], 19.5(b) [motion to
change or extend time limits, etc.], 19.10 [notice of charges and hearing, or notice of
hearing and answer], 19.14 [motions], 19.14(d) [objections to motions], 19.15 [motion
for interlocutory review], 19.30(a) [motion for prehearing conference], 19.31 [prehear-
ing exchange of information], 19.32 [stipulations and admissions of fact], 19.33(b)(1)
[application to take oral deposition], 19.34(a) [request for issuance of subpoena(s)],
19.34(d) [motion to quash subpoena], 19.40-19.45 [formal hearing], 19.40(c) [objec-
tions to evidence], 19.43(d) [motion for public hearing], 19.50 [proposed findings of
fact and conclusions of law], 19.51 [submissions by limited participants], 19.52 [initial
decision of presiding officer], 19.60(a) [notice of appeal], 19.60(b), (c) [exceptions to
initial decision; briefs], 19.61 [request for oral argument], 19.62 [notice of submission
to agency for final decision], 19.64 [final decision], 19.65 [stay of proceeding or final
order].

Rules of practice for formal hearings before the Board of Governors of the Federal
Reserve System, 12 CFR §§ 263.3 [appearance and right to practice], 263.4 [notice of
hearing], 263.5 [answer to allegations in notice of hearing; informal settlement], 263.6
[conduct of hearing], 263.7 [subpoenas], 263.8 [depositions], 263.9 [rules of evidence],
263.10 [motions], 263.11 [proposed findings and conclusions; recommended decision],
263.12 [exceptions], 263.13 [briefs], 263.14 [oral argument before board], 263.16–
263.18 [filing papers; service; number of copies], 263.19 [computation of time], 263.20
[confidentiality of documents], 263.21 [formal requirements], 263.22 et seq. [additional
rules relating to assessment and collection of civil penalties], 263.30 et seq. [additional

---

91. Note: The rules listed under this heading relate specifically to required or permitted
   actions of counsel in representing his client in an administrative proceeding. For a

Background Material

Each chapter, or part thereof, contains textual discussion of the relevant procedural aspects of the particular topic. Included are such matters as jurisdiction, venue, parties, statutes of limitation, discovery, attorneys' fees, and, where applicable, aspects of state remedies and procedures.

BANKING AND FINANCING   § 8:121

12 CFR §§ 308.99-308.103 [procedures and standards applicable to application to engage services of individual convicted of criminal offense involving dishonesty or breach of trust].

RESEARCH REFERENCES

The following references pertain to administrative proceedings involving banks and banking.

Texts

4 Fed Proc, L Ed, BANKING AND FINANCING §§ 8:126-8:164.

10 AM JUR 2d, Bank, § 427.

Annotations

INDEX TO ANNOTATIONS: Banks and Banking, Federal Deposit Insurance Corporation.

Digests

L ED DIGEST: Banks.

ALR DIGESTS: Banks.

§ 8:112 Annotation references

Annotations pertaining to applications before the FDIC are listed below. Additional annotations are listed in pertinent sections of this division and in the notes after particular forms.

ALR Federal annotations:

What is a "deposit" or "insured deposit" in a bank under 12 USCS § 1813 for Federal Deposit Insurance Purposes. 84 ALR Fed 331.

Reminder: For additional annotation material, consult the Index to Annotations.

2. GENERAL APPLICATION PROCEDURES

§ 8:121 Procedural guide—investigation

The FDIC, which has responsibility for insuring the deposits of all banks and savings associations entitled to the benefits of insurance under

---

3A Federal Forms   **359**

TYPICAL FORM WITH
NUMBERED BLANKS FOR
EASY DICTATION AND
FILL IN

---

§ 8:104   Petition—For review—Application for acquisition of stock denied [12 USCS § 1848; FRAP 15(a)]

[Caption, see 8:102]

PETITION FOR REVIEW

The __1____ *[name]* National Bank respectfully represents:

1. That petitioner is a national bank with its principal place of business located at __2____.

2. That it has entered into an agreement with __3____, of __4____ *[place of business]*, a bank holding company, whereunder all of its voting shares would be acquired by said bank holding company.

3. That pursuant to 12 USC § 1842(a)(3), application was made to the respondent Board for approval of said acquisition.

4. That on __5____, 19_6_, the respondent Board issued an order denying said application. A copy of said order is attached hereto.

5. That said order is erroneous, null and void, and contrary to law, in that __7____ *[specify, such as:* it was not issued within the time prescribed by 12 USC § 1842(b) *or* it is not supported by substantial evidence].

6. That petitioner is a party aggrieved by said order and brings this petition pursuant to 12 USC § 1848.

WHEREFORE, petitioner prays that the Court review, vacate and set aside said order of the respondent, and order that said application for the acquisition of petitioner's stock be granted.

Dated __8____, 19_9_.

[Signature and address]
Counsel for Petitioner

NOTES

(See notes in § 8:102)

3A Federal Forms   **355**

NOTES FOLLOWING FORMS

Notes Following Forms

Notes that follow each form contain case notes, statutory and rule notes, comments, cross-references, and reminders, as well as references to Federal Procedure, Lawyers Edition, Am Jur, ALR, and U.S. Supreme Court Reports, L Ed 2d, and other TCSL publications.

Tables of Statutes, Rules, and Regulations

At the back of each volume there are tables that set forth the constitutional and statutory provisions, court rules, and administrative regulations and rules of practice that are cited in the volume. This provides an easy way to locate particular forms and text materials.

Supplementation

To keep Federal Procedural Forms current, annual pocket parts are issued. These contain new and updated forms; statute, regulation, and court rule citations; and references to related material in other publications, including Federal Procedure and ALR.

TABLES OF STATUTES, RULES, AND REGULATIONS

PART ONE

STATUTES AND REGULATIONS

Table No. 1

UNITED STATES CODE SERVICE

5 USCS §	Section	5 USCS §	Section
252(b)(5)	§ 8:642		8:201, 8:221, 8:391, 8:621,
532a(e)(7)	§ 7:342		8:631
551 et seq	§ 8:201	701–706	§ 7:221, 8:219
551(4)	§ 8:391, 8:411	701(a)	§ 8:221
551(5)	§ 8:391	701(a)(2)	§ 8:83
552	§ 7:341, 7:342, 7:343, 8:651, 8:672	702	§ 7:242, 7:243, 7:244, 8:397
552(a)(2)	§ 7:341, 8:641	706	§ 8:418, 8:631
552(a)(3)	§ 7:361, 8:641, 8:642, 8:656,	706(2)(A)	§ 8:596
	8:658, 8:671	1348	§ 8:443
552(a)(4)(B)	§ 7:342, 7:343, 7:346, 8:641,		
	8:658	7 USCS	Section
552(a)(4)(C)	§ 8:658	1828(c)	§ 8:221
552(a)(4)(E)	§ 7:342, 7:343, 8:641, 8:642,	12 USCS	Section
	8:658	1 et seq	§ 8:414
552(a)(4)(G)	§ 8:658	21 et seq	§ 8:241, 8:261, 8:281, 8:282,
552(a)(6)	§ 7:345, 8:641		8:283, 8:284, 8:285, 8:287,
552(a)(6)(A)	§ 8:672		8:288, 8:301, 8:321, 8:341,
552(a)(6)(C)	§ 7:342		8:361, 8:391, 8:415, 8:417,
552(b)	§ 7:342, 8:641		8:431, 8:443, 8:463, 8:467,
552(b)(1)	§ 7:342, 8:642		8:591, 8:611
552(b)(2)	§ 7:342, 8:642	21	§ 8:232
552(b)(3)	§ 7:342, 8:642	22	§ 8:263

United States Supreme Court Reports, Lawyers' Edition

First and second series

Beginning with the organization of the United States Supreme Court in 1789, every case decided by the United States Supreme Court can be found in United States Supreme Court Reports, Lawyers' Edition. It is also the only privately published series of supreme court cases that goes back to 1789. L Ed is the only supreme court reports that has annotations. But the Lawyers' Edition (often referred to as "Law. Ed", "US L Ed" or "L Ed") is not just another set of complete court reports.

Because of the importance and widespread effect of the Court's decisions, special care and attention is given to the method of presentation of the decisions, as well as the ancillary works and features that are a part of the service.

L Ed—The reported case

In addition to a careful and prompt publication of the decisions and opinions of the Supreme Court, the Lawyers' Edition includes editorial features designed to provide the most efficient use of the set.

A valuable Summary of the decision precedes the case, giving a quick overview of the points decided by the court.

Each point of law supported by a majority of the participating members of the court is summarized in a separate headnote, classified to the U.S. Supreme Court Digest, L Ed.

A box contains references to the Total Client-Service Library.

Annotations in L Ed, ALR Fed, and ALR highlighted separately where users can find articles analyzing all cases ever decided on a point of law.

NEW YORK v HARRIS
(1990) 495 US 14, 109 L Ed 2d 13, 110 S Ct 1640

HEADNOTES

Classified to U.S. Supreme Court Digest, Lawyers' Edition

Evidence § 681.5 — exclusionary rule — statement of suspect at police station — effect of warrantless, nonconsensual entry of home

1a-1d. The Fourth Amendment exclusionary rule does not bar a state's use in a criminal trial of a written inculpatory statement made by a murder suspect at a police station—even though the statement was taken after the suspect was arrested by the police in his home without a warrant and without consent to their entry, in violation of the rule of Payton v New York (1980) 445 US 573, 63 L Ed 2d 639, 100 S Ct 1371 (holding that the Fourth Amendment prohibits the police from making a warrantless and nonconsensual entry into a suspect's home in order to make a routine felony arrest)—where (1) the statement was not the product of being in unlawful custody, inasmuch as the police had probable cause to arrest the suspect; (2) the police had a justification to question the suspect prior to his arrest, so that the suspect's subsequent statement was not an exploitation of the illegal entry into the suspect's home; and (3) the statement was not the fruit of having been

---

TOTAL CLIENT-SERVICE LIBRARY® REFERENCES

5 Am Jur 2d, Arrest § 116; 29 Am Jur 2d, Evidence §§ 415, 416

5 Am Jur Trials 331, Excluding Illegally Obtained Evidence

USCS, Constitution, Amendment 4

US L Ed Digest, Evidence § 681.5

Index to Annotations, Arrest; Exclusion and Suppression of Evidence: Fourth Amendment; Fruit of the Poisonous Tree Doctrine; Search and Seizure

Auto-Cite®: Cases and annotations referred to herein can be further researched through the Auto-Cite® computer-assisted research service. Use Auto-Cite to check citations for form, parallel references, prior and later history, and annotation references.

ANNOTATION REFERENCES

Admissibility of pretrial confession in criminal case. 1 L Ed 2d 1735, 4 L Ed 2d 1833, 16 L Ed 2d 1294, 22 L Ed 2d 872.

Admissibility of evidence obtained by illegal search and seizure. 93 L Ed 1797, 96 L Ed 145, 98 L Ed 581, 100 L Ed 239, 6 L Ed 2d 1544.

"Fruit of the poisonous tree" doctrine excluding evidence derived from information gained in illegal search. 43 ALR3d 385.

The decisions of the Supreme Court are kept current by the issuance of Advance Reports which are published twice a month while the court is in session.

CASES OF SPECIAL INTEREST ARE HIGHLIGHTED

MAIN HOLDINGS OF CASE ARE SUMMARIZED IN ONE SENTENCE

ADVANCE

UNITED STATES SUPREME COURT REPORTS

LAWYERS' EDITION

Volume 120 L Ed 2d, No. 1 • August 10, 1992 • Pages 1–925

CROSS BURNING CASE, p 305
CIGARETTE LIABILITY CASE, p 407
GRADUATION PRAYERS CASE, p 467
PENNSYLVANIA ABORTION CASE, p 674

American National Red Cross v S. G. 201
Original federal court jurisdiction over all cases to which American National Red Cross is party held conferred by "sue and be sued" provision (36 USCS § 2) of Red Cross' federal corporate charter.

(Continued on next page)

Lawyers Cooperative Publishing
Aqueduct Building, Rochester, New York 14694

Each Advance Report contains a Current Awareness Commentary which provides comprehensive, up-to-date information concerning issues in cases scheduled for argument, cases accepted for review, and cases in which review is summarily denied.

In the back of certain Advance Report issues (also published in the bound volume) will be found a division entitled "Miscellaneous Proceedings" which covers such activities of the court as assignment orders, and orders such as those prescribing amendments to Court Rules and Forms.

The Advance Report also contains cumulative tables of cases reported and federal statutes and regulations cited, as well as a cumulative index.

An outstanding and exclusive editorial feature of U.S. Supreme Court Reports, Lawyers' Edition, is the annotations on points of law covered in decisions of the Supreme Court. Written with the same care and expertise found in the ALR annotations (see discussion ALR, supra), the L Ed annotations have been a popular research tool through the years.

In the first series of L Ed, each annotation directly follows the case reported in the volume. In the Second Series, the annotations and the summaries of the briefs of counsel are grouped together in a separate division at the end of each volume. Cross references link the pertinent cases and annotations together.

"POISONOUS TREE"—REMOTE EVIDENCE   § 1[a]
109 L Ed 2d 787

ANNOTATION

**WHEN IS EVIDENCE WHICH IS OBTAINED AFTER UNCONSTITU-
TIONAL SEARCH OR SEIZURE SUFFICIENTLY REMOTE FROM
SUCH SEARCH OR SEIZURE SO AS NOT TO BE TAINTED BY, AND
NOT TO BE INADMISSIBLE AS FRUIT OF, SUCH SEARCH OR
SEIZURE—SUPREME COURT CASES**

by

Daniel A. Klein, J.D.

I. Preliminary Matters

§ 1. Introduction
   [a] Scope
   [b] Related matters
§ 2. Summary and comment
   [a] Generally
   [b] Practice pointers

II. Attenuated Connection

A. In General

§ 3. View that evidence obtained as remote result of unconstitutional search
   or seizure is admissible where taint or causative nature of such
   search or seizure is purged or sufficiently attenuated
   [a] Generally
   [b] View with respect to live-witness testimony

"POISONOUS TREE"—REMOTE EVIDENCE   § 3[a]
109 L Ed 2d 787

witness, (2) whether the witness' identity or relationship with the accused were discovered only as a result of the illegal search, and (3) whether the application of the exclusionary rule under the circumstances would have any deterrent effect on improper police behavior (§ 4[f], infra).

In applying attenuation analysis in any given case, whether involving evidence obtained after an illegal seizure of a person (§§ 5[a], 5[b], infra) or evidence obtained after an illegal search or seizure of property (§ 6, infra), the Supreme Court has followed a highly fact-specific approach in weighing all the circumstances, and has said that no single fact is dispositive (§ 3[a], infra).

[b] Practice pointers

Although the prosecution bears the burden of proof that the causal connection between an unconstitutional search or seizure and the acquisition of evidence is sufficiently remote to render the evidence admissible,[4] a motion to suppress such evidence as "fruit of the poisonous tree" must be supported by factual proof,[5] and thus if counsel for the accused chooses to pursue suppression, counsel may find it advisable to conduct a thorough investigation beforehand to gather such proof. By interviewing the accused and all available witnesses and utilizing whatever judicial discovery procedures may be provided,[6] counsel may be able to obtain the information necessary to establish a sufficiently close connection between the illegal search or seizure and the acquisition of the evidence at issue. If the available proof points to no more than a tenuous "but for" connection, counsel may find it unadvisable to pursue suppression on Fourth Amendment grounds.

Counsel should bear in mind that even if more than a "but for" connection can arguably be shown, the prosecution may attempt to counter the fruit of the poisonous tree defense in other ways. Thus, it may be prudent for counsel to anticipate such tactics by gathering proof that the evidence would not have been "inevitably" discovered eventually by lawful means,[7] and that the police officers concerned did not in fact have a lawful "independent source" for the evidence besides their illegal conduct.[8]

II. Attenuated Connection

A. In General

§ 3. View that evidence obtained as remote result of unconstitutional search or seizure is admissible where taint or causative nature of such search or seizure is purged or sufficiently attenuated

[a] Generally

The following cases support a general rule that, notwithstanding the exclusionary rule, under which evidence obtained as an indirect result of a Fourth Amendment violation is generally deemed inadmissible "fruit of the poisonous tree," there are circumstances under which the causal connection between an illegal search or seizure and the acquisition of evi-

---

4. See Brown v Illinois (1975) 422 US 590, 45 L Ed 2d 416, 95 S Ct 2254, infra § 3[a].

ery" rule, see the annotation at 81 ALR Fed 331.

Summaries of Briefs of Counsel are helpful
in analysis of decisions.

**MAIN HOLDINGS
OF CASE ARE
SUMMARIZED
IN ONE SENTENCE**

NEW YORK v HARRIS

109 L Ed 2d 13

NEW YORK, Petitioner

v

BERNARD HARRIS

Reported in this volume: p 13, supra.

Holding: Fourth Amendment exclusionary rule held not to bar use at trial of statement made by suspect at police station after police had entered suspect's home without warrant or consent and had arrested him there.

Annotation: p 787, infra.

BRIEFS AND APPEARANCES OF COUNSEL

Peter D. Coddington, of Bronx, New York, argued the cause and, with **Robert T. Johnson,** District Attorney, **Anthony J. Girese, Susan L. Valle, Stanley R. Kaplan,** and **Karen P. Swiger,** Assistant District Attorneys, all also of Bronx, New York, filed briefs for petitioner:

The New York Court of Appeals erroneously construed the Fourth Amendment to require the exclusion from evidence of a murder suspect's voluntary confession, given with full comprehension of the Miranda warnings at a police precinct, solely because, about 1 hour before, the police, acting on probable cause, had arrested him in his home without first obtaining a warrant for his arrest.

Barrington D. Parker, Jr. of New York City, by invitation of the court, 492 US 934, 106 L Ed 2d 631, 110 S Ct 18, argued the cause as amicus curiae in support of the judgment below and, with **Ronald G. Blum, Debra Freeman,** and **Charles L. Kerr,** filed a brief for respondent.

Solicitor General **Kenneth W. Starr,** Assistant Attorney General **Edward S.G. Dennis,** Deputy Solicitor General **William C. Bryson, Michael R. Dreeben,** and **Robert J. Erickson** filed a brief for the United States as amicus curiae urging reversal; **Gregory U. Evans, Daniel B. Hales, George D. Webster, Jack E. Yelverton, Fred E. Inbau, Wayne W. Schmidt,** and **James P. Manak** filed a brief for Americans for Effective Law Enforcement, Inc. et al. as amici curiae urging reversal; and **John D. O'Hair** and **Timothy A. Baughman** filed a brief for the Office of Prosecuting Attorney, Wayne County, Michigan, as amicus curiae urging reversal.

L Ed Citator Service In the US L Ed supplement there is a citator service which consists of summaries of pertinent holdings of subsequent Supreme Court decisions to the cases in the bound volume. The citator service analyzes these later decisions as they affect the cases in the volume.

UNITED STATES
SUPREME COURT REPORTS
LAWYERS' EDITION
SECOND SERIES

CITATOR SERVICE

This Service consists of brief summaries of the pertinent holdings from other Supreme Court decisions making significant references to the Supreme Court holdings published in this L Ed 2d volume. The nature of the Supreme Court's reference in the citing case to the holding published in this L Ed 2d volume is disclosed precisely, through the use of such language as "Cited in," "Quoted in," "Discussed in," "Followed in," "Explained in," "Distinguished in," or "Overruled in," and the nature of the citing case's holding relating to the cited case is summarized concisely yet comprehensively. Cases and annotations referred to herein can be further researched through the **Auto-Cite®** computer-assisted research service. Use Auto-Cite to check citations for form, parallel references, prior and later history, and annotation references.

104 L Ed 2d 58

(Amerada Hess Corp. v Director, Div. of Taxation, New Jersey Dept. of Treasury)

Discussed in Trinova Corp. v Michigan Dept. of Treasury (1991, US) 112 L Ed 2d 884, 111 S Ct 818, 91 CDOS 1278, 91 Daily Journal DAR 2066, holding that state's value added, single business tax, as applied to particular foreign corporation during particular tax year, did not violate Federal Constitution's commerce clause (Art I, § 8, cl 3) or due process clause of Constitution's Fourteenth Amendment.

104 L Ed 2d 86

(California v ARC America Corp.)

Cited in Kansas v Utilicorp United, Inc. (1990, US) 111 L Ed 2d 169, 110 S Ct 2807, 1990-1 CCH Trade Cases P 69064, holding that utility alone, and not states on behalf of utility customers, had standing to bring antitrust suit under § 4 of Clayton Act against natural gas suppliers allegedly overcharging utility.

104 L Ed 2d 250

(Skinner v Mid-America Pipeline)

Cited in Rust v Sullivan (1991, US) 114 L Ed 2d 233, 111 S Ct 1759, 91 CDOS 3713, 91

Daily Journal DAR 6006, holding that provision of Controlled Substances Act (21 USCS § 811(h)) permitting temporary expedited designation of controlled substance by United States Attorney General was not unconstitutional as improper delegation of legislative authority.

104 L Ed 2d 487

(United States v Halper)

Quoted in Jones v Thomas (1989, US) 105 L Ed 2d 322, 109 S Ct 2522, holding that imposition of separate consecutive sentences for felony-murder and underlying felony, in violation of double jeopardy, was remedied by vacating completed felony sentence and crediting time served to felony-murder sentence.

Distinguished in Browning-Ferris Industries, Inc. v Kelco Disposal, Inc. (1989, US) 106 L Ed 2d 219, 109 S Ct 2909, 1989-1 CCH Trade Cases P 68630, holding that Eighth Amendment's excessive fines clause is inapplicable to punitive damage awards between private parties.

104 L Ed 2d 526

(Rodriguez de Quijas v Shearson/American Express, Inc.)

Distinguished in Patterson v McLean Credit Union (1989, US) 105 L Ed 2d 132, 109 S Ct 2363, 49 BNA FEP Cas 1814, 50 CCH EPD P 39066, declining to overrule prior United

There are two series of L Ed. The first series covers the period 1789-1956. The second series covers 1956 through the current term.

L Ed Quick Case Table pamphlet
This pamphlet is the quickest access to all U.S. Supreme Court cases by the name of the case. Also included are all ALR, ALR Fed and U.S. L Ed annotations that analyzed the case listed.

Pocket Supplements
The annotations in Volumes 1-31 of L Ed 2d are supplemented in a two-volume Later Case Service, updated by annual, cumulative pocket supplements. Beginning with Volume 32 of L Ed 2d, each volume is equipped with a pocket in the back of the volume. In addition to providing later cases for annotations appearing in the volume, this pocket supplement includes a list of corrections in the decisions made by the Justices after the volume was published.

Citator Service
This service consists of brief summaries of the pertinent holdings from other Supreme Court decisions, making significant references to the Supreme Court holdings published in the volume. The nature of the Supreme Court's reference in the citing case to the holding published in the volume is precisely disclosed through the use of such language as "Cited in", "Quoted in", "Discussed in", "Followed in", "Explained in", "Distinguished in", or "Overruled in", and the nature of the citing case's holding relating to the cited case is summarized.

L Ed General Index
The L Ed General Index is a six volume comprehensive topical index of the U.S. Supreme Court cases. Also included is a Table of Justices, statutory table and a history table of past annotations. This comprehensive index helps a user find cases and annotations by the thing, act, person or place of the issue.

United States
Supreme Court
Digest, L Ed

States Supreme Court Digest, Lawyers' Edition. The L Ed Digest, which contains over 40 volumes, is composed of three basic parts: the Digest proper; finding aids providing entry into the Digest proper; and the rules governing practice in federal courts.

Traditional Digest Method
The primary method of entry into L Ed is the A to Z digest covering nearly 400 Digest topics from Abandoned Property to Zoning.

The Digest topics are designed to allow the user to find the law on a desired point without delay.

Finding the Law in L Ed
A primary research tool for finding the opinions and annotations in L Ed is the United

DIGEST

OF THE

UNITED STATES

SUPREME COURT REPORTS

EVIDENCE

Scope of Topic: This topic covers the principles and rules of evidence applicable in civil and criminal cases; including judicial notice; presumptions, inferences, and burden of proof; the relevancy, materiality, competency, admissibility, weight, effect, and sufficiency of evidence; and variance between pleading and proof.

Treated elsewhere are evidence in administrative proceedings (see ADMINISTRATIVE LAW and such other topics as LABOR; WORKMEN'S COMPENSATION; etc.); proof in extradition (see EXTRADITION) and habeas corpus (see HABEAS CORPUS) proceedings; matters as to witnesses (see WITNESSES), discovery and inspection (see DISCOVERY AND INSPECTION), or depositions (see DEPOSITIONS); constitutionality of statutes (see CONSTITUTIONAL LAW), conflict of laws (see CONFLICT CONTRACTS), or appellate matters (see APPEAL AN of judgment to proof (see JUDGMENT); new trial of, or for newly discovered, evidence (see NEW conform to proof (see PLEADING); and matters of as the offer and reception of, demurrer to, comm of amount of, or striking out of, evidence, or th require submission of the case to the jury (see TR

Statutory references
Federal Rules of Evidence, 28 USCS Appendix
Federal Rules of Civil Procedure, Rules 43, 44, 44
Federal Rules of Criminal Procedure, Rule 26.1
18 USCS §§ 3491–3504 (criminal proceedings)
Jencks Act, 18 USCS § 3450
28 USCS §§ 1731–1746 (documentary evidence)
Federal Business Records Act, 28 USCS § 1732

SCOPE OF TOPIC AND RELATED TOPICS ARE NOTED

[For fact-word approach see Word Index to this Digest]

I. IN GENERAL, § 1.

II. JUDICIAL NOTICE.

  (A) IN GENERAL, § 2.

  (B) CONSTITUTION AND LAWS, §§ 3–17.

  (C) PROCLAMATIONS, § 18.

  (D) OFFICIAL AND JUDICIAL CHARACTER, AUTHORITY, DUTIES, ACTS, DOCUMENTS, AND RECORDS, §§ 19–30.

  (E) POLITICAL, HISTORICAL, AND GEOGRAPHICAL MATTERS, §§ 31–39.

  (F) OTHER MATTERS, §§ 40–87.

III. PRESUMPTIONS, INFERENCES, AND BURDEN OF PROOF.

  (A) IN GENERAL, §§ 88–90.

  (B) LAWS, CONSTITUTION, §§ 91–102.

  (C) ESTABISHING ALLEGATIONS OR CLAIMS, §§ 103–106.

  (D) DEFENSES, §§ 107, 108.

  (E) EXCEPTIONS, EXEMPTIONS AND NEGATIONS, §§ 109–114.

  (F) CONCERNING PERSONS, §§ 115–200.

  (G) CORPORATIONS; PARTNERSHIPS, §§ 201–208.

  (H) CONTINUANCE, §§ 209–211.

  (I) CAUSE, §§ 211.3–213.

  (J) AS TO SKILL; NEGLIGENCE; CARE, §§ 214–242.

SCHEMES DEFINE LOCATION OF SPECIFIC POINTS

Evidence § 681.5

ment facility—at the direction of a state highway patrol trooper—force open a locked suitcase found in the car's trunk, is properly suppressed, where the highway patrol has no policy whatever with respect to the opening of closed containers encountered during an inventory search. Florida v Wells (US) 110 S Ct 1632.

109 L Ed 2d 1

The Fourth Amendment exclusionary rule does not bar a state's use in a criminal trial of a written inculpatory statement made by a murder suspect at a police station—even though the statement was taken after the suspect was arrested by the police in his home without a warrant and without consent to their entry, in violation of the rule of Payton v New York (1980) 445 US 573, 63 L Ed 2d 639, 100 S Ct 1371 (holding that the Fourth Amendment prohibits the police from making a warrantless and nonconsensual entry into a suspect's home in order to make a routine felony arrest)—where (1) the statement was not the product of being in unlawful custody, inasmuch as the police had probable cause to arrest the suspect, (2) the police had a justification to question the suspect prior to his arrest, so that the suspect's subsequent statement was not an exploitation of the illegal entry into the suspect's home; and (3) the statement was not the fruit of having been arrested in the home rather than someplace else. (Marshall, Brennan, Blackmun, and Stevens, JJ., dissented from this holding.) New York v Harris (US) 110 S Ct 1640.

109 L Ed 2d 13

The exclusionary rule relating to evidence obtained through a violation of the Fourth Amendment does not require the adoption of a "per se" or "but for" rule that would make inadmissible any evidence, whether tangible or live-witness testimony, which somehow comes to light through a chain of causation which begins with an illegal arrest; the penalties visited by the exclusionary rule upon the government, and in turn upon the public, because its officers have violated the law must bear some relationship to the purposes which the law is to serve; and the rule that the Fourth Amendment prohibits the police from making a warrantless and nonconsensual entry into a suspect's home in order to make a routine felony arrest is designed to protect the physical integrity of the home and is not intended to grant a criminal suspect protection for a statement made outside the premises where the police have probable cause to arrest the suspect for committing a crime. New York v Harris (US) 110 S Ct 1640.

109 L Ed 2d 13

For purposes of determining whether the Fourth Amendment precludes admission of a suspect's statement made at a police station, after the police had entered the suspect's home without a warrant and without consent and had arrested him there, a suspect who is removed to a police station, given Miranda warnings, and allowed to talk is not unlawfully in custody where police officers had probable cause to arrest the suspect for a crime, and the legal issue is the same as it would be if the police had arrested the suspect on his doorstep, had illegally entered the suspect's home to search for evidence, and had later interrogated the suspect at the police station; similarly, if the police make a warrantless entry into the suspect's home, do not find him there, but arrest him on the street when he returns, a later statement made by him after proper warnings is admissible. New York v Harris (US) 110 S Ct 1640.

109 L Ed 2d 13

The warrant requirement for an arrest in the home imposed by the rule of Payton v New York (1980) 445 US 573, 63 L Ed 2d 639, 100 S Ct 1371 (holding that the Fourth Amendment prohibits the police from making a warrantless and nonconsensual entry into a suspect's home in order to make a routine felony arrest), is imposed to protect the home, and, where anything incriminating gathered by the police from arresting a suspect in his home, rather than elsewhere, in violation of the rule is excluded from evidence, the purpose of the rule is vindicated; the Constitution does not require the United States Supreme Court to go further and suppress statements later made by the suspect in order to deter police from violating the Payton rule. New York v Harris (US) 110 S Ct 1640.

109 L Ed 2d 13

In the case of a search incident to a lawful arrest, if the police stray outside the permissible scope of the search, they are in violation of the Fourth Amendment, and evidence so seized will be excluded. Horton v California (US) 110 S Ct 2301.

110 L Ed 2d 112

An object—later found to be crack cocaine when discovered by the police—discarded by a person who is being pursued by a police officer, and who is immediately thereafter tackled by the officer, is abandoned and is not the fruit of a "seizure" of the person within the meaning of the Federal Constitution's Fourth Amendment, and therefore—even if, as conceded by the state, the officer's pursuit of the person was not based on reasonable suspicion—is not suppressible under the Fourth Amendment as the fruit of an unlawful seizure, where the officer did not touch the person before the object was discarded, and where, assuming that the officer's pursuit of the person constituted a show of authority enjoining him to halt, the person

**CAREFULLY
WRITTEN
HEADNOTE
FORMS DIGEST
PARAGRAPH**

**DIRECT ACCESS
TO THE CASE IN L ED
WITH PARALLEL CITES
TO THE REPORTS**

Table of Cases as Research Tool

Where the title of a U.S. Supreme Court case is known, its location in Lawyers' Edition may be learned through use of the Table of Cases in Volumes 15-15D of the L Ed Digest. This table provides the forward and reverse title of every U.S. Supreme Court case in one alphabetical sequence with the citation (and digest references) under the forward title.

New York v Harris (US) 109 L Ed 2d 13, 110 S Ct 1640
Cited in:
42 L Ed 2d 946 (What issues will the Supreme Court consider, though not, or not properly, raised by the parties)
22 L Ed 2d 872 (Admissibility of pretrial confession in criminal case—Supreme Court cases)

New York, Havnor v

mental factors in their planning and decision making)
78 L Ed 2d 780 (Considerations affecting grant or vacation of stay or injunction by individual Justice of Supreme Court)

New York, Kunz v

New York, La Marca v

New York, Lanza v

New York v Latrobe, 279 US 421, 73 L

US L Ed Quick Case Table Pamphlet with annotation references: Another entry method by case name is the L Ed quick case table pamphlet. This entry sends the user to the case by name and annotation that have cited that case.

New York, Bock v
New York, Bond v
New York, Bowen v •
New York, Brand v
New York, Brown v
New York v Burger, 479 US 812, 93 L Ed 2d 20, 107 S Ct 61
New York v Burger, 482 US 691, 96 L Ed 2d 601, 107 S Ct 2636—search & s §§ 5, 7, 8, 25; statutes § 145.4
New York, Burr v
New York, Butts v
New York, Carbone v
New York, Carrion v
New York, Carter v
New York, Cartier v

New York, Guarino v
New York v Guzman (US) 114 L Ed 2d 477, 111 S Ct 2234
New York, Halloran v
New York, Hardy v
New York v Harris, 490 US 1018, 104 L Ed 2d 178, 109 S Ct 1741
New York v Harris, 490 US 1105, 104 L Ed 2d 1017, 109 S Ct 3153
New York v Harris, 492 US 903, 106 L Ed 2d 562, 109 S Ct 3211
New York v Harris, 492 US 934, 106 L Ed 2d 631, 110 S Ct 18
New York v Harris (US) 109 L Ed 2d 13, 110 S Ct 1640—arrest §§ 1, 2; ev §§ 681, 681.5, 683, 684; search & s § 9

The Rules Volumes of the L Ed Digest
As an aid to research of federal law, Volumes 17-22 include the text of the U.S. Constitution as well as the various rules governing practice in the federal courts. Included are:

Supreme Court Rules
Appellate Procedure Rules
Bankruptcy Rules
Civil Procedure Rules
Criminal Procedure Rules
Magistrates' Rules
Federal Rules of Evidence

Also included are Court of Appeals Rules and rules for such special courts as the Judicial Panel on Multidistrict Litigation, the Court of International Trade, the Tax Court, the Court of Military Appeals, and the Claims Court.

Bringing the Law Up-to-Date
All units of the L Ed Digest are kept up-to-date annually by pocket supplements. Replacement volumes are issued as needed.

Rule 34.   Arrest of Judgment

The court on motion of a defendant shall arrest judgment if the indictment or information does not charge an offense or if the court was without jurisdiction of the offense charged. The motion in arrest of judgment shall be made within 7 days after verdict or finding of guilty, or after plea of guilty or nolo contendere, or within such further time as the court may fix during the 7-day period.

ADVISORY COMMITTEE NOTES

Notes of Advisory Committee on Rules. This rule continues existing law except that it enlarges the time for making motions in arrest of judgment from 3 days to 5 days. See Rule II (2) of Criminal Appeals Rules of 1933, 292 USC 661 [18 USC formerly following § 688].

Notes of Advisory Committee on 1966 Amendments to Rules. The words "on motion of a defendant" are added to make clear here, as in Rule 33, that the court may act only pursuant to a timely motion by the defendant.

The amendment to the second sentence is designed to clarify an ambiguity in the rule as originally drafted. In Lott v United States, 367 US 421, 6 L Ed 2d 940, 81 S Ct 1563 (1961) the Supreme Court held that when a defendant pleaded nolo contendere the time in which a motion could be made under this rule did not begin to run until entry of the judgment. The Court held that such a plea was not a "determination of guilt." No reason of policy appears to justify having the time for making this motion commence with the verdict or finding of guilt but not with the acceptance of the plea of nolo contendere or the plea of guilty. The amendment changes the result in the Lott case and makes the periods uniform. The amendment also changes the time in which the motion may be made to 7 days. See the Advisory Committee's Note to Rule 29.

RESEARCH GUIDE

US Supreme Court Digest:
Criminal Law §§ 64, 65.

Federal Procedure L Ed:
Criminal Procedure, Fed Proc, L Ed, §§ 22:27, 22:28, 22:569, 22:824, 22:957, 22:958, 22:959, 22:960, 22:1199, 22:1207, 22:1230, 22:1237.

HOW TO USE
UNITED STATES SUPREME COURT REPORTS,
LAWYER'S EDITION

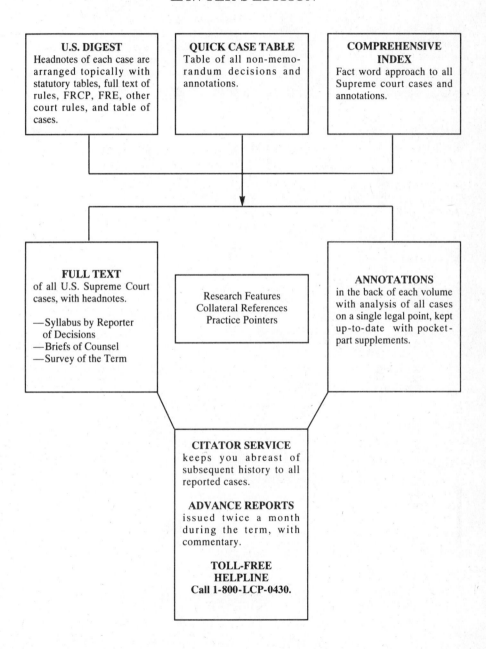

U.S. DIGEST
Headnotes of each case are arranged topically with statutory tables, full text of rules, FRCP, FRE, other court rules, and table of cases.

QUICK CASE TABLE
Table of all non-memorandum decisions and annotations.

COMPREHENSIVE INDEX
Fact word approach to all Supreme court cases and annotations.

FULL TEXT
of all U.S. Supreme Court cases, with headnotes.

—Syllabus by Reporter of Decisions
—Briefs of Counsel
—Survey of the Term

Research Features
Collateral References
Practice Pointers

ANNOTATIONS
in the back of each volume with analysis of all cases on a single legal point, kept up-to-date with pocket-part supplements.

CITATOR SERVICE
keeps you abreast of subsequent history to all reported cases.

ADVANCE REPORTS
issued twice a month during the term, with commentary.

TOLL-FREE HELPLINE
Call 1-800-LCP-0430.

The "How-To-Do-It" Units of the Total Client-Service Library

Once a lawyer has thoroughly researched the substantive law on any given problem, there remains the essential and often delicate task of applying this research intelligently and effectively to the real-life situation that confronts his client. Knowing how to use the law is just as crucial as knowing what the law is. Many confident lawyers, with the "law on their side," have lost cases simply because they did not know what to do or how to do it. It has often been said that such knowledge "cannot be learned from a book." But such a myth cannot withstand scrutiny, for it is precisely this kind of practical, how-to-do-it knowledge that is contained in the "How-To-Do-It" units of the Total Client-Service Library.

This portion of the TCSL consists of four sets of books:

*Am Jur Legal Forms 2d
*Am Jur Pleading and Practice Forms, Revised
*Am Jur Proof of Facts, 1st, 2d, and 3d Series
*Am Jur Trials

Together, these books provide such things as forms, checklists, guidelines, strategies, practice pointers, and illustrations...virtually everything a lawyer needs to know in order to prepare for and present a winning case.

Students as well will find these "How-To-Do-It" units of the TCSL extremely helpful in their trial practice courses, drafting courses, seminars, clinical programs, and the like.

Am Jur
Legal Forms 2d

Comprehensive Coverage

Am Jur Legal Forms 2d is a collection of thousands of forms, carefully edited and checked for validity, that are designed to aid the attorney in the preparation of "office practice" documents needed for a client's personal and business affairs. These forms are designated as "legal" forms to distinguish them from those that assist the attorney in preparing papers used in court proceedings.

Am Jur Legal Forms 2d consists of three basic elements: (1) the 35 volumes of forms and accompanying text and materials, organized under approximately 268 topics or chapters; (2) the two-volume general index pamphlets; and (3) the two-volume Federal Tax Guide to Am Jur Legal Forms 2d.

In all, Am Jur Legal Forms 2d provides the professional with forms and other drafting aids that cover practically every situation requiring a document outside of litigation. Thus, in addition to those forms that have been classified under basic legal titles such as Agency, Bailments, Descent and Distribution, Waters, and Wills, coverage will also be found under such modern titles as Condominiums; Co-operative Apartments; Consumer Credit Protection Acts; Housing Laws and Urban Development; and Premises and Products Liability.

Special Feature:
Federal Tax Guide to Legal Forms

The drafting of legal documents in today's practice requires a careful consideration of the tax consequences that will result when a document becomes operative. To alert and assist the attorney in this important area, Am Jur Legal Forms 2d includes two self-contained binders filled with discussions of federal tax problems, called Federal Tax Guide to Am Jur Legal Forms 2d. Copious references are made to the material in these binders at all appropriate places in Am Jur Legal Forms 2d. In addition, and for in-depth coverage, specific references are made in the Federal Tax Guide itself to the Federal Tax Coordinator 2d, the Tax Guide, and the Tax Action Coordinator published by the Research Institute of America (RIA), as well as to the article on Federal Taxation in Volumes 33, 34 and 34A of American Jurisprudence 2d.

The Federal Tax Guide to Am Jur Legal Forms 2d contains hundreds of paragraph title lines covering legal and business transactions in which a tax question may arise. The Federal Tax Guide is kept current through the replacement of individual pamphlets when necessary as well as through the issuance of conventional-style supplements appearing behind "Current Matter" tabs. This updating process covers new statutes, new regulations and rulings, court decisions, and the like.

¶ 105. Corporations.

A corporation is a legal entity separate from its stockholders and is treated as such for tax purposes. It is taxed on its gross income less certain deductions and credits, except for S corporations, which pass their taxable income through to their stockholders. Virtually all corporate transactions involve technical tax rules affecting the corporation and its stockholders.

Agreements, instruments and clauses used in connection with various corporate activities are discussed in the following section under these headings:

SAMPLE PAGES FROM THE FEDERAL TAX GUIDE TO AM JUR LEGAL FORMS 2d

CLAUSES COVERING	TAX POINTS

conduct of a trade or business in a U.S. possession and is received from an unrelated person. Hence a Code Sec. 936 corporation should provide for payment to it outside the U.S. in all its sales agreements, service contracts, and invoices, calling for payment to the corporation for transactions outside the U.S.

Authorities: Code Sec. 936(b); Fed Tax Coord 2d ¶ O-1503.

Inactive Corporations

67. Even though all the requirements of applicable corporate law have been complied with in order to organize a corporation, the corporation may be disregarded by IRS, for tax purposes, if it lacks a business purpose, or if it is merely an inactive "dummy" or "straw man" corporation. But it may be difficult for the *taxpayer* to establish that a corporation was an inactive "dummy" that should be disregarded. Where a corporation is disregarded, its income is taxed to its owners.

A corporation set up solely to avoid state usury laws will generally *not* be disregarded for tax purposes. However, if a corporation formed to avoid state usury laws, holds title to property as an agent, it will be disregarded for tax purposes if the facts demonstrate that a true agency relationship exists.

Authorities: Com. v. Bollinger Jr., Jesse, (1988) 485 US 340, 99 L Ed 2d 357; Burnet v. Commonwealth Improvement Co, (1932) 287 US 415, 77 L Ed 399; Fed Tax Coord 2d ¶ D-1200 et seq.

Real Estate and Mortgage Investment—Corporation with Over 99 Shareholders

75. A corporation that is engaged principally in investing in real estate and mortgages and has 100 or more shareholders may find it advantageous taxwise to convert into a business trust or association qualifying as a real estate investment trust. A real estate investment trust is taxable under more favorable rules than ordinary business corporations.

Authorities: Code Sec. 856 *et seq.*; Fed Tax Coord 2d ¶ E-7000 *et seq.*

Stocks and Other "Passive" Investments

81. Investments in stock of other corporations subject to U.S. taxes are attractive taxwise to corporate taxpayers because of the dividends-received deduction allowed to corporate taxpayers. This is generally 70% of dividends received from domestic corporations (100% for affiliated corporations filing separate returns and small business investment corporations), and 70% of the U.S. source portion of dividends received from certain foreign corporations that are 10%-owned by the U.S. corporate taxpayer. However, to the extent the stock investment is debt-financed, the dividends-received deduction is lost.

The dividends received deduction is 80% if the dividend is received from a "20% owned corporation." A "20% owned

The Features of Am Jur Legal Forms 2d
In addition to the vast collection of model
legal forms, each chapter in the set contains
several important features designed to guide
the user in the preparation and execution of
the desired document.

Preliminary Guides
Every chapter in Am Jur Legal Forms 2d begins
with a number of brief but important paragraphs
that should be scanned before going any further.
The Scope of Chapter paragraph states concisely
what the chapter covers; the Treated Elsewhere
paragraph leads to related subjects in other chapters of the set; citations to the federal tax guide

volume and to the federal tax coordinator 2d are
given under Federal Tax References; the
Federal Research References paragraph alerts
the user to other sets of books in the TCSL where
relevant federal law is discussed; ALR System
References leads to appropriate annotations on
the subject; and finally, the Practice Aids paragraph directs attention to other "How-To-Do-It"
units of the TCSL that may be helpful in the
preparation of the desired document.

To assist in the location of specific forms and
other definitive material, each chapter contains
a general or "skeleton" outline, followed by a
detailed outline listing each section in the chapter.

**STATEMENTS
OF SCOPE AND
RELATED TOPICS**

**FEDERAL TAX
AND RESEARCH
REFERENCES**

**ALR
REFERENCES**

Condominiums

Scope of Chapter: This chapter contains forms for the establishment of
"apartment" ownership in condominium projects; the purchase and
sale of condominium units and their financing; and the management,
operation, and permitted uses of the condominium project and
individual condominium units.

Treated Elsewhere: Related subjects treated elsewhere are associations
and clubs (see Ch 27), cooperative apartments (see Ch 70), deeds
(see Ch 87), mortgages and trust deeds (see Ch 179), real estate
sales (see Ch 219), and real property (see Ch 220).

Federal Tax References: FEDERAL TAX GUIDE TO LEGAL FORMS,
Associations ¶¶ 189-A et seq.; Clubs ¶ 189-H-11 et seq.; Cooperative
Housing and Condominiums ¶ 165-I; Mortgages ¶ 140-S-61;
Property ¶ 165 et seq.; 34 AM JUR 2d, Federal Taxation ¶¶ 4263,
7039, 7410; RIA TAX COORDINATOR, Sales and Exchanges ¶¶ I-3105,
I-3206, I-3207; Taxes, Interest, Medical Expenses, etc. ¶¶ K-5206, K-
5805, K-5807.

Federal Research References: US L ED DIGEST, Associations and Clubs;
Federal Housing Administration; Real Property; Sales; US L ED
INDEX TO ANNOTATIONS, Associations and Clubs; Deeds; Federal
Housing Administration; Mortgages.

ALR System References: ALR INDEX TO ANNOTATIONS, Apartments and
Apartment Houses; Co-operative Apartments; Covenants; Deeds;
Easements; Homesteads; Mortgages; Property; Sale and Transfer of
Property; ALR DIGESTS, Associations and Clubs; Cooperative
Associations; Corporations; Vendor and Purchaser.

5 Am Jur Legal Forms 2d (Rev)   **249**

The Outlines

To speed the user to the specific forms
and materials needed, each chapter contains
a general or "skeleton" outline, followed by a
detailed outline listing the section headings in
the chapter.

I. GENERAL CONSIDERATIONS (§§ 64:1, 64:2)

II. PLAN OF OWNERSHIP
   A. IN GENERAL (§§ 64:11 TO 64:15)
   B. FORMS (§§ 64:16 TO 64:19)

III. SUBSCRIPTION AND PURCHASE
   A. PURCHASE AGREEMENT (§§ 64:31 TO 64:44)
   B. CONVEYANCES (§§ 64:51 TO 64:61)

IV. MANAGEMENT AND OPERATION
   A. ASSOCIATION OF OWNERS (§§ 64:71 TO 64:89)
   B. MANAGEMENT AGENT (§§ 64:101 TO 64:113)

V FINANCING
   A. MORTGAGES (§§ 64:121, 64:122)
   B. COMMITMENT TO INSURE (§§ 64:131 TO 64:144)

VI. COVENANTS, CONDITIONS, AND RESTRIC-
TIONS
   A. IN GENERAL (§§ 64:151, 64:152)
   B. FORMS (§§ 64:161 TO 64:164)

VII. LEASE OF UNIT (§§ 64:171, 64:172)

**SKELETON OUTLINE
OF MAIN CHAPTER
DIVISIONS**

**DETAILED OUTLINE OF
SECTIONS CONTAINING
FORMS AND OTHER
PERTINENT MATERIAL**

CONDOMINIUMS

II. PLAN OF OWNERSHIP

   A. IN GENERAL

§ 64:11 Scope of division
§ 64:12 Form drafting guide
§ 64:13 —Checklist—Matters to be considered in drafting a
       master deed or enabling declaration
§ 64:14 Formal requirements—Execution
§ 64:15 —Acknowledgment

   B. FORMS

§ 64:16 Plan of ownership—Master deed
§ 64:17 —Enabling declaration
§ 64:18 Lease agreement—Recreational facilities—Between
       developer and condominium association
§ 64:19 Pledge agreement for recreational facilities—By unit
       owner—For use in connection with lease agree-
       ment

III. SUBSCRIPTION AND PURCHASE

   A. PURCHASE AGREEMENT

      1. IN GENERAL

§ 64:31 Scope of division
§ 64:32 Form drafting guide—Federal Housing Authority
§ 64:33 —Federal Truth in Lending Act

Background Material

The opening section of each chapter and each major subdivision in the chapter contains a clear, concise statement of the applicable substantive law, with definitions of important terms, govern- ing the form or forms that follow. In the event that a more exhaustive analysis of the law is necessary, these sections are thoroughly cross-referenced to Am Jur 2d, ALR, and other sources.

I. GENERAL CONSIDERATIONS

§ 64:1 Introductory comments

The term "condominium" refers to a type of group ownership of multiunit property in which each member of the group has title to a specific part of the improvements to the real property, and an undivided interest with the whole group in the common areas and facilities.[1] Each condominium owner in a multiunit structure has title to the "family unit" in fee simple, while holding an undivided interest in stairways, halls, lobbies, doorways, and other common areas and facilities.[2]

The primary characteristics of condominium ownership are:

(1) Individual ownership of a unit or apartment,

(2) An ownership interest in certain designated common areas or facilities that serve all units in the condominium, and

(3) An agreement among the unit owners regulating the administration and maintenance of the property.[3]

1. *Text references:* Definitions and terminology of "condominium" and related terms. 15A Am Jur 2d (Rev), Condominiums and Cooperative Apartments § 1.

Legal periodicals: The new Uniform Condominium Act. 64 ABAJ 1370.

—Government regulation of condominium conversion. 8 Boston College Environmental Affairs LR 919.

—Community Apartments: Condominium or Stock Cooperative? 50 Cal LR 299.

—Kids allowed—Children may not be excluded from apartments or condos. 3 Calif Lawyer No. 11, p 22.

—Condominium: Shelter on a statutory foundation. 63 Colum LR 987.

—The "Model Condominium Code"—A blueprint for modernizing condominium legislation. 78 Colum LR 587.

(For Tax Notes and Notes on Use, see end of form)

254   **5 Am Jur Legal Forms 2d (Rev)**

Form Drafting Guides

In keeping with the thoroughly practical nature of Am Jur Legal Forms 2d, a Form Drafting Guide is included in every major subdivision of each chapter in the set. Here the user will find step-by-step guidance for the preparation of each form, along with healthy words of caution to ensure the avoidance of hidden pitfalls. As is the case with all of the textual material in Am Jur Legal Forms 2d, the Form Drafting Guides are completely cross-referenced to the TCSL and other appropriate legal sources for detailed discussions of the applicable law.

Checklists

Following the Form Drafting Guide is a Checklist of matters that should be considered in the drafting of the desired document. These Checklists help to ensure that nothing is overlooked.

Tax Notes

Following many of the forms in the set is a section entitled Tax Notes. These notes, which are keyed to the appropriate sections of the preceding form, refer the user to specific paragraphs in the Federal Tax Guide volume where the tax implications and authorities are covered.

Notes on Use

To ensure that the user is alerted to every possible legal consideration affecting a particular form, a Notes On Use section appears at the end of the forms. Here the user is referred to related material in other units of the TCSL, as well as to relevant law review articles.

II. PLAN OF OWNERSHIP

A. In General

§ 64:11 Scope of division

Some material in this division consists of forms setting forth the essentials of plans of apartment ownership. Included in this division are pertinent form drafting guides, checklists, federal tax references, and annotations for use in drafting such plans.

§ 64:12 Form drafting guide

The "master deed," or enabling declaration, is the primary document by which property is committed to the condominium form of ownership.[4] Generally, condominium statutes apply only to such property as is specifically submitted to the provisions of the statute, by recordation of the declaration with the proper designated county official.[5] In some states condominiums may be established only in they may be established in either an existir

☑ **Caution:** Counsel should consult the c condominium statutes with which counsel

(For Tax Notes and Notes on Use

256   5

---

§ 64:13 Form drafting guide—Checklist—Matters to be considered in drafting a master deed or enabling declaration

☑ **Checklist** of matters that should be considered in a master deed or enabling declaration:

- Location of property.
- Legal description of entire property (survey map of land included within condominium project).
- Floor plan of building or buildings existing or to be built.
- Description of land and facilities to be owned in common by all unit owners.
- Description of facilities of common nature that are to be limited to particular apartments, if any.
- Legal description of each unit or apartment.
- Percentage of ownership interest in common area and facilities allocated to each unit.
- Provision for association of owners.
- Provision for board of directors or managing agent to act for association of owners in managing building.
- Rights, liabilities, privileges, and duties of owners.
- Rights, liabilities, privileges, and duties of management.

(For Tax Notes and Notes on Use, see end of form)

5 Am Jur Legal Forms 2d (Rev)   257

The Forms

Each of the model forms in Am Jur Legal Forms 2d is thoroughly accurate, correctly worded, and legally sound. The forms were selected and drawn with the assistance of leading law firms, corporate legal departments, and state and federal agencies. Special attention was given to appropriate state and federal statutes and judicial decisions. In addition, many of the forms offer the flexibility of optional clauses and alternate language should the facts warrant special tailoring. Thus, Am Jur Legal Forms 2d provides the most comprehensive and practical form-drafting aids available today.

---

§ 64:17 Plan of ownership—Enabling declaration

ENABLING DECLARATION
ESTABLISHING A PLAN FOR
CONDOMINIUM OWNERSHIP

Grantor, its successors and assigns, by this declaration, and all future owners of the family units, by their acceptance of individual deeds, covenant as follows:

SECTION ONE
OWNERSHIP OF PROPERTY

__1____ *[Name]*, referred to as grantor, owns certain real property described in this instrument.

SECTION TWO
DESCRIPTION OF PROJECT

Grantor has improved the described property by constructing on it a __2____-unit multifamily structure known as __3____ *[name of condominium]*, which was constructed in accordance with plans and specifications prepared by __4____ *[architect]*, on record in the __5____ *[city office]* of the City of __6____, State of __7____, and styled __8____ *[characterization or class of project]*, FHA Project No. __9__, and consisting of sheets __10____ *[number]* through __11____ *[number]*, __12____ *[number]* through __13____ *[number]*, and the like, all inclusive.

Attached and made a part as Exhibit "A" is a survey consisting of __14____ *[number]* sheets prepared by __15____ *[surveyor]*, dated __16____, 19__17__.

SECTION THREE
ALLOCATION OF AREAS

Grantor, in order to establish a plan of condominium ownership for the

(For Tax Notes and Notes on Use, see end of form)

266   **5 Am Jur Legal Forms 2d (Rev)**

TYPICAL FORM WITH NUMBERED BLANK

BRACKETED WORDS INDICATE NATURE OF MATERIAL TO BE INSERTED IN BLANK

Finding the forms

Each form or related editorial topic in Am Jur Legal Forms 2d carries a section number. The first number in the section designation is the number of the chapter; this number is followed by a colon and the individual section number. Thus, a reference to 64:1 is the first section in Chapter 64 on Condominiums.

The topical approach

If the user knows the general topic area in which a desired form is likely to appear, he or she may proceed directly to the appropriate chapter in the set and find the form by using the general and detailed outlines at the beginning of the chapter. To assist with this approach, the first and last chapters contained in each volume are stamped on the spine of the volume itself, and a complete list of the chapters in the volume is printed on the inside of the front cover. For detailed discussion of the Topical Approach to legal research, see pages 6-8, dealing with Am Jur 2d.

The indexes

A two-pamphlet General Index covers the forms in all topics in a single alphabetical arrangement. In addition, a single alphabetical fact-word index in the back of each pamphlet covers the material in that volume. Both indexes apply the TAPP-rule, allowing the user to look for descriptive words that suggest the Thing, Act, Person or Place involved in the particular form needed. The references in the indexes are to section numbers only (see above) and these section numbers are carried on the outer top edges of each page of the text volume. If a reference is obtained from the General Index, the section numbers appearing on the spine of the text volumes will indicate the volume containing the desired material. A separate volume index appears in the Federal Tax Guide to Legal Forms 2d.

Supplementation

Am Jur Legal Forms 2d is kept up-to-date with cumulative pocket supplements. New forms, Tax Notes, Notes On Use, and other pertinent material, including new index lines, are added regularly to keep the set current with developing law and practice.

Am Jur Pleading and Practice Forms, Revised

Sources and Coverage

Comprised of 36 volumes of forms and 2 pamphlet indexes, Am Jur Pleading and Practice Forms, Revised, contains more than 25,000 expertly drawn and court-proven practice documents covering all phases of a court proceeding. For example, there are such pretrial forms as petitions and complaints; demurrers; bills of particulars and interrogatories. Also, there are forms needed during the progress of a trial, such as notices, orders, writs, and jury instructions. Furthermore, there are post-trial forms such as judgments, motions for a directed verdict or new trial, and forms required for appeal or review. Thousands of forms have been taken from the files and court records of practitioners in every jurisdiction, including the federal jurisdiction. As a result of the careful planning in the collection and collation of these forms, Am Jur Pleading and Practice Forms, Revised, provides a depth of coverage that could not be equalled in a collection of forms that have been "localized" wherever appropriate by specific references to state statutes or procedural rules.

The 363 main legal topics under which the forms in this set are classified include the usual "practice" topics such as Appeal and Error; Appearance; Certiorari; Coram Nobis and Allied Statutory Remedies; Deposition and Discovery; Parties; and Venue. The greater number of forms, however, are comprehensive collections under substantive law topics, such as Automobiles and Highway Traffic; Conflict of Law; Corporations; Executors and Administrators; Insurance; Products Liability; and Zoning and Planning.

Features of Am Jur Pleading and Practice

In this set, the editors have added many useful features to assist the attorney in meeting the needs of modern courtroom practice. A Procedural Timetable in the front of each volume lists the principal procedural steps to be followed in chronological order. In addition, each topic contains specifically keyed time-saving features.

Statutory and procedural rules references

Where applicable, Statutory References appear in each division of a topic, directing the user to the law in his or her own jurisdiction, thus allowing any local adaptation needed in the document. Changes in the statutes or rules are duly noted in the periodic pocket supplements.

BAIL AND RECOGNIZANCE

BAIL AND RECOGNIZANCE

COLLATERAL REFERENCES

The Auto-Cite® computer research system allows case citations to be checked for form, parallel references, later history, and annotation references.

ANNOTATIONS

Validity of statute abolishing commercial bail bond business, 19 ALR4th 355.

Bail: effect on surety's liability under bail bond of principal's subsequent incarceration in same jurisdiction, 35 ALR4th 1192.

Failure of person, released pursuant to provisions of Federal Bail Reform Act of 1966 (18 USCS §§ 3141 et seq.), to make appearance as subjecting person to penalty provided for by 18 USCS § 3150, 66 ALR Fed 668.

Propriety of denial of pretrial bail under Bail Reform Act (18 USCS §§ 3141 et seq.), 75 ALR Fed 806.

STATUTORY REFERENCES

Ala C §§ 15-13-1 et seq.;
Alaska Stat §§ 09.40.120 et seq., 12.30.010 et seq.;
Ark C §§ 16-109-104 et seq.;
Cal CCP §§ 515.010; Pen C §§ 1268 et seq.;
Conn Gen S §§ 52-313 et seq.;
11 Del C §§ 2101 et seq.;
DC C §§ 16-704 et seq.;
Fla Stat §§ 903.02 et seq.;
Ga C §§ 17-7-90;
Hawaii RS §§ 804-1 et seq.;
Idaho C 8-109 et seq.;
Ill RS ch 16 §§ 51 et seq.;
Ind C 34 1-6-6 et seq.;
Kan Stat 22-2801 et seq.;
Ky RS 434E.2-070, 434E.2-280;
La RS 15:81 et seq.;
Me RS tit 14 § 5544; tit 15 § 942;
Md C art 27 §§ 12B, 638A;
Mass Gen L ch 224 §§ 6 et seq.;
Mich Comp L §§ 600.6075 et seq. [MSA §§ 27A.6075 et seq.];
Minn Stat 629.41 et seq.;
Miss C §§ 99-5-1 et seq.;
Mo RS §§ 544.420 et seq.;

Mont C 27-16-101 et seq.; 46-9-201 et seq.;
Neb RS §§ 29-302 et seq.;
Nev RS 31.550 et seq.;
NH RS 597:1 et seq.;
NJ Stat 2A:15-43 et seq.;
NM Stat 31-3-1 et seq.;
NY CPL §§ 500.10 et seq.;
NC Gen S §§ 1-409 et seq., 15A-531 et seq.;
ND CC 29-08-01 et seq.;
Ohio RC §§ 2713.09 et seq.;
22 Okla Stat §§ 1101 et seq.;
Or RS 29.560 et seq.;
Pa 42 PS §§ 5701 et seq.;
RI Gen L 10-11-1 et seq., 12-4-1 et seq.;
SC C §§ 17-15-10 et seq.;
SD CL 21-27-17 et seq., 23A-43-2 et seq.;
Tenn C §§ 40-11-101 et seq.;
Tex CCP art 17.01 et seq.;
US 18 USCS §§ 3141 et seq.;
Vt RS tit 12 §§ 3471 et seq.; tit 13 §§ 7551 et seq.;
Va C §§ 19.2-119 et seq.;
W Va C §§ 53-7-2 et seq., 62-1C-1 et seq.;
Wis Stat 969.01 et seq.;
Wyo Stat 1-288 et seq.

PROCEDURAL RULES REFERENCES

Ala RJA 2;
Alaska RCP 41;
Ariz RCP 7.1 et seq.;
Cal RC 32(b), 801;
Colo R Crim P 46;
Conn PB §§ 2060 et seq.;
Del Com P Crim R 46; J. P. Crim R 28; Super Ct Crim R 46;
DC SCR Crim 46;
Fla RCrP 3.130;
Hawaii RPP 5(a), 38, 46;
Idaho CR 46;
Ill (ch 110A § 553) Rule 553;
Ky CR 4.00 et seq.;
La C Cr P arts 311 et seq.;
Me RCrP 46;
Md Rules 721, 722;
Mass R Crim P 7(a)(1);
Mich GCR 712.17;

Mo Rule 32.01 et seq.;
NJ Rule 3:26-1 et seq., 7:5-1 et seq.;
NM R Crim P 22 et seq.; Crim App Rule 204, 401;
NY CPLR Rule 7201(c);
ND R Crim P 46;
Ohio Crim R 46;
Okla Rule of Ct of Crim A 3.7;
Pa RCP 1481; R Cr P 4001 et seq.;
RI Super R Crim P 46; Dist R Crim P 46;
SC Cir Ct R 9, 10, 35;
Tex RCP 2, 180;
US Fed RCP 46; FRAP 9, 41; Sup Ct Rule 49;
Vt Cr P 5, 46; RAP 9, 41;
Va Sup Ct Rule 3A:29;
Wash CrR 3.2; JCrR 2.09;
Wyo R Cr P 8, 39.
[Local statutes or rules should be examined]

REFERENCES TO STATE AND FEDERAL STATUTES AND PROCEDURAL RULES

STATUTORY CHANGES ARE COVERED IN SUPPLEMENT

23 Am Jur Pl. and Pr Forms (Rev)

CHECK LIST

To state a cause of action for trespass to real property, a complaint, petition, or declaration, should allege:

+ Jurisdictional facts, if required.

+ Facts fixing venue, when required, especially county in which real property is located.

+ Facts concerning diversity of citizenship and amount in controversy, if complaint is to be filed in federal court as a diversity action.

+ A description of the property sufficient to identify and locate it (need not be the legal description).

+ Plaintiff's actual or constructive possession (right to immediate possession) of property.

+ Facts showing that a trespass was committed.

+ Time during which trespass was committed (great leeway is permitted respecting this allegation).

+ Injury to property, if any, resulting from the trespass (not an essential allegation since trespass is an intentional tort from which the law imports damage, but necessary if substantial damages are to be recovered).

+ Facts showing the case to be a proper one for exemplary or multiple damages if such damages are justified on the grounds of malice, fraud, wilfulness, or wantonness, and, if applicable, the statutory authority for such an award.

+ Damages:
— General
— Special
— Exemplary.

If injunction is sought instead of, or in addition to, damages, facts showing inadequacy of remedy at law, such as:

+ Continuance or repetition, or threat to continue or repeat, trespass.

+ Irreparable injury
— Destruction or injury to land or to use and enjoyment amounting to virtual dispossession;
— Danger defendant's acts may ripe ment;
— Insolvency or financial irresponsi

+ Impossibility or extreme difficulty of

+ Need for multiplicity of actions to o

504

Check Lists enumerate points to be considered for adequate coverage in the document and guard against errors and omissions.

Governing Principles affecting the legal rights or procedural steps involved are stated at all appropriate places within a topic. Cross references lead to in-depth treatment of the applicable law.

I. PRELIMINARY PROCEEDINGS

A. Placement of Cases on Calendar and Setting of Trial Dates

Governing Principles

Statutes and rules of court provide for the placing of actions on the trial calendar and the order in which cases thereon shall be tried. Certain cases are given preference over others on the calendar. Many jurisdictions provide for a short cause calendar on which may be placed cases which can be tried within certain time limits. (Am Jur 2d *Trial;* 53 Am Jur *Trial* [1st ed] §§ 5, 6.)

An action must be brought to issue by the pleadings or by a pre-trial order before trial can be had. The fixing of a time for trial rests in the discretion of the trial court, and a case is set for trial by entering an order fixing a certain day on or after which the case may be called for trial. Statutes or rules frequently require that notice of trial be given, but in the absence of such statute or rule notice need not be given a party. In some jurisdictions notice of trial should be given to the party and not just to his attorney. (Am Jur 2d *Trial;* 53 Am Jur *Trial* [1st ed] §§ 8–10.)

532

Finding the forms

The forms in Am Jur Pleading and Practice Forms, Revised, are numbered in sequence within each topic, beginning with Form 1. Thus, a reference to "Trusts 16" refers to the 16th form in the topic on Trusts.

The index pamphlets

Each volume contains a single, alphabetical fact/word index covering all the forms included in such volume. In addition, there are two General Index pamphlets to all the forms in the entire set. In each of the indexes, the TAPP-rule is followed, allowing the user to search for descriptive words that suggest the Thing, Act, Person or Place involved in the needed form.

The topical approach

Use of the general and detailed outlines preceding each topic is another means of locating special forms. This method is usually called the "topical approach".

Supplementation

To keep Am Jur Pleading and Practice Forms current, annual pocket parts are issued. These include new forms, as well as updated statutory references, new case notes, new annotation references and other pertinent new material.

Am Jur
Proof of Facts

*First, Second
and Third Series*

Am Jur Proof of Facts (commonly referred to
as POF) fills a most important role in the structure
of "how-to-do-it" publications. Concisely stated,
it is a synthesis of substantive law, elements of
damages, elements of proof, and sample testimony
designed to assist in the preparation for, and the
proving of facts that may be at issue in, judicial
or administrative proceedings.

Am Jur Proof of Facts consists of three series
of books. Am Jur Proof of Facts 3d (POF3d)
is a continuation of the second series (Vols. 1-50),
which is a continuation of the first series (Vols.
1-30). Each new series reflects various improvements. The articles in all three series cover a wide
range of topics describing and illustrating proof
of ultimate facts essential to either plaintiff or
defendant.

The material in POF, POF2d, and POF3d can
be used for a variety of purposes, such as initial
client interview; interviewing prospective witnesses; taking depositions; preparing for settlement

negotiations; introducing documentary and other
evidence; and examining and cross-examining
witnesses.

The following is a list of generic categories that
reflect the wide range of topic coverage in POF,
POF2d, and POF3d:

Banks
Building Construction
Business Enterprises
Commercial (including UCC)
Contracts
Criminal Law
Damages
Defamation
Eminent Domain
Employment
Family Law
Insurance
Landlord-Tenant
Malpractice
Municipalities
Personal Injury/Wrongful Death
Products Liability
Real Property
Securities
Taxation
Trial
Unemployment/Workers' Compensation
Vendor/Purchaser
Water
Wills, Trusts, and Estates
Zoning

Each article in POF 2d consists of four main parts: (1) Prefatory material; (2) background material; and (3) the Proofs and their accompanying materials; and (4) damages for all possible types of recovery for an injury.

1. Prefatory material
Topic of Article:

Similar to the "scope note" found at the beginning of the encyclopedic articles in Am Jur 2d, a "fact in issue" or "topic of article" statement appears at the beginning of each POF article.

This concise statement reveals precisely what the article deals with and enables the user quickly to determine if it covers a fact situation involved in a case under consideration.

TEMPOROMANDIBULAR JOINT INJURIES*

*DALE M. FOREMAN, J.D.,** and DONALD M. ROLFS, D.D.S.***

Topic of article: Proof of the nature and extent to which a person has suffered an injury to the temporomandibular joint. This issue may arise in a personal injury or dental malpractice action, or in an action under a workers' compensation statute.

I. BACKGROUND

§ 1. Anatomy and physiology of the temporomandibular joint
§ 2. TMJ disorders—Overview
§ 3. —Causative factors
§ 4. —TMJ internal derangement—Stage I
§ 5. —TMJ internal derangement—Stage II
§ 6. —TMJ internal derangement—Stage III
§ 7. —TMJ internal derangement—Stage IV
§ 8. Diagnosis—Overview

* Portions of this article are adapted from WHIPLASH AND THE JAW JOINT: A MANUAL FOR LAWYERS, DENTISTS, AND INSURANCE ADJUSTERS: TMJ INJURY, by Dale M. Foreman and Donald A. Rolfs, D.D.S.; published by Book Publishing Company, 201 Westlake Avenue North, Seattle, Washington 98109; copyright 1985, Dale M. Foreman and Donald A. Rolfs, D.D.S.

** Mr. Foreman, who graduated from the Harvard Law School, is a member of the firm of Jardine, Foreman & Appel with offices in Seattle, Spokane, and Wenatchee, Washington, and Los Angeles, California. He is a member of the bar in the states of Washington and California, and a member of the Association of Trial Lawyers of America, Washington State Trial Lawyers Association, and American Bar Association. He has settled and tried numerous TMJ cases and has been a speaker at many continuing education seminars for lawyers and dentists.

*** Dr. Rolfs is a periodontist in Wenatchee, Washington. He is a graduate of the University of Washington Dental School and is the author of scientific articles and book chapters. He has been a speaker at dental conventions throughout the United States and Europe.

1 Am Jur Proof of Facts 3d   123

Topical Outline
Each article is divided into sections. Section headings are listed in the topical outline (table of contents) preceding each article furnishing immediate reference to sections meeting specific needs.

TCSL References

Every POF article contains references that will guide the user to sources of additional information. In addition to references to related POF articles and to the various units of the TCSL, there are also references to other authoritative legal and medical texts and periodicals. In the first and second series these references are found in the prefatory material. In the third series the TCSL references are in the prefatory material and the additional references are in a Bibliography at the end of the article.

TMJ INJURIES   **1 POF3d 123**

TOTAL CLIENT-SERVICE LIBRARY®

AM JUR PROOF OF FACTS

Anatomy of Facial Skeleton, POF FACT BOOK § I:137
Damages for Headaches, 3 POF 491, Proof No. 27
Dental Injuries, 4 POF 315
Dental Malpractice, 36 POF2d 1
Depression Following Trauma, 29 POF 529
Jaw and Facial Fractures, 6 POF 553
Malingering, 7 POF 427
Neck Injuries, 37 POF2d 223
Pain and Suffering, 23 POF2d 1
Traumatic Cause or Aggravation of Condition Affecting Mobility of Joints, 30 POF2d 511

AM JUR 2d

Damages for injuries to face and jaw, 22 AM JUR 2d, Damages § 378 (1965)
Workers' compensation for particular injuries or disabilities, 82 AM JUR 2d, Workmen's Compensation §§ 289-337 (1976)

AM JUR TRIALS

Dental Malpractice Litigation, 25 AM JUR TRIALS 495
Determining the Medical and Emotional Bases for Damages, 23 AM JUR TRIALS 479

Article Index

Each article in POF is preceded by a fine-point subject index that allows the user to locate specific material at a glance.

TMJ INJURIES   **1 POF3d 123**

INDEX

Acute lock, §§ 4, 5	Crepitus, § 7
Acute trauma, § 3	Damages, §§ 20, 21
Advances	Defense considerations, § 18
– technology, § 12	Definitions, §§ 1, 19
– treatment, § 17	Degenerative arthritis, § 7

---

2. Background Text

Each article contains background textual
discussion setting forth the underlying law
relating to the "Proofs" presented in the article.
Leading case and text authorities are cited,
together with collateral research references.

I. BACKGROUND

§ 1. Anatomy and physiology of the temporomandibular joint

The temporomandibular joint (TMJ) is the articulation between the lower jaw, or mandible, and the base of the skull. (See Diagram 3 at the end of this section.) Frequently referred to as the "craniomandibular articulation," the TMJ is comprised of a unique and complex joint system.

One unique aspect of the craniomandibular articulation is that the mandible has a joint at both ends, each of which is affected by the other. No movement can take place at either end of the two joints without affecting the other end, although, under most circumstances, the movement is different in direction and magnitude.

3. The Proofs

The main part of each article is the "Proofs." At least one proof is included in every article; many contain two or more.

Preceding each proof, the Elements of Proof section furnishes a convenient guide and checklist for the planning of a case and serves as an invaluable reminder of the necessary or possible points involved in establishing the facts in issue.

---

1 POF3d 123
§ 22

TMJ INJURIES

III. ELEMENTS OF PROOF

§ 22. Checklist—Elements of proof of TMJ injury

The following facts and circumstances tend to establish that the plaintiff has suffered temporomandibular joint dysfunction due to trauma caused by the defendant's negligence:

☐ Injury sustained by plaintiff [§ 25]

☐ Condition of plaintiff's temporomandibular joint prior to trauma [§§ 26, 33]

☐ Symptoms of TMJ dysfunction
—Headache [§§ 25, 26, 29, 31, 33]
—Clicking in jaw during opening [§§ 5, 8]
—Popping in jaw during opening [§ 29]
—Grating in jaw on opening [§§ 7, 8]
—Pain in jaw [§§ 26, 29, 31]
—Inability to open jaw fully [§ 29]
—Locking of jaw [§ 33]
—Ringing in ears [§ 33]
—Blurred vision [§ 33]
—Irritability [§ 33]

☐ Diagnosis of plaintiff's condition as TMJ problem
—Medical and social history of patient [§ 29]
—Review of previous medical and dental records [§ 9]
—Interview of patient [§ 9]
—Physical examination of patient [§§ 9, 29]
— —Vital signs
— —Auscultation
— —Postural irregularities
— —Dentition of patient
— —Evidence of bruxism
— —Malocclusion
— —Palpation of jaw joint
— —Manipulation of mandible revealing rotational or translation phase abnormality
— —Head and neck screening
— —Dental and periodontal examination
—Diagnostic anesthetic blocks [§ 9]
—Intraoral and extraoral photographs [§ 9]
—Centric relation records [§ 10]
—Plaster models of mouth [§ 31]

4. Elements of Damages
Here there is a list of all potential damages
to maximize recovery.

II. DAMAGES

§ 20. Elements of damages checklist

Testimony as to the following elements of damages should be elicited, when applicable, from the plaintiff and his witnesses in a personal injury action arising from an injury to the temporomandibular joint:

Damages recoverable by or on behalf of injured person—

☐ Necessary and reasonable medical expenses
　　—Actual past expenses for physician, hospital, nursing, and laboratory fees; medicines; prosthetic devices; etc.
　　—Anticipated future expenses [69 ALR2d 1261]

☐ Necessary and reasonable dental expenses
　　—Actual past expenses for consultation, diagnosis, treatment, prescriptions, orthotic devices, etc.
　　—Anticipated future expenses

☐ Necessary and reasonable chiropractic and physical therapy expenses
　　—Actual past expenses for treatment
　　—Anticipated future expenses

☐ Loss of past and future earnings [15 POF2d 311]
　　—Actual loss of wages or salary
　　—Loss of existing vocational skill
　　—Loss of capacity to earn increased wages [18 ALR3d 88]
　　—Loss of profits or net income by person engaged in business [45 ALR3d 345]

☐ Cost of hiring substitute or assistant [37 ALR2d 364]

☐ Pain and suffering from physical injuries [23 POF2d 1]

☐ Pain and suffering reasonably likely to occur in the future [18 ALR3d 10]

☐ Mental anguish
　　—Anxiety, depression, and other mental suffering or illness [29 POF 529; 30 POF 1; 29 POF2d 571]
　　—Physical injuries caused by mental anguish

☐ Harm from loss of sleep [28 POF 1]

☐ Sexual dysfunction

☐ Past and future impairment of ability to enjoy life [24 POF 171; 34 ALR4th 293]

Damages recoverable by dependents of injured person—

Supplementation

POF is supplemented in two ways. First,
because POF is a serial publication, new volumes
containing current articles are continually added
to the set, usually at the rate of three volumes per
year. Second, all of the articles in existing volumes
are brought up-to-date by the regular issuance of
pocket supplements, which appear inside the back
cover of each volume. Together, these methods
assure the most complete coverage available of
developing law and practice in the proof of facts.

POF Fact Book

A unique special volume, the POF Fact Book
with Medical Glossary places at the fingertips
of the attorney a broad range of legal, medical,
and technical information drawn from many
sources. The data is invaluable in understanding
and proving various types of accidents and injuries,
as well as in identifying experts for purposes of
consultation or testimony.

POF Medical Dictionary

The newest feature of POF is the Medical
Dictionary, introduced with the third series.
Taber's Cyclopedic Medical Dictionary has
been reprinted to provide the POF user with
the definitions, illustrations, and additional appendix material of an established and distinguished
medical dictionary. The dictionary is styled and
bound to match the most recent POF series while
retaining the wealth of medical information that
health practitioners have relied on for decades.

Finding the Proofs
The POF Pamphlet Index

Comprehensive, detailed, yet simple-to-use
three index pamphlets provide the user with
much greater depth of coverage and only one
place to look for POF articles from the 1st,
2nd and POF 3d series.

At the end of the last index volume are lists of
POF articles by volume; also included is a table
of authors and diagrams in the POF articles.

Am Jur
Trials

Am Jur Trials is a unique set of books designed to acquaint the lawyer with court-proven techniques for every aspect of successful preparation and presentation of his case at the trial level. It is an encyclopedic guide to the modern practices, procedures, and strategies used in preparing and trying cases, with model programs for the handling of all types of litigation. More than 180 lawyers, all busy and successful practitioners, have participated in the preparation of Am Jur

Trials. These lawyer-authors were selected on the basis of specialty experience, and reputation, as well as for their willingness to disclose, frankly and completely, those methods that have proved most successful in their own litigation. The result is a comprehensive, lawyer-to-lawyer publication that reveals, on a step-by-step basis, the proper procedures and tactics involved in winning lawsuits, from the client interview through the final judgment.

The Format of Am Jur Trials

The articles in Am Jur Trials have been arranged in two main divisions. Volumes 1-6 are devoted to office and courtroom procedural issues that are common to most types of litigation. These volumes are known as the "Practice, Strategy, and Controls" division. The balance of the volumes is known as the "Model Trials" division, and is devoted to expert "how to do it" aspects of particular kinds of criminal and civil actions.

Practice, Strategy, and Controls

Volumes 1-6 of Am Jur Trials consist of comprehensive articles discussing every phase of trial preparation and presentation, from interviewing the client to the return of the verdict. Each article is written by an expert, and the textual discussion is supplemented by forms, charts, diagrams, photographs of actual evidence, checklists, illustrations, and other aids to guide the reader toward successful litigation, be it civil or criminal. Among the dozens of such articles in Volumes 1-6 are: Interviewing the Client, Setting the Fee, Investigating the Criminal Case, Investigating the Civil Case, Locating and Interviewing Witnesses, Selecting the Forum, Discovery, Settling the Case, Tactics and Strategy of Pleading, Selecting the Jury, Courtroom Semantics, and Summations. Many of the articles feature separate treatments of the subject from the point of view of both defendant and plaintiff. And, of course, throughout Am Jur Trials are helpful references to all other units of the TCSL. The following illustrations will serve to demonstrate just some of the features of the "Practice, Strategy, and Controls" division of Am Jur Trials.

172

**SKELETON
ARTICLE OUTLINE
ANALYZES THE
TOPIC**

**ALL AUTHORS
ARE EXPERTS
IN THEIR FIELD**

JORDAN S. GRUBER

Videotape Evidence

JORDAN S. GRUBER is president of LexTech Consulting, a
research and communications firm emphasizing legal, technological, and psychological innovation, located in Menlo Park,
California. Mr. Gruber received a bachelor's degree with honors
in philosophy (Phi Beta Kappa) from the State University of
New York at Binghamton and a master's degree in public policy
analysis and administration from the same institution. He
obtained his law degree from the University of Virginia School
of Law, where he was elected to the Order of the Coif and served
as Research and Projects Editor of the *Virginia Law Review.* Mr.
Gruber was an associate attorney at the law firm of Cooley,
Godward, Castro, Huddleson & Tatum in Palo Alto, California.
He is also the former managing editor of *Gnosis* magazine, a
scholarly journal of religion and psychology.

The author wishes to thank Anthony Pellicano, Forensic Audio
Labs, Ltd., 9200 Sunset Boulevard, Los Angeles, California, for
serving as technical consultant on the development of the article
and for reviewing the article for technical accuracy.

171

44:171
§ 2   44 AM JUR TRIALS

evidence, including "day-in-the-life" videotapes,[21] child testimony
by videotape or closed-circuit television in alleged child-abuse
cases,[22] videotape reenactments and reconstructions,[23] and videotape depositions.[24]

Within the category of contemporaneous videotape evidence, a
detailed discussion of staged evidence[25] constituting legally operative agreements such as videotaped wills[26] or videotaped prenuptial agreements is beyond the scope of this article. Similarly, no
attempt will be made to cover the important constitutional issues
that arise in criminal matters when videotape is used for law
enforcement surveillance, confessions, lineups, and the like.[27]

21. **Am Jur Trials:** Planning and Producing a "Day-in-the-Life" Videotape in a
Personal Injury Lawsuit, 39 AM JUR TRIALS 261; Using or Challenging a "Day-in-
the-Life" Documentary in a Personal Injury Lawsuit, 40 AM JUR TRIALS 249.

22. See, for example, Maryland v Craig (1990, US) 111 L Ed 2d 666, 110 S Ct 3157,
30 Fed Rules Evid Serv 1, on remand Craig v State (1991) 322 Md 418, 588 A2d
328.

Other Aids: Symposium on Child Sexual Abuse Prosecutions, 40 U Miami L Rev
135 (1985).

23. **Am Jur Trials:** See Videotaped Settlement Brochure, 43 AM JUR TRIALS 239.

Other Aids: See, for example, Comment, Videotaped Reenactments in Civil Trials:
Protecting Probative Evidence from the Trial Judge's Unbridled Discretion, 24 John
Marshall L Rev 433 (1991); Comment, Computer Simulations and Video Re-Enact-
ments: Fact, Fantasy and Admission Standards, 17 Ohio Northern U L Rev 145
(1990).

24. **Am Jur Trials:** The Use of Videotape in Civil Trial Preparation and Discovery, 23
AM JUR TRIALS 95.

ALR Annotation: Use of videotape to take dep
state court, 66 ALR3d 637.

Other Aids: See also Uniform Audio-Visual
ANNOTATED 10-16 (1991 Supp).

25. See §§ 5-7.

26. **Other Aids:** See Beyer & Buckley, Videotape
Grows, 42 Okla L Rev 43 (1989).

27. These constitutional issues include violation
tion, violation of protection against unlawfu
process, and denial of rights to a public trial.

ALR Annotations: Admissibility of videotape
ALR3d 333; Admissibility of visual recordi
litigation or prosecution, 41 ALR4th 812; Adr
or matter other than that giving rise to litigatio

192

**COMPREHENSIVE
TEXTUAL
DISCUSSION
OF THE TOPIC**

**HELPFUL
CROSS-REFERENCES
TO OTHER TCSL
SOURCES**

§ 37. CHECKLIST OF USES IN CRIMINAL CASES
What follows is a checklist of the ways in which videotape
evidence has been used thus far in criminal cases.[92]

☑

☐ *Contemporaneous recording of criminal event.* A relatively large body of case law has built up with respect to
surveillance pictures, and an increasing number of cases
based on camcorder-generated evidence is expected, especially with respect to so-called hate crimes. The poor
quality of tapes made with low-cost or ill-placed surveillance equipment has been a frequent issue here.

☐ *Child's testimony by closed-circuit broadcast, or prere-
corded by videotape, in child-abuse case.* The Supreme
Court, in *Maryland v Craig,*[93] held that provided a trial
court makes a case-specific finding of necessity, the Sixth
Amendment's confrontation clause does not prohibit a
state from using closed-circuit television for receiving
testimony from an alleged child-abuse victim. Justice
O'Connor pointed out that the majority of states allow
videotaped testimony of child-abuse victims, that almost
half of the states allow the use of one-way closed-circuit
television, and roughly a dozen states allow the use of
two-way, closed-circuit testimony in such cases.

☐ *Crime scenes.* Like accident scenes, these can include
immediately subsequent or retrospective views of an accident scene, and the admissibility requirements are similar
but usually stricter because of the constitutional implications.

91. See § 63.

92. This list, and accompanying comments, are derived mainly from Scott, 3 PHOTO-
GRAPHIC EVIDENCE §§ 1312-1340 (2d ed Supp 1991), and Joseph, Videotape
Evidence in the Courts, 26 So Tex L J 453 (1985).

93. (1990, US) 111 L Ed 2d 666, 110 S Ct 3157, 30 Fed Rules Evid Serv 1, on remand
Craig v State (1991) 322 Md 418, 588 A2d 328.

254

**AIRTIGHT
CHECKLISTS
LEAVE NOTHING
TO CHANCE**

SAMPLE FORMS

Figure 1: Petition to NLRB (Form NLRB 50...)

SUGGESTED DIAGRAM PREPARATION

§ 20   23 AM JUR TRIALS

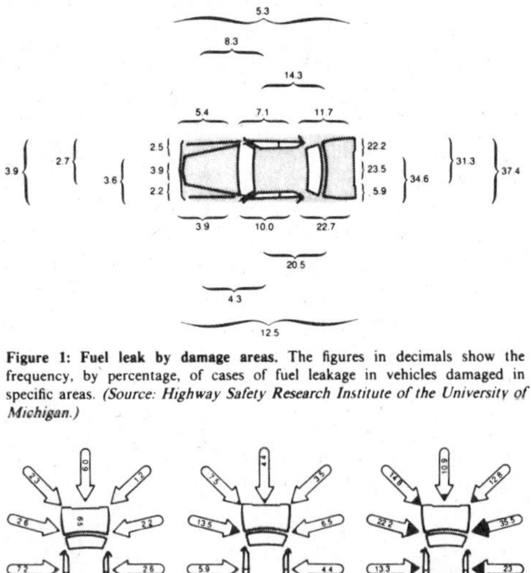

Figure 1: Fuel leak by damage areas. The figures in decimals show the frequency, by percentage, of cases of fuel leakage in vehicles damaged in specific areas. *(Source: Highway Safety Research Institute of the University of Michigan.)*

MINOR   MODERATE   SEVERE

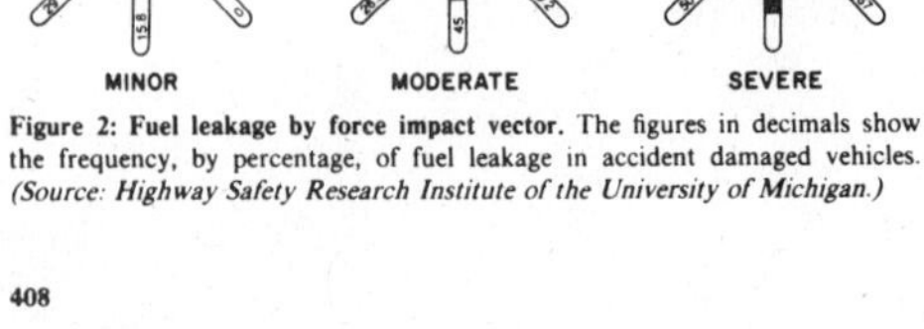

Figure 2: Fuel leakage by force impact vector. The figures in decimals show the frequency, by percentage, of fuel leakage in accident damaged vehicles. *(Source: Highway Safety Research Institute of the University of Michigan.)*

408

Model Trials

The balance of Am Jur Trials, Volumes 7 et seq., is devoted mainly to in-depth examinations of particular kinds of litigation. Articles such as Medical Malpractice Cases, Divider Line Automobile Cases, Will Contests, Condemnation of Real Property, and Homicide, exemplify the wide range of topics which receive expert treatment in this division of Am Jur Trials. Most articles cover all facets of the subject from the beginning to the end of the litigation, and the text is supported by helpful aids similar to those used in the "Practice, Strategy, and Control" division discussed above. The following illustrations exhibit some of the many features available in the "Model Trials" division.

§ 33   23 AM JUR TRIALS

§ 33. —MANUFACTURER'S ENGINEER AS DEPONENT

Counsel should not expect to achieve maximum success insofar as the testimony elicited from the manufacturer's engineer on deposition is concerned. An extensive deposition may result in establishing only one or two essential points, and perhaps only a single essential point can be established from several of the depositions taken of defendant's technical personnel.

Following is a portion of the deposition of a manufacturer's engineer taken by plaintiff's counsel, which, after establishing that the witness was a member of the engineering staff of the defendant manufacturing company and had had extensive experience over the previous 20 years, including development-design product improvement, proceeded as follows:

Q. Do you have an opinion whether the gasoline tank assembly of a vehicle struck from the rear by another vehicle of like size and weight at a differential speed of approximately 28 to 30 miles per hour, was properly designed, if, upon impact, it was caused to rupture and spew gasoline into its own passenger compartment?

A. Yes, I have an opinion.

Q. What is that opinion?

A. I would not be surprised in some models that the fuel tank was ruptured by an impact of such severity, but I would not expect fuel to be spewed into the passenger compartment.

Q. Then as I understand it, you are saying it is not an unexpected or uncommon thing for fuel tanks to rupture upon rear-end collisions under the circumstances I have given you.

A. It is not uncommon depending on the model and year of the vehicle. Automotive design is an evolutionary process in which each year the designer and manufacturer attempts to make next year's car better. A 1928 vehicle impacted under those conditions undoubtedly would result in having the fuel tank rupture. It is expected that cars today are designed better than in 1928 and that they will be designed even better in the future. It is an evolutionary process.

Q. Referring specifically to an automobile built in the year 19 , which is the year when the automobile involved in

436

**EXEMPLARY
EXAMINATION
OF WITNESSES**

§ 20   23 AM JUR TRIALS

Principal classes of motor-vehicle deaths

About two out of three deaths in 1974 occurred in places classified as rural. In urban areas, nearly two out of five of the victims were pedestrians; in rural areas, the victims were mostly occupants of motor vehicles. Slightly over half of all deaths occurred in night accidents, with the proportion somewhat higher in urban areas than in rural areas.

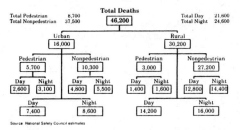

Source: National Safety Council estimates

Trends in death rates

Motor-vehicle deaths decreased 17 per cent in 1974 from 1973, vehicle mileage decreased 2 per cent, the number of vehicles increased 5 per cent, and population increased 1 per cent. As a result of the large decrease in motor-vehicle deaths, the three death rates below declined in 1974 from 1973. The rates were as follows: **Mileage death rate** — 3.61 from 4.24 (see chart on page 40); **Registration death rate** — 3.40 from 4.28; **Population death rate** — 21.9 from 26.5 (see chart below). See page 59 for all rates

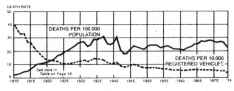

MOTOR-VEHICLE   41

Figure 4: Table and chart showing areas, time and trends in motor vehicle deaths. *(Source: Accident Facts, 1975, Edition, National Safety Council.)*

410

Supplementation

All of the articles in Am Jur Trials are kept current by pocket supplements appearing in the back of each volume. Thus, you are conveniently and quickly made aware of recent developments that may affect your case.

Index Pamphlet

Comprehensive and easy-to-use, it gives full access to the entire set, enhancing its scope and usefulness. Index entries on any point have been gathered in one place. Thousands of topics and groups have been created in order to place entries under a variety of terms descriptive of specific things, acts, persons, and places. The descriptive word approach embraces both legal and factual terms and concepts. Collateral and interrelated material are tied together by the use of cross-references and legends to facilitate ready access to material within this index.

Index entries are pinpointed to volume and page. For example, the entry "3:616" refers to volume 3, page 616.

AUSMAN & SNYDER'S MEDICAL LIBRARY, L Ed

Ausman & Snyder's Medical Library, L Ed
is a comprehensive medical encyclopedia written
especially for attorneys. It provides a thorough yet
easy to understand discussion of the medical
terms, conditions, and procedures that attorneys
encounter in their practices.

Summary of Ausman & Snyder's Medical Library, L Ed Features

* Comprehensive coverage of medicine—
  organized according to the 30 recognized
  medical specialties, the medical library
  provides total coverage of the practice
  of medicine.

* Up to the minute coverage—each volume
  will be supplemented annually to provide
  coverage of the most recent medical developments and techniques.
* Easy to use organization—each chapter
  covers a different medical specialty. Medical terms, conditions, procedures, drugs,
  and techniques are set out in a logical order
  within each chapter.
* TCSL References—each chapter has a separate section for legal references to the Total
  Client-Service Library. In addition, relevant
  ALR annotations and POF articles are footnoted in the medical text.
* Medical References—related medical texts,
  journals, and periodicals are noted at the end
  of each chapter for the user's convenience.
* Illustrations and charts throughout each
  volume highlight and exemplify the text.
* Expert commentary—in addition to the
  text, illustrations and references, the authors
  have added their own practical pointers
  where appropriate.

* Individual volume Indexes—in the back of
  each volume are indexes for the chapters in
  that volume. The index for each volume provides detailed descriptions of the volume's
  contents in alphabetical order.

Medical Specialties

Ausman & Snyder's Medial Library, L Ed
discusses the following specialties in separate
chapters:

Gynecology
Obstetrics
Pulmonary Diseases
Dermatology
Nephrology
Infectious Diseases
Anesthesiology
Oncology
Rheumatology
Orthopedics
Surgery
Pediatrics
Ophthalmology
Otolaryngology
Neurology
Radiology
Neurological Surgery
Nuclear Medicine
Psychiatry
Radiation Therapy
Cardiology
Emergency Medicine
Gastroenterology
Clinical Pathology
Allergy/Immunology
Rehabilitation
Endocrinology
Podiatric Medicine
Hematology
Chiropractic
Dentistry

Each section within a chapter is divided into
subsections setting out the information pertinent
to the term, condition, procedure, drug or technique under discussion. In addition, medical
words and phrases are highlighted, and the text
includes cross references and footnotes.

AUSMAN & SNYDER'S MEDICAL LIBRARY

I. PRE-SURGERY CONSIDERATIONS

A. GENERALLY

§ 20:1. Anesthesia

a. General

Preparing a patient for surgery requires considerable interaction between the anesthesiologist and the operating surgeon. They must ring the expertise and training of each laborating in all aspects of patient care. difficulties develop, there must be a anesthetist, surgeon, and nurses who are patient risk.[1]

s of general anesthesia are loss of con-iesia.

roves surgery by rendering the patient iained awake during most procedures in move unless paralysis were induced, a : additional undesirable effects.

:h there is no sensitivity to actions which patient is rendered pain-free even though mally produce even unbearable pain.

§ 20:11

CHAPTER TWENTY

Figure 20:11-1

Abdominal Cavity

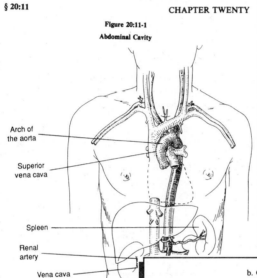

Arch of
the aorta

Superior
vena cava

Spleen

Renal
artery

Vena cava

Abdominal
aorta

Kidney

48

b. Clinical Features

The CLASSIC SIGN OF APPENDICITIS usually is mild, diffuse abdomi-nal pain, sometimes described by the patient only as a discomfort accompanied by loss of appetite. The classic shift and localization of pain in the right, lower quadrant follows.

An atypical pain pattern occurs in approximately half of the patients with the disease. An atypical pattern may include failure to localize the pain, failure to have or recognize the diffuse component, and failure to develop intense pain.

Nausea is nearly an invariable symptom, but vomiting is less customary. Occasionally, diarrhea is present.

If allowed to progress to perforation, the pain of appendicitis usually changes, but it rarely disappears, even temporarily (contrary to popular belief). The patient develops diffuse abdominal pain and abdominal distention.

The traditional physical signs found when examining a patient with appendicitis are local tenderness, rebound tenderness, muscle spasm (abdominal muscle), right-sided tenderness on rectal exam, and low-grade fever. Not all of these signs need be present to make a diagnosis of appendicitis. In an advanced state of the disease, the patient prefers to stay quietly in bed with the right hip flexed slightly.

c. Diagnosis

In any discussion of appendicitis, it is important to point out that

FEDERAL RULES SERVICE

DIGEST

The Federal Rules Digest classifies cases from all levels of the federal court system that interpret the Federal Rules of Civil and Appellate Procedure. Headnotes are organized under the unique Findex system of rule subdivisions. The Findex system lets you pinpoint the aspect of the rule you're interested in and go directly to the Digest section listing pertinent cases.

* Covers decisions from the U.S. Supreme Court, Courts of Appeal, District Courts, Court of Claims, Court of Military Appeals, Tax Court, and other Federal courts.

* Cites to Federal Rules Service (2d & 3d), Federal Rules Decisions, Federal Supplement, Federal Reporter 2d Series, federal specialty reporters, and U.S. Supreme Court cases.

* Features the exclusive Findex finding aid, which provides full text of each Rule followed by numbered rule subdivisions keyed to specific Digest sections.

* Provides Case Tables to help you quickly locate treatment of any cited case.

* Furnishes a detailed Word Index to the Rules as an alternate means of entry into the Rules and Digest.

REPORTER

Includes headnotes and relevant sections of all cases construing the Federal Rules of Civil and Appellate Procedure, linked by rule-based Findex numbers to the Federal Rules Digest. Monthly Advance Sheets bring you the latest cases.

HOW TO USE THE FEDERAL RULES SERVICE

*Suppose you're looking for a Court of Appeals decision on **Prerequisites to a Class Action** (Rule 23a of the Federal Rules of Civil Procedure) pertaining to attorneys' fees...*

1. FINDEX

The *"Attorneys' fees"* Findex number (23a.16) directs you to the appropriate Digest section.

Rule numbers are subdivided in the Findex to help you pinpoint your specific area of interest. Cases in the Digest are organized by Findex number for easy reference.

2. DIGEST

Federal Rules Service 3d cite leads you to the case you need. Parallel citations are also provided.

Headnotes focus on interpretations of the Rules and clearly identify courts and dates of decisions for your convenience.

3. REPORTER

Reporter includes case headnotes and court opinion that has interpreted rule 23a in the Federal Rules of Civil Procedure.

FEDERAL RULES OF EVIDENCE SERVICE

DIGEST

The Federal Rules of Evidence Digest classifies civil and criminal cases from all levels of the federal court system that interpret the Federal Rules of Evidence. Headnotes are organized under the unique Findex system of rule subdivisions. The Findex system lets you pinpoint the aspect of the rule you're interested in and go directly to the Digest section listing pertinent cases.

* Covers civil and criminal cases from the U.S. Supreme Court, Courts of Appeal, District Courts, Court of Claims, Court of Military Appeals, Tax Court, and other Federal Courts.

* Cites to Federal Rules of Evidence Service, Federal Supplement, Federal Reporter 2d Series, federal specialty reporters, and U.S. Supreme Court cases.

* Features the exclusive Findex finding aid, which provides full text of each Rule followed by numbered rule subdivisions keyed to specific Digest sections.

* Provides Case Tables to help you quickly locate treatment of any cited case.

* Furnishes a comprehensive State Correlation Table which compares the Federal Rules of Evidence to similar state evidence provisions.

* Supplies a detailed Word Index to the Rules as an alternate means of entry into the Rules or Digest.

REPORTER

Includes headnotes and relevant sections of all cases construing the Federal Rules of Evidence, linked by rule-based Findex numbers to the Federal Rules of Evidence Digest. Monthly Advance Sheets bring you the latest cases.

HOW TO USE THE FEDERAL RULES OF EVIDENCE SERVICE

*Suppose you're looking for a Court of Appeals decision on **Character Evidence Not Admissible to Prove Conduct; Exceptions; Other Crimes** (Rule 404b) pertaining to the credibility of a witness...*

1. FINDEX

The *"credibility of accused or other witnesses"* Findex number (404b.35) directs you to the appropriate Digest section.

Rule numbers are subdivided in the Findex to help you pinpoint your specific area of interest. Cases in the Digest are organized by Findex number for easy reference.

2. DIGEST

Federal Rules of Evidence Service cite leads you to the case you need. Parallel citations are also provided.

Headnotes focus on interpretation of the Rules and clearly identify courts and dates of decisions for your convenience.

3. REPORTER

Reporter includes case headnotes and court opinion that have interpreted rule 404b in the Federal Rules of Evidence.

Americans with Disabilities
Practice and Compliance Manual

It's the Law

The American with Disabilities Act (ADA) is the most significant civil rights legislation enacted since the Civil Rights Act of 1964, which prohibited discrimination on the basis of race, national origin, sex, etc. This all-encompassing piece of legislation prohibits discrimination on the basis of disability and seeks to remove "barriers" to public places, services, transportation, telecommunications, and employment.

Make no mistake about it, there will be a great deal of activity under the new Act. The ramifications of this Act will be felt for years to come. Over 40 million Americans with disabilities are protected by the ADA—such as those Americans who are hearing impaired, totally or legally blind, epileptic, partially or completely paralyzed, wheelchair users, speech impaired, developmentally disabled, mentally retarded, and HIV infected—and many are prepared to enforce its provisions. Depending on the violation, remedies, such as injunctive relief, compensatory and punitive damages, and civil fines of up to $100,000, will now be allowed.

Americans With Disabilities: Practice and Compliance Manual is a source on the ADA and other related statutes. It gives you all the information you need for proceeding with any action related to this area. The set comprehensively collects all the legislation and regulations on the topic. It's designed to provide you with all the information you'll require when dealing with businesses, transportation carriers, schools and municipalities, and other institutions that must comply with the ADA.

This publication is comprised of 4 tab-divided binders with chapter pamphlets and contains forms, textual analysis, trial strategy, ALR annotations, primary source materials (i.e. statutes and regulations) and much more. Various federal agency compliance guidelines are also thoroughly examined. References to CFR, USCS, and other related sources guarantee complete coverage. Topics treated include employment, public accommodations, education, housing, transportation, state and local government services, telecommunications, and much more. The set will be kept up to date with monthly newsletters, annual supplements, and replacement pamphlets as needed. *Americans With Disabilities* will undoubtedly ease the confusion that is inherent in this burgeoning field of law.

Chapter List

Binder 1:   Programs, Services and Accommodations

Chapter 1   Section 504: Nondiscrimination Under Federal Programs or Activities
Chapter 2   State and Local Government Services
Chapter 3   Transportation
Chapter 4   Public Accommodations
Chapter 5   Telecommunications Relay Services
Chapter 6   Programs, Services and Accommodations Forms

Binder 2: Employment

Chapter 7   Americans with Disabilities Act
Chapter 8   Employment by Federal Government and Federal Contractors
Chapter 9   Veterans
Chapter 10   Employment Forms

Binder 3: Education

Chapter 11   Individuals With Disabilities Education Act (IDEA)
Chapter 12   Suits Under Section 1983
Chapter 13   Education Forms

Binder 4: Housing

Chapter 14   Fair Housing
Chapter 15   Housing Forms

UNITS OF THE NATIONAL TOTAL CLIENT-SERVICE LIBRARY®

	AMERICAN JURISPRUDENCE 2d	AM JUR LEGAL FORMS 2d	AM JUR PLEADING & PRACTICE FORMS, REV.	AM JUR TRIALS	AM JUR PROOF OF FACTS	UNITED STATES CODE SERVICE
	The Law in Breadth State & Federal Coverage	Drafting Legal Documents	Drafting Pleadings	Preparing the Case	Proving the Facts	The Laws Enacted By Congress
FINDING TOOLS	Index Pamphlets Indexes and Tables in each volume The Annotated Reports System Table of Statutes, Rules, and Regulations Cited Am Jur 2d Desk Book including List of Titles Ballentine's Law Dictionary 3d	Index Pamphlets	Index Pamphlets	Index Pamphlets	Index Pamphlets	General Index—6 vols. (Supplemented in General Index Update Service Binder) Tables volumes (USCS)—3 vols. The Annotated Reports System
LAW PRACTICE	American Jurisprudence, Second Edition (Am Jur 2d) 1962-Present Vols. 1-82 (105 books) Plus Desk Book New Topic Service Federal Taxation Volumes	American Jurisprudence Legal Forms, Second Edition (AJLF 2d) 1971-1986 Vols. 1-20 (30 books) Plus Federal Tax Guide to AJLF2d (2 binders)	American Jurisprudence Pleading and Practice Forms, Revised (AJP & P Rev.) 1986-Present Vols. 1-25 (39 books)	American Jurisprudence Trials (AJT) 1964-Present Vols. 1-	American Jurisprudence Proof of Facts (AJPOF) 1959-1973 Vols. 1-30 / American Jurisprudence Proof of Facts, Second Series (AJPOF2d) 1974-1988 Vols. 1-50 / American Jurisprudence Proof of Facts, Third Series (AJPOF3d) 1988-Present Vols. 1- / POF/POF2d Fact Book with Medical Glossary 1 vol. 1983 / Am Jur POF3d Medical Dictionary 1 vol., 1988	United States Code Service (USCS) 1972-Present 50 Titles Plus Constitution, Court Rules, Rules of Bankruptcy, Administrative Rules, Uncodified Laws, and Tables
UPDATING TOOLS	Pocket Part Supplements published annually for each volume New Topic Service volumes and pamphlets published as required. Current articles are: Alternative Dispute Resolution / Comparative Negligence / Consumer and Borrower Protection / Consumer Products Warranty Acts / Energy / Pension Reform Act / Real Estate Time-Sharing / Right to Die: Wrongful Life / Uniform Probate Code	Pocket Part Supplements published annually for each volume	Pocket Part Supplements published annually for each volume	Pocket Part Supplements published annually for each volume	Pocket Part Supplements published annually for each volume	Pocket Part Supplements published for each volume Later Case and Statutory Service pamphlets issued in January, June and September each year Advance Service pamphlet published monthly

THE ANNOTATED REPORTS SYSTEM

	UNITED STATES SUPREME COURT REPORTS LAWYERS' EDITION	
L A W F I N D E R S	L Ed Quick Case Table Pamphlet (General Index vol) US L Ed Digest – 22 vols. (42 books) USCS Am Jur 2d Fed Proc. L Ed	
T H E L A W	US L Ed UNITED STATES SUPREME COURT REPORTS LAWYERS' EDITION First Series 1789-1956 vols. 1-100	US L Ed 2d Second Series 1956-Present vols. 1-
U P D A T I N G T O O L S	US L Ed Annotation History Table located in back of US L Ed Index to Annotations	
	US L Ed First Series Annotations supplemented as required only through later annotations	Vols. 1-31 of US L Ed 2d supplemented by two Later Case Service volumes which are supplemented annually; vols. 32 et seq. annually supplemented by pocket parts for each volume

THE ANNOTATED REPORTS SYSTEM

AMERICAN LAW REPORTS ANNOTATED (ALR)

A Quick Command Of All Case Law in Point
With Additional References To Law Reviews And Other Legal Authority

Index To Annotations - 5 vols.
(Includes Table of Statutes, Rules, and Regulations cited, and is supplemented quarterly)

AMERICAN LAW REPORTS ANNOTATED

	ALR	ALR 2d	ALR 3d	ALR 4th	ALR 5th	ALR Fed
LAW FINDERS	ALR First Series Quick Index Alternates: Word Index - 4 vols. Digest - 12 vols. Am Jur 2d	Alternates: ALR 2d Word Index - 3 vols. ALR 2d Digest - 7 vols. Am Jur 2d Fed Proc. L. Ed	Alternates: Digest to ALR 3d, 4th & Fed Am Jur 2d Fed Proc. L. Ed	Alternates: Digest to ALR 3d, 4th & Fed Am Jur 2d	Alternates: Digest to ALR 3d, 4th & Fed Am Jur 2d Fed Proc. L. Ed	Alternates: Digest to ALR 3d, 4th & Fed Am Jur 2d Fed Proc. L. Ed
THE LAW	First Series 1919-1948 Vols. 1-175	Second Series 1948-1965 Vols. 1-100	Third Series 1965-1980 Vols. 1-100	Fourth Series 1980-1992 Vols. 1-90	Fifth Series 1992-present Vols. 1 -	ALR Federal 1969-Present Vols. 1 - Since the publication in 1969 of ALR Fed, annotations based on questions of Federal law are covered in ALR Federal. Prior to this, such annotations are covered in ALR, ALR 2d and vols. 1 thru 27 of ALR 3d.

Annotation History Table for ALR, ALR 2d, ALR 3d, ALR 4th, ALR Fed (located in Volume 5 of the Index To Annotations)

	ALR	ALR 2d	ALR 3d	ALR 4th	ALR 5th	ALR Fed
UPDATING TOOLS	ALR Blue Book of Supplemental Decisions 6 Volumes plus Paperback supp. published annually	ALR 2d Later Case Service 26 Volumes Supplemented on an annual basis by pocket parts	ALR 3d Pocket Part Supps. Published annually for each volume	ALR 4th Pocket Part Supps. Published annually for each volume	ALR 5th Pocket Part Supps. Published annually for each volume	ALR Fed Pocket Part Supps. Published annually for each volume

STATE TOTAL CLIENT-SERVICE LIBRARY

Alabama
   Alabama Pattern Jury Instructions-Civil
   Trial Handbook for Alabama Lawyers
Arkansas
   Trial Handbook for Arkansas Lawyers
California
   California Personal Injury Digest
   California Condominium Handbook 2d with Forms
   California Drunk Driving Defense
   California Criminal Forms and Instructions
   California Reports & Appellate Reports
   California Judges Benchbook
   California Litigation Techniques
   Alternative Dispute Resolution News Alert
   Gilfix California Elder Law News Alert
   California Criminal Law 2d
   California Digest of Official Reports Third Series
   California Evidence, 3d
   California Family Law Service
   California Forms, Legal and Business
   California Jurisprudence 3d
   California Negotiation and Settlement Handbook
   California Personal Injury Forms
   California Civil Practice
   Current Law of California Real Estate
   Deering's Annotated and Unannotated California Codes
   Miller & Starr California Real Estate 2d
   Modern California Discovery 4th
   Trial Handbook for California Lawyers 2d
   Witkin California Procedure 3d
   Witkin California Evidence 3d
   Witkin Summary of California Law, 9th Edition
   Witkin Significant Developments in CA Substantive Law
Colorado
   Colorado Corporate Forms
   Colorado Jury Instructions 3d-Civil
   Colorado Law Annotated, 2d Edition
   Colorado Real Estate Transactions
Connecticut
   Connecticut Estates Practice: Commitment, Placement, Conservatorship, Guardianship, Adoption 2d
   Connecticut Estates Practice: Death Taxes, 2d Edition
   Connecticut Estates Practice: Jurisdiction and Procedure
   Connecticut Estates Practice: Probate Litigation
   Connecticut Estates Practice: Settlement of Estates
   Connecticut Estates Practice: Trusts
   Connecticut Estates Practice: Wills
   Connecticut Probate Deskbook
   Trial Handbook for Connecticut Lawyers
Florida
   Florida Code Research Guide
   Florida Corporations
   Florida Dissolution

Florida Evidence 2d
Florida Jur Forms Legal and Business & Disc Version Available 10/92
Florida Jurisprudence, 2d Edition
Florida Lawyer's Guide
Florida Pleading and Practice Forms
Florida Practice Guide: Personal Injury
Florida Real Estate
Read's Florida Evidence
Trial Handbook for Florida Lawyers 2d
Florida Uniform Commercial Code

Georgia
Georgia Code Research Guide
Georgia Divorce
Trial Handbook for Georgia Lawyers

Illinois
Callaghan's Illinois Civil Practice Forms
Callaghan's Illinois Legal Forms
Counseling the Elderly Client in Illinois
Righeimer Eminent Domain in Illinois
Estate Planning and Administration in Illinois, 2d Edition
Horner Probate Practice and Estates-Illinois
Illinois Evidence Manual, 2d Edition
Illinois Forms, Legal and Business & Disk Version Available 12/92
Illinois Jurisprudence
Illinois Lawyers Manual 3d
Illinois Non-Pattern Jury Instructions, 2nd Edition & Disk Version
Illinois Official Reports 2d
Illinois Official Appellate Reports 3d
Illinois Personal Injury
Illinois Products Liability
Illinois Practice Guide: Personal Injury
Personal Injury Forms: Illinois
Illinois Real Estate
Illinois Real Property Service
Illinois Tort Law and Practice, 2d Edition
Law of Medical Practice in Illinois
Nichols Illinois Civil Practice with Forms
Trial Handbook for Illinois Lawyers 6th

Indiana
Appellate Handbook for Indiana Lawyers
Indiana Medical Malpractice
Trial Handbook for Indiana Lawyers

Iowa
Iowa Practice
McCarty Iowa Probate 3d

Kansas
Kansas Code of Civil Procedure 2d Annotated
Pattern Instructions for Kansas 2d (Civil)

Kentucky
Kentucky Collections
Kentucky Divorce
Kentucky Jurisprudence
Kentucky Probate
Kentucky Workers' Compensation
Trial Handbook for Kentucky Lawyers

Louisiana
    Estate Planning in Louisiana
    Louisiana Appellate Practice Handbook
    Louisiana Civil Practice Forms 2d
    Louisiana Code of Evidence Practice Guide
    Louisiana Code Research Guide
    Louisiana Construction Law Manual
    Louisiana Corporations
    Louisiana Divorce
    Louisiana Environmental Handbook
    Louisiana Real Estate Transactions
    Louisiana Successions
    Trial Handbook for Louisiana Lawyers
Maine
    Trial Handbook for Maine Lawyers
Maryland
    Maryland Criminal Procedure Forms
    Trial Handbook for Maryland Lawyers, 2nd Edition
Massachusetts
    Annotated Laws of Massachusetts
    Estate Taxation in Massachusetts with Forms
    Law of Chapter 93A, (The Massachusetts Consumer and Borrower Protection Act)
    Massachusetts Code Research Guide
    Massachusetts Collection Law 2d
    Massachusetts Conveyancers' Handbook, with Forms 3d
    Massachusetts Corporations
    Massachusetts Domestic Relations
    Massachusetts Jurisprudence
    Massachusetts Landlord-Tenant Law
    Massachusetts Real Estate
    Proof of Cases in Massachusetts 2d
    Settlement of Estates and Fiduciary Law in Massachusetts 4th
    Trial Handbook for Massachusetts Lawyers 2d
Michigan
    Callaghan's Michigan Civil Practice Forms
    Callaghan's Michigan Pleading and Practice
    Counseling the Elderly Client in Michigan
    Evidence: A Trial Manual for Michigan Lawyers
    Gillespie Michigan Criminal Law & Procedure with Forms
    Gillespie Michigan Criminal Law and Procedure: Practice Deskbook
    Michigan Civil Jurisprudence
    Michigan Evidence
    Michigan Construction Accident Litigation
    Michigan Lawyers Manual
    Michigan Litigation Forms and Analysis
    Michigan Probate
    Michigan Statutes Annotated
    Michigan Reports
    Michigan Court of Appeals Reports
    Michigan Statutes Annotated-Related Criminal Statutes
    Michigan Statutes Annotated-Research Guide
    Michigan Torts
    Planning for Estates and Administration in Michigan
    Trial Handbook for Michigan Lawyers, 2d Edition

Minnesota
Minnesota Collections
Minnesota Dissolution of Marriage
Minnesota Probate
Minnesota Real Estate
Trial Handbook for Minnesota Lawyers
Mississippi
Mississippi Code of 1972
Summary of Mississippi Law
Trial Handbook for Mississippi Lawyers
Missouri
Missouri Evidence
Missouri Lawyers Guide
Missouri Tort Law
Missouri Workers' Compensation
Trial Handbook for Missouri Lawyers
New Jersey
Law of Medical Practice in Pennsylvania & New Jersey
Law of Zoning in New Jersey
New Jersey Code Research Guide
New Jersey Criminal Procedure
New Jersey Forms-Legal and Business
New Jersey Pleading and Practice Forms
Trial Handbook for New Jersey Lawyers 2d
New York
Bench Book for Trial Judge-New York
Bills of Particulars in New York-Revised
Callaghan's Criminal Law in New York
Carmody-Wait 2d: Cyclopedia of New York Practice with Forms
Carmody-Wait Surrogates Court and Estates Practice
Charges to the Jury and Requests to Charge in a Criminal Case in New York
Criminal Law of New York
Criminal Procedure in New York Parts I (Practice & Forms) and II (Evidence)
Examination Before Trial and Other Disclosure Devices
Family Court Law and Practice in New York -Revised
Law and the Family New York 2d
Lien Priorities in New York
Modern New York Discovery
Mortgage Liens in New York
Mortgages and Mortgage Foreclosure in New York-Revised
New York Collections
New York Condominium and Cooperative Law
New York Consolidated Laws Service-Annotated Statutes with Forms
New York Court of Appeals on Criminal Law
New York Driving While Intoxicated
New York Estates Practice Guide, 4th Edition
New York Evidence-Proof of Cases 2d
New York Forms-Legal and Business & Disk Version Available 10/92
New York Jurisprudence 2d
New York Landlord and Tenant, Summary Proceedings 3d
New York Landlord and Tenant-Rent Control and Rent Stabilization 2d
New York Law and Practice of Real Property 2d
New York Matrimonial Law and Practice
New York Matrimonial Practice
New York Pattern Jury Instructions-Civil

New York Probate
New York Products Liability
New York Reports Official Edition, 2nd Series
New York Real Property Service
New York Standard Civil Practice Service Deskbook
New York Vehicle and Traffic Law 2d
New York Wills
New York Zoning Law and Practice 3d
Secured Transactions in New York
Trial Handbook for New York Lawyers 2d
North Carolina
North Carolina Code Research Guide
North Carolina Commercial Financing Forms
North Carolina Real Estate Forms
North Carolina Tort Law
Strong's North Carolina Index 4th
Ohio
Law of Medical Practice in Ohio
Ohio Code Research Guide
Ohio Forms-Legal and Business & Disk Version Available Nov. '92
Ohio Jurisprudence 3d
Ohio Probate
Ohio Uniform Commercial Code
Ohio Workers' Compensation Claims
Trial Handbook for Ohio Lawyers 3d
Pennsylvania
Goodrich-Amram 2d Procedural Rules Service
Law of Medical Practice in Pennsylvania and New Jersey
Law of Zoning in Pennsylvania
Pennsylvania Appellate Practice
Pennsylvania Crimes Code Annotated
Pennsylvania Criminal Practice
Pennsylvania Estates Practice
Pennsylvania Matrimonial Practice
Pennsylvania Real Estate
Standard Pennsylvania Practice 2d
Summary of Pennsylvania Jurisprudence 2d
Trial Handbook for Pennsylvania Lawyers 2d
South Carolina
Code of Laws of South Carolina, 1976
South Carolina Workers' Compensation Laws Annotated
Tennessee
Tennessee Corporation
Tennessee Probate
Trial Handbook for Tennessee Lawyers
Texas
Black's Texas Evidence Manual
McDonald Texas Civil Practice
Modern Texas Discovery
Texas Annotated Penal Statutes with Forms
Texas Encyclopedia of Criminal Law
Texas Family Law Service
Texas Forms, Legal and Business
Texas Jurisprudence 3d
Texas Jurisprudence Pleading and Practice Forms 2d

Stevenson's Texas Legal Practice Forms 2d
Texas Practice Guide: Personal Injury
Texas Trial Handbook
Virginia
Trial Handbook for Virginia Lawyers
Virginia Code Research Guide
Virginia Corporations
Washington
Trial Handbook for Washington Lawyers
Washington Court Rules Annotated with Forms
West Virginia
Trial Handbook for West Virginia Lawyers
Wisconsin
Callaghan's Wisconsin Digest
Official Wisconsin Reports
Trial Handbook for Wisconsin Lawyers
Wisconsin Civil Practice Forms
Wisconsin Corporations
Wisconsin Pleading and Practice
Wisconsin Probate Law and Practice
Wisconsin Real Estate

APPENDIX D

The University of Chicago Manual of Legal
Citation

THE UNIVERSITY OF CHICAGO
MANUAL OF LEGAL CITATION

EDITED BY

THE UNIVERSITY OF CHICAGO
LAW REVIEW
AND
THE UNIVERSITY OF CHICAGO
LEGAL FORUM

1989

THE LAWYERS CO-OPERATIVE
PUBLISHING COMPANY
BANCROFT-WHITNEY COMPANY
AND
MEAD DATA CENTRAL, INC.

The editors of *The University of Chicago Law Review* and *The University of Chicago Legal Forum* gratefully acknowledge the assistance of the Advisory Committee in developing this manual.

Jerome M. Marcus, Chairman
  Member, Pennsylvania Bar
Ann T. Fessenden
  Circuit Librarian United States Court of Appeals, Eighth Circuit
Henry C. Lind
  Retired Reporter of Decisions United States Supreme Court
Frederick A. Muller
  Deputy State Reporter New York Court of Appeals
Jean Maclean Snyder
  Member, Illinois Bar

We also thank Douglas G. Baird, Gerhard Casper, Richard A. Epstein, Larry Kramer, Jo Desha Lucas, Geoffrey P. Miller, Richard A. Posner, A.W.B. Simpson, and Nelson Lund for helpful comments on earlier drafts.

To order copies of *The University of Chicago Manual of Legal Citation,* please write to:
  Executive Editor
  The University of Chicago Law Review
  1111 E. 60th St.
  Chicago, IL 60637

Table of Contents

Introduction

The following set of guidelines provides a simple, workable system of citation for legal writing. The guidelines are intended to cover all varieties of legal writing, including but not limited to briefs, legal memoranda, judicial opinions, and academic writing.

These rules provide a basic framework: they suggest the essential elements of any citation and how they most clearly can be presented. However, because it is neither possible nor desirable to write a particular rule for every sort of citation problem that might arise, the rules leave a fair amount of discretion to practitioners, authors, and editors. Users of this manual are encouraged, where no specific rule covers a situation, to cite authority in a clear, sensible manner. See Rule 4.11.

We believe that consistency within a brief, opinion, or law journal is important but that uniformity across all legal materials is not. We hope and expect that writers and editors will adapt the rules to the particular needs of their formats. The rules leave this responsibility to users of this manual editors without imposing on them the burden of conforming exactly to the rest of the legal world.

RULE 1:   TYPEFACES

All material should appear in roman type except the following, which should be italicized (or underlined if only roman typeface is available):

(a) case names;
(b) titles of periodical articles and articles in edited books;
(c) book and treatise titles;
(d) uncommon foreign words;
(e) words to be emphasized in text or notes.

Common legal phrases, such as ex parte or de facto, need not be italicized.

RULE 2:   ABBREVIATIONS

Rule 2.1:   General Rule

In general, abbreviations should only be used if they are easily recognized without reference to this manual.

For abbreviations not familiar or recognizable from context (for example, those in specialized fields) spell out the word or phrase on first reference and note the chosen abbreviation in parentheses.

Periods may be omitted from abbreviations in citations, with the exception of abbreviations of case names or book or treatise titles. The period following the "v" in case names may be omitted. Periods are generally inserted in abbreviations in text. When referring to an organization or other entity that is usually referred to by an abbreviation (for example, "SEC," "NLRB," "UCC"), periods may be omitted, even in text or case name abbreviations. For example,

SEC v Texas Gulf Sulphur Co., 401 F2d 833 (2d Cir 1968).

Rule 2.2:   Reporters, Statutes, and Other Sources

Appendix 2 is a list of recommended abbreviations of reporters and other legal sources. Appendix 3 is a list of recommended abbreviations of statutory sources. These lists are not exhaustive; writers and editors should use their own unambiguous abbreviations, consistent with the style of this manual, for sources not listed. Appendix 5, a more general list of recommended abbreviations, should facilitate this process.

Rule 2.3:   Periodicals

Appendix 4 is a list of recommended abbreviations of periodicals. Again, authors and editors should use their own unambiguous abbreviations where necessary.

Rule 2.4:   Geographical Terms

(a) Directions. Use "N," "S," "E," and "W" for all forms of these directions (for example, "N" for "Northern" as well as "North").

(b) Foreign Countries. Generally, use the first three or four letters of each word, but use more letters if a shorter form would be ambiguous: for example, do not use "Aust" because it might stand for Austria or Australia. Where the country's name includes a direction, abbreviate as above: for example, "E Ger" or "S Kor". Use of a common name ("E Ger" instead of "Ger Dem Repub") is encouraged; thus, omit such terms as "The Republic of."

(c) States and Similar Subdivisions.

For U.S. states, abbreviate in citations as follows:

Ala	DC	Ky	Mont	Ohio	Utah
Alaska	Fla	La	Neb	Okla	Vt
Ariz	Ga	Me	Nev	Or	Va
Ark	Hawaii	Md	NH	Pa	Wash
Cal	Idaho	Mass	NJ	RI	W Va
Colo	Ill	Mich	NM	SC	Wis
Conn	Ind	Minn	NY	SD	Wyo
Del	Iowa	Miss	NC	Tenn	
	Kan	Mo	ND	Tex	

Textual abbreviations should include periods.

For U.S. territories, spell out the name except for common abbreviations such as "N" or "Am".

For Canadian provinces, Australian states, and other non-American subdivisions, some limited abbreviation may be possible (for example, the first three or four letters, as in "Ont" for Ontario or "Vict" for Victoria). Depending on the intended audience, however, it may be advisable to include the name of the country parenthetically.

Names of counties, cities, and smaller subdivisions should generally be spelled out.

Rule 2.5:   Ordinal Numbers

For ordinal numbers in citations, use 1st, 2d, 3d, 4th, 5th, etc. Spell out ordinal numbers appearing in text.

RULE 3:   CITATION SENTENCES

Rule 3.1:   Introducing Authorities

An authority may be introduced either:

(a) without any words of introduction, only when the authority directly supports the statement in the text; or,

(b) by an ordinary English phrase explaining its force and or purpose.

Thus, for example, citations might be introduced by:

"See"
"But see"
"See, for example,"
or other descriptive language.

For example,

See *Board of Osage County Comm'rs v Burns*, 242 Kan 544, 747 P2d 1338 (1988).

Contrast *K.M.C. Co., Inc. v Irving Trust Co.*, 757 F2d 752 (6th Cir 1985) with *Centerre Bank of Kansas City v Distributors, Inc.*, 705 SW2d 42 (Mo App 1985).

For the evolution and present state of legal doctrine, see Douglas Laycock, *A Survey of Religious Liberty in the United States*, 47 Ohio St L J 409 (1986).

Rule 3.2:   Punctuation of Citation Sentences

Multiple authorities following a single introductory phrase or sentence should be separated by semicolons. When a new phrase introduces another group of citations, a new citation "sentence" should begin.

Rule 3.3:   Order of Authority

Authorities may be organized in any manner that seems desirable. The most important authorities, or those most supportive of the argument being made in text, should usually appear first. Authority that supports the text only by analogy, or indirectly, should appear next, in a separate citation sentence introduced by language explaining how the authority supports the proposition made in text. Sources that provide only tangential support for the proposition in text should be omitted.

Rule 3.4:   Explanatory Information

Additional information should be provided if it is helpful in

explaining the force or meaning of the authority cited or if the authority makes a point different from that in the text. This information may be presented in parentheses or in a separate phrase as seems appropriate. For example,

United States v Benjamin, 328 F2d 854 (2d Cir 1964), affirming the conviction of an attorney for conspiracy.

General Trade Policy, Hearings on HR 794, HR 1571, and HR 2203 before the Subcommittee on Commerce, Transportation, and Tourism of the House Committee on Energy and Commerce, 98th Cong, 1st Sess 234 (1983) (statement of U.S. Trade Representative William E. Brock).

When citing to a dissenting or concurring opinion, so indicate using the last name of the justice or judge. For example,

Owen Equipment & Erection Co. v Kroger, 437 US 365, 379 (1978) (White dissenting), citing *Aldinger v Howard,* 427 US 1 (1976).

For quoted material with alterations not otherwise indicated in the quotation itself, use a descriptive parenthetical. For example,

Lochner v New York, 198 US 45, 56 (1905) (emphasis added).

RULE 4: INITIAL REFERENCE TO AUTHORITIES

Rule 4.1: General Matters

(a) Internal Citation. Citation to a specific part of a work should correspond to the internal ordering system the work uses. Indicate the precise location of the supporting statements within the authority, using the page number (no symbol, or preceded by "at" if necessary to distinguish other subdivisions), section number (§), paragraph number (¶), chapter number (ch), or note number (n), or any combination of these. For example,

E. Allan Farnsworth, *Contracts* § 7.1 at 445 (Little Brown, 1982).

Internal identifiers standard for many or all editions of a work should be used. For example, a few well known works indicate the pagination of a specific earlier edition with an asterisk at the appropriate place in the margin or text. Thus,

William M. Blackstone, 1 *Commentaries* *12.

The particular edition used may be cited if desired.

(b) Authors' and Editors' Names. Cite to the author's or editor's full name as given on the first page or the title page of the source cited. (In subsequent references give only the last name, as indicated in Rule 5.3(b) and (c)).

Where there are two or three authors, list them all in the same fashion; if there are more than three, it is adequate to list the first author and then "et al". For example,

Paul M. Bator, et al, *Hart and Wechsler's The Federal Courts and the Federal System* (Foundation, 3d ed 1988).

When citing to *The Federalist Papers,* it is customary to indicate the author of the particular paper cited. For example,

Federalist 42 (Madison) in Clinton Rossiter, ed, *The Federalist Papers* 264, 270 (Mentor, 1961).

For student written works in law journals, the author's name should be replaced by the designation used in the journal, such as "Note," "Comment," or "Case Note". For example,

Comment, *Jurisdiction over Interstate Felony Murder,* 50 U Chi L Rev 1431 (1983).

(c) Authority Included in Another Source. When an authority is collected, reprinted, or otherwise included in whole or in part in another source, cite by joining the citation clauses for the two works with an appropriate descriptive phrase. Indicate the page of the

larger source at which the included work begins as well as the page being cited. Thus, for example,

Mark Tushnet, *Corporations and Free Speech,* in David Kairys, ed, *The Politics of Law* 253, 256 (Pantheon, 1982).

The Civil Rights Attorney's Fees Awards Act of 1976, S Rep No 94-1011, 94th Cong, 2d Sess 6 (1976), reprinted in 1976 USCCAN 5908, 5913.

Goldberg v Kelly, 397 US 254 (1970), excerpted in Stephen G. Breyer and Richard B. Stewart, *Administrative Law and Regulatory Policy* 719 (Little Brown, 2d ed 1985).

Rule 4.2:   Cases

(a) Reported Cases. Use the following form, with the indicated punctuation:

{*case name*}, {volume number} {reporter} {1st page}, {cited page} ({court} {year}).

For example,

Iowa Elec. Light & Power v Local Union 204, 834 F2d 1424, 1427 (8th Cir 1987).

Profit Sharing Plan v MBank Dallas, N.A., 683 F Supp 592 (ND Tex 1988).

(i) Case Name. Use the case name as reported in the Table of Cases Reported in the first reporter cited, dropping or abbreviating words at the end of each party's name if necessary to keep the case name reasonably short. The running head may be used if it is sufficiently descriptive of the case name that the reader will be able to locate the case through the Table of Cases Reported, a case name citator, or a law digest in the event of miscitation.

If a party named in the running head is commonly known by a name other than that in the running head, use the more familiar name. For example, "Am. Civ. Lib. U." should instead appear as "ACLU".

(ii) Reporter. Recommended abbreviations are listed in Appendix 2.

When citing to a state case, indicate the volume and first page of the case for both the official and commercial reporters. For example,

Henningsen v Bloomfield Motors, Inc., 32 NJ 358, 161 A2d 69 (1960).

Where the official reporter reprints an earlier editor's collection of cases and renumbers the volumes, it is not necessary to indicate the name of the earlier reporter's editor. For example, use either

Marbury v Madison, 5 US 137 (1803), or

Marbury v Madison, 5 US (1 Cranch) 137 (1803).

Some early state reports are named after their reporters and have no parallel state-named volumes. Such reports must be cited to the reporter-named volumes. For example,

Case v Hotchkiss, 3 Keyes 334 (NY 1867).

A looseleaf service or other source containing opinions is treated the same as any other reporter, but the publisher should be indicated parenthetically at the end of the looseleaf's name to facilitate location of the volume. For example,

In re Saberman, 3 Bankr L Rptr (CCH) ¶ 67,416 (Bankr N D Ill 1980).

United States v Belgard, 1 Fed Sent Rptr (Vera) 55 (D Or 1988).

(iii) Cited Page. Indicate the particular pages of the case that support the proposition in text.

When citing to state cases, however, it is permissible to give the particular pages supporting the text for one reporter only. For example,

Yanow v Seven Oaks Park, 11 NJ 341, 348, 94 A2d 482 (1953).

Dunwoody Country Club v Fortson, 243 Ga 236, 253 SE2d 700, 703 (1979).

(iv) Court. Indicate the name of the court that decided the case, unless the court's identity is clearly indicated by the name of the reporter. For example,

Burney v Children's Hospital, 169 Mass 57, 47 NE 401 (1897).

Aetna Life Ins. Co. v Lavoie, 470 S2d 1060 (Ala 1985).

Bohmfalk v Linwood, 742 SW2d 518 (Tex App 1987).

(b) Pending and Unreported Cases. Use the slip opinion, the citation employed by a computer research service, or both. For slip opinions, use the following forms:

(i) Federal Cases.

{case name}, {docket or action number}, slip op at {cited page} ({court}, {date and year}).

For example,

Gioda v Saipan Stevedoring Company, Inc., No 86-2435, slip op at 10026 (9th Cir, Aug 18, 1988).

Rogers v Consolidated Rail Corp., No 88-CV-1061, slip op at 2 (N D NY, July 29, 1988).

(ii) State Cases.

{*case name*}, {docket, appeal, indictment, claim, or index number, if available}, slip op at {cited page} ([state], {court}, {date and year}).

For example,

People v Moody, No 4582-84, slip op at 3 ([NY] Supreme Ct, NY County, June 27, 1986).

For computer research service citations, follow the form used by the service. For example,

Gioda v Saipan Stevedoring Company, Inc., 1988 US App LEXIS 11248, *16 (9th Cir).

Gioda v Saipan Stevedoring Company, Inc., 1988 WL 8494, 13 (9th Cir).

Use any reasonable abbreviation of the case name. Usually, the names of the first named plaintiff and first named defendant—separated by "v"—will suffice.

(c) Prior and Subsequent History. Indicate a case's prior or subsequent history only when it clarifies the strength of the case's authority or shows whether the case is continuing.

Use the following form:

{citation to main authority}, {type of prior/subsequent action} {citation to subsequent/prior authority}.

Use reasonable abbreviations ("aff'd," "rev'd," "aff'g," "rev'g") to indicate type of prior or subsequent action. For example,

Delaware Valley Citizens' Council v Com. of Pa., 762 F2d 272 (3d Cir 1985), aff'd in part, rev'd in part, and restored to docket for reargument, 478 US 546 (1986).

Indicate a grant of review ("cert granted," "appeal filed") but do not indicate a denial of review ("cert denied," "appeal denied") that has no precedential authority (for example, a denial of certiorari by the United States Supreme Court) unless it is particularly recent and thus indicates finality.

A substantially different case name in prior or subsequent history should be indicated. For example,

Great Western United Corp. v Kidwell, 577 F2d 1256 (5th Cir 1978), rev'd as *Leroy v Great Western United Corp.,* 443 US 173 (1979).

Leroy v Great Western United Corp., 443 US 173 (1979), rev'g *Great Western United Corp. v Kidwell,* 577 F2d 1256 (5th Cir 1978).

Rule 4.3: Periodical Articles

Articles in journals, newspapers, and services should be cited as follows:

{author}, {*title*}, {volume number} {periodical} {1st page}, {cited page} ({date}).

For example,

Herbert Wechsler, *Toward Neutral Principles of Constitutional Law,* 73 Harv L Rev 1, 9 (1959).

(a) Author. See Rule 4.1(b).

(b) Title. A very long title may be shortened as seems appropriate. Article titles should be italicized (or underlined if only roman typeface is available).

(c) Volume Number. Some periodicals are frequently identified by date rather than by volume. If so, the volume number may be omitted:

Albert Gore Jr., *Stability for Two,* New Republic 19 (Nov 17, 1986).

(d) Periodical. Recommended abbreviations are listed in Appendix 4.

(e) Date. Where the issues of a periodical are paginated consecutively throughout a volume, only the year is needed. Where issues are not consecutively paginated, give the date of the issue being cited, for example, "(Summer 1983)" or "(June-July 1983)" or "(June 13, 1983)".

If the volume number or title clearly indicates the year of publication, the date should be omitted. For example,

E. Donald Elliott, *Constitutional Conventions and the Deficit,* 1985 Duke L J 1077.

Rule 4.4: Books and Treatises

Books and treatises should be cited in the following form:

{author}, {volume number} {*title*} {subdivision} ({publisher}, {edition} {year}).

For example,

Roger J. Magnuson, 2 *Shareholder Litigation* § 15.02 at 4 (Callaghan, 1984).

James J. White and Robert S. Summers, *Handbook of the Law Under the Uniform Commercial Code* § 14-6 at 563 (West, 2d ed 1980).

(a) Author. See Rule 4.1(b). When referring to an edited collection of works by different authors, place the editor's name in the author's position, followed by "ed". For example,

David Kairys, ed, *The Politics of Law* (Pantheon, 1982).

(b) Volume Number. Replace roman numerals with arabic numerals.

(c) Title. Generally, use the title of the book as it appears on the title page. If the title is very long, it may be shortened by omitting subtitles or otherwise as appropriate. Book and treatise titles should be italicized (or underlined if only roman typeface is available).

(d) Subdivision. See Rule 4.1(a).

(e) Publisher, Edition, and Date. The name of the publisher may be abbreviated in any unambiguous manner; periods are not needed. Give the number of the edition cited unless citing to a first or single edition. Thus one would cite to "(Publisher, 2d ed 1978)" but only indicate "(Publisher, 1978)" for a first edition. If an edition is commonly identified by the editor's name rather than by the number of the edition, the editor's name may be substituted, or added if there are multiple editions by that editor.

If a supplement is being cited, the year of its publication should be indicated. For example,

Steven M. Brent and Sharon P. Stiller, *Handling Drunk Driving Cases* § 12:2 (Law Co-op, Supp 1988).

Rule 4.5:   Constitutions

Cite to constitutions in the following form:

{state or country} Const, {subdivisions}.

For example,

US Const, Art I, § 9, cl 2.
NM Const, Art IV, § 7.
US Const, Amend XIV, § 2.

If the constitution cited has been superseded, indicate the year of its adoption and, parenthetically, the year it was superseded. For example,

Ark Const of 1868, Art III, § 2 (superseded 1874).

Rule 4.6: Statutes

(a) Which Source to Cite. There are two citation sources for most statutes: the codification, which collects statutory language after enactment; and the act, which is the original source of the statutory language. For federal statutes, the codification appears in the official United States Code ("USC") as well as United States Code Annotated ("USCA") and United States Code Service ("USCS"); original acts appear in United States Statutes at Large ("Stat"). For state statutes, see Appendix 3.

Always cite to the codification if available. Wherever possible, cite to the official codification (for example, USC, not USCA or USCS).

The act may be cited in addition, and it should be cited if the material relied upon is not contained in the codification (for example, statements of legislative findings or purposes often are not codified).

If neither the codification nor the act is available, cite to a legislative looseleaf service or to another secondary source, such as United States Code Congressional and Administrative News ("USCCAN").

(b) Citation to a Codification. Use the following form:

{name of act}, {title or volume number} {codification} {subdivision} ({year}).

For example,

National Labor Relations Act, 29 USC §§ 151-169 (1982).

Subdivided Lands Act, Cal Bus & Prof Code § 11000 (West 1964).

(i) Name of Act. Give either the official or popular name of the act or title, as desired, with or without abbreviating. This part of the citation may be omitted if the name is not helpful.

(ii) Codification. Give the title or volume number, the name of the codification, and all necessary subdivisions of the statute cited (articles, sections, etc.). Recommended abbreviations for federal and state codifications are listed in Appendix 3.

(iii) Year. Indicate the year of the most recent version that

contains the language cited. If the codification is unofficial, give the publisher's name in the parenthetical before the date. For example,

Cal Civil Code § 1511 (West 1982).

If amendments are contained only in a supplement to a codification, cite to the supplement. For example,

Employee Retirement Income Security Act, 29 USCS §§ 1001 et seq (1982 & Supp 1988).

(c) Citation to an Original Act. Use the following form:

{name of act}, {source} ({year of passage}), codified at {codification}.

(i) Name of Act. As with citation to a codification, give the official title of the act or a popular or common name. If there is no official or popular name, it is customary to identify the act by "Act of {date of passage}". For U.S. statutes since 1957 and some state statutes, it is customary to indicate "Pub L No xxx" after the name.

(ii) Source. Recommended abbreviations for collections of federal and state acts are listed in Appendix 3.

(iii) Year of Passage. The year may be omitted when clearly indicated in the name of the act.

(iv) Codification. If the act is or will be codified, cite the codified version after the date.

For example,

National Environmental Policy Act, Pub L No 91-190, 83 Stat 853 (1970), codified at 42 USC § 4332 (1982).

Act of May 28, 1981, 1981 Minn Laws 1307, to be codified at Minn Laws § 260.

(d) Other Information. Indicate if a law is no longer in force as cited. For example,

Antidumping Act of 1921, 19 USC § 160 (1947), repealed by the Trade Agreements Act of 1979, § 106(a), Pub L No 96-39, 93 Stat 144, 193.

When citing to sections of widely known acts, it is often helpful to indicate the section number in the original act as well as the section number in the codification. For example,

Taft-Hartley Act § 301(a), 29 USC § 185(a) (1982).

(e) Model Codes and Uniform Acts. When citing to a state law that is an adaptation of a uniform act, cite to the state statute, although it may be helpful to indicate parenthetically the corresponding

uniform act section. When citing the uniform act directly, it is helpful to give the name of the author parenthetically with the date. For example,

See Fla Stat § 672.615 (1967) (UCC § 2-615 (ALI 1962)).

Rule 4.7: Legislative Materials

(a) General Rule. For legislative materials other than those specified below, cite as follows:

{title}, {legislature}, {session} {subdivision} ({date}).

The session may be omitted if the legislature only has one session, and the publication may be omitted where there is no published volume containing the material (for example, for unenacted bills).

(b) Federal Sources. Federal bills and resolutions often can be cited to the Congressional Record ("Cong Rec"). Federal reports and documents often can be cited to the United States Code Congressional and Administrative News ("USCCAN"). Forms for such citations are:

(i) Bills and Resolutions.

{title and/or bill number}, xxth Cong, x Sess ({month, day, and year introduced}) in {citation to source, if any}.

For example,

S 2404, 97th Cong, 2d Sess (April 13, 1982), in 128 Cong Rec 7091 (April 20, 1982).

(ii) Committee or Subcommittee Reports.

{title of the report}, {S or HR} Rep No xx, xxth Cong, x Sess {page} ({year}).

For example,

Martin Luther King, Jr. Federal Holiday Commission, HR Rep No 98-893, 98th Cong, 2d Sess 4 (1984).

(iii) Committee or Subcommittee Hearings.

{title, including bill number and committee name}, xxth Cong, x Sess {page} ({year}).

For example,

Service Industries Commerce Development Act of 1982, Hearings on HR 5519 before the Subcommittee on Commerce, Transportation and Tourism of the House Committee on Energy and Commerce, 97th Cong, 2d Sess 69 (1982) (statement of Gordon J. Cloney, II, Chamber of Commerce of the United States).

Rule 4.8:   Executive and Administrative Materials

(a) General Rule. Cite by issuing agency, title, official source, page, and date, for both federal and state materials.

(b) Federal Regulations and Rulemakings. Federal agency regulations appear in two sources: the Code of Federal Regulations ("CFR"), which collects final rules; and the Federal Register ("Fed Reg"), which publishes both proposed and final rules. Notices of proposed rulemakings appear only in the Federal Register.

Cite to the Code of Federal Regulations if available, and otherwise to the Federal Register. For example,

10 CFR § 10.12 (1986).

National Bureau of Standards, Amendment to Procedures for the Development of Voluntary Product Standards, 51 Fed Reg 22496, 22502 (1986) (amending 10 CFR § 10.13).

Some specialized regulations are often cited according to the convention of the agency promulgating them. For example, the Treasury's regulations under the Internal Revenue Code are cited simply as "Treas Reg § xx."

(c) Federal Adjudications. Cite to the official source used by the agency, if available. Where applicable, follow the rules for citing court cases (see Rule 4.2); for example, use the name in the Table of Cases Reported if there is one. Thus,

Hollywood Ceramics Company, Inc., 140 NLRB 221 (1962).

Some official sources are specific to particular agencies. For example, Treasury rulings and procedures for the Internal Revenue Code are cited to the Cumulative Bulletin ("Cum Bull") or its advance sheet, the Internal Revenue Bulletin ("Int Rev Bull").

(d) Presidential Documents. Executive Orders, Presidential Proclamations, and Reorganization Plans should ordinarily be cited only to Title 3 of the Code of Federal Regulations. If a particular document is not yet published in CFR, cite to the Federal Register. Other Presidential documents may be cited either to Public Papers of the President ("Pub Papers Pres") or to Weekly Compilation of Presidential Documents ("Weekly Comp Pres Doc").

(e) Administrative Materials Not Contained in Official Reporters. Examples of such materials include IRS private letter rulings and SEC no-action letters. If the agency maintains a numbering scheme, use it. Alternatively, or as a parallel citation, the form used by Lexis, Veralex, or Westlaw is permissible.

Rule 4.9:   Rules of Practice

A special form is used for court rules and rules of evidence or procedure, which are cited simply by name and number of the rule. For example,

FRCP 12.
FRCrP 12.
FRE 403.
Tex Rule Evid 803(a)(1).
US S Ct Rule 7.

Rule 4.10:   Treaties and Other International Agreements

Treaties and agreements to which the United States is a party should be cited with both the official and unofficial citation.

(a) Official Citation. For treaties signed prior to 1949, the official citation is to the Statutes at Large. Treaties signed since 1949 are officially published in United States Treaties and Other International Agreements ("UST"). Treaties in UST are cited as follows:

{name of treaty}, [{year of UST volume}] {volume number} UST {subdivision} ({year signed}).

(b) Unofficial Citation. For treaties signed prior to 1945, the unofficial citation is to the Treaty Series ("Treaty Ser") or Executive Agreement Series ("Exec Agr Ser"), each of which assigns a number to treaties covered. Treaties signed since 1945 should be cited to the Treaties and Other International Acts Series ("TIAS"), which also assigns a number to treaties covered.

For example,

Treaty with Iraq on Commerce and Navigation, 53 Stat 1790, Treaty Ser No 960 (1939).

Postal Agreement with the Gold Coast Colony, [1952] 2 UST 1859, TIAS No 2322 (1951).

Rule 4.11:   Other Sources

Sources not included in one of the previous categories may be cited in any unambiguous form consistent with the general practice of this manual. For example,

Annotation, *Intoxicating Liquors: Employer's Liability for Furnishing or Permitting Liquor on Social Occasion,* 51 ALR4th 1048 (1987).

16 Am Jur 2d Conflict of Laws § 75 (1979).

Black's Law Dictionary 543 (West, 5th ed 1979).

Restatement (Second) of Contracts § 205 (1979).

RULE 5: SUBSEQUENT REFERENCE TO AUTHORITIES

Rule 5.1: General Rule

When citing an authority for the first time, give the full citation according to Rule 4 above. Thereafter, references to the same authority should be made as follows:

(a) by another full citation, if the full citation has not appeared for several pages;

(b) by "id", only if the authority is the only one cited in the immediately preceding sentence or footnote;

(c) by a short form, if one exists (see Rule 5.3); or

(d) to avoid ambiguity, by a name specifically designated in parentheses in the initial reference. For example, the initial reference might read

> Gerald Gunther, *Constitutional Law* 14 (Foundation, 11th ed 1985) *("Gunther Casebook"),*

and the later references

> *Gunther Casebook* at 292 (cited in note 16).

Rule 5.2: Cross References

Reference to authorities and materials cited elsewhere in the document in which the reference occurs may be made by a short phrase such as "cited in note x," "cited at x," or "see p x." "Supra" and "infra" are redundant in such phrases and need not be used.

Rule 5.3: Short Forms

(a) Cases. For a case cited previously, use the following form:

> {*shortened case name*}, {volume number} {reporter} at {page}.

For example,

> *Iowa Elec.,* 834 F2d at 1429.

(i) Shortened Case Name. The shortened form of the case name is usually the name of the first non-governmental party (for example, *"Watson"* for *"United States v Watson,"* and *"Hardwick"* for *"Bowers v Hardwick").* Popular names for cases (for example, *"The Lottery Cases")* may be used when desired. If the case is cited several times in close proximity, even the shortened case name may be omitted.

(ii) Reporter and Page. For state cases, cite to either the official or commercial reporter or both, but be consistent. For example, if the first internal citation was to the official reporter, use only the official reporter in subsequent references.

(b) Periodical Articles. Use the following form:

{author's last name}, {volume} {periodical} at {page} (reference to previous full citation).

For example,

Ackerman, 98 Harv L Rev at 725 (cited in note 10).

Recall that for student written works, the name of the author is replaced by a designation such as "Comment" or "Note."

If citations to an article appear several times in close proximity, the reference to a previous full citation may be omitted.

(c) Books and Treatises. Use the following form:

{author's last name}, {volume number } {*shortened title*} {subdivision} at {page} (reference to previous full citation).

For example,

Davis, 3 *Administrative Law* at 357 (cited in note 41).

Again, if the book is cited several times in close proximity, the reference to a previous full citation may be omitted.

(d) Statutes. Use either of the following forms, according to the source used in the initial reference:

(i) Citation to a Codification:

{title or volume number} {codification} {subdivision}

For example,

42 USC § 4332.

(ii) Citation to an Original Act:

{shortened name of act} {subdivision}, {source}.

For example,

National Environmental Policy Act § 201, 83 Stat at 854.

(e) Legislative Materials. Use the following form:

{shortened title or bill/report number} {subdivision} at {page} (reference to previous full citation).

For example,

HR Rep No 96-304 at 9 (cited in note 94).

(f) Executive and Administrative Materials. Cite to a codified regulation as to a statute, to a regulation appearing in the Federal Register as to a periodical, and to an adjudication as to a case.

For example,

49 CFR § 73.607.

50 Fed Reg at 2530 (cited in note 23).

Hollywood Ceramics, 140 NLRB at 221.

Appendix 1: General Rules of Style

In matters not peculiar to legal writing, general rules of style are observed. We recommend use of *The Chicago Manual of Style* (Chicago, 13th ed 1982) to resolve those questions of style not addressed in this manual. For convenience, however, this appendix offers a few rules of style frequently needed in editing legal writing.

Quotations: Quoted materials may be indicated by a block quotation (indented left and right, without quotation marks and generally single-spaced) or by quotation marks surrounding material in text. The choice is left to the discretion of the writer or editor. Generally, quotations running more than six lines in text should be in block form.

If the source for a block quotation is given in text (as in briefs, memoranda, or footnote text), it should begin on a separate line after the quotation, flush with the (original) left margin.

Alterations of Quoted Texts: All alterations of quoted text should be noted. When a letter must be changed from lower to upper case or vice versa, enclose it in brackets. Substituted words or letters also should be bracketed. Significant mistakes in the original should be followed by "[sic]," but otherwise left as in the original.

Omissions in Quoted Materials: Omissions must be noted. Omissions should be indicated by three ellipsis points (" . . . "). There should be a full space between each point, and between the points and the text on either side. Punctuation may be used on either side of the ellipsis points. For example,

> Moreover, the language of the various declarations of rights . . . indicates that the authors of those documents believed that they were merely declaring existing, inalienable rights. . . . The Declaration of Independence "declared" "self-evident truths."

For more detailed rules see *The Chicago Manual of Style.*

Omissions may also be noted by including a brief statement in brackets in place of the omitted material. For example, [citations omitted], or [Madison] in place of or to explain a pronoun of ambiguous reference.

Capitalization: Capitalize nouns referring to people or groups (for example, "the Administrator" or the "Board," etc.) only when they

Appendix 1   UNIVERSITY OF CHICAGO

identify specific persons, officials, groups, or government offices. Similarly, capitalize such phrases as "the Act," "the Code," "the Circuit," and so forth only when the referent is unambiguously identified.

Names of parts of a constitution or statute may be capitalized when used in an English sentence as proper nouns, as in "First Amendment," "Article III," or "Section 8(e)." This practice should be consistent within a journal, article, brief, or memorandum. The phrases "the Court" and "the Constitution" should be capitalized only when referring to the United States Supreme Court and Constitution.

Appendix 2: Recommended Abbreviations of Reporters and Other Sources

Agriculture Decisions	Ag Dec
Alabama Appellate Court Reports [1910-1976]	Ala App
Alabama Reports [1840-1976]	Ala
Alaska Reports [1884-1959]	Alaska
American Maritime Cases	Am Marit Cases
Appellate Division Reports (NY)	AD, AD2d
Arizona Court of Appeals Reports [1965-1976]	Ariz App
Arizona Reports	Ariz
Arkansas Reports	Ark
Atlantic Reporter	A, A2d
Bankruptcy Law Reporter	Bankr L Rptr (CCH)
Bankruptcy Reporter	Bankr
California Appellate Reports	Cal App, Cal App 2d, Cal App 3d
California Reporter	Cal Rptr
California Reports	Cal, Cal 2d, Cal 3d
Claims Court Reporter	Cl Ct
Code of Federal Regulations	CFR
Colorado Reports [1864-1980]	Colo
Commodity Futures Law Reporter	Comm Fut L Rptr (CCH)
Congressional Record	Cong Rec
Connecticut Appellate Reports	Conn App
Connecticut Reports	Conn
Connecticut Supplement	Conn Supp
Court of Claims Reports [1857-1982]	Ct Cl
Criminal Law Reporter	Crim L Rptr (BNA)
Cumulative Bulletin	Cum Bull
Customs Bulletin and Decisions	Cust Bull
Customs Penalty Decisions	Cust Pen Dec
Customs Rules Decisions	Cust Rules Dec
Customs Service Decisions	Cust Serv Dec
Delaware Reports [1832-1966]	Del
Delaware Chancery Reports [1814-1968]	Del Chanc
District of Columbia Appeals	DC App
Employee Retirement Income Security Act Opinion Letters	ERISA Op Let
Employment Practice Decisions	Empl Prac Dec (CCH)
Environmental Reporter	Envir Rptr (BNA)

Appendix 2   UNIVERSITY OF CHICAGO

Environmental Law Reporter	Envir L Rptr
Equal Employment Opportunity Commission Decisions	EEOC Dec (CCH)
European Treaty Series	Eur Treaty Ser
Executive Agreement Series	Exec Agr Ser
Fair Employment Practice Cases	FEP Cases (BNA)
Federal Cases	F Cases
Federal Communications Commission Reports	FCC, FCC2d
Federal Register	Fed Reg
Federal Reporter	F, F2d
Federal Rules Decisions	FRD
Federal Rules of Civil Procedure	FRCP
Federal Rules of Criminal Procedure	FRCrP
Federal Rules of Evidence	FRE
Federal Rules Service	Fed Rules Serv, Fed Rules Serv 2d
Federal Securities Law Reporter	Fed Secur L Rptr (CCH)
Federal Sentencing Reporter	Fed Sent Rptr (Vera)
Federal Supplement	F Supp
Florida Reports [1846-1948]	Fla
Florida Supplement	Fla Supp, Fla Supp 2d
Georgia Appeals Reports	Ga App
Georgia Reports	Ga
Hawaii Appellate Reports	Hawaii App
Hawaii Reports	Hawaii
Idaho Reports	Idaho
Illinois Appellate Court Reports	Ill App, Ill App 2d, Ill App 3d
Illinois Court of Claims Reports	Ill Ct Cl
Illinois Reports	Ill, Ill 2d
Immigration and Naturalization Service Decisions	INS Dec
Indiana Appellate Court Reports [1891-1971]	Ind App
Indiana Court of Appeals Reports [1971-1979]	Ind App
Indiana Reports [1848-1981]	Ind
Internal Revenue Bulletin	Int Rev Bull
International Legal Materials	Intl Legal Mat
Interstate Commerce Commission Reports	ICC
Iowa Reports	Iowa
Kansas Court of Appeals Reports	Kan App, Kan App 2d
Kansas Reports	Kan
Kentucky Reports [1879-1951]	Ky
Labor Cases	Labor Cases (CCH)
Labor Relations Reference Manual	Labor Rel Ref Man (BNA)
Lawyer's Edition U.S. Supreme Court Reports	L Ed, L Ed 2d

Louisiana Annual Reports [1846-1900] .... La Ann
Louisiana Courts of Appeal Reports [1924-1932] . La App
Louisiana Reports [1900-1972] .... La

Maine Reports [1820-1965]..................... Me
Maryland Reports .... Md
Maryland Appellate Reports .... Md App
Massachusetts Appeals Court Reports .... Mass App
Massachusetts Reports .... Mass
Michigan Court of Appeals Reports .... Mich App
Michigan Reports............................. Mich
Minnesota Reports [1851-1977]................. Minn
Miscellaneous Reports (NY) .... Misc, Misc 2d
Mississippi Reports [1818-1966] .... Miss
Missouri Appeal Reports [1876-1952] .... Mo App
Missouri Reports [1821-1956] .... Mo
Montana Reports .... Mont

National Labor Relations Board................ NLRB
National Labor Relations Board Decisions .... NLRB Dec (CCH)
Nebraska Reports............................. Neb
Nevada Reports .... Nev
New Hampshire Reports .... NH
New Jersey Equity Reports .... NJ Eq
New Jersey Law Reports [1790-1948]............ NJ L
New Jersey Miscellaneous Reports [1923-1949]... NJ Misc
New Jersey Reports........................... NJ
New Jersey Superior Court Reports .... NJ Super
New Mexico Reports.......................... NM
(NY) Appellate Division Reports .... AD, AD2d
(NY) Miscellaneous Reports .... Misc, Misc 2d
New York Reports .... NY, NY2d
New York Supplement .... NYS, NYS2d
North Carolina Reports .... NC
North Carolina Court of Appeals Reports .... NC App
North Dakota Reports [1890-1953].............. ND
Northeastern Reporter .... NE, NE2d
Northwestern Reporter........................ NW, NW2d

Ohio Appellate Reports .... Ohio App, Ohio App
                                                       2d, Ohio App 3d
Ohio Circuit Court Reports [1885-1901]......... Ohio Cir Ct
Ohio Opinions [1934-1982] .... Ohio Op, Ohio Op 2d,
                                                       Ohio Op 3d
Ohio Reports [1821-1851]..................... Ohio
Ohio State Reports .... Ohio St, Ohio St 2d,
                                                       Ohio St 3d
Oklahoma Reports [1890-1953]................. Okla
Oklahoma Criminal Reports [1908-1953] .... Okla Crim
Opinions of the Attorney General (U.S.) .... Op Atty Gen

Appendix 2   UNIVERSITY OF CHICAGO

Oregon Reports	Or
Oregon Court of Appeals Reports	Or App
Pacific Reporter	P, P2d
Pan-American Treaty Series	Pan Am Treaty Ser
Pennsylvania Commonwealth Court Reports	Pa Commw
Pennsylvania District and County Reports	Pa D & C, Pa D & C 2d, Pa D & C 3d
Pennsylvania District Reports [1892-1921]	Pa Dist
Pennsylvania State Reports	Pa
Pennsylvania Superior Court Reports	Pa Super
Public Papers of the President	Pub Papers Pres
Revenue Procedure	Rev Proc
Revenue Ruling	Rev Rul
Rhode Island Reports [1828-1980]	RI
Securities and Exchange Commission	SEC
South Carolina Reports	SC
South Dakota Reports [1890-1976]	SD
Southeastern Reporter	SE, SE2d
Southern Reporter	S, S2d
Southwestern Reporter	SW, SW2d
Supreme Court Reporter	S Ct
Tax Cases [1913-1982]	Tax Cases
Tax Court Memorandum Decisions	Tax Ct Mem Dec (CCH)
Tax Court Reports	Tax Ct
Tennessee Court of Appeals Reports [1925-1971]	Tenn App
Tennessee Reports [1791-1971]	Tenn
Texas Criminal Reports [1876-1963]	Tex Crim
Texas Reports [1846-1962]	Tex
Trade Cases	Trade Cases (CCH)
Trade Regulation Reports	Trade Reg Rep (CCH)
Treasury Decisions	Treas Dec
Treaties and International Agreements Series	TIAS
Treaty Series [1778-1945]	Treaty Ser
Unemployment Insurance Reporter	Unempl Ins Rptr (CCH)
United Nations Treaty Series	UN Treaty Ser
United States Code Congressional and Administrative News	USCCAN
United States Law Week	USLW
United States Reports	US
United States Treaties and Other International Agreements	UST
Utah Reports [1855-1974]	Utah, Utah 2d
Vermont Reports	Vt
Virginia Court of Appeals Reports	Va App

Virginia Reports............................... Va

Washington Court of Appeals Reports........... Wash App

Washington Reports .... Wash

Weekly Compilation of Presidential Documents... Weekly Comp Pres
                                               Doc

West Virginia Reports [1863-1973].............. W Va

Wisconsin Reports............................. Wis, Wis 2d

Wyoming Reports [1870-1959] .... Wyo

Appendix 3: Recommended Abbreviations of Statutory Sources

United States (Federal)

Codification:
United States Code .... {title} USC § x (19xx)
United States Code Annotated .... {title} USCA § x (19xx)
United States Code Service .... {title} USCS § x (19xx)

Original Acts:
United States Statutes at Large .... {volume} Stat x (19xx)

Alabama

Codification:
Code of Alabama .... Ala Code § x (19xx)

Original Acts:
Acts of Alabama .... 19xx Ala Acts x

Alaska

Codification:
Alaska Statutes .... Alaska Stat § x (19xx)

Original Acts:
Alaska Session Laws .... 19xx Alaska Sess Laws x

Arizona

Codification:
Arizona Revised Statutes Annotated .... Ariz Rev Stat Ann § x
                                          (West 19xx)

Original Acts:
ArizonaLegislative Service .... 19xx Ariz Legis Serv x
                                          (West)
Arizona Session Laws .... 19xx Ariz Sess Laws x

Arkansas

Codification:
Acts of Arkansas .... 19xx Ark Acts x

Original Acts:
Arkansas Statutes Annotated .... Ark Stat Ann § x (19xx)

California

Codification:
Annotated California Code .... Cal [subject] Code § x
                                          (Deering 19xx) or (West
                                          19xx)

Appendix 3 UNIVERSITY OF CHICAGO

California General Laws Annotated...........Cal..Gen.Laws..Ann..§ x
(Deering 19xx)

Original Acts:
Statutes of California .... 19xx Cal Stat x
Calfornia Advanced Legislative Service .... 19xx Cal Adv Legis Serv x
(Deering)
California Legislative Service .... 19xx Cal Legis Serv x
(West)

Colorado

Codification:
Colorado Revised Statutes................. 19xx Colo Rev Stat § x
Original Acts:
Session Laws of Colorado .... 19xx Colo Sess Laws x

Connecticut

Codification:
General Statutes of Connecticut........... Gen Stat Conn § x (19xx)
Connecticut General Statutes Annotated ... Conn Gen Stat Ann § x
(West 19xx)

Original Acts:
Connecticut Public and Special Acts .... 19xx Conn Acts x (Reg [or
Spec] Sess)
Connecticut Public Acts [1650-1971] ...... 19xx Conn Pub Acts x
Connecticut Special Acts [1789-1971] ..... 19xx Conn Spec Acts x
Connecticut Legislative Service .... 19xx Conn Legis Serv x
(West)

Delaware

Codification:
Delaware Code Annotated................ {title} Del Code Ann § x
(19xx)

Original Acts:
Laws of Delaware........................ {volume} Del Laws x
(19xx)

District of Columbia

Codification:
District of Columbia Code Encyclopedia ... DC Code Encyc § x (Equity
19xx) or (West 19xx)
District of Columbia Code [1940-1981] .... DC Code § x (19xx)
Original Acts:
United States Statutes at Large .... {volume} Stat x (19xx)
District of Columbia Statutes at Large ..... 19xx DC Stat x
District of Columbia Register .... DC Reg x (19xx)

Florida

Codification:
Florida Statutes .... Fla Stat § x (19xx)

Florida Statutes Annotated .... Fla Stat Ann § x (Harrison
                                          19xx) or (West 19xx)

Original Acts:
Laws of Florida......................... 19xx Fla Laws x
Compiled General Laws of Florida .... 19xx Comp Gen Laws Fla x
                                          (Harrison)

Florida Session Law Service .... 19xx Fla Sess Law Serv x
                                          (West)

Georgia

Codification:
Official Code of Georgia Annotated .... Ga Code Ann § x (Michie
                                          19xx)

Original Acts:
Georgia Laws .... 19xx Ga Laws x

Hawaii

Codification:
Hawaii Revised Statutes .... Hawaii Rev Stat § x (19xx)
Original Acts:
Session Laws of Hawaii .... 19xx Hawaii Sess Laws x

Idaho

Codification:
Idaho Code .... Idaho Code § x (19xx)
Original Acts:
Session Laws, Idaho .... 19xx Idaho Sess Laws x

Illinois

Codification:
Illinois Revised Statutes .... Ill Rev Stat ch x, § x (19xx)
Illinois Annotated Statutes ....,.. Ill Ann Stat ch x, § x
                                          (Smith-Hurd 19xx)

Original Acts:
Laws of Illinois........................ 19xx Ill Laws x
Illinois Legislative Service .... 19xx Ill Legis Serv x
                                          (West)

Indiana

Codification:
Indiana Code .... Ind Code § x (19xx)
Annotated Indiana Code .... Ind Code Ann § x (West
                                          19xx)

Indiana Statutes Annotated Code Edition .. Ind Code Ann § x (Burns
                                          19xx)

Original Acts:
Acts, Indiana.......................... 19xx Ind Acts x

Iowa

Codification:
Code of Iowa .... Iowa Code § x (19xx)

Iowa Code Annotated................... Iowa Code Ann § x (West 19xx)

Original Acts:
Acts and Joint Resolutions of the State of
Iowa .... 19xx Iowa Acts x
Iowa Legislative Service .... 19xx Iowa Legis Serv x (West)

Kansas

Codification:
Kansas Statutes Annotated .... Kan Stat Ann § x (19xx)
Kansas Statutes Annotated (Vernon) ...... Kan [subject] Code Ann § x (Vernon 19xx)

Original Acts:
Session Laws of Kansas .... 19xx Kan Sess Laws x

Kentucky

Codification:
Kentucky Revised Annotated Statutes...... Ky Rev Ann Stat § x (19xx)
Kentucky Revised Statutes Annotated...... Ky Rev Stat Ann § x (Baldwin 19xx)

Original Acts:
Kentucky Acts......................... 19xx Ky Acts x
Kentucky Revised Statutes and Rules Service .... 19xx Ky Rev Stat & Rules Serv x (Baldwin)

Louisiana

Codification:
Louisiana Revised Statutes Annotated ..... La Rev Stat Ann § x (West 19xx)
Louisiana Civil Code Annotated........... La Civ Code Ann § x (West 19xx)

Original Acts:
State of Louisiana: Acts of the Legislature . 19xx La Acts x
Louisiana Session Law Service .... 19xx La Sess Law Serv x (West)

Maine

Codification:
Maine Revised Statutes Annotated .... {title} Me Rev Stat Ann § x (19xx)

Original Acts:
Laws of the State of Maine .... 19xx Me Laws x
Acts, Resolves and Constitutional Resolutions of the State of Maine [1820-1899].. 18xx Me Acts x
Maine Legislative Service................. 19xx Me Legis Serv x

Maryland

Codification:

Annotated Code of Maryland (subject matter) .... Md [subject] Code Ann § x (19xx)

Annotated Code of Maryland (otherwise) .. Md Ann Code art x, § x (19xx)

Original Acts:

Laws of Maryland .... 19xx Md Laws x

Massachusetts

Codification:

Annotated Laws of Massachusetts .... Mass Ann Laws ch x, § x (Michie/Law Co-op 19xx)

Massachusetts General Laws Annotated.... Mass Gen Laws Ann ch x, § x (West, 19xx)

Original Acts:

Acts and Resolves of Massachusetts .... 19xx Mass Acts x

Massachusetts Advanced Legislative Service 19xx Mass Adv Legis Serv x (Law Co-op)

Michigan

Codification:

Michigan Compiled Laws................. Mich Comp Laws § x (19xx)

Michigan Compiled Laws Annotated....... Mich Comp Laws Ann § x (West 19xx)

Michigan Statutes Annotated .... Mich Stat Ann § x (Callaghan 19xx)

Original Acts:

Public and Local Acts of the Legislature of the State of Michigan .... 19xx Mich Pub Acts x

Michigan Legislative Service .... 19xx Mich Legis Serv x (West)

Minnesota

Codification:

Minnesota Statutes .... Minn Stat § x (19xx)

Minnesota Statutes Annotated .... Minn Stat Ann § x (West 19xx)

Original Acts:

Laws of Minnesota...................... 19xx Minn Laws x

Minnesota Session Law Service .... 19xx Minn Sess Law Serv x (West)

Mississippi

Codification:

Mississippi Code .... Miss Code § x (19xx)

Appendix 3   UNIVERSITY OF CHICAGO

Original Acts:
General Laws of Mississippi ....   19xx Miss Laws x

Missouri

Codification:
Missouri Revised Statutes ....   Mo Rev Stat § x (19xx)
Annotated Missouri Statutes ....   Mo Ann Stat § x (Vernon 19xx)

Original Acts:
Laws of Missouri ....   19xx Mo Laws x
Missouri Legislative Service..............   19xx Mo Legis Serv x (Vernon)

Montana

Codification:
Montana Code Annotated ....   Mont Code Ann § x (19xx)
Original Acts:
Laws of Montana ....   19xx Mont Laws x

Nebraska

Codification:
Revised Statutes of Nebraska ....   Neb Rev Stat § x (19xx)
Original Acts:
Laws of Nebraska........................   19xx Neb Laws x

Nevada

Codification:
Nevada Revised Statutes ....   Nev Rev Stat § x (19xx)
Original Acts:
Statutes of Nevada......................   19xx Nev Stat x

New Hampshire

Codification:
New Hampshire Revised Statutes Annotated
....   NH Rev Stat Ann § x (Equity 19xx)

Original Acts:
Laws of the State of New Hampshire ......   19xx NH Laws x

New Jersey

Codification:
New Jersey Revised Statutes ....   NJ Rev Stat § x (19xx)
New Jersey Statutes Annotated...........   NJ Stat Ann § x (West 19xx)

Original Acts:
Laws of New Jersey ....   19xx NJ Laws x
New Jersey Session Law Service...........   19xx NJ Sess Law Serv x (West)

New Mexico

Codification:
New Mexico Statutes Annotated .... NM Stat Ann § x (19xx)

Original Acts:
Laws of New Mexico .... 19xx NM Laws x

New York

Codification:
McKinney's Consolidated Laws of New York
.... NY [subject] Law § x (Mc-
Kinney 19xx)
Consolidated Laws Service .... NY [subject] Law § x (Law
Co-op 19xx)

Original Acts:
Laws of New York .... 19xx NY Laws x
New York Session Laws .... 19xx NY Sess Laws x (Mc-
Kinney) or (Law Co-op)

North Carolina

Codification:
General Statutes of North Carolina .... NC Gen Stat § x (19xx)

Original Acts:
Session Laws of North Carolina .... 19xx NC Sess Laws x
Advanced Legislative Service to the General
Statutes of North Carolina .... 19xx NC Adv Legis Serv x

North Dakota

Codification:
North Dakota Century Code .... ND Cent Code § x (19xx)

Original Acts:
Laws of North Carolina .... 19xx ND Laws x

Ohio

Codification:
Ohio Revised Code Annotated .... Ohio Rev Code Ann § x
(Baldwin 19xx) or (Page
19xx)

Original Acts:
State of Ohio: Legislative Acts Passed and
Joint Resolutions Adopted .... 19xx Ohio Laws x
Ohio Legislative Bulletin .... 19xx Ohio Legis Bull x
(Anderson)
Ohio Legislative Service .... 19xx Ohio Legis Serv x
(Baldwin)

Oklahoma

Codification:
Oklahoma Statutes .... Okla Stat § x (19xx)

Appendix 3 UNIVERSITY OF CHICAGO

Oklahoma Statutes Annotated .... {title} Okla Stat Ann § x
(West 19xx)

Original Acts:
Oklahoma Session Laws .... 19xx Okla Sess Laws x
Oklahoma Session Law Service .... 19xx Okla Sess Law Serv x
(West)

Oregon

Codification:
Oregon Revised Statutes .... Or Rev Stat § x (19xx)
Original Acts:
Oregon Laws and Resolutions .... 19xx Or Laws x
Oregon Laws and Resolutions, Special Ses-
sion .... 19xx Or Laws Spec Sess x
Oregon Laws Advanced Sheets .... 19xx Or Laws Adv Sh No x

Pennsylvania

Codification:
Pennsylvania Consolidated Statutes Anno-
tated .... {title} Pa Cons Stat Ann
§ x (Purdon 19xx)

Pennsylvania Statutes .... {title} Pa Stat § x (Purdon
19xx)

Original Acts:
Laws of the General Assembly of the Commonwealth of Pennsylvania .... 19xx Pa Laws x
Pennsylvania Legislative Service.......... 19xx Pa Legis Serv x (Purdon)

Rhode Island

Codification:
General Laws of Rhode Island .... RI Gen Laws § x (19xx)
Original Acts:
Public Laws of Rhode Island............. 19xx RI Pub Laws x

South Carolina

Codification:
Code of Laws of South Carolina Annotated SC Code Ann § x (Law Co-
op 19xx)

Original Acts:
Acts and Joint Resolutions, South Carolina. 19xx SC Acts & Resol x

South Dakota

Codification:
South Dakota Codified Laws .... SD Cod Laws § x (19xx)
Original Acts:
Laws of South Dakota................... 19xx SD Laws x

Tennessee

Codification:
Tennessee Code Annotated .... Tenn Code Ann § x (19xx)

Original Acts:
Public Acts of the State of Tennessee......	19xx Tenn Pub Acts x
Private Acts of the State of Tennessee.....	19xx Tenn Priv Acts x

Texas

Codification:
Texas Codes Annotated..................	Tex [subject] Code Ann § x (Vernon 19xx)
Texas Revised Civil Statutes Annotated....	Tex Rev Civ Stat Ann § x (Vernon 19xx)
Texas Business Corporation Act Annotated	Tex Bus Corp Act Ann art x (Vernon 19xx)

Original Acts:
General and Special Laws of the State of Texas	19xx Tex Gen Laws x
Texas Session Law Service	19xx Tex Sess Law Serv x (Vernon)

Utah

Codification:
Utah Code Annotated...................	Utah Code Ann § x (19xx)

Original Acts:
Laws of Utah..........................	19xx Utah Laws x

Vermont

Codification:
Vermont Statutes Annotated..............	{title} Vt Stat Ann § x (Equity 19xx)

Original Acts:
Laws of Vermont	19xx Vt Laws x

Virginia

Codification:
Code of Virginia	Va Code § x (19xx)
Virginia Statutes at Large [1619-1807].....	Va Stat ch x (17xx)

Original Acts:
Acts of the General Assembly of the Commonwealth of Virginia	19xx Va Acts x

Washington

Codification:
Revised Code of Washington	Wash Rev Code § x (19xx)
Revised Code of Washington Annotated ...	Wash Rev Code Ann § x (West 19xx)

Original Acts:
Laws of Washington	19xx Wash Laws x

West Virginia

Codification:
West Virginia Code.....................	W Va Code § x (19xx)

Original Acts:
    Acts of the Legislature of West Virginia ...   19xx W Va Acts x

Wisconsin

Codification:
    Wisconsin Statutes.......................   Wis Stat § x (19xx)
    Wisconsin Statutes Annotated ....   Wis Stat Ann § x (West
        19xx)

Original Acts:
    Laws of Wisconsin.......................   19xx Wis Laws x
    Wisconsin Legislative Service ....   19xx Wis Legis Serv x
        (West)

Wyoming

Codification:
    Wyoming Statutes ....   Wyo Stat § x (19xx)

Original Acts:
    Session Laws of Wyoming ....   19xx Wyo Sess Laws x

Appendix 4: Recommended Abbreviations of Periodicals

Adelaide Law Review	Adel L Rev
Administrative Law Review	Admin L Rev
Air Force Law Review	AF L Rev
Akron Law Review	Akron L Rev
Alabama Law Review	Ala L Rev
Albany Law Review	Albany L Rev
American Bankruptcy Law Journal	Am Bankr L J
American Bar Association Journal	ABA J
American Bar Foundation Research Journal	Am Bar Found Res J
American Business Law Journal	Am Bus L J
American Journal of Criminal Law	Am J Crim L
American Journal of International Law	Am J Intl L
American Journal of Jurisprudence	Am J Juris
American Journal of Legal History	Am J Legal Hist
American Journal of Trial Advocacy	Am J Trial Advoc
American University Law Review	Am U L Rev
Anglo-American Law Review	Anglo-Am L Rev
Antioch Law Journal	Antioch L J
Arizona Journal of International and Comparative Law	Ariz J Intl & Comp L
Arizona Law Review	Ariz L Rev
Arizona State Law Journal	Ariz St L J
Arkansas Law Review	Ark L Rev
Atomic Energy Law Journal	Atom Ener L J
Auckland University Law Review	Auck U L Rev
Australian Law Journal	Austl L J
Banking Law Journal	Bank L J
Baylor Law Review	Baylor L Rev
Black Law Journal	Black L J
Boston College Industrial and Commercial Law Review	BC Indust & Comm L Rev
Boston College Law Review	BC L Rev
Boston College Third World Law Journal	BC Third World L J
Boston University International Law Journal	BU Intl L J
Boston University Law Review	BU L Rev
Bracton Law Journal	Bracton L J
Brigham Young University Law Review	BYU L Rev
Brooklyn Law Review	Brooklyn L Rev
Buffalo Law Review	Buff L Rev
Business Lawyer	Bus Law
California Law Review	Cal L Rev

Appendix 4 UNIVERSITY OF CHICAGO

California Western Law Review	Cal W L Rev
Cambridge Law Journal	Camb L J
Campbell Law Review.....................	Camp L Rev
Capital University Law Review	Cap U L Rev
Cardozo Arts & Entertainment Law Journal ..	Cardozo Arts & Enter L J
Cardozo Law Review......................	Cardozo L Rev
Case and Comment.......................	Case & Comm
Catholic Lawyer	Cath Law
Catholic University Law Review	Cath U L Rev
Chicago Kent Law Review	Chi Kent L Rev
Chicano Law Review......................	Chicano L Rev
Cleveland State Law Review	Cleve St L Rev
Colorado Lawyer	Colo Law
Columbia Business Law Review	Colum Bus L Rev
Columbia Human Rights Law Review........	Colum Hum Rts L Rev
Columbia Journal of Environmental Law	Colum J Envir L
Columbia Journal of Law and the Arts	Colum J L & Arts
Columbia Journal of Law & Social Problems .	Colum J L & Soc Probs
Columbia Journal of Transnational Law	Colum J Transnatl L
Columbia Law Review	Colum L Rev
Common Market Law Review	Common Mkt L Rev
Comparative Labor Law	Comp Labor L
Connecticut Journal of International Law	Conn J Intl L
Connecticut Law Review	Conn L Rev
Constitutional Commentary	Const Comm
Conveyance and Property Lawyer	Conv & Prop Law
Cooley Law Review	Cooley L Rev
Cornell International Law Journal	Cornell Intl L J
Cornell Law Review	Cornell L Rev
Creighton Law Review	Creighton L Rev
Criminal Justice Journal	Crim Just J
Criminal Law Journal	Crim L J
Criminal Law Quarterly	Crim L Q
Criminal Law Review	Crim L Rev
Cumberland Law Review	Cumb L Rev
Dalhousie Law Journal	Dalhousie L J
DePaul Law Review......................	DePaul L Rev
Delaware Journal of Corporate Law	Del J Corp L
Denning Law Review	Denning L Rev
Denver Journal of International Law and Policy	Denver J Intl L & Policy
Denver University Law Review	Denver U L Rev
Detroit College of Law Review.............	Detroit Coll L Rev
Dickinson Law Review	Dickinson L Rev
Drake Law Review.......................	Drake L Rev
Duke Law Journal	Duke L J
Duquesne Law Review	Duquesne L Rev
Ecology Law Quarterly...................	Ecol L Q

Appendix 4

Emory Law Journal	Emory L J
Energy Law Journal.....................	Energy L J
Environmental Law	Envir L
Family Law Quarterly	Family L Q
Florida State University Law Review	Fla St U L Rev
Food Drug Cosmetic Law Journal	Food Drug Cosm L J
Fordham Law Review	Fordham L Rev
Fordham Urban Law Journal	Fordham Urban L J
George Mason University Law Review	Geo Mason U L Rev
George Washington Law Review	Geo Wash L Rev
Georgetown Immigration Law Journal	Georgetown Immig L J
Georgetown Law Journal	Georgetown L J
Georgia Journal of International and Comparative Law	Ga J Intl & Comp L
Georgia Law Review	Ga L Rev
Glendale Law Review	Glendale L Rev
Golden Gate University Law Review	Golden Gate U L Rev
Gonzaga Law Review	Gonzaga L Rev
Hamline Law Review	Hamline L Rev
Harvard Civil Rights-Civil Liberties Law Review...............................	Harv CR-CL L Rev
Harvard Environmental Law Review	Harv Envir L Rev
Harvard International Law Journal	Harv Intl L J
Harvard Journal of Law and Public Policy	Harv J L & Pub Pol
Harvard Journal on Legislation	Harv J Leg
Harvard Law Review	Harv L Rev
Harvard Women's Law Journal	Harv Women's L J
Hastings Constitutional Law Quarterly.......	Hastings Const L Q
Hastings International and Comparative Law Review	Hastings Intl & Comp L Rev
Hastings Law Journal	Hastings L J
Hofstra Labor Law Journal	Hofstra Labor L J
Hofstra Law Review	Hofstra L Rev
Houston Law Review	Houston L Rev
Howard Law Journal....................	Howard L J
Idaho Law Review	Idaho L Rev
Illinois Bar Journal	Ill Bar J
Indiana Law Journal	Ind L J
Indiana Law Review	Ind L Rev
Institute on Federal Taxation	Inst Fed Tax
Institute on Securities Regulation	Inst Sec Reg
International and Comparative Law Quarterly	Intl & Comp L Q
International Journal of Law and Psychiatry ..	Intl J L & Psych
International Review of Law and Economics..	Intl Rev L & Econ
International Tax & Business Lawyer	Intl Tax & Bus Law
International Lawyer....................	Intl Law

Appendix 4

Iowa Law Review	Iowa L Rev
JAG Journal	JAG J
John Marshall Law Review	John Marshall L Rev
Journal of Air Law and Commerce	J Air L & Comm
Journal of Business Law	J Bus L
Journal of College and University Law	J Coll & Univ L
Journal of Contemporary Health Law and Policy	J Contemp Health L & Policy
Journal of Contemporary Law	J Contemp L
Journal of Corporation Law	J Corp L
Journal of Corporate Taxation	J Corp Tax
Journal of Criminal Law and Criminology	J Crim L & Criminol
Journal of Energy Law and Policy	J Energy L & Pol
Journal of Environmental Law and Litigation .	J Envir L & Litig
Journal of Family Law	J Family L
Journal of Law and Commerce	J L & Commerce
Journal of Law & Economics	J L & Econ
Journal of Law and Politics	J L & Pol
Journal of Legal Education	J Legal Educ
Journal of Legal History	J Legal Hist
Journal of Legal Studies	J Legal Stud
Journal of Legislation	J Legis
Journal of Maritime Law and Commerce	J Marit L & Comm
Journal of Products Liability	J Prod Liab
Journal of Taxation	J Tax
Juridical Review	Jurid Rev
Jurimetrics Journal	Jurimet J
Justice System Journal	Just Sys J
Kentucky Law Journal	Ky L J
Labor Law Journal	Labor L J
Labor Lawyer	Labor Law
Land and Water Law Review	Land & Water L Rev
La Raza Law Journal	La Raza L J
Law and Contemporary Problems	L & Contemp Probs
Law and Human Behavior	L & Human Beh
Law and Psychology Review	L & Psych Rev
Lincoln Law Review	Lincoln L Rev
Louisiana Law Review	La L Rev
Loyola Law Review	Loyola L Rev
Loyola of Los Angeles Law Review	Loyola LA L Rev
Loyola University of Chicago Law Journal	Loyola U Chi L J
Maine Law Review	Me L Rev
Manitoba Law Journal	Manitoba L J
Marquette Law Review	Marq L Rev
Maryland Law Review	Md L Rev
Massachusetts Law Review	Mass L Rev

MANUAL OF LEGAL CITATION   **Appendix 4**

McGill Law Journal . . . .   McGill L J
Melbourne University Law Review. . . . .   Melb U L Rev
Memphis State University Law Review . . . .   Memphis St U L Rev
Mercer Law Review . . . .   Mercer L Rev
Michigan Law Review . . . .   Mich L Rev
Military Law Review . . . .   Milit L Rev
Minnesota Law Review . . . .   Minn L Rev
Mississippi Law Journal . . . .   Miss L J
Missouri Law Review . . . .   Mo L Rev
Modern Law Review . . . .   Mod L Rev
Monash University Law Review . . . .   Monash U L Rev
Montana L Review . . . .   Mont L Rev

National Black Law Journal . . . .   Natl Black L J
Nebraska Law Review . . . .   Neb L Rev
New Law Journal . . . .   New L J
New Mexico Law Review . . . .   NM L Rev
New York Law School Journal of International
    and Comparative Law . . . .   NY L Sch J Intl & Comp L
New York Law School Law Review . . . .   NY L Sch L Rev
New York University Journal of International
    Law and Politics . . . .   NYU J Intl L & Pol
New York University Law Review . . . .   NYU L Rev
New York University Review of Law and So-
    cial Change . . . .   NYU Rev L & Soc Change
North Carolina Central Law Journal . . . .   NC Cent L J
North Carolina Journal of International Law
    and Commercial Regulation . . . .   NC J Intl L & Comm Reg
North Carolina Law Review . . . .   NC L Rev
North Dakota Law Review . . . .   ND L Rev
Northern Illinois University Law Review . . . . .   NIU L Rev
Northern Kentucky Law Review . . . .   N Ky L Rev
Northwestern University Law Review . . . .   Nw U L Rev
Notre Dame Law Review . . . .   Notre Dame L Rev
Nova Law Review . . . .   Nova L Rev

Ohio Northern University Law Review . . . .   Ohio N U L Rev
Ohio State Law Journal . . . .   Ohio St L J
Oklahoma City University Law Review . . . .   Okla City U L Rev
Oklahoma Law Review . . . .   Okla L Rev
Oregon Law Review . . . .   Or L Rev
Osgoode Hall Law Journal . . . .   Osgoode Hall L J
Otago Law Review . . . .   Otago L Rev
Ottawa Law Review . . . .   Ottawa L Rev
Oxford Journal of Legal Studies . . . .   Oxford J Legal Stud

Pace Law Review . . . .   Pace L Rev
Pacific Law Journal . . . .   Pac L J
Pepperdine Law Review . . . .   Pepperdine L Rev
Potomac Law Review . . . .   Potomac L Rev

Practical Lawyer	Prac Law
Probate Law Journal	Prob L J
Real Estate Law Journal	Real Est L J
Review of Litigation	Rev Litig
Rutgers Computer and Technology Law Journal	Rutgers Computer & Tech L J
Rutgers Law Journal	Rutgers L J
Rutgers Law Review	Rutgers L Rev
St. John's Law Review	St John's L Rev
Saint Louis University Law Journal	SLU L Rev
St. Mary's Law Journal	St Mary's L J
San Diego Law Review	San Diego L Rev
San Fernando Valley Law Review	San Fernando V L Rev
Santa Clara Law Review	Santa Clara L Rev
Securities Regulation Law Journal	Sec Reg L J
Seton Hall Law Review	Seton Hall L Rev
Seton Hall Legislative Journal	Seton Hall Legis J
South Carolina Law Review	SC L Rev
South Dakota Law Review	SD L Rev
South Texas Law Journal	S Tex L J
Southern California Law Review	S Cal L Rev
Southern Illinois University Law Review	SIU L Rev
Southern University Law Review	S U L Rev
Southwestern Law Journal	Sw L J
Southwestern University Law Review	Sw U L Rev
Stanford Law Review	Stan L Rev
Stetson Law Review	Stetson L Rev
Suffolk Transnational Law Journal	Suffolk Transnatl L J
Suffolk University Law Review	Suffolk U L Rev
Supreme Court Review	S Ct Rev
Sydney Law Review	Sydney L Rev
Syracuse Journal of International Law and Commerce	Syracuse J Intl L & Comm
Syracuse Law Review	Syracuse L Rev
Tax Adviser	Tax Adviser
Tax Law Review	Tax L Rev
Temple Environmental Law & Technology Journal	Temple Envir L & Tech J
Temple Law Quarterly	Temple L Q
Tennessee Law Review	Tenn L Rev
Texas International Law Journal	Tex Intl L J
Texas Law Review	Tex L Rev
Texas Tech Law Review	Tex Tech L Rev
Thurgood Marshall Law Journal	Thurgood Marshall L J
Trial Lawyers Quarterly	Trial Law Q
Tulane Law Review	Tulane L Rev

MANUAL OF LEGAL CITATION   **Appendix 4**

Tulsa Law Journal ....   Tulsa L J

U.C. Davis Law Review.....................   UC Davis L Rev
UCLA Journal of Environmental Law & Policy   UCLA J Envir L & Policy
UCLA Law Review ....   UCLA L Rev
UCLA Pacific Basin Law Journal ....   UCLA Pac Basin L J
UMKC Law Review ....   UMKC L Rev
Uniform Commercial Code Law Journal .....   UCC L J
University of Arkansas at Little Rock Law
   Journal ....   U Ark Little Rock L J
University of Baltimore Law Review ....   U Balt L Rev
University of Bridgeport Law Review ....   U Bridgeport L Rev
University of Chicago Law Review...........   U Chi L Rev
University of Chicago Legal Forum..........   U Chi Legal F
University of Cincinnati Law Review.........   U Cin L Rev
University of Colorado Law Review ....   U Colo L Rev
University of Dayton Law Review ....   U Dayton L Rev
University of Detroit Journal of Urban Law ..   U Detroit J Urban L
University of Detroit Law Review ....   U Detroit L Rev
University of Florida Law Review ....   U Fla L Rev
University of Hawaii Law Review............   U Hawaii L Rev
University of Illinois Law Review............   U Ill L Rev
University of Kansas Law Review............   U Kan L Rev
University of Miami Inter-American Law Re-
   view...................................   U Miami Int-Am L Rev
University of Miami Law Review ....   U Miami L Rev
University of Michigan Journal of Law Reform
   ....   U Mich J L Ref
University of Pennsylvania Journal of Interna-
   tional Business Law.....................   U Pa J Intl Bus L
University of Pennsylvania Law Review ......   U Pa L Rev
University of Pittsburgh Law Review.........   U Pitt L Rev
University of Puget Sound Law Review ......   U Puget Sound L Rev
University of Richmond Law Review.........   U Richmond L Rev
University of San Francisco Law Review .....   USF L Rev
University of Toledo Law Review ....   U Toledo L Rev
University of Toronto Faculty of Law Review.   U Toronto Fac L Rev
University of Toronto Law Journal ....   U Toronto L J
University of West Los Angeles Law Review..   U W La L Rev
Urban Lawyer ....   Urban Law
Utah Law Review ....   Utah L Rev

Valparaiso University Law Review ....   Valp U L Rev
Vanderbilt Law Review.....................   Vand L Rev
Vermont Law Review ....   Vt L Rev
Villanova Law Review.....................   Vill L Rev
Virginia Journal of International Law ....   Va J Intl L
Virginia Law Review ....   Va L Rev

Wake Forest Law Review...................   Wake Forest L Rev

Appendix 4   UNIVERSITY OF CHICAGO

Washburn Law Journal	Washburn L J
Washington & Lee Law Review	Wash & Lee L Rev
Washington Law Review	Wash L Rev.
Washington University Journal of Urban and Contemporary Law	Wash U J Urban & Contemp L
Washington University Law Quarterly	Wash U L Q
Wayne Law Review	Wayne L Rev
West Virginia Law Review	W Va L Rev
Western New England Law Review	W New Eng L Rev
Western State University Law Review	W State U L Rev
Whittier Law Review	Whittier L Rev
Willamette Law Review	Willamette L Rev
William & Mary Law Review	Wm & Mary L Rev
William Mitchell Law Review	Wm Mitchell L Rev
Wisconsin International Law Journal	Wis Intl L J
Wisconsin Law Review	Wis L Rev
Yale Journal of International Law	Yale J Intl L
Yale Journal of World Public Order	Yale J World Pub Ord
Yale Journal on Regulation	Yale J Reg
Yale Law and Policy Review	Yale L & Policy Rev
Yale Law Journal	Yale L J

Appendix 5: Other Abbreviations To Be Used in Citations

American	Am
Amendment	Amend
Annotation	Ann
Annotated	
Appeal	App
Appellate	
Article	Art
Board	Bd
Business	Bus
Cases	Cases
certiorari	cert
Circuit	Cir
chapter	ch
Civil	Civ
clause	cl
Congress	Cong
Constitution	Const
Contract	Cont
Corporation	Corp
Court	Ct
Decisions	Dec
District	D
East	E
Eastern	
edition	ed
editor	ed
Employment	Empl
Employee	
Employer	
Environmental	Envir
Evidence	Evid
Federal	F or Fed
idem (the same)	id
International	Intl
Journal	J
Law(s)	L
Legal	Legal
Legislation	Legis
Legislature	
Legislative	
Manual	Man

Appendix 5   UNIVERSITY OF CHICAGO

Maritime	Marit
Materials	Mat
National	Natl
North	N
Northern	
note	n
Number	No
Opinions	Op
page	p
Politics	Pol
Political	
Public	Pub
Quarterly	Q
Record	Rec
Reference	Ref
Regulation	Reg
Report(s)	Rep
Reporter	Rptr
Review	Rev
Revised	Rev
School	Sch
Security	Sec
Series	Ser
Service	Serv
Session	Sess
slip opinion	slip op
South	S
Southern	
Statutes	Stat
Supplement	Supp
University	U
West	W
Western	

INDEX

INDEX

INDEX

INDEX

INDEX

INDEX

INDEX